Heinrich Schenker's Conception of Harmony

Eastman Studies in Music

Ralph P. Locke, Senior Editor
Eastman School of Music

Additional Titles of Interest

Analyzing Atonal Music: Pitch-Class Set Theory and Its Contexts
Michiel Schuijer

Analyzing Wagner's Operas: Alfred Lorenz and German Nationalist Ideology
Stephen McClatchie

Aspects of Unity in J. S. Bach's Partitas and Suites: An Analytical Study
David W. Beach

August Halm: A Critical and Creative Life in Music
Lee A. Rothfarb

Explaining Tonality: Schenkerian Theory and Beyond
Matthew Brown

Explorations in Schenkerian Analysis
Edited by David Beach and Su Yin Mak

Greek and Latin Music Theory: Principles and Challenges
Edward Nowacki

Music Theory in Concept and Practice
Edited by James M. Baker, David W. Beach, and Jonathan W. Bernard

The "Musica" of Hermannus Contractus
Edited by Leonard Ellinwood
Revised by John L. Snyder

A Theory of Music Analysis: On Segmentation and Associative Organization
Dora Hanninen

A complete list of titles in the Eastman Studies in Music series
may be found on our website, www.urpress.com.

Heinrich Schenker's Conception of Harmony

Robert W. Wason and
Matthew Brown

UNIVERSITY OF ROCHESTER PRESS

The University of Rochester Press gratefully acknowledges generous support from the General Publications Fund of the American Musicological Society, supported in part by the National Endowment for the Humanities and the Andrew W. Mellon Foundation.

Copyright © 2020 by Robert W. Wason and Matthew Brown

All rights reserved. Except as permitted under current legislation, no part of this work may be photocopied, stored in a retrieval system, published, performed in public, adapted, broadcast, transmitted, recorded, or reproduced in any form or by any means, without the prior permission of the copyright owner.

First published 2020
Reprinted in paperback 2025

University of Rochester Press
668 Mt. Hope Avenue, Rochester, NY 14620, USA
www.urpress.com
and Boydell & Brewer Limited
PO Box 9, Woodbridge, Suffolk IP12 3DF, UK
www.boydellandbrewer.com

ISBN-13: 978-1-58046-575-5 (hardcover)
ISBN-13: 978-1-64825-115-3 (paperback)
ISSN: 1071-9989 ; v. 163

Library of Congress Cataloging-in-Publication Data

Names: Wason, Robert W. (Robert Wesley), 1945– author. | Brown, Matthew, 1957– author.
Title: Heinrich Schenker's conception of harmony / Robert W. Wason, Matthew Brown.
Other titles: Eastman studies in music ; 163.
Description: Rochester : University of Rochester Press, 2020. | Series: Eastman studies in music, 10719989 ; 163 | Includes bibliographical references and index.
Identifiers: LCCN 2020010715 | ISBN 9781580465755 (hardback) | ISBN 9781787449763 (epub) | ISBN 9781787446694 (pdf)
Subjects: LCSH: Schenker, Heinrich, 1868-1935. Harmonielehre. | Harmony.
Classification: LCC ML444 .W25 2020 | DDC 781.2/5—dc23
LC record available at https://lccn.loc.gov/2020010715

Contents

	Abbreviations	vii
	Preface	xi
	Note on Online Material	xxvii

Part I. *Harmonielehre*

1	The Eclectic Intellectual Methodology of Schenker's Theory of Harmony (1906)	1
2	The Music-Theoretical Content of Schenker's Theory of Harmony (1906) and the Status of Harmony in His Later Work	83

Part II. *Harmonielehre*: The Past

3	Schenker's Theory of Harmony (1906) in Historical Perspective: The Theory of Harmony from the Ancient Greeks to the Early Nineteenth Century	177
4	Sources of Schenker's Intellectual Methodology in 1906: The Conflict between the Human and Natural Sciences in Schenker's Education, Music Theory in the Later Nineteenth Century, and His Reaction to Both	246

Part III. *Harmonielehre*: The Future

5	A "New Edition" for a New Audience and an "American Version" for a New Country: Problems of Editing and Translating *Harmonielehre* (1906)	311

6 The Twilight of the Masters: Schenker's Reinterpretation of the
   Classical Concept of Harmony   376

   Appendix A: "The Path to Likeness." OC/83, 2–43   397
   Introduction and Translation by Robert W. Wason

   Appendix B: "[Foundations of Tonal Systems.]"
   OC/31, 360–417   425
   Introduction and Translation by Robert W. Wason

   Bibliography   455

   Index   477

Abbreviations

Archives

AW   Arthur Waldeck papers related to Heinrich Schenker MP.0008.01; The New School Archives and Special Collections. The New School, New York, New York. Sources are cited in the form AW/box number, folder number.

FS   Felix Salzer Papers, JPB 07-1, New York Public Library. Sources are cited in the form FS/box number, folder number.

OC   Oster Collection: Papers of Heinrich Schenker, New York Public Library. *ZB-2237 [Microfilm]. Sources are cited in the form OC/file number, folder number (if applicable), item number[s].

OJ   Oswald Jonas Memorial Collection, University of California, Riverside. MS 067. Sources are cited in the form OJ/box number, folder number, document number[s] (if applicable).

SDO   *Schenker Documents Online* (Schenkerdocumentsonline.org). Sources are cited in the form *SDO*: archival location; description and date; transcriber; translator.

Schenker's Main Works

Titles of Schenker's main works appear here in chronological order of his writing of the originals, translations following immediately regardless of publication date. The biography and correspondence also appear here. See the full bibliography at the end for additional works by Schenker, also in chronological order. All other books and articles cited appear in the full bibliography in alphabetical order.

GEIST	"Der Geist der musikalischen Technik," *Musikalisches Wochenblatt* 26 (1895), 245–46, 257–59, 273–74, 285–86, 297–98, 309–10, 325–26. Reprint in Hellmut Federhofer, *Heinrich Schenker als Essayist und Kritiker: Gesammelte Aufsätze, Rescensionen und kleinere Berichte aus den Jahren 1891–1901*. Hildesheim: Olms, 1990, 135–54.
SPIRIT	"The Spirit of Musical Technique." Translated by William Pastille. *Theoria* 3 (1988), 86–104; revised translation by Pastille in Nicholas Cook, *The Schenker Project*, 319–32. Oxford: Oxford University Press, 2007.
WEG	"Der Weg zum Gleichniss." Titled but unfinished and unpublished essay in Schenker's hand (written ca. 1904–5); handwritten MS only. OC/83, 2–43.
PATH	"The Path to Likeness." Translation of "Der Weg zum Gleichniss," Appendix A.[1]
[DTS]	Untitled, unpublished, and incomplete essay in Schenker's hand (written ca. 1904–5), generally known as "Das Tonsystem." OC/31, 360–417. Fair copy in Schenker's hand (360–87) and typescript (388–417).
[FTS]	"[Foundations of Tonal Systems]." Translation of [Das Tonsystem], Appendix B.
EBO	*Ein Beitrag zur Ornamentik*. Vienna: Universal Edition, 1903, rev. 1908.
CSO	"A Contribution to the Study of Ornamentation." Edited and translated by Hedi Siegel. *The Music Forum* 4, edited by Felix Salzer. New York: Columbia University Press, 1976, 1–139.
NdK	"Über den Niedergang der Kompositionskunst: eine technisch-kritische Untersuchung" (ca. 1904–5). OC/31, 28–153. Untitled, undated typescript that is all but certain to be the work bearing the title given here, to which Schenker referred several times.
DAC	"The Decline of the Art of Composition: A Technical-Critical Study." Translation of NdK by William Drabkin, with introduction. *Music Analysis* 24 (2005), 3–129.

---

[1] *Gleichniss* is an antiquated spelling of *Gleichnis*. Except in the case of the title, we use the modern spelling whenever the German word is called for.

HL   *Harmonielehre. Neue musikalische Theorien und Phantasien 1.*
      Stuttgart and Berlin: Cotta Verlag; distributed in Vienna by
      Universal Edition, 1906.

HA   *Harmony.* Abridged edition with introduction by Oswald Jonas,
      translated by Elisabeth Mann Borgese. Chicago: University
      of Chicago Press; Toronto: University of Toronto Press;
      London: Cambridge University Press, 1954. Paperback reprint,
      Cambridge, MA: MIT Press, 1974, 1980; now available through
      University of Chicago Press.

CFF (1910) *J. S. Bach, Chromatische Fantasie und Fuge.* Edited by Heinrich
      Schenker. Vienna: Universal Edition, 1910.

CFF (1984) *J. S. Bach's Chromatic Fantasy and Fugue: Critical Edition with
      Commentary.* Edited and translated by Hedi Siegel. New York:
      Longman, 1984.

KP1   *Kontrapunkt I. Neue musikalische Theorien und Fantasien II.I.*
      Stuttgart and Berlin: Cotta Verlag, 1910.

CP1   *Counterpoint 1: A Translation of Kontrapunkt by Heinrich Schenker;
      New Musical Theories and Fantasies; II.I: Cantus Firmus and Two-
      Voice Counterpoint.* Translated by John Rothgeb and Jürgen Thym.
      Edited by John Rothgeb. New York: Schirmer, 1987. Corrected
      edition, Ann Arbor, MI: Musicalia Press, 2001.

TW   *Der Tonwille,* vols. 1–10, 1921–24, "published" by Universal (via
      a fictitious publisher called *Tonwilleflugblätterverlag* (Will-of-
      the-tone pamphlet publishing), distributed in Vienna by Albert
      Gutmann.

WT   *Der Tonwille* [The Will of the Tone] Pamphlets in Witness of
      the Immutable Laws of Music, Offered to a new Generation of
      Youth by Heinrich Schenker, William Drabkin, ed., Volume 1
      (Issues 1–5), and II (Issues 6–10). Oxford: Oxford University
      Press, 2004 and 2005.

KP2   *Kontrapunkt II. Neue musikalische Theorien und Fantasien* II.II.
      Vienna: Universal Edition, 1922.

CP2   *Counterpoint 2: A Translation of Kontrapunkt by Heinrich
      Schenker. New Musical Theories and Fantasies II.II: Counterpoint
      in Three and More Voices; Bridges to Free Composition.* Translated
      by John Rothgeb and Jürgen Thym; Edited by John Rothgeb;
      New York: Schirmer Books, 1987.

MW	*Das Meisterwerk in der Musik*, vols. 1–3. Munich: Drei Masken Verlag, 1925, 1926, 1930.
MM	*The Masterwork in Music*. 3 vols. Edited by William Drabkin. Translated by Ian Bent, Alfred Clayton, William Drabkin, Richard Kramer, Derrick Puffett, John Rothgeb, and Hedi Siegel. Cambridge: Cambridge University Press, 1994, 1996, 1999; New York: Dover, 2014.
FT	*Fünf Urlinie-Tafeln / Five Analyses in Sketchform*. Printed in Vienna, but supported by the David Mannes Music School, New York, 1932.
FGA	*Five Graphic Analyses*. Photo-reprint of *Fünf Urlinie-Tafeln / Five analyses in sketchform* (without Schenker's Foreword). Introduction and glossary of English terms by Felix Salzer. New York: Dover, 1969.
DfS	*Der freie Satz*. Neue musikalische Theorien und Phantasien 3. Vienna: Universal Edition, 1935.
FC	*Free Composition (Der freie Satz): New Musical Theories and Fantasies, III*. Edited and translated by Ernst Oster. New York: Longman, 1979; Hillsdale, NY: Pendragon Press, 2001.

Other Primary Sources

Biography

HS	Federhofer, Hellmut. *Heinrich Schenker nach Tagebüchern und Briefen in der Oswald Jonas Memorial Collection, University of California, Riverside*. Hildesheim: Georg Olms Verlag, 1985.

Correspondence

SC	*Heinrich Schenker: Selected Correspondence*. Edited by Ian Bent, David Bretherton, and William Drabkin. Woodbridge: Boydell & Brewer, 2014.

Preface

Heinrich Schenker (1868–1935) is generally regarded as the leading music theorist of the twentieth century. He was born of German-speaking, Jewish parentage in Wisniowczyk, Galicia, a small town in a Polish-, Ukrainian-, and German-speaking province that was part of Poland for four hundred years before its annexation by the Habsburgs in 1772.[1] During the first half of the nineteenth century, that annexation produced the Germanized culture in which Schenker grew up; but the uprisings of 1848 unleashed a nationalistic fervor that led to a resurgence of Polish language and culture, to the extent that Schenker declared Polish his native language in the first seven out of his ten semester registrations at the University of Vienna.[2] Surely one reason for his declaration is that between the ages of eight and sixteen, Schenker, two years younger than his cohort, was educated at three different *Gymnasien* in which the Polish language and its culture were dominant.[3] After graduating from the Brzezany (English, "Berezhany") *Gymnasium* in the spring of 1884, he moved in the fall to Vienna, the cultural center and capital of what was by that time the Austro-Hungarian Empire, to study law at the university (1884–88) and music at the conservatory (1887–90).[4] Although Schenker took his *Dr. juris* at the university in 1890 and stayed in Vienna for the rest of his life, he never practiced law; instead, he devoted

---

1. Wisniowczyk, Galicia (Polish, "Galicja"; German, "Galizien") is now in the Ukraine, on the border of Poland.
2. See Rothfarb, "Henryk Szenker" for a full account of Schenker's early education. This opening passage and continuing discussion in chapter 2 are based on Rothfarb's ground-breaking archival research.
3. Rothfarb, "Henryk Szenker," 24.
4. With government support, the Conservatory of the Society of Friends of Music became the k. k. Academy for Music and the Performing Arts in 1909. After World War I it was renamed the "State Academy," becoming the "Hochschule" in 1970. It took its present name, the University for Music and the Performing Arts, Vienna, in 1998. We refer to it throughout simply as the "conservatory."

himself entirely to music, working in the 1890s as a composer, music critic, and piano accompanist, and, starting a decade or so later, as a music editor and teacher of piano and theory. It is for his extraordinarily productive career as editor and music theorist that Schenker is remembered today.[5]

Though this project has grown considerably, it began as a book about a book—or, more accurately, a book about two interrelated books. Our first—*Harmonielehre* ("Theory of Harmony" and hereafter *HL*, when referring to the published German text)—is Schenker's first major work about music theory and his link with the most important music-theoretical genre of the past, the history of which we begin to explore in part I and will develop in greater depth in chapter 3 in part II.[6] Our second book is one entitled *Harmony* (hereafter, *HA*), the only English translation of Schenker's *HL* presently available.[7]

Schenker was surely aware of the status of harmony as he deliberated over which of his music-theoretical works to publish first (see *HL*, "Vorwort"). Should it be the first volume of his theory of counterpoint, the theory of a compositional technique that certainly took historical precedence and was, even at this early point in his career, more fundamental to his conception of tonal music? Or should it be *HL*? The overlap in content between the two books shows that he must have been thinking about (and very likely writing) both books at the same time. Though he claims to have decided to publish *HL* first principally for pedagogical reasons—in order "not to delay the necessary reforms" he describes—Schenker certainly knew that publishing a treatise on harmony would place his music-theoretical ideas in a long tradition of a subject regarded, particularly in the nineteenth century,

---

5. For a fuller biographical sketch in English, see Cook, *The Schenker Project*, 15–28. See Federhofer, *HS*, 1–47 for the most complete biography to date, and 5–7 for more details on Schenker's conservatory study.

6. Throughout the present work, "Theory of Harmony," in capitals, refers specifically to Schenker's theory, and represents an English translation of the German title of Schenker's book, though the theory itself is to be found as well in other ancillary documents covered in detail in chapter 1. Meanwhile, "theory of harmony" refers to the general meaning of the phrase.

7. Schenker, *HA*. First appearing when the original text was forty-eight years old and Schenker studies were brand new in America, it was published in one edition only, though that edition was taken over for a time by MIT Press before it returned to University of Chicago Press. Neither the translation nor its sparse critical apparatus have been revised or updated since, and its critical reception has been checkered at best.

as the "science" (*Wissenschaft*) of music.[8] Such a text would also provide a forum for discussing one of his most original ideas: the theory of essential harmonies (*Stufen*), or what he would eventually regard as harmonies "prolonged" contrapuntally—phenomena of great musical importance largely unrecognized by theorists of the past. At the same time, the need to reform music theory and music theory pedagogy was equally pressing, and Schenker was hardly alone in calling for it.[9] Publishing *HL* as soon as possible would allow him not only to denounce recent speculative works on the theory of harmony and propose a coherent alternative, but also to criticize the moribund pedagogues of the day and replace their textbooks rich in artificially constructed examples with an up-to-date volume illustrated by examples from significant tonal compositions. In short, a book on harmony that had to do with real music.

In describing Schenker's motivations for writing *HL*, it is important to stress that this is by no means the only text relevant to his early Theory of Harmony; on the contrary, crucial insights can also be found in a cluster of at least seven other documents from the period 1895–1910. Of the published works, *Kontrapunkt 1* (hereafter *KP1* when referring to the published German text) contains much that is relevant to the discussion of *HL* and thus will be cited in this book with some frequency. Mention will likewise be made of *Ein Beitrag zur Ornamentik* (hereafter *EBO* when referring to the published German text) and Schenker's edition of J. S. Bach, *Chromatische Fantasie und Fuge* (hereafter *CFF* (1910) when referring to the published German text). And, though wide-ranging and not particularly technical, Schenker's earliest essay touching on music theory—"Der Geist der musikalischen Technik" (GEIST)—forecasts the unusual direction his Theory of Harmony would take, and had a clear and important impact on the opening of *HL*.[10] Of the works unpublished during Schenker's lifetime, three stand out as particularly significant. An unpublished essay by Schenker entitled "Der Weg zum Gleichniss" (hereafter, WEG) links, if somewhat distantly, with GEIST, and bears on issues brought up at the very beginning of *HL*, engaging repetition and motives; these prove to be essential in understanding Schenker's personal

---

8. As regards the delays, see Schenker, *HL*, VI–VII and 223–35; *HA*, xxvi and 175–82. On the translation of *Wissenschaft*, see chapter 4 below.
9. See, for example, the *Harmonielehren* by Rudolf Louis and Ludwig Thuille, and by Arnold Schoenberg.
10. See Cook, *The Schenker Project*, 319–32.

version of the theory of harmony.[11] It is presented here in English translation as "The Path to Likeness" for the first time in appendix A (hereafter, PATH, when referring specifically to the English translation). This work appears to be approximately contemporaneous with another unpublished and incomplete essay on tonal systems, which, though untitled, has come to be known as "Das Tonsystem" ([DTS]). It is likewise presented here in English translation for the first time as "Foundations of Tonal Systems" (or [FTS], when referring specifically to the English translation).[12] It may be Schenker's first effort in technical harmonic theory, and is the document most intimately related to *HL* as a "harmony book" in that tradition. Complementing WEG and [DTS], which extend the beginning of *HL* backwards, is a source that Schenker mentions at the end of the "Vorwort" to *HL* ("Preface" in the English translation; see below) and towards the beginning of *KP1*; he calls it "Über den Niedergang der Kompositionskunst: eine technisch-kritische Untersuchung" (NdK), and promises to publish it later.[13] NdK extends *HL* forward, presenting what Schenker, at least, thought were *HL*'s critical implications—and more. Indeed, NdK also links with important ideas on form presented in *HL*, part II. Given Schenker's holistic approach to music analysis—an approach that is clear from the very beginning of his career in music theory—harmony, repetition, motive, counterpoint, and form are linked, and his ideas on the latter topic are of all the more interest due to the revival of *Formenlehre* pursued by many music theorists today. Arguably this cluster of documents represents Schenker's "real" Theory of Harmony, at least in its early stage, though, as we demonstrate below, even Schenker's philological and editorial projects link with it. The new direction that Schenker's career took after about 1900 is thus more unified than it might appear at first. For purely practical reasons, however, our primary focus must remain on the theory of harmony—the ostensible topic of his first book, a work which was to take its place in a crowded field of books so titled.

Our second book, as mentioned, is *Harmony* (*HA*), the only English translation of Schenker's *HL*. Why "Harmony" and not "Theory of Harmony," as

---

11. OC/83, 2–43. See the lecture by Nicholas Marston on this work at: https://www.youtube.com/watch?v=7GC2xIEZwlU&t=5s, accessed January 19, 2019. Also see Marston, "'. . . nur ein Gleichnis,'" A transcription of Schenker's essay appears as appendix 1 in Hooper, "Schenker's Early Approach to Form," 364–95.
12. OC/31, 360–417. See appendix B.
13. NdK, OC/31, 28–153, translated by William Drabkin as "The Decline of the Art of Composition: A Technical-Critical Study" (hereafter, DAC).

Harmonielehre is rendered in our title? The German *Harmonielehre* (literally "teaching of harmony") can be translated as "treatise on harmony," "theory of harmony," or simply "harmony," depending on the nature of the text in question. "Harmony" is the customary rendering for a pedagogical book on the topic, while the phrases "theory of harmony" or "treatise on harmony" are more appropriate to a full-scale academic work, as Schenker's original text was. *HA*, on the other hand, was clearly designed for the American commercial textbook market, is thus correctly titled, and, given these circumstances, is not surprisingly a considerably abridged version of the original text.[14] Unfortunately, it also contains significant errors in translation, and offers little in the way of annotation to set the original text in historical and music-theoretical perspective, or to help the reader in interpreting it. Yet, from another point of view, *HA* is also a "historical document" to be added to the *HL* cluster, and many passages are well translated and continue to be of use (see chapter 5); and, despite its many flaws, it remains of value in ongoing discussions about the history of Schenker's Theory of Harmony and its Anglo-American reception—ironically, even more so, since the book is not an accurate rendering of *HL*. Indeed, read in isolation, *HA* is far from sufficient for the reader interested in Schenker's Theory of Harmony as he actually conceived it in 1906.

The aim of the present book is to provide a firmer foundation for the study of Schenker's work by correcting and expanding the context within which to understand his thinking about harmony throughout his career. We believe this context to be especially necessary to the reader dependent on the present abridged translation, *HA*, but helpful even to the reader of some future, improved (perhaps even scholarly) translation, or even of the original German-language edition. The big question is, of course, just how much context? This question has occasioned some reordering of the present book's contents. In earlier drafts, the actual reading of *HL* was postponed considerably by chapters that presented historical background, the present chapters 3 and 4. Thus, they preceded chapters 1 and 2, in the order 3 (history of harmony), 4 (Schenker's education), 1 (methodology in Schenker's Theory of Harmony), 2 (music-theoretical content of Schenker's Theory of Harmony). We have settled on the final ordering because we believe that most readers

---

14. At least thirty-seven passages of text, seventy-five musical examples, and fourteen tables with associated explanation were cut, resulting in a considerably shorter book. The excised texts and tables may be found on the companion website to the present work as appendix C, and a list of musical examples is given as appendix D.

will want us to get to the point as early as possible. Still, some readers may prefer to retain the original order, reading the background first, though it delays the reading of *HL* itself. In that case, they can simply read part II, in order, before part I. Or they may choose to read the final ordering, but to consult the index in the event that problems arise.

In our final chapter ordering, part I concentrates first on Schenker's Theory of Harmony as it was in 1906. Chapter 1 begins directly with a reading of the book, but one whose point of view may be surprising: it contends that Schenker's ideas on harmony constitute a "theory," but a most unusual one. Here Schenker's clear debt to the Classical theory of harmony, is, we believe, exposed for the first time. The discussion then turns to the documents that comprise Schenker's Theory of Harmony in its original state. The body of the chapter analyzes the original published text with the aid of the ancillary documents from the point of view of its eclectic intellectual methodology. Schenker's Theory of Harmony is thus unusual both by virtue of its point of departure, and its methodology—not to mention its music-theoretical conclusions, explored in the next chapter.

Chapter 2, in many ways the linchpin of this book, takes a more conventional route into the treatise by viewing it as a work in the history of harmonic theory, but doing so with the treatise itself always kept front and center throughout the reading. However, while Schenker's debts go back very far indeed, *HL* also carries the seeds of his later work, and thus chapter 2 ultimately moves on to Schenker's view of harmony as it evolved in works from the 1920s and 1930s, including *Der Tonwille* (1921–24, henceforth *TW*), *Kontrapunkt II* (1922, henceforth *KP2*), *Das Meisterwerk in der Musik* (1925, 1926, 1930, henceforth *MW1–3*), and *Der freie Satz* (1935, henceforth *DfS*). By that time, *HL* did not represent Schenker's thinking without considerable revision, as the latter part of chapter 2 makes clear.

In examining *HL*'s "past," part II of the book presents more detailed historical background on the main ideas in part I. Chapter 3 may be read as a continuation of chapter 2, for in recounting a brief history of the theory of harmony, it continues the examination of *HL*'s ties to traditional music theory, this time getting into the actual sources themselves. Chapter 4 explores Schenker's education and the intellectual milieu he inhabited in his early years, as well as German-language music theory that was current while he prepared for the writing of *HL*: this is essentially the historical background for the unusual intellectual methodology explored in the first chapter. The reader will learn that Schenker took a completely different view of his topic than that presented in any contemporaneous work.

Indeed, at few points in the history of music theory do we find a text that is such an outlier.[15]

Looking into the "future" of Schenker's Theory of Harmony, chapter 5, the first in part III, investigates developments that took place largely after Schenker's death, but not entirely so. By the early 1930s it looked as though a full-time teaching job at the conservatory was finally going to materialize (Schenker had long coveted such a position). Presumably, for such teaching Schenker would need a textbook. Controversy arose among his students, however, as to whether *HL* was in fact still usable at all in this capacity, or whether a revision and abridgement of it was appropriate. Having worked through *HL* in great detail before studying with Schenker in 1911–12, the composer and musicologist Otto Vrieslander (1880–1950) suggested and ultimately spearheaded the effort to revise *HL* into a text for Schenker's teaching. Thus the revised edition was first conceived to be for German speakers. But the conservatory teaching position never materialized, Vrieslander never completed the edition, Schenker died in 1935, and the annexation of Austria by the Nazis in 1938 and World War II brought *HL*'s European history to an abrupt end.[16] During this same time, however, Schenker's ideas were beginning to generate passionate interest in the US. Thus we take up the problem first of editing *HL* into something from which Schenker could teach a class in Vienna, and then of translating a theory whose vocabulary, while richly resonant in its original language (though apparently not the native language

---

15. Some may argue that Schoenberg's *Harmonielehre* is as much an outlier, but in fact, completely unlike Schenker, who heaped criticism on the traditional theory of harmony and its proponents, Schoenberg sought to emphasize his connection to the current theory and the music it purported to represent. Indeed, before the crucial chapter rejecting the notion of "non-harmonic" tones (chapter 17), the book is really quite conventional. Only then does it turn out that virtually any pitch-class collection-type can be a "chord." Schenker presents a view of "harmony" totally different from any source after Rameau of which we know, right from the beginning of his book.

16. *HL* continued to be available sporadically after its initial appearance. Universal Edition (UE) reissued the book in 1921, but from unsold stocks they had received from Cotta. The book seems to have gone out of print by the late 1920s, one reason for the interest in a new edition. More than thirty years after the end of the war, in 1978, UE finally issued a photo-reprint of the original (except for the title page and advertising material at the end) along with an introduction by Rudolf Frisius. This version went through further printings in 1992 and 2003, indicating continued demand for the work.

of its author!—a potential cause of difficulties in translation), was sufficiently far removed from traditional music-theoretical discourse that the whole matter of translation became problematic: it used some of the same words, but their meanings had changed considerably. The big question was—and still is—should one translate such words, preserve them as new terms, or coin yet more terms to denote the concepts behind them? We take up the problem of translation in the latter part of chapter 5, though we cannot claim to have solved it once and for all.

In broaching this topic, a note on the translations in this book is appropriate. Whenever we have used a passage from *HL* translated by Elisabeth Mann Borgese, the section number in *HL* is given, along with the precise page in *HA*; if we use a translation of hers, but edit it beyond her translation of terms (e.g., changing "scale step" to "essential harmony" for *Stufe*), that is also indicated. If no citation of an English-language source is given, the translation is ours. Though Wason assumes ultimate responsibility for all translations in this book, otherwise uncredited, the authors often considered controversial matters of translation together. The translation of terms is an excellent case in point. Both authors are convinced that such terms must be translated, rather than passing off the interpretation to the poor reader, who is turning to a translation, after all, in hopes of learning what the author "meant" by the text in question! It is our contention that the most important role of the translator is to offer the reader a comprehensible interpretation of the text in idiomatic English that stays as close to the original as possible. There are two further points in the translation of terminology to emphasize. Firstly, Wason believes that the translation of terms must be flexible, based upon the different shades of meaning that the term may assume in the original text, particularly in an early text like *HL*, in which Schenker had yet to develop a large repertoire of terms: a one-to-one equivalence may not—and likely is not—possible. The most egregious example of an all-purpose term is *Stufe*, to which we devote extended discussion. Secondly, Brown is convinced that the translation of a term must take into account the role that the term plays in the overall theory in which it appears. Surprisingly, we were often able to honor both points of view in our translation of terms. Readers will have to judge for themselves whether we are successful as they consider the discussion of translation in chapter 5.

Beyond the matter of translation, chapter 5 also recounts the convoluted story of *HA*, the existence of two different translations and their very different approaches, and the eventual publication of *HA*. In our assessment, we get to see our remarks on translation in action in comparison and judgement of the two. For the participants, the question of just what should be translated was of great importance: the original *HL*, or a revised (i.e., abridged) edition?—a question that provoked great controversy between *HA*'s editor and its first translator. Schenker's student Oswald Jonas (1897–1978) took charge of the project in the US and produced the final edition. Either he or his student Ernst Oster (1908–77) engaged the first translator, Arthur Waldeck (1899–1965). An acquaintance of Oster's clearly steeped in Schenker's ideas, Waldeck surely was brought to Jonas's attention by Oster. Waldeck seems to have been against the idea of producing an abridgement from the beginning, for his letters to Jonas are filled with impassioned pleas to reinstate his favorite passages that Jonas had cut. This disagreement is certainly one reason—though not the most important one—that a second translator, Elisabeth Mann Borgese (1918–2002), was ultimately engaged to redo the whole project, starting, apparently, from Waldeck's marked-up complete translation—marked with circled passages of text, examples and tables and the remark "omit." The content of *HA* as it finally emerged in published form was thus strongly influenced by the editorial philosophy espoused by Jonas's "interventionist" editing of text, and was consistent with his and his teacher's editing of music, which may be gleaned from musical editions made by both. Thus Schenker and Jonas may have agreed to a considerable extent with the latter's plans for *HL*, but it is unlikely that Schenker would have liked the end result.

Chapter 6 rounds off the volume by continuing to explore the connection between Schenker's efforts to revive the Classical definition of harmony and Aristotle's defense of organicism and associationism in the *Poetics*. In particular, it shows how Schenker applied such ideas to instrumental music of the common-practice period, works that do not have any obvious extramusical or "extrinsic" associations. He did so by suggesting that musical material becomes associative by means of motives and repetition. The chapter then shows how Schenker used these ideas not only to shed light on what he saw as a decline in the state of musical composition at the turn of the twentieth century, but also on what he regarded as a similar decline in the explanatory power of contemporary music theory. Music theorists are still grappling with the implications of such bold ideas.

Finally, the two appendixes present, for the first time, English translations of two unpublished essays by Schenker that are essential to an understanding of the earlier stages of Schenker's Theory of Harmony as it existed in 1906.

To paraphrase the opening of Schoenberg's *Harmonielehre*, we have learned this book from one another.[17] We cannot guarantee that our very different interests in Schenker's work and areas of research do not occasionally come into conflict, but we believe that our different points of view have made this a much more interesting book than it would have been had one of us written it alone.

The project has been long in the making. While our interest in *HL* reaches back to work we have both done since the late 1970s and early 1980s (see the bibliography), the more immediate origin of the project is the paper that Wason presented at the International Conference on the dissemination of Schenker's Theories ("*Schenker-Traditionen*"), held in Vienna in June 2003. We thank Martin Eybl for conceiving and organizing that conference, and for suggesting to Wason that he return to *HL* as a topic for it.[18] It was during preparation of that presentation that Wason first confronted [DTS] as a result of reading Robert Kosovsky's introduction to the microfilm of OC (as well as his article in *Schenker Studies II*).[19] We thank him for that work and for further help in accessing the original manuscripts. In writing about the origin of *HA* in the article that arose from the conference presentation, Wason was aided immeasurably by an extensive critique of his account by Heribert Esser. That corrected history formed the basis of the one presented in his earlier article, and is elaborated considerably now in chapter 5.[20] Not only did Esser fill out missing events in the history, but he also granted his permission to quote from materials in his possession, for which we also owe him our heartfelt thanks. Hedi Siegel, a fellow participant in the Vienna Conference, who apparently knows where to find most anything having to do with Schenker in New York City, provided many invaluable suggestions

---

17. Schoenberg, *Harmonielehre*, Vorwort, "Dieses Buch habe ich von meinen Schülern gelernt." This sentence opens the discussion of some of the pitfalls of translating from German to English that we take up in chapter 5.

18. Eybl also brought the Hinterberger catalogue of Schenker's personal library to our attention by reprinting it in his book, *Ideologie und Methode*. It demonstrates that Schenker was well aware of important works in the history of harmonic theory, and we refer to it frequently in this book. Two copies of the catalogue also may be found in OJ.

19. Robert Kosovsky, "Levels of Understanding"; see 7–8 in particular.

20. Cf. Wason, "From *Harmonielehre* to *Harmony*." Though beholden to this earlier essay in some respects, chapter 5, mainly conceived by Brown, updates the older account by adding new historical background available more recently. Further, its topical organization and discussion of editing (Brown) and translating (Wason) are completely new, as is the comparison of the two translations of *HL*.

regarding this work then and beyond, alerting Wason to the Waldeck translation of *HL*, for example. The translation of [DTS] began to take shape in 2007 as a class assignment in a research seminar Wason gave at the Eastman School of Music of the University of Rochester. Our thanks go to that class for their work on the first draft of the translation, and for prompting Wason to think through the problems of both translation and content that arose from it. In the summer of 2011, he began to study the handwritten version and its relationship to the typescript more carefully. This stage of the work turned out to be a family affair: his wife, Barbara McIver, transcribed the typescript, and his daughter, Julia Cook (now his editor!), compared the handwritten copy and the typescript closely and developed the annotated transcription on which the final translation is based. A "thank you" is hardly sufficient for the time they spent on this. The companion to [DTS], WEG, only came to our attention late in this project. Fortunately, it fitted right in with prior research, confirming many of the ideas we had begun to develop regarding Schenker's research on melody. We thank Nicholas Marston here and again in appendix A because without his generous offer to let us use his transcription as the basis of our translation, the project would have been delayed, and the translation would surely have been inferior to what we present here. He also sent us a pre-publication proof of his essay "'. . . nur ein Gleichnis'" that helped greatly in our work, and he offered wise counsel (and warnings) concerning Schenker's essay. During various stages of the work on the many German-language sources cited in this book Wason was able to call on colleagues for advice regarding translation; in particular, we thank Wolf Kittler, Michael Metzger, and Hartmut Schick for their advice on various problematic passages. Lytton Smith generously offered suggestions of sources on the art of translation. Our Eastman colleague, Reinhild Steingröver, has tackled numerous problems of translation throughout the writing of this book (and earlier), and deserves our special thanks for always being there when we needed her. Finally, Lee Rothfarb, a friend and colleague of Wason's for more than forty years, continues to provide advice to him on German translation as he has throughout their friendship. Besides that topic, he offered other ideas that improved all aspects of this book, right down to a pre-publication review of the completed manuscript. We cannot think him enough for his numerous—and generous—suggestions.

Ian Bent read much of the material on [DTS], written earlier, and provided valuable advice then, as he continues to do now. As one of the "editors-in-chief" of *SDO* and an extraordinarily prolific editor and translator in the project himself, he has a vast knowledge of the context for *Harmonielehre* that we are all very lucky to be able to draw on. The other editor in charge of *SDO*, William Drabkin, the editor of the translations of *TW* and *MW* that are essential to our work, was earlier to be a part of this project, but was forced to withdraw due to very difficult personal circumstances. He wrote a helpful review of [FTS], and provided advice in formative stages of this project. We miss his presence here. John Koslovsky's dissertation work (which we co-advised) prompted us both to think about many of the relevant problems, and the resulting dissertation made us even more aware of the importance of Felix Salzer to Anglo-American Schenker reception. It was vital to our work in the history of early twentieth-century musicology as well. Wason's advising of Rothfarb's excellent translation of Ernst Kurth's first work proved to be essential to his work in the history of music theory as a whole: the advisor learned at least as much as the advisee.[21] At the end of that career, Daphne Tan's PhD dissertation work with him on Kurth's last work, *Musikpsychologie*, his other "bookend" to advising, brought him back to the history of psychology at the turn of the twentieth century, which he had engaged briefly in a translation of Hugo Riemann's classic essay on the topic.[22] The work with Tan proved to be excellent preparation for considering many of the issues that Schenker faced in this area, which we take up in chapters 1 and 4.

Our Eastman colleague, William Marvin, read many partial drafts and offered excellent advice. We thank Daniel Ketter for his research and reading of drafts. Our profound thanks also go to Frank Samarotto, who, on reading an earlier version of the manuscript, suggested some excellent strategies for reorganization that heavily influenced the final form of the book. This would not have been the book that it is now without his reading.

We thank the staff of the University of Rochester Press, and especially Ralph Locke and Julia Cook, for their patience, counsel, and excellent work on a large and demanding project. The staffs of the archives, libraries, and publishers we consulted were of great assistance in our work. David Peter Coppen, Special Collections Librarian and Archivist at the Sibley Library of the Eastman School graciously made arrangements to photograph sources used in chapter 3, and the tables and examples from *HL* in appendix C. This work was carried out excellently by Gail Lowther, with additional photography by Michelle

---

21. "Ernst Kurth's *The Requirements for a Theory of Harmony*: An Annotated Translation with an Introductory Essay," master's thesis, Hartt College of Music, University of Hartford, 1979.
22. Robert W. Wason and Elizabeth West Marvin, "Riemann's "Ideen zu einer 'Lehre von den Tonvorstellungen': An Annotated Translation."

Martorell. Permission to print these tables and other sources held under copyright by Universal Edition was secured with the kind assistance of Caroline Kane, Vice President of Licensing and Administration of Schott Music Corporation & European American Music Distributors Company. We also thank Christine Busch and Olms Verlag, who granted us permission to paraphrase parts of Wason's earlier article on the genesis of *HA*. Jenny Swadosh, Associate Archivist of Archives and Special Collections at the New School went well beyond the call of duty, actively engaging in the comparison of the two copies of the Waldeck translation of *HL* in their possession, for which we thank her with great pleasure. We thank the staff of the Library of University of California, Riverside, for excellent work providing reproductions of items from OJ. Thanks should also go to Christopher Winders for engraving many of the examples for us and to the Eastman Professional Development Committee and the Department of Music Theory for their generous financial support.

The following figures and examples are used with the kind permission of European American Music Distributors Company, US and Canadian agent for Universal Edition Vienna: figure 2.1a, from Heinrich Schenker, *Harmonielehre* (Vienna: Universal Edition, 1906), par. 88, p. 204; figure 2.10, from J. S. Bach, *Chromatische Phantasie und Fugue*, ed. Heinrich Schenker (Vienna: Universal, 1909), example 30; and example 2.15a and b, from Heinrich Schenker, *Der freie Satz*, figures 154.4 and 114.8, copyright 1935 by Universal Edition Vienna, copyright renewed, all rights reserved.

Figure 3.6b appears as figure 2 (p. xviii) in Gioseffo Zarlino, *On the Modes; Part Four of "Le Istitutioni Harmoniche,"* 1558, Vered Cohen, tr. and Claude V. Palisca ed. and intro. (New Haven: Yale University Press, 1983), copyright 1983 by Yale University. Figures 5.9, 5.10a and b, 5.11, and 5.12a and b are from "Arthur Waldeck Papers Related to Heinrich Schenker," at The New School Archives and Special Collections, The New School, New York, NY.

Finally, we owe a huge debt to modern computing, the world wide web (without which the indispensable—and seemingly inexhaustible—*Schenker Documents Online* would not exist), and the extraordinarily large number of primary sources available in original texts on the web, often computer-searchable. This study would have been impossible without it—and them.

꧁ ꧁ ꧁

The main purpose of this book is to provide context we regard as necessary for the reading of *HA*, much of which has not been available to now. This, in itself, may need justification, for there has been some controversy over the broader context—if any—in which Schenker's works should be read. Obviously, we would not have written this book if we completely agreed with John Rothgeb, who "urge[s] the reader to recognize that however much Schenker may have regarded his musical precepts as an integral part of a unified world-view, they are, in fact, not at all logically dependent on any of his extramusical speculations. *Indeed, no broader philosophical context is necessary—or even relevant—to their understanding.*"[23]

Of course, Rothgeb is reacting to Schenker's more infamous political asides that embarrassed Rothgeb's teacher Oswald Jonas (and others of the first generation of Schenker's students), and did little to endear Schenker and his work to a skeptical musicological community in the US. In the present work we confine ourselves to Schenker's music theory, and agree with Rothgeb that a book on harmony, since it emerges from a relatively clear tradition—and Schenker was well up on many works in that tradition, as we shall see—has many components that are directly understandable without extramusical context. Indeed, Schenker would urge that we "let the tones speak for themselves" through his theory. Nonetheless, we hope that the history of the theory of harmony presented in chapters 2, 3, and 4 sets these technical elements in greater perspective, and that we have pointed out some newly discovered resonances throughout the historical discussion. With this discussion, we also hope to have demonstrated just how original Schenker was in *HL*—a point often lost, as he is regarded as a "conservative" (or worse) who only wrote about music "of the past."

The language in which a theory of harmony is presented is another matter, however, and *HL* does present such a theory. That language is often resonant with other intellectual endeavors of the time or earlier. Here we definitely need context to read the book as an educated reader at the time would have—particularly in the case of *HL*, which, for a book on "harmony," is intellectually eclectic and unusually structured in the extreme. Since about 1980, scholars have been exploring many influences on Schenker's work as a whole in an attempt to build that context, and this scholarship has been vital to us in our preparation for writing this book. However, we do not summarize the work here (though it certainly informs our discussion), for it has already been synthesized most ably.[24] Rather, we explore contexts that are less familiar. Since we are particularly interested in Schenker's early work in a

---

23. Schenker, *CP1*, Translator's introduction (our emphasis).
24. See Cook, *The Schenker Project*, passim. Also see the review by Korsyn, "Schenker's Vienna."

traditional genre, we explore the book's status within the history of harmonic theory. Just what effect might that history have had on his own thinking? *HL* is also his first major work of music theory, written when his student years were not that far behind him, and thus we delve into his Austrian education as part of his preparation for writing it.[25] Finally, our book is directed to Anglo-American readers, many of whom are familiar only with *HA*, and thus the discussion of *HL*'s transformation into *HA* is an essential part of the story. Investigation of the position *HL* holds in the history of harmonic theory and the birth of *HA* probably need no further defense here. But what may seem to some to be a rather narrow focus on Schenker's education perhaps needs some additional justification.

In that regard, the work of the German philosopher and educational reformer, Johann Friedrich Herbart (1776–1841), Kant's successor in Königsberg, and the philosopher "most widely taught in Austria between 1820 and 1880," was fundamental, and not nearly as well known as it should be by scholars of music outside of German-speaking lands.[26] Schenker's *Gymnasium* education included a course in Herbart's work in psychology in the final year. The coursebook Schenker studied is known, and connections of his music theory to it are also apparent. In fact, psychology was one of the most important parts of Herbart's educational philosophy, permeating the (state-mandated) Austrian *Gymnasium* curriculum throughout. Talk of psychology certainly continued during Schenker's legal training, for Herbart's student Robert Zimmermann, the writer of a *Gymnasium* text on psychology himself, was Schenker's professor of "practical philosophy," and the primary Austrian Herbartian.[27] Moreover, the whole psychologically oriented

---

25. We know quite a bit about Schenker's education now through the work of Alpern and, most recently, Rothfarb. See Alpern, "Music Theory as a Mode of Law," and "The Triad of the True, the Good, and the Beautiful," and Rothfarb, "Henryk Szenker."

26. See Johnston, *The Austrian Mind*, 281. We have only found one English translation of Herbart, and a dated one at that, though it is certainly relevant to Schenker's education: see Herbart, *A Text-Book in Psychology*. For an introduction to Herbart, Brentano, and the beginnings of empirical psychology, see Huemer and Landerer, "Mathematics, experience and laboratories."

27. To the extent that Zimmermann is known in the English-speaking world, it is mainly for his pioneering history of aesthetics, and his treatise on aesthetics as a "theory of forms." See his *History of Aesthetics,* and *General Aesthetics.* Also see the translation of selections from the latter work in Bujić, *Music in European Thought*, 40–50. Rothfarb, "Nineteenth-Century Formalism," focuses on Herbart as a formalist, and the development of his ideas by Zimmermann; see especially 176–86.

philosophy of Franz Brentano, the main philosopher at the University of Vienna (and co-founder of the University of Vienna Philosophical Society where Schenker read GEIST as a lecture), very likely suggested the move into psychology of the famous physicist Ernst Mach (the other co-founder of the society), and certainly led to Christian von Ehrenfells and early gestaltism.[28] All of this forms an important backdrop to Schenker's thinking in *HL*.[29] On the other hand, Schenker's historicist legal education helped in the forming of a mind that always thought of the historical implications of a music theory.[30] And from the music-theoretical point of view, it provided Schenker with a way of thinking about music-theoretical "laws" in *HL* that was quite different from the notion of "law" other theorists of the time drew from the natural sciences. Even Schenker's anthropomorphizing of the tones can be understood in light of his legal studies. Following Hanslick in his belief that music was about the "tones themselves," he attempted to formulate laws governing their behavior that were likewise intramusical, often drawing ideas from the historical school of jurisprudence to inform his music theory, thereby transforming social theory into music theory. In short, Schenker's Austrian education left a deep mark on his music theory.

Schenker's work in music theory got underway with GEIST five years after he had completed his law degree, and thus during a time in which his secondary and university education—and post-university "continuing education" in Vienna—if not fresh in his memory, were still arguably of importance in influencing the language of his music theory. Some of that influence wore off the farther Schenker got from those events, and the more he developed his own ideas about music theory and a technical language in which to express them. But in the reading of Schenker's first work, there can be little doubt of the importance of the context we explore below.

---

28. Korsyn has made extremely significant contributions in this area, regarding both Schenker's connection to Ernst Mach and to psychological research at the University of Vienna. See his "Schenker's Organicism Reconsidered," section V, 109–16, and his review of Cook, 164–69.

29. For Brentano's thinking in the context of the Vienna Circle and the dominant fields of phenomenology and analytical philosophy, see Huemer, "Brentano's Conception of Philosophy as Rigorous Science."

30. We are indebted to Blasius, *Schenker's Argument*, for pioneering work in both psychological and historical thinking in *HL*.

Note on Online Material

Three additional appendixes to our book can be found online at https://boydellandbrewer.com/series/eastman-studies-in-music/heinrich-schenker-s-conception-of-harmony-hb.html. Appendixes C and D are designed to provide the material excised from *HL* in the preparation of *HA*. Appendix C consists of all text, musical examples that go with that text and are discussed in detail, and the missing tables. The points at which these text segments may be inserted into *HA* are clearly marked. Appendix D is a list of the many musical examples in *HL* missing in *HA*, perhaps the main reason for the striking difference in size of the two books.

Appendix E contains Heinrich Hinterberger's catalogue of Schenker's books on music, among which is listed his books on music theory. All too often it has been assumed that Schenker had minimal interest in works on music theory other than the canonical texts he mentions, such as Fux's *Gradus ad Parnassum* or C. P. E. Bach's *Versuch*. Appendix E shows that his interests were far broader than previously assumed, and that he owned a number of books that are quite suggestive in light of his own theorizing, including, for example, all of the most important works of Kirnberger, and even of Sechter. We consult Hinterberger's Catalogue frequently in the text below.

Part One

Harmonielehre

Figure 1.1. E. De Morgan, *Cadmus and Harmonia*, 1877. © akg-images. Used with permission.

Chapter One

The Eclectic Intellectual Methodology of Schenker's Theory of Harmony (1906)

Introduction: Schenker's Reaction to the Classical Theory of Harmony

The original notion of "harmony"—the Classical idea—and the word denoting it, descend from "Harmonia" (Roman counterpart, "Concordia"), who, according to ancient Greek legend, was the illegitimate child of Aphrodite, the beautiful goddess of love and pleasure, and the handsome Ares, god of war and warriors.[1] She was the progeny of this stormy "union of opposites," and in that sense epitomizes this ancient idea: the element or elements that hold a complex system—such as a piece of tonal music, to place the notion in a modern context—together and make it work. She appears here in a wonderfully idealized rendering by the British painter, Evelyn De Morgan (1855–1919), the painting entitled *Cadmus and Harmonia*. According to one version of the legend, Cadmus, Harmonia's husband, was turned into a snake by Ares, though of course this pairing of the beautiful maiden with the snake surely suggested Eve in the Garden of Eden as well in nineteenth-century Britain. When De Morgan, some thirteen years Schenker's senior, painted this work (one of her earliest, done in 1877), she was associated with the later phase of the Pre-Raphaelite movement. In its synthesis of antiquity and modernity it was not unlike the later Viennese *Jugendstil* movement in the fine arts, crafts, and architecture that surrounded Schenker during the period

---

1. Robert Graves, *The Greek Myths*, 18.a.9 (67); 198–99: "Cadmus and Harmonia." Also see Simon Hornblower, Antony Spawforth, and Esther Eidinow, eds., *Oxford Classical Dictionary*, s.v. "Ares."

he was contemplating his research in melody and writing his *Harmonielehre*. Nor is Schenker's book, in *its* approach to harmony, unlike this synthesis.

The word *harmonia* (ἁρμονια) was also present in the everyday language of ancient Greece. In common parlance, it came to mean a joining of things, such as the planks of a ship, or even the joint itself. By extension, the word could refer to a framework, thereby giving rise to its philosophical meaning of a framework for the universe itself. In a similar vein, *harmonia* was also used to refer to a social or political consensus (cf. Latin, *concordia*), a meaning well known to Schenker, the lawyer.[2] This usage, which encompasses the process of joining and that of a framework, is analogous to the word's musical meaning—an analogy basic to much of Schenker's language in *HL*. Like Harmonia herself, musical harmony to the Greeks was the means by which disparate (and perhaps even *contradictory*) parts of a larger whole were made to work in harmony with one another, and thus the idea is closely related to Schenker's notions of "synthesis," "unity," or even the much-debated "organicism," all of which stress the cohesion of compelling works of art, and certainly of the musical works in the Schenkerian canon.[3]

Yet, it is a commonplace that the theory of harmony today is centered on the study of "chords." How did that happen? What harmony book is not? Indeed, what musician has not studied from one of these chord books? After all, counterpoint, we are often told, deals with simultaneously occurring melodies, while harmony deals with chords. But in fact neither of these definitions is historically correct: counterpoint (a term that only arose in the middle ages) originally had to do with the regulation of successions of intervals, or two-part chords that controlled the melodies, while *harmonia*, for the ancient Greeks, had to do, in a musical context, with tones in "harmonious relationships"—specifically, favored ratios and proportions between measurements of tones, *in melodies*. This is what we call, in the present work, the

---

2. Liddell and Scott, *A Greek-English Lexicon*, 244. The primary meanings are set out more directly in Liddell and Scott's *An Intermediate Greek-English Lexicon*, 118.
3. Pastille writes that he finds only one instance each of the words *organisch* and *Organismus* in *HL*. (See Pastille, "Heinrich Schenker, Anti-Organicist," 33.) Twenty-five years later, a computer search of the text yielded four instances of *organisch* and two of *Organismus*, but we take Pastille's point. We contend that more important than the use of these terms is, as Marston points out ("'. . . nur ein Gleichnis,'" 7), Schenker's emphasis on the "biological nature of tones," which he emphasizes near the beginning of the "Vorwort" of *HL*. Indeed, the anthropomorphizing of the tones—providing them with agency—is essential to Schenker's argument almost everywhere.

"Classical theory of harmony," sometimes attributed to Pythagoras (sixth century BCE), and passed along and developed further by Plato (late fifth to mid-fourth century BCE), and various later writers heavily indebted to both. The notion of a chord of more than two parts did not arise until the sixteenth century, with the dawning of "triadic consciousness," and the idea that the "harmonic series" was influential on musical structure.[4] The "chord of nature" had arrived—almost. With the advent of the figured bass in the seventeenth century and the Modern Theory of Harmony in the eighteenth, the new theory of chords based on triads attempted to account for "dissonant chords" as well—usually chords of four or more notes. This was a particularly controversial turn of events—and one that Schenker soon rejected—given that harmony originally referred to the ratios of consonant intervals and their conjoining into consonant proportions. Dissonant harmonies? Certainly an oxymoron to many, and especially to Schenker.

That the Classical *idea* of harmony also had a much broader currency was not lost on Schenker, who went through a thorough Classical education at the *Gymnasium* level, reinforced by his legal education in Vienna, which centered on Roman law (all read in the original Latin texts) for the first two years (see chapter 4).[5] But, we might counter, Schenker's Classical education did not center on music, though the topic may have arisen occasionally. Did he *know* that the Classical theory of (musical) harmony was completely

---

4. The notion of sympathetic resonance is adumbrated in the fourth-century BCE Aristotelian "Problems," book XIX, 4.20–24. But it was not until the beginnings of the Scientific Revolution in the mid-sixteenth century that the mysteries of the harmonic series really began to be unraveled. The final proof of its existence via experimentation did not occur until the end of the seventeenth century.

5. Of course, this was a standard public education (in the *Gymnasium* track) in the German-speaking countries during the nineteenth century (and elsewhere on the continent), but easy for us to forget in the twenty-first, as language-learning and knowledge of Classical culture have declined considerably. The education in Classical languages and literatures was basic in Britain as well, of course, going well into the twentieth century. W. H. Auden writes in his introduction to *The Portable Greek Reader* (New York: Viking Press, 1948), 2: "Until near the end of the eighteenth century, Europe thought of itself less as Europe than as Western Christendom, the heir to the Roman Empire, and its educational system based on the study of Latin. The rise of Hellenic studies to an equal and then a superior position was a nineteenth century phenomenon and coincided with the development of European nations and nationalist feelings."

different from the one he was taught by Bruckner in the late 1880s? In fact, we know that he did by 1895 at the latest:

> I am prepared to restore to the word harmony (which the Greeks were the first to use) what was and still is its original and finest meaning. By harmony the imaginative Greeks understood *the melody itself*, that is, the succession of tones as a whole, *together with all the particular elements at work in that succession* [our emphasis]. In this broad sense, the concept of harmony ceased to exist quite some time ago, yet even today the concept seems to strive innately toward the broad significance that it had for the Greeks at the start of its existence. All too often we forget that every succession of tones, every melody, carries its own harmonic credo within itself, and that it expresses this conviction autonomously.[6]

Thus, to understand harmony, one must search for it first in melody, and that is exactly what Schenker does when he introduces the concepts of the triad and essential harmony (*Stufe*) in *HL*.[7] But what exactly are "all the particular elements at work in that [melodic] succession"? Here it becomes clear that Schenker does not reject the modern theory *in toto*, for in *HL* the melody's clear projection of a (major) *triad* (but *not* a minor triad—the product of the artist, and not nature) is the most important element that may be attributed to nature. This is something the Greeks totally ignored in their melodic analyses (though triads do occur occasionally in ancient Greek melodies), for their favored ratios did not include those of thirds and sixths, and the structure of the explanation was vital to their thinking. Moreover, Schenker's "essential harmonies" are necessarily consonant triads as well (both major and minor), and a melody may "compose out" (a term used for the first time in *HL*) a triad, forming an essential harmony. And then there is the generation of triads of the key, embodied in the "system" in which a piece is composed. That idea of system—a topic broached at the beginning of *HL*—goes back to the Greeks too, but without triads, the essential piece of the musical puzzle they were missing. Nor did they have the notion of the motive, invented by the artist—the phenomenon of the greatest importance for the historical development of music as an art, and the other topic with which Schenker opens *HL*. The consequence is that Schenker announces immediately in no uncertain terms (*HL* §1) that while poetry and the visual and

---

6. SPIRIT, 325.
7. *HL*, §§76–83, "Stufe und Harmonielehre," 176–98; *HA*, 133–53. See chapter 2 and chapter 5 for discussion of our translation of the problematic *Stufe*.

dramatic arts of the ancient Greeks survived as models for later art forms, ancient Greek music did not rise to the level of art—a point on which he had vacillated in GEIST, though, in WEG, he comes to the idea that music as an art only began to develop in the sixteenth century, admitting, however, that there were "positive signs" earlier. In his view, the primary problem with Greek music was that it remained associated with poetry and dance and never developed independently.[8] Nonetheless, though neither the triadicity of melody nor the motive stem from the Greeks, both are essentially melodic, and, in that sense, in the Greek tradition, updated with the triad drawn from the modern theory: Schenker's *HL* is only coincidentally about chords, to coin an apt phrase; they are byproducts of melodic phenomena.[9]

Not surprisingly, Federhofer writes that GEIST was part of a "History of Melody" (*Geschichte der Melodie*), a project Schenker worked on in the 1890s, intending to propose it to Hanslick, with whom he was on good terms.[10] Federhofer also cautions that the whereabouts of the part of that study not taken over into GEIST are unknown.[11] Notwithstanding his caution, we claim that Schenker never really gave up on the idea, but rather transformed it—and probably at least some of his *Geschichte der Melodie* text—into the basis of *HL*. Recognizing the melodic basis of *HL* is essential in sorting out the early history of Schenker's turn to music theory.

The broader philosophical context of the Classical theory also finds its way into *HL*. For example, Schenker embraced the mimetic theory of art,

---

8. There are in fact examples of ancient Greek "absolute music," though they are associated with programs, the musical support of which is essentially onomatopoeic. Schenker likely would not have approved, had he known them.

9. We note the agreement with Hanslick, who writes that "*melody* rules primarily as the fundamental form of musical beauty." See Hanslick, *On the Musically Beautiful*, 40.

10. Evidence that he actually did so is lacking. It is clear from correspondence from Hanslick to Schenker in OJ they were on good terms, but correspondence from Schenker to Hanslick is lacking, and apparently Hanslick's *Nachlass* was destroyed by his widow. See Federhofer, *HS*, 12.

11. A note on both the first installment of the serialized publication of GEIST and on an offprint of the whole essay says that part of it formed the contents of a lecture given to the University of Vienna Philosophical Society (see chapter 4), and that the rest of it "remains in manuscript." Federhofer continues, "Whether the remaining section of the essay as indicated, which has not been bequeathed to us by the *Nachlass*, has been worked into his later publications, can only be conjectured." *HS*, 12ff.

transmitted most famously and influentially by Aristotle (fourth century BCE) in the *Poetics*: art is an "imitation" (or "representation") of nature.[12] In WEG, Schenker investigates the notions of model and "imitation" (or "likeness"—even "analogy"), thereby setting up the technical requirements of motivic composition, a product of the artist. Indeed, in WEG he emphasizes the pride that humanity should take in their creation of music, which does not depend on any likeness with nature, but rather internalizes the use of likeness. Music is thus a "second nature" (a point also made in [DTS]), that enhances nature. In *HL* he broadens this to the notion that art consists of "ideas *associated* with nature *or* reality" (our emphasis), thereby providing room for the motive in the aesthetic world of the *Poetics*, for the motive is not the product of nature, but of human reality—and most importantly, of the artist. The basic idea of "association" likewise comes ultimately from Aristotle, though Schenker would have been thoroughly indoctrinated in it as a result of going through the Austrian educational system, where it was ubiquitous: all elements of an art must be associated with corresponding elements in nature or reality. And all education takes place through association. The problem, of course, is music's association with the external world. Schenker discusses this throughout the first four sections of WEG, concluding that music's use of likeness is purely internal, brought about by motives.[13] In the last section he turns to program music, but demands that the technique of internal likeness be maintained for music to achieve the status of art; external, programmatic likenesses are thus an add-on to absolute music.

The notion that likeness or association in music is a purely intramusical affair, and thus very different from such phenomena in any of the other arts, is the main reason why Schenker must provide the tones with agency: thus the motive, in Schenker's view, often behaves like the protagonist of a drama. Indeed, Schenker's notion of the motive and its treatment often invokes the drama. And his preference for unity in motivic writing is consistent with Aristotle's advice about construction of a dramatic plot.[14] In writing about the appropriate treatment of the motive and its associations, Schenker emphasizes that "from the infinity of situations into which his motive could conceivably fall, [the composer] must choose only a few. These, however, must be so chosen that the motive is forced to reveal in them its

---

12. Aristotle, *Poetics*, tr. and ed. Heath. See "Poetry as a Species of Imitation," section 2, 3–6.
13. Appendix A.
14. Aristotle, *Poetics*, tr. and ed. Heath, 15.

character in all its aspects and peculiarities."[15] The parallel with Aristotle's ideas is clear: "When [Homer] wrote the *Odyssey*, he did not include everything which happened to Odysseus ... instead he constructed the *Odyssey* about a single action of the kind we are discussing."[16] Schenker goes on to provide examples of just what Schiller did not include in his "Wallenstein" trilogy to make the analogy between the motive and the protagonist of a play that much clearer. His concentration on compositions of the "geniuses" also parallels Aristotle's concentration only on works of Homer, Aeschylus, and Sophocles. Moreover, the list of historical figures associated with Greek music that Schenker provides in WEG, who were nonetheless unable to rescue music from its inferior status, runs Orpheus, Marsyas,[17] Homer, Aeschylus, Sophocles, Pythagoras, Aristotle and Aristoxenus.[18] Given that Schenker cites "Homer, Aeschylus, and Sophocles" as the only three literary figures, he remembered his Aristotle exceptionally well.

Though Aristotle accepted the dependence on ratios and proportions of the Classical theory of harmony,[19] he was skeptical of its extension to the

---

15. *HL*, §6, 20; *HA*, 13. Schenker follows Hanslick in this regard: "Like the principal character of a novel, the composer places the theme into the most diverse contexts and environments, into the most varying outcomes and moods" (*On the Musically Beautiful*, trans. Rothfarb and Landerer, 113–14). See Maus, "Hanslick's Animism," especially p. 279, and the surrounding discussion. Also see below, particularly our treatment of the psychological and legal arguments in HL. It is beyond the scope of this study to review the sizable literature on action and agency, but Monahan's "Action and Agency Revisited" is particularly helpful.
16. Aristotle, *Poetics*, tr. and ed. Heath, 15.
17. "Marsyas found the aulos (double pipe) that the goddess Athena had invented and thrown away and, after becoming skilled in playing it, challenged Apollo to a contest with his lyre. The victory was awarded to Apollo, who tied Marsyas to a tree and flayed him." *Encyclopedia Britannica,* https://www.britannica.com/topic/Marsyas-Greek-mythology (accessed May 7, 2019).
18. See appendix A.
19. "For ... one cannot prove by ... any other science the theorems of a different one, except such as are so related to one another that the one is under the other—e.g. optics to geometry and harmonics to arithmetic." From "Posterior Analytics," Bekker 75b14–17, Barnes, ed., *Aristotle*, vol. 1, 122. "Neither [optics nor harmonics] considers its objects *qua* light-ray or *qua* voice, but *qua* lines and numbers; but the latter are attributes proper of the former." From *Metaphysics*, book XIII, Bekker 1078a13–16; Barnes, ed., *Aristotle*, vol. II, 1704.

celestial realm.[20] No writing dedicated exclusively to music by him has survived, but many comments on music exist in works dealing nominally with other subjects.[21] Most important, the first treatise on music theory in the Western canon that we have is an *Elementa Harmonica* (Elements of Harmonics) by Aristoxenus of Tarentum (b. ca. 375 BCE; fl. 335 BCE), Aristotle's student. Its subject is essentially *melos* (melodic composition), of which *harmonia* forms an important part.[22] In contrast to his teacher, Aristoxenus actually rejects the application of mathematics to music, which would have appealed to Schenker, who wrestles with acoustical theory in [DTS] as the primary element of nature, but dedicates most of his theorizing to the products of the artist, and outgrowths of his motivic theory. Aristoxenus also takes a psychological tack in his analysis of *melos* (melody) that Schenker would surely have appreciated. Indeed, Schenker greatly develops that approach to harmony, starting by declaring on the first page of *HL* that "I conceive of the theory of harmony . . . as a world purely of the mind [*eine bloß geistige Welt*], as one of ideally moving forces."[23]

Aristoxenus is the last Greek historical figure on Schenker's list, of course, so it is certain that he was well aware of his importance. In fact, Schenker very likely read his treatise in either the original Greek or German translation (or both) as part of his research in the history of melody: a study by the well-known classicist and writer on ancient Greek music, Rudolf Westphal (1826–92), appeared in 1883, containing a German translation by the author. The second volume containing the original Greek and a Latin

---

20. "It is clear that the theory that the movement of the stars produces a harmony, i.e., that the sounds they make are concordant, in spite of the grace and originality with which it has been stated, is nevertheless untrue." Bekker 290b 12–14. After disposing of the explanation that we are so used to these sounds from birth that we fail to notice them, Aristotle goes on to write that "if the moving bodies are so great, and the sound which penetrates to us is proportionate to their size, that sound must needs reach us in an intensity many times that of thunder, and the force of its action must be immense. Indeed the reason why we do not hear, and show in our bodies none of the effects of violent force, is easily given: it is that there is no noise." From "On the Heavens," Bekker 291a1–6; *Aristotle*, Barnes, ed., vol. 1, 479.
21. For an excellent collection, see Barker, *Greek Musical Writings*, vol. 2, chapter 3, "Aristotle."
22. Aristoxenus, *Elementa Harmonica*, tr. Andrew Barker, in Barker, *Greek Musical Writings*, vol. 2, 126–84; also see Macran, tr., in his *Harmonics of Aristoxenus*, 165–222.
23. *HL*, "Vorwort," V.

translation appeared in 1893, while Schenker's research was probably well underway.[24] In general, Classical thought is one important place to start when studying *HL*, for in rejecting much of the Modern Theory of Harmony, Schenker essentially updated the Classical theory.

The Documents

Schenker's earliest Theory of Harmony is contained in a series of eight documents written between 1895 and 1910, beginning with GEIST, and ending with *KP1*. GEIST, though relatively short on technical music theory, nonetheless is essential in understanding the whole trajectory that *HL* took from its inception for three main reasons. First, it announces Schenker's intention to revisit ancient Greek musical thought; second, it promises to return melody to its central role in the theory of harmony; and third, it devotes considerable attention to the role of repetition, a vital component of motivic and hence melodic activity, which Schenker treats at length in *HL*.[25] Placed in the context of other contemporaneous *Harmonielehren*, all three actions are revolutionary. The second document, WEG, though unrelated to historical theories of harmony, is an investigation into the nature of likeness that very quickly begins to concentrate on the motive as the means of producing it. That topic had come up inevitably in the section on repetition in GEIST, while both motive and repetition are important topics taken up in *HL* §§1–7. Thus, as Marston has pointed out, WEG forms an important intermediary stage between GEIST and *HL*.[26] Parts of the fragmentary and unpublished third document, [DTS], were transformed into the opening chapter of *HL*, §§8–19, and the essay, which contains much of

---

24. See Westphal, *Aristoxenus of Tarentum*. The second volume was edited and published after the author's death by Franz Saren. It contains a Latin translation of the treatise by Antonio Gogava (originally published in Venice in 1562), and the original Greek text. (On problems with Gogava's translation and its reception, see Palisca, *Humanism*, 148–57.) An edition of the original text with English translation, both still well-regarded today, appeared in 1902 (Macran, *Harmonics of Aristoxenus*). Aristoxenus's work was clearly an important topic for classicists of that time.
25. SPIRIT, part II (Cook, *The Schenker Project*, 320–22); *HL*, §4, §5, and passim.
26. Marston starts right off with this claim (with which we certainly agree): "to put it somewhat sensationally, we are dealing with what might well be considered a 'missing link' between [GEIST and *HL*] separated by the decade straddling 1900." See his "'. . . nur ein Gleichnis,'" 1.

interest that was not transferred to *HL*, is the most closely related to the historical theory of harmony. *EBO*, the fourth document on our list, is relevant because it focuses on ornamenting melodies and introduces the concept of group construction (*Gruppenbildung*), a very important component of *HL*, part II. The fifth document is the centerpiece: the finished and published *HL*, the main body of the theory. Sixth is Schenker's edition of J. S. Bach, *Chromatische Phantasie und Fuge*, since Schenker's theory of harmony began with his research on the harmonic structure of melody, the importance of which comes to the fore in the opening sections of *HL*. The explanatory notes in *CFF* (1910) not only analyze extended passages of the music, but also hint at the concept of an essential melody or *Urlinie*, the outgrowth of Schenker's career-long research on melody. The seventh, *KP1*, though not published until 1910, contains ideas, particularly in its opening pages, that were clearly on Schenker's mind while he was writing *HL*, and that may be characterized as addenda to his thinking about harmony: these include his views on other contemporaneous theories of harmony and his thinking about systematic matters of music theory in general.

The document most tenuously related to *HL* as a harmony book is the eighth one, NdK. Schenker's goal in writing this text was to highlight the achievements of the tonal masters (e.g., J. S. Bach, Handel, C. P. E. Bach, Haydn, Mozart, Beethoven, Schubert, Schumann, Mendelssohn, Chopin, and Brahms) and denounce the music of late nineteenth-century composers (e.g., Berlioz, Liszt, Dvořák, Wagner, Bruckner, Wolf, and Richard Strauss). In particular, Schenker criticized the latter on two counts. On the one hand, he held that they had failed to master the intrinsic techniques of composition, especially the principles of diminution, composing "groups" of themes, and cyclic composition (i.e., sonata form). These principles relate directly to *HL*, part II (§§129–30).[27] On the other hand, Schenker rebuked late nineteenth-century composers for resorting to programs and other extrinsic associations in order to provide their music with a semblance of unity. Although he certainly believed that music could be programmatic, Schenker insisted that it should nonetheless be coherent in purely intrinsic terms at the same time; this is something that he had made perfectly clear in WEG,[28] and in *HL*, §§1–7.

Schenker had modestly called NdK an "afterword" to *HL* when he submitted the manuscript to the publisher, Cotta Verlag, in late November of

---

27. We treat Schenker's thoughts on form from *HL* and DAC in chapters 2 and 6.
28. See appendix A.

1905, but by May 1906, when he sent Cotta proofs for the first half of *HL* and an estimate of NdK's size, the manuscript seems to have grown considerably, to the point where it corresponded in size to the untitled manuscript in OC that is almost certain to be NdK (published by Drabkin as DAC).[29] By 1907, he called it the "capstone" of his *New Musical Theories and Creative Ideas* (*Neue musikalische Theorien und Phantasien*), the title he originally envisioned for *HL*.[30] By that time, however, *HL* was published as such,[31] and Schenker saw NdK as volume 3 of the series. Indeed, Schenker was clearly enamored of NdK, continuing to promise—right at the beginning of *KP1* (1910)—to publish it (*CP1*, xvii). But there were problems then and there remain problems with NdK as part of the *HL* cluster. NdK is irrelevant to the traditional theory of harmony. Further, it is the most polemical of any of the documents we are considering, and *HL* already contained attacks on Reger and Strauss, both of whom had been published by Universal Edition, the publisher of *HL* in Vienna![32] Perhaps neither Schenker nor his potential publishers ever found exactly the right place for this essay (which the publishers were clearly not fond of anyway) in work that was beginning to develop along the lines of the comprehensive music theory books of the nineteenth century, but with a completely new approach.[33]

---

29. Drabkin's transcription runs eighty-two print pages, at forty-two lines per page, averaging eight to ten words per line. 34,000 words (rounded down to the nearest thousand) is quite a sizable essay.

30. On the title of *HL* see *SC*, 75–76, footnote 2. "Capstone" (Drabkin's translation of *Pointe*) comes from a letter of September 13, 1907 to Cotta Verlag, in which Schenker tries to interest them in publishing NdK after *KP1*. See William Drabkin, "Schenker's 'Decline': An Introduction," *Music Analysis* 24 (2005), 10. On our translation of *Neue musikalische Theorien und Phantasien* see chapter 4.

31. *SC*, 76, footnote 2.

32. Drabkin, "Schenker's 'Decline': An Introduction," 6. Much of this paragraph is drawn from this source.

33. Multi-volume *Kompositionslehren* by Weber, Marx, Lobe, Sechter and Riemann appeared in the nineteenth century (accompanying the rise of the conservatories). Schenker's book—and indeed his lifelong project of *Neue musikalische Theorien and Phantasien*—may be seen as part of that trend towards a comprehensive treatment of the pedagogy of composition. In these works, form and instrumentation always appeared in later volumes, after first volumes on harmony, and only then counterpoint. Schenker follows this order with *HL* and *KP1/2*, and indeed, NdK might be seen as a kind of premature third volume, were it not for its heavily polemical tone. On the other hand, the Viennese organist-theorist and teacher of Bruckner,

Of uncertain provenance, [DTS] and WEG are clearly the most closely related to *HL*.[34] Both manuscripts are undated and unsigned. Yet in appearance at least, they seem related. Both are written in Schenker's *Lateinschrift*, which is characteristic of his writing after 1902.[35] We agree with Marston that the probable date of WEG is 1904–5, where we place [DTS] as well (see below). Of the two, [DTS] is surprisingly irrelevant to Schenker's other pre-*HL* writings, and may be his very first attempt to deal with the theory of harmony. It is constructed in sections of varying length separated by § signs, as are *HL*, *KP1*, *KP2*, and *DfS*. The two halves of the essay (on the "natural" and "compositional" systems, though the second also deals more briefly with the "practical" system) bear headings inserted in colored pencil at a later stage of composition; but neither the essay nor any of its subsections is titled (hence our square brackets). WEG, on the other hand, is titled, but Roman numerals are used to mark the first four sections, titles marking the last two: "On Likeness Itself" (the central discussion of motives), and "The Second and Less Important Likeness: the Poetic Element," the second originally called "Conclusion and Transition." The big question is transition to what? Schenker answered that one by crossing out this last heading and superimposing the new heading, which far better reflects the actual content of the next segment (the last). Here, after a brief summary of some of his previous points, he gets to his contention that music is the most "abstract" of the arts, an "art by analogy," since it essentially leaves nature behind. Yet it can convey "feelings," "emotions," "bodily movements," etc.—in other words, it can approach the external world, as all the other arts do, despite its abstractness. In that attempt, however, music must deal with two sets of likenesses—internal and external. The internal may not be abandoned, as happens all too often today, Schenker warns, if music is to remain art. Indeed, Beethoven

---

Simon Sechter, limits his sights to topics closely related to harmony and counterpoint throughout his three-volume treatise. Schenker studied the contents of the first volume on harmony with Bruckner, and personally owned the second and third volumes. The second contains a section entitled "On One-Part Structure: The Art of Finding the Harmony of a Given Melody" that likely would have been of particular interest to Schenker.

34. Philological details of the two manuscripts of [DTS] and additional remarks on it are included in the introduction to the translation in appendix B, as are speculations on how it may have been revised to produce *HL*, §§8–19. For details on the manuscripts of WEG, see Marston, "'. . . nur ein Gleichnis,'" especially 8–10.

35. Schenker "writes things that he sees as possible public material entirely in *Lateinschrift* from 1902 on" (email by Ian Bent to Wason, August 5, 2006).

has already written program music at a much higher level than present-day music because he managed to balance the two sets of likenesses.

Several pages later there appears an unnumbered page, entitled "Überleitung."[36] It reads as follows:

Transition [*Überleitung*]

However, in order to fulfill the task of the art of music, the tonal material had to be created first. The tonal system had to be found, in which it was possible to demonstrate musical as well as poetic likenesses. To find this was almost more difficult than to find the internal musical principle [of likeness], and centuries went by—indeed millennia—until what we have was finally created.[37]

But the text stops abruptly here, all of it is crossed out, and Schenker continues on the next page (if indeed the unnumbered page is in the right place!) with the previous section, which turns out to be the last. To judge from the handwriting, the page was crossed out at a later time (in broader and larger strokes in green pencil), as Schenker added a reminder (hastily scrawled with the same green pencil) to discuss the relationship between music and words in the finale of Beethoven's Ninth Symphony. The reminder is consistent with the topic of the continuation of the last section, though he never followed it: in the essay as we have it, Schenker continues to discuss program music, but his analysis is of Op. 81a. The crossed-out text is most suggestive, however: could this stray page relate to the previous "Schlüsswort u. Überleitung" (conclusion and transition)? Could Schenker have taken time off from WEG to develop his thoughts on the birth of the tonal system in [DTS]? Consistent with that speculation, could the use of § signs put [DTS] closer in time to *Neue musikalische Theorien und Phantasien* than WEG might be? Could [DTS] have been a false start of the opening section of *HL*?

Whether or not Schenker began to write [DTS] after he crossed out the text, we believe that the crossed-out text strongly implies that, firstly, the topic of [DTS]—the document most related to the historical theory of harmony—only arose as Schenker continued his work on theory of melody (of

---

36. The page is OC/83, 29, which appears between Schenker's pages 26 and 27 of the essay. The "Schlüsswort u. Überleitung" page was page 22. Clearly the unnumbered page does not belong here. The question is where it does belong.

37. See appendix A.

which motive and repetition are clearly a part), and secondly, that consequently WEG pre-existed [DTS], though the two were probably written so close to one another as to be essentially contemporaneous. And most important, the idea that a topic in harmony was suggested as a consequence of working with melody is perfectly in keeping with Schenker's thinking at that time—and later.

These speculations aside, it is perfectly clear that WEG relates directly to *HL* §§1–7, the "likenesses" having been transformed into "associations," while [DTS] is another treatment of the material presented in *HL*, §§8–19, in approximately the same order, but with significant differences in content: the "natural" and "compositional" systems of [DTS] have become "natural" and "artificial," for example, and the "practical system" is covered under "mixture" in *HL*. Indeed, the most likely scenario is that WEG predates [DTS], slightly, and that both predate *HL*—though not by much—and that they either were written in preparation for the treatise or were abortive drafts of *HL*, §§1–19, chapter 1, "The Natural System." In fact, once Schenker decided to write a theory of harmony, the off-topic [DTS] may well have become the book's beginning (temporarily). Why else would he have titled the opening large section (*Abschnitt*, translated as "Division" in *HA*): "Systems, Their Foundation and Their Differentiation with Respect to Transposition and Purity or Mixture"?[38] Not only would that explain the heading and subheading (the subheading is "Foundation of Systems," *HL*, 3), but we later find out that Schenker's history of modality includes the contention that the other modal systems went out of use and the Ionian and Aeolian achieved their hegemony by virtue of the fact that they offer the most complete possibilities for motivic imitation on I, IV, and V (*HL*, §26). Motive thus determines the surviving systems. Indeed, motive and system are intimately linked for Schenker, but to say that motive is an existential condition of system seems to go too far: system is linked with "neutral" or even "empty" techniques of harmony that exist in the abstract independently of pieces, while motive is linked with melodic "content," which is quite piece-specific and malleable. The two more often seem to be in an oppositional, yet symbiotic, relationship.

---

38. As is often the case, *HA*'s literal translation tells us little: "Position and Purity" for "Lage und Reinheit." *Lage* is "[registral!] position" or "[pitch] level," and clearly refers to which transpositional level a system may assume, while *Reinheit* refers to whether the system is "pure" (i.e., major or minor) or a "mixture" of major and minor.

On the other hand, if the off-topic [DTS] became the opening of *HL* and WEG was inserted later, it is not surprising that "Systems" is the title of *HL*'s first large section. Moreover, "tonal system" is surely a topic on which a young music theorist would have had to take a position at the beginning of a career, when the tenability of Riemann's dualistic conception of the tonal system was the burning music-theoretical question of the day. The Riemann problem emerges quite clearly in [DTS], and is taken up at the climax of the "Vorwort" to *HL* ("Preface" in *HA*). Yet, it is not until *HL*, §§8–19 that Schenker eventually gets to this nominal topic. Here the reader finds out that there are "pure" systems—i.e., a "natural" (major) versus an "artificial" (minor) system—and that these as well as certain modal inflections can be combined into "mixed systems," and all may be transposed.[39] All of this amounts to a continuation of the investigation begun in [DTS] that solves some of the problems there, but not all of them. The point here is that GEIST and WEG plus [DTS], all in more developed form, may be said to present the contents of *HL*, §§1–19, or, in other words, precisely the whole of part I, chapter 1, no less and no more—additional evidence that GEIST/WEG and [DTS] were developed together into the opening of the *HL* text. They also present the modes of argumentation of the book as a whole—GEIST and WEG are predominantly "historical" (though the latter at times also invokes the psychological argument), while [DTS] presents the psychological and legal arguments. All three—particularly [DTS] and WEG—present music theory as well. It may simply be that beginning *HL* with the discussion of motive turned out to be necessary, for Schenker's historical and music-theoretical argument was, to him, the crux of the matter; because of his modal-to-tonal evolutionary theory, historical evolution as Schenker imagined it would determine theory, or at least the order in which it is presented.

---

39. Schenker's use of the term "system" is not that far removed from the ancient Greek usage, but the meaning is a bit broader: it too indicates the total repertoire of pitches *within a key*, and the order in which they are generated; but there are now a major, minor and "mixed" system, and temperament allows for a much greater range of transpositions. It is worth noting that many theorists of the nineteenth century, before the rise of dualism, would have agreed on the notion of "mixing" major and minor, but that the precise way Schenker does it seems to be original with him. Still, there is a near precedent for it in the work of Immanuel Faisst and his far better-known student, Percy Goetschius.

Under such circumstances, the agent of discovery, the artist, would likewise be necessary to the argument. The opening discussion of the artist's invention of the motive eventually moves to a history of the artist's discovery of a musical "hint" given by nature in the form of the harmonic series, and his invention of both compositional techniques that follow that hint, and many others that are suggested by it, but depart from it. (This ordering of events follows WEG.) In investigating the series, Schenker does more than simply abstract a just major triad, as most natural-base theorists had done. In one sense, the natural base is more important to him than to the others, for he considers both the upward "directionality" of the series, which forms the basis of his notion of generation, and the importance of the bass generator (Rameau's "fundamental bass," transformed), which serves as the foundation of his notion of essential harmony. But in another sense, it is less important, for he is much less beholden to the natural base, once the book really gets underway: now that he has taken care of the notion of "generation" and the bass as foundation of essential harmonies, he focuses on his investigations of techniques invented by the artist that far outweigh those dictated by the series. Indeed, he writes quite explicitly that "my task here is to demonstrate that to which artists may lay claim as their own achievements," and proceeds to develop a 460-page book largely devoted to that task.[40]

In the following discussion we concentrate on *HL*—the material on harmony that Schenker chose to publish—while drawing in the unpublished [DTS], and occasionally GEIST, WEG, and even *KP1* as ways of deepening our reading and expanding our knowledge of Schenker's early thinking. We begin with brief remarks on the structure of *HL*. Next, we approach both *HL* and [DTS] from perspectives largely tangential to the history of music theory, discussing Schenker's "borrowed" modes of argumentation—i.e., his revision of the Classical theory of harmony by recourse in particular to contemporaneous thinking about psychology, legal theory, and history.

---

40. *HL*, last sentence of §19. Schenker reiterates this in regard to one of those techniques in an unpublished essay, "On Musical Causality": "Musical synthesis, like every synthesis, is the bringing together of tones for the purpose of a higher unity, from the point of view only of art, and not nature." OC/51, 9, 1385. See the transcription by William Rothstein in Hooper, "Schenker's Early Approach to Form," 433.

The Layout and Organization of *HL*

The story of the publication of *HL* (and the fate of NdK) is well documented by Drabkin and Bent;[41] moreover, all of the relevant correspondence with the eventual publisher, Cotta Verlag, is now available.[42] Thus our historical summary here will be very brief, as we proceed directly to the matter of the book's methodology.

Before going to Cotta Verlag, the book's eventual publisher, Schenker wrote in May of 1905 to the publisher of his compositions, Breitkopf & Härtel, offering his first large theoretical work, without actually sending the manuscript. Breitkopf replied that they could not take such a work sight unseen, asking him to send in the manuscript, and assuring him "that neither Herr Professor Riemann nor Dr. Mandyczewski would get to see it before it was published."[43] Schenker sent the manuscript, but Breitkopf wrote "that the published works by Riemann on the same topics make any sure success of the work questionable," and proceeded to turn it down. Cotta Verlag in Stuttgart first turned it down, but then accepted it, because of the intercession of Schenker's student and patron, Baron Alphons von Rothschild (who also bore the costs of production), as well as that of the well-known composer and virtuoso pianist, Eugen d'Albert (1864–1932).[44] After some discussion of the form the book would eventually take, and whether NdK would appear in it, the work appeared as a single volume without NdK late

---

41. See Drabkin, DAC, "Introduction," 5–13. For a shorter and more recent account that presents the most important points, see Ian Bent's account in *SDO*/Profiles/Work by Schenker/Harmonielehre.

42. See *SC*, 74–87.

43. OJ/59, 9. Eusebius Mandyczewski (1857–1929) was a musicologist who had studied with Hanslick, and thus one of the *Musikwissenschaftler*—a potential strike against him for Schenker. He was also a conductor, composer, editor, and perhaps most important, archivist and librarian of the Gesellschaft der Musikfreunde—a powerful position in Viennese musical life. Why Schenker did not want his manuscript to be sent to Mandyczewski is not entirely clear, but a diary entry written not long after *HL* had been published (*SDO*: OJ/1, 7; April 10, 1908?; transc. Ian Bent; transl., Ian Bent) elaborates on Schenker's unfavorable impression of his "arrogance." On the other hand, the *SDO* profile (*SDO*/Profiles/Person/Mandyczewski) portrays them as being on cordial terms. Very likely this was true of at least their public behavior, for Schenker was surely a frequent user of the library for his philological work. Schenker's private opinion seems quite different.

44. See Cotta's letter to d'Albert of November 4, 1905 (*SC*, 77).

in 1906, titled *Harmonielehre*, Universal Edition distributing it in Vienna.[45] Universal has continued to publish it, reprinting it periodically, to the extent that 2055 copies were printed between the years 1906 and 2003,[46] evidence that demand continues to exist for the original edition in German.

In writing to Cotta Verlag about his book, Schenker called it "a harmony *textbook* [his emphasis] with a continuously reasoned scholarly text subdivided into short paragraphs."[47] But if he really intended it as a textbook, it is certainly a most unusual exemplar of the genre: a superficial perusal reveals a book replete with 379 musical examples displayed in just under 500 pages. Of these, only about 130 are artificial instructional examples designed to make specific music-theoretical or analytical points. Most of the remaining nearly two-thirds of the total—some of them quite extensive—consist of real music from acknowledged masterworks of the eighteenth and nineteenth centuries, a small number of excerpts from minor composers, and five excerpts from contemporaneous works by Bruckner, Reger, and Strauss. There are also eighteen tables, many lists, and many small and unnumbered examples run into the text. The result is what must have been for the time a kind of multimedia text that had to have been a typesetter's nightmare. Even in the abridged translation, the general impression is of a book centered on examples.[48] That impression is only heightened when Schenker's work is compared with the "classics" of the period: Hauptmann (no musical examples), Sechter (no examples from actual, composed pieces), or with the

---

45. When *HL* appeared, Schenker collected a number of citations and brief reviews (OC/2, pp. 19, 20, 22, 24, 38, 46, 57). However, it is telling that August Halm's two-part 1920 review of *HL* and *KP1* is preceded by this editorial statement: "Schenker's work appeared half a generation ago published by Cotta Verlag [Volume 1, *HL*], and has been more or less ignored. We are thus that much happier to publish this essay by the distinguished music scholar August Halm." Halm, two-part review of Schenker's *HL* and *KP1*.
46. Email of Ian Bent, June 8, 2019.
47. *SC*, 75.
48. In this respect, Schenker's work is probably most comparable to Gottfried Weber's *Attempt at an Ordered Theory of Musical Composition*, in which the author analyzes musical examples from real pieces, or criticizes other theorists' analyses. Weber attempts to formulate his theory through analysis, though certain *a priori* theoretical tenets emerge nonetheless. Perhaps not coincidentally given the critical and non-didactic approaches of both writers, Weber was also trained as a lawyer. The musical examples seem like exhibits, as he argues the case (rather naively) for a completely empirical method.

perennial schoolbooks of the day, Richter and Jadassohn (no real music in either). Schenker's book essentially stands alone in the number and size of the musical examples discussed, though there is historical precedent for his approach.[49] As he says at the outset of the preface: "the present work is an attempt to build a bridge, a real and practical bridge from composition to theory—in contrast to those works of other authors, who present their theories as completely remote from art, as self-contained, so to speak."

The table of contents in *HL* gathers together the headings of the series of numbered sections, becoming, in effect, a detailed outline of the book, a feature that unfortunately was discarded in *HA* (though the headings fortunately were preserved at the beginnings of the relevant sections within the book). [DTS] is organized in the same manner. In the case of *HL*, this organization makes sense when we remember that it was conceived when Schenker had just begun to develop his private teaching, and whether or not he intended it as a textbook, it is unlikely that it was ever intended as a series of lessons: there are no exercises at any point in the book, and, given his relegation of the study of voice leading to separate books on counterpoint, it is difficult to imagine just what form or content such exercises would have taken. Certainly they would have to have been purely analytical, and thus largely conceptual. This aspect of the book would emerge as a topic of controversy with the later discussion of a revised edition, though *HA* shows that the matter was ultimately dropped.

The basic organization of the book is, Schenker claims, a division into a "theoretical part," and a "practical part," an organizational strategy that may be seen at least as far back as Zarlino (see chapter 3). But the practical part,

---

49. The only comparable example of the period is the Louis and Thuille *Harmonielehre*, which focuses mainly on contemporaneous musical examples that are relatively brief. Musical examples first came to great prominence within technical books on music in the early days of music printing. See, for example, Judd's discussion of Glarean's *Dodecachordon* (Basel: 1546) in her *Reading Renaissance Music Theory*, part III. But during the period of Rameau and beyond, as common-practice harmony arose, they became less prominent. Weber's book is an exception. Perhaps the most striking exception, however, is Jelensperger's *Harmony at the Beginning of the Nineteenth Century*, which attempts to move beyond "school harmony" through close examination of examples of music of the time. However, the most influential harmony treatises of the nineteenth century tended to be self-contained, preoccupied with developing a didactic approach to harmony and voice leading, and teaching it through laboratory examples removed from real music, with minimal theory to support their teaching.

without study of voice leading, is essentially analytical, and the whole enterprise has become much more abstract than most pedagogical works on harmony. As Schenker remarks in the preface, part I, the theoretical part handles the "topography of the material"—systems, intervals, chords, etc., and most important, Schenker's concept of the essential harmony—all techniques abstracted from real music. The practical part implements these techniques in real time, but also moves into more advanced techniques of harmony, such as "tonicization" (Schenker's coinage), chromaticism, and modulation. Most important, it demonstrates how the abstract structures described in part I are, first, realized motivically, and in the case of essential harmonies, elaborated via voice leading and lower-level harmonies beyond the duration of single vertical slices. Thus, even in this first work, Schenker offers an alternative to the prevailing theory of harmony.

Psychology, Law, and History: Three Modes of Argumentation in *HL*

In order to get a sense of Schenker's eclectic style of argumentation right off, we discuss the "Vorwort" (*HA*, Preface) in some detail, assuming a general understanding of the three modes of argumentation we contend he uses, drawn directly from his education, as demonstrated in chapter 4. Sometimes he uses them independently, sometimes in combination, and sometimes drawing on other ancillary modes to support them. We then turn to more detailed discussion of each type of argument in turn. Needless to say, there are also music-theoretical arguments that we address in the last section of this chapter and in the next chapter, and other modes of argumentation that we find less important (or that may have escaped our attention). Limitations of space preclude further blow-by-blow analysis beyond the preface, but readers will find that our discussion provides a useful perspective on the "intellectual style" of the book.[50]

---

50. Lawrence Gushee coined the term to describe the ways in which early treatises on music theory fit in with other intellectual currents of their time and earlier, and it is apt here. See his "Questions of Genre." The term indicates the "sum of overt and covert beliefs and traditions as to what is knowable, how it is knowable, and what knowledge is worthwhile, significant and interesting" (366). In brief, the intellectual style of Schenker's treatise is that of a work written on the technical subject of harmony and well within that tradition, but conceived by a creative, practicing

The Preface, and the Eclectic Mode of Argumentation

The preface lays out, with impressive economy, a number of the most important issues on Schenker's mind, and calls up the various modes of argumentation he will use to support his points. Paragraphs 1 and 2 describe the compositional irrelevance of books of the time, his book's relegation of all observations on voice leading to another work on counterpoint (as yet unpublished), and the organizational consequences this latter feature entails. The first and most dramatic instance of the psychological argument occurs almost at the outset in paragraph 2 when Schenker rejects the practical element of voice leading—the primary contribution to harmony of the middle ages, the longest period in its history—by placing harmony squarely in the mind of the creator, perceiver, and interpreter: no actual sounding piece in the outer world would appear to be necessary. Thus all of harmony is "psychological," voice leading apparently irrelevant. We "think" harmony, for it "represents a world purely of the mind, a world of ideally moving forces, whether born of nature or art."[51] The distinction of nature versus art will prove to be of great importance: harmony is fundamentally a psychological matter—a matter of interpretation, whether certain of its materials and techniques may be seen as derived from natural phenomena, or as invented by the "artist," reinterpreting natural models. Here, the psychological argument and argument by law converge: that is, the process by which the systems are formed is essentially modeled on natural versus positive law. Interestingly, there exists a music-historical parallel with the development of legal theory in the nineteenth century that Schenker must have noticed: both witnessed the decline of "natural law" (in music, approximately Fétis's *ordre transitonique*, in which modulation was confined to diatonic systems), and rise of "positive law" (viz., Fétis's *ordre pluritonique*, in which modulation via chromatic and enharmonic techniques became increasingly prominent—processes Schenker essentially rejects when their clear sublimation to a tonal center becomes questionable).[52]

---

musician who was also a scholar of the late nineteenth-century human sciences. Our studies below elaborate this characterization.

51. The metaphor of "ideally moving forces"—the way we think harmony—may be found at least as far back as Rameau's invocation of Newtonian imagery; see Christensen, *Rameau*, 7–11, but especially 187–93. The metaphor also places Schenker in the company of other contemporaneous "energeticists," such as Ernst Kurth. See Christensen, ed., *Cambridge History*, chapter 30, by Rothfarb.

52. On natural and positive law, see chapter 4.

The third paragraph of the preface emphasizes the biological nature of the tones, moving out from the listener to the "society of tones." In anthropomorphizing the tones, Schenker, as many of his contemporaries, was surely influenced by evolutionary theory, but most importantly, this strategy enables him to call again upon his legal theory in the creation of laws by which to curb the "natural impulses" of the tones and to "socialize" them (e.g., the law of tonality that exerts ultimate control on the society of tones). This is the primary purpose and importance of this technique: Schenker, consciously or unconsciously, is not merely anthropomorphizing tonal material out of some naive animistic proclivity, but attributing agency to the tones in order to avoid the superimposition of extramusical theory, and most importantly, to engage his legal thinking about just what a "law" is. That Schenker regards anthropomorphizing of the tones as metaphoric is clear in [DTS], §[3], as is shown below.

The fourth paragraph notes the importance of musical examples in building a bridge from theory to composition, while paragraph 5 enumerates Schenker's other projects and the problem of ordering their publication. Finally, the climactic paragraph 6 isolates the most important music-theoretical problem of the day, Riemann's dualism. The critique of Riemann and the derivation of minor from the "undertone series" in the preface is music-theoretical, but the linchpin of the argument is historical. After claiming that regarding the fifth of the minor triad as its "root" and the root as its "fifth" in itself demonstrates "the untenability of the theory," Schenker launches into the historical argument, which he claims would stand even if the reality of the undertones were to be proven:

> For if theory has the task of explaining art as it came about and is—and not the reverse—then it must respect the fact that from time immemorial artists have based the progression of essential harmonies in principle on roots in the bass, and have done so with equal verve everywhere, with no regard for the appearance of the minor triad as such, and indeed in the major as well as the minor key.

Finally, Schenker presents a theoretical argument, appealing to the superfluity of Riemann's theory. He writes that since the root and fifth of the minor triad are secure in the harmonic series and the compositional treatment of the minor triad is analogous to that of the major triad, in effect, the only difference between a major and minor triad is the inflection of the third. Is that sufficient reason to extract the minor triad from the secure model of the harmonic series and to invent a new—and highly questionable—explanation of it? In imagery that obviously alludes to Riemann's theory, Schenker notes that the effect is to place all three components "on the shaky ground" (*auf den schwankenden Boden*) of a hypothesis, and to substitute the idea of a "root in the air" (*Grundton in der Höhe*) that contradicts both the instincts and practice of the artist with respect to the progression of essential harmonies. Schenker's transformation of Rameau's *basse fondamentale* into the progression of essential harmonies continues to call upon the bass as an important determinant of its interpretation, even as Schenker broadens the duration of such vertical "slices" into "tonal areas." The presentation and development of "essential harmony" (*Stufe*) will turn out to be the most important new idea in *Harmonielehre*.

Curiously, Schenker never brings up Riemann or his theory again in the body of the book; rather, the version of minor presented there is itself an implicit rebuttal of Riemann's theory. Yet, in [DTS], §[21] he had gotten much closer to Riemann's ideas in his discussion of the "practical system," in which resources of an expanded "compositional system" are freely available, mixed with the natural system. Here he wrote that

> in practical composition [in C major], B♭, E♭, A♭ and all other roots that may be found through the process of reversion[53] return—in short, everything returns that the tonal system could not demonstrate within its narrow framework. *What occurred upward can also occur downward* [our emphasis]. The freedom is the same; only the directions are different, as implied by generation and reversion, which run in different directions.

---

53. "Reversion" is our translation of Schenker's *Inversion*, the process by which pitches are produced by *descending* fifths. When he means "inversion," he uses the standard German word, *Umkehrung*. Our translation of *Entwicklung*, the process by which pitches are produced through ascending fifths, is "generation." Both are attempts to avoid confusion with the standard music-theoretical definitions of "development" and "inversion," the literal translations of these words. The terms *Entwicklung* and *Inversion* are ubiquitous in *HL*, and unfortunately confusion between the standard definitions and Schenker's idiosyncratic definitions—particularly in the case of *Inversion*—is ubiquitous in *HA* as well. The "natural" generative process is via ascending fifths; reversion is thus the invention of the artist, on the model of the natural process, but "reverting" to the source. See chapter 5 (on translation), and the notes to [FTS] (appendix B) for further explanation.

The Psychological Argument

In *HL, KP1*, occasionally in *WEG*, and particularly [*DTS*], an important ancillary mode of argumentation is the argument via psychology. The evidence for its importance in Schenker's early work amounts to more than the circumstances of his education and general cultural surroundings we discuss in chapter 4. Both Riemann and Louis/Thuille attempted to engage contemporary psychology in their work, and Schenker was certainly steered in this direction by competition from his competitors as well as dissatisfaction with their ideas.[54] Riemann's "musical logic" was hardly a psychological view of "musical hearing" Schenker could endorse, after all, and his criticism of Louis and Thuille in *KP1* shows that their conception of the tonal system alone put them too close to the Riemann axis.[55]

As early as GEIST Schenker had promised "to explain the nature of harmonic and contrapuntal prescriptions almost solely in terms of their psychological origins and impulses."[56] In his later criticism of Sechter in *KP1*, he would claim superiority for his own presentation of "the psychology of the progression of essential harmony" (*Psychologie des Stufenganges*) and write of the "psychology of intervals," the "psychology of the deceptive cadence," and the "psychology of mixed species."[57] But *HL* is the source where explicit appeals to psychology appear in the greatest abundance,[58] and are apparently

---

54. Oettingen and Helmholtz had already made the explicit appeal to psychology. Indeed, controversy over the epithet "psychologism" arose late in the nineteenth century, indicating just how widespread such claims were becoming. See Ash, *Gestalt Psychology*, 74ff. Obviously, we believe that the argument as used by Schenker at this time is more than that.

55. See *CP1*, 22–24 for Schenker's criticism of Louis and Thuille's explanation of "system": "how can we understand the 'system' if its individual degrees, except for I, IV, and V, are deprived of their independence and thus of their attractive capability of assuming various functions?" (23).

56. SPIRIT, 324.

57. *KP1*, XXXIII, 16, 39, and 374.

58. There are eleven appearances of the word *Psychologie* in *HL*. These can be reduced quickly to eight that are of interest, since two are in headings in the Table of Contents that are repeated and explained in the text proper, and one is a mention of Schenker's soon-to-appear "Psychology of Counterpoint." The techniques of harmony that he speaks of are: 1. "the psychology of progression by fifth" (§125, 311); 2. "the psychology of the abstract essential harmony" (§90, 226); 3. "the psychology of the progression of essential harmonies and its realization"; 4. "the psychology of

most important: in the second half of the book the abstract harmonic techniques of the first half are realized motivically (given "content" or *Inhalt*, as the German puts it) in practice, and the interpreting mind becomes essential in the process: "The Psychology of Step Progression and Its Realization" is the large heading for all of §§115–32, "The Psychology of Chromaticism and Alteration" is the heading for all of §§133–62. Schenker entitles a section "The Psychology of the Use of the Pedal Point" (§170), and speaks of the "free progression of essential harmonies with their idiosyncratic psychology," certainly referring to the freer sense, in the prelude, of harmonic suspension versus expectation (§§171–82). Most of the second half of the book thus appeals explicitly to the "psychology" of these three large topical areas, though there is essentially no further explanation. Yet almost all of these appeals come down to the necessity of interpretation when any of these techniques is engaged. Agency—of the composer, performer, theorist, or even the tones themselves—is always necessary, and thus the psychology of some human or anthropomorphized non-human is important to consider: harmony is much more than a cataloging of techniques and exercises. In the second half of *HL* Schenker is vitally interested in the interaction of these agencies using the abstract techniques described in the first half.

But there is also psychology in *HL* and [DTS] that Schenker never calls attention to as such, though it is arguably more interesting than his overt appeals. Indeed, he does not mention the word psychology even once in [DTS], though he writes from that point of view for much of the essay— perhaps his most interesting effort in this regard. Thus, we must be sensitive to both implicit and explicit appeals to psychology. If the latter arise in part because of Schenker's reaction to competitors in the harmony-book marketplace, in the former we engage Schenker's education and general culture. He never explicitly claims that associationism is psychological, for example, though we know it is. The word and idea are simply embedded in his way of thinking. Nor does he mention the law of least action. Yet associationism as well as human perceptual and cognitive limitations (which may well be the foundation of the law of least action as a psychological law) prove to be core arguments in Schenker's Theory of Harmony.

---

chromaticism and alteration"; 5. "the true psychology of the altered chords" (§146, 367); 6. "the psychology of registral voicing of intervals that are decisive for alteration" (§153, 374); 7. "the psychology of the use of the pedal point" (§170, 415); and 8. "the psychology of free harmonic progression [in an improvised prelude]" (§181, 445).

In the following section, we begin by discussing the question of method in psychology and "tone psychology" of Schenker's time. We then turn to the implicit appeals, to associationism, as well as Schenker's investigation of human perceptual and cognitive limitations as a means of developing the artist's role in the construction of a theory of harmony. Schenker's explicit appeals to psychology, on the other hand, are tied very closely to particular harmonic techniques; we leave that discussion until we take up the techniques themselves in chapter 2.

The Emergence of Psychology as a Human Science and the Question of Method

If psychology is an important component in the understanding of *HL*, it seems fair to begin by asking just what kind of psychology, and just what Schenker's method was in carrying out this work. There exists a lengthy history of thinkers who asked fundamental questions about psychological matters long before the formal discipline of psychology began to take shape in the mid- to late nineteenth century.[59] The birth of the later movement is often set in 1879 with the establishment of Wundt's research laboratory, a product of the German university system, though, as Kurt Danziger remarks, the irony is that much of the development of the discipline after 1879 was a reaction against Wundt's ideas.[60] With respect to the earlier history, it is important to differentiate between the asking of introspective questions, and the conscious use of such interrogation as a "method of introspection," which Danziger dates to about the beginning of the nineteenth century, though it does not become a general method until the latter half.[61] We start with Immanuel Kant (1724–1804), whose insistence that a true science have a mathematical basis caused him to reject any "science" of psychology, though he nonetheless accepted it as a purely empirical field of study.[62] Unfortunately, empirical psychology could not become a science because "its special method of introspection would have to yield to mathematical treatment in the way that the visual data of astronomy, for example, yielded to

---

59. See, for example, Leahey, *Psychology*, chapter 7, 189–219.
60. See Danziger, *Constructing the Subject*, 34.
61. Ibid., 18.
62. Kant, *Metaphysical Foundations of Natural Science*, 8; cited in Danziger, *Constructing the Subject*, 19 and 205.

mathematical treatment."[63] That was not about to happen any time soon, though Herbart proved it was not impossible.[64]

Kant also influenced the birth of psychology by distinguishing between it and philosophy—this in an era in which academic "philosophers" were fast becoming arbiters of the epistemologies of new disciplines vying for university status. The grounds on which they made their decisions were largely methodological, thus directing much more attention to that aspect of any discipline. Kant's distinction is described particularly clearly by Danziger: "there is a huge difference between examining the factors involved in particular spatial perceptions and examining the implications of the fact that our perceptions are characterized by spatiality."[65] Schenker did both: in many locations in *HL* he worked from the ground up by discussing interpretive approaches to specific musical examples (particularly in the discovery and interpretation of essential harmonies), while in [DTS], he tended more often to work from the top down: in particular, he speaks at some length about human perceptual and cognitive limitations and their implications for construction of musical systems. The former is part of empirical psychology, the latter, arguably a part of philosophy. Again we find additional evidence of [DTS] predating *HL*: Schenker almost certainly asked the philosophical questions before getting down to work in interpreting the answers in musical practice.

Once psychology was at last declared separate from philosophy, the "introspective method" was available to the investigation of the "'inner sense,' in the same way that the various natural sciences based themselves on the evidence of the external senses."[66] [DTS] demonstrates that introspection must be regarded as Schenker's method in the realm of empirical music psychology as well as philosophy of music, and, given what he chose to publish in *HL*, his approach was more properly psychological, not philosophical. Yet Schenker was first of all a music theorist—and one on a crusade to correct what he regarded as wrongheaded music theory at that. Thus, just because he did not align himself specifically with (or even cite) Wundt, Stumpf and other empirical psychologists of the time, who conducted basic research in the perception of musical sound, this does not mean that his music theory

---

63. Danziger, *Constructing the Subject*, 21.
64. J. F. Herbart, *Psychologie als Wissenschaft* (Psychology as a Science), cited in Danziger, *Constructing the Subject*, 22 and 206.
65. Danziger, *Constructing the Subject*, 20.
66. Ibid., 20.

was not "psychological." These others were researchers truly working "from the bottom up," and the basic perceptual questions they were asking would not have interested Schenker. Though Riemann surely considered his music theory to be "psychological," and even cited Stumpf, he differed with him strongly on important points, and clearly considered Stumpf's *Tonpsychologie* naive from the music-theoretical point of view. Schenker would have strongly agreed, had he known the work. Schenker's invention of the artist announces the high artistic level and aims of his musical research: this was clearly an alter ego—his creative ideas and artistic personality. In this sense it represented Schenker interrogating himself, and by extension the history of the artist, before sitting down to formulate "theories." He then proceeds to develop "principles," "laws," and to ask interpretive questions in order to test and teach them. The order of Schenker's title notwithstanding, creative ideas (*Phantasien*) generally precede theories (*Theorien*), though his ordering of the two connects him directly with the long tradition of music theory we review in chapter 3.

Associationism

At the outset of the main text of *HL* we land in foreign territory compared to the books of Schenker's competitors. There is simply no other book on harmony we know of that starts like this one:

> All of the arts, with the exception of music, consist basically of associations of ideas [*Ideenassoziationen*]—great and universal associations of ideas, to be sure, drawn from nature and reality. In all cases, nature is the model, art its imitation, whether in word, color, or sculpted form. We know immediately to which part of nature the word, the color, or the sculpted form applies. But the situation is different with music. Here, the unambiguous relationship to nature is entirely lacking.

In making his argument Schenker uses the linguistically borrowed words *Ideen* and *Assoziationen* twice in this first sentence (fused into the compound *Ideenassoziationen*). The Latin-derived "ideas" and, especially, "associations," demonstrate that Schenker, a product of the Herbartian educational system in which "associationism" was fundamental to the teaching process, has brought it into the realm of art, as all of his teachers would have.[67] Fur-

---

67. Taken from the singular noun *Associationem*, from the verb, *associare*. See the *Oxford Dictionary*, 129 (First Edition: vol. 1, 513). He could have written, for

ther, in claiming that the arts are based on associations of ideas "drawn from nature [*Natur*] and reality [*Wirklichkeit*]," Schenker clearly subscribes to the traditional mimetic theory of art, in which art "imitates" (or "represents," depending on the translation of *mimesis*) reality. He surely knew the *locus classicus* of the idea: Aristotle's response to Plato in his *Poetics*. Plato's abstract "ideas" were his ultimate object of imitation, and thus he claimed that imitation in art was twice removed from the "idea" of a thing—that reality stood in the way, so to speak, and thus that art was necessarily a diminishment of the ideas.[68] Aristotle had a much higher regard for art, believing it imitated "reality," adding to our understanding of it rather than merely describing it, as history did—essentially the form of the theory that was passed to later generations through the *Poetics*.[69] Though it became controversial in the nineteenth century, the mimetic theory continued to hold currency for many thinkers of that time. But Schenker seems to have interpreted it according to his own thinking, for the notions of nature [*Natur*] and reality [*Wirklichkeit*] are of particular interest here: we claim that the two words are necessary because Schenker reinterprets the traditional theory in light of the distinction between natural and positive law—i.e., some of "reality" is not natural, but "human-made," and, in that sense, "artificial," but as Schenker will maintain, in following nature, its construction is a "second nature," and thus available to imitation.[70] The distinction is vital, and ubiquitous in Schenker's thinking. Of course, the big question is, as influential and apparently effective as the mimetic theory is in the visual, literary and dramatic arts in which human-made objects can certainly imitate real phenomena, just what, if anything, is music imitating?

Schenker begins, surprisingly, by claiming that music is exceptional, and presumably devoid of "associations of ideas" (§1), but he reverses himself almost immediately (§2). It turns out that in differentiating between nature and reality, Schenker had been preparing the way for the human-made "motive": "The motive and it alone is absolutely the only means of associating

---

example, the German *Verbindungen der Begriffe* to indicate the "connection" of ideas. Schenker tends to use Latin cognates when he announces new "principles" as well—certainly a consequence of his legal study.

68. Republic X: 595ff.
69. Aristotle, *Poetics*, tr. and ed. Heath, section 4.
70. Schenker goes into this at length in [DTS], §[1], calling his "compositional system less a contradictory force than a continuation and extension—a second nature, so to speak." Cf. WEG, 8; Marston, "'. . . nur ein Gleichnis,'" 23.

ideas that music possesses. It is the first and most basic means; and most important, it is the form of association *intrinsic* to music" (§2). Thus the very raw material of music is human-made; only the process—and not all of that—is natural: the human-made motive associates only with versions of itself. Though Schenker does not say so explicitly, music, as an association of motives, would appear to be entirely self-referential, internal motivic associations replacing the imitation of nature and reality essential to the other arts (we hear echoes of Zimmermann[71] and Hanslick here). This is certainly his position in WEG. The process by which such association takes place is repetition: "Any succession of tones can be a motive, but it can only be recognized as such when a repetition follows *immediately* . . . Only repetition may elevate a succession of tones into something definite; only it can explain what the succession is and what it seeks, just as the previously mentioned association of ideas from nature and works of art does in the other arts" (*HL*, §4).[72] In chapter 4, we will see that the psychology textbook Schenker studied in the *Gymnasium* passes along Herbart's notion of "reproduction" as a way of extending a Kantian mental image or *Vorstellung* in time; certainly repetition is the musical equivalent.[73] Once again, it is worth remembering that such Herbartian ideas were deeply embedded in the Austrian educational system. We need not claim that Schenker modeled his ideas on specific references to Crüger or Herbart, but rather that he was a product of that system. Such repetitions (and hence the associations they foster) need not be literal, for "freer repetitions and imitations that also include manifold small contrasts do not cancel the wonderful effect of association."[74] This is precisely the case in reproductions, which take different forms. Moreover, rhythm, melody, and harmony may all be called upon to articulate repetitions—to "demarcate various motivic phenomena individually" (*HL*, §4). (Again, Schenker holds the same position with respect to likenesses in WEG.) Repetition is also the

---

71. For more on Schenker's teacher, Robert Zimmermann, see chapter 4.

72. Schenker had already made nearly these exact points in his remarks on "repetition" in SPIRIT, 321.

73. See Johannes Crüger, *Grundriß der Psychologie*, 36–68, for the complete discussion of the topic. See also Herbart, *Lehrbuch der Psychologie*, 44–47.

74. Schenker of course would pursue the topic of "freer repetitions" throughout his career, first opening *TW1* (1921) with the motto, "semper idem sed non eodem modo" (always the same, but not in the same way), which appeared periodically in his works and personal correspondence from then on, and was the motto of his last work, *DfS*.

basis of larger-scale form, the means by which formal components are associated, and even the basis of formal structures that apparently are dependent on "contrast," since return is essential to such forms: a true A B C form is "unthinkable" (*HL*, §5). Thus, Schenker finds "contrast" in its musical manifestation to be derived from the more basic processes of association, as Hume did in the realm of ideas.[75] In the case of the three-part form, it is derived from the interrupted association of the two like parts, A1 B A2.[76] Schenker was already headed in this direction when writing WEG, where he finds contrast to be a part of "likeness" (repetition), and a companion to repetition, writing that "by motive, we understand all and everything in music that may be raised to the level of a model for an imitation [*Nachbild*], or counter-image [*Gegenbild*]."[77]

Schenker generally reserves the term *Assoziation* for repetition and relationships between various transformations of a motive, but at one point he draws it into a description of his theory of essential harmony. Here it applies to our need for associations in general, which are the psychological property of the artist. Thus art is essentially a synthesis of nature and *Assoziationen*:

> Precisely in its higher, abstract nature, the *essential harmony is the distinctive characteristic of the theory of harmony* [emphasis in original]. For the teaching of harmony has the task of instructing the aspiring artist in the abstract powers that in part correspond with nature, and in part with our need for associations (*Assoziationsbedürfnisse*), as determined by the purpose of art. The theory of harmony is thus an abstraction that brings with it the most mysterious psychology.[78]

---

75. Hume wrote that "to me, there appear to be only three principles of connexion among ideas, namely, Resemblance, Contiguity in time or place, and Cause or Effect ... Contrast or Contrariety is also a connexion among Ideas: but it may perhaps, be considered as a mixture of Causation and Resemblance." Hume, *An Enquiry Concerning Human Understanding*, 22.
76. In DAC, 44, Schenker defines his notion of "cyclic form," the three-part sonata form, as an outgrowth or A1 B A2 form: "If a movement of instrumental music can be divided into three parts, it has cyclic form."
77. See appendix A.
78. *HL* §83. Schenker uses both meanings of *Harmonielehre*.

Music Theory and Human Perceptual and Cognitive Limitations

The Law of Least Action and the Principle of Generation

In [DTS], §[4], Schenker asks the big philosophical questions, developing his most extensive interrogation of the law of least action (though he never announces a name for this "law" or "principle"), and using it as a way to formulate the "principle of generation" that describes how we abstract the basics of the tonal system from the harmonic series:[79]

> In general, a consequence of our limited capacity to comprehend is that we give preference to simple relationships as opposed to complicated ones merely because we comprehend the former better and more easily. If, for example, a length or an area has only few units so that we can orient ourselves right away to its number, then that strikes us more agreeably than the reverse, when the feeling of orientation abandons us because the length or area is too large or complicated to be estimated on first glance. And there will be a substantial distinction for us in the first and more favorable case when the length measures 4 meters, not 5; or 8 meters, not 7, etc. Likewise, it causes us greater pleasure when we quickly assess, for example, thoughts or artworks as complete wholes, or the organizational plan of buildings, animal- or plant-forms; on the other hand, our aesthetic perception is perplexed and thus unsatisfied when complexity prevents us from quickly grasping these phenomena. Not taxing our senses is thus a higher life-principle for us than straining them, from which arises the necessity of an easier and quicker view of all things and relationships, respectively, and for the fulfillment of this necessity as an aesthetic rule, and as a condition of pleasure in general. This describes our state as we confront the phenomena of the tonal universe described in the previous section (§[3]). That is, here we also tend, for innate reasons, to prefer the simple to the complicated, as, so to speak, closeness to distance, an earlier

---

79. Whether or not Schenker's ideas were prompted by the early Gestaltists at the University of Vienna, as we strongly suggest in chapter 4, it is clear that in [DTS] the appeals to psychology—or, in this case, philosophy of music—are more obvious than they are in *HL*. But why is the psychological argument so much less apparent in *HL*? If [DTS] was originally a part of *HL*, perhaps Schenker later regarded these "introspective" inquiries as preliminary. Perhaps this is why he never included them in his "textbook," which may have been conceived—at least in the beginning—as a more "practical" work, given the tradition from which it emerged. Or Schenker may have removed them to help keep the size of the book down—one reason why NdK was never included (Cotta more than once counseled against adding to the bulk of *HL*).

generation to a later one, or the stronger to the weaker. And we even went so far that we accepted only the first three species of overtones—the first and most strongly generated—into our practical tonal system. (We did this unconsciously, of course, which demonstrates the dependability of our instincts as well as the overwhelming force of nature.) These species result from the law of generation [*Zeugungsgesetz*], 2, 3 and 5—and thus, to take the cosmos of C as an example, would be the octave C, fifth G and third E.

Schenker concludes ([FTS], §[3]): "The laws of generation regarding the species of overtones are contained in the prime numbers (1, 2, 3, 5, 7, 11, 13, 17, etc.)." A bit later ([FTS], §[5]) he claims that the fifth partial of the harmonic series is the limit of generation; further generative roots yield results that are "too difficult to understand."[80] The laws of generation come down to (1), 2, 3, 5, and their doubles, powers and products.[81]

In [FTS], §[6] Schenker continues the discussion of psychological restrictions on the principle of generation from yet another angle, offering more "proof" of this point, this time effectively invoking "natural law," though he never abandons the psychological argument. He maintains that the generative process is essentially "successive" (*Nacheinander*), not "simultaneous" (*Nebeneinander*): nature moves forever forward, oblivious to what occurs "sideways." Treating such relationships as simultaneities stems once again from our psychological limitations, from "our way of seeing, according to which we readily project onto a plane that which conceptually has nothing to do with it" ([FTS], §[6]). The musical purpose of this discussion is to discredit the view that the interval of the minor third (for example, E/G, as generated by C) can be evaluated *on its own* as a "minor third." Rather, the two pitches are generated by C, to which they continue to relate as successive generations; the interval's "minor-thirdness" (taken as a simultaneity) is a secondary byproduct of a generator that is still present psychologically. Schenker transfers much of this discussion to *HL*, developing it further in §10 with another anthropomorphic analogy: a lengthy discussion of the Bach family tree, unfortunately with far less psychological context.[82] He ends *HL*, §10 with a critique of those theorists who availed themselves of a "shoddy

---

80. Many followed Zarlino, limiting harmonic generation to the "senary number" or 6. But 6, not a prime, is merely the octave of the fifth (2 x 3), and thus not really "new."

81. For a discussion of the mathematics of tuning, see chapter 3.

82. For more detail on the possible transformation of [DTS] into *HL*, §§ 9–11, see the preface to [FTS], appendix A, below.

method" of generating the tonal system by accepting the primes 7, 11, 13 as "approximations" of our scale-degrees 7, 4, and 6.⁸³ The music-theoretical purpose of §[6] is to disenfranchise those pretenders to "first-level" tonal citizenship: , , , and any chromatic tones, none of which may be directly generated by the fundamental.⁸⁴

The Law of Least Action, Human Perceptual and Cognitive Limitations, and the Law of Abbreviation

Though some kinship of the law of least action to *HL*'s "law of abbreviation" seems clear, Schenker apparently had not yet come to abbreviation in [DTS], though he does mention it in a final note added at the end of WEG (perhaps added later?). It is only in *HL* that he announces that abbreviation limits the otherwise infinite generation of overtones. Preoccupied as he was with overtone generation, and faced with many topics as he wrote *HL*, he clearly saw the extensive potential of the law of least action. That abbreviation, a new (and, to our knowledge, original) music-psychological law, is also new to its creator, is shown by its status: most often Schenker refers to it simply as "abbreviation," but sometimes it is a "law," and in two sections it becomes a "principle."⁸⁵

Early on, the subject of larger-scale form in *HL* brings up more anthropomorphizing (*HL*, §6), for motives are essentially like personae in a drama, the extended musical composition a depiction of the "life of the motive." Schenker details various episodes in the life of a hypothetical character in a drama, and concludes that there are too many of them—and too many of those are trivial—for the artist to present them all.⁸⁶ Thus he announces for the first time the law of abbreviation (*Abbreviationsgesetz*): the life of the motive must be compressed, allowing the artist to choose only its most interesting events. Again, Schenker uses the unusual (and

---

83. Such explanations largely died out by the early nineteenth century. Certainly the most influential continental music theorists of the time did not accept them.

84. 2 (whose origin Schenker later reads as 9 = 3 x 3) is an interesting case. Neither is it a "first-level" member, but it is the first (other than octaves) of the doubles, powers or products of Schenker's chosen generators (1), 2, 3, 5. Schenker goes on to work extensively with these.

85. *HL*, §13, 41; *HL*, §36, 105.

86. He chooses the hero of Friedrich Schiller's "Wallenstein" trilogy of plays (completed 1799), familiar fare for his audience, and thus incompletely identified by Schenker. With no editorial help, the reader of *HA* is most likely at a complete loss.

lawyerly) Latin cognate (from *abbreviare*) not *Abkürzungsgesetz*, as he could have, had he wished *not* to draw special attention to it: "Among the endless, countless situations into which his motive may fall, the composer has to choose only a few, which, however, must be characteristic enough that they reveal the clearest peculiarities of the motive's nature. Thus, because of the law of abbreviation, it is not admissible to bring the motive into situations that do not contribute something new to the exploration of its character."[87]

A bit later, that law becomes a principle, and collapses the *Naturklang* into three triadic pitches within the span of an octave: "What we call a triad [is] always much more correctly conceived of as a conceptual abbreviation of nature; basically, all of the arts consist only of abbreviations, and their stylistic principles may be derived from the principle of abbreviation alone, if one wants to reach an explanation perfectly consistent with nature."[88]

And later still, Schenker calls on abbreviation to confine the indefinitely ascending fifths within the span of an octave.[89] Reversion[90] is likewise the product of abbreviation, as the available diatonic pitches within the octave are filled out by $\hat{4}$.[91] Becoming a principle again, abbreviation also explains the advent of equal temperament used to close the complete "circle" of twelve fifths, which also limits the phenomenon of transposition, the products of which Schenker identifies closely with the infinite progeny of the fundamental.[92] Abbreviation limits the technique of enharmonic modulation as

---

87. *HL*, §6, 20.
88. Ibid., §13, 41.
89. Ibid., §15, 43.
90. This is our translation of Schenker's *Inversion*. See ibid., §16, and chapter 5 below.
91. Ibid., §16, 44.
92. *HL*, §36, 105. Beware the incorrect translation at the bottom of *HA*, §18, 44: *Temperierung des Systems* as "outcome of the system," when it should be "tempering of the system." This error is all the more curious, since the translation of *HL*, §36, 105; *HA*, 82–3—a section devoted entirely to temperament—contains no significant errors. Indeed, someone silently corrected Schenker, who confused the syntonic (= ditonic) comma (22 c.) with the Pythagorean comma (24 c.). As the translation says, each fifth in equal temperament is 1/12 of the Pythagorean comma smaller than 3 : 2. Another passage seems to involve temperament, but in fact does not: §26 (*HL*, 70; *HA*, 55). The translator has confused "gleichmäßig" with "gleichschwebend." When Schenker says that the triads on I, IV, and V in the major and minor keys "eine gleichmäßige Dur- oder Molltemperatur haben, die sich zur Durchführung motivischer

well.⁹³ Finally, Schenker calls upon it to explain the "incomplete" figures of the figured bass in his discussion of the inversion (*Umkehrung*—not *Inversion*) of chords.⁹⁴

The Law of Least Action, or the Number Five?

It is important to remember that the main point with which Schenker took issue in the work of music theorists of his time was their efforts to construct complete harmonic systems based solely upon nature ([DTS], [§1 and §2]). Schenker lays out his view right at the very beginning of WEG, writing that unlike the other arts that are designed to bring an image from nature to the perceiver, "to a greater extent than the other arts, music has earned the right to be understood and valued as the most fundamental creation of humanity." Indeed, continuing on in this vein later, he writes "what a triumph . . . that nature, finally conquered by the spirit of man, was now made to place this art-like art alongside the other arts, as child of its own children!"⁹⁵ Admittedly, Schenker's theory remained in touch with the tradition of natural base, but he was vitally interested in finding the reason that the human mind accepted so little of the harmonic series, and so much of the system and the compositional techniques underlying music were, in his view, the property of the artist. We recall that even the opening of *HL* is far from "conventional," discussing as it does the fundamental role of the motive in the construction of a theory of harmony—clearly, in an effort to set the property of the artist in high relief from the outset.⁹⁶ Indeed, the overall purpose of

---

Probleme besonders gut eignet," he apparently means that these chords in each mode "possess equivalent major or minor quality [i.e., intervallic structure] that is especially well suited for working through motivic problems." One might substitute "tuning" for "quality" to get closer to the original, or Schenker could be referring (as a result of his study of Sechter with Bruckner) to the fact that all three are tuned just. It seems most likely that he simply means that these triads are all major in the major key, and all minor in the minor key (true only of the major and minor modes). This is of course a corollary of his claim that major and minor systems offered the greatest possibilities for motivic working-out, and hence emerged victorious over the modes.

93. *HL*, §179, 441.
94. Ibid., §98, 240–41.
95. WEG, 9; tr. Marston, "Schenker and the Path to "Likeness," 12.
96. We have a fundamental disagreement with Suzannah Clark, who claims that the opening of *HA* "involves a conventional beginning," which we find puzzling. The brief history of harmony presented in chapter 3 shows it to be quite unconventional. See her "Schenker's Mysterious Five," 86. Reading on, we see that she recognizes the

HL is not to detail the natural base of the system, but to explore its artistic features. For example, in describing the basics of the tonal system, Schenker writes that:

> It never occurred to them to entertain the idea that a substantial part of the system is the complete and original property of the *artist* [emphasis in the original], as is, for example, reversion and its consequences, the first lower (subdominant) fifth, and the tempering of the system. Thus, the system as a whole must only be regarded as a compromise between nature and art—as a mixture of the natural and the artistic, though with the predominating force of the natural, which was the point of departure. *My task here is to demonstrate that to which artists may lay claim as their own achievements.*[97]

In the opening of *KP1* Schenker laments the death of the music he loved, and is even more insistent on the tonal system as the property of the artist: "the very tonal material—that foundation of music which artists, transcending the spare clue provided by the overtone series, *created anew in all respects from within themselves* [our emphasis]—is demolished."

In using the notion of psychological limits to keep the role of nature within bounds and clear a space for the artist, Schenker was hardly a dispassionate natural-base music theorist or music psychologist. His most

---

importance of human agency in Schenker's system and is certainly on the right track by emphasizing the importance of generation, abbreviation, reversion, and the number five. But she misses the psychological origins of abbreviation and the number five, and the extreme limitations placed on "natural" generation by our perceptual and cognitive limitations. This is in part because she was unaware of [DTS], and too dependent on *HA*, which, given Jonas's editing, puts Schenker closer to nature than *HL* did (he cut significant passages on Schenker's view of minor; see appendix C). Ultimately, citing the familiar Babbitt critique, she reads Schenker in the long line of natural-base theorists, and his fascination with the number five as yet another attempt to found the theory of harmony on a mystical "natural" principle outside the domain. We argue the opposite point of view: that five was an attempt to find a psychological principle that limits the role of nature in his system. True, Schenker is always deferential to nature, but we hear a subtle tone of irony when he writes that "somewhere Heine speaks of poetry as an 'enhancement of nature.' Without wishing to make myself complicit in the same disrespect for Mother Nature—whom I certainly hold to be the greater—I would nonetheless recommend, without hesitation, viewing the Aeolian system as such an 'enhancement of nature.'" (*HL*, §24, missing from *HA*).

97. Our emphasis. *HL*, §19, 59.

ambitious attempt to formulate a psychological law may have been his "principle of the number five" (*HL*, §113), which he seems to have believed—or at least hoped—was a deeper reason for the limitations on our understanding of tone generation and reversion than the law of least action. At one point he even says that, with regard to the ascending fifth progression in C, we could never hear it starting on F, because interpreting more than five ascending fifths "oversteps our limits."[98] Borgese turns the sentence around, translating it—too freely, we would think (though in keeping with our argument!)—as interpreting *only* five fifths "is inherent in our subconscious."[99] She was a native German speaker, after all, familiar with all instances of the number five in *HL*. Surely the translation is an attempt to render what Schenker "actually said," for the sentence is quite straightforward. Still, we add the modal "may" to our claim because *HL* demonstrates ambivalence about the exact status of five: Schenker calls it "mysterious" many times, referring to it only once as a *Prinzip*, his highest-level law (see below). Nonetheless, it is clear from the sources that he was convinced that such limits on the power of the human mind did exist, regardless of whether he truly understood the status of five. Thus, despite the fact that Schenker's invocation of five seems to lurk somewhere between superstition and science, we believe its purpose is clear: that it is not a latter-day naturalized Zarlinian justification of the tonal system (for it adds nothing to Zarlino in this respect), but is more likely to be Schenker's attempt to find, once and for all, a clear and reliable psychological limit on our ability to perceive and cognize natural musical processes (and hence a reason to limit the natural base)—an attempt comparable to later efforts to enlist the number seven in a similar cognitive cause.[100]

Given the Riemann problem confronting Schenker at the beginning of his work in harmony, the harmonic series was the first item on the agenda, and its limitations clearly brought five to his attention first, though, interestingly, he does not single the number out for commentary and speculation in [DTS].[101] In *HL*, on the other hand, five quickly emerges as the last prime from the harmonic series that is "comprehensible" to us: all further tones

---

98. *unsere Grenze überschreitet*; ibid., §17, 54.
99. *HA*, §17, 40.
100. Miller, "The Magical Number Seven, Plus or Minus Two," 81–97.
101. This is all the more interesting, since he devotes a section to speculations on whether a "genius" would one day liberate us from our confinement to the lower reaches of the harmonic series ([DTS] §[5]).

generated are derivatives of 1, 2, 3, or 5.[102] After the application of abbreviation, which confines the tones generated to a one-octave span, the artist gains exactly five diatonic tones in addition to the fundamental (*HL* §15, 44). Thus five quickly becomes the limit of the practical process of generation, and would be equally applicable to reversion, for that matter, since, in [DTS] the subdominant and four additional lower fifths emerge through this process in "practical composition," via five fifths generated downwards.[103] Thus we have the fundamental and 5 + 5 tones generated from it—all very neat. Moreover, we have a memory of the tonic that locates us in the 7-pitch-class diatonic space, or even the 11-pitch-class, "[modally] mixed" space—a basic feature of the hearing of common-practice tonal music. Only ♭5/♯4 are unattainable via the cycle of ascending or descending fifths, since diatonic 5 and 4 arrive first, allowing them no room.[104] Indeed, "♭$\overset{8}{5}$" is unattainable in virtually any harmonic system of the late nineteenth century, and to get any of the "sharp spellings" of the non-diatonic pitches in Schenker's system, the chromatic processes of modulation or tonicization will turn out to be necessary.

Schenker might appear to skate on some thin ice when he claims that five helped to determine the five-line staff, but it is clear that, having just spoken of the limitations on the ear as analogous to those on the retina's processing of light, he is attempting to extend the limits on hearing to those on vision.[105] The skeptic would do well to read through some English and Dutch seventeenth-century keyboard music in original editions, in which the line filling the space between treble and bass clefs creates a single—and

---

102. *HL*, §11, 37–38.

103. Cf. *HL* §38–52, *Mischungen* ("Mixture," which Borgese renders as "Combinations"). Schenker comes to the same conclusion here through the mixture of modes. He rejects the "Lydian Mode," and thus #4.

104. Thus #IV must be generated via tonicization or alteration, processes that Schenker calls "chromatic." See Brown, Dempster, and Headlam, "The #IV Hypothesis."

105. *HL*, §11, 37–38. Curiously, Schenker's editor and student, Oswald Jonas, chastises his teacher for his reliance on the number five, which "is bound to remain more or less doubtful," while in the very next footnote he is sympathetic to his view of notation, taking the opportunity to criticize the attempts to construct a twelve-tone notational system that arose at the beginning of the twentieth century, though in doing so he only refers vaguely to "self-styled 'reformers' of our notational system" (*HA*, §11, 26, footnotes 16 and 17).

quite bewildering—eleven-line staff.[106] Surely the limits on our abilities to orient ourselves visually in a "staff field" had some effect on the development of the five-line staff from the old four-line staff, as did the limitation on an (untrained) vocal range of a tenth or eleventh, the total number of lines and spaces available around the five-line staff.[107] Admittedly, the principle of five fails in delimiting chord-types, however, for the alleged ninth chord is not a chord (*HL*, §113).

But can the importance of five—or seven, for that matter—be proven? On that subject we turn briefly to Miller and more recent reaction to his article. Given the development of information theory, early computing, and cognitive psychology in the 1950s, it is not surprising that Miller's work was entirely focused on the limitations of human memory. While others conceived of it essentially as they did computer memory, treating it as a processing of impossibly long strings of binary choices, Miller recognized the resulting "informational bottleneck," and recommended creating larger "chunks" of data (and correspondingly fewer of them) through the information-theoretic process of "recoding":

> The input is given in a code that contains many chunks with few bits [binary choices] per chunk. The operator recodes the input into another code that contains fewer chunks with more bits per chunk. There are many ways to do this recoding, but probably the simplest is to group the input events, apply a new name to the group, and then remember the new name rather than the original input events.[108]

Thus Miller takes ideas from information theory and computing, and uses them to "automate" processes that begin to approach human language, its processing, and memory. This is the core of the article, for ironically, his report regarding the number seven is ultimately dismissive, the title appearing to have been a hook to get the reader into his more original ideas. At the end he asks one last time about the status of seven, citing many examples, two of which would have interested Schenker—the seven primary colors and the seven diatonic pitches. But he finishes by writing: "Perhaps there is

---

106. See Shannon, *Evolution of Organ Music*, appendix, 219.
107. Cf. Schenker's "Vocal Principle" (*HL* §13, 41; *HA*, 28), which limits the range to an octave, and implies that vocal limitations are one source of what we call "pitch class."
108. Miller, "The Magical Number Seven, Plus or Minus Two," 93.

something deep and profound behind all these sevens, something just calling out for us to discover it. But I suspect that it is only a pernicious, Pythagorean coincidence."

The latest update on the topic seems to move a little closer to Schenker's implicit question and to an answer, however.[109] And its opening abstract is remarkably sympathetic to the notion that seven or any other number might serve as a rule of thumb in determining limitations on perception and cognition:

> This chapter began by discussing a simple answer to the question of what primary memory capacity is: that primary memory can hold seven chunks or meaningful units. This answer was shown to have some basis in the facts, but overall it was shown not to be a general rule, and therefore was said to be a legend. However, it should be said that simple answers are not, in principle, bad. One of the goals of science is to find simple rules to explain the available evidence in a comprehensible manner. What makes the simple rules unacceptable is just when they are shown not to match the facts. What is likely to advance people to the next level is a better understanding of the long-term memory processes involved in chunking.

The authors then look at studies of the brain's processing of diverse stimuli (digits, letters, words, colors, etc.), citing, for example, one study that ties visual memory to neural functioning by using fMRI testing (functional magnetic resonance imaging). Indeed, they write that "there are many different experimental procedures and each one has to be analysed carefully before we will know whether a similar 'magical number' truly applies to all of them, and for the same reason."[110] The focus is still primarily on memory, the techniques of chunking and recoding leading to a more efficient memory of data and smaller number of packets thereof. Thus, five and seven have become, now, three or four. The authors conclude that

> just as the more comprehensive understanding of gravity by Albert Einstein eventually displaced the simpler gravitational law of Newton, a more comprehensive understanding of primary memory capacity is bound to come along and replace the simple generalization that people can remember on average three or four chunks of information. Until that time, however, the limit of

---

109. Cowan et al., "Magical Number Seven."
110. Ibid., 19.

three or four serves as a useful guideline for research and theory, as did the gravitational constant for many years.[111]

We still have not come to questions of "cognitive limits" on our perceptual apparatus in general, but we are getting closer. And whatever the limits on the processing power of the human brain may be, Schenker's motivation for embracing the "principle of five" is all-important: it was his conviction that there was a deepest-level limitation on our cognitive capability, and thus a foundation for the artist's contributions to the system, not a justification of the "natural system."

The Jurisprudential Argument

Schenker's Legal Training and His Earliest Music Theory

Near the opening of [FTS] §1, Schenker asserts that the "natural" and the "compositional" systems he has developed "relate to one another as nature does to culture, and completely so. Just as culture, basically, can never deny nature (and should not be permitted to do so), just as little can the compositional system deny the natural system. Therefore, the compositional system represents, in relation to nature, what culture does: it is less a contradictory force than a continuation and extension—a second nature, so to speak." This argument immediately calls to mind the distinction between natural law (available to all) and positive law (law "posited" by a particular society): for Schenker, culturally determined laws—musical or otherwise—surely could not "deny" natural law. In this sense, he remained a legal and musical theorist of the Enlightenment. Translating this back into music theory, it is clear that in the ongoing debate between theorists who insisted on the natural basis of music-theoretical systems (e.g., Rameau), and those who saw them as culturally determined (e.g., Fétis), Schenker managed to find a synthesis of both the natural and the cultural, his legal study helping in this pursuit. This solution to the problem figures into his critique of music theory of the time: instead of a subtle equilibrium (a "harmony") between conflicting natural and cultural forces, Schenker finds an oversimplified and strained attempt to derive whole systems from thinking drawn from the natural sciences; thus, the problem with the work or Helmholtz, Oettingen, Riemann, et al. is essentially misinterpretation of the *range of application* of natural law—not

---

111. Ibid., 21.

its relevance or irrelevance.[112] The argument also has profound implications for Schenker's own music theory, for the notion of positive law underlies the compositional system of [DTS], the extensive "property of the artist" in *HL* (including "practice"—the subject of the second half of the book), and, ultimately "free composition." Thus, Schenker took in the basics of natural law, but spent his whole career developing musical positive law—a theory for the "property of the artist."

But how do the laws that Schenker studied in his law training relate to the laws of his music theory? Towards the end of the first large section of [FTS] §12 he presents what is probably his earliest attempt at an answer. It is surely the most eloquent and all-encompassing legal/musical argument of the essay:

> Tonality, and along with it, the musical artwork as a whole, is, in the final analysis, very much comparable to the state. The state also forms, in a similar manner, a powerful unity and indeed a unity of human beings, to each of which it grants (or at least should grant) individual growth, whose independence it even desires ... How beautiful it is when equilibrium prevails between the demands of the individual on the state and, vice versa, those of the state on the individual. Likewise, it is beautiful when a similar equilibrium emerges between the rich expansion of the independent overtone generations on the one hand and the collective idea of tonality on the other.[113]

As will become apparent in chapter 4, Georg Jellinek (1851–1911), a proponent of the balance between personal freedom and state control in medieval Teutonic law and one of Schenker's law professors, was a strong influence on Schenker's thinking. Jellinek's delicate balance is clearly recognizable behind Schenker's analogy; it is safe to say that Schenker would have stood by the analogy throughout his career, at least as he states it here with respect to tonality in free composition.[114] Given the close relationship between [DTS] and *HL*, it is not surprising to see the argument's return, this time in

---

112. In [DTS] §2, his critique is directed specifically at "die Physiker," so it is not part of a wholesale condemnation of scientific approaches to music, Schenker's opinion of which has sometimes been read too negatively.

113. See appendix B.

114. The influence of Jellinek can be found elsewhere too. In DAC, for example, Schenker almost literally quotes "The Rights of Minorities" (5f.) when, concerning the expansion of audiences as a result of the rise of program music, he writes that "verily, the point has been reached at which voices are counted instead of being weighed." This is precisely Jellinek's criticism of democracy.

less grandiose terms, focused specifically on the tonal system, which restrains the "procreative urge" of the tones: "The tonal system, particularly the natural [major] one, could be seen as a sort of higher collective order, similar to a state, based on its own social contracts by which the individual tones are bound to abide ... In this sense a system resembles, in anthropomorphic terms, a constitution, regulation, statute, or whatever other name we use to grasp conceptually the manifold relationships we enter."[115] The argument works in this guise for *HL*, which deals with many more specific compositional techniques than [DTS]: in *HL* the "system" is the controlling element of generation and reversion in the theoretical part of the book, and, in the practical part, the "interpreter" of the motive's tonal meaning. In part II the reader also learns to interpret the motive at the musical surface, or even the essential harmony at a deeper level, against the backdrop of the system. Such interpretation is a primary feature of the jurisprudential model.

In discussing the nitty-gritty of voice-leading detail a few years later, however, a much more autocratic regime seems to have taken over; there now seems little room for interpretation. Schenker describes his view of laws at the start of *KP1*:

> In this study, the beginning artist learns that tones, organized in such and such a way, produce one particular effect and none other, whether he wishes it or not. One can predict this effect: it *must* follow. Thus tones cannot produce any desired effect just because of the wish of the individual who sets them, for nobody has the power over tones in the sense that he is able to demand from them something contrary to their nature. Even tones must do what they do.[116]

Apparently, they have a "nature"—i.e., a psychology—unlike the inanimate phenomena of the exact sciences. Nonetheless, they must "do what they do"—at least, in the "contrapuntal laboratory."[117] Prediction is thus a desir-

---

115. *HL* §38; *HA*, 84.
116. *KP1*, "Introduction," part IV; *CP1*, 14.
117. Schenker continued to hold this strict view of law. "In a footnote pasted into the manuscript [of *KP1*], Schenker speaks of removing his examples of free composition from parts 1 and 2 if he were ever to prepare a revised edition of the first book of *Kontrapunkt*. Parts 1 through 5 [most of the contents of *KP1/2*] would thus form a true "Strenger Satz" section—devoted to strict counterpoint alone." He would then transfer the examples of free composition to later discussion of that topic. See Siegel, "When 'Freier Satz' was a part of *Kontrapunkt*," 21.

able attribute of law, for Schenker; and the lofty existences of the citizens of his tonal state in [DTS] that began to fade in *HL* seem to have become much more restricted. Of course, we must remember that these are tones in the laboratory, where they are forced into prescribed formations whose effects are well known and clearly demonstrated, a notion of law perhaps inspired by empirical psychology of the period, in that grey area between the human and natural sciences. Still, while Schenker started his career with the analogy between the jurisprudential notion of law he had been taught and musical laws, by 1910, with some pedagogical experience, he seems to have wanted both the flexibility of application of jurisprudential law, and the absolute predictive power more at home in the natural sciences. These apparent extremes—in chronology as well as approach to the law—will determine the limits of our further investigation.

Explanation and Prediction

To understand Schenker's concern for laws, it is important to remember that he regarded music theory as an explanatory pursuit: he wanted to explain what happens to tones in specific situations and why those tones behave in some ways but not in others. Thus, in addition to prediction, the related notion of "explanation" places his laws closer to those of the natural sciences than it does to jurisprudential laws, or at least this is the case by 1910. This much is clear from the start of *KP1*, where he claims that theory teachers must tell students not only what contrapuntal rules they should follow, but also why they should do so:

> All of the contrapuntal rules must be supported by good reasons. This, certainly, is the most difficult matter; and because of the difficulty, it is fully understandable that until now most theorists have avoided providing a basis for counterpoint. If even religion has had to cope with the fact that mankind asks "why," isn't it all the more understandable that contrapuntal theory, which in fact has long enjoyed almost the reputation of a musical religion would meet the same fate?[118]

Of course, the reasons for well-wrought jurisprudential laws should be clear as well, but the goal of such laws is not explanation, but to keep the public order, after all, which translates to enforcement of rules of tonal behavior. But Schenker, the theorist and pedagogue, wanted more. Elsewhere he also

---

118. *KP1*, "Einleitung," part III, 18–19; *CP1*, "Introduction," 12.

appealed to the explanatory nature of music theory when he criticized C. P. E. Bach's guidelines for improvising a free fantasy: "it is not that the musical facts of the case are falsely represented, but that his language was as yet inadequate to supply the right words to explain the deeper relationships."[119]

Yet, since they generalize about what normally happens to specific things in specific contexts, Schenker's laws also allow music theorists to predict the behavior of musical tones. Such predictions, unlike those that result from laws in human societies, suggest law in the natural sciences. Nonetheless, Schenker recognized that some laws, especially the laws of counterpoint, are often transformed in profound and unique ways in specific tonal compositions. This is in keeping with the necessity of interpretation in jurisprudential law. As he explains in *KP1*:

> How great the distance even in language from the first principles concerning subject, predicate, object, and the like, and from a simple sentence based on these elements, to the proud free architecture of an actual work of art in language! In music, however, this great gulf has simply been overlooked and the contrapuntal rules, elevated immediately to the status of rules of composition—that is, to principles that would be binding in free composition as well.[120]

Later, Schenker illustrates the point by quoting a sophisticated sentence from Goethe's *Faust*.[121] Although Goethe's sentence freely alters "the normal ordering of the sentence components," Schenker insists that it "does not constitute an offense against German grammar: "Who can miss the fact that this sentence, in spite of kinds of departures from normal organization, basically manifests only prolongations [i.e., transformations] of the most ordinary grammatical laws?"[122] He adds: "In a similar way, the new forces that accompany free composition in music form an apparently new order, yet those who have true understanding see the fundamental contrapuntal principles profoundly and mystically at work in the background. The phenomena of free composition, then, are invariably to be understood only as the prolongations

---

119. Schenker, "The art of improvisation," 8. Note that Schenker's reading of the inadequacy of C. P. E. Bach's explanation is couched in lawyerly prose, as Alpern would say.
120. *KP1*, "Einleitung," part I, 2–3; *CP1*, "Introduction," 2.
121. *KP1*, "Einleitung," part III, 19–20; *CP1*, "Introduction," 12–13.
122. *KP1*, "Einleitung," part III, 19; *CP1*, "Introduction," 13.

[i.e., transformations] of those principles."[123] Schenker makes similar claims in *HL*, as in his discussion of the analogy between reversion and word order in §16 and in his discussion of the relationship between essential harmonies and strict counterpoint in §§84–89.[124] Here, again, he stresses that "free composition, then, appears as an extension of strict composition: an extension with regard to both the quantity of the tone material and the principle of its motion. What is responsible for all these extensions is the concept of the essential harmony. Under its aegis, counterpoint and free composition are wedded."[125] A couple of paragraphs later, Schenker again claims that a rule of voice leading in strict counterpoint might be prolonged or extended in free composition.[126]

Causality

Schenker's concern with laws is matched by a similar concern with the notion of causality [*Kausalität* or *Ursächlichkeit*]. Whereas, in the *Poetics*, Aristotle had only considered music with extramusical associations—that which accompanied a text or a dance—Schenker, as we know, insists that autonomous music can imitate nature by virtue of its motivic associations. He clarifies this process of cause and effect in the following equation:

In nature: procreative urge ——> repetition ——> individual kind;
and, in music: procreative urge ——> repetition ——> individual motive.[127]

Schenker concludes: "The musical image created by repetition need not be, in all cases, a painstakingly exact reproduction of the original series of tone. Even freer forms of repetition and imitation, involving manifold little contrasts, will not cancel the magical effects of association."[128] Schenker also invokes the concept of musical causation in his account of so-called ninth chords in *HL*.[129] Instead of regarding dominant-ninth chords as essential harmonies and ninths as harmonic intervals, he insists that they arise

---

123. *KP1*, "Einleitung," part III, 20; *CP1*, "Introduction," 13.
124. *HL*, §16, 44–51, §§84–89, 198–223; *HA*, 31–37, 154–74.
125. *HL*, §88, 204; *HA*, 159.
126. *HL*, §91, 228–29; *HA*, 177–78.
127. *HL*, §4, 6; *HA*, 6–7.
128. *HL*, §4, 6; *HA*, 7.
129. *HL*, §107–114, 249–77; *HA*, 190–208.

contrapuntally, either as byproducts of passing motion over a pedal tone or as suspensions. In the first case, Schenker gives a beautiful example from Wagner's *Faust* overture, in which the upper voices project strings of passing diminished-seventh sonorities over a pedal tone A. In the second case, he quotes a passage from Wagner's *Rheingold*, scene 4.[130] According to him, both examples demonstrate that ninth chords do not have the "individual nature" [*eigene Natur*] of a triad or a seventh chord.[131] Schenker concludes: "Such a conception and a way of hearing its cause [*Ursache*] is incomparably more artistic than a merely theoretical clumping of the intervals with no demonstrable common cause [*Ursache*]."[132] Interestingly, he also notes that Rameau was correct to regard the ninth chord "as an *accord par supposition*."[133] By the time he completed *KP1*, of course, Schenker would offer a similar causal explanation of seventh chords as well.

Causality can be quite complex in free composition, in particular, because various laws may operate simultaneously, and it takes knowledge of these laws and careful listening to understand the music as it should be understood:

> In music it is important—indeed, very important—to observe every phenomenon, even the smallest, and to listen to every detail, even the slightest, according to the cause specifically associated with it. Listening in this manner not only does justice to the artist, but to music in general. This unique mode of listening allows multiple laws to have their effect at the same time, though one will be stronger than the others, such that the strongest attracts our attention as the law most in need to be obeyed; yet in no sense does it silence those laws that preserve the order of the smaller and narrower associations of tones. If one learns to listen in this artistic manner—that is, to listen to the various tonal events that happen at the same time and in the same place, each according to its many and manifold causes—one will frequently be spared the disappointed clamoring after new harmonies and new theories, as many do so often today, as they suddenly stand before a complex phenomenon and search in vain for a single cause.[134]

For Schenker, the nature of the subject of *KP1* clearly called for a stricter approach to causality than that implied by the interpretive model of law of

---

130. See *HL*, ex. 228 and ex. 234–35; *HA*, ex. 167 and ex. 173–74.
131. *HL*, §112, 268; *HA*, 204.
132. Ibid.
133. Ibid.
134. *HL*, §34. Cf. Borgese's translation, *HA*, 82, paragraph 2.

HL, particularly in part II. Near the end of *KP1*, for example, he suggests that dissonant syncopes provide "a means of establishing a purely musical causality [*Kausalität*]."¹³⁵ According to him, "the artistic instinct discovered in the *compulsion* to prepare and resolve a dissonance is a most welcome means of feigning a kind of musical causality [*Kausalität*] and necessity at least from harmony to harmony. Considering that a seed of such propulsion was contained even in the simplest passing motion (the issue of developing length should be kept always in mind in investigating the nature and history of our art!), it is clear that the compelling force of the dissonant syncope must be viewed as incomparably stronger and more urgent."¹³⁶ Through them "harmonies appear linked more intimately and with seemingly greater necessity the more drastically and obtrusively a tone of one harmony hooks into the flesh of the following one. The higher degree of structural necessity as well as length is then further provided by essential harmonies (including all that derives from them, such as tonality, chromaticism, modulation etc.) and *form*!"¹³⁷

Years later, in preparing *KP2* for publication Schenker essentially held the same views. In fact, he wrote specifically about causality in an unpublished essay completed on August 31, 1917, "On Musical Causality—Review and Epilogue," originally planned as the ending of *KP2*.¹³⁸ Here, he even cites the very passage we just quoted from *KP1*. Contrapuntal laws are inviolable, and in that sense, inevitably cause particular musical—i.e., voice-leading—consequences. It is almost as though the logic that Riemann heard in harmony had been transferred to counterpoint. In trying to solve the problem of just what the driving forces of absolute music were, Riemann and Schenker faced the same problem, but came up with opposite solutions: thus Schenker formulates his "tonal logic" in the context of counterpoint, not harmony, where, being an "affair of the mind," interpretive leeway is essential: "Under causality one has to imagine a drive, a compulsion that legitimizes the tone

---

135. *KP1*, part II, chapter 4, §12, 376; *CP1*, 291.
136. Ibid.
137. Ibid.
138. OC/51, 9, 1378–91; Hooper, "Schenker's Early Approach to Form," 423–39. The transcription that appears in Hooper—and to which we refer here—is by William Rothstein. On the plan for the essay to be the end of *KP1*, see Siegel, "When 'Freier Satz' was part of *Kontrapunkt*," 12–25.

as a quasi living, logically thinking being, as a logical motor, so to speak, as we use causality analogously in our language."[139]

Not surprisingly, given the planned position of the essay, Schenker gives a summary of contrapuntal devices near its beginning, to each of which he attributes a causal property. The first is consonance, the attractive state constantly strived for; the second, dissonance, the phenomenon causing that striving; the third, properties of individual intervals that provide each with a unique identity, and so forth. This is followed by a list of specific types of dissonance and their causal behaviors. Schenker goes into voice-leading detail at that point. He does not stop there, however, but presents the devices of harmony as well, in less detail, recalling our quotation from *HL*, §34:

> In the world of the vertical direction, countless forces are active, determined, pressing forward, compellingly and inexorably unique. Thus it appears to us most importantly that the *essential harmony* itself is the ultimate foundation of the causality of composing out. Just as it translates its essence causally into the synthesis of composing-out, so tonality bears in itself the causality of harmonic progression.[140]

Schenker goes on to claim causal status for mixture, modulation, chromaticism, thematic working-out, and ultimately, form:

> And on top of all of this, [we add] form as a causal force! What an enormous sum of motor forces here in this world . . . And thus from the smallest to the largest, small formal components up to whole movements know to raise claims, which at the same time are directional markers for tones. Much of this is told in various instruction manuals on form, but unfortunately once again unsatisfactorily, completely ignoring the most mysterious causal forces.[141]

Principles and Laws in Schenker's Music Theory

The law may be defined as the body of principles recognized and applied by the state in the administration of justice.[142]

---

139. OC/51, 9, 1378; Hooper, "Schenker's Early Approach to Form," 427. Cf. *KP1*, part II, chapter 4, §12, 376; *CP1*, 290–91.
140. OC/51, 9, 1382; Hooper, "Schenker's Early Approach to Form," 431.
141. OC/51, 9, 1383; Hooper, "Schenker's Early Approach to Form," 433.
142. Salmond, *Jurisprudence*, §13, 33; quoted in Patterson, *Jurisprudence*, 117.

Schenker's legal vocabulary in [DTS] is simple: the two large sections of the essay are headed by "I. The Principle of Generation (*Entwicklung*)," and "II. The Principle of Reversion [*Inversion*]," the only instances of the word *Prinzip* in the essay—both added by hand to the typescript at a later stage of editing. This could mean that the words were added as part of the process of editing that produced *HL*. There Schenker invokes a principle for the first time near the beginning (*HL* §4). Otherwise, in [DTS] he speaks of the "laws [*Gesetze*] of generation," assigning 2 (the octave), 3 (the fifth) or 5 (the third) to them, and applying them frequently.

The extraordinary topical breadth of *HL* makes this hierarchy less clear, and Schenker never says anything about it. The legal definition of a principle—of which Schenker invokes many in *HL*—is essentially the general definition: "a fundamental truth or proposition that serves as the foundation for a system of belief or behavior or for a chain of reasoning."[143] As one nineteenth-century jurisprudential source explains it, principles are plain truths that do not need to be proven.[144] Schenker's principles are in fact generally clear, far-reaching, self-evident, and require little further explanation. Given this status, they are analogous to the axioms of an exact science, famously illustrated by such statements as "a straight line may be drawn between any two points" from Euclidean geometry. Like principles, axioms are accepted as primitives of the system without proof. But unlike axioms that give rise to theorems under ideal circumstances, principles may be applied to a vast number of real and individual cases that appear very different from one another in "tonal life." The breadth of application of the principle of abbreviation is particularly impressive in this regard: Schenker begins by invoking it to collapse the infinite number of partial tones corresponding to a "major triad" into three pitch classes, while ultimately, he claims that "all art is abbreviation." Unfortunately, he fails to list all of his principles and laws in one place. The closest we get is the table of contents of *HL*, in which topical headings are occasionally principles. Other principles are explained, or sometimes merely applied, as they first enter the text, independent of the section headings.

Schenker's use of the word "law" (*Gesetz*), on the other hand, is surprisingly informal in *HL*. He is sometimes inconsistent in his vocabulary,

---

143. New Oxford American Dictionary.
144. *Unumquodque principiorum est sibimetipsi fides: et, perspicua vera non sunt probanda.* Co. Lit. Il. (Whatever is accounted as a principle is taken for granted to be founded in truth, and plain truths are not proved.) Wharton, *The Law Lexicon*, 1028.

calling the "principle of abbreviation" (§13) the "law of abbreviation" during another section of the text (§6), though it is always a "principle" elsewhere in the book. At other locations in the text he uses "law" vaguely: i.e., in the manner of "contrapuntal laws" (§87), or "mysterious laws" (§88). Thus law is the more general term. See table 1.1 for an annotated list of all principles and laws that occur in *HL*.

Schenker's ideas on the status of musical laws were likely just forming as he wrote [DTS] and *HL*: the jurisprudential model is strongly represented in the early [DTS], but then the paper is quite limited in scope, if important nonetheless. *HL* is the opposite: topically vast and sprawling, it engenders a bewildering list of principles and laws, as table 1.1 makes clear.[145] At the same time though, there is no real explanation of the nature of these laws. The status of law seems to have evolved by the time Schenker published *KP1*, though surely the subject matter has much to do with it. Unlike Schenker's abstract notion of harmony, his conception of counterpoint is of a collection of laws that are quite specific: "Contrapuntal theory, which is nothing but a theory of voice leading demonstrates tonal laws [*Gesetze*] and tonal effects in their absolute sense. Only contrapuntal theory is able to do so, and therefore it should do so. This is its greatest value and, at the same time, its significance for all eternity."[146]

The Jurisprudential and Scientific Models, and the Status of Schenker's Musical Laws

The *generality* of jurisprudential law is a requirement—that is, "its capacity to serve as a rule, a measure, a guide for an indefinite number of varied situations."[147] Of course, it shares this property with scientific law, but with an important difference: "both physical formulas and political laws are

---

145. This figure, the result of a computer search of *HL* for "Prinzip" and "Gesetz," lists unique principles and laws individually, in order of appearance, with minimal commentary. The search for the former yielded ninety-two matches (some of which are the plural form, and many of which are repetitions). A search for "Gesetz," on the other hand, yields forty-nine matches, many irrelevant to our purposes, since, as a true Germanic word, it is often embedded in longer words with quite different meanings. Thus "Prinzip" prevails by a wide margin. The table collates both principles and laws; the bolded principles are translations of the relevant sectional headings; standard Roman typeface indicates principles; italic type indicates laws.
146. *KP1*, "Einleitung," part IV, 21; *CP1*, "Introduction," 14.
147. Patterson, *Jurisprudence*, 98.

Table 1.1. A Summary of the Principles and Laws in *HL*

Principle of Association of the Motive (§3)

Repetition as the Principle of the Motive (§4)

Repetition as the Principle of Form (§5)

Principle of String Division, which yields the individual principles of generation (2, 3, 5) (§10) [These are called "laws" in [FTS]]

The Fifth Partial as the last Principle of Division for Our System (§11)

Vocal Principle, causing us to conceive of pitch within approximately a one-octave range (§13)

Principle of Abbreviation (§13); referred to as "Law of Abbreviation" in §6

Principle of the Fifth Relation (§18)

Principles of Generation and Reversion: defined in §16; referred to as "principles" but as "laws" in §21 and §71

Principle of Progression of Essential Harmonies (§21)

The Principle of Transposition by Fifth (§31)

§34 contains an especially interesting claim that more than one "law" may be operative at a time in music. Though one is stronger, and takes our primary attention, it does not cancel the effects of the more limited and weakly represented laws.

Law of fifth generation of accidentals (§37)

The Biological Basis of the Principle of Mixture (§38) (also cf. §52)

Principles of Derivation of Intervals (§63)

Principle of Mixture of Intervals and Harmonies (which gives rise to modulation) (§69)

Principle of Harmony in a Horizontal (Melodic) Line (§76)

Principle of Natural Resolution (§84)

The Principle of Voice-Leading in Counterpoint without Essential Harmonies, even in Free Composition (§85)

Laws of Counterpoint (§87)

Natural Law of Growth (§88)

Laws of Voice-Leading (§88)

Law of Harmony (§88)

Principle of the Creation of Horizontal Limitation on the Vertical via Reform of the Fundamental Bass Voice (Italian Monody) (§88)

Mysterious Laws of the Essential Harmony (§88)

(continued)

Table 1.1.—*(concluded)*

Principle of Imitation and Canon (§88)
Principle of Inversion [Umkehrung] (§98)
Principle of Construction in Thirds (§107)
Principle of Passing Chord [over a Pedal] (§110)
Law of the Fifth Degree (§110)
Principle of the Number Five (§113)
Law of Harmony (§116)
Principle of the Third Partial [the Fifth] (§126)
Principle of Cyclic Composition (§130)
Principle of Combination (§130)
Natural Law of Generation (§131)
Natural Law of the Upper Fifth (§131)
Law of the Resolution of a Passing Dissonance by Step in the Same Direction (§163)
Principle of the Fantasia (§182)

---

generalizations which only human beings can understand and apply. They differ in that the latter can be disobeyed. This difference explains why (political) law has other attributes: political authority and political sanction."[148] The potential for violation of political law is important to emphasize, for the institutionalization of "political authority and political sanction" has given rise to a vast profession of lawyers and jurists dedicated to advocacy, and interpretation of the law, both of which Schenker understood well, and transformed into vital features of his music theory: he advocated strongly for his principles and laws, and interpreted them when their application was not obvious. A scientific law, on the other hand, is either inviolable, or inadequate and in need of revision or replacement: scientific laws are also presumed to be applicable in all relevant situations by any possible observer.

Schenker claims that the laws of *KP1* enable us to *predict* the behavior of tones. Is prediction a property of law in jurisprudence? In fact, no less an authority than Oliver Wendell Holmes proclaims that the whole point of studying the law is prediction: "When we study law, we are studying what we shall want in order to appear before judges, or to advise people in such a way

---

148. Ibid., 97.

as to keep them out of court. The object of our study, then, is prediction, the prediction of the incidence of the public force through the instrumentality of the courts."[149] Developing this line of thought further, Patterson writes that "a line of decisions of a court, displaying a specific regularity down to the present time, is a basis for predicting what the court will do in the future, is generally accepted in Anglo-American law, and to some extent in the European systems."[150]

This evokes the familiar refrain of *stare decisis* in the American court system, and it also means that prediction would very likely have come up as a topic during Schenker's law training. But are the courts predictable in an absolute sense, as the "behavior" of water, on earth, at 30 degrees Fahrenheit is? The answer is "no," of course, since they *may* rule differently, for example, in a case that at first appears subject to precedent, but presents crucial differences in detail later on. The behavior of individuals is even more difficult to predict, since not all members of a human citizenry living under law follow that law in practice, violators ranging from individuals who cruise unwittingly through stop signs, to criminals who do far worse, intentionally. Judgement in the application of political law is therefore of the greatest importance, and it must be flexible, the judge constantly ready for the unexpected and apparent exceptions. Certainly, Schenker sees this as a most important aspect of his view of law: the music theorist becomes advocate, arbiter and interpreter of the laws of strict composition when they are brought over into the realm of free composition.

On the other hand, prediction, in its scientific sense, is closely related to the concept of explanation via that of causality, according to Carl Hempel:[151]

> Quite generally, prediction in empirical science consists of deriving a statement about a certain future event ... from (1) statements describing certain known (past or present) conditions, and (2) suitable general laws ... Thus the logical structure of a scientific prediction is the same as that of a scientific explanation ... The customary distinction between explanation and

---

149. Quoted ibid., 119.
150. Ibid., 118; Patterson continues: "Holmes' prediction theory of law has had a pervasive influence upon legal thinking in the United States" (119).
151. Hempel, *Aspects of SCIENTIFIC EXPLANATION*. It is important to point out here that Hempel's viewpoint is that of the "logical empiricist," and consistent with ours: "The terms 'empirical science' and 'scientific explanation' will here be understood to refer to the entire field of empirical inquiry, including the natural and the social sciences as well as historical research" (333).

prediction rests mainly on a pragmatic difference between the two: While in the case of an explanation the final event is known to have happened, and its determining conditions have to be sought, the situation is reversed in the case of a prediction: here, the initial conditions are given, and their "effect," which, in the typical case, has not yet taken place—is to be determined.[152]

A certain event or set of events can be said to have caused a specified "effect" only if there are general laws connecting the former with the latter in such a way that, given a description of the antecedent events, the occurrence of the effect can be deduced with the help of the laws.[153]

That being said, however, scientific laws are not easy things to pin down precisely: on the one hand, it is not clear that all generalizations are law-like; on the other, it is debatable whether law-like generalizations are always necessary and sufficient for scientific explanations.[154] And yet, there is good reason to suppose that arguments involving scientific laws will stand up as being explanatory.

Thus scientific law is explanatory specifically in this sense. But can the same be said of jurisprudential law? In fact, does jurisprudential law ultimately explain anything? Certainly not in the scientific sense of the word. First of all, the three concepts of prediction, causality and explanation appear not to be closely related as they commonly occur in jurisprudence. *Stare decisis* is a predictive rule of thumb, but ultimately unreliable. Causality is essentially retributive: usually an effect is known, raising the suspicion (or even certainty) that a law has been violated (an impossibility in science). The cause must be sought, in the form of an action and agent, and when found, culpability is assigned and an appropriate legal sanction imposed. The cause cannot be deduced from the effect merely by a law or laws; rather, such "deduction" depends on careful investigation and observation of the circumstances, after which persuasive evidence of the cause and culpability must be shown. Do these proceedings constitute an explanation? They certainly explain what happened in a single case, but no more.

So where does this leave us with respect to the competing models of jurisprudential and scientific law when Schenker invokes a law or principle? We can probably only answer this question on a case-by-case basis, a procedure Schenker surely would have applauded. Nonetheless, it seems safe to say that the more the context is strict composition, the closer Schenker gets to the

---

152. Ibid., 234.
153. Ibid., 301.
154. For a general discussion of these issues, see Brown, *Explaining Tonality*, 1–12.

scientific model; the more the context is free composition with its necessity for interpretation and extension of law, the closer he gets to the jurisprudential model.

The Historical Argument

> A history of music would above all have to show precisely the unity in the geniuses. However, to write it presupposes that the unity has first been verified in the primordial laws, in the material. The requirement to be fulfilled is, as you see, my most fervent aspiration, and you should believe that I would gladly like to show the destiny of the laws as it was experienced by artists over the course of the centuries.[155]

That Schenker was a "historicist" is clear from virtually everything we know about him. At the very least, we know it from his education and the environment in which it took place, his pioneering work in music philology, his preference for authentic performance of the music he loved, and most of all, from the music-theoretical perspective, his return to "authentic" music theory, which he combined with his original insights in an attempt to "correct" the pedagogy of theory and the course of music history. He clearly thought of music theory as intimately tied to and influential on the history of music, as well as our understanding of it. *HL* demonstrates that throughout. Indeed, an idiosyncratic combination of music theory and, to a lesser extent, history, its "plot," especially when one considers the descent into decadence recounted in DAC, is a tragedy.[156] Much grander in conception than a harmony book, the work is essentially an introduction to Schenker's whole research program as it existed at the beginning of his career, recounted via the tale of the artist, his discoveries, and inventions.

As a spokesman for the apparent end of the common practice, as he saw it, his approach to history served a practical purpose as well. Schenker was a performer and composer who faced the problem of composition in the twentieth century: he was therefore concerned with understanding the history of compositional technique that culminated in the works of Brahms, and the implications that history had for the future of music composition.

---

155. Letter from Schenker to August Halm, *SDO*: DLA [Deutsches Literaturarchiv] 69.930 9; January 18, 1920; transc. Ian Bent and Lee Rothfarb; transl. Lee Rothfarb. This is also transcribed by Federhofer in *HS*, 142.
156. See White, *Metahistory*, particularly his remarks on Burckhardt, 262–64.

It is no accident that his first essay containing music theory is called "The Spirit of Musical Technique."[157] Thus, his research in the history of music focused not on recounting the lives and styles of particular composers, discovering and deciphering hitherto unknown repertoires, or connecting particular musical idioms to those in the other arts or to some general *Zeitgeist*, etc., but rather on shedding light on the development of particular compositional techniques used by the great composers of the common-practice period. For him, the nature of those techniques was inseparable from their historical genesis.

This is all, of course, consistent with Schenker's continual emphasis on the tones "leading their own lives"—the conviction that no extramusical context is necessary to understand music; rather, we must endeavor to understand the reasons not only why the tones behave as they do, but also how they came to do so. And it is consistent with his work in musical philology—that is, his efforts to let composers' manuscripts speak for themselves rather than through the intervention of other documents either by the composers themselves, such as their essays, letters, etc., or by other secondary sources. Such documents are important, but they have their place: they are there to serve the music: "it is a mistake to believe that one must . . . understand the tones above all from the life. No! the tones are first of all to be grasped only of themselves; and if we can do this, then we can, on the other hand, also better understand the life of the creator."[158]

During the course of *HL*, Schenker is quite clear about which topics should be the subject of historical investigation: "the penetration of the harmonic principle into the horizontal line of the melody has its own history. It certainly would be worthwhile to trace that history, if only because this would facilitate the solution of many a difficult problem of music history."[159] A few pages later, he adds: "one might even write a history of the essential harmony, V. The other tones of the system—with the exception of the tonic—did not encourage the concept of the essential harmony, at least not to the same extent and at so early a time as did the V."[160] But these topics

---

157. Given the substance of the essay, the title might be translated more accurately as "The Essence of Musical Technique." *Cassell's German Dictionary* (1962)—often quite reliable for academic prose of this vintage—gives "essence" as a possible translation of *Geist* (182).
158. Schenker, *Die letzten fünf Sonaten, op. 109*, 7.
159. *HL*, §76, *Anmerkung*; *HA*, 134, footnote.
160. *HL*, §78, 183; *HA*, 141.

were part of a history still to be investigated; when Schenker wrote *HL*, he was not yet ready to write *the* history of compositional technique. Indeed, he never wrote that history as a separate entity, in large part because his theoretical work and private teaching ultimately took all of his time. But *HL* contains a partial history, often recounted in the "epochal style"—i.e., language designed to match the grandeur Schenker perceived in the musical language itself. His Promethean artist accepts (steals?) nature's hint, and invents the fundamental compositional techniques of Western art music with no further help, a momentous task that took centuries to complete: "In broad terms, mankind should take more pride in its development of music than in that of any [of the] other arts. For the other arts, as imitations of nature, have sprung more spontaneously—one might even say, more irresistibly—from the innate human propensity to imitate."[161]

Schenker's History of Compositional Technique

> Repetition, this ancient and original musical discovery, probably provides the best evidence that even millennia ago music *carried in its own womb a unique and reliable principle of organization,* and, following this line of thought, was *emancipated from language much earlier* than music historians suppose. It also shows, in my opinion, the great antiquity of instrumental music, which had been operating according to purely musical principles long before the beginning of the sixteenth century, when musicians began that epochal cultivation whose fruits we enjoy today.[162]

But just what was to be repeated, as purely instrumental music arose? In Schenker's view, it had to have been the motive. The kind of evidence he offers for this assertion is interesting: it is not external documentary evidence of whatever sort, but a music-theoretical "deduction" from the "notes themselves." Though it is clear throughout *HL* that Schenker was aware of a considerable amount of external musicological evidence, he continued to concentrate on what the notes themselves could tell us. According to him, the problem of how to create purely instrumental music compelled musicians to follow an inevitable path, since the (presumably inevitable) motive "is nothing more and nothing less than itself":

---

161. *HL* §8, 32f.; *HA*, 20; cf. opening paragraph of PATH.
162. SPIRIT, 321.

People must have become thoroughly convinced of this deficiency on the part of music as soon as instrumental music began to arise. For as long as music clung to language, it believed itself to be comprehensible, although it was only language that ensured comprehensibility; but when it ventured out alone into the world, it must have realized its self-deception rather quickly and recognized its inability to solicit understanding in any other way than by clarifying individual motives and tonal successions through repetition and imitation.[163]

Schenker develops this line of thought further in *HL*. There he starts immediately by arguing that the artist's invention of the motive and its psychological associations through repetition create "imitations" that make music as an art possible (*HL*, §§1–7). The argument is richer and more convincing in two respects than the corresponding passage in GEIST: first, Schenker emphasizes the notion of "associations" in *HL*, making musical motivic repetition part of a much larger psychological process,[164] and second, he connects the notion of imitation from GEIST with the arts in general, which depend on the mimetic theory for comprehensibility—also missing from GEIST. The internal motivic imitations of music are sufficient to insure instrumental music a place in the high arts, which, he emphasizes in the very first section, ancient Greek music did not achieve.

Clearly, something had dampened Schenker's enthusiasm for ancient music, and ancient Greek music in particular. The relatively large number of discoveries of remnants of the music itself may have been that event. The late nineteenth century witnessed crucial discoveries of Greek melodies, in 1883 (the famous "Song of Seikilos," discovered by Sir William Ramsey), 1890 (C. Wessely's discovery of a papyrus fragment), and 1893–94 (H. Weil and T. Reinach's discovery of two paeans). Counting all sources known earlier as well, "the corpus was now of respectable size, and C. von Jan [who published the volume of Greek technical writing on music in 1895] collected the remains of Greek vocal music known by 1899 in a small Teubner volume,"[165] the *Musici scriptores graeci*, supplementum, *melodiarum reliquiae*. It is not impossible that Schenker knew of this activity, and that perusal of the Teubner volume prompted him to revise his belief in "the great antiquity of instrumental music" to the negative view of Greek music he writes at the

---

163. Ibid.
164. In GEIST Schenker uses the word *Ideenassociationen* only once (139), ascribing music's use of repetitive associations to the association of words in language, which, he had stressed earlier, do not depend on repetition. It is ideas that are "associated."
165. See Introduction to Pöhlmann and West, eds., *Documents*, 5.

outset of *HL*. He is no less enthusiastic about melody as the driving force of music, but he claims that what was then known to musicologists as ancient Greek music—largely vocal and text-driven, as it was—never achieved the status of true art. Thus Schenker seems to retreat from the claim that there was instrumental music "operating according to purely musical principles long before the beginning of the sixteenth century," or, if he continued to believe this, he did not place that music in ancient Greece and chose to be silent on the issue in *HL*,[166] never providing an alternative. Indeed, in WEG,[167] Schenker places the beginnings of "our music" quite specifically at the opening of the sixteenth century. The history of polyphony before the Renaissance is conspicuously absent from his account in any of the sources.

The motive can be articulated by simple rhythmic repetition (*HL*, §4), but "even freer forms of repetition and imitation, including manifold little contrasts, will not cancel the magical effects of association."[168] Repetition is the basis of form as well, even forms that apparently depend on "contrast" (§5). Combining the motive with the tonal system (§8) brings the means of creating melodic content and musical systems together:

> The creation of the *system of tones*, within which the associative drives of the motives, finally discovered, could be expressed, proved to be as difficult as the discovery of the motive, the original seed of music. [Cf. the unnumbered *Überleitung* page in WEG.] Basically, the two experiments were reciprocal: learning the pathways by which to explore the motive led at the same time to work on the system, and vice versa: as the system was built, new results and pathways by which to explore the motive arose.

For Schenker, the intimate connection of motive and system is so important that it ultimately led to the decline of the modal system, and the emergence of the major and minor systems, which are optimal for motivic

---

166. As yet, neither literary nor music-theoretical sources provide evidence of motivic repetition or even melodic variation form in ancient Greek music. (The latter might seem a likely transitional phase between texted and purely instrumental music that Schenker, focused on motivic repetition, does not pursue.) Nonetheless, virtuoso instrumental music came into its own by the sixth century BCE. Not surprisingly, there is evidence of instrumental "program music," which passes the mimetic test. See Martin West's account of the five-part *Pythikos Nomos* in West, *Ancient Greek Music*, 212–15. The piece describes Apollo's victory over a monstrous serpent.
167. See appendix A.
168. *HL*, §4; *HA*, 7.

development (§§26–30). Instrumental music and repetition may have earlier origins, but given the date when modality waned, we infer that the motive came into its own starting in the late sixteenth century.

Nonetheless, Schenker does in fact present the modes, which are largely absent from books on harmony of the late nineteenth and early twentieth centuries. His modal system consists of six permutations of the white-note diatonic series (*Reihe*), Ionian (on C), Dorian (on D), Phrygian (on E), Lydian (on F), Mixolydian (on G), Aeolian (on A)—actually the final state of a long historical evolution in theory and practice that he scarcely mentions, but was evidently aware of (*HL*, §20).[169] The ultimate rejection of the modal system was inevitable, though the modes were necessary "stages of development" (§30). Indeed, they were "false theory" (§28), based upon misunderstandings of Greek theory and propped up by the church (§30)—essentially failed "experiments," out of touch with practice (§28). The existence of *musica ficta*, often used to correct Lydian and Mixolydian modes to Ionian, for example, is proof that true musicians of talent (or even genius) could rise above such false, prescriptive theory and find the right way (§29).[170] The minor mode, as it occurs in "primitive music" and early Western music was a "stepping stone" to the major mode, and is not to be identified with the minor mode as the product of the artist.[171] Much of this account concurs with the one Guido Adler gives (see the end of this chapter), and was probably held by many.

Yet traces of the modes survived into the tonal era (though clearly under the aegis of the major and minor systems) through the process of "mixture," by which certain pitches from the "minor modes" may replace their major counterparts and be mixed with the remaining pitches from the parallel major (*HL*, §38). Schenker demonstrates this by transposing the modes over C. The process yields the six possible combinations of five or six letter-name classes from major, with one or two replacements drawn from the parallel

---

169. These are the six authentic modes (from a twelve-mode system, six authentic, and six plagal) of the Swiss theorist, Heinrich Glarean (1488–1563), presented in his ΔΩΔΕΚΑΧΟΡΔΟΝ *(Dodecachordon)*. (The seventh permutation (B–B) presents a tritone from the first to fifth scale degree, so Glarean rejects it as a potential authentic mode; the F–F permutation is likewise rejected as a possible plagal mode, since it presents a tritone from the first to fourth degree.)

170. It was Glarean who first pointed out that *musica ficta* used in this way turned the "Lydian" and "Mixolydian" modes into his Ionian mode, though he was hardly the "discoverer" of the major/minor system, as has been alleged in the past.

171. *HL*, §25; *HA*, 52–54.

minor (*HL*, §39).[172] Most importantly, none of these six resulting series is a system on its own, as has been claimed in the singling out of the ♭3 + ♭6 (non-diatonic!) "scale" by Hauptmann (as "minor–major") and Riemann (as "major–minor") (*HL* §40, footnote). Two of the six series are recognizable as modes: ♭$\hat{7}$ (Mixolydian) and ♭$\hat{3}$ + ♭$\hat{7}$ (Dorian). This raises the question of whether the Phrygian and Lydian modes might have survived (*HL*, §50). In fact, the Phrygian survives in the use of ♭$\hat{2}$ in minor, its true home—Schenker is skeptical of its use in major (*HL*, §50). The Lydian series remains as unusable as ever (*HL*, §51).

In investigating the modes in practice, Schenker analyzes examples of Gregorian chant, claiming that they show no clear tonal, motivic or formal organization. Indeed, the melodies appear "to have been thrown together in a haphazard and irrational fashion,"[173] and are essentially controlled by the words. He finds that they lack the necessary motivic repetition, and theorizes that variants in their transmission may well have been caused by the difficulty of memorizing them. He examines these examples, however, in the section entitled "The Realization of the Triad" (*HL*, §76), which comes just after the section on intervals, and introduces his theory of the essential harmony. The student learns early on that melody projects its own harmony without the necessity of polyphony, or homophonic chordal accompaniment, and the chant examples, text-driven as they are, demonstrate just how far removed they were from the melodic projection of harmony. "It may be assumed, however, that [folk songs and "liturgical jubilations"[174]] have contributed to the development of harmonic feeling, as manifested, for example, in the melodic unfolding of a major or minor triad or in the discovery of the Ionian and Aeolian systems themselves."[175] But regarding very early polyphony, which Schenker gets to in the large section on "Essential Harmony and Counterpoint," he claims that any extension of the melody (a necessary first

---

172. Thus, taking the three possible replacements, ♭3, ♭6, ♭7, the possibilities are, ♭3, *or* ♭6, *or* ♭7, added to 6 tones from major; and ♭3 + ♭6, *or* ♭3 + ♭7, *or* ♭6 + ♭7 added to five tones from major. Schenker presents these six possibilities as intervening stages between major and (Aeolian) minor systems, yielding eight in all. He calls each a "series" (*Reihe*), not a "scale" (*Skala* or *Tonleiter*). Indeed, he never uses the term *Skala* even once in *HL* (despite the ubiqitous "scale-step" in *HA*).
173. *HL*, §25; *HA*, 52–54.
174. Cf. the Latin *iubilate*, "be joyful," from the opening line of Psalm 66: "Make a joyful noise unto the Lord."
175. *HL*, §88; *HA*, 164.

step in realizing harmony through melody) was probably impeded by the Church's "ownership" of the melodies; moreover, the use of these melodies as cantus firmi in constructing the first experiments in polyphony probably doomed any effort to find harmony in this music from the start.[176] For one thing, it confined the length of the polyphonic music that resulted. "It was out of the question to extend the length of a melody, which is what ought to have been done most urgently."[177]

According to Schenker, it took centuries for composers to "reflect the harmonic point of view in the melody itself."[178] Certain decisive steps were finally taken in Italy around 1600.[179] Schenker is particularly impressed by the ways in which composers of monody, such as Giulio Caccini and Lodovico Viadana, ornamented their melodies in an almost improvised manner: "The melody had to be unfolded and to become ever richer; it was to gain a fresher tempo, uninhibited by any overburdening; it was to learn how to run. All this was achieved by the Italian monody . . . The individual harmony learns, so to speak, to dictate a vast melodic project and to support and carry it as long as it lasts."[180]

Through their use of continuo, Caccini and Viadana also liberated the bass melodically: "the bass voice gets emancipated from the stiff technique, noticeable until then, of over strict dependence on the melody, on the one hand, and, on the other, on a voice-leading which rests almost throughout on the principle of the triad, and it thus acquires an independence, lifting it almost to the rank of a line in its own right, almost coordinated, with the melody itself." In this respect, the bass asserts itself as an independent melodic line: "Thus the bass, too, becomes melody, and its projection undergoes the influence of the harmonic principle no less

---

176. *HL*, §88, *Anmerkung*; *HA*, 163–64.

177. *HL,* §88; *HA*, 164–65.

178. *HL*, §76, 180; *HA*, 137.

179. "The vocal era came to an end. Composers learned in the next stage—and this is the most significant revolution in the field of musical technique—to fertilize the sonority itself in a new way. The sonority was, in a sense "set free" by a longer series of tones, whose multiplicity in succession is grasped precisely through the sonority's unity. The sonority was *composed out*, and thereby represented through the horizontal line. And thus the first step was taken on the way to the final goal of reducing a longer succession of sonorities, each with its own multitude, according to a new principle special to those sonorities alone." *CP1*, xxvi.

180. *HL*, §88, 218; *HA*, 172.

than the melody; the bass, too, unfolds harmonic ideas; i.e., together with the other voices, it becomes a link in an unrolled harmonic concept."[181]

Still, Schenker maintains that many late sixteenth- and seventeenth-century musicians had difficulty balancing the horizontal and the vertical in their compositions. According to Schenker, the passage from measure 1 to measure 9 of example 1.1 may lead to an E major triad, but it does so in a manner that is nonetheless obscure harmonically: "What a lack of proportion there is between this orphaned triad, on the one hand, and, on the other, the sum total of manifold triads attached to the individual tones of the melody! Without any further explanation it must be obvious to anybody that this abundance of chords is bound to retard the inner momentum of the melody." Furthermore, the individual harmonies "suffer from a lack of purposiveness" with each one becoming "a purpose in itself" and each one expressing "things of which the melody knows nothing."[182]

The new melodic nature of the bass that arose in the continuo in the seventeenth century leads Schenker to analyze a figured bass from J. S. Bach's *Generalbassbüchlein*, which demonstrates a "bass line, showing rich rhythmical articulation. Its development could constitute part of a real live composition."[183] This is in stark contrast to the exercise Schenker had just criticized from Richter's *Lehrbuch*, in which the bass line consisted merely of chord roots.[184] Thus, from the point of view of the historical narrative, all parts have now achieved the freedom and potential melodic profile to participate in an essential harmony, and a mature compositional technique is

---

181. *HL*, §88, 218; *HA*, 172–73. Schenker recycles his comments about Caccini and the role of monody later on. See Schenker, "Yet Another Word on the Urlinie," Robert Snarrenberg, tr. (*WT2*, 53–54). Also see *FC*, §251, 94 and *FC* §254, 99ff.: here Schenker not only discusses the nature of repetition in detail, especially as regards imitative music and the role of the German chorale (though he fails to admit that many chorales were adapted from plainchants), but he also focuses on the idea of expanding content (something that comes from the improvisatory spirit). This balance between repetition and the creation of new material resurfaces in his discussion of fugue in *FC* §322, 143–44, notably in his comparison between Bach's treatment of his material and Handel's approach, which explores "even more hidden paths than Bach" that "are monuments to a freedom which seems to scorn all organic bonds."
182. *HL*, §88, 211–12; *HA*, 166.
183. *HL*, §92; *HA*, 179. See Poulin, *J. S. Bach's Precepts and Principles*, 29.
184. Richter, *Lehrbuch*, 20.

Example 1.1. *HL*, Example 169, J. P. Sweelinck, Psalm 1

possible, though other transpositions of the key systems will be explored in the nineteenth century, sometimes at the expense of over-arching tonal control.

But though Bach's compositional technique, even in relatively modest chorales, represented a giant stride forward compared to Sweelinck's, composers struggling with the nascent phenomenon of the essential harmony were, unfortunately, helped little by theorists, for the "figured bass," the new theoretical genre of the time, was also in its infancy. Much as Schenker valued figured-bass theory as a guide for teaching keyboard players how to accompany melodies, he nonetheless questioned its capacity to explain the behavior of late seventeenth- and eighteenth-century Baroque polyphony. As he made clear in *KP1*, he believed theorists must not only describe what contrapuntal rules the student should follow, but they must also offer reasons for following them. And it was precisely C. P. E. Bach's reasons that Schenker found wanting: "The figured-bass theory of Bach was faulty because, unfortunately, problems are shown there not in their origin but in an already advanced state. Thoroughbass theory shows us prolongations of fundamental forms [*Urformen*] without having first familiarized the reader with the latter in any way."[185] As seen above, he made the same point in his response to Bach's description of his free fantasy.

Such are the main points of the history of compositional technique and its understanding by theorists as conceived by Schenker at the time he wrote *HL*. During its presentation in *HL*, often placed in digressive "remarks" (*Anmerkungen*), Schenker also manages to cover some of the main topics of a harmony course, though he presents the most prominent of these—i.e., triads and seventh chords, and a rejection of ninth chords—as a kind of afterthought in a brief final section—after the history has been presented! (*HL*, 236–77) The message to the student is clear: the psychology of harmony is an interpretive process that evolved historically, communicable by the melody alone, and with other "cooperative" contrapuntal voices, even in transparent textures. Learning to write and connect chords is not the point. But is this really a book on common-practice harmony, given that it started with a discussion of motives, does not get to chords in any real detail until the end of part I (and then, there is apparently nothing on seventh chords[186]), while part II ends with an exhortation to improvise preludes—to improvise real music rather than write harmony exercises, of which there are none in the book? Certainly all of this places the book in extremely rarified company—if any at all.

A Larger Context for Schenker's History of Compositional Technique

It is important to remember that Schenker began writing about music during the infancy of musicology: there was not yet a "normal science" of music scholarship, if indeed there ever would be one, but it was particularly rudderless at this point.[187] To use Kuhn's definition, there was not yet any

---

185. *CPI*, "Author's Preface," xxviii.
186. In fact, there is a discussion of seventh chords and their inversions, but it was excised by Jonas in the editing of *HA*. See appendix C.
187. "'Normal science' means research firmly based upon one or more past scientific achievements, achievements that some particular scientific community acknowledges for a time as supplying the foundation for its further practice." Thomas Kuhn, *Structure of Scientific Revolutions*, 10.

established "foundation" for writing the history of music—to say nothing of one for a critique of speculative or pedagogical music theory. And while the research university seemed to offer a locus for this activity, *Musikwissenschaft* had yet to establish a secure home there. On the music-historical front, the first "history of harmony" had appeared, and historic musical sources were beginning to open up, though the theoretical texts relating to medieval music were available before the music itself, which remained in short supply until near the end of the century.[188] At the same time, the writing of history itself was in turmoil, as the old "epoch style," in which the reader "was meant to sense the nearness of actual events," gave way, in some quarters, to a more "analytic and discursive style," in response to the rise of the *Naturwissenschaften* we discuss in chapter 4.[189]

Schenker's pathway through the history of music may seem to be a personal one, but it was not unprecedented. Indeed, a famous and influential nineteenth-century history, penned not by a musicologist but by a composer, starts with Greek monody, has little good to say about text-driven Gregorian chant, after which monody returns in transformed state with a bassline embellished harmonically in Italian opera of the seventeenth century, then on to the Lutheran chorale, Bach, his treatment of the chorale and the whole polyphonic edifice based upon it, and finally the culmination: Beethoven. This is in fact Wagner's history of music, and clearly it had a strong impact on Schenker.[190] And like Wagner's history, Schenker's had a "message": namely, the prehistory, birth and evolution of the essential harmony, an extraordinarily—even shockingly—original notion. Some will object that it is history at the service of theory—like Wagner's—but it is history nonetheless: history *interpreted* by theory, no longer fashionable. As outside the norm as his historical scholarship might seem now, it likely would have been viable in this larger context of the period, if he had managed to secure a teaching position in a university or *Musikhochschule*, which he never did, and perhaps to temper

---

188. See Fétis, *Esquisse*. Also see Coussemaker's *Scriptores*, which published later medieval treatises, continuing the work that Martin Gerbert had started in the eighteenth century.
189. See Dahlhaus, *Foundations of Music History*, 129.
190. Wagner, "The Artwork of the Future." See section 4, "The Art of Tone" (*Das Kunstwerk der Zukunft; Tonkunst*).

his polemical writing—which also never happened.[191] It was left to his students to make a home for his ideas in the American college and university system, and to the "music theory movement" that began in the US during the post–World War II era to demonstrate the viability of his work as a direction for future research, though the historical argument would remain the most controversial aspect of it.

Heinrich Schenker, Guido Adler, Felix Salzer, and the Beginnings of Musicology

When, in about 1900, Schenker began his scholarly work in music theory, editing, and private teaching, Guido Adler (1855–1941) was in charge of musicology at the university. Like Schenker, Adler was also Jewish and a provincial, but from Moravia, in the eastern part of the present-day Czech Republic. Thirteen years Schenker's senior, he likewise had studied music (with Bruckner, among others) at the conservatory (1868–74; diploma, 1874) and law at the university, completing his law degree in 1878 (at age twenty-three; Schenker was twenty-two on completion). But from there on, Schenker's and Adler's paths diverged.

For example, it is clear that Schenker saw Bruckner as a personification of the crisis in the theory of harmony when he quoted him as having said: "Look gentlemen, this is the rule. Of course I don't compose that way."[192] If anything, Bruckner, about whom Schenker also had positive things to say, inspired his effort to reform music theory.[193] The remark, allegedly uttered during a class at the conservatory (though Bruckner's classes at the university were, by all reports, similar), was surely, for Schenker, one strike against the higher academic study of music, of which Bruckner had become an unlikely and controversial part.[194] Adler, on the other hand, seems to have struck up a

---

191. This suggests a point of comparison with Aristoxenus, also a famously abrasive personality, who was passed over in favor of Theophrastus when Aristotle was looking for a replacement to head his Lyceum.
192. See *HL* §90; *HA*, 177.
193. For a textured portrait of the Bruckner–Schenker relationship see Federhofer, "Heinrich Schenkers Bruckner-Verständnis."
194. We must also factor in Bruckner's additional years of teaching from the time he taught Adler, during which he stood by Sechter's increasingly antiquated system nearly chapter and verse. See Bruckner, *Vorlesungen*, ed. Schwanzara, Also cf. Flotzinger's claim that "Bruckner always delivered the same material in the

friendship with Bruckner, or at least an active correspondence.[195] And while Schenker turned to music criticism and performance after his studies at the university, Adler remained in the university, moving on to the Musicology Department after his law degree, where he wrote a PhD dissertation entitled "The Basic Historical Types of Christian-Western Music up to 1600,"[196] receiving the PhD in 1880. After a start as an unsalaried lecturer (*Dozent*), he began to teach full-time at the university in 1883. After a lengthy stint as professor of musicology at the Charles University in Prague (1885–98), he returned to Vienna in 1898 with the retirement of Hanslick and transformed what must have been a relatively modest operation into the Institute of Musicology (Musikwissenschaftliches Institut), a model for others that followed. One of modern musicology's "inventors," Adler's recommendations for the nascent field appeared in a foundational paper, "The Scope, Method, and Aim of Musicology" (1885), which, to a great extent, has continued to determine the structure of musicology down to the present day. Adler's plan divided the new study into two parts: I. "historical musicology" and II. "systematic musicology":

I. Historical musicology: the "history of music according to period, ethnic group, larger political organization [in an era of empires], country, province, city, artistic school, artist." Areas of study were: A. Notation; B. Basic historical classes (grouping of types of music); C. Historical succession of [musical] laws: 1. how they were executed in each period; 2. How they were taught by theorists of the period; 3. Types of performance practice of the period; D. Organology, the study of musical instruments.
II. Systematic musicology: "the establishment of *the primary laws* of the individual aspects of music composition." Areas of study were: A. "investigation and justification of the laws of harmony, rhythm, and melody"; B. Aesthetics; C. Pedagogy and teaching methods (principally of the standard topics of pedagogical music theory of the time); D. Ethnomusicology.[197]

---

same order with the same musical examples in his lectures." See his "Bruckner als Theorielehrer," 44. Also see Wason, *Viennese Harmonic Theory*, chapter 9.
195. See Rosenthal, "Reminiscences of Guido Adler (1855–1941)," 19: "Among [Adler's] many friends were such musical giants as Brahms, Bruckner, Mahler, Schoenberg, Wolf, et al."
196. "Die historischen Grundklassen der christlich-abendländischen Musik bis 1600," *Allgemeine Musikzeitung* 15, 1880.
197. Adler, "Umfang, Methode und Ziel der Musikwissenschaft." Also see the excerpt in *Music in European Thought 1851–1912*, ed. Bujić, 348–55. Adler summarized the

We could go on at length regarding Schenker's probable objections to this plan, starting with the separation of the historical and systematic, and the lesser position given to the latter. (And of course *HL* details many of his objections to II. C.) Riemann in fact developed a plan that sets theory out front, and the history of music last.[198] But it was Adler's that held sway in Vienna.[199] As Karnes shows, Adler was preoccupied with finding a place for *Musikwissenschaft* within the university, and adopting a completely historicist, positivist, and data-driven plan of research surely seemed to him the best way to go about doing it. Analysis was the focus of the discussion, and Adler started with real music, a point of agreement with Schenker, one might think. The question is the kind of analysis. The reader will gain a sense of Adler's approach from the following excerpt:

> When a work of art is to be examined, it is first identified *paleographically* [Adler might have used the musical term, notation, straightaway, but he knew the power of words associated with the study of ancient languages]. If not in our notational system, it will need to be transcribed. This activity itself will provide important criteria regarding the time when it originated. Next, the work will be investigated according to the nature of its construction. We begin with its *rhythmic* characteristics: whether there is a time signature and of which type; which temporal relationships are to be found among the parts; how these are to be grouped and arranged into periods. We may begin with the *tonality*, and indeed the tonal nature of the individual parts, and only then with that of the whole, as was the usual practice for a long period during the Middle Ages, but today, correctly, no longer normal procedure. The individual

---

plan in tabular form; a photocopy and translation of the original appear on 354–55. Also see Mugglestone, "Guido Adler's 'The Scope, Method, and Aim of Musicology' (1885)." The translation here is our own.

198. Not surprisingly, Riemann's plan, the plan of a music theorist, takes a much more "structuralist" approach, assuming that one must understand musical processes before worrying about systems of classification. Thus Riemann starts with 1. acoustics (the naturalized and streamlined Classical theory of harmony); 2. tone-psychology (presumably a précis of Stumpf); 3. aesthetics; 4. the standard practical music-theoretic disciplines; 5. the history of music. See his *Grundriß der Musikwissenschaft* (Outline of Musicology), first published in 1908.

199. For a very interesting perspective on Adler's vision for musicology, its many evolutionary metaphors, and its relationship to work by the German biologist Ernst Haeckel (1834–1919), see Breuer's "The Birth of Musicology from the Spirit of Evolution." The similarity of Haeckel's tabular summary of his work to Adler's summary is striking.

parts are then investigated according to their cadential structure, transitions, accidentals, and placed in the context of the whole. Now the construction of the polyphony is described: range and division of the voices, the imitation of themes and motives, each according to the entrances at various intervals, and their various temporal succession; whether the themes are augmented, diminished, inverted or retrograded; and further, the voice leading and use of consonance or dissonance, their preparation and resolution.[200]

The description continues at some length past this point, but this excerpt is sufficient for us to see that in its flat, passive construction, it attempts to be as neutrally descriptive as possible. But can a recitation of data alone, with no guiding theory—or at least some articulated purpose—satisfy the demands of a "human science"? To invoke the legal argument that would have been familiar to these fellow lawyers, there is evidence, but no "charge"—apparently no purpose to this cross-examination. Moreover, the description does not—and cannot—succeed in avoiding all judgements of "value," for the mere selection of the material to be analyzed is itself laden with value: it obviously assumes a polyphonic piece from some time in the later Middle Ages or early Renaissance (worthy of study, we presume—though that is not beyond question); however, the analytical terms and categories seem to be anachronistically those of harmonic and formal theory of Adler's time.[201] This is not surprising: knowledge of the early repertoire was new and largely undeveloped, while the terminology of common-practice harmony was the lingua franca of most educated musicians. The work described might well have been a candidate for Adler's *Denkmäler der Tonkunst in Österreich* (*DTÖ*, Monuments of Music in Austria), a project that Hanslick, and Adler, his star student, conceived in 1888, and that Adler edited for more than forty years (from its start in 1894 to 1938). About *DTÖ* and the parallel project in Germany, *DDT, Denkmäler Deutscher Tonkunst* (Monuments of German Music), which began in 1892, Schenker wrote:

> In our time—this time of "historical monuments of music"—the signs are increasing in favor of the assumption that old works are good *eo ipso* [in

---

200. Adler, "Umfang, Methode und Ziel der Musikwissenschaft," 6.
201. Was Adler looking for the right things? He was evidently conscious of this problem. A number of early dissertations from the University of Vienna deal with the history of music theory, as does his own work, as we shall see. This is where the study of the history of music theory as a handmaiden to transcription and the production of editions began, but also as an aid in "authentic" analysis.

themselves] and merely on account of their age and that they deserve to be saved and reproduced at great expense. Oh no! The committee in charge of such decisions ought to make up its mind whether it wants to represent the archivist point of view, according to which all works, no matter whether good or bad, ought to be reproduced . . . or whether they want to adopt the criterion of goodness or badness as decisive for the inclusion of a work into new volumes . . . The historical approach has the advantage of strict neutrality; its disadvantage is that of misleading public opinion . . . The critical approach, on the other hand, has the advantage of systematic sifting of the whole material. Its disadvantage is that this sifting depends on the whim of some editors who are not in all cases as gifted and as learned as is required by the task.[202]

In his worry about an uncritical printing of works based purely upon age, Schenker voices a fear similar to that expressed by the young Friedrich Nietzsche in the 1870s in works that achieved wide circulation in Vienna, and were the subject of discussion at the university. Karnes writes that "as Nietzsche argued, 'everything old and past that enters one's field of vision . . . is in the end blandly taken to be equally worthy of reverence, while . . . everything new and evolving is rejected and persecuted.'" Schenker's fear of "misleading public opinion" also resonates with Nietzsche's thinking. Karnes continues, quoting Nietzsche: "More important, should the antiquarian tendency 'grow too mightily and overpower the other modes of regarding the past,' it can pose a great danger not only for the present and future of art, but for the future of one's culture as a whole."[203]

The voice of Jellinek, the professor of law who had the greatest impact on Schenker, also emerges here: Schenker is no "democrat" in his philological work. Rather, he believed strongly that the purpose of such historical editions was not only the preservation of historical sources, but also the support and encouragement of actual performance of the work—that a balance between the two had to be achieved. Since one cannot perform everything (or indeed edit and preserve everything), the judgement and formulation of criteria for preservation devolve to the editor (and editorial board), and they must be up to the task of making hard musical choices. Schenker and Adler may not have been so far apart in this goal, but they certainly disagreed on the means to achieve it. For Schenker, musicianship was at least as important as scholarship.

---

202. *HL*, §30; *HA*, 69, footnote 5, modified.
203. Karnes, *Music, Criticism and the Challenge of History*, 72.

However, probably the biggest disagreement Schenker had with Adler concerned his notion of "style," which Adler had borrowed from art historians, and which was his current project while Schenker was starting his career in music theory, teaching, and editing.[204] Schenker regarded the idea as superficial—to the extent that there was any stable idea behind the term, which, when Adler popularized it in musicological writing, was already overused and underdefined.[205] Schenker writes in his diary about a conversation that his student Hans Weisse, also a PhD student at the university, had with Adler concerning a paper he had written (which certainly contained ideas indebted to Schenker):

> Weisse appeared for his lesson and told me the following: that Adler . . . had made numerous "objections," among which, for example, was that he did not understand the concepts "causality" and "synthesis" . . . The most amusing thing is the way Adler wants to replace the words "causality" and "synthesis"—that is, the very expressions that I use in teaching students and in my own work—with "style," which he propagandizes in his own work. Adler's attempt is all the more grotesque, as he has not the slightest idea what Weisse or I mean by "causality" or "synthesis." The inevitable conclusion is that Adler is clearly not connecting the notion of "style" with anything well-defined or true, for otherwise he would have known whether the idea of style was permissible, in any sense, in those places where I speak of "musical causality" and "synthesis."[206]

As we have seen, even at the very beginning of his new career, Schenker wanted to get below the surface of the music, to demonstrate compositional techniques and their history, unrecognized by the *Musikwissenschaftler*. Thus avoiding the Musicology Department under Adler, whom he accused of lacking any artistic instinct,[207] Schenker identified himself with his hero of

---

204. See his *Der Stil in der Musik* (Style in Music).
205. Nonetheless, "style analysis" continues to live on. See Crocker, *A History of Musical Style*, or the most descriptive version, LaRue, *Guidelines for Style Analysis*; LaRue even goes so far as to summarize his "guidelines" à la Adler in his "Cue Sheet for Style Analysis." But also see the approach of Meyer, *Style and Music History, Theory and Ideology*, which raises the notion of "style" to a much higher level, due in no small measure to Meyer's uncovering of non-obvious stylistic debts beneath the immediate surface of the music.
206. Federhofer, *HS*, 52; taken from diary entries of February 27, March 12, and May 12, 1915.
207. Ibid., 49.

HL, and not as a "music-scientist," which, at least according to Adler's job description, was entirely too positivist for his taste. Yet, despite Schenker's falling out and disagreements with Adler, they shared musical interests, and, in fact, students. Four of Schenker's students had doctorates in musicology from the University of Vienna, and the first three had written dissertations under Adler.[208] But that activity came to an end when Adler was pushed out in 1927 by Robert Lach, largely because Adler was Jewish.[209] To get a sense of the positive effect Adler's musicological training may have had on these students, we need a fuller knowledge of his scholarship.

As Karnes points out, Adler had first made his reputation as a medievalist before "The Scope, Method, and Aim of Musicology" achieved great notoriety as the lead article in the *Musicology Quarterly* he had founded with Friedrich Chrysander and Philip Spitta. Adler's dissertation was in fact consistent with ideas he later set out in that article—namely, that the way into a study was a descriptive setting up of "categories." But it also prepared the way for two analytical papers that amounted to studies in the history of music theory as well: Adler's 1881 *Habilitationsschrift*, "Studie zur Geschichte der Harmonie" (A Study on the History of Harmony), that got him started full-time in Vienna, and the job in Prague, and its sequel "Repetition and Imitation in Polyphony" (1886).[210] Needless to say, the titles immediately suggest inter-

---

208. Hans Weisse (1892–1940): "On the Historical Basis of the Instrumental *Kunstwalzer*, with Special Consideration of the Works of Schubert, Chopin, and Brahms" (PhD, 1919); Viktor Zuckerkandl (1896–1965): "Principles and Methods of Instrumentation in Mozart's Works" (PhD, 1927); Felix Salzer (1904–86): "Sonata Form in Schubert" (PhD, 1926). See Martin Eybl and Evelyn Fink-Mennel, eds., *Schenker-Traditionen: Eine Wiener Schule der Musiktheorie und ihre internationale Verbreitung* (A Viennese School of Music Theory and Its International Dissemination), Vienna: Böhlau Verlag, 2004, 251, for a complete list; for the individual biographies, see 236–52, and *SDO*/Profiles/Person.

209. See Antonicek, "Musikwissenschaft in Wien zur Zeit Guido Adlers," as cited in Koslovsky, "From *Sinn und Wesen* to *Structural Hearing*," 21.

210. "Die Wiederholung und Nachahmung in der Mehrstimmigkeit." A poor but marginally servicable transcribed digital copy is available at: http://www.archive.org/stream/diewiederholung00unkngoog/diewiederholung00unkngoog_djvu.txt, accessed January 23, 2020. Both of these Adler studies have been reprinted by Forgotten Books: https://www.forgottenbooks.com/de/Musik/Musik_Theorie_und_Geschichte.

ests shared with Schenker, and very likely with his students.[211] They also suggest that these interests were part of a larger historical agenda of scholars of the period—that Schenker was hardly an outlier in the questions he was trying to answer.

To demonstrate Adler's approach and the questions with which he was preoccupied, we look briefly at his "Study on the History of Harmony," the one most germane to our topic. Here, Adler proves to be just as much a "presentist" as Schenker, holding essentially the same opinion—that medieval music will always be "strange" because of his culture's deeply ingrained sense of major–minor tonality. "Sacred tonality [*Kirchentonalität*] rebels against polyphony, and this is the reason why today we confront polyphonic sacred song even by the greatest masters with admiration, but also often with alienation, which may be attributed to the fact that these works cannot be brought into accord with our modern tonal sense. The whole modern academic argument over whether and when semitones should be applied to polyphonic compositions, and the insecure attempts in this regard, only betray the opposition of our harmonic tonality to sacred tonality."[212]

But where did that tonal sense come from? This is what concerns Adler. First, to define the notion of "harmonic singing" as opposed to "contrapuntal singing" Adler provides two familiar, but nonetheless ingenious, voice-leading prototypes: the lower voice of the first is a "harmonic filling voice," and "accommodates harmonic tonality, in that the harmonies tonic, dominant, tonic succeed one another."[213] The second features a "coequal [second] voice." In example 1.2a, the new voice is "*sub*ordinated" *to* the first; in 1.2b, the new voice is "*co*ordinated" *with* the first.

The first immediately appears to be the famous "horn fifths" combination, in which a triad is arpeggiated against the stepwise filling in of the same triadic root and third. Just as quickly we note that the second is the "voice-exchange"—the contrapuntal framework of the "passing chord," which will become familiar to us in chapters 3 and 4 via Kirnberger, Sechter, and Bruckner (and likely familiar to Adler via the same sources), in which the same structural third is filled in by step. In the first example, that third is inverted to a sixth, as the voices exchange, and the upper voice takes a new, lower register; in the second, the registers are retained. In Adler's "literalist"

---

211. Also see Karnes *Music, Criticism and the Challenge of History*, 161–6 on both of these studies.
212. Adler, "Harmonie," 782.
213. Ibid., 781.

Example 1.2. Adler's Voice-leading Paradigms for Harmony and Counterpoint

a.

b.

harmonic reading, all three vertical intervals are given harmonic meaning in the first example as "tonic, dominant, tonic," but not in the second (which could certainly be forced to accept the same interpretation). To Adler, the two prototypes suggest origins in two different musical genres as well, the first secular, and the second sacred.

Thinking a little more about this, our informal description of the first example turns out to have profound implications, for the horn in "horn fifths" is the natural horn or *Alpenhorn*, which Adler never mentions.[214] Indeed, the words *Alpenhorn* or *Alphorn* never appear anywhere in the essay, and we can only wonder why Adler did not consider that the origin of "harmonic singing" might not in fact be vocal at all, but rather, instrumental. Instruments of all four of the standard organological families are found already in the Tombs of Ur (3000 BCE), after all![215] Surely the *Alpenhorn* is of great antiquity, having been used first as a means of communication, and only later put to musical purposes; regardless of the purpose, two horns played together (and based on the same fundamental) could barely avoid horn fifths. Here is an instance where the "natural base" of harmonic theory can be of perhaps the greatest significance, for the harmonic series is inescapable in instrument building, and if the origin of harmony is instrumental instead of vocal, that would explain a lot. And, if this thoroughly Alpine

---

214. The horn fifths emerge directly from the harmonic series, 3rd and 4th octaves: 5th, 6th, 8th, 9th, and 10th harmonics.
215. "Aerophones" (Sachs-Hornbostel system) in the form of "flutes" are found there.

instrument were the origin of the "harmonic sense," it also has important political implications that could have been useful in Adler's argument as to who those with the harmonic sense were.[216]

But, as Adler frames it, the question is: did both modes of singing exist from time immemorial—from the very beginning of two-part singing? Questioning Edmond de Coussemaker's claim that there is no polyphonic folksong, Adler's rejoinder is that

> two things clearly speak against this claim. First, with a closer look at the history of music, a battle confronts us that cannot support this view as correct; it is the conflict between sacred tonality and secular major–minor tonality, the latter emerging victorious . . . The second factor, which has been almost completely overlooked, and is not to be underestimated, is that our natural melody (*Naturgesang*), which we find preserved in its purest form in the high mountains—that this melody suggests the conjecture that the manner of accompaniment of the primary voice, or, better said, this way of linking the two voices—results solely from the *harmonic instinct* of the natural singer.[217]

Historically, the two opposed manners of singing are epitomized for Adler by the practical notions of "discant" (more often contrapuntal singing) and "fauxbourdon" (more often harmonic singing), as they were interpreted in the fourteenth and fifteenth centuries, though he details a number of techniques that amount to mixing these genres. He then turns to a close reading of a late fifteenth-century treatise on the topic to examine this distinction.[218] According to current views, the treatise is a composite (Adler agrees), with an assortment of many examples ranging over many years (though Adler probably dates the earliest of these too early), offering a short history of polyphony

---

216. In Karnes's view (*Music, Criticism and the Challenge of History*, 161–66), "Adler's essays on the history of harmony evince palpable tension between the positivist methodologies advocated in his disciplinary polemics and the Greater German nationalist ideologies so deeply ingrained in his society." In Adler's defence, however, "he conceded that the historical record also makes clear that the Germans shared their innate aptitude for harmonic expression with a diverse array of other peoples residing throughout the world" (166).

217. Adler, "Harmonie," 782–83.

218. Adler gets the main document he examines from the recently appearing Coussemaker, *Scriptorum*, vol. 3 (1869), chapter 23, 273: Guillelmi Monachi, *De Praeceptis Artis Musicae et Practicae Compendiosus Libellus*, which is on "gymel" and "fauxbourdon."

in examples. After translating and discussing the treatise and the examples, Adler concludes that

> *the development of harmony* (in the sense described in the introduction to this study) *proceeded independently alongside the development of polyphonic composition*, and when a common basis for both types of multi-voice composition is assumed ... harmony was not *produced artificially from counterpoint, as has been accepted up to now*, but rather produced by an original desire for harmony born of the muse of the people (*Volk*), as a child of folksong, reared to full independence by the rod of counterpoint. Thus harmony, united with counterpoint, forms at the same time the foundation and craft of polyphonic music, under whose roof melody freely operates and rules.

The substance of this—particularly the last sentence—would have been applauded by both Wagner *and* Schenker.

Indeed, Schenker was substantially in agreement with Adler, and well aware of the questions the *Musikwissenschaftler* were asking when he wrote "it may be assumed ... that [folksong] ha[s] contributed to the development of harmonic feeling, as manifested, for example, in the melodic unfolding of a major or minor triad or in the discovery of the Ionian and Aeolian systems themselves" (*HL*, §88; *HA*, 164). But though aware of and certainly able to read and understand all of the primary and secondary sources in theory that were available, he was preoccupied with the repertoire he loved, and hardly an expert on medieval music.

But one of the shared students would develop that expertise. Of Schenker's three students who studied with Adler, the most significant for the further history of Schenkerian theory—and Schenker's incomplete history of compositional technique—was Felix Salzer (1904–86). Raised in a privileged household with a native English-speaking governess, the bilingual Salzer would become *the* representative of "Schenkerian Theory and Analysis" for the English-speaking world in the middle of the twentieth century with his *Structural Hearing* (1952), but his first large project after his dissertation was quite different: a combination of a thesis heavily influenced by Schenker, but a research technique certainly well-informed by study with Adler. It was a historical project, guided, as Schenker's compositional history was, by theory, undertaken and completed while Salzer was studying with Schenker in the early 1930s, not very long after his study with Adler. Indeed, this book, *Sinn und Wesen der abendländischen Mehrstimmigkeit* (The Sense and Essence of Western Polyphony, 1935), was dedicated precisely to filling the lacunae in

Schenker's knowledge of polyphony to which we pointed earlier, and which even in the early 1930s remained unfilled. Schenker must have had something to do with Salzer's turn to a radically different topic from that of his dissertation on Schubert (in which he would surely have had great interest), though Salzer's new direction may also have been suggested by Adler and the general abundance of Medieval and Renaissance studies appearing at that time. The topic and scope of the study would have been perfect for a *Habilitationsschrift* (its likely purpose), had the deteriorating political situation not interfered. Schenker's correspondence of the period and his diary entries show that the master was well aware of the student's work, and closely monitored its progress.[219] Though he did not live to read the final version, evidence points towards Schenker's having read earlier drafts.[220]

In *Sinn und Wesen*, Salzer's main strategy was to take Schenker's idea of "composing-out" (*Auskomponierung*)—which, along with essential harmony, had already appeared numerous times in *HL*, though the actual noun itself does not appear—and trace the history of that technique through the history of Western polyphony. According to Salzer, "composing-out is the ultimate sense of Western art music; therefore, the central problem of the history of Western music lies in understanding the development of composing-out."[221] Trying to distance himself from the other *Musikwissenschaftler*, Salzer claimed in the preface that his method as a historian was influenced by Spengler's in *The Decline of the West*, certainly a history driven by theory—agree with it or not. This was not the standard assemblage of data, pidgeon-holed into Adler's style categories:

> Like Spengler, Salzer wished to act as an observer who came at the end of a cultural epoch, and, by using his intuitive capabilities, could capture Western Culture's physiognomy and its morphology through time. Spengler likens the "method" of the historian to that of the Artist: he does not calculate or process the facts of history "logically," but rather grasps the essence of it, just as an Artist grasps the essence of his art form . . . Spengler thus allows Salzer to release himself from the shackles of mainstream music history to become a historian of a different sort: a prophet.[222]

---

219. See http://www.schenkerdocumentsonline.org/search/?fq=all&kw=salzer+sinn+und+Wesen, accessed September 4, 2018.
220. Koslovsky, "From *Sinn und Wesen* to *Structural Hearing*," 164f.
221. Salzer, *Sinn und Wesen*, 239–40; tr. Koslovsky, ibid., 205f.
222. Koslovsky, "From *Sinn und Wesen* to *Structural Hearing*," 206.

Like Schenker, both Spengler and Salzer are convinced of the decline of Western culture. And methodologically, all three are essentially unrepentant *Geisteswissenschaftler*, rejecting positivist history; indeed, Spengler and Salzer, almost like Schenker's "New Theories and Creative Ideas of an Artist," even verge on *Künstler*. But unlike Schenker, for Salzer the historian has the upper hand, and thus he can range through history, of which the period of the "great composers" is its summit, but only a part nonetheless. A culture has an "organic" trajectory, from birth to DAC, and it is assessing that process itself that demands his attention. "At the same time, Salzer could not completely divorce himself from [Adlerian] *Musikwissenschaft*, since so many of his claims relied on musicological sources and transcriptions."[223] To that extent, he was a positivist musicologist despite his best intentions. Koslovsky concludes: "*Sinn und Wesen* is a musicological writing, though one that deliberately sets itself against the norms of musicology in order to redefine what it is musicology should do as a discipline."[224] Whatever genre one assigns it to, it is important to point out that *Sinn und Wesen* is derived from *HL* both in its view of history and in its concentration on "composing-out" as the key to that "morphology" of Western music.[225] Thus it is a continuation of the work begun by Schenker in *HL*.[226]

However, when Salzer arrived in the US just before the war, as an émigré to the New World who brought a new music theory with him, he succeeded his first teacher, Hans Weisse (who had died unexpectedly), and began to teach at the David Mannes Music School (subsequently Mannes College of Music, and now absorbed by the New School University). Among the

---

223. Ibid., 161.
224. Ibid., 163.
225. This also relates it to Oswald Jonas's contemporaneous revision of the content of *HL* that appears in the first two chapters of *Das Wesen des musikalischen Kunstwerkes* (The Essence of the Musical Artwork, 1934). The subtitle, *Einführung in die Lehre Heinrich Schenkers* (Introduction to the Theory of Heinrich Schenker) does not appear on the dust jacket! The title suggests the competition for Schenker's favors that was rising between Salzer and Jonas. See chapter 5. (The title and subtitle were reversed in the 1972 edition by Universal, and the English translation by Rothgeb.)
226. In 1922, Schenker returned to this topic: after remarking that "a history of the art of music has yet to be written," he went on to list the questions that should be central to such a project. See *TW2* (1922); *WT2*, 52, "History of the Art of Music," tr. Snarrenberg. See also Koslovsky, "From *Sinn und Wesen* to *Structural Hearing*," 119, which turns Schenker's narrative into a list of fifteen questions.

students he attracted were composers, surely nurtured by Weisse, an active composer. This prompted him to begin the study of music of his own time according to Schenker's theory, now modified considerably in an attempt to extend its purview on both historical ends.[227] Thus arose the provocative analyses of modern music that began to attract immediate attention with the appearance of *Structural Hearing* in 1952, and to influence at least a generation of music analysts to follow suit, and push the tonal boundaries further still. It was little known that Salzer's adventures beyond the common practice had begun at the other end of the historical continuum in an attempt to fill the biggest gap in Schenker's historical account, investigating what he regarded as the birth of deeper structure in early polyphony, an interest he maintained throughout his career.

Until the works of Schenker himself began to appear in English in the form of scholarly translations in the late 1970s and beyond, *Structural Hearing* was "Schenker theory" in the Anglo-American world. Given that the ideas of the real Schenker had been reduced to a few slogans, except among the initiates who had direct contact with the émigrés or could read—and get hold of—the original texts, *HA* was an orphan that many found disappointing, if not downright inscrutable—even though Jonas had tried valiantly, with his annotations, to make up for what it apparently lacked.[228] Had history—and Schenker's health—been different, we wonder what projects he and his students would have turned to after *DfS*, as he continued the seminars in his apartment that produced *FGA*. To judge from Salzer's work in *Sinn und Wesen*, and Schenker's supportive reaction to it, his history of tonality might well have been one topic of interest that he and his students would have continued. It is not difficult to imagine a subsequent volume of *FGA* containing pieces that included a seventeenth-century Italian lute song, or an early Lutheran chorale setting, perhaps suggested by Salzer. But unfortunately, this will remain mere conjecture.

---

227. In Koslovsky's estimation, "even *Structural Hearing* . . . is by and large a commentary on the nature of music history, specifically on the history of tonality and the future of the Western musical language" ("From *Sinn und Wesen* to *Structural Hearing*, 8).

228. What it lacked at the time had nothing to do with the deletions from *HL*, of course, but rather any overt relationship to the Schenker of *DfS*, which appeared in a new German edition by Universal in 1956 (edited by Jonas and, once again, expurgated). Word of the real Schenker got around, but slowly, sporadically, and at secondhand to non-German-readers.

Chapter Two

The Music-Theoretical Content of Schenker's Theory of Harmony (1906) and the Status of Harmony in His Later Work

The Viennese Theory of Harmony at Mid-Century

Schenker's harmony teacher during the time he studied at the conservatory in the late 1880s was the Austrian composer and organist, Anton Bruckner (1824–96). Simon Sechter (1788–1867), the leading theorist in Vienna in the first half of the nineteenth century, had been Bruckner's teacher between 1856 and 1861, the lessons consisting entirely of exercises in harmony, not composition.[1] Indeed, Sechter forbade Bruckner to compose during the time he studied with him. Apparently, no archival material remains from Schenker's study with Bruckner, but Bruckner's teaching at the university has been well documented. It was essentially Sechter's system of harmony that Bruckner taught (in a lightly edited version), recently published when Bruckner studied with him.[2] Schenker's study with Bruckner,

---

1. Sechter, *Grundsätze*, vol. 1 of 3. See the bibliography for Sechter's descriptive titles of the individual volumes.

2. The most complete source describing Bruckner's university lectures is his *Vorlesungen über Harmonie und Kontrapunkt* (Lectures on Harmony and

however, was more than thirty years later, and Bruckner was famous for recycling the same lecture notes year after year. It is almost certain that he would have concentrated his teaching at the conservatory, where Schenker studied with him, on the same material he taught at the university. By the time Schenker studied Sechter's system, it was thirty-five years since its publication date. Heavily indebted to eighteenth-century sources as it was—and Rameau in particular—it had become that much more out of date by the late 1880s.

Sechter was an organist and composer of great industry, if not originality, steeped in the sacred music tradition of "strict composition" set forth most famously by his Viennese predecessor of the early eighteenth century, Johann Josef Fux (ca. 1660–1741).[3] Sechter, from Bohemia (the westernmost region of the present-day Czech Republic), was highly regarded in Vienna as a composer and teacher of counterpoint by the 1820s, to the extent that Schubert had a lesson with him on the fugal answer.[4] One of his first published works was a "figured-bass" book, apparently in the eighteenth-century tradition.[5] In reality, however, it also looked forward to his main work, the *Grundsätze*.[6] Sechter finally ascended to a position at the conservatory in

---

Counterpoint), ed. Schwanzara. Also see Wason, *Viennese Harmonic Theory*, chapter 9. Bruckner always spoke of Sechter in tones of reverence; such was the faith in harmony as the *Wissenschaft* of composition. Bruckner's lesson books are preserved in the Library of the Gesellschaft der Musikfreunde in Vienna. On the sources of Sechter's system, see chapter 3, below.

3. Fux wrote one of the "monuments" in the history of Western music theory, *Gradus ad Parnassum*.

4. For a transcription of the contents of the manuscript that survived the lesson, as well as Sechter's fugue on Schubert's name, written in his memory, see Mann, "Schubert's Lesson with Sechter," in his *Theory and Practice*, 143–51.

5. Simon Sechter, *Practische Generalbaß-Schule* (Practical Figured-Bass School), 1830.

6. Zeleny notes many points on which the exercises in Sechter's book on figured bass are consistent with and suggestive of the rules he laid down twenty-three years later in his *Grundsätze*. See Zeleny, *Die historischen Grundlagen des Theoriesystems von Simon Sechter* (The Historical Basis of the Theory System of Simon Sechter), 94–100, and Wason, *Viennese Harmonic Theory*, 32. Figured-bass books continued to be produced in Vienna through the first half of the nineteenth century: see Thomson, *Voraussetzungen und Artungen der österreichischen Generalbaßlehre zwischen Albrechtsberger und Sechter* (Assumptions and Typology of Austrian Figured-Bass Books between Albrechtsberger and Sechter).

1851; very likely the *Grundsätze* emerged from his teaching there. He was thus at the top of his profession both as a musician (working as Principal Court Organist) and theory pedagogue when Bruckner, a fellow organist well-known for his improvisations, came to him.

In essence, it was Sechter who brought Rameau's laws of progression and theory of the fundamental bass, as modified by Kirnberger, to Vienna, implicitly in his earlier works, but explicitly in his *Grundsätze*.[7] Sechter begins with the diatonic scale (the knowledge of which he assumes), as many figured-bass theorists did. This is obvious from the first section's title: "Diatonic Progression in the Major Scale." Indeed, the word *Stufe*, or "scale degree," which will become the most problematic of Schenker's terms to translate, is ubiquitous in Sechter's writing. In fact, Sechter never really leaves the scale, as the titles of the other three sections demonstrate: "Diatonic Progression in the Minor Scale," "Diatonic Modulation and Chromatic Progression in the Major Scale," and "Chromatic Progression in the Minor Scale and Enharmonic Modulation." To be sure, Sechter does not concentrate on the scale *qua* scale, but uses it merely as a source of intervals first, and then chords. There are no surprises here. Once he defines the basic chords he gets right to what the treatise is really about, again indicated in the section titles: a theory of chord progression.

The "correct succession" (or, as we say, "progression") of harmonies presented in volume 1 is according to Rameau's laws, still taught in many harmony classes today. These come down to preference rules for motion by triadic intervals: prefer descending fifths or ascending fourths (less frequently, ascending fifths and descending fourths); only then accept thirds (or sixths); seconds may occur, but they are "licenses" derived from inversions of chordal sevenths. The one that stands out in Sechter's work particularly is the last: Rameau's prohibition of stepwise progressions, with which he wrestled throughout his career. Such was not the case with Sechter. The explanation

---

7. As expected (see chapter 3), Sechter picked up his Rameau at second hand, essentially from Kirnberger's *Kunst des reinen Satzes* and *Die wahren Grundsätze*. See Johann Philipp Kirnberger, *The Art of Strict Musical Composition*, tr. Beach and Thym, and "*The True Principles for the Practice of Harmony* by Johann Philipp Kirnberger: a Translation," tr. Beach and Thym. Johann Abraham Peter Schulz, Kirnberger's star student, actually wrote the latter book, in close consultation with Kirnberger. See Wason, *Viennese Harmonic Theory*, 62 for Sechter's own testimony on the music theory books he had read. As Zeleny, *Simon Sechter* shows (386), Sechter in effect underscores the importance of these two works to him by mentioning them in the first sentence of his memoir.

of progression by seconds brings out Sechter's dogmatic streak: he never even entertains the possibility that such familiar progressions as IV–V and V–VI might suggest the "license" to use stepwise progressions, as Rameau had. Instead, he lays down the law, developing essentially three ways to explain them away. While the "inversions" of the fundamental bass in his title are nothing new, by "substitutes" (*Stellvertretern*) Sechter refers to chords whose "real" roots are "concealed"—e.g., VII, a rootless V7, in Sechter's estimation, VII–I is thus an incomplete V7–I. Thus the idea is essentially the simplest explanation of "apparent" stepwise progressions. In other contexts, other substitutes emerge that are not necessarily thirds apart; the idea is not as simple as it will later re-emerge in the work of Riemann, where all substitutes are by third. The second way of banishing stepwise progressions is via the "intermediate fundamental" (*Zwischenfundament*), an interpolated chord, imagined by the analyst. In writing about the cadential progression IV–V–I, for example, Sechter insists that a fundamental on II be inserted between IV and V (with doubling of the harmonic rhythm), an explanation again invented by Rameau.[8] The chord may be explicitly stated, or appear "with concealment of the second fundamental" (example 2.1).[9] Sechter, however, surely got the idea from a work from Kirnberger–Schulz, who remark that the fundamental bass of example 2.2 is not as in 2.3a, but 2.3b.[10] While Sechter manages to come up with an explanation of descending stepwise progressions as well through the same device, they are truly exceptional. It was Bruckner who made them normative.

Sechter fails to name his third explanation, leading the reader to wonder if he recognized it for what it was: progressions containing a prolonged harmony suggest the *extension* of the first fundamental, resulting in suspension-, passing- or neighboring-chords.[11] This idea does not come from Rameau, but from Kirnberger, though it seems that Kirnberger's ghost-writer, Schulz, may have had some influence on his thinking, since the idea is more prominent in the work written by Schulz than it is in *Kunst des reinen Satzes*,

---

8. Sechter did not use Roman numerals, but rather stayed with notes as Rameau had, though he notated them as letter names, and thus avoided Rameau's use of another staff.
9. Sechter, *Grundsätze*, vol. 1, 19.
10. Kirnberger–Schulz, *The True Principles for the Practice of Harmony*, 206–7.
11. See Wason, "Schenker's Notion of Scale-Step."

Example 2.1. Sechter's "Concealed Fundamental"

 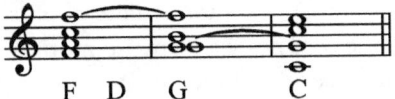

with concealment of the
second fundamental:

F D G C

Example 2.2. The Apparent Progression of IV–V

Example 2.3. (a) The Apparent Fundamental Bass of Example 2.2; (b) The Real Fundamental Bass of Example 2.2

(a)   (b)

Example 2.4a and b. Sechter's Passing Chords (from Kirnberger–Schulz)

(a)   (b)

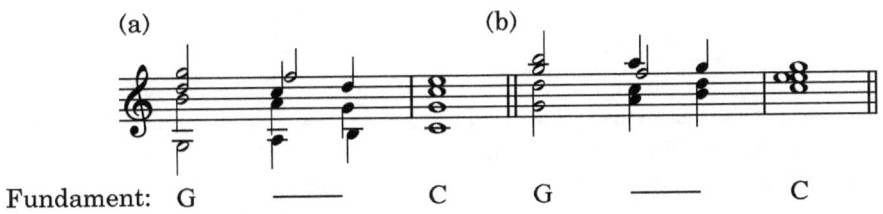

Fundament: G   ——   C   G   ——   C

Kirnberger's magnum opus.[12] In fact the authors coin a term for these chords: intermediate chords [*Zwischenakkorde*], and an explanation that Sechter, curiously, fails to provide: "Thus the passing chords [*durchgehende Akkorde*] are intermediate chords [*Zwischenakkorde*], in which one or more voices passes via stepwise motion and generally consonant progression from a preceeding fundamental chord [*Grundakkord*] to the following one."[13] See the passing chords in examples 2.4a and b from Sechter, drawn directly from Kirnberger–Schulz.[14]

All of this theory designed to explain away apparent progression by step means that the cadential model of chord progression gets very short shrift. Sechter speaks of the "reciprocal effect" of progressions involving the subdominant (e.g., I–IV–I–V–I, etc.), but IV or any of its derivatives are essentially unavailable as *direct* dominant preparations. Thus, as he had in his *Generalbaß-Schule*, he concentrates on various sequences of progressions by third and fifth, the foremost among them being the cycle of fifths, which drives the first volume as a whole. When Sechter goes on to present a section on "chromatic progression," it turns out to be cycle-of-fifths progressions of secondary dominants (a term he does not use), and all chromatic alterations are applied to the upper notes of the chord, never to the fundamental bass. Thus, though he devotes a considerable portion of the book to chromatic and enharmonic techniques—one of the first theorists to do so—the theory remains diatonic to the core. See examples 2.5a and b, which show the diatonic basis of the augmented sixth chord: Sechter's *Zwitterakkord* (hybrid chord), so called because he derives its two leading tones from two different keys, the minor tonic and the dominant. Schenker will essentially follow suit in his explanation of these chords, though he takes such chords into his larger notion of "tonicization."[15]

---

12. Like Sechter, Kirnberger too never coined a term for "non-essential chords." In that sense, Schenker follows in the tradition, playing down the "incidental" harmonies, and concentrating on the "essential" ones.
13. Kirnberger–Schulz, *Die wahren Grundsätze*, 34. Schulz uses the term "essential" (*wesentlich*) only once, and with regard to an "essential seventh." This corresponds to Kirnberger's use of the term in *Kunst des reinen Satzes*.
14. Sechter, *Grundsätze*, vol. 1, 40; cf. Kirnberger–Schulz, *Die wahren Grundsätze*, 36.
15. *HL*, §§146–54, 366–78; *HA*, 277–87.

Example 2.5a. Sechter's Diatonic Basis of a Chromatic Sequence

Example 2.5b. Sechter's Chromatic Sequence Derived from Diatonic Basis

Both the defects of the theory and its dogmatic presentation in print—and in person by Bruckner—certainly had a largely negative effect on Schenker, who was famously critical of his teacher's approach to harmony, though he had quite a positive impression of his gentle personality and sincere religious belief. The case of Schenker demonstrates the twists and turns that Rameau reception underwent: during his student years Schenker studied Bruckner's version of Sechter, a mechanization of Kirnberger, the more authentic source of Rameau, while in his maturity he knew "Rameau" through Marpurg's translation of d'Alembert—an impoverishment of the original, translated by someone with fundamental misunderstandings of Rameau's work.[16] Given Schenker's own theory education and

---

16. Schenker owned all of the important works of Kirnberger, including the complete *Kunst des reinen Satzes* and *Die wahren Grundsätze*. He also owned a copy of Marpurg's translation of d'Alembert. For further background on all of this, see chapter 3.

the watered-down conservatory manuals around him that others studied, it is little wonder that he reacted so strongly against "harmony" as conventionally taught.[17]

Schenker's Early Theory of Harmony

Although Schenker's derivation of the tonal system (*HL*, §§8–52) stands out in its attempt to balance the natural properties of the harmonic series with the basic instincts of the artist, the music-theoretic content of his Theory of Harmony as a whole does not represent a major departure from the tradition. On the contrary, most of the details of Schenker's Theory of Harmony resonate with ideas whose origins can be traced back to the seventeenth century, and sometimes, much earlier. Yet Schenker's interpretation of these details is often very new, for even the most trivial of them seem to be contingent on his brilliant overarching idea—the "essential harmony" (*Stufe*).[18] His views about harmony were far more abstract and expansive than those of his predecessors, even at the beginning of his career, as is made perfectly clear when, in GEIST, he promises to return harmony to the meaning that the ancient Greeks had given it, and at the outset of *HL*, he describes the theory of harmony "as a world purely of the mind." According to him, this mental universe can be studied from a theoretical as well as a practical perspective: the former allows him to discuss "intervals, triads, seventh chords, and so on," whereas the latter covers "the truly functional, the driving force of the fundamental musical ideas: namely, the progression of essential harmonies, chromatic change

---

17. Nonetheless, Schenker owned volumes 2 and 3 of Sechter's *Grundsätze*, which he was not required to buy for Bruckner's instruction. Indeed, the presence of these volumes in his personal library suggests that he may have wanted to follow out Sechter's ideas beyond volume 1. The detailed titles in the bibliography speak for themselves: all would have been of considerable interest to Schenker.

18. In all of the quotations which follow, *Stufe* is rendered as "essential harmony," if indeed it is "composed out" to some extent. It is rendered as "chord" or "degree" in more limited contexts. In quotations from Borgese's translation, "scale degree" has been changed, silently, to one of these alternatives, as appropriate. In quotations from her translation that have been more heavily edited, "tr. Borgese, modified" has been added. For detailed discussion of the translation of *Stufe*, see chapter 5.

(*Chromatisierung*) and modulation, etc."[19] In fact, however, the notion of essential harmony is there from beginning to end.

Essential Harmonies (*Stufen*), and Their Effects on Intervals and Chords (*HL*, §§53–73 and 93–114)

The venerable Aristotelian distinction between "essence" and "accident" became the basis of the distinction between "essential" and "non-essential"[20] harmonies in the thinking of Kirnberger, and was picked up by Sechter to become the Viennese theory Schenker inherited. But Schenker goes much further with the idea even in *HL*: in a sense, certain chords are just that—chords, while others are the product of counterpoint that are not really there as chords. This kind of thinking is characteristic of the work of Ernst Mach, a topic we pursue further in chapter 4. Given Mach's interest in the role perception plays in our understanding of the world, it is not surprising that he drew attention to the opposition of reality and appearance. A couple of examples immediately spring to mind. Consider, for a moment, our perception of color. A pencil may be painted a specific color, but that color will seem different depending on the color of the light by which it is illuminated. Similarly, there is the case of refraction. Our pencil may be perfectly straight, but, due to differences in the refractive index of air and water, it will look bent if it is placed in water.[21] The distinction between appearance and reality is one that features prominently

---

19. Schenker, *HL*, "Vorwort," V–VI; *HA*, xxv.
20. *Zufällig* means literally "accidental," or "incidental," the latter quite an acceptable rendering of harmonies that are better thought of as products of voice leading. But "non-essential" (or, as it sometimes appears, "nonessential") is in general use, so we maintain it here. Since Schenker's emphasis is on the "essential harmony" as a prolonged harmony, to use his later terminology, we need not be detained by a discussion of the translation of *zufällig*.
21. According to Blackmore: "In fact, Mach's 'holistic' impressions seem to go back at least to the age of three when he 'saw' tables as rectangular, and refused to accept either direct visual images or wall-picture representations that tapered at one end as legitimate. His first adult concern with 'visual holism' may well have been his 1861 analysis of visual symmetry." Blackmore, *Ernst Mach*, 47. Musicians listening to a recording and imagining themselves playing the piece will identify with this immediately.

Example 2.6. Example of Essential Harmony

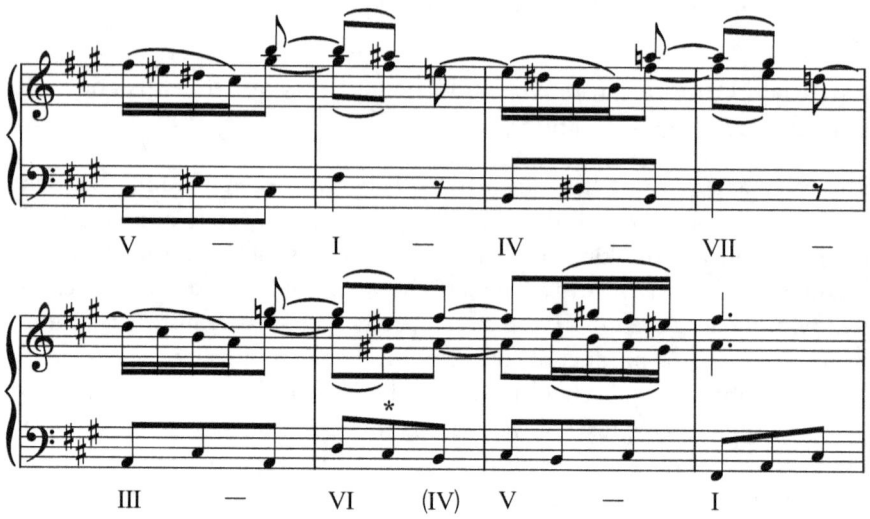

in Schenkerian thought, especially in his distinction between essential harmonies or *Stufen* and non-essential harmonies. Consider the triadic tones C♯-E♯-G♯ marked with an asterisk in the following passage from Bach's St Matthew Passion (see example 2.6).[22]

Although this sonority might appear to serve as a dominant to the upcoming tonic F♯ two measures later, it is really a passing chord between VI and IV, and as such "a chance product of contrapuntal movement." Note that the "contrapuntal movement" is not the simple contrary-motion passing tones taken from strict counterpoint by Kirnberger, Sechter, et al., and that the prolongation of the dominant through the whole following bar would be inconceivable in their theories. Rather, it is surely the harmonic rhythm of the passage, the weak metric placement of the chord, and the clear prolongation of the dominant throughout the succeeding bar (articulated clearly by the bass) that determine this compelling analytical interpretation.

We have started this section with the idea of essential harmony because it motivates virtually every detail in the book as a whole—even what would appear to be the standard topics of most any harmony book that appear of necessity. For example, there is the obligatory discussion of intervals. Perhaps the most

---

22. *HL*, §79, ex. 153, 187; *HA*, ex. 119, 144–45.

remarkable aspect of Schenker's thinking is his belief that essential harmonies need not appear purely vertically as local chords but can also be projected horizontally through melodic lines, motivic patterns, and even polyphonic textures.[23] Thus he motivates the discussion of intervals as part of the discussion of essential harmony, since the student will need to be able to read harmony in "incomplete chords." Schenker's point of departure in discussing intervals is figured-bass theory.[24] He notes that, although figured-bass treatises such as C. P. E. Bach's focus their attention on intervals that are the "most usable in harmony," they nonetheless classify intervals into well over twenty types.[25]

As Schenker points out, the figured-bass theorists showed examples of how all of these intervals might occur in practice. Indeed, a pedagogy designed to prepare the continuo player to realize any possible vertical combination had to have all possible intervals available. Schenker's approach, on the contrary, is through harmonic theory, and he is interested in the essential. This is not a continuo course. Thus, in his view, it is high time to "correct" and "purify" the "all-encompassing" approach to intervals by defining them in terms of their harmonizability[26]—in effect, another invocation of the distinction between appearance and reality.[27]

One might expect Schenker to begin the discussion of intervals with consonance and dissonance, in order to place each interval (and later, each chord) into one of these two categories—or to discuss the problems in doing so. But surprisingly, he takes up that topic only at the end of his discussion.[28] There, rather than putting intervals on a continuum ranging from consonant to dissonant, Schenker is a proponent of the naturalized version of Pythagorean theory— Zarlino's theory of intervals. In that sense too he returns to the Greeks.[29] For him, there is a categorical difference between consonance and

---

23. *HL*, §§53–114, 151–277; *HA*, 117–208.
24. *HL*, §53, 151; *HA*, 117.
25. *HL*, §53, 153; *HA*, 119. C. P. E. Bach, *Versuch*; ed. and tr. Mitchell, *Essay*.
26. *HL*, §54, 153, §55, 155; *HA*, 119.
27. *HL*, §§54–57.
28. *HL*, §§73–75, 174–76.
29. Though the harmonic series, discovered during the Scientific Revolution of the seventeenth century, could be interpreted as the "natural" justification of Pythagorean theory (and its extension by Zarlino), at the same time the Zarlinian theory of a categorical distinction between consonance and dissonance was subjected to intense criticism, from which it did not emerge unscathed. See Cohen, *Quantifying Music*, passim, and see chapter 3 of the present study for a discussion of the matter. The

dissonance, though he seems to embrace it with some hesitation when he writes that "*perhaps* [our emphasis] the only intervals to be called consonant are those that may be reduced to the simple ratios involving 1, 2, 3, or 5 in the harmonic series, either directly or through inversion, while those intervals that are to be designated as dissonant are the ones that lack this characteristic."[30] Fortunately, all of these intervals can be inverted without altering their status as consonances or dissonances: unisons, octaves (as inversions of unisons), fifths, fourths (as inversions of fifths), thirds, and sixths (as inversions of thirds) are consonant; seconds, sevenths, and all augmented and diminished intervals are dissonant.[31] The one problematic interval is the fourth. Schenker writes that "among the perfect consonances, the *perfect* fourth assumes a special status, in that it becomes a dissonance in counterpoint, and indeed only in one situation there."[32] Later in his career Schenker would account for all chords that include dissonant intervals as products of voice leading, and in that sense, embrace the naturalized Zarlinian theory of consonance as the structure of the deeper levels of a work.

---

nineteenth-century solution of Stumpf, Riemann, et al. was to separate the scientific from the artistic notion of consonance as "concordance" vs. "consonance," but that did not stop the controversy, which continues to the present day. As Cohen writes at the end of his study (258–59): "Time and again the problem of consonance has been proclaimed solved. Yet always the solution has turned out to be highly problematical . . . We have seen it tackled on the basis of number, of geometric figures, of physical and of physiological principles . . . Each of these approaches has taken the analysis closer to the seat of our perceptions—none has reached it."

30. *HL*, §73, 174–75. Schenker had discussed inversion in §72. On the nature of consonance, see [FTS], passim. By adding "through inversion," Schenker manages to account for the minor third (5: 6), which under such tight restrictions must be derived as the inversion of the major sixth (3: 5), the main reason Zarlino included the senary number 6 in his preferred group. Zarlino did not have the concept of interval inversion available to him.

31. *HL*, §§72–73, 175; *HA*, 130–31.

32. *HL*, §75, 176. But if the fourth is the problematic consonance, the tritone is the problematic dissonance. Zarlino and his followers (e.g., Fux) admitted the diminished fifth as a "resolution" of the passing fourth in their two-part counterpoint instruction, and in the early nineteenth century Fétis christened it his "consonance appellative"—likewise because it could assume the duration of a consonance.

But at the time he wrote *HL*, Schenker believed that the triads and seventh chords extracted from the six *Reihen* he had constructed via mixture[33] were the basic harmonies of tonal music. He thus proposed that the only possible intervals were the ones contained within these sonorities: "According to the present-day standards of art, the concept of an interval is bound to and limited by its harmonic capability. In other words, the ability to occur in a triad or seventh chord is the conceptual requirement of the interval."[34] Column a of table 2.1 provides a list of intervals typical in figured-bass theory;[35] column b is a list of the eighteen intervals that satisfy Schenker's criterion for intervallic status.[36]

We might ask, what of chromatic triadic intervals such as the diminished third/augmented sixth or diminished fifth/augmented fourth that figure prominently in other books of the period? For Schenker, chromaticism is simply not part of essential structure. Nonetheless he deals quite extensively with the topic of "altered" (i.e., diminished third/augmented sixth) chords in part II of *HL*, since they, in particular, originate in "tonicization." These two intervals bring the sum total of intervals to twenty, and close the system to further possibilities.[37]

Almost at the outset of his discussion of intervals, Schenker offers some advanced examples of the complex ways in which composers articulate the

---

33. *HL*, §57.

34. *HL*, §55, 155–56. See also §§107–14, 249–77. Hauptmann and Riemann would have been in complete agreement. The idea is indicative of the status the Modern Theory of Harmony had achieved as a way to "hear music." The banishment of intervals other than these also undercuts the modernists (e.g., Schoenberg) who would form "chords" of any intervals. While Schoenberg wrote a chapter in his harmony book that derides the notion of "non-harmonic tones" (*harmoniefremde Töne*) and attempts instead to admit all tonal combinations as "harmonic," Schenker dismissed intervals that cannot be found in conventional chords as irrelevant to a book on harmony.

35. *HL*, §53, 153; *HA*, 119.

36. *HL*, §62, 160; *HA*, 123.

37. *HL*, §147. See *HL*, §§136–45 for tonicization via conventional chords; see §§146–54 for tonicization via diminished third/augmented sixth chords.

Table 2.1: Lists of Intervals from Figured Bass Theory, and the List of Intervals in *HL*

	a. List of intervals from figured-bass theory	b. List of intervals in *HL*
Unison	(not mentioned by Schenker)	perfect
Seconds	major, minor, augmented	major, minor, augmented
Thirds	major, minor, diminished	major, minor
Fourths	perfect, diminished, augmented	perfect, augmented, diminished
Fifths	perfect, diminished, augmented	perfect, augmented, diminished
Sixths	major, minor, diminished, augmented	major, minor
Sevenths	major, minor, diminished	major, minor, diminished
Octaves	perfect, diminished, augmented	perfect
Ninths	major, minor, etc.	none
Total	24 +	18

constituent intervals of a given essential harmony: they show how those intervals are sometimes "heard merely horizontally" with no reference to the vertical and sometimes "the vertical component is far more important."[38] Example 2.7 gives a short passage from Variation IX of Beethoven's *32 Variations in C minor* WoO 80 in which Schenker adds arrows to indicate both possibilities: "the first arrow indicates the horizontal direction in which the D♯ must be heard; the second one, the vertical context of the E."[39] D♯ related vertically to certain other tones in proximity forms intervals that are not on the chart: the "augmented third" (D♯/B♭), "doubly augmented unison" (D♭/D♯) simply do not exist.

Schenker comments: "Apart from the fact that it is surely more correct to hear it this way musically, this will do away with all sorts of theoretical apparitions and utopian [harmonic] schemes. Particularly these days when people love to believe that they hear new harmonies merely when they see peculiar notes piled atop one another, it is doubly important to accent the

---

38. *HL*, §54, 155; *HA*, 121.
39. Ibid.

Example 2.7. A Verticality that is not a "Chord" (last measure)

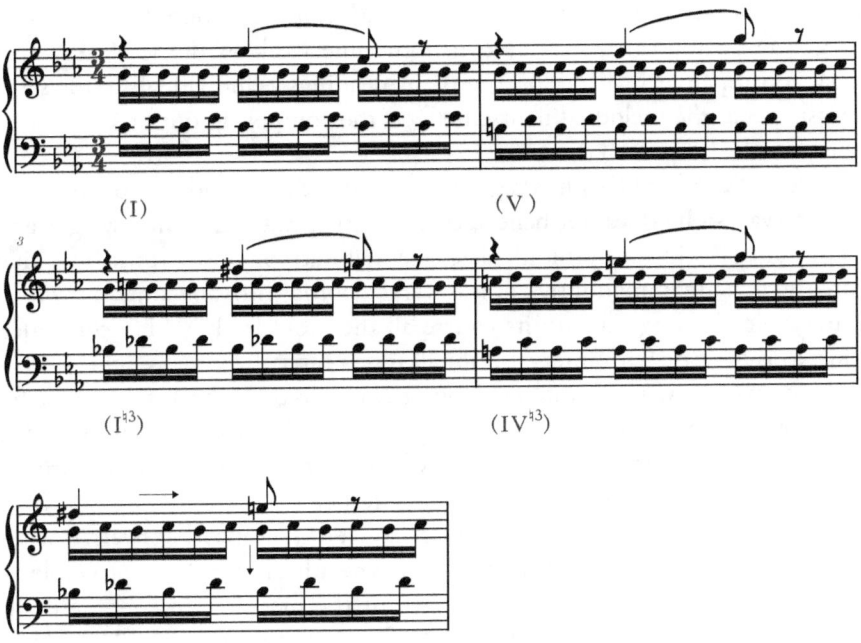

obligation to hear clearly and with good musical sense."[40] Schenker develops this idea further in *KP2*. Indeed, just as the pre-existence of the cantus firmus necessarily had its consequences even in two-voice counterpoint—for example, the fact that certain traces of subservience were imprinted on the added voice—it likewise manifests consequences in three-voice counterpoint as well, specifically in that the sonorities of the vertical dimension in their significance as individual entities must yield before the significance of the horizontally expressed sonority. The horizontal harmony proves to be stronger than the relationships of the vertical sounds to one another. This effect, to which our attention is drawn for the first time in three-voice counterpoint—three-voice counterpoint is the first to do so because it is the first to introduce such three-voice polyphony as the content and corporeality of the essential harmonies —weaves, as it will be shown shortly, like a "red thread"

---

40. *HL*, §54, 155. In the second sentence, Schenker surely refers to the profusion of non-essential chromatic "harmonies" in music of his day, particularly in Reger's music.

through all similar phenomena of strict counterpoint as well as free composition.[41] Schenker concludes "as a main principle, it might rightly be expressed in general as follows: Any closed melodic line weakens the vertical chords [that accompany it] with respect to their meanings as individuals in the same measure that the melodic line itself effects the composing-out of a particular chord in the horizontal direction."

Just as Schenker does not regard "every vertical coincidence of tones" as an interval, so he does not believe that "all triads have the same weight and importance."[42] In his opinion: "The essential harmony now constitutes that force which unambiguously joins several chords into one unit, in whose frame voice-leading can run its course all the more freely."[43] He continues: "Just as is the case with intervals, not all triads carry the same weight. It matters not what circumstantial evidence is presented to the listener—as, for example, the retention of a tone, a rhythm, or a likeness and various other triggers—the essential harmony always remains the higher compositional factor, having priority over individual phenomena."[44]

Again, like intervals, the members of a given triad may be inverted without altering the identity of a triad or a seventh chord: "The principle of inversion, which we used with intervals for the first time in §72, naturally finds its extension here to triads, which also consist of intervals."[45] And yet, Schenker immediately accepts that second inversion triads are in some sense problematic since they "may give rise to misunderstandings" from a contrapuntal perspective.[46] More remarkably, however, Schenker concedes that ninth, thirteenth, and augmented-sixth chords arise contrapuntally. In the case of dominant ninth chords, he remarks:

> Because we have rejected the usual interpretation of the so-called dominant ninth chord as mistaken, and have explained it not as a true chordal formation—and thus not as an independent one—but merely as a reflex basically of an unconsciously sensed relationship of all chords build on the fifth degree (and only on the fifth!), it remains only for us to describe where the

---

41. *HA*, 152; *KP2*, chapter 1, §15, 18; *CP2*, 15–17.
42. *HL*, §81, 197; *HA*, 152. The echo of George Jellinek's preference for the Teutonic synthesis of Roman law and Anglo-American democracy is clear.
43. *HL*, §88, 203; *HA*, 158.
44. *HL*, §81, 197.
45. *HL*, §98, 240.
46. *HL*, §98, 241; *HA*, 187. See also *HL*, §§78, 125, and 127.

interdependent substitution of the latter occurs in practice, and where that idea may be dispensed with.[47]

Towards the end of part I (*Theoretischer Teil*) of *HL*, Schenker criticizes a standard simplified realization of a harmonic progression from Richter's harmony book.[48] Schenker claims that in a lesson in harmony, the author should not drill on (or in) one "correct" contrapuntal realization of a harmonic progression, but more properly give a lesson in the "psychology of the *abstract* essential harmony." (The emphasis in the original is unfortunately lacking in *HA*). What does he mean by psychology in this context? Obviously, the emphasis shows that essential harmony is an "empty" harmonic technique—a product of the mind that will only later be realized. This is in keeping with the first half of *HL*, which presents techniques that will be realized musically in the second half. The student of *HL* is given lessons in *how to interpret* the influence of harmony on melody and counterpoint, instead of being pushed through a regimen of "harmony exercises," which amount to "techniques" devoid of melodic or motivic content. This is the essence of the "psychology of essential harmonies": the interpretation of passages of varying length that demonstrate one prevailing harmony, a melody itself that composes-out that harmony, and one that is composed-out, a harmony along with a subsidiary melody, or three- or four-part counterpoint.

Melody (*HL*, §§76–83)

One of the most important consequences of claiming that essential harmonies can be projected horizontally as well as vertically is that it allows Schenker to highlight the fact that tonal composition is ultimately melodically driven:

> The principal [component] in music, even after the addition of the vertical direction, remains the horizontal line, and thus the melody itself . . . Furthermore, in this sense, the vertical direction is secondary (which, incidentally, corresponds at the same time to the chronology of history), in which case, the harmonic imagination is perhaps only called upon to allow further melodic lines to originate according to a plan, and to organize them.[49]

---

47. *HL*, §109, 251–52.
48. Richter, *Lehrbuch*, 90.
49. *HL*, §88, 214.

In particular, Schenker focuses on the inherent triadicity of tonal melodies, and the connections that the ear makes between triadic tones, even when other structural features may seem to outweigh them.[50] He supports his case by quoting the opening phrase of the popular German tune "Muß i denn, muß i denn, zum Städtele hinaus" (see example 2.8), the tune that Christian von Ehrenfels (1859–1932) had used in his influential essay, "On *Gestalt* Qualities" (1890):[51]

> I have already shown in §13 how the association with nature, in the form of the acoustical phenomenon 1:3:5, lies at the basis of the appearance in reality of our triad. It need not always be three voices that cause the three consonant intervals to sound. That is to say, the *idea* [*Idee*] of the triad is not, as some believe, bound to three sounding voices. The idea may be realized all the more in two voices, or even with one. In the latter case, nature as well as art are satisfied, when, in the course of a melody, the ear gradually groups a single tone with its third and fifth in whatever manner they occur. For example, in the folk tune,

Example 2.8. "Muß i denn?" ("Must I?")

the ear, according to the demands of nature, instinctively groups the first tone G with the B of the first quarter as its third, and with the D, the first quarter of the second bar, as its fifth. Likewise, the ear will group the first G with the

---

50. *HL*, §76, 176–77. He reiterated this idea in *MW1*: "There are no other tone spaces than those of 1-3, 3-5, 5-8. There is no other origin for passing progressions, or for melody." Schenker, "Elucidations," *MW1*, 203; tr. Bent *MM1*, 112.

51. For more on Ehrenfels and the content of his essay, see chapter 4. We would like to thank Daniel Ketter for his additional research on this tune. Although its origins are unknown, the melody became popular after the publication of Friedrich Silcher's *Volkslieder, gesammelt und für vier Männerstimmen gesetzt*, Op. 8, No. 12, in 1827. Schenker's choice of this tune in particular as the very first example in his discussion of essential harmony was clearly designed as a corrective of a naive discussion by a philosopher and psychologist who had also studied composition with Bruckner (see chapter 4). Schenker's choice of a German (or Austrian) folk tune is also consistent with Guido Adler's opinion regarding the origin of the "harmonic impulse," as discussed in chapter 1.

C and E, both of which occur in the second half of the first bar, as a triad. No possible triadic relationship escapes the ear, even if it lies in the background of consciousness and standing behind more important relationships in the plan of the piece.

Thus one must follow the element of harmony in both directions—the horizontal as well as the vertical.[52]

By way of contrast, Schenker quotes several plainchant melodies and the Phrygian cantus firmus from Fux's *Gradus ad parnassum* to show that they lack the sense of triadicity that he perceives in "Muß i denn?" In his opinion, the modal orientation of these other tunes emphasizes the horizontal at the expense of the vertical:

> This explains the well-known fact that the original systems applied only to the horizontal direction, and thus only to the melody, which tendency remained with them later, though the technique of counterpoint had long since accustomed the ear to hearing harmonies in a vertical direction, to the extent that even in the fifteenth and sixteenth centuries it appeared not to be nonsensical to assume, for example, a four-part structure interpreted simultaneously according to four different systems.[53]

Counterpoint (*HL*, §§84–89)

Once Schenker has shown how tonal melodies are constrained harmonically, he proceeds to explain how essential harmonies likewise control the behavior of tonal counterpoint. This point is important because his arguments were based on the notion that the principles of strict counterpoint must be extended in order to explain the idiosyncrasies of tonal voice leading: "[Tonal] composition, then, appears as an extension of strict [counterpoint]: an extension with regard to both the quantity of [tonal] material and the principle of its motion. All these extensions derive from the concept of

---

52. *HL*, §76, 176–77.
53. *HL*, §76, 179–80; *HA*, 137. Perhaps Schenker has misunderstood Pietro Aron, the leading modal theorist of the beginning of the sixteenth century, who proposed that the tenor and soprano would be in one mode, and the alto and bass would be in the plagal counterpart of that mode. See Strunk, *Source Readings*, revised edition, ed. Treitler, 420–22. The attempted adaptation of the modes (an innately melodic theory) to polyphony was and remains controversial.

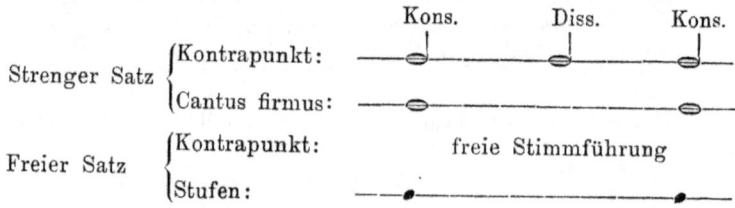

Figure 2.1a. Basic Textures of Strict versus Free Composition

Strict Composition:	Counterpoint:	Cons.	Diss.	Cons.
	Cantus Firmus:			
Free Composition:	Counterpoint:	Free Voice-leading		
	Essential Harmonic Progression:			

Figure 2.1b. Translation of Figure 2.1a

the essential harmony."[54] It extends both "the quantity of tonal material and the principle of its motion."[55] Schenker illustrates this idea in a diagram reproduced in figure 2.1a and b, which was cut from HA. The impact of these extensions is, in fact, profound. Strict counterpoint is a world of pure intervals in which essential harmonies simply do not exist: "where in strict [counterpoint], we have notes consonant to those of the cantus firmus, we have, in tonal composition, the essential harmony" that "articulate[s] its content" and "allow[s] for a much wider range of freedom in voice-leading."[56] In short: "essential harmonies resemble powerful searchlights—in their illuminated sphere the parts go through their evolution in a higher and freer contrapuntal sense, uniting in [discrete harmonies], which, however, never become ends in themselves but always result from the free movement."[57]

There are several important differences in the ways in which melodies behave in strict counterpoint as opposed to tonal composition. First, strict counterpoint limits the number of possible diminutions to a maximum of just four notes against one, whereas tonal composition permits more florid

---

54. *HL*, §88, 204; *HA*, 159; tr. Borgese, modified.
55. *HL*, §88, 204; *HA*, 159.
56. *HL*, §88, 203–4; *HA*, 158. See also §84, "Abwesen der Stüfen im strengen Satz" or "The Lack of Essential Harmonies in Strict Counterpoint," *HL*, 198–99.
57. *HL*, §85, 199–200; *HA*, 155; tr. Borgese, modified.

configurations. Second, strict counterpoint constrains the number, size, and successive use of melodic leaps, whereas tonal composition treats leaps more liberally, allowing them to appear repeatedly one after another. Third, strict counterpoint encompasses a very small number of non-harmonic tones (i.e., unaccented passing tones, the *nota cambiata*, unaccented neighbor tones, and suspensions) and prohibits them from appearing successively, whereas tonal composition includes a broad range of options (e.g., escape tones, accented passing and neighbor tones, appoggiaturas, and anticipations) and also allows them to occur in succession. Fourth, strict counterpoint forbids parallel perfect octaves and fifths between adjacent tones, whereas tonal counterpoint admits them in special circumstances through doublings and figuration or through combinations of harmonic and non-harmonic tones.[58] And fifth, strict counterpoint forbids repeated tones, pedal tones, motives, sequences, modulations and most chromatic tones, whereas tonal composition exploits these devices as a matter of course.

Schenker was perfectly aware of the historical implications of his arguments: he knew full well that they resonated with his earlier observations about the melodic and contrapuntal innovations of Caccini and Viadana. Indeed, the tendency for monodic pieces to superimpose elaborate melodic diminutions over simple sustained bass tones not only contradicts the precepts of strict counterpoint, but it also foreshadows later tonal practices. And yet, Schenker acknowledges that incipient essential harmonies can sometimes be found in strict counterpoint. In *HL*, §78, for example, he cites a fourth species passage from Fux's *Gradus ad parnassum* (see example 2.9).[59] According to him: "This construction, as is well known, is generally considered as a precursor of our pedal point. But what is of even greater interest to us in the present context is the technique which enables a tone to gather, so to speak, a large sequence of contrapuntal parts into a unity, this being the proper function of an essential harmony."[60] Just a few years later, Schenker described an even more elaborate

---

58. In *DfS*, Schenker lists the following combinations of harmonic and non-harmonic tones: "a principal note with an accented or unaccented passing tone or with a neighboring note; a passing tone with an anticipation, with an accented passing tone, or with a neighboring note; a neighboring note with another neighboring note, with the concluding turn of a trill, or with a suspension; the resolution of a suspension with a passing tone, with another suspension, and so forth." *DfS*, §164, 98; *FC*, 59.
59. *HL*, §78, 183; *HA*, 141. Fux, *Gradus ad parnassum* and *The Study of Counterpoint*, figure 142, 99.
60. *HL*, §78, 183; *HA*, 141.

Example 2.9. Incipient Essential Harmony ("V") in Fux

Example 2.10. Tonic pedal at the ending of J. S. Bach, Chromatic Fantasy and Fugue, BWV 903

pedal tone in J. S. Bach's Fantasy, in example 30 of *CFF* (1910) (see example 2.10). In this particular case, he notes that "we find a chain of diminished seventh chords, descending by half steps... While moving through so many diminished seventh chords, who else would give any thought to IV and I and their need for expression as pure, serene, and complete triads? Let us kneel in devotion before Bach's majestic spirit."[61]

Motives (*HL* §§1–7 and 115–17)

As we know, Schenker was a firm proponent of the mimetic theory of art when he was writing *HL*. In his words, all art "rests on the association of ideas" and is ultimately a form of imitation, "imitation by word or color or form."[62] He also assumes that, in musical contexts, ideas become associative when they are repeated: "Only repetition can demarcate a series of tones and its purpose. Repetition is thus the basis of music as an art. It creates musical form, just as the association of ideas from a pattern in nature creates the other forms of art."[63] When writing *HL*, Schenker believed that

---

61. *CFF*, 40.
62. *HL*, §1, 3; *HA*, 3.
63. *HL*, §4, 5; *HA*, §4, 5.

motives offered composers the only means of associating ideas, that it was only through the discovery of the motive and its use that "music became an art in the real sense of this word."[64] Although any series of tones—melodic, rhythmic, chordal—can be regarded as a motive, they will only do so if they are repeated, preferably immediately: "as long as there is no immediate repetition, the series, even if belatedly raised to the rank of a motive in the work in question, must be considered for the time being as a dependent part of a greater unity."[65] Motives can also be varied: "The musical image created by repetition need not be, in all cases, a painstakingly exact reproduction of the original series of tones. Even freer forms of repetition and imitation, including manifold small contrasts, will not cancel out the magical effects of association."[66]

Schenker also presumes that through motives, essential harmonies can be transformed from abstract entities into concrete ideas that express the unique content of a given composition: "To the extent that the harmonic concept uses as its interpreter the motive, which, as we saw earlier, constitutes the primal part of content—to this extent harmony and its realization become one."[67] He supports this claim by quoting the opening of Chopin's Prelude in B minor, Op. 28, No. 6 (see example 2.11) in which the motive in the left hand "gives life" to the triad, B-D-F♯.[68] "The mutual organic influence between musical content and harmony cannot be emphasized enough, especially in times like ours, when composers often heap chords upon chords without enveloping them in motivic substance and thereby clarifying the progression of essential harmonies."[69]

Towards the end of *HL*, Schenker offers a particularly fascinating example of ways in which different surface patterns can arise from fundamental ideas (*Urideen*).[70] Examples 2.12a–e show his analysis of measures 16–20 of J. S.

---

64. *HL*, §§2–3, 4; *HA*, 4.
65. *HL*, §4, 5. Schenker also admits that rhythmic patterns and even harmonic details can be repeated and create associations: see *HL*, §4, 6–10; *HA*, 7–9; and Hooper, "Schenker's Early Conception of Form," 41–47.
66. *HL*, §4, 6; *HA*, 7.
67. *HL*, §116, 282.
68. *HL*, §115, 281; *HA*, 211.
69. *HL*, §116, 282–83, footnote; *HA*, 212.
70. For the record, Schenker invoked the concept of *Urideen* in his analysis of the first movement of Beethoven's String Quartet, Op. 132, in *EBO*, 19; tr., Siegel, *CSO*, 42.

Example 2.11. Chopin, Prelude No. 6 in B Minor, Op. 28

Example 2.12a. J. S. Bach, Fugue in D Minor, BWV 851

Example 2.12b–e. J. S. Bach, Fugue in D Minor, BWV 851

b)

c)

d)

e)

Bach's Fugue in D minor in the *Well-Tempered Clavier*, part I.[71] In this case, the fluid string of harmonic tones, passing tones, changing tones, and auxiliary tones in the melody in measures 16–17 stem (example 2.12a) from the fundamental idea C-B-A (example 2.12b) and its derivative (example 2.12c).[72] Similarly, the lower counterpoint in measures 19–20 elaborates a similar fundamental idea (example 2.12d) through another intermediate version (example 2.12e).[73] It is also worth noting that Schenker finds parallels between the use of chromaticism and that of motives. Having claimed that the listener's perception of diatonic tones can be enhanced through chromatic contrast, he adds: "The harmonies behave in this respect much like motives. If the latter, in order to crystalize in our minds, need an association such as a single repetition, a contrast, or any juxtaposition whatsoever, the harmonies likewise welcome contrast as a most desirable means of association, and not only in the sphere of a small diatonic fragment but also in large form complexes."[74]

---

71. *HL*, §164, 404–5; *HA*, 306–7.
72. *HL*, §164, Exx. 308, 347–48.
73. *HL*, §164, Ex. 349.
74. *HL*, §155, 380; *HA*, 189.

Progressions of Essential Harmonies (*HL*, §§117–28)

In the second large part of *HL* (*Praktischer Teil*), Schenker attempts to realize the abstract tonal materials he has introduced in part 1. The German heading is "Von der Psychologie des Inhalts und des Stufenganges." Unfortunately, the dictionary equivalent for "Inhalt," "content," simply does not work in English, as Borgese's translation of the title, "On the Psychology of Contents and of Step Progression," demonstrates. In fact, Schenker attempts here to separate the abstract notion of the progression of essential harmony from the concrete notion of "musical content," which, we claim, is rendered more idiomatically in English as "musical realization," or simply "realization."[75] "To make real" is essentially what Schenker has in mind for *Inhalt*, and "realization" has the additional benefit of its connection to figured-bass theory, where it performs the same function. Obviously, the duality is akin to the form versus content duality of much literary theory, or even Aristotle's form (*eidos* or *morphē*) versus matter (*hulē*). But Schenker clearly identifies *Stufengang* quite restrictively with the "world purely of the mind" of harmony, while *Inhalt* is necessary to the outer, practical world of composition (or, as it will turn out, an idealized world of composition): a harmonic concept is essentially "empty" until it is "filled," or "realized" musically. For Schenker, the progression of essential harmonies is the abstract succession of essential harmonies; both it and its realization are intimately tied to interpretation, and are in that sense psychological. But perhaps surprisingly, the music "interprets" itself, for it is the motive (the extension of the artist) that turns out to be the interpreter of otherwise empty forms:

> To the extent that harmony uses the motive, which forms the primary part of its realization, as its interpreter, the two adhere to one another. From this point on, only a particular element of the realization from the complete organism brings the triad or the seventh chord to our consciousness; and vice versa, the laws of harmony influence the formation of the realization. Accordingly, a particular harmony is not merely asserted, but also composed out, and only thereby made definitive. It is from the bonding of

---

75. See the informative discussion by J. B. Robinson, who ends up rendering the pair *Form* and *Inhalt* as "technique" and "expression," in his translation of Dahlhaus's *Foundations*, x.

the harmonic element and its realization that the sensation of the essential harmony is felt within us.[76]

Here it becomes clear just what Schenker is getting at with his notion that this part of the book deals with "practical application." That is, harmony is only made "definitive" (*erwiesen*, or literally "proven") when it is "composed out" (*auskomponiert*) in the real world. Such a "composing out" need not be extensive or complex, as we saw with the simple arpeggiations of the tonic in Chopin's B minor Prelude, Op. 28, No. 6. We and our reaction to the process are the ultimate focus of the argument, not our conception of harmony. Hence Schenker's language gets intensely personal, his metaphors bringing us to the inner world of feeling rather than the intellect. Music evokes a "feeling" (*Gefühl*) within us, as the realization of an essential harmony interprets it for us: with the synthesis of harmony and its realization, our feeling for the essential harmony manifests itself in us (literally "blooms" in us [*in uns erblüht*], a common metaphor of Romantic poetry). Indeed, examples of appeals to the psychology of the listener and the composer are legion in part II: "Thus harmony by itself calls for a further clarification, which, in turn, creates in us the need and expectation of a continuation—in us, and naturally, in the composer as well."[77]

The bond of progression of essential harmony and its musical realization is also the origin of form: "If we follow the further stages of this union, the form of the piece gradually becomes clear to us, and, conversely, only from the basic features of the form does the essential meaning of the psychology of the progression of essential harmony emerge so emphatically."[78]

Thus a "form" is not some abstract structure in a textbook, but something that "becomes clear to us" through our interpretation of essential progression, the basics of which are put in place by motivic interpretation of harmony. Schenker's insights about the interconnections between harmony and motive inevitably led him to consider situations in which motives can be used to express a string of essential harmonies (or essential progressions). He cites a couple more passages from Chopin's Prelude in B minor, Op. 28, No. 6 (see example 2.13a). The piece established the tonic B in measures

---

76. *HL*, §116, 282; *HA*, 212. In the first sentence Schenker uses the old Austrian word "Dolmetsch" for "interpreter," and thus means "interpreter" in the sense of "translator" or "spokesperson."
77. *HL*, §117, 283; *HA*, 213.
78. *HL*, §117, 282; *HA*, 212.

1–4 through repetitions of the main motive, but Schenker notes that this single essential harmony "calls for further clarification." Although the subsequent progression of degrees—VI–II♯3–V–I–IV–V—is familiar enough, it not only ends with a half cadence on the dominant rather than an authentic cadence on the tonic, but it also injects a new motive in measures 6–8.[79] Schenker then shows how Chopin clarifies this motion in measures 9–18 (see example 2.13b). The new chain of degrees I–VI7–II (phryg.)–V–I–VII (=V)–IV–V–VI recalls the motive from measures 6–8 in measures 15–18 in the left rather than the right hand.[80] Remarkably, Chopin stopped short of providing "absolute satisfaction" by ending on a deceptive cadence on VI rather than an authentic cadence on I.[81]

One of the reasons why Schenker was so interested in passages like those shown in examples 2.13a–b is that they illustrate some of the different "feelings of satisfaction" induced at the end of formal units. Schenker then uses this idea as a pretext for discussing cadences, especially full closes, half closes, deceptive cadences, plagal cadences, and related patterns. Not surprisingly, perhaps, Schenker underscores the fact that, whatever their formal function, each type of cadence relies on a distinctive progression of degrees: full closes articulate the progression (IV)–V–I; half closes the progression (I)–IV–V; deceptive cadences the progression (IV)–V–VI, plagal cadences the progression IV–I.[82] Significantly, most of these progressions involve motion by a fifth, one of the basic triadic intervals and the progenitor of the tonal system.

Triadic intervals also play a determining role in other harmonic progressions. Indeed, as he points out in *HL*, §§125–28, Schenker believes that degrees are usually arranged into progressions that project triadic intervals, namely, the fifth and third.[83] Since those intervals stem from the harmonic series, he classifies progressions by these intervals as "natural."[84] Even

---

79. *HL*, §117, 284–85; *HA*, 214.
80. *HL*, §118, 285–87; *HA*, 215–16.
81. *HL*, §118, 287; *HA*, 216.
82. *HL*, §119, 290; *HA*, 218. Schenker discusses full closes in §119; half closes in §120; deceptive cadences in §121; plagal cadences in §122. He considered other forms of cadence and certain modifications to cadences in §§123 and 124 respectively.
83. *HL*, §125, 311 and §126, 314; *HA*, 232 and 225 respectively.
84. For progressions by fifth, see *HL*, §125, 311–13; *HA*, 232–34. For progressions by third, see *HL*, §126, 314–15; *HA*, 235–36.

Example 2.13a–b. Chopin, Prelude No. 6 in B Minor, Op. 28, mm. 1–8 and 9–18

when degrees follow one another by step, a possibility that he regarded as "artificial," Schenker proposes that they are still contingent upon those intervals.[85] For example, he explains an upward progression from I to II as an abridged motion of two ascending fifths I–V and V–II and a downward progression from II to I as an abridged motion of a descending fifth followed by a descending third I–IV and IV–II.[86] In other words, Schenker not only maintains that tonal harmony is intrinsically triadic, but he also proposes that harmonic progressions project triadic intervals horizontally.

Mixture (*HL*, §§38–52 and 155–62)

Besides allowing degrees and essential harmonies to appear in diatonic form, Schenker invokes the principle of mixture (*Mischung*) to make the resources of the minor system available to major and vice versa.[87] For him, this was a natural process: "The tone lives a richer life, it satisfies its vitality all the better the more it revels in these relationships—that is, first, when it unites major and minor—and second, the more intensely it revels in each [system]. Thus every tone must fight for such wealth and life-force."[88] He adds that it is hard to find a work that does not contain mixture of one sort or another: "Properly speaking, I think that any composition moves within a major–minor system. A composition in C, for example, should be understood as in C major–minor (Cmajor/minor); for a pure C major, without any ingredients from C minor, or, vice versa a pure C minor, without any elements from C major, hardly ever occurs in reality."[89] In short: "The expansive urge of the tone demands the use of both systems as well as of all their possible combinations."[90]

---

85. Schenker classified progressions by second as artificial in *HL*, §125, 311 and §127, 314; *HA*, 232 and 236.

86. *HL*, §127, 315–18; *HA*, 236–39. Interestingly, neither of these interpretations corresponds to Sechter's reading of the same progressions, but the general principle—to regard the stepwise progression as a combination of two progressions by third or fifth (or combinations thereof)—is the standard one in fundamental bass theory.

87. *HL*, §§38–52 and 106–50.

88. *HL*, §38, 107.

89. *HL*, §40, 109.

90. Ibid.

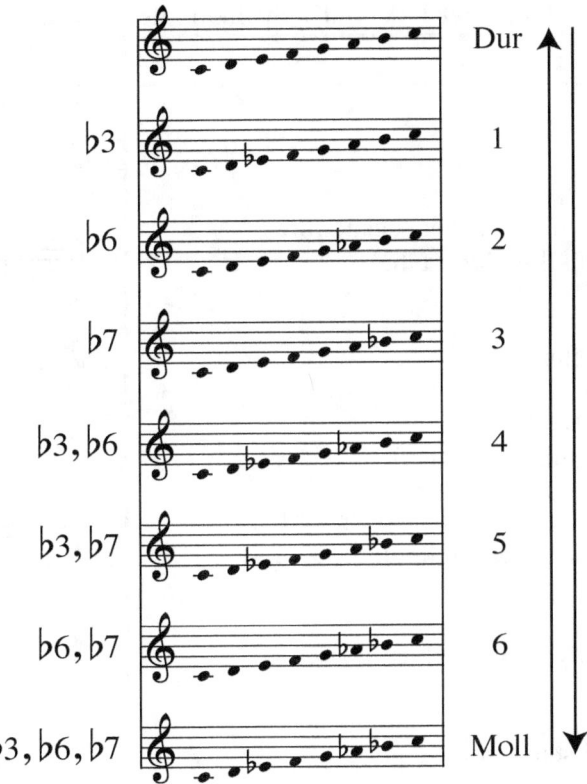

Figure 2.2a. Possible Series Created via Mixture of Major and Minor Systems

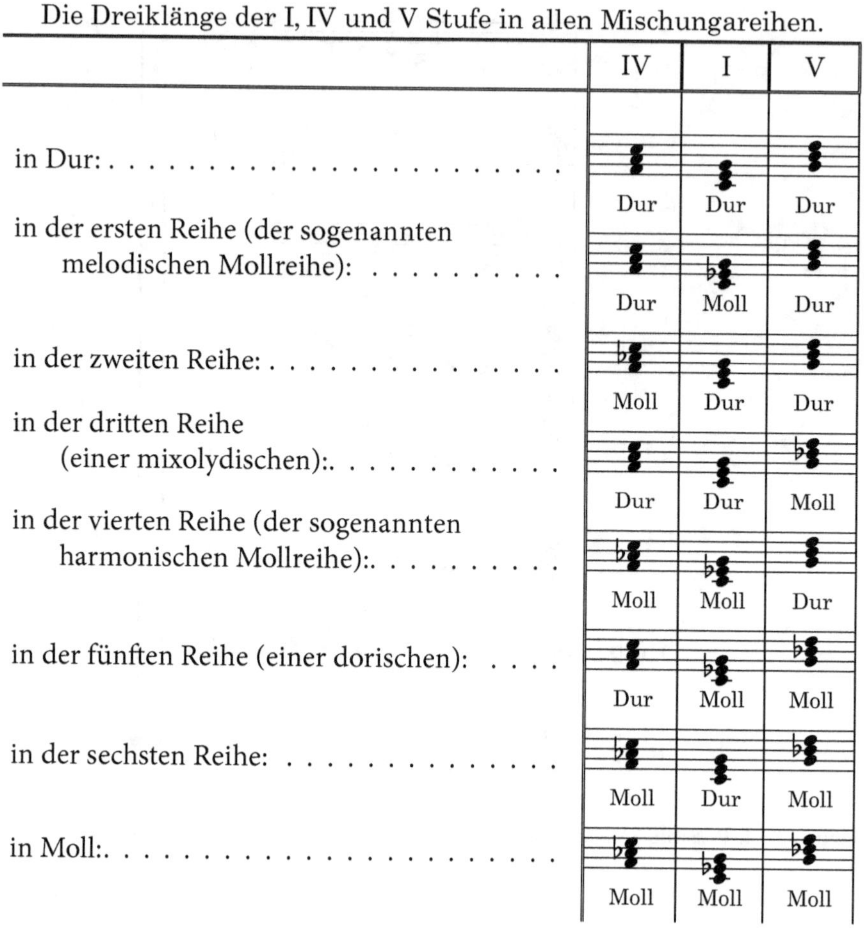

Die Dreiklänge der I, IV und V Stufe in allen Mischungareihen.

	IV	I	V
in Dur:..................	Dur	Dur	Dur
in der ersten Reihe (der sogenannten melodischen Mollreihe):..........	Dur	Moll	Dur
in der zweiten Reihe:...............	Moll	Dur	Dur
in der dritten Reihe (einer mixolydischen):............	Dur	Dur	Moll
in der vierten Reihe (der sogenannten harmonischen Mollreihe):.........	Moll	Moll	Dur
in der fünften Reihe (einer dorischen):	Dur	Moll	Moll
in der sechsten Reihe:..............	Moll	Dur	Moll
in Moll:....................	Moll	Moll	Moll

Figure 2.2b. The Chords on I, IV, and V in Major (Top) and Minor (Bottom), and in the Six "Mixed" Series (Middle), from Figure 2.2a

To show the different ways in which mixture operates within the tonal system, Schenker in *HL*, 110 constructs an elaborate chart given here as figure 2.2a. The chart places the major system at the top and the natural minor system—with its lowered third, sixth, and seventh degrees—at the bottom. Between these two poles, he includes six series (or *Reihen*), corresponding to the six possible combinations of natural and lowered degrees: series 1, 2, and 3 present the lowered third, sixth, and seventh degrees individually within an otherwise major context; while series 4, 5, and 6 present the different pairs of lowered third, sixth, and seventh degrees within an otherwise minor context. The arrows along the right-hand side of figure 2.2a emphasize that mixture can occur to varying extents between the purely major and the purely minor.[91] Schenker then underscores the harmonic implications of figure 2.2a in another chart that lists the subdominant, tonic, and dominant degrees for each series (see figure 2.2b, from *HL*, 117). This new chart indicates that the triads from series 1 correspond to the ascending melodic minor, series 3 to Mixolydian mode, series 4 to harmonic minor, and series 5 to Dorian mode. Near the end of *HL*, Schenker finally gives a complete list of degrees in the C major–minor system (see figure 2.3).[92] By referring to the mixed third, sixth, and seventh degrees with a single Roman numeral, Schenker's list shows that the combined major–minor system still has only seven degrees, but that the second, third, sixth, and seventh degrees have two distinct forms with two distinct roots. The latter point becomes all the more significant in the next stage of derivation in which Schenker claims that each of these degrees can appear as major and minor triads: "Nothing stands in the way of projecting an 'apparent' key chromatically on each of these degrees: in so doing, mixture, as an ever present compositional procedure, could penetrate even these pseudo-keys as well."[93] Schenker adds these extra forms to his previous list, thereby producing the chart given in figure 2.4a.[94] This figure clearly shows that each degree can appear in several different forms: in C major–minor,

C	Des	D	Es E	F	G	As A	B H
I	♭II	♮II	III	IV	V	VI	VII

Figure 2.3. Complete List of Degrees of the Key of C Major–Minor

---

91. These arrows are cut from *HA*.
92. *HL*, §160, 395. In German, "s" is added to the letter name to indicate a flat, unless the letter name is a consonant, in which case "es" is added. In addition, B = B♭ and H = B natural (probably derived from the medieval "hard B," though one theorist claimed that it was merely the next letter in the alphabet after the terminal G).
93. *HL*, §160, 395.
94. Ibid. This chart is absent from *HA*. Thus figure 2.4b provides a translation.

C-$\frac{dur}{moll}$ (selbstverständlich),

Des-$\frac{dur}{moll}$, wenn die zweite phrygische Stufe als scheinbare Tonart chromatisch (also auch mit Zuhilfenahme anderer Stufen) präpariert wird,

*Es-$\frac{dur}{moll}$ entsprechend einer chromatischen Tonart auf der dritten Stufe,

E-$\frac{dur}{moll}$ dto. auf der dritten Stufe,

F-$\frac{dur}{moll}$ dto. auf der vierten Stufe,

G-$\frac{dur}{moll}$ dto. auf der fünften Stufe,

As-$\frac{dur}{moll}$ } dto. auf der sechsten Stufe,
A-$\frac{dur}{moll}$

B-$\frac{dur}{moll}$ } dto. auf der siebenten Stufe.
H-$\frac{dur}{moll}$

*should include D-$\frac{dur}{moll}$

Figure 2.4a. Possible Keys Related to C Major–Minor, Created via Mixture

C major-minor (obviously)
D♭ major-minor (when the Phrygian Second Degree is chromatically prepared as an apparent key—with the assistance of another chord)
E♭ major-minor (corresponding to the chromatic key on the third degree, ([according to the prevailing mode]))
E major-minor (the same on the third degree)
F major-minor (the same on the fourth degree)
G major-minor (the same on the fifth degree)
A♭ major-minor (the same on the sixth degree)
A major-minor
B♭ major-minor (the same on the seventh degree)
B major-minor
Note that D maj./min. is conspicuously absent.

Figure 2.4b. Translation of Figure 2.4a

for example, the III degree can appear as major and minor triads on E♭ as well as major and minor triads on E. Mixture, then, refers to two different processes: that of interchanging roots and chord qualities of degree between the major and minor systems, but also that of altering the quality of any triad from major to minor and vice versa.

Figure 2.5 clarifies Schenker's argument.[95] Figure 2.5a presents the major system with major triads on I, IV, and V, minor triads on II, III, and VI, and a diminished triad on VII. Meanwhile, figure 2.5b gives the minor system with minor triads on I, IV, and V, major triads on ♭II, ♭III, ♭VI, and ♭VII, and a diminished triad on II. Secondary systems for the major and the minor are given in figures 2.5c and 2.5d respectively: the former consists of major triads on I, II, III, IV, V, VI, and VII, and a minor triad on VII; the latter consists of minor triads on I, ♭II, ♭III, IV, V, ♭VI, and ♭VII. Simple mixture is the process by which composers borrow triads from the parallel key: this amounts to switching between figures 2.5a and 2.5b. This process involves changing the quality of the I, IV, and V degrees and the roots of the II, III, VI, and VII degrees. Secondary mixture then allows them to borrow two triads from the secondary system: in the case of figure 2.5a, they can borrow triads from figure 2.5c; in the case of figure 2.5b, they can borrow triads from figure 2.5d. This process involves changing the qualities of II, III, VI, and VII in major, and ♭II, ♭III, ♭VI, and ♭VII in minor. Double mixture then allows composers to borrow triads from the parallel key and then to change the quality of that triad: in the case of figure 2.5a, this means that they can borrow the triads from figure 2.5d; and in the case of figure 2.5b they can borrow triads from figure 2.5c.

	Major	Minor	
a. Diatonic	I, ii, iii, IV, V, vi, vii°	i, ♭II, ii°, ♭III, iv, v, ♭VI, ♭VII	b. Diatonic
c. Secondary	I, II, III, IV, V, VI, vii, VII	i, ♭ii, ii°, ♭iii, iv, v, ♭vi, ♭vii	d. Secondary

Figure 2.5. Triads Available on All Degrees of Pure Diatonic (a and b) and Secondary (c and d) Systems, Available for Mixture

---

95. Brown, *Explaining Tonality*, 44.

Tonicization (*HL*, §§133–54)

Chromatic alteration (*Chromatische Alterierung*) and altered chords (*alterierte Akkorde*) were standard topics of later nineteenth and early twentieth-century harmony books. Schenker uses the terms chromaticism and alteration in the section heading "Von der Psychologie der Chromatik und der Alteration," but quickly qualifies them so that his restricted approach to the topic becomes clear: he implicitly rejects the standard treatments of these topics, which often lead quickly to chords containing chromatic intervals.[96] Instead, in the section entitled "The Theory of Interpretation of Essential Harmonies" ("Werttheorie der Stufen," §133),[97] Schenker calls upon the behavior of the tones he had been emphasizing all along—namely, their urge to be interpreted as a tonic. He bases this whole section on our interpretation of the initial onset of single chords, which he then transfers to their entrance within more complicated contexts. Once again, this brings to mind the "law of least action," since interpretation of a major or minor triad out of context as a potential tonic is the most obvious choice.[98] The essence of the "psy-

---

96. The Louis and Thuille *Harmonielehre* stands out as the most sophisticated attempt of the time to construct a theory of "chromatic harmony," for the two halves of their book are not devoted to theory vs. practice, but rather to "diatonic harmony" (part 1) and "chromatic harmony" (part 2), and are of nearly equal lengths. While the dominant seventh is (not surprisingly) the model dissonant chord in the diatonic system, its enharmonic twin, the diminished third/augmented sixth chord, plays that role in the chromatic system. Schenker eventually deals with these chords in *HL*, §146.

97. The reader confined to *HA* will have a difficult time getting this argument from the literal translation, "Scale-Steps and Valuation Theory (*Werttheorie*)" (*HA*, 251). Just what is "valuation theory"? In fact, Schenker means "value" in the sense of "interpretation," or perhaps, the function that a tonal formation assumes upon interpretation. Unfortunately, "function" is already so overused in theories of harmony that it is essentially unavailable. In Borgese's defense, *Wert* is most often translated as "value." Moreover, *Werttheorie* is close to *Wertlehre*, which has a place in philosophy as "theory of values"—those phenomena that were banished from "pure reason" by Kant and placed in aesthetics and ethics, and later became the subject of treatises that sought to explain their philosophical basis, thereby raising their status. See, for example, Kraft, *Foundations for a Scientific Analysis of Value*. Perhaps this is the source of Schenker's idea. In a book on the theory of harmony, however, our translation gets much closer to telling the reader just what this section is about.

98. This suggestion of the law of least action is yet another point of comparison with Weber, whose protagonist in his analysis of the introduction to Mozart's

chology of chromaticism and alteration" thus turns out to be tied intimately to our interpretation of a triad out of context, and within various contexts Schenker described. This sets up his view of chromaticism, which is confined to diatonic entities that are *chromatic in the context in which they are found*: an E major triad in the overall key of C major, for example, even if it is clearly the dominant of the temporary key of A minor, and thus intrinsically diatonic, is interpreted as chromatic because it is found in the larger context of C major. Thus, in essence, Schenker attempts to explain all "chromaticism" and "alteration" via modulation, and modal mixture, and in that respect does not depart significantly from the nineteenth-century Viennese party line.[99] In the former case, the modulation may be transitory and of very limited duration, for which he coins his own term, "tonicization" (*Tonikalisierung*). Such a modulation may also be chromatic in the more broadly held sense that there is no diatonic "pivot chord": i.e., the leading tone of the tonicizing chord is introduced directly by chromatic inflection. By confining himself mainly to eighteenth- and relatively early nineteenth-century examples, Schenker is successful with this strategy.

Still, there are certain chromatic intervals, the existence of which must be acknowledged, namely, the augmented second/diminished seventh, diminished third/augmented sixth, and diminished fourth/augmented fifth: chromatic alterations of chordal intervals that became more and more common through the nineteenth century. Such intervals and the chords in which they are found turn out to be further products of tonicization for Schenker. In part II of *HL*, Schenker discovers another important principle that allowed composers to expand the content of degrees and guide the formal structure of a tonal composition, for which he invents the term "tonicization" (*Tonikalisierung*).[100] Whereas mixture allows composers to borrow

---

"Dissonance Quartet" is "the ear" (*das Gehör*), which always seeks the most obvious analytical interpretation, and is constantly surprised or disappointed, given the clear difficulties of the passage in question. See Ian Bent's translation in his *Music Analysis in the Nineteenth Century*, 157–83, and especially the first two pages of Bent's introduction.

99. Wason, *Viennese Harmonic Theory*, chapter 7. See Sechter, *Grundsätze*, vol. 1, 146f., in which Sechter agrees that an augmented sixth/diminished third chord is simultaneously a V7 (of the tonic) and II7 (of the minor subdominant), though he would more likely phrase it as II7 (of the minor tonic) and V7 (of the dominant), the latter being the more likely transposition in which it normally occurs. This is his "hybrid chord" (*Zwitterakkord*).

100. Schenker, *HL*, §§136–45; *HA*, 256–76.

triads whose roots and qualities belong to the major and minor systems, tonicization allows them to borrow individual notes (i.e., microtonicization) and even triads whose roots and qualities belong to another major–minor system.[101] Such notes and triads are often referred to now in English as secondary or applied tones and chords, but the distinction by theorists between modulations of significant duration and brief references to related keys was hardly common when Schenker invented the term. This procedure is ubiquitous in tonal composition and, according to Schenker, is ultimately a natural process: "Not only at the beginning of a composition, however, but also in the midst of it, each degree displays an irresistible desire to attain for itself the value of the tonic as the strongest essential harmony. If the composer surrenders himself to this desire to attain the strongest value of tonic within the diatonic system, I call the process 'tonicization' and the phenomenon itself 'chromaticism.'"[102]

As it happens, the ways in which particular degrees are tonicized depends on the role that the degree plays within a particular key. Tonicizing the subdominant degree, for example, involves lowering 7 in the original key so that it functions locally as 4 in the new key. Figure 2.6a shows this process in the key of C major. In this particular case, the tritone E/B♭ functions as $\frac{7}{4}$ in F major whereas the tritone F/B functions as $\frac{4}{7}$ in the original tonic C.[103] Tonicizing the dominant, however, involves raising 4 in the original key so that it functions locally as 7 in the new key. This process is shown in figure 2.6b: the tritone F♯/C functions as $\frac{7}{4}$ in G major, whereas the tritone F/B functions as $\frac{4}{7}$ in the original tonic C. The patterns shown in figures 2.6a–b can even be used sequentially: as shown in figures 2.6c–f, they can be used to generate diatonic and chromatic sequences that ascend (figures 2.6c–d) and descend (figures 2.6e–f).

For his part, Schenker discusses several different types of tonicization: direct tonicization; indirect tonicization; tonicization by fifth; tonicization by descending third; tonicization though upward progression by a second.[104] Schenker even suggests that tonicization helps to explain the function of the ♭II degree.[105] Take, for example, the progression VI–II–V♯3–I in D minor given in example 2.14a. If, however, the penultimate dominant is tonicized

---

101. For Schenker's discussion of microtonicization, see *HL*, §144.
102. *HL*, §136, 337; *HA*, 256; tr. Borgese, modified.
103. *DfS*, fig. 79.5.
104. *HL*, §137, §138, §§139–140, §141, and §§142–3 respectively.
105. *HL*, §145.

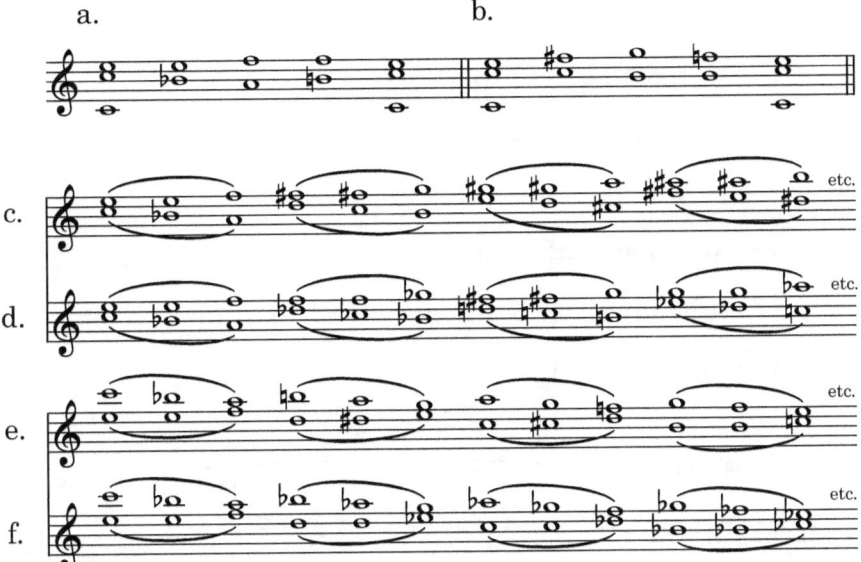

Figure 2.6a–f. Tonicization Patterns

with its own applied dominant (E–G♯–B), the first three degrees might be reinterpreted as ♭II–V♯3–I in A major or major–minor (see example 2.14b). According to Schenker, this procedure was specifically used by Chopin in *Etude* in A minor, Op. 10, No. 4 (see example 2.14c).

Just as Schenker claims that tonicization was an essential feature of the tonal system, so he also insists that there is no limit to its use: "the composer's leeway with regard to chromatic changes indeed seems unlimited."[106] Schenker's comment can, however, be interpreted in two slightly different ways. Obviously, it can be interpreted qualitatively to mean that even the most abstruse harmonies can be tonicized. Example 2.15 shows a good case in point from Bach's Prelude in E-flat minor in the *Well-Tempered Clavier Part I*. According to Schenker, the appearance of the B♭♭ in measure 2 makes the supporting Phrygian II sound locally like the tonic: "Here again it is a II (Phrygian) essential harmony in E-flat minor, the major triad, F-flat, A-flat, C-flat—see the B-double-flat in measure 2—that confers upon itself, without further ceremony, the rank of a tonic. It would be idle, in this case too, to speak of a real F-flat major key: much simpler is to sympathize with the II degree in its yearning for the higher value of a I essential harmony—

---

106. *HL*, §156, 381–92; *HA*, 290.

Example 2.14a–c. Chopin, *Etude* in A Minor, Op. 10, No. 4

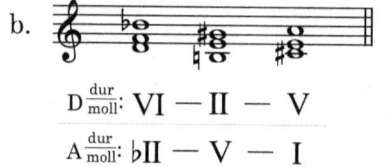

F-flat major, as it were. Note the exquisite effect resulting from the contrast between the B-double-flat and the diatonic B-flat!"[107]

Alternatively, Schenker's comment can be interpreted quantitatively to mean that every chord in a progression can be tonicized. For example, figure 2.7a presents the simple progression I–vi–IV–ii–V–I in C major. Figure 2.7b then tonicizes every member of the chord progression: the upper string tonicizes D near the cadence with the chromatic passing tone C♯; the middle

---

107. *HL*, §136, 340; *HA*, 258.

Example 2.15. J. S. Bach, Prelude in E-flat Minor, BWV 853

string tonicizes A at the start with the chromatic passing tone G♯ and with the upper neighbor tone B♭; and the lower string tonicizes G at the cadence with the F♯. Besides adding passing tones to the original bass line, figure 2.7b shows how the new bass line not only becomes more melodic, but also how it projects a variant of the Rule of the Octave, C-B-A-G-F-E-D-(G)-C. The resulting texture confirms Schenker's general observation that in tonal contexts "one can never write too chromatically."[108]

The preceding remarks make it clear that Schenker was able to explain how essential harmonies need not be expressed in purely diatonic forms: whether they derive from mixtures or from tonicizations, these altered essential harmonies "do not destroy the diatonic system" but "rather emphasize and confirm it."[109] In his words:

> Even in its chromatic state, the essential harmony retains its ability to be the same higher intellectual unity that we have already defined for the diatonic form. That is, the obligation to return to the diatonic system [major or minor] does not imply any restrictions as far as the duration of the chromatic degree

---

108. *HL*, §155, 380; *HA*, 289.
109. *HL*, §155, 380; *HA*, 288.

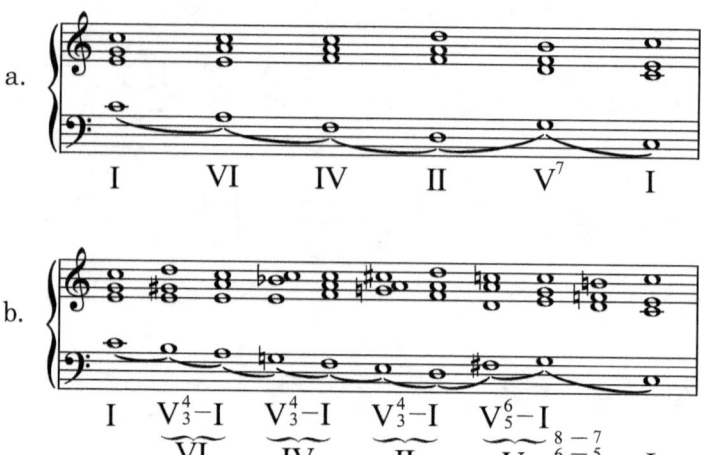

Figure 2.7a–b. Variant of the Rule of the Octave

is concerned; its duration remains variable just like that of the diatonic degree and varies from a minimum to the greatest conceivable maximum.[110]

And yet, Schenker claims that "we do not lose the feeling for the underlying diatonic relationships between degrees."[111] For him, "there remains in us the expectation of a return of the Artistic system; and in most cases, in fact, the minor thirds, major thirds, etc., soon re-enter victoriously, and the triumph of the system thus alternates with the triumph of Nature."[112]

Local Form (*HL*, §§129–32)

Even at the beginning of *HL*, Schenker draws attention to the fact that motivic repetition plays a vital role in creating musical forms: "The principle of repetition, once successfully applied to an understanding of the microcosm of musical composition, could now be applied on a larger scale as well."[113] After explaining how tonal motives (and for that matter tonal melodies and counterpoint) are constrained harmonically, Schenker returns to formal

---

110. *HL*, §159, 388.
111. *HL*, §155, 379; *HA*, 288.
112. Ibid.
113. *HL*, §5, 10; *HA*, 9.

issues in *HL*, §129 in an effort to demonstrate the connections between harmony and motives of a "higher order."[114] His reference to "higher order" relations recalls the distinction that he made in *HL*, §77 between foreground (*Vordergrund*) and background (*Hintergrund*).[115] In *HL*, §129, however, Schenker uses it to broach the topic of *Gruppenbildung*—the formation of thematic groups.[116] This term refers to the ways in which composers create diversity within a formal unit by changes not only in the harmony and motives, but also in rhythm and dynamics.[117]

Schenker illustrates the concept of *Gruppenbildung* in a close reading of measures 23–47 from the first movement of Beethoven's String Quartet in F minor, Op. 95 (see example 2.16).

The passage in question corresponds to the entry of the second group in D. According to Schenker, Beethoven presents a new motive in measures 23–7: although it is supported by I and V degrees, the passage requires some sort of continuation. The following measures (28–34) seem to satisfy this demand by developing the motive, but end unexpectedly with a weak half cadence on V. The lack of harmonic closure on I calls for more material. After sustaining the dominant for four bars with an independent motive (measures 34–37), the music takes a dramatic turn in measures 38–43: a number of new motives and a startling turn to ♭II (measures 38–39) finally lead to the anticipated cadence V–I in the local tonic D♭ (measures 42–43). The passage ends with a four-measure tonic pedal that features the subordinate motive from measures 34–37. Although Schenker does not say so, Beethoven immediately presents a varied counterstatement of the theme in measures 47–59. Convoluted as it may seem to modern readers, Schenker's discussion of this remarkable passage does not detract from his more basic point, namely that Beethoven created the impression of a closed formal unit through an array of motives and rhythmic elements but a limited number of degrees.[118] As he explains:

---

114. Schenker attacks traditional *Formenlehre* at several points: see *HL*, §§131–32, 246–50, esp. 250; *HA*, 246–50.
115. *HL*, §77, 181; *HA*, 138.
116. *HL*, §§129–32. Schenker previously discussed the concept of *Gruppenbildung* in *EBO*, 11–14 (*CSO*, 28–33). See also Ian Bent and Anthony Pople, "Analysis" (part II, History; §4, 1910–45) and Koslovsky, "Tracing the Improvisatory Impulse."
117. It is worth noting that Schenker had already described the ways in which composers join successive phrases motivically in *HL*, §5. He later referred to this phenomenon as linkage technique. See *HL*, §5, 17–19; *HA*, 11–12.
118. Koslovsky discusses this point in detail in "Tracing the Improvisatory Impulse," 66–76.

Example 2.16. Beethoven, String Quartet in F Minor, Op. 95, First Movement, mm. 23–47

Example 2.16.—*(concluded)*

Table 2.2. Examples of Group Construction

C. P. E. Bach	Collection 1, Sonata IV, in *Kenner & Liebhaber*, #5 in Schenker edition, 1st mvt. 2nd group
	Collection 1, Sonata IV, *K&L*, #5 in Schenker edition, 3rd mvt. 2nd and 3rd group
	Collection 1, Sonata VI, *K&L*; #9 in Schenker edition, 1st mvt. 1st group and so on
Haydn	Symphony D major, Hob. I:104, 1st mvt. 1st group and bridge
	Symphony D major, Hob. I:104, 4th mvt. bridge and 2nd group and so on
	String Quartet D major, Op. 20 #4, Hob. III:34, 1st mvt. 1st group, bridge and 2nd group
	String Quartet D major, Op. 20 #4, Hob. III:34, 4th mvt. 1st group, bridge and 2nd group
	String Quartet D major, Op. 50 #6, Hob. III:49, 1st mvt. 1st group
	String Quartet A major, Op. 55 #1, Hob. III:60, 1st mvt. 1st group, bridge and 2nd group
	String Quartet E flat major, Op. 64 #6, Hob. III:64, 1st mvt. 1st, 2nd, and 3rd group
	String Quartet D major, Op. 71 #2, Hob. III:70, 1st mvt. bridge and 2nd group and so on
	Piano Sonata E flat, Hob. XVI:52, 1st mvt. 2nd and 3rd group
	Piano Sonata A flat major, Hob. XVI:46, 1st mvt. 2nd group and so on
Mozart	Symphony E-flat major, K. 543, 1st mvt. 2nd and 3rd group
	Symphony G minor, K. 550, 1st mvt. 2nd and 3rd group
	Symphony C major, K. 551, 1st mvt. 2nd and 3rd group
	Symphony C major, K. 551, Finale, 1st group, bridge (fugato) from m. 36 and 2nd group from m. 74 on and so on
	String Quintet C major, K. 515, 1st mvt. 1st group, bridge and 2nd group
	String Quintet G minor, K. 516, 1st mvt. 1st group, bridge (!!), 2nd group and 3rd group and so on
	String Quartet E flat major, K. 428?, 1st mvt. bridge and 2nd group

(continued)

Table 2.2.—*(concluded)*

	String Quartet C major, K. 465?, 1st mvt. bridge and 2nd group and so on
	Piano Sonata C major, K. 309? 1st mvt. 1st group (mm. 13 and 14!)
	Piano Sonata C major, K. 330?, 1st mvt. 2nd and 3rd group and so on
Beethoven	Symphony No. 3, Op. 55, 1st mvt. 2nd and 3rd group
	Symphony No. 4, Op. 60, 1st mvt. 2nd group
	Symphony No. 4, Op. 60, 4th mvt. 1st group
	Symphony No. 5, Op. 67, 1st mvt. 2nd and 3rd group
	Symphony No. 6, Op. 68, 1st mvt. 2nd group
	Symphony No. 7, Op. 92, 1st mvt. bridge, 3rd and 2nd group [*sic*]
	Symphony No. 8, Op. 93, 1st mvt. 2nd group
	Symphony No. 9, Op. 125, 1st mvt. 2nd and 3rd group
	String Quartet F major, Op. 59 #1, 1st mvt. 1st group
	String Quartet E minor, Op. 59 #2, 1st mvt. 2nd group and so on
	Piano Sonata A flat major, Op. 110, 1st mvt. 1st group and so on
Schubert	String Quintet C major, D. 956, Op. posth. 163, 1st mvt. 2nd and 3rd group
	Octet, D. 803, Op. 166, 1st mvt. 2nd group and so on
Mendelssohn	Symphony No. 3 A minor, Op. 56, 1st mvt. bridge, 2nd and 3rd group
	String Quintet No. 1 A major, Op. 18, 1st mvt. 1st group, bridge and 2nd group
	String Quintet No. 3 D major, Op. 44 #1, 1st mvt. 1st group, bridge and 2nd group
	String Quintet No. 5 E flat major, Op. 44 #3, 1st group, bridge and 2nd group and so on
Brahms	Symphony No. 2 D major, Op. 73, 1st mvt. 2nd group
	Symphony No. 3 F major, Op. 90, 1st mvt. 2nd and 3rd group
	Symphony No. 4 E minor, Op. 98, 1st mvt. bridge, 2nd and 3rd group and so on
	String Quartet C minor, Op. 51 #1, 1st mvt. 1st and 2nd group
	Piano Quartet G minor, Op. 25, 1st group and so on

Source: *HL*, 325–6. We thank Frank Samarotto for sharing his transcription of Schenker's list.

> [Beethoven] achieved this effect by using few, relatively few degrees for each single element while attempting to make the most, motivically, out of each given degree. This technique—more content, less harmonic dispersion—thus allows for a variety of characterization. It exhausts the content of each degree by interpreting it conceptually. By never wasting any harmony, it spares each one for whatever effect it may yet yield.[119]

Schenker adds: "The degrees and the themes motivated by them are assured, in any case, their desired effect, and there arises the image of organic unity."[120] He then points the reader to an extensive list of analogous passages from works by C. P. E. Bach, Haydn, Mozart, Beethoven, Schubert, Mendelssohn, and Brahms (see table 2.2).[121] Unfortunately, Jonas subsequently cut this list from *HA*.

The idea of *Gruppenbildung* prompted Schenker to discuss sonatas forms, or what he referred to as cyclic movements (*zyklische Sätze*). Cyclic movements typically establish a certain pattern of material across a large section and bring it back at one or more points later in the piece. Schenker cites the example of those that use three themes, one for the "main" section or strain I, another for the "subsidiary" section or strain II, and another the "closing" section.[122] Such movements also stand out because they generate this wealth of motivic content out of a limited number of harmonic areas:

> This technique—more content, less harmonic dispersion—thus allows for a variety of characterization. It exhausts the content of each degree by interpreting it conceptually. By never wasting any harmony, it spares each one for whatever effect it may yet yield. The essential harmonies and the motivic content [*Gedanken*] motivated by them are assured, in any case, their desired effect, and there arises the image of organic unity which is so essential to a cyclic movement.[123]

According to Schenker, the idea of making "the most, motivically, of each degree," is one from which the classical masters rarely deviate: rather they join together a "splendid plurality of ideas" in ways that are both unique

---

119. *HL*, §129, 325; *HA*, 244–45.
120. *HL*, §129, 325; *HA*, 245.
121. *HL*, §129, 325–26.
122. *HL*, §130, 326; *HA*, 245.
123. *HL*, §129, 325; *HA*, 245.

and organic.[124] This allowed him to articulate the following principle: "Spare your harmonies and develop out of them as much thematic content as possible."[125]

Global Form (*HL*, §§155–62, 171–82, and NdK)

Even at the opening of *HL*, Schenker expresses his concern for the overall form of tonal compositions.[126] He claims not only that repetition is the primary means by which ideas are associated in music thereby defining it as art, but also that repetition plays a vital role in creating musical forms. As he explains in *HL*, §5: "The principle of repetition, once successfully applied to an understanding of the microcosm of musical composition, could now be applied on a larger scale as well."[127] The simplest cases are so-called two-part forms (a^1: a^2) in which specific musical material is repeated immediately either exactly or in some varied form.[128] But Schenker immediately notes that the repetition can also be delayed by the intrusion of other new material: such violations of the law of immediate repetition give rise to other forms, such as three-part forms—for example, those associated with so-called *Lied* form (a^1: b^1: a^2), fugues (exposition, modulation, development), and sonata (or *zyklische*) form (exposition, development, and recapitulation), and even four-part forms (a^1: b^1: a^2: b^2).[129] According to him, these other forms are all adaptations of the basic two-part model: by delaying the repetition, composers create a sense of tension and increase the effect of the repeated material.[130]

Schenker was not only concerned with the large-scale repetitions of motivic material; at the end of *HL*, he also considers the global implications

---

124. *HL*, §130, 326; *HA*, 245.
125. Ibid.
126. For a general discussion of Schenker's approach to form before WW I, see Hooper, "Schenker's Early Conception of Form," 35–64.
127. *HL*, §5, 10; *HA*, 9.
128. *HL*, §5, 10; *HA*, 9–10.
129. *HL*, §5, 12–15; *HA*, 10–11. Hooper shows how Schenker even represented such schemes using tree diagrams, see Hooper, "Schenker's Early Conception of Form," 51–56. These diagrams, which appear in OC 83/255 and apparently date from 1912–14, also include plans for five-part forms (a1: b1: a2: c1: a3, or a1: b1: a2: c1 (+b2): a3) and six-part forms (a1: b1: c1 (df) a2: b2: c2 (= a1: b1: a2).
130. *HL*, §5, 12; *HA*, 10.

of changing key or modulating within a tonal composition. The idea of changing key is something that he had already touched upon in his account of tonicization. After all, there is no way to change key without tonicizing a new one. The difference between tonicization and modulation is therefore a matter of degree rather than kind: whereas any note or degree in a particular progression or formal unit can be tonicized without altering the prevailing key, modulation involves "the complete change from one key to another."[131] Such changes can be achieved in three main ways: by modifying the meaning of a harmony; by chromatic alterations; and by enharmonic shifts.[132]

But while Schenker clearly endorses the concept of modulation, he regarded each secondary key as an essential harmony within the context of the global tonic (i.e., as *Stufen der Tonalität als Tonarten*) and treated the progression of secondary keys in qualitatively the same ways as the progression of local chords. In his words:

> The psychological nature of the progression of essential harmonies, which we have described so far in the context of form in the narrow sense, manifests itself in a marvelous and mysterious way also in the context of form in a wider sense—on the way from thematic complex to thematic complex, from group to group. In the form of clearly articulated secondary key areas (*ausgesprochene Tonarten*) clearly stated earlier, we have simply the same progression of degrees, albeit at a superior level [now as essential harmonies].[133]

He adds: "Thus for the sake of the bias towards extensive building of content, the natural progression of degrees is elevated correspondingly."[134] Given Schenker's claim that degrees are usually arranged into progressions that project triadic intervals, this means that modulations will ultimately be governed by the intervals of a fifth or a third.[135] He reinforces this last point by citing the development section from the first movement of Beethoven's Emperor Concerto in E-flat major, Op. 73. This analysis suggests that the section projects a string of just three degrees: E♭, G♭, and C♭.[136] In other words: "the principle of the fifth and of the third not only affects the form

---

131. *HL*, §171, 423; *HA*, 321.
132. *HL*, §§171–76, §§177–78, and §§179–80 respectively.
133. *HL*, §131, 327; *HA*, 246; tr. Borgese, modified.
134. *HL*, §131, 327; *HA*, 246.
135. *HL*, §125, 311 and §126, 314; *HA*, 232 and 225 respectively.
136. Schenker, *HL*, §131, 327; *HA*, 246.

in so far as the extension of an individual idea or even a group of ideas is concerned, but it affects the form in so far as form is the sum total of all ideas brought to play, i.e., the form of the whole."[137]

Schenker extends this point to explain the harmonic structure of sonata or "cyclic" movements. On the one hand, he reinforces the idea that those in major keys tend to modulate to the dominant: "We see how in most cyclic movements the content is developed from the starting point of the main key to that of the dominant: the complexes of the subsidiary section and closing section, i.e., the second and third thematic complexes, are usually set in the key of the dominant. [Meanwhile], the recapitulation brings an inversion of the dominant back to the tonic. Most compositions in the major mode take this turn."[138] On the other hand, Schenker maintains that cyclic movements in minor keys usually follow a different strategy because the minor system is an artificial construct. Instead of satisfying the "natural law of development," which demands that works in minor keys modulate to the dominant minor, tonal composers often prefer major keys "the third above or the third below" to the dominant minor.[139] And he suggests that key changes that proceed by second "are far more frequent" in formal sections that are modulatory and developmental.[140]

Although such claims seem to be perfectly in line with familiar approaches to *Formenlehre*, Schenker is quick to distance himself from such traditions. For one thing, he notes that numerous exceptions can be found: "Art would not be free art, however, if it insisted always and under all circumstances on a development of a composition in the major toward the fifth and of a composition in the minor toward the third. Both in the progression of degrees, as they complete a thematic complex, and in the succession of keys, as they produce the sum total of the content, we therefore find deviations from the development of the fifth or the third."[141] For another, Schenker argues that the tendency for the masters to modulate by fifth or third stems not from their desire to follow some stable set of formal types but from the natural properties of the tonal system: "instead of understanding that Nature must penetrate all forms of music—be they sonatas or waltzes, symphonies or potpourris—the layman will mistake the command of Nature for a quality

---

137. Ibid.
138. *HL*, §131, 328; *HA*, 247.
139. *HL*, §131, 329; *HA*, 247.
140. *HL*, §131, 331; *HA*, 249.
141. *HL*, §131, 329; *HA*, 248.

of form."[142] He concludes: "Before arousing himself to hurl the insult of formalism in the face of the masters, would he not be well advised to study more closely the truly distinctive qualities of form in cyclic movements, apart from such common qualities?"[143]

In a final rejection of traditional *Formenlehre*, Schenker rounds off *HL* by proposing that the most efficient way for musicians to learn how to modulate is not by mastering an array of voice-leading drills, like those offered by Salomon Jadassohn in his *Die Kunst zu modulieren und zu präludieren* (1890) or Max Reger in his *Beiträge zur Modulationslehre* (1903), but rather by improvising their own fantasies, preludes, and cadenzas.[144] He suggests that to do so, the budding composer must be able to integrate "a freely invented motive, free and variegated rhythm, as well as the harmonic tools offered by the diatonic system, the principle of mixture, chromatic change and alteration, and finally free progression of essential harmonies, with the singular psychology obtaining within it."[145] This amounts, of course, to learning how to transform degrees melodically, motivically, contrapuntally, and formally and how to synthesize each element into a single organic whole: "It is the task of harmony to instruct the discipline of art about the abstract forces which partly correspond to Nature [and] partly surge from our need for mental association, in accordance with the purpose of art. Thus the theory of harmony is an abstraction, enclosed in the most secret psychology of music."[146] It is small wonder, then, that Schenker made essential harmonies the hallmark of his harmonic theory.

Although Schenker certainly touches on the issue of global form at various points in *HL*, he tackles the issue head on in his supplementary essay NdK (DAC). In part sonata form is central to the success of Haydn, Mozart, Beethoven, Mendelssohn, and Brahms; the decline of musical composition during the nineteenth century stemmed from their misunderstanding of how their forebears set about composing in sonata or cyclic forms. According to Schenker: "The inner workings of the structure of a cyclic movement

---

142. *HL*, §132, 331; *HA*, 249.
143. *HL*, §132, 331–32; *HA*, 250.
144. *HL* §181, 445–47; *HA*, 336–38. See also Jadassohn, *Die Kunst zu modulieren und präludieren* (The Art of Modulating and Improvising a Prelude) and Max Reger, *Beiträge zur Modulationslehre*; tr. John Bernhoff, *On the Theory of Modulation*, 3 and 4.
145. *HL*, §181, 445; *HA*, 336.
146. Ibid.

are based . . . on the principle of three-part construction [*Dreiteiligheit*]. As I have already mentioned in *HL*, §5, musical ideas are in a sense divisible by two or three; this divisibility may be applied to a single theme, or to the entire movement. If a movement of instrumental music can be divided into three parts, it has cyclic form. The three parts being: the first three thematic groups [i.e., first group, second group, closing material], the development, and the recapitulation."[147] However, Schenker insists that it is a mistake to infer that there is a schematic plan to sonata form: "For the three-part construction is not present for sake of the form in general; rather it is its own specific organization of the musical content, something quite different from two-part construction. For just because they may share a three-part construction, sonata movements do not all have the same form."[148]

The Development of Schenker's Theory of Harmony after 1906

Once Schenker had completed *HL* in 1906, he continued to embrace its main arguments throughout the remainder of his career. Those arguments, which were grounded in the general principles of Aristotelian aesthetics, presuppose that each element of an artwork is in perfect harmony with each other so that the whole is greater than the sum of the parts. Schenker insisted that such a balance is only possible because chords, melodies, motives, counterpoint, rhythm, and form are causally related to one another: these causal relationships made it possible for tonal masters to synthesize each individual element of a musical composition into a single organic entity. Through their capacity to generate musical content and associate different musical ideas, these causal processes guaranteed that the particular work would attain the status of great art. It was for this reason that Schenker primarily used examples taken from real music from the most distinguished composers of tonal music.

But while Schenker did not retract the main positions outlined in *HL*, he spent the next three decades refining and extending them in some significant ways. For one thing, he came up with a more precise explanation of how essential harmonies are actually constructed. This task forced him to reconcile the rules of strict counterpoint with the principles of harmonic progression (or progression of essential harmonies). For another, Schenker began

---

147. NdK, 14–15, DAC, 44.
148. NdK, 15, DAC, 44.

to classify more precisely the specific ways in which essential harmonies are horizontalized in tonal contexts. This meant, among other things, introducing the concept of a fundamental line (or *Urlinie*) and enumerating a finite set of voice-leading transformations (or *Stimmführungsverwandlungen*). And Schenker developed more sophisticated accounts of the causal connections between each element of a piece—harmony, melody, motive, counterpoint, rhythm, and form. Those accounts hinge on the principles of composing out or *Auskomponierung*. By the 1930s, he claimed that each element is created by composing out prototypical strings of essential harmonies (or *Ursätze*) at a succession of different voice-leading levels (or *Stimmführungsschichten*).

To understand just how much the ideas presented in *HL* shaped Schenker's later work, it is helpful to consider two interrelated texts published in the early 1930s: Oswald Jonas's *Das Wesen des musikalischen Kunstwerks: Einführung in die Lehre Heinrich Schenkers* (1934) and Schenker's own treatise *DfS* (1935). The former stands out both because it was the first single-volume survey of Schenkerian theory and because it was enthusiastically received by Schenker himself.[149] Schenker even inscribed a copy to his wife Jeanette in the summer of 1934: "To my dear LieLie, grandmother of this grandchildbook."[150] Meanwhile the latter stands out because, published a few months after Schenker's death in 1935, it was not only the final installment of his monumental triptych *Neue musikalische Theorien und Phantasien*, but it was also his final and most ambitious contribution to music theory.

Art, Nature, and the Tonal System

Nowhere is the lasting impact of *HL* more readily apparent than in chapter 1 of Jonas's *Das Wesen des musikalischen Kunstwerks*: the chapter is basically an updated version of *HL*, §§1–30 (see comparison below). There are good reasons why this is the case. As it happens, Jonas had known *HL* at least since 1915, when he took piano lessons with Schenker's friend Moritz Violin. Jonas would surely have discussed the book in person with Schenker when he studied with him in 1918–19 and 1919–20 and with Hans Weisse after that. Since *HL* had "long been out of print" and was "a prerequisite to

---

149. Oswald Jonas, *Das Wesen des musikalischen Kunstwerks: Einführung in die Lehre Heinrich Schenkers*; ed. and tr. John Rothgeb, *Introduction to the Theory of Heinrich Schenker*.
150. Rothgeb, "Foreword to the English Edition," *Introduction to the Theory of Heinrich Schenker*, xi–xii.

Table 2.3. Comparison of *HL* and Jonas, *Das Wesen*, Chapter 1

Art, Association, Repetition, and Motives *HL*, §§1–7, 3–32; *HA* 3–20. *DfS*, §§251–66, 150–74; *FC*, 93–107.	Jonas, *Das Wesen*, Sec. 1–2, 9–20; *Intro*, 1–10.
The Tonic Triad and the Overtone Series *HL*, §§8–12, 32–39; *HA*, 20–26. *DfS*, §§1–26, 30–33; *FC*, 10–16.	Jonas, *Das Wesen*, Sec. 4, 29–38; *Intro*, 15–20.
The Major System *HL*, §§13–19, 39–59; *HA*, 26–44. *DfS*, §§1–4, 30–32; *FC*, 10–12.	Jonas, *Das Wesen*, Sec. 5, 38–46; *Intro*, 21–26.
The Minor System *HL*, §§20–25, 59–70; *HA*, 45–54.	Jonas, *Das Wesen*, Sec. 6, 47–55; *Intro*, 27–31.
Modes *HL*, §§26–30, 70–97; *HA*, 55–76. *KP1*, 30–40; *CP1*, 20–32. *DfS*, §4, 30–32, §251, 150–56; *FC*, 11–12, 93–96.	
Transposition *HL*, §§31–37, 98–106; *HA*, 77–83.	
Mixture *HL*, §§38–52, 106–50; *HA*, 84–115. *DfS*, §§102–3, 71, §193, 115; *FC*, 40–41, 70–71.	
Tonicization *HL*, §§136–62, 337–99; *HA*, 256–301. *DfS*, §§248–50, 146–48; *FC*, 91–93.	Jonas, *Das Wesen*, Sec. 7, 55–61; *Intro*, 31–36.

the understanding of [Schenker's] work," Jonas remedied the situation in *Das Wesen des musikalischen Kunstwerks* by presenting a brief survey of its main contents.[151] This tactic did not, however, prevent him from acknowledging the conceptual distance between *HL* and *DfS*. On the contrary, as Jonas explained: "[Schenker's] theory itself, naturally, has undergone its own development, which extends over twenty years and more. It could not have been otherwise, because the theory is not an intellectually manufactured system

---

151. Jonas, *Das Wesen*, 6; *Introduction*, xv.

made to fit certain initial assumptions, but is derived rather from intimate knowledge of the masterworks."[152]

Using *HL* as his model, Jonas begins *Das Wesen des musikalischen Kunstwerks* by discussing the status of music as art, and emphasizing the importance of associationism. His remarks, echoing those of Schenker, reinforce the Aristotelian principle that artworks involve associating sounds, images, or words with specific ideas: "As expression of a specific conceptual realm, [every work of art] needs to communicate by some means intrinsic to its material if it is to make contact with the recipient's power of comprehension."[153] According to Jonas, poets find such connections between material and specific ideas "in language," the visual artist "in the world of figures that surrounds both him and us," and musicians in "the principle of repetition."[154]

It is clear from *HL*, chapter 4 that Schenker originally conceived of repetition primarily in motivic terms: "the motive, and the motive alone, creates the possibility of associating ideas, the only one of which music is capable."[155] He likewise acknowledged that motivic repetition plays a decisive role in determining a work's form: "repetition creates musical form, just as the association of ideas from a pattern in nature creates the other forms of art."[156] These were claims that Schenker continued to reiterate in the 1930s: "Repetition . . . is a biological law of life, physical life as well as spiritual, like the contrast and repetition of day and night. Even the life of pure ideas moves in repetitions, for each of the individual manifestations of such ideas represents a repetition."[157] And they were sentiments that Jonas likewise echoed in *Das Wesen des musikalischen Kunstwerks*.

Nevertheless, Schenker's approach to repetition broadens in *DfS* in at least two respects. First, he starts to use the concept of voice-leading levels to show how surface motives can be enlarged across large swathes of music. Schenker usually refers to such expansions as concealed repetitions (*verborgene Wiederholungen*).[158] He explains this idea as follows: "concealed repe-

---

152. Jonas, *Das Wesen*, 6; *Introduction*, xiv–xv.
153. Jonas, *Das Wesen*, 9; *Introduction*, 1.
154. Jonas, *Das Wesen*, 9–11; *Introduction*, 1–2.
155. *HL*, §2, 4; *HA*, 4.
156. *HL*, §4, 5; *HA*, 5.
157. *DfS*, §285, 192; *FC*, 118 and appendix N. Cf. *HL*, §4ff.
158. See also *DfS*, §30 and §§251–66, 42 and 150–74; *FC*, 18–19 and 93–107; and "Von der Diminution," 93–98. For a general discussion of the concept, see Charles Burkhart, "Schenker's 'Motivic Parallelisms,'" 145–75.

titions are not merely imagined by the ear, nor are they the result of fantasy. They could, in fact, even be grasped visually, if the music were able to see without being guided by the ear."[159] Schenker adds: "Repetitions of this kind have nothing to do with 'motive' repetitions; they are so simple and so minute that they often do not fall within the concept of a motive."[160] Jonas was clearly impressed by his teacher's insight, noting that "associations function not only with respect to the small motive but also over the long span, where they help to shape the form of a work and to bind it together securely."[161] To amplify the point, he presents some compelling examples of his own, including several from Mozart's Fantasy in D minor, K. 397 (see example 2.17).

Second, by the time of *DfS*, Schenker no longer assumes that motives are the prime agents of repetition; he now assigns that role to voice-leading spans, something that Jonas likewise accepts: "during the later stage of his development Schenker would hardly have defined the motive as an association of ideas *intrinsic* to music ... According to Schenker, music was elevated to the rank of art only by the unfolding of the chord."[162] This shift in focus manifests itself in several ways. In *DfS*, for example, Schenker describes voice-leading spans in the same ways as surface motives: for example, he uses the terms "leader" and "follower" to describe the order in which motives enter at the surface of a piece, as well as to the order in which voice-leading spans are generated, with leaders being generated at earlier levels than followers.[163] And when he considers the behavior of bass diminutions at the deep middleground, Schenker observes not only that they constantly "imitate" the stepwise motion of the *Urlinie*, but also that their ascending trajectory could be inverted at later levels so that it descends.[164] Significantly, this more abstract view of repetition also allows Schenker to classify musical form in terms of voice-leading transformations rather than of motives. To quote from *DfS*: "Who could have suspected, at that time, that these phenomena, through the process of diminution, were to become form-generative and

---

159. *DfS*, §254, 162–63; *FC*, 99–100.
160. *DfS*, §254, 163; *FC*, 100.
161. Jonas, *Das Wesen*, 13; *Introduction*, 3.
162. *HA*, §2, 4, footnote 1.
163. *DfS*, §221 and §308, 127–28 and 212; *FC*, 78 and 132.
164. *DfS*, §63, 57; §§186–91; *FC*, 31 and 68–70.

Example 2.17. Mozart, Fantasy in D minor, K. 397

Example 2.17.—*(continued)*

Example 2.17.—*(concluded)*

would give rise to entire sections and large forms!"¹⁶⁵ In short: "differences in prolongation lead to differences in form."¹⁶⁶

Jonas's debts to *HL* were not, however, confined to his general comments about the status of music as art: he also recycled its derivation of the tonal system.¹⁶⁷ That derivation is based on the premise that the overtone series "constitutes Nature's only source for music" and that the root, fifth, and third of the major triad stem from the first, third, and fifth partials.¹⁶⁸ To highlight the fact that triads provide the consonant basis of the tonal system, Jonas maintains that *"the dissonance does not belong to the domain of harmony as it is presented to us by Nature,* but is derived from voice leading, which is an essential constituent of Art."¹⁶⁹ Jonas may well have had chapter 2 of *DfS* in mind when penning this passage because his statements reaffirm that

---

165. *DfS*, §301, 207; *FC*, 128.
166. *DfS*, §308, 212–13; *FC*, 131.
167. *HL*, §§8–12, 32–39; *HA*, 20–26. Jonas, *Das Wesen*, 29–38; *Introduction*, 15–20.
168. Schenker, *HL*, §8, 33; *HA*, 20, cited by Jonas, *Das Wesen*, 29; *Introduction*, 15.
169. Jonas, *Das Wesen*, 36; *Introduction*, 19.

Urlinien fill the horizontal intervals of a third, fifth, or octave with passing tones: "The *Urlinie* must contain the linear progression of at least a third; the step of a second as fundamental line is unthinkable. The traversal of the *Urlinie* is *the most basic of all passing motions*; it is the necessity (derived from strict counterpoint) of continuing in the same direction which creates coherence, and, indeed, makes this traversal the beginning of all coherence in a musical composition."[170]

Since each tone potentially asserts itself as a major triad, Jonas follows Schenker's lead in proposing that the artist inverts the natural outward tendency of the harmonic series by construing another cycle of fifths that descends back through the fundamental tonic to the subdominant. Again, like Schenker, Jonas proposes that the artist allows a diminished fifth on the leading tone "in order to close the cycle" by precluding "an unchecked ascent through the upper fifths."[171] Such adjustments show how the major system "represents a marvelous compromise between Art and Nature."[172] He concludes with a brief discussion of cadences that specifically recalls Schenker's account of cadences in *HL*, §§118–24.[173]

Jonas even supports Schenker's decision to dismiss the minor system and Church modes as artificial; he consciously reworked *HL*, chapters 2–3 in chapter 1, section 6 of *Das Wesen des musikalischen Kunstwerks*.[174] Above all, Jonas insists that the minor system provides further confirmation of the compromise between art and nature.[175] He adds: "The leading tone is a borrowed accidental, which, despite its frequent occurrence, is not expressed in the key signature."[176] To underscore the harmonic implications of the minor system and the Church modes, Jonas borrows a table from *HL* in which Schenker lists the subdominant, tonic, and dominant triads in the Ionian,

---

170. *DfS*, §5, 32–33; *FC*, 12. As Koslovsky points out, Jonas had already replaced figure 1 of *DfS* in the short extract of the book reprinted in *Der Dreiklang* 1 (1937), 12–13. See Koslovsky, "The Early Schenkerians," 180, footnote 44.
171. Jonas, *Das Wesen*, 39; *Introduction*, 22.
172. Jonas, *Das Wesen*, 40; *Introduction*, 22.
173. *HL*, §§118–24, 285–306; *HA*, 215–31. Jonas, *Das Wesen*, 41–46; *Introduction*, 23–26.
174. *HL*, §§20–25 and §§26–30, 59–70 and 70–97; *HA*, 45–54 and 55–76. Jonas, *Das Wesen*, 47–55; *Introduction*, 27–31.
175. Jonas, *Das Wesen*, 50; *Introduction*, 29.
176. Ibid.

Dorian, Phrygian, Lydian, Mixolydian, and Aeolian systems.[177] By drawing attention to the harmonic implications of each system, Schenker's chart conveys his skepticism about the value of scales as explanatory concepts. As he made clear in *KP1*, Schenker believed that scales at best describe purely linear relationships and are incapable of explaining how voice leading and harmony interact in musical contexts: "The so-called systems—again exactly as in the earliest period of Western music—are of value at most only as mechanical descriptive tools and can, of course, apply only to the horizontal dimension at that."[178]

Having modeled his accounts of the major system, the minor system, and the Church modes on *HL*, §§8–30, Jonas jettisons Schenker's discussion of transposition and mixture entirely.[179] His decision to omit the former is not especially remarkable because transposition is clearly a fundamental feature of the tonal system and can be taken as given. But omitting the latter is very surprising because it prevents Jonas from discussing some familiar nondiatonic triads (e.g., the Phrygian ♭II) and because it contradicts Schenker's account of the topic in *DfS*. Indeed, as mentioned earlier, mixture allows for interchange of materials between major and minor systems. In *DfS*, Schenker insists that, while *Ursätze* may be strictly diatonic, upper middleground levels might include mixtures of all types.[180]

Although Jonas ignores Schenker's discussions of transposition and mixture, he is less cavalier about his teacher's account of tonicization and offers a handy summary of this all-important principle.[181] Chapter 4 of *DfS* describes how tonicization allows composers to borrow individual notes and triads from one major–minor system and present it in another. Those notes and triads may serve several different purposes: sometimes they are used by composers to color a particular line or chord; sometimes they are introduced in order to facilitate a modulation from one local key to another. According

---

177. Jonas, ex. 38 = Schenker, §26, table 1, 56. See Jonas, *Das Wesen*, 29. Jonas also recycled Schenker's chart from *HL*, §20, ex. 42, 59–60, as his ex. 37: Jonas, *Das Wesen*, 47; *Introduction*, 27.
178. *KP1*, section 1, chapter 1, §5, 32; *CP1*, 21.
179. Schenker discussed transposition in *HL*, §§31–37, 98–106; *HA*, 77–83, and mixture in *HL*, §§38–52, 98–150; *HA*, 84–115; *DfS*, §§102–5 and §§193–95, 71–72 and 115–16; *FC*, 40–42 and 70–71.
180. Matthew Brown, "The Diatonic and the Chromatic."
181. *HL*, §§136–46, 337–71; *HA*, 256–76. Jonas, *Das Wesen*, chapter 1, section 7, 55–61; *Introduction*, 31–36.

to Schenker, the difference between the former and the latter is a matter of degree rather than of kind: he believed that secondary keys function as essential harmonies within a tonal work in the same ways as surface notes and chords function within a tonal phrase. As noted earlier, Schenker even went so far as to refer to secondary keys as "*Stufen der Tonalität als Tonarten*," and claimed that, like surface notes and chords, they arise contrapuntally. In his words: "Essential harmonies *are inextricably bound up with counterpoint.*"[182]

Essential Harmony and Its Progression

Whereas chapter 1 of *Das Wesen des musikalischen Kunstwerks* updates Schenker's remarks in *HL* about the status of music as art, the role of repetition in music, the origins of the major, minor, and modal systems, and the impact of tonicization, chapter 2 takes a very different tack and replaces Schenker's account of triads and seventh chords from *HL*, §§53–114 with a general survey of triads and their capacity to be composed out over time. This dramatic shift in outlook was necessary in part because Schenker changed his mind about the nature of essential harmonies and the principles of the progression of essential harmonies, and in part because it challenges several widely held beliefs about the nature of tonal harmony, many of which stemmed from the work of Rameau and his successors.

It is important to note in this regard that when Schenker wrote *HL*, he still promoted certain ideas whose origins can be traced back to Rameau. Rameau is famous, for example, for promoting the claim that major and minor triads and seventh chords are the fundamental building blocks of tonal music: every harmony "is a perfect chord, a seventh chord, an inversion of these, or a derivative of a seventh chord (the added sixth chord and chords by *subposition*)."[183] According to him, triads (or *accords parfaits*) represent the basic form of consonance and seventh chords are the basic form of dissonance.[184] Rameau also distinguished *basso continuo*, which refers to the lowest sounding note in a chord, from *basse-fondamentale*, which designates the root of the chord. According to him, the effects of the fundamental bass are always implied even when the triad or seventh chord is inverted and the root

---

182. Schenker, *DfS*, §79, 63; *FC*, 35.
183. Lester, *Compositional Theory in the Eighteenth Century*, 100.
184. To quote Joel Lester: "the perfect chord (or *accord parfait*; Rameau never used the term *triad*) or consonant harmony, and the seventh chord or dissonant harmony." Joel Lester, *Compositional Theory in the Eighteenth Century*, 100.

does not appear in the bass of the chord: "If the fundamental bass is removed [from the bottom voice] and one of the other parts is put in its place, all of the resulting chords will be inversions [*renversements*] of the original chords. The harmony will always remain good, for even when the fundamental bass is removed, it is always implied."[185] Rameau and his followers also proposed that chord progressions are controlled by a succession of fundamental bass tones and that the seven degrees can be reduced to just three basic functions—tonic (T), subdominant (S), and dominant (D).

Rameau's influence can be felt at several points in *HL*. Schenker, for example, presumes that major and minor triads are self-contained entities and that they are the source of consonance in tonal contexts. He also accepts that inversion "does not alter the identity of the triad," though he conceded that second inversion triads "may give rise to misunderstandings" from a contrapuntal perspective.[186] And, though he acknowledges that ninth, thirteenth, and augmented-sixth chords arise contrapuntally, Schenker still maintains that essential harmonies could be expressed by independent seventh chords: "The reader may have understood by now that, in the present phase of our art, the concept of [an] interval has become bound to and limited by the concept of its harmonizability. In other words, the possibility of being used in a triad or seventh chord has become a conceptual prerequisite of the interval."[187]

Just four years after the publication of *HL*, Schenker starts to distance himself from Rameau's theories in *KP1* (1910), the second installment of his *Neue Theorien und Phantasien*. Certainly, he still recognized his forebear's contributions to music theory and even credited him with "creat[ing] the theory of the harmonic degree" as "the complement of voice leading."[188] But Schenker immediately criticizes Rameau for treating harmonic degrees "too narrowly" and for failing to "specify the true laws according to which [they] move."[189] In particular, he realizes that Rameau's theory of harmony was incompatible with the rules of strict counterpoint. Since those rules presuppose that the interval of a fourth is always unstable when it appears above the bass, inverting triads does not, in fact, preserve their identity and, unlike

---

185. Rameau, *Traité de l'harmonie*, book 2, chapter 5. Cited by Lester, *Compositional Theory in the Eighteenth Century*, 104.
186. *HL*, §98, 241; *HA*, 187. See also *HL*, §§78, 125, and 127.
187. *HL*, §55, 155–56. See also *HL*, §§107–14, 249–77.
188. *KP1*, "Vorwort," XXIX; *CP1*, "Author's Preface," xxviii.
189. *KP1*, "Vorwort," XXIX–XXX; *CP1*, "Author's Preface," xxix.

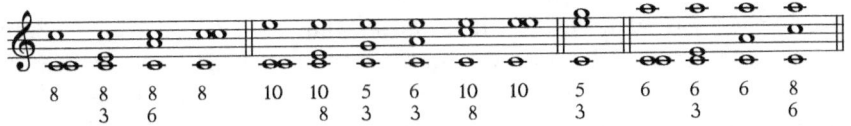

Figure 2.8. Catalogue of Every Complete and Incomplete Triad

root and first inversion triads, second inversion chords are seldom, if ever, stable. He made this point clear in *KP2* (1922) in a catalogue of every complete and incomplete triad (see figure 2.8).[190] Except for cadences that end on a tripled root, each triad contains at least one third or sixth, between the root and third or between the third and fifth.[191] Significantly, the list contains no $^6_4$ sonorities.[192]

Schenker likewise repudiates his earlier view that seventh chords can exist as free-standing harmonies:

> The essential harmony exists in our perception only as a triad; that is, as soon as we expect an essential harmony, we expect it first of all only as a triad, not as a seventh chord. In this sense, the seventh is absolutely not an a priori element of our perception comparable to the fifth or the third; it is rather an event a posteriori, which we understand best of all with reference to the function associated with it; that is, we understand it in retrospect as a passing tone, or as a means of chromaticization, or the like.[193]

He expresses the same idea in *MW2* as follows: "The seventh is either a suspension or a passing tone which comes from the octave of the chord and either continues on to another chord or remains in the fourth-space of the same chord, and the ninth is either a suspension or a neighbor tone. Hence they are not at all seventh or ninth chords in the sense of triads,

---

190. *KP2*, part III, chapter 1, §14, 11–12; *CP2*, 10.
191. Schenker did not include the tripled root on his list in §14, but he subsequently includes it in ex. 68, noting "because of its complete perfection, it is better suited to the close than $^8_3$." Schenker, *KP2*, part III, chapter 1, §27, 58; *CP2*, 46.
192. Elsewhere, $^6_4$ sonorities are sometimes stable or consonant provided that it "manifests true character of a essential harmony, thereby expressing the harmonic degree itself." See *KP2*, part III, chapter 1, §3, 2; *CP2*, part III, chapter 1, §3, 2–3.
193. *KP1*, "Vorwort," XXXIII; *CP1*, "Author's Preface," xxxi.

i.e., completely equal-valued alongside the others."[194] In other words: "the unfurling of a triad is music—it is music's sum and substance."[195] Since Schenker also accepts that intervals are defined by their harmonizability, this new observation effectively denies that sevenths ever serve as essential intervals. One benefit of this move is that it resonates with his other claim that degrees behave qualitatively in the same ways whether they appear as surface chords or as secondary keys.

And Schenker now uses the links between degrees and counterpoint to reject Rameau's account of chord function. Near the start of *KP1*, for example, he dismisses any idea that chord progressions are controlled by the motion of the fundamental bass and that the seven degrees can be reduced to three functions—tonic (T), subdominant (S), and dominant (D). He continues: "How can one claim to have understood the [tonal] 'system' if its individual degrees, except I, IV, and V, are deprived of their independence and thus of their attractive capability of assuming various functions?"[196] For him, "it is the functional versatility of the degree that is the basis of tonal practice, and this, of course, at least presupposes its independence!"[197] By the time he completes *DfS*, Schenker is adamant that essential harmonies are guided by the rules of counterpoint: "As a consequence of voice-leading constraint[s], all those individual harmonies that arise from the progression of the various voices are forced to move forward. All the transient harmonies which appear in the course of a work have their source in the necessities of voice-leading."[198]

Once Schenker determines that harmonic function is a byproduct of tonal voice leading, he is able to offer his most devastating critique of Rameau's theories. Since fundamental bass theory presupposes that the function of each note in a bass line is primarily harmonic, it is not equipped to explain how bass lines function melodically, let alone motivically. According to Schenker, this shortcoming is especially serious in imitative textures where the bass is ultimately melodic and motivic in conception: "One has only to see the out-and-out Rameauification of the B minor Fugue from book I

---

194. Schenker, "Fortsetzung der Urlinie-Betrachtungen II," tr. John Rothgeb, "Further considerations of the Urlinie II," *MM2*, 15.
195. Schenker, "Fortsetzung der Urlinie-Betrachtungen I," *MW1*, 187; tr., John Rothgeb, "Further considerations of the Urlinie I," in *MM1*, 104.
196. *KP1*, part 1, chapter 1, §5, 36; *CP1*, 23.
197. *KP1*, part 1, chapter 1, §5, 37; *CP1*, 24.
198. *DfS*, §84, 64; *FC*, 35.

[of the *Well-Tempered Clavier*] of J. S. Bach, and the A minor Prelude from book II, in Kirnberger's *The True Principles of Harmonic Practice* (see pp. 55ff and 107ff), to be persuaded of the impracticality of Rameau's principles."[199] As noted earlier, Schenker overcomes these deficiencies by treating bass lines in melodic terms: instead of labeling each chord with a Roman numeral, he proposes that bass tones might arise as passing tones, neighboring tones, suspensions, and so on. Not surprisingly perhaps, Schenker regards J. S. Bach as the greatest exponent of the melodic bass line: "Altogether J. S. Bach remains the master teacher of a genuinely contrapuntal bass: even with the most extensive unfolding of diminutions he never exceeds the limits set by the bass."[200]

Given Schenker's radically different conception of degrees and the principles of degree progression, it is hardly surprising that Jonas ignores Schenker's account of intervals, degrees, triads, seventh, and ninth chords from *HL*. Instead, he uses chapters 2 and 3 of *Das Wesen des musikalischen Kunstwerks* to present material akin to that found in *DfS* and to offer his own attack on Rameau's theory of harmony.[201] During the course of these chapters, Jonas pays special attention to the ways in which functional progressions can be created by composing out essential harmonies contrapuntally: he shows, for example, how the progression I–V–I could be generated by passing motion $\hat{3}$-$\hat{2}$-$\hat{1}$.[202]

Unfortunately, however, Jonas does not spell out precisely how more complex functional progressions arise contrapuntally. In an effort to fill this gap, figures 2.9–2.10 show how subdominant functioning harmonies (S) fit into the progression T–D–T. These figures show these harmonies arising contrapuntally to support $\hat{6}$, the common tone among II, IV and VI degrees.[203] Figure 2.9a, for example, displaces the upper voices against one another to create a variety of functional progressions: I–II$^6_5$–V–I (figure 2.9b);

---

199. Schenker, "Rameau oder Beethoven?," 14; tr. Bent, "Rameau or Beethoven?," 3.
200. *DfS*, §257, 166; *FC*, 102. He anticipated this point in *HL*: "The paragon of composition founded magnanimously and securely on *Stufen* (even in fugues), whatever the audacity in voice-leading—the paragon of such composition, it seems to me, is still the work of J. S. Bach." See *HL*, §89, 221–22; *HA*, 174.
201. For Jonas's critique of Rameau's theory of harmony, see Jonas, *Das Wesen*, chapter 3, 166–74; *Introduction*, 122–28.
202. Jonas, *Das Wesen*, 80; *Introduction*, 52.
203. *DfS*, §79, 62–63; *FC*, 34–35.

Figure 2.9. Contrapuntal Origins of Harmonic Progressions

Figure 2.10. Further Contrapuntal Origins of Harmonic Progressions

I–II^6–V–I (figure 2.9d); I–II^6–V–I (figure 2.9f); and I–IV^7–V–I (figures 2.9h and 2.9j). Similarly, figure 2.10 elaborates the soprano with escape tones or incomplete neighbor tones to create other progressions: I–IV–V–I (figures 2.10b and 2.10f), I–II–V–I (figure 2.10d), and I–VII^6–I^6–II$^6_5$–V–I (figure 2.10h). To paraphrase Schenker, subdominant functioning harmonies (S) derive from the necessities of voice leading.

Horizontalizing Essential Harmonies Melodically and Contrapuntally

Implicit in the derivations outlined in figures 2.9–2.10 is Schenker's claim that the constituent intervals of a given degree can be articulated horizontally as well as vertically: the upper voices compose out the space between the third and the root of the tonic chord whereas the bass fills out the space between the root and the fifth. This crucial idea, which Schenker presents so forcefully in *HL*, is one that he continues to advance in all of his later writings. In *MW1* (1925), for example, he declares: "Translation from the vertical to the horizontal is effected by means of linear progressions [*Züge*]: in the succession of the horizontal dimension, it fills the given tonal spaces of the third and fifth with third- and fifth-progressions, and moreover adds, in the sense of inversions, the sixth- and fourth-progressions."[204] A decade later he reiterates this idea in *DfS* (1935): "Throughout the [transformational] levels it is sometimes the horizontal that determines the particular course and meaning of the vertical, sometimes the vertical which by its own voice-leading dictates the horizontal. So, in one instance we can speak of the horizontalization of the vertical, in another instance of the verticalization of the horizontal."[205] What changed, however, between 1906 and 1935 were Schenker's explanations of how vertical intervals can be reconfigured horizontally. Those explanations appeared incrementally in his writings from the 1920s, especially in his essays for *TW* and *MW*. Jonas was, of course, well aware of Schenker's achievements in this regard and expounded on them at length in chapter 3 of *Das Wesen des musikalischen Kunstwerks*.

The first signs of progress can be found as early as 1910 in the pages of *KP1* and its remarks about the triadicity of tonal melodies. Schenker is especially interested in the idea of melodic fluency (*fliessender Gesang*). This term, which Schenker borrows from Albrechtsberger, Bellermann, Forkel, and others,

---

204. Schenker, "Fortsetzung der Urlinie-Betrachtungen I,"; tr. Rothgeb, "Further considerations of the *Urlinie* I," *MM1*, 107.
205. *DfS*, §277, 182; *FC*, 111. Cf. Schenker, *HL*, §54, 155.

Example 2.18a. J. S. Bach, Prelude from *English Suite* in D minor, BWV 811, mm. 1–15

Example 2.18b. Guiding Line of Example 2.18a

refers to the sense of equilibrium that is characteristic of good melodic writing.[206] According to him, this sense of equilibrium is achieved locally when composers strike a balance between their use of repeated tones, pedals, step motion, and melodic leaps, and globally by anchoring the melody triadically and by allowing it to rise and fall in a fluid and purposeful manner.[207] Above all, Schenker associates melodic fluency with passing motion: "we recognize in the dissonant passing tone the most dependable—indeed the only—vehicle of melodic content."[208]

Significantly, Schenker even uses the concept of melodic fluency to explain the structure of extended segments of music from the common-practice repertory. Figure 2.18a gives a perfect case in point: measures 1–15 from the Prelude from Bach's *English Suite* in D minor, BWV 811. Example 2.18b shows how, according to Schenker, the elaborate figurations of the musical surface are guided by two chains of passing tones, the first descending an octave from D to D in measures 2–6, the second descending a sixth from F to A in measures 6–15.[209] In his words: "In free composition, therefore, lines that are not balanced in their melodic discourse and thus do not express a unified goal will be noticed by the ear as poor." The concept of melodic fluency also provides Schenker with a way of explaining so-called polyphonic or compound melodies. These are melodies that

---

206. See Rothgeb's footnote in Schenker, *CP2*, tr. John Rothgeb and Jürgen Thym, revised edition, part 6, chapter 2, §1, 196.
207. *CP1*, tr. John Rothgeb and Jürgen Thym, revised edition, part 1, chapter 2, §20, 94–95. As regards the second point, Schenker noted: "such procedures yield a kind of wave-like melodic line which as a whole represents an animated entity, and which, with its ascending and descending curves, appears balanced in all its individual components." *CP1*, part I, chapter 2, §20, 94.
208. *CP2*, part III, chapter 2, §3, 58.
209. *CP1*, 96. See William Pastille, "The Development of the *Ursatz*." Morgan offers a nice account of Schenker's discussion of *Urlinien* in the essays from *TW* and *MW* in his *Becoming Heinrich Schenker*, 117–55.

appear as a single horizontal line but that actually project several implied/ latent voices (*latente Stimmen*): "We see that the requirement of melodic fluency—to mention something special and little noticed—fulfilled also in, for example, the lines of a composition for piano. Such a line may be based on the postulates of polyphony and thus may tend to express, through itself, several latent voices in a unified fashion."[210] Schenker gives a couple of examples of this phenomenon, appearing here as examples 2.19a–b.[211] To account for the disjunct nature of both lines, he insists that the various leaps arise when the conceptual upper line skips between several latent strands of counterpoint. In example 2.19a, he proposes that Handel's sixteenth-note melody projects three separate contrapuntal threads: a stepwise motion C-B♭-A-B♭ in the soprano accompanied by stepwise descents from G to F and E♭ to D in the inner voices. Much the same can be said of example 2.19b: this soprano voice descends by step E-D-C-B♮, while the inner voices fall B-A-G and F-E♭-D. As Schenker pondered the concepts of melodic fluency and latent voices in his editions of Bach's *Chromatic Phantasie und Fuge* (1909) and Beethoven's late piano sonatas (1913–20), he gradually came up with the concept of a fundamental melodic line or *Urlinie*: "A musical work comes into being as an interweaving of *Urlinie*, essential harmonies, and voice-leading. All of these fundamental fluids and forces—motive and melody spring from the *Urlinie*—constantly interpenetrate one another."[212] According to him, *Urlinien* generally proceed by step motion, repetition, rising and falling, "as inhaling and exhaling."[213] He adds: "It is the Artist's work to evoke, by means of this particular number of [step motions], these particular kinds of repetitions, this particular kind of rise and fall, unique tensions: to elicit from the rise and fall, and simultaneously from the fundamental laws of voice leading and degrees, ever new modes of play of individual motives and melodies, and thus to imbue each case with the stamp of the particular . . . ever the same, but not in the same way."[214]

Schenker demonstrates the power of *Urlinien* at several places in these editions. In the second volume, for example, he shows how the development

---

210. *KP1*, part I, chapter 2, §20, 135; *CP1*, 95.
211. Example 2.19a is from Schenker, *KP1*, examples 48 and 49; example 2.19b from Schenker, *KP1*, example 76.
212. Rothgeb, ed. and tr., *Beethoven: The Last Piano Sonatas*, vol. 4, 9.
213. Ibid.
214. Schenker quoted this phrase in Latin: *semper idem, sed non eodem modo*. He would later use it as a motto for *TW*, *KP2*, *MW*, and *DfS*. The origins of the phrase are unclear: William Pastille points to a line from St Augustine's *Confessions*, book 8, chapter 3 and William Helmcke to a passage in Iranaeus's *Adversus Haereses*.

Example 2.19. (a) G. F. Handel, "Air and Variations," *Suites de pièces*, 2nd collection, Variation No. 1, last measure; (b) J. S. Bach, Prelude from *English Suite* in D minor, BWV 811, m. 165.

section of the first movement of Op. 110 projects a long stepwise descent in the soprano voice from measure 38 to measure 56 (see figure 2.11a).[215] Similar patterns appear in the second movement (see figures 2.11b–c).[216] Schenker specifically coins the term *Urlinie* in the fourth volume. Figures 2.12a–b present his reading of measures 1–8 from the second movement of Op. 101.[217] The upper system, marked *Urlinie*, contains several descending fourth-spans marked with brackets: F-E-D-C in the lowest register (measures 1–4); F-E-D-C in the upper register (measures 2–6); B♭-A-G-F in the soprano register (measures 4–5); B♭-A-G-F in the middle register (measures 6–7); and F-E-D-C in the lowest register (measures 7–8). The lower system, marked *Ausführung*, shows how the essential voice leading is fleshed out to produce the progressions I–IV–V⁷–I in measures 1–5; I–V–I in measures 5–7; and I–VI♯3–II♮3–V–I in measures 7–8. Figures 2.13a–b

---

215. For more details, see William Pastille, "The Development of the *Ursatz*," 74–75.
216. Pastille, "The Development of the *Ursatz*," 75.
217. Rothgeb, ed. and tr., *Beethoven: The Last Piano Sonatas*, vol. 4, 46–50.

Figure 2.11a. Beethoven's Piano Sonata in A-flat Major, Op. 110, Line Projected in the First Movement, mm. 38–56

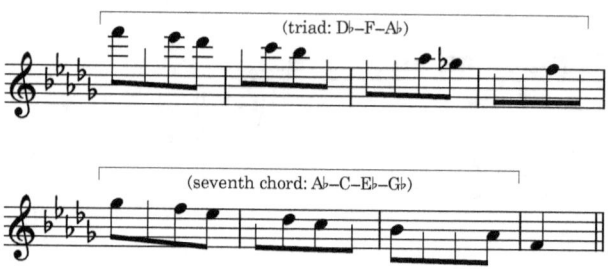

Figure 2.11b. Beethoven's Piano Sonata in A-flat Major, Op. 110, Second Movement, mm. 41–8.

give Schenker's sketch of measures 28–38 from the first movement of the "Moonlight" sonata from his facsimile edition of the autograph.[218] The lower staff suggests that the *Urlinie* of this passage prolongs the dominant G♯ by elaborating the leading tone with upper neighbor tones: B♯-C♯-B♯-C♯-B♯. The upper staff then shows how Beethoven ornamented the final C♯-B♯ with a descending pattern C♯-E-D♯-C♯-B♯.[219]

Besides highlighting the generative capacity of the *Urlinie*, figures 2.12 and 2.13 also demonstrate the extent to which Schenker had clarified his views about the causal links between harmony, counterpoint, and motives. It is clear from his commentaries, for example, that he interpreted the function of each surface sonority within the harmonic context of the passage as a whole: in the case of figure 2.12 that context is an eight-measure antecedent phrase which shifts from the tonic essential harmony to the dominant essential harmony; in the case of figure 2.13 it is a ten-measure dominant pedal. Both analyses show that the surface sonorities are contrapuntal phenomena and that they stem from the particular ways which Beethoven composed out

---

218. Schenker, ed., L. Van Beethoven, *Sonate Op. 27, Nr. 2* Facsimile (Vienna: Universal Edition, 1921).
219. Ibid., IV.

the *Urlinie*. Figures 2.12 and 2.13 also show that Schenker no longer thought of repetition in purely motivic terms: the former shows how Beethoven created content by numerous repetitions of a descending fourth-span; and the latter shows how he generated material from repetitions of an upper neighbor tone.

During the 1920s and early 1930s, Schenker also devoted much of his time to cataloging the many ways in which essential harmonies can be transformed melodically and contrapuntally. To quote William Benjamin: "One of the reasons his theory incorporates so many, seemingly redundant, operations is that they give the theory the flexibility to reflect the particulars of melodic design."[220] Indeed, by the time he finished *DfS* and Jonas completed *Das Wesen des musikalischen Kunstwerks*, Schenker had come up with the list shown in table 2.4. The transformations themselves can be classified into four main types.[221] To begin with, a given essential harmony can be horizontalized either by transforming a single essential voice through repetition (*Wiederholung*), register transfer (*Höherlegung, Tieferlegung, Koppelung*), arpeggiation (*Brechung*), or more than one essential voices through unfolding (*Ausfaltung*), voice exchange (*Stimmentausch*), and reaching over (*Übergreifen*). Once they have been horizontalized, the members of a given essential harmony can be linked by step to create non-harmonic tones: neighbor motion links repeated tones with neighbor tones (*Nebennoten*); linear progressions (*Züge*) or motion to or from an inner voice (*Untergreifen* and *Übergreifen*) link arpeggiations, unfoldings, and the like, with passing tones. Next, the resulting non-harmonic tones can be harmonized by new diatonic or chromatic essential harmonies (i.e., *Mischung, Tonikalisierung*) and by new contrapuntal lines. Finally, the members of a given essential harmony can be substituted (*Vertretung*) or deleted and displaced to create "non-intervals" (*uneigentliche Intervalle*), the latter creating other non-harmonic tones, e.g., suspensions, anticipations, and appoggiaturas.

Modulation

As Schenker cultivated the idea that chords are byproducts of voice leading, so he combined it with his understanding of structural levels to conclude that modulations are ultimately contrapuntal phenomena that arise horizontally from passing tones, neighbor tones, and similar devices. Such

---

220. Benjamin, "Schenker's Theory and the Future of Music," 162–63.
221. See Brown, *Explaining Tonality*, 76–83.

Figure 2.11c. Structural Points in Beethoven, Piano Sonata in A-flat Major, Second Movement

Figure 2.12a–b. Beethoven's Piano Sonata in A Major, Op. 101, Second Movement, mm. 1–8

Figure 2.13a–b. Beethoven's Piano Sonata in C-sharp Minor, Op. 27, No. 2 ("Moonlight"), First Movement, mm. 28–38

voice-leading phenomena can appear both in the upper voices or in the bass. A particularly nice example can be found at the start of the first movement of Beethoven's "Waldstein" sonata, Op. 53, when the music modulates from the global tonic C for the first theme to the local tonic E major for the entry of the second theme (see figure 2.14). As Carl Schachter has pointed out, the passage modulates from the global tonic C to the local tonic E major by means of a stepwise motion from G to B and from B to G♯. As he explains: "The bridge section begins in measure 14 and reestablishes the main upper

Table 2.4. Schenkerian Voice-Leading Transformations

Transformation	Domain	Schenker's Discussion
a. Horizontalizing Transformations		
Repetition (*Wiederholung*)	single line single harmony	none but implied *DfS*, Fig. 21
Register transfer (*Höherlegung, Tieferlegung, Koppelung*)	single line single harmony	*DfS*, §§147–54, 238–41 Figs. 47–49, 106–8
Arpeggiation (*Brechung*)	single line single harmony	*DfS*, §§125–28, 230 Figs. 40, 100
Unfolding (*Ausfaltung*)	multiple lines single harmony	*DfS*, §§140–44, 234 Figs. 43–45, 103
Voice exchange (*Stimmentausch*)	multiple lines single harmony	*DfS*, §§236–37 Fig. 105
Reaching over (*Übergreifen*)	multiple lines multiple harmonies	*DfS*, §§129–34, 231–32 Figs. 41, 101
b. Filling in Transformations		
Neighbor motion (*Nebennote*)	single line	*DfS*, §§106–12, 196–202 Figs. 32, 76–80
Linear progression (*Zug*)	single line	*DfS*, §§113–24, 203–29 Figs. 33–39, 81–99
Motion from inner voice (*Untergreifen*)	multiple lines multiple harmonies	*DfS*, §§135–39, 233 Figs. 42, 102
Motion to inner voice	multiple lines multiple harmonies	*DfS*, §203
c. Harmonizing Transformations		
Harmonize	single/multiple lines single harmony	none but implied *DfS*, §§93, 115
Addition	single tone single/multiple lines	*DfS*, §§221–29, Figs. 95–99
Mixture (*Mischung, Phrygische II*)	single/multiple lines single/multiple harmonies	*DfS*, §§102–5, 193–95 Figs. 28–31, 73–75 *HL*, §§26–30, 38–52
Tonicization (*Tonikalisierung*)	single/multiple lines single tone/harmony	*HL*, §§132–62

(continued)

Table 2.4.—*(concluded)*

Transformation	Domain	Schenker's Discussion
d. Reordering Transformations		
Substitution (*Vertretung*)	single line	*DfS*, §§145–46, 235, 244–46 Figs. 46, 104, 110–11
Realignment (*uneigentliche Intervalle*)	single/multiple lines	*DfS*, §§158, 261
Delete (Implied tones)	single/multiple lines	none*

* See William Rothstein, "On Implied Tones."

voice tone G in measure 16. From there, the line ascends—G♮-G♯-A♮-A♯-B—arriving on B over the dominant of E major (m. 23)."[222] This process is shown in figure 2.14a. Schachter also notes that the ascent A♯-B in measures 22–3 "relates back to the B♭-B♮ within the first theme."[223] Figure 2.14b then shows how the dominant B in measure 23 eventually resolves onto the tonic E in measure 35 for the second theme. Notice, too, how this resolution involves transforming the dominant sonority into a seventh by means of the passing tone A. This diatonic passing tone A stands in direct contrast with the string of chromatic passing tones G♯ and A♯ that set up the arrival on B just a few measures earlier: these tones both serve to tonicize the upcoming note, with G♯ tonicizing A and A♯ tonicizing B.[224]

Next, figure 2.15 shows an even more complex example of how modulations arise contrapuntally, in this case in the development section of the first movement of Beethoven's "Appassionata" sonata, Op. 57. Figure 2.15a shows how Schenker derived the movement from a $\hat{5}$-line *Ursatz* in which the development modulates from III back to V as the *Urlinie* descends from $\hat{3}$ to $\hat{2}$.[225] He clarified the contrapuntal structure of this passage in another sketch, given here as figure 2.15b.[226] This sketch shows how the underlying progression in the bass from A♭ (m. 65) through E♮ (mm. 67, 79) and C♮ (m. 83)

---

222. Carl Schachter, *The Art of Tonal Analysis*, ed. Joseph N. Straus, 252.
223. Ibid., 253.
224. Ibid., 254.
225. *DfS*, Fig. 154.4.
226. *DfS*, Fig. 114.8.

Figure 2.14a–b. Beethoven's Piano Sonata in C Major, Op. 53 ("Waldstein"), First Movement, Beginning

to A♭ (m. 87), the latter serving locally as V of VI. Although Schenker drew attention to the fact that this bass line projects a string of major thirds, he did not suggest that it arpeggiates the augmented triad A♭/E♮/C♮/A♭. Instead, he suggested that the modulation was actually generated by the upper voices in an effort to avoid the direct chromatic succession C♭ to C♮. In the surrounding text, Schenker explained how composers often avoid such infelicities by interpolating neighbor tones and enharmonic tones.[227] In one voice, C♭ is enharmonically respelled as B♮ and succeeded by its upper neighbor tone C♮; in another, A♭ is enharmonically respelled as G♯ and succeeded by

---

227. Schenker, "Der chromatische Schritt wird durch Einschaltung einer Nebennote vermieden, werde sie im Durchgang konsonant oder sonstwie gestützt oder überhaupt nicht ... Unter Umständen führt die Enharmonie zu einem Chromen-Austausch: die Einschaltung eines enharmonischen Zustandes gibt Gelegenheit zu reizvollen Auskomponierungen, wobei man eine Art Anspielung auf das Kommende genießt." *DfS*, §249, 147–48.

its lower neighbor tone G♮ before returning back to A♭.[228] The bass tones E♮ (mm. 67, 79) and C♮ (m. 83) simply provide consonant support for the contrapuntal motion of the upper voices. Although the resulting chain of major thirds subdivides the octave A♭ to A♭, Schenker does not suggest that it in any way challenges the principles of common-practice tonality, at least as he understood them.[229]

It was precisely because Schenker regarded modulation as a byproduct of voice leading because many writers equate tonicization with modulation, that in his later writings he came to reject existing accounts as "the most baleful error" of conventional theory: in his opinion, it prompted them to posit "an absurd abundance of 'keys' at the surface of a composition."[230] In the case of figure 2.15a, there is no doubt that the only modulation in the passage is the one from C to E, the chromatic tones F♯, G♯, and A♯ simply tonicize the upcoming tones G, A, and B, respectively. Similarly, in the case of figure 2.15b, although E in measure 65 and 79 is tonicized by an applied dominant B-D♯-F♯-A and C is tonicized in measure 83 by an applied dominant G-B-D-F♮, neither point of articulation marks a modulation: they are simply stepping stones within a larger modulation back from A♭ (III) to C (V of F). Schenker's antipathy towards conventional approaches to modulation also extended to his rejection of traditional concepts of key relations: although he still relied on the idea of parallel keys, Schenker dispensed with the concept of relative keys and downplayed traditional explanations of so-called closely and distantly related keys. The concept of relative keys is made redundant because no two keys actually contain the same notes: C major and A minor may both have the same key signatures but A minor needs G♯ and possibly F♯ in order for A to be tonicized. The concepts of close and distant keys is rendered obsolete by the fact that Schenkerian theory does not include any mechanism for measuring the distance between key areas.

Tonal Prototypes

Schenker's discussions of melodic bass lines and *latente Stimmen*, as well as his distinction between transformations that apply to a single voice and

---

228. See also Schenker, "Beethovens Sonate Op. 57"; tr. Robert Snarrenberg, "Beethoven's Sonata in F minor, op. 57," 45–46.
229. For a very different interpretation of this passage, see Gregory Proctor, "Technical Bases of Nineteenth-Century Chromatic tonality," 171–75.
230. *FC*, 8.

Figure 2.15a–b. Beethoven's Piano Sonata in F Minor, Op. 57 ("Appassionata"), First Movement

those that apply to multiple voices, leave no doubt that he always imagined *Urlinien* as being supported by other contrapuntal voices. In the years leading to the publication of *DfS*, Schenker uses this idea to support his claim that complex tonal surfaces can be derived from prototypical strings or *Ursätze*. He takes over a decade to bring this remarkable idea to fruition; during that time he vacillates about how many voices are necessary and how extensive the prototypes should be. In *DfS*, Schenker reaches the conclusion that complete, continuous monotonal compositions can be derived from a single all-embracing prototype. It was this final stage in Schenker's thought that Jonas championed in chapter 4 of *Das Wesen des musikalischen Kunstwerks*.

Although Schenker begins to toy with the idea of tonal prototypes in his editions of Beethoven's late piano sonatas, he develops them more systematically in *TW* and *MW*. In *TW*, for example, Schenker pays increasing attention to a work's outer-voice counterpoint (or *Außensätze*): "Elaboration [*Auskomponierung*] brings to fruition a bass line that, in view of the fact that the roots of essential harmonies operate in the depths of the mind, is just as much an upper voice in the soprano with respect to the behavior of the line, its undulating play, and its consonances and passing [tones]."[231] He notes, however, that *Außensätze* generally include at least one other implied or latent inner voice: "Thus the setting of the outer voices [*Außensätze*] is to be understood as a counterpoint of two upper voices above the structural bass, a two-voice setting the quality of which determines the worth of the composition."[232] These ideas soon prompt Schenker to introduce the concept of a tonal prototype (or *Ursatz*) that projects simple string of essential harmonies comprised of at least three essential voices. He sometimes uses the term as a contraction of the phrase *Urlinie-Satz*.[233]

There were, in fact, pressing theoretical reasons why Schenker focuses his attention on stacks of lines and strings of *Stufen* rather on successions of individual tones and chords. Since he maintains that tonal motion is controlled contrapuntally and that the rules of tonal voice leading are extensions of the rules of strict counterpoint, Schenker acknowledges that behavior of individual tones and essential harmonies depends upon the context in which those tones and essential harmonies appear. For example, the rule prohibiting

---

231. Schenker, "Noch ein Wort zur Urlinie," *WT2*, 4–6; tr. Robert Snarrenberg, *WT1*, 53–54. For further details, see Lubben, "Schenker the Progressive," 65.
232. Ibid.
233. See Schenker, "Beethoven's Sonata in F minor," *TW7*, 41.

parallel perfect octaves and fifths determines what happens between two adjacent tones and essential harmonies. Similarly, the rules of dissonance treatment presuppose the basic scheme consonance–dissonance–consonance.[234] The processes of *Auskomponierung* follow analogous rules and are likewise context-dependent.[235]

This much is apparent from Schenker's graphic analysis of J. S. Bach's Little Prelude No. 5 in D minor, BWV 926 from *TW5*, given here as figure 2.16.[236] According to Schenker, the structure of the *Urlinie*, which is given in figure 2.16a, may "not be enough for a cantus firmus setting," but the succession of intervals that it forms with the bass of the *Ursatz* (3–6–5–8) are "in accordance with the [modified] precepts of strict counterpoint."[237] He explains how figure 2.16b composes out the headtone (or *Kopfton*) of the *Urlinie* with an octave descent supported by 5–6 patterns in the lower voices. The octave span from D to D "provides an opportunity to increase the musical content, to generate motives, to express small-scale multiplicity and unity—in short, to bring a stationary note to life."[238] In his opinion, the voice-leading spans within the octave descent also comply with the rules of counterpoint. Next, Schenker notes that figure 2.16c replaces certain diatonic tones in figure 2.16b with chromatic tones that "give the appearance of cadential closure"; these tones are permissible in tonal music but "are forbidden in strict counterpoint." Indeed, if the voice leading of figure 2.16d–f had not been grounded in the rules of tonal counterpoint and the overall arc of the *Urlinie*, then the piece "would not have the cogency and perfection that we admire in it."

Although Schenker invokes the concept of an *Ursatz* in his writings from the early 1920s, he develops it considerably over the next decade. Early on, he tends to associate the number of *Ursätze* with the scale of the piece in question: short pieces may be derived from a single *Ursatz* and large pieces from a string of separate *Ursätze*, each one encompassing a discrete segment of music. Schenker's aforementioned graph of Bach's Little Prelude No. 5

---

234. *KP1*, part 2, chapter 1, §2; part 2, chapter 2, paragraph 6; part 2, chapter 4, §4; *CP1*, 112, 184, 261.
235. For details, see Brown, *Explaining Tonality*, 83–98 and 99–139.
236. *TW5*, 8–9 and tr. Dubiel, J. S. Bach's Little Prelude No. 5 in D minor, BWV 926, *WT1*, 180–81. The commentary appears in "Vermischtes," Schenker, *TW5*, 45–46 and tr. Lubben, "Miscellanea," *WT1*, 212–13.
237. "Miscellanea," *WT1*, 212–13.
238. "Miscellanea," *WT1*, 213.

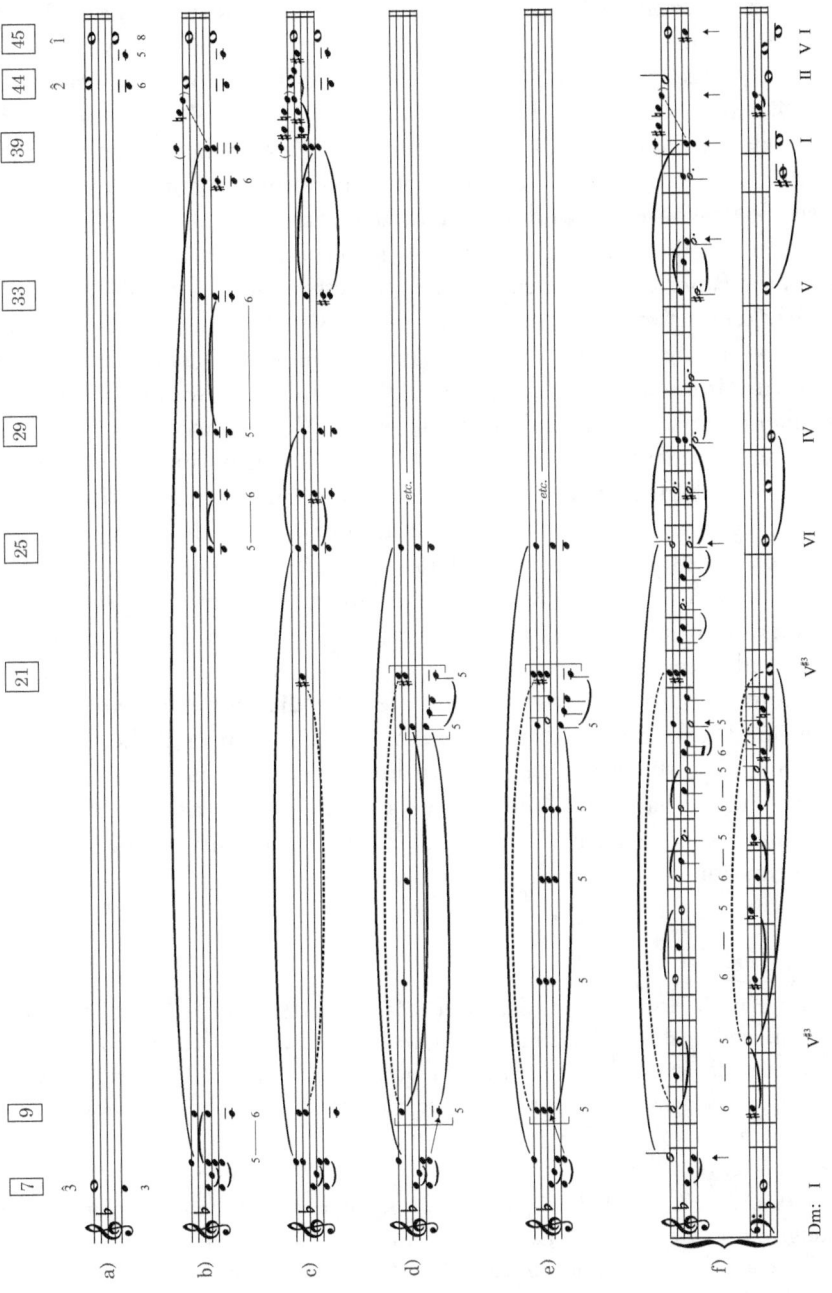

Figure 2.16a–f. Graphic Analysis of J. S. Bach's Little Prelude No. 5 in D minor, BWV 926, from *TW5*

in D minor BWV 926 is a good case in point. His decision to derive the piece from a single *Ursatz* seems entirely appropriate given that it is just 48 bars long and has a simple harmonic architecture: a tonic pedal (measures 1–8), a long sequence (measures 9–20), an elaborated dominant pedal (measures 21–38), a short cadenza and cadence pattern (measures 39–45), and a final tonic pedal (measures 45–48). By the 1930s, however, Schenker realized that he could derive all complete, continuous, monotonal works from a single global *Ursatz* whose *Urlinie* descends by step from $\hat{3}$, $\hat{5}$, or $\hat{8}$ to $\hat{1}$; at the same time, an inner line eventually ascends by step from $\hat{7}$ to $\hat{1}$, and a bass arpeggiation (or *Baßbrechung*) articulates the progression of *Stufen* I–V–I.

Schenker's claim that complete, continuous, monotonal works are controlled by a single global *Ursatz* has several important ramifications. To begin with, it underscores the abstract, all-embracing view of harmony that Schenker endorsed at the end of his life. Hans Weisse emphasizes this point in a letter to Schenker dated March 30, 1933. Exaggerating somewhat, he claims that Schenker treated *Stufen* as local phenomena in *HL*: "The *Stufen* in the foreground (in fact, you yourself usually indicate these, in parenthesis) are only illusory *Stufen*."[239] In *DfS*, however, Weisse declares: "the concept of the *Stufe* belongs above all to the middleground and background."[240] Schenker drew attention to such differences between background and foreground in the opening example of *DfS*.[241] As shown in figure 2.17, this innocuous trapezoid clearly differentiates the diatony (*Diatonie*) of the background from the tonality (*Tonalität*) of the foreground: the former is represented by "the content of the *Urlinie*, counterpointed by the *Baßbrechung*," and the latter by "the sum of all occurrences, from the smallest to the most comprehensive."[242] The middleground consists of the "levels of transformation."

---

239. See Hans Weisse's letter to Schenker (March 30, 1933) in *SC*, 472. This claim is contradicted by some of Schenker's analyses in *HL*: for example, his analysis of the development from the first movement of Beethoven's Emperor Concerto in E-flat major, op. 73 suggests that the section projects just three essential harmonies: E♭, G♭, and C♭. *HL*, §131, 327.

240. *SC*, 472.

241. *DfS*, 17; *FC*, 4. This figure does not appear in Schenker's gloss "Vom Hintergrund in der Musik," 12–13 and was subsequently removed from Oswald Jonas's second edition of *DfS* and from Ernst Oster's translation *FC*.

242. *DfS*, 17; *FC*, 5 (1st edition only).

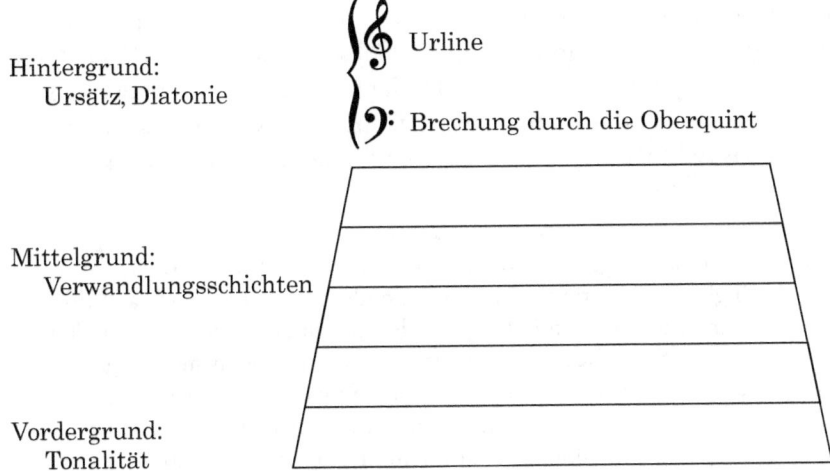

Figure 2.17. Graphic Display of Relationship of Foreground and Background, *DfS*, 17 (First Edition Only)

It is likewise clear from Schenker's discussion of figure 2.17 that the harmonic content of the *Ursatz* controls not only a work's surface chord progressions and successions of secondary keys, but its melodic, motivic, contrapuntal, rhythmic, and formal structure as well. His concept of harmony had now become so abstract that it encompassed an entire piece or movement. More specifically, Schenker claims that by composing out the tonic *Stufe*, the *Urlinie* summarizes "the primal design of melodic content."[243] This idea reinforces his faith in the inherent triadicity of tonal melodies. Schenker also insisted that the *Ursatz* provides a contrapuntal framework for each piece: "Neither the *Urlinie* nor the *Baßbrechung* can stand alone. Only when acting together, when unified contrapuntal structure, do they produce art."[244] And he maintains that the harmonic content of the *Ursatz* dictates a work's rhythmic and formal structure as well: "All rhythm in music comes from counterpoint and only from counterpoint. In the middleground every individual level has its own specific rhythm, according to the extent of its contrapuntal content. Thus rhythm, too, progresses through various transformational stages until it reaches the foreground, just as do meter and form, which also represent end-results of a progressive contrapuntal

---

243. *DfS*, 17; *FC*, 5.
244. *DfS*, §3, 31; *FC*, 11.

differentiation."[245] And, although part 3, chapter 5 of *DfS* discusses a number of specific formal types already mentioned in *HL*, §5 (e.g., undivided forms (*DfS*, §307), song forms (§§308–10), sonata forms (§§311–16), four-part forms (§317), rondo (§§318–21), fugue (§322), and variations (§323), Schenker nonetheless rejected traditional approaches to understanding form and emphasized that the form of a work ultimately depends on its derivability from an *Ursatz*:

> Coherence in language does not arise from a single syllable, a single word, or even a single sentence; despite the correspondence between words and things, every coherent relationship in language depends upon the meaning hidden in a background. Such meaning achieves no fulfillment with mere beginnings. Similarly, music finds no coherence in a "motive" in the usual sense [*DfS*, §50]. Thus, I reject definitions which take the motive as their starting point and emphasize the manipulation of the motive by means of repetition, variation, extension, fragmentation and dissolution. I also reject those explanations which are based upon phrases, phrase-groups, periods, double-periods, themes, antecedents, and consequents.[246]

Schenker continues: "My theory of form replaces all of these with specific concepts of form which, from the outset, are based upon the content of the whole and of the individual parts: that is, differences in prolongations lead to differences in form."[247] This applies to all of the formal types mentioned in *HL*, §5: "Be they two-, three-, four-, or five-part forms, all receive their coherence only from the fundamental structure, from the fundamental line in tone-space."[248] Schenker added: "the fundamental significance of the particular prolongation is always of paramount importance; the prolongation assigns each part its task with great exactness. The composer is thus spared the anguish of aimlessness, of happenstance, and of the continual search for the means to go on. [§§83, 254, and 264]."[249] In other words, Schenker proposes that a work's surface chords, secondary keys, as well as its melody, counterpoint, rhythm, motives, and formal structure are emergent properties: they are contingent on the distinctive harmonic and contrapuntal structure

---

245. *DfS*, §21, 38; *FC*, 15.
246. *DfS*, §308, 212–13; *FC*, 131.
247. *DfS*, §308, 213; *FC*, 131.
248. *DfS*, §25, 39; *FC*, 16.
249. Schenker, *DfS*, §308, 213; *FC*, 132.

of the *Ursatz* and take shape in the middleground through the process of *Auskomponierung*. Although figures 2.17 and 2.18 underscore the close attention Schenker pays to the behavior of the *Urlinie* and the *Baßbrechung*, it would be wrong to assume that *Ursätze* are necessarily two-voice constructs. There are, in fact, good reasons to suppose that they require at least one other essential voice.[250] For one thing, Schenker sometimes marks these inner voices in his graphs (see figure 2.18). These inner voices are important because they provide the third of the opening tonic *Stufe* in *Urlinien* beginning on $\hat{5}$ and $\hat{8}$ and the third of the penultimate dominant *Stufe*: the former determines whether the opening tonic is major or minor; the latter helps to define the final sonority as the global tonic. For another, when Schenker explains how *Ursätze* can be prolonged at the first level middleground, he includes unfolding (*Ausfaltung*), voice exchange (*Stimmentausch*), reaching over (*Übergreifen*), and other polyphonic transformations in his list of options. Such transformations are only possible if there is an inner voice below the *Urlinie*.

When comparing the *Ursatz* in figure 2.18 with that in figure 2.16, it is clear that the former is harmonically simpler than the latter: it projects a string of three essential harmonies (I–V–I) rather than four: I–II(6)–V–I. This difference arises because Schenker became increasingly aware of the fact that the characteristics of a particular tonal surface depend not only on what types of transformation are involved, but also on the order in which those transformations are applied. This order is indicated by a string of transformational levels (*Verwandlungsschichten*). Transformational levels specify the order in which the members of the *Ursatz* are elaborated. As shown in figure 2.17, Schenker classifies them into three types. The background (*Hintergrund*) corresponds to the *Ursatz*. The middleground (*Mittelgrund*) identifies various intermediary stages of transformation. As mentioned earlier, this process is constrained by the rules of tonal voice leading. Finally, the foreground (*Vordergrund*) then presents an analytical interpretation of the score itself, though that score can potentially be composed out even further in performance through by the addition of ornaments, cadenzas, and so forth. According to this scheme, the *Ursatz* given in figure 2.16 is typical of the deep middleground rather than the background: by including the

---

250. For further arguments in support of adding inner voices in the *Ursatz*, see David Neumeyer, "The Three-Part *Ursatz*"; Matthew Brown, *Explaining Tonality*, 72–76; Channan Willner, "The Polyphonic *Ursatz*"; and Geoffrey Chew, "The Spice of Music."

Figure 2.18. Fundamental Lines through a Third, Fifth, and Octave, with Inner Voices Marked (Brown, *Explaining Tonality*, 73)

additional *Stufe* II(6), it represents the first stage in the development of the piece and conforms not only to the sorts of procedures described in figures 2.9–2.10, but also to the deep middleground paradigms shown in figures 15.5b and figure 15.6 of *DfS*.

Following Aristotelian precepts, Schenker spent his career cultivating a theory of harmony which presupposes that each element of a tonal masterwork is in perfect harmony and causally related with one another. These properties require a balance between elements from nature, e.g., the overtone series, the generative capacity of the fifth, and the tendency for tones to assert themselves as tonics, and those that stem from art, e.g., the desire for repetition, the recognition of the subdominant, and the invention of the minor system. During the thirty or so years between *HL* and *DfS*, however, he developed ever more sophisticated ways of explaining how the tonal masters are able to achieve this balance both locally across individual phrases and periods, and globally across complete, continuous, monotonal compositions. Those explanations required him to refine and extend his understanding of *Stufen* by finding new ways to reconcile the rules of strict counterpoint with the principles of harmonic progression (*Stufengang*), by using the concepts of the *Urlinie* and voice-leading transformations to specify how *Stufen* are horizontalized in tonal contexts, and by introducing *Ursätze* and

Stimmführungsschichten to clarify the processes of *Auskomponierung*. In this way Schenker was able to show tonal masters were able to synthesize individual elements of a musical composition into an organic whole and create some of the greatest artworks of all time. It is hard to imagine a more worthwhile goal for any music theory.

Part Two

Harmonielehre: The Past

Chapter Three

Schenker's Theory of Harmony (1906) in Historical Perspective

The Theory of Harmony from the Ancient Greeks to the Early Nineteenth Century

When Schenker wrote his Theory of Harmony, he engaged the most important music-theoretical topic of the time. As one contemporary source made clear, it referred to:

> the study of the meaning of harmonies (chords)—that is, the explanation of the mental processes of musical hearing. By classifying the various types of simultaneities, delineating their relationships to one another, and attempting as well to develop the natural laws of musical design—in particular those of harmonic structure—the theory of harmony *cultivates the mental imaging of music in a systematic manner*, and develops the capability of the mind *to understand musical works more quickly as well as to think productively in tones.*[1]

---

1. Hugo Riemann, *Musik-Lexikon* (5th edition, 1900), s.v. *Harmonielehre*, 457. Emphasis in the original. That work, written entirely by Riemann himself, first appeared in 1882. Except for his addition of emphasis (which highlights the psychological angle), this definition is unchanged from its appearance in the first edition. Schenker owned a copy of the third edition (1887).

The ambitious leap from the "meaning of harmonies (chords)" to "musical hearing" in this passage is striking. That leap and the further claim that "the theory of harmony cultivates the mental imaging of music" demonstrate that as early as the 1880s, the "scientific" aspirations of harmony that were often couched in language of the physical sciences in mid-century now could be found in language drawn from human psychology, the recently rising field vying for scientific status. At the beginning of his career, Schenker likewise believed that harmony was fundamentally a matter of psychology. But the notion that an *artistic* hearing of music could come down to a psychological processing of successions of surface "chords" was one he rejected entirely, right from the outset of his career.

The above definition also underscores the central position that harmony held in music theory throughout the late eighteenth and nineteenth centuries, when something like a "common practice" reigned—the "science of music," many would have called it. Thus Schenker's entrée into the field was a high-stakes gambit. But as the repertoire has aged and pressing music-theoretical problems of twentieth-century modernism have emerged, the theoretical treatise on (now "traditional") harmony has appeared more rarely, so much so that today's English definition is purely practical: "the combining of notes simultaneously, to produce chords, and successively, to produce chord progressions."[2] Though no longer the science of music, harmony, now usually packaged in practically oriented books, remains a staple of theory pedagogy: it still refers to triads, occasional seventh chords, and their progressions found in tonal music of the common-practice period, and assumes that the latter are constrained by the principles of tonal voice leading, especially as regards the triadicity of melodies, the treatment of non-harmonic tones, and the prohibition of parallel perfect octaves and fifths.[3] Essentially no echoes of the Classical theory remain.

Ironically, while Riemann could claim exalted status for the theory of harmony, its practical teaching in conservatories was in decline at the turn of the last century. Schenker knew full well that the prevailing notion of "harmony" he was taught in the 1880s was of fairly recent vintage and that the practical instructional manuals of the time had lost touch with both works of the

---

2. *Grove Music Online.*

3. Admittedly, there are occasional peculiarities of usage, as when Allen Forte speaks of "atonal harmonies," an oxymoron if there ever was one, possible only when the word means merely "pitch-class simultaneity." See Forte, *The Harmonic Organization*, 148 and passim.

great eighteenth-century masters and contemporary music alike.[4] He also knew—and never tired of proclaiming—that the basis of the pedagogy of the master composers of the eighteenth and early nineteenth centuries—both what they learned and what they taught—was not the theory of harmony taught to him, but the study of counterpoint and figured bass. And finally, he knew that "harmony" had quite a different meaning in Classical antiquity—probably during his student years, but definitely by the time he wrote GEIST.

Yet, in surveys of music theory of the middle ages and beyond, what we refer to as the "Classical theory of harmony" often makes a cameo appearance at best.[5] There is surely justification for this, since what we think of as "music" was primarily seen by the ancients as a reification of structures that obtained in higher realms, all the way to the level of the cosmos (the so-called "harmony of the spheres"). Consequently, *musica theorica*, which included the Classical theory, was seen by many as divorced from practical music making, and grouped with the other mathematical sciences—arithmetic, geometry, and astronomy—ultimately institutionalized in the medieval university as the *quadrivium*. Was the "Classical theory" (also known as "harmonics") in any sense of use to musicians? True, Andrew Barker writes of the "science" of harmonics. And the work of Aristoxenus (fourth century BCE), which we shall have more to say about shortly, is justly regarded as an attempt to make harmonics a science along Aristotelian lines. But Barker's work convincingly ties Aristoxenus to earlier fragmentary writings that are clearly empirical, practical and musical in nature. In short, Barker provides convincing evidence of the purely musical importance of the Classical theory as well.[6]

While the middle ages witnessed a steady rise in works on *musica practica*, the Renaissance marked a rapprochement between *musica theorica* and *musica practica*. And a streamlined version of the Classical theory became the epistemological basis of practical theory at least as early as the late fifteenth and certainly by the mid-sixteenth century. Once the Classical theory was naturalized by the discovery of the harmonic series in the seventeenth

---

4. For his critique of current pedagogy of harmony, see *HL*, 223–35; *HA*, 175–81.
5. This is to be distinguished from the "modern theory of harmony" that essentially began in the early eighteenth century with the work of Jean-Philippe Rameau (1683–1764).
6. Barker, *The Science of Harmonics*. See especially chapter 9, "Contexts and purposes of Aristoxenus' harmonics."

century, it became that much more interconnected with practical harmony—and aesthetics, in which the all-important concept of nature ruled. It was during the nineteenth century that controversy regarding the relevance of the naturalized Classical theory arose and other potential epistemological bases of the theory of harmony emerged. Schenker came of age in a period in which this questioning came to a head, and proposed a unique synthesis. Thus, it is essential to study the basis of the Classical theory and its naturalization as elementary acoustical theory to understand harmony as Schenker understood it. The attempts to disconnect the two had little effect on Schenker, who wrestled mightily with the questions of such "natural-base" theorizing, as is apparent in his account of tonal systems, [DTS].

The present chapter considers the changing meanings of the word harmony and the content of the field of study it denoted, from its ancient Greek origins through the beginning of the nineteenth century, describing in the process some of the major conceptual turning points and the most important works that appeared as the field evolved. For practical reasons, the survey is highly compressed, selective, and teleological, headed unapologetically to Schenker. A much longer and more nuanced story could, of course, be told. But despite these limitations, the chapter provides important background for our music-theoretical discussion of Schenker's Theory of Harmony in chapter 2.

The Ancient Greeks and the Classical Theory of Harmony

The connection of *harmonia* with music is, in fact, extremely old: as early as the seventh century BCE the Greeks differentiated the musical styles of various ethnic groups, later associating them with particular types of tonal organization or *harmoniai* that took the form of *melodic prototypes*, or "scales."[7] A *harmonia* was not a "harmony," as we think of it, but a framework of the available pitches: a "pattern of attunement over the span of an octave," and

---

7. Though the term "scale" only arose in the middle ages, we use it informally here and below to denote a particular linear sequence of intervals and the pitches produced thereby. Interestingly, Schenker avoided it entirely. So far, the earliest known Western source of these scales is a cuneiform tablet from ancient Mesopotamia (from around 2000 BCE) containing instructions for playing the harp. See Wulstan, "Tuning of the Babylonian Harp." For a larger context, see Kilmer, "Music Tablet from Sippar (?)." Kilmer also wrote the article in *Grove Music Online* (revised by Sam Mirelman), which provides an excellent overview of this fascinating area of research.

thus the pitch structure of a melody.[8] Since the patterns were rotations of one constant pattern of intervals, this usage is close to our notion of mode. That idea, which also involves "pitch centers," appeared in the fourth century with the advent of the "tones" (*tonoi*), or "transposition scales," sometimes given the familiar Greek ethnic names in the sources.[9] Some of these names are still used today (Ionian, Dorian, Phrygian, Lydian, Aeolian, and Locrian), though the precise intervallic successions they denoted evolved considerably through history.[10] The simple notion of rotation of an interval pattern within an octave survived as the "form" (*eidos*) or "species" of that octave. *Harmonia* as a designator of scales seems to have fallen out of fashion by the late fourth century BCE.

During the Classical period (ca. 400–323 BCE), the framework signified by *harmonia* was desirable in music because it was thought to mirror that of both the universe and the human body: it was the "goal of the musician, through which he affect[ed] the soul of the listener."[11] This is yet another parallel with the conception of music propounded by Schenker, who always emphasized its moral dimension. The term's derivative *harmoniké* (or "harmonics") referred to a "system of principles and procedures through which *harmonia* [was] codified," and thus is roughly equivalent to our modern use of the term "harmony" to denote a subject of study, though the content of that study was very different from the Modern Theory.

To the Greeks, the notion of "good attunement" demanded that the component parts of a well-formed structure relate to one another in simple arithmetic ratios and proportions. This idea dominated ancient Greek medicine, architecture, visual arts, and cosmology. According to tradition, it was applied to music by Pythagoras (sixth century BCE) and subsequently transmitted by his disciples, the "Pythagoreans," Plato (late fifth to

---

8. See Barker, tr. and ed., *Greek Musical Writings*, vol. 2, 14.
9. The *tonoi* have been controversial, but M. L. West goes so far as to translate "tones" quite explicitly as "keys." See West, *Ancient Greek Music*, 228–33 and passim.
10. The Greek prefix "hypo" ("under," "beneath"), affixed to one of the ethnic names, refers to a lower-pitched version (or an extended lower range) of that mode. See *Grove Music Online*, s.v. "Mode."
11. Mathiesen, "Problems of Terminology," argues that the narrower, strictly music-theoretical, definition of *harmonia* is a product of the Hellenistic Period, after the death of Alexander the Great in 323 BCE.

mid-fourth century BCE), his followers, and the later "Neo-Platonists."[12] Pythagoras allegedly discovered that three musical intervals could be represented by the ratio between the lengths of two vibrating strings: 2:1 = the perfect octave; 3:2 = the perfect fifth; and 4:3 = the perfect fourth.[13] The notion that musical intervals can be represented by the ratio of two measurements is of enormous significance, representing one of the two basic ways in which intervals have been conceived in Western music theory.[14] It also had a direct impact on Schenker's categorical distinction between consonance and dissonance, another feature of the Classical theory that began to draw considerable criticism with the beginnings of the Scientific Revolution in the mid-sixteenth century.

The Pythagoreans also used the *simplicity* of the ratios for the octave, fifth and fourth to explain the unique effect of those intervals. This is the biggest difference between the Mesopotamian and later Greek use of this arithmetic. As Morris Kline writes, "that the methods worked was sufficient justification to the Babylonians for their continued use. The concept of proof, the notion of a logical structure based on principles warranting acceptance on one ground or another, and the consideration of such questions as under

---

12. A brief presentation of "harmony of the spheres" is in Plato's *Timeaus* (34b–36d); see Barker, *Greek Musical Writings,* vol. 2, 58–61. Also see his second chapter, passim.

13. According to legend, Pythagoras heard the sound of anvils emitting the basic consonances, and continued "experimentation" with strings under different tensions, glasses filled with different amounts of water, flutes, and bells of different sizes, all of which were thought to relate to one another by the same ratios. But the legend was debunked during the Scientific Revolution of the seventeenth century, when it was found through failed attempts to replicate these experiments that the ratios only worked for strings of the same thickness under the same tension. The ratios were more complex for air columns, solid bodies (like anvils!), etc. Most scholars think that Pythagoras was experimenting with a single-string instrument called the "monochord" (Greek for "one string," though the instrument often had more than one), also known as the "canon" ("rule," or "ruler").

14. Since string length and frequency are reciprocally related, a given ratio *or* its reciprocal can represent the same interval. The choice depends on the phenomenon being measured: the octave, for example, measured low to high via the traditional string length (or the modern notion of wavelength) is 2:1 (a string sounding an octave higher is half the length of a string sounding the lower octave; the same is true of the period of a wavelength); measured low to high by frequency, or its position in the harmonic series (see below), it is 1:2. Consistency in calculations is essential.

what conditions solutions to problems can exist, are not found in Babylonian mathematics."[15]

The notion of "explanation" is, of course, fundamental to ancient Greek thinking, and the Greeks found the numbers 1–4 especially efficacious in explaining the consonances.[16] The Pythagoreans assigned great mystical significance to ten, the sum of these four integers, which they represented by the so-called *tetraktys* (see figure 3.1). When arranged in their natural succession, the second and fourth numbers form the interval of an octave, just like the first two, but this time in "composite" form—i.e., as the interval of a fifth joined to that of the fourth; similarly, the first and fourth numbers form the double octave—the only time in the series of natural numbers that this happens.[17] From the practical point of view, they present the structural framework of a two-octave range that became the boundaries of ancient Greek pitch space (see figure 3.2), which, when divided tetrachordally, was known as the Greater Perfect System (see figure 3.3).[18] Thus, for the Greeks, the first four numbers represent all of the structural intervals, the larger intervals mediated by the smaller ones.

---

15. Kline, *Mathematical Thought from Ancient to Modern Times*, vol. 1, 14. The Babylonians flourished in Mesopotamia between approximately 2000 and 1000 BCE. Pythagorean mathematics may come from Mesopotamia as well. There exists a cuneiform tablet with the Pythagorean theorem inscribed on it at Yale University (YBC 7289, "Old Babylonian Period Mathematical Text"). And the Mesopotamian source inscribed with scales described earlier also contains mathematical notations. Thus the linking of mathematical and musical theory was practiced in ancient Mesopotamia, where Pythagoras is alleged to have traveled.
16. The numbers 1–4 form the ratios in simplest terms. In order to produce these ratios in practice on the monochord, the smallest whole numbers that can represent them are 12, 6, 4, 3. (12:6 = 2:1; 6:4 = 3:2; 4:3 = 4:3).
17. Richard Crocker, "Pythagorean Mathematics and Music," 193.
18. This *system* (from the Greek, *systema*; plural, *systemata*) and its later forms were two-octave *intervallic structures*, notated purely for convenience of reading as modern "pitches." It is not until the eighteenth century that we can start to talk about any reliable relationship between note names and their positions in pitch space (frequencies). Before this point, a system was usually conceived on a monochord (as here), whose precise pitch reference could change while preserving intervallic structure. Schenker's essay presented in appendix A engages this topic as it relates to common-practice music and its theory.

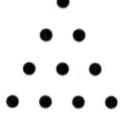

Figure 3.1. The *Tetraktys* of the Decad

Pitch names:	A2		A3		E4		A4
Monochord measurements:	12	(12:6)	6	(6:4)	4	(4:3)	3

Ratios in simplest terms:

4:1		
2:1	4:2	
2:1	3:2	4:3

Figure 3.2. Ancient Greek Two-Octave Range

A ratio consisting of two consecutive natural numbers was designated an epimore (*epimorios*) in Greek. More commonly known as "superparticular" (from the Latin *superparticularis*), it had an exalted status. In Pythagorean tuning, aside from the octave, fifth and fourth, superparticular ratios include the whole step (9:8), formed by subtracting a fourth from a fifth.[19] The "half

---

19. Operations on ratios are logarithmic (logarithm means "ratio-number"), and thus "addition" = multiplication, "subtraction" = division. To "add" two ratios, multiply the corresponding terms: $\frac{3}{2}$ "+" $\frac{4}{3} = \frac{12}{6} = \frac{2}{1}$ (a fifth "added" to a fourth = an octave). To "subtract" them, divide the terms, or multiply the first ratio by the reciprocal of the second: $\frac{2}{1}$ "−" $\frac{4}{3} = \frac{2}{1}$ "+" $\frac{3}{4} = \frac{6}{4} = \frac{3}{2}$ (an octave minus a fourth = a fifth). For "division," take the root of the divisor, for "multiplication" the power of the multiplier. In essence, we hear intervals logarithmically: as frequencies rise or fall, and *distances between* the two notes of the interval become larger or smaller, it is the constant proportion between them that identifies an "interval."

From this point on, when speaking of interval ratios, we will provide translations into the "cents" measurements of the British physicist Alexander J. Ellis (1814–90), whose logarithmic scale based on twelve-tone equal temperament (hereafter, "EQ") allows for easy comparison of the intervals formed by the ratios with their counterparts in EQ. For Ellis, there are 1200 cents ("c.") in an octave: the half step = 100 c., whole step = 200 c., etc. The "pure" intervals (i.e., those that result from the simple ratios) are *all incommensurate with the corresponding intervals in EQ, except for the*

step" formed by subtracting two 9:8 whole steps from a fourth is not superparticular (256:243 = 90 c.); it thus had a lower status still, and was referred to simply as the "remnant" or "leftover" (*leimma*)—leftover when two 9:8 whole-steps (= 490 c.) were removed from a 4:3 fourth. In this process, the fourth, fifth and octave were structural (since they were superparticular *and* occur within the *tetraktys*), while the other intervals were derivative. Greek theorists were able to construct complete tetrachords comprised of a semitone and two tones (STT): when combined with an "extra" 9:8 whole step at the bottom, these tetrachords produced a two-octave pitch range filled with "steps."[20] That pitch range formed the basis of the diatonic scale through the middle ages, though it was extended above and below (only to G or Γ, below the Greek range; see figure 3.5a–b).

Greek arithmeticians also compared ratios via the notion of *proportion*: "a situation in which four numbers, when arranged as pairs, determine the same ratios."[21] When, in a proportion, the second term of the first ratio is the same as the first term of the second ratio, it is said to be the "mean" between

---

octave. Thus all Ellis measurements are rounded to the nearest whole number, except for the 2:1 octave that equals 1200 cents. For example, the 3:2 fifth will be notated as 702 c., not 701.9550009 . . . (the pure fourth, the remainder from the octave, 4:3 = 498 c.): Ellis's cents make it easy to see that the 3:2 fifth is slightly wider than the same interval in EQ, the fourth slightly narrower. On the other hand, the just major third (386 c.) is *considerably* narrower (and quite audibly so) than the major third of EQ (400 c.) An interval measurement in the form a:b can be converted into an Ellis measurement via the formula: $1200(\log a - \log b)/\log 2$.

20. The system could be tuned as a "diatonic system," which we concentrate on here exclusively, since it was most influential historically. But it could also be tuned as a "chromatic system," in which the top interval of the tetrachord was stretched to about the span of today's minor third (leaving the bottom intervals at about the size of two minor seconds). And it could be retuned as the "enharmonic system," in which the bottom interval sizes were further reduced to around the size of quartertones, while the upper interval was extended to slightly larger than the size of a major third. (It is important to emphasize that these "thirds"—a term that only arose in the middle ages—were conceived as larger, indivisible, "steps.") The terms "chromatic" and "enharmonic" have survived in modern music theory, but with radically altered meanings, since EQ has become the basis of most art music. Indeed, the idea of "retuning" systems for expressive purposes, and as an integral structural process, essentially fell out of common-practice music until abortive attempts to revive it in the sixteenth century, and its more successful revival in some music of the twentieth and twenty-first centuries.

21. See Corry, *A Brief History of Numbers*, 35.

A₂	B₂	C₃	D₃	E₃	F₃	G₃	A₃	B₃	C₄	D₄	E₄	F₄	G₄	A₄
9:8		4:3				4:3		9:8		4:3				4:3

Figure 3.3. Two-Octave Range Divided Tetrachordally

the extreme terms of the proportion—"a third number that satisfies some additional, well-defined condition."[22] In the expression a:b :: b:c the mean of "a" and "c" is "b."[23] The Greeks catalogued ten types of mean proportions, three of which were used in the development of harmony: the geometric mean, and—especially important as our story unfolds—the arithmetic and harmonic means:[24]

Three Musical Means

1. The geometric mean is the square root of the product of the extremes. (Two-octave spans on the monochord are structured via the geometric mean: 4:2 :: 2:1)
2. The arithmetic mean is one half the sum of the extremes, the "arithmetic average." (An octave divided on the monochord by a fourth on the bottom and a fifth on top is structured via the arithmetic mean: 4:3 :: 3:2)
3. The harmonic mean is twice the product of the extremes divided by their sum. (An octave divided on the monochord by a fifth on the bottom and a fourth on top is structured via the harmonic mean: 12:8 [=3:2] :: 8:6 [=4:3].)

This is yet another important property of the Greater Perfect System: it embodies these three types of mean proportions—particularly the harmonic and arithmetic means, represented multiply. See figure 3.4, in which only one example of each is bracketed off.

Harmony and Monophony

Anyone familiar with modern discussions of harmony will be surprised that in our historical account there has yet to be any mention of polyphony, or "chords." This is because, as Schenker well understood, ancient Greek music

---

22. Ibid., 35–36.
23. Here we follow the notation used ibid., 35, which shows clearly that a proportion compares two ratios.
24. Ibid., 37.

A₂	B₂	C₃	D₃	E₃	F₃	G₃	A₃	B₃	C₄	D₄	E₄	F₄	G₄	A₄
12							6				3 ($\sqrt{(12 \times 3)}$ = 6 = Geometric)			
		8					6			4 (8:6 :: 6:4 = 4:3 :: 3:2 = Arithmetic)				
							6			4		3 (6:4 :: 4:3 = 3:2 :: 4:3 = Harmonic)		

Figure 3.4. Example of Each of the Means Within the Two-Octave Range

was essentially monophonic. The complete corpus of ancient Greek music theory and fragments of notated music make this clear.[25]

The monophonic texture of ancient Greek music is confirmed by the focus on melody in the oldest extant music theory treatise, the *Elementa Harmonica* (Elements of Harmonics) by Aristoxenus of Tarentum (b. ca. 375; fl. 335 BCE). Having grown up in an environment in which Pythagorean theory reigned, Aristoxenus went to Athens to study with Aristotle (384–322 BCE), and subsequently became a critic of Pythagorean methodology, though there can be little doubt that he was an expert in it. Drawing on Aristotelean methods, he claimed that mathematical approaches to music were irrelevant (despite—or perhaps because of—his background in Tarentum and Aristotle's support of them!).[26] Instead, he attempted a rigorous logical analysis of musical phenomena and our perception and cognition of them, strongly influenced by Aristotle—though not his thinking on music.[27] Most importantly, Aristoxenus is usually credited with the authorship of the competing

---

25. See Barker, *Greek Musical Writings*, vol. 2, passim. Drones and the strumming of the lyre likely were added, but all writing on the music concerns only the melodic line. The surving notation is also purely monophonic: as of 2001, sixty-one ancient Greek melodies had been found. See Pöhlmann and West, eds., *Documents*.

26. Nonetheless, Aristoxenus cannot escape "mathematical approaches to music" entirely when dealing with the proportionality of rhythm, as is clear in the surviving fragment of his writing on that topic. See Barker, *Greek Musical Writings*, vol. 2, 185–89.

27. As Crocker points out, Aristoxenus's notion of the "motion of the voice in place" is indebted to "Aristotle's definitions of motion and place in books III and IV of the *Physics*, and to his classification and continuity of movement in books V and VI. In particular, Aristoxenus's discussion of continuity and consecution is a direct application to music of chapter 3, book V of the *Physics*, 'Succession, Contact, Continuity and Related Distinctions.'" See Crocker, "Aristoxenus and Greek Mathematics," 100. Aristoxenus's structure of an argument, particularly in book III, is indebted to Aristotle's thinking on the topic as presented in *Posterior Analytics*. See Barker, *Greek Musical Writings*, vol. 2, 67–68.

way of conceptualizing the relationship of the interval: as a distance between two (dimensionless) points on an imaginary line.

Active at a time when Greek mathematicians were developing so-called Euclidean geometry (ca. 320 BCE), Aristoxenus endorsed a geometric approach to intervals: instead of viewing them as ratios of natural numbers, he imagined a continuous "space" between tetrachordal boundaries.[28] This view is intuitively attractive as a metaphor for the intervallic "moves" that we make mentally, that our vocal chords make as we sing, and that our fingers make as we play instruments. It is also consistent with Aristoxenus's decision to make melodic composition (*melos*) the initial focus of his treatise and his claim that whereas *harmonia* is inherently static, *melos* takes place in time, and can therefore teach us to recognize (appropriate) character and action.[29]

Persuasive as Aristoxenus's views may be, however, Pythagorean and Platonic approaches to intervals dominated later thinking, thanks to two of antiquity's most important treatises, the authors of which were not musicians, so far as we know. The first was the *Harmonics* of Claudius Ptolemy (fl. second century CE). A polymath and the most famous proponent of the geocentric view of the universe, Ptolemy anticipated features of the scientific method (and thus the science of acoustics) by constructing experiments on the monochord to prove ideas arrived at theoretically.[30] Much of Ptolemy's work was passed on by Anicius Manlius Severinus Boethius (ca. 480–524) in his *De institutione musica* or *Institutes of Music*.[31] For him, the "musical institutes" were essentially the Pythagorean and Platonic theory of harmony as codified by Ptolemy and, to a somewhat lesser extent, Nichomachus (early second century CE), a Pythagorean.[32] Probably because of

---

28. Crocker, ibid., passim.
29. For Aristoxenus's interpretation of the terms, See Barker, *Greek Musical Writings* vol. 2, 126. Also see Fiecconi, "*Harmonie, Melos,* and *Rhythmos.*"
30. See Barker, *Scientific Method in Ptolemy's "Harmonics,"* especially chapter 2, "Reason and perception."
31. The title is in the tradition of Quintillian (first century CE), *Institutio Oratoria*. An archaic definition of the literal English translation, "institutes" reads "a commentary, treatise, or summary of principles, especially concerning law" (*New Oxford American Dictionary*). Boethius's work *institutione* is the first in a line of musical treatises using this title. We use the literal translation in all cases to make that tradition clear.
32. Bower reads the source of the earlier part of Boethius as a lost treatise by Nichomachus, while Ptolemy comes out later in *institutione*. See Bower, "Boethius and Nicomachus," 1–45.

Boethius's extraordinary influence in the middle ages—more full or partial manuscripts survive than for any music treatise before the advent of printed books—*musica* eventually became the usual mantle under which the Classical theory of harmony was taught in the medieval university, using *De institutione musica* as a "textbook."

The Theory of Harmony in the Middle Ages

Although there are no extant musical treatises from the seventh and eighth centuries, sources from the ninth century show that the term *harmonia* not only survived in the middle ages, but also continued to be associated with monophony and melody.[33] This is clearly the case for the late ninth-century writer Hucbald (840/50–930), whose "Musica" was given the Boethian title *De harmonica institutione* (On the Institutes of Harmony) by an eighteenth-century cataloger.[34] Hucbald discussed more than seventy plainchant melodies through a mixture of the Classical theory of harmony inherited from Boethius and a strain of practical theory associated with Byzantine chant. Essential to the latter were eight scales (the *okto echoi*) that centered on four tonal centers or "finals" related by tone, semitone, tone, and rendered by convention as D, E, F and G (see figure 3.5a.).[35] Equally important, however, was Hucbald's revision of the Greek pitch system via this "tetrachord of finals" (see figure 3.5b for the Greek system, and figure 3.5c for Hucbald's revision of it). As opposed to the Greek tetrachord semitone, tone, tone (STT), the TST tetrachord cleverly shifts the whole range (including the low A, which was "the note added" in the Greek system) to conjunct and disjunct concatenations of these tetrachords. In other words, Hucbald continued to use both the two-octave Greek pitch range, and the tetrachordal division of that range as a constructive device, but revised it according to medieval chant practice. This, and variants of it, became the "medieval system."

Another pair of treatises of the time, the anonymous *Musica Enchiriadis* and its companion the *Scolica Enchiriadis*, also presents a system, but one built of stacked fourths that are *only* disjunct—that is, TST tetrachords that start on G2, D3, A3, and E4. Though the system never caught on, the

---

33. See Dahlhaus, *Studies*, 19.
34. Gerbert, *Scriptores*, 104.
35. On these finals as "tonal centers," see McAlpine, *Tonal Consciousness and the Medieval West*.

```
       D   E   F   G
           T   S   T
```

Figure 3.5a. Medieval Tetrachord of Finals

```
+A   B   C   D   E   F   G   A   B   C   D   E   F   G   A   (B)
   T   S   T   T   S   T   T   T   S   T   T   S   T   T   T
     (Disjunct)   (Conjunct)       (Disjunct)   (Conjunct)   (Disjunct)
```

Figure 3.5b. Ancient Greek System

```
+Γ   A   B   C   D   E   F   G   A   B   C   D   E   F   G   (A)
   T   T   S   T   T   S   T   T   T   S   T   T   S   T   T
     (Disjunct)     (Conjunct)       (Disjunct)    (Conjunct)   (Disjunct)
```

Figure 3.5c. Hucbald's "Modern System"

anonymous authors had begun to understand the significance of transposition in the construction of a system. More important, they began to recognize the significance of polyphony, and thus the treatises contain the first surviving accounts of organum.[36] The language they use to describe the intervals of the fourth, fifth and octave betrays, for the first time, a vertical conception of these intervals.[37] This move not only marked a subtle shift of emphasis away from the Classical theory, but it also indicated that the real growth genre of the middle ages was not *musica theorica* at all, but rather *musica practica*, a genre best exemplified by Guido's *Micrologus* (early eleventh century), the second most widely circulated treatise after Boethius's *De institutione musica*.[38] Guido still depended on Pythagorean divisions of the

---

36. Gerbert incorrectly attributed both to Hucbald. The critical edition is Schmid, *Musica et scolica enchiriadis*. The English translation is Erikson, tr., intro, and notes, *Musica Enchiriadis and Scolica Enchiriadis*.
37. Fuller, "Theoretical Foundations."
38. See Palisca, ed., *Hucbald, Guido, and John*, 49–83. Guido's *Micrologus* survives in ca. 70 MMS. Other treatises on organum introduced elaborations of and departures from this simplistic structure, but the "perfect intervals" remained structural until

monochord to produce his pitch repertoire, however, translating the largely abstract reasoning of Boethius into a practical aid in teaching aural skills; and he also felt obligated to pass along the story of Pythagoras in his last chapter. The enthusiastic reception of Guido's solfège system, attested to by numerous diagrams of Guidonic hands in treatises, is of the greatest importance. Indeed, it was used at least through the sixteenth century to map the uncharted reaches of pitch space and to do so as a system of transposed hexachords producing early forms of the key areas of common-practice music.[39]

After Guido, many anonymous authors wrote small tracts on practical problems associated with polyphony. Starting in the thirteenth century, such texts show how the term *harmonia* was often applied to simultaneous combinations of tones.[40] The frequent recommendation to seek variety in the succession of these simultaneities likely emerged from the demands of maintaining *harmonia* as well. Some scholars have designated the rules that began to appear in these treatises as "interval-succession theory," and have seen them as the first theories of voice leading.[41] The texts were sensitive to sonority and encouraged composers to write chiefly with consonant intervals, though some gradations were certainly possible. For example, writing in the late thirteenth century, John of Garland even developed a continuum of interval consonance to dissonance, calling the fourth and fifth "intermediate consonances," and thirds "imperfect" consonances.[42] Perfect consonances—the unison or octave—had to appear only at the end of a work. By the middle of the fourteenth century, sixths had joined the thirds as imperfect consonances, and the fourth had become a dissonance. Meanwhile, discant treatises advocated the use of contrary motion between the two parts: a

---

at least the mid fifteenth century. The immediate precursor of Guido's work is the "Dialogue on Music," formerly thought to have been written by an "Odo," but now regarded as an anonymous northern Italian treatise from the eleventh century. See Treitler, ed., *Strunk's Source Readings*, 198–210.

39. See Berger, *Musica Ficta*, 29–55. For a transcription of a chart that shows such transpositions of the hand, see figure 4 (p. 35), from Anonymous, *Tertius liber musicae* (1464).

40. Dahlhaus, *Studies*, 19.

41. See Eggebrecht et al., eds., *Die mittelalterliche Lehre von der Mehrstimmigkeit*. Also see Sachs, "Zur Tradition der Klangschritt-Lehre," 233–70.

42. Crocker, "Discant, Counterpoint and Harmony." John goes on to classify dissonances in the same manner, creating a complete scale of intervallic consonance and dissonance: perfect (M7, tritone and m2); imperfect (M6 and m7) and intermediate (M2 and m6). See his *Concerning Measured Music*, tr. Birnbaum, chapter 9, 15–18.

major sixth should proceed to an octave in contrary motion, a minor sixth to a fifth in oblique motion, a minor third to a unison in contrary motion, and a major third to a fifth in contrary motion (or fourth, if consonant, in oblique motion), though specific exceptions to these rules were tolerated. But in general, imperfect consonances should be inflected to approach their intended perfect-interval resolutions as closely as possible.

By the early fifteenth century, whole books were devoted to practical composition: these not only catalogued possible pitch materials (i.e., consonances in two parts), but also discussed methods for choosing pitches in interval successions. Prosdocimo de Beldomandis (d. 1428) used the term *harmonia* for two-part dyadic composition in his *Contrapunctus* (Montagnana: 1412), one of the first books devoted exclusively to two-part polyphony.[43] As early as the thirteenth century, however, dissonances were allowed if mixed with consonances "at the proper places."[44] By the mid- to late fifteenth century, Johannes Tinctoris (ca. 1435–1511) and others even developed rules to govern the resolution of dissonant intervals to consonant ones in measured music.[45]

Franchino Gaffurius (also Franchino Gaffurio, Gafurius, Gafori, 1451–1522) may have been the first to use the term *harmonia* to describe sonorities of three voices, as we do today with our notion of "three-part harmony." He reserved the term consonance for two-part combinations.[46] Clearly the notion of the union of diversity—the combining of two different intervals—played an important role in his choice of terms.

The High Renaissance: The Revision of the Classical Theory of Harmony in *Le istitutioni harmoniche* of Zarlino

One writer influenced by Gaffurius was Gioseffo Zarlino (1517–90), whose approach to three-part sonorities via the Greek theory of proportions may have been taken from Gaffurius's use of that theory in his bisection of intervals into their constituent ratios. Gaffurius points out the division of the

---

43. Dahlhaus, *Studies*, 20.
44. Crocker, "Discant, Counterpoint and Harmony," 10.
45. Tinctoris, *The Art of Counterpoint*. On Tinctoris's reform in rhythmic notation, see Christensen, ed., *Cambridge History*, 648ff.
46. Dahlhaus, *Studies*, 9–20. Dahlhaus cites Gaffurius's *De harmonia musicorum instrumentorum opus* (Milan: 1518).

fifth, for example, into a major third and minor third as an example of the "harmonic mean," adumbrating the close relationship of the later concept of "chord of nature" or "major triad" and "harmony."[47]

Zarlino wrote one of the most important treatises in the history of music theory: *Le istitutioni harmoniche* (The Harmonic Institutes). He conceived the work during a time when printing was well underway, and wrote in the vernacular Italian. Surely these are important reasons why his influence on subsequent music theory—in Italy and beyond—was massive. Another was surely the ingenuity of Zarlino's synthesis of an extraordinarily cohesive view of *musica theorica* together with lessons in musical composition penned by a master composer of the period. Zarlino's book is thus the first known work in the form that Schenker would eventually adopt for *HL*. The theoretical part begins with an abstract presentation of Zarlino's revision of the arithmetic associated with the Classical theory in part I, followed in part II by a discussion of "sounds," in which Zarlino implements the theory, using the voice, the monochord, and ultimately the (mean-tone) tempered keyboard. In the second half of the book, part III sets up the rules of counterpoint that would evolve into "species counterpoint," and addresses such topics as use of a "subject" (soggetto), use of rhythm, and chromaticism. Part IV discusses the modes and gives advice on text setting.

The title represents an underlying theme of the treatise as a whole: *harmonic proportion*.[48] In part I, Zarlino extends the range of possible natural numbers from the Greek *tetraktys* to the senary number, six, thereby justifying the "imperfect consonances," the major third (5:4) and minor third (6:5) in just intonation (part I, chapters 13 and 15). Thirds so intoned extend the possibilities of harmonic proportioning: for example, the (5:4) major third is divided harmonically into the "large whole tone" (9:8) and the "small whole tone" (10:9), while the (6:5) minor third is divided harmonically into the large whole tone and the large semitone (16:15). Zarlino has problems with

---

47. See Gaffurius, *Practica musicae*, book III, chapter 2, "De Natura & denominatione specierum contrapuncti." See Miller, tr., "Nature and Terminology of Contrapuntal Species," 119–24.

48. On the other hand, Dahlhaus has claimed that Zarlino's reference to *harmonia* in the title of his treatise demonstrates that the term's meaning had grown considerably so that it now included "all the factors of polyphonic composition: the combining of tones into a sequence of tones; the agreement of the two tones in a dyad; the connection between successive dyads; the compounding of dyads into a triad; and the relationship among the melodies and rhythms of different voices." See Dahlhaus, *Studies*, 21.

the two other imperfect consonances. The major sixth (5:3) lies within the *scenario* but is not superparticular; his justification is that it is a composite interval, consisting of the fourth plus the major third—full-fledged superparticular consonances in the *senario* (part I, chapter 15)—essentially Gaffurius's analysis. The minor sixth (8:5) is neither superparticular nor completely within the *senario*, and thus has to be considered composite—as a combination of the minor third and fourth (part I, chapter 16). Justifying thirds and sixths allowed Zarlino to talk about triads (without the term), which used the Greek consonances as well as his newly justified thirds and sixths. In composition in three or more parts Zarlino recommends using fifths mediated by thirds (or their octave compounds) as often as possible in either harmonic or arithmetic proportion, occurring so as to create "perfect harmony" (*harmonia perfetta*: part III, chapter 31). He also prefers major triads to minor triads because the former are harmonically proportioned (part III, chapter 10), with the 5:4 major third on the bottom and 6:5 minor third on top (= 15:12 :: 12:10); minor triads are arithmetically proportioned (part III, chapter 31). Yet, Zarlino thought of musical textures as a theorist of counterpoint, in which two-part counterpoint was always formative of terminology in counterpoint in more voices. Nonetheless his harmonically mediated fifths soon became known as "harmonic triads" and featured prominently in German treatises of the later sixteenth and early seventeenth centuries, such as those by Siegfried Harnisch (ca. 1568–1623) and Johannes Lippius (1585–1612).[49] It was Lippius who spoke of the "trias harmonica," justifying it theologically: its "threeness" combined with harmonic proportioning made it the perfect Neo-Platonic entity, a union of Christian theology and Classical thinking. Lippius also introduced the notions of a triadic "root" (*radix*) and the invertibility of the triad, though alleging his influence on later theory—either figured bass, or Rameau—is problematic.

Harmonic proportioning proved to be an important part of Zarlino's overall argument, turning up not only with the greater frequency of occurrence of major triads as components of the vertical texture, but in such apparently unrelated domains as tuning and modal structure. Preference for harmonic division of the octave, fifth and the major third prompted Zarlino to pick "syntonic diatonic" tuning for vocal music.[50] For keyboard music he chose mean-tone temperament, a tuning system designed to preserve as many just-tuned triads as possible, while still allowing movement to closely

---

49. See Lester, *Between Modes and Keys*, 28–36, 39–43.
50. The term is taken from Ptolemy, and is synonymous with just intonation.

related transpositions of modes.[51] And the harmonic division of the octave with its (3:2) fifth on the bottom and (4:3) fourth above (= 6:4 :: 4:3) was fundamental to Zarlino's view of the structure of so-called "authentic" modal scales.[52] Meanwhile, the octave divided such that the fifth is on top and the fourth on the bottom, the octave partitioning of "plagal modes" for lower voice ranges, is in arithmetic proportion. And the minor triad (6:5 :: 5:4), in which the 6:5 minor third is *beneath* the 5:4 major third is likewise in arithmetic proportion. Both plagal modes and minor triads are of secondary

---

51. It will suffice for us to understand that "1/4 comma mean-tone temperament" preserves just major and minor triads in eight transpositions, allowing free circulation through the commonly used keys. However, if tuned from C, the "major thirds" A♭/C, D♭/F, and B/D♯ and F♯/A♯ are really diminished fourths of 428 c. (G♯/C, C♯/F, B/E♭ and F♯/B♭, respectively). Thus transpositions that use them are considerably out of tune. We might suspect that minor triads that use these major thirds will suffer from excessively small "minor thirds" (really augmented seconds of 269 c.). In fact, three "minor" modal scales are so affected: those on F, B♭, and E♭. Scales on G♯ are a special case, since its "wolf fifth" (really a diminished 6th), constructed from the extremes of a line of fifths (G♯ on the sharp side and E♭ on the flat side) is intolerably wide to modern ears (738 c.) for an interval we expect to be "perfect." (Whether it was actually used as a "special effect" at the time, however, remains controversial.) Zarlino also recommends "$\frac{2}{7}$ comma meantone," in which the major thirds are a little more than 3 c. smaller than pure, but, as a consequence, more transpositions are available.

52. It will be remembered (note 14) that the use of ratios as a notation for intervals is possible in either reciprocally related order. The arithmetic and harmonic mean proportions are also reciprocally related. The harmonic series (a series of ascending frequencies) clearly demonstrates *arithmetic proportion*: any middle term of a succession of three consecutive natural numbers is the arithmetic mean of the two on either side. The measurements of string lengths producing the overtones (measured from the fundamental of "1"), amount to the *reciprocals* of the natural numbers (1/1, 1/2, 1/3, 1/4, 1/5 . . .), and demonstrate *harmonic proportion*. Zarlino is thinking of string lengths, which are easiest to understand by taking a series of whole-number measurements, rather than fractions of 1. If the length of the whole string producing the fundamental measures 120 cm, its second harmonic (or "first overtone") will measure 60 cm (octave = 1/2 the whole length), its third, 40 cm (twelfth = 1/3 the whole length), its fourth, 30 cm (fifteenth = 1/4 the whole length), and its fifth, 24 cm (seventeenth [octave + tenth] = 1/5 the whole length), etc. 60 is the harmonic mean of 120 and 40; 40 is the harmonic mean of 60 and 30; and 30 is the harmonic mean of 40 and 24. All sets of three adjacent measurements of strings producing successive overtones are in *harmonic proportion*.

importance. This thinking extends to cadence structure in the modes as well. Zarlino claims that the "regular" cadence degrees of any modal pair are the first, third and fifth degrees of the authentic mode (thus adhering to harmonic or arithmetic division of both the octave and lowest fifth), exactly the same degrees as used in the corresponding plagal mode: thus there is, in effect, one and only one "structural" set of cadence degrees for each modal pair. Zarlino makes this claim despite overwhelming empirical evidence to the contrary in music of his time. Indeed, it contravenes the dictates of most other modal theorists. Zarlino offers no evidence from the repertoire of the time, but instead composes his own set of duos to demonstrate. Clearly, it is Classical proportioning that determines his thinking here.

Having investigated harmonic relationships further in an intervening work, Zarlino renumbered the modal scales in the 1573 edition of *istitutioni* so that their order started on C for the first time, for he discovered that if the interval ratios of string segments were related to the greatest extent possible via the harmonic mean, the C–c' scale would result. In effect, it was Zarlino who first treated the "C major scale" as the progenitor of other scales, though he did not call it that, and certainly was *not* promulgating a major–minor tonal system.[53] Yet many musicians certainly learned the idea from Zarlino, for, having written his book in the vernacular Italian for dissemination via the relatively new technology of printing, its influence was vast. The significance of this fundamental axiom of tonal harmony—the origin of which is ancient—would not be explored until more than a century and a half later (see figure 3.6a–b).[54]

Towards the Modern Theory of Harmony in the Seventeenth Century

The late sixteenth and early seventeenth centuries was a period of music-theoretical gestation of the greatest importance, for the later seventeenth

---

53. Nonetheless, he placed the twelve modes into two general categories, depending on whether the triad formed from the first degree was major or minor.
54. Figure 3.6 is a diagram of the C–C octave tuned according to Zarlino's instructions, from the second edition of *l'istitutioni* (1573), 140. Figure 3.6b is Claude V. Palisca's transcription of the most important parts of Zarlino's diagram, taken from Zarlino, *On the Modes*, xviii. For discussion of the transcription and further context, see Palisca's introduction, xvi–xix.

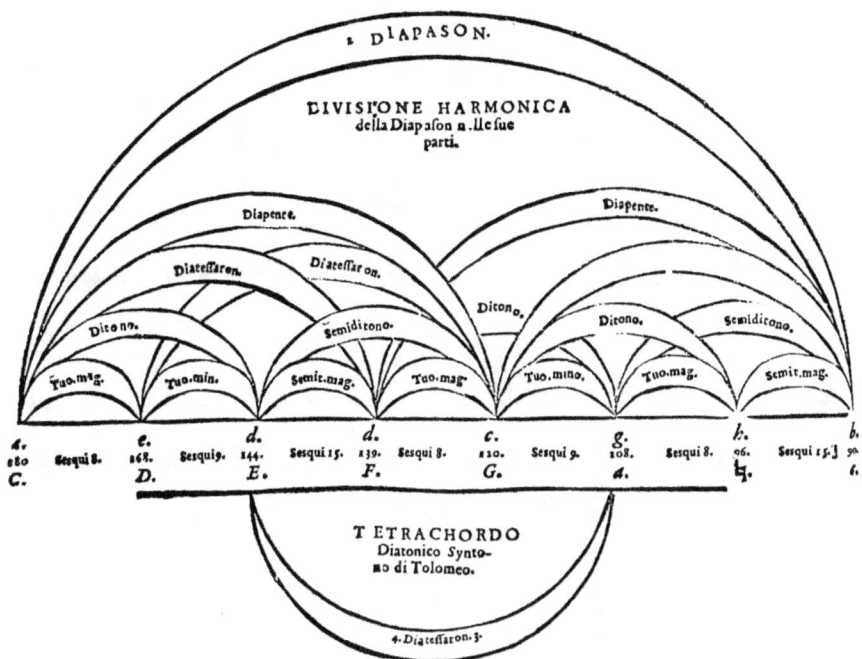

Figure 3.6a. Zarlino's C3–C4 Octave

century ultimately would witness the birth of new genres of music theory. While experimental physicists started to transform the Classical theory of harmony into the new science of acoustics, practical musicians continued to write about and teach counterpoint as part of their larger efforts to teach the art of music composition. Indeed, *musica practica* began to enter its greatest period of growth.

The biggest single event for the *theory* of harmony, however, was the discovery of the harmonic (or overtone) series—the series of partial vibrations that occurs any time an acoustic sound source emitting a pure musical pitch is set in motion.[55] Figure 3.7 provides only the first sixteen partials from an infinite series. The arrows above four notes signify that they are considerably flat of those notated pitches in our system, tuned as just or EQ. The other twelve partials are correct in just intonation (but only the fundamental and its octaves correspond to these pitches in EQ). The ancient Greeks had asked questions that show they were aware of the existence of sympathetic

---

55. This statement excludes experimental instruments designed to emit fundamentals only, such as tuning forks.

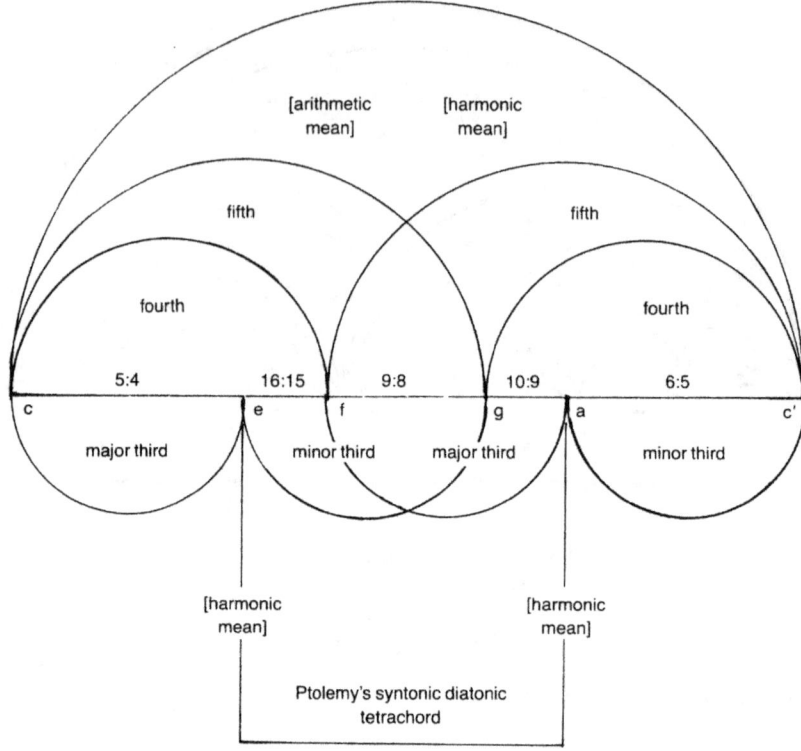

Figure 3.6b. Palisca's (Selective) Transcription of Zarlino's C3–C4 Octave

vibration (resonance), but there is no indication that they knew its cause.[56] That had to wait for the experimental ingenuity of seventeenth-century scientists, though basic tenets of acoustics were proposed very shortly after the appearance of Zarlino's *istitutioni*. By the mid-sixteenth century, the scientist Giovanni Battista Benedetti (1530–90) noted in a private communication of 1563 to the composer Cipriano de Rore (1515/16–65) that string length

---

56. See the Aristotelian *Problemata*, book XIX, "Problems Connected with Music" (Barnes, ed., *Aristotle*, 1430–31). See, e.g., 8, "Why does the low note contain the sound of the high note? Is it because the low note is greater and resembles an obtuse angle, while the high note resembles an acute angle?," or 13, "Why is it that the low note in the octave gives the effect of unison with the high, but not vice versa? Is it because, if possible, the sound of both notes is in both notes, but failing that, in the low note, since it is greater?" Also see Barker, *Greek Musical Writings*, vol. 2, chapter 4.

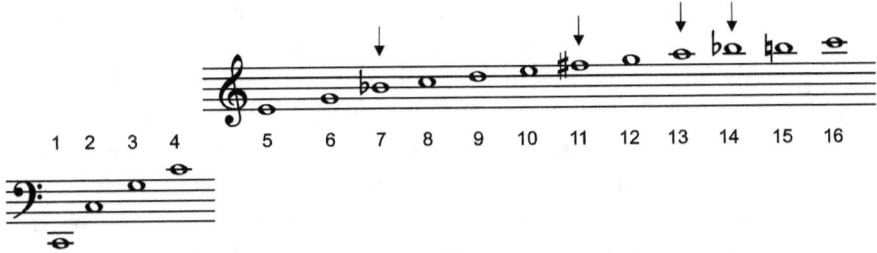

Figure 3.7. Harmonic Series

and frequency were reciprocally related. Working independently early in the seventeenth century, the Dutch scientist Isaac Beeckman (1588–1637) was aware of the vibrational nature of pitch, but advocated a corpuscular theory of sound transmission instead of the wave theory. A friend of René Descartes (1596–1650), Beeckman communicated his researches to him. In the *Compendium of Music* (1618, dedicated to Beeckman), Descartes wrote that the sounds of higher strings were "contained" in lower ones, and *not* vice versa—essentially the Aristotelian view.[57] Around the same time, Marin Mersenne (1588–1648) proposed a continuum of consonance to dissonance and introduced the experimental method into acoustics to investigate overblowing in wind instruments. Yet he never could accept the reality of overtones without reservations.[58] The final proof of the existence of overtones through experimentation with slips of paper pinned to vibrating strings is usually credited to John Wallis at the end of the seventeenth century.[59] The result of all this was the certain knowledge that any acoustic source of pitch vibrates simultaneously in successively smaller integral proportions: 1:1, 1:2, 2:3, 3:4, etc., indefinitely.

This discovery shifted the focus from an abstract view of pitch combinations generated from string divisions to an actual sounding entity that vibrated simultaneously in parts related to the fundamental pitch by those same hallowed superparticular ratios. Experimentation had proven the reality of an ancient theory! Whereas the Greeks took the simplicity of the numerical relationships as an aesthetic desideratum, seventeenth-century scientists demonstrated that it was a law of nature. The discovery played right

---

57. See Christensen, *Rameau*, 71–90, for an admirably concise yet complete account of this development.
58. Cohen, *Quantifying Music*, 114.
59. Ibid., 236.

into prevailing mimetic aesthetic theory—the notion that art was an imitation of nature, an aesthetic view held since the Greeks, and by Schenker, among many, many others. Since the fundamental and lowest five partial tones of the harmonic series form a just major triad, the "harmonic triad" became the "chord of nature"—the *Naturklang*—of the greatest importance for Schenker, determining, among other things, his categorical distinction between consonant and dissonant intervals. At the same time, the systems of composition were apparently shifting from (arguably) twelve modes to only two, major and minor, and it now seemed possible to demonstrate that music composition was a direct product of nature, at least with respect to the major mode. Accordingly, theorists began the attempt to generate the major and minor systems from the harmonic series.

Our previous discussion has prepared us for working with the harmonic series, for the reciprocals of the familiar interval ratios created via the standard technique of string division used by the ancient Greeks correspond to the positions of those intervals in the harmonic series (measured low to high, and counting the fundamental). Conveniently, these positions provide terms of the ratios: for example, 1:2 = the octave, 2:3 = the fifth, and so on.[60] The numbers need not be in consecutive numerical order: the third and fifth partial produce 3:5 = major sixth; the fifth and eighth produce 5:8, the minor sixth, etc.

In actually using the series to generate the materials of major and minor tonality, however, we are in for some disappointment. We saw, for example, that the Greeks, not confined to a single generating tone, were able ultimately to generate a complete two-octave diatonic scale via mathematical manipulation of intervals. But in trying to generate a major scale from a harmonic series, it turns out that we are limited to taking successive aliquot parts (1/2, 1/3, 1/4, etc.) of a string sounding a single "fundamental." And only the partial tones that correspond to tones of the major triad built on that fundamental are in our system, as are their products and powers (1, 2, 3, 4, 5 = triadic partials; 6, 8, 9, 10, 12, 15, 16, etc. = products and powers); most of the latter are merely octave duplications of tones of the triad.[61] The

---

60. Each position in the harmonic series is a "partial" (vibration). First partial : first partial = 1:1 (the unison); first partial : second partial = 1:2 (octave), second partial : third partial = 2:3 (the fifth), etc. From now on, our ratios will generally be in the form a : a+x.

61. New intervals arise, but not measured from the fundamental. For example, 4 and 6, composite numbers (the product of two or more integers greater than one—in this case, 2 x 2 and 2 x 3), produce the fourth partial, the double octave (1:4),

number 9 is an interesting borderline case: it *is* new (familiar to us from the 9:8 tone of the Greeks, if we subtract the octave), but more easily heard as a "secondary generation": 3 x 3 = "the fifth of the fifth." Beyond that, it is true that the just minor triad is formed by the remaining "in-tune" harmonics of the first sixteen shown in figure 3.7, the tenth, twelfth and fifteenth partial tones, but the "root" of the triad they form is *not* the fundamental. Unless we are willing to continue climbing the extreme heights of the harmonic series and making multiple octave adjustments, we have exhausted overtone generation directly from a fundamental. Now we must speak of "secondary" and "tertiary" generations. Thus $\hat{7}$ can be the "fifth of the third" or the "third of the fifth" (3 x 5 = 5 x 3 = fifteenth partial), but $\hat{6}$ has to be the "fifth of the fifth of the fifth" (27th partial!) for we still have no $\hat{4}$, and thus $\hat{6}$ cannot be "third of the fourth." Indeed, $\hat{4}$ is simply absent from the harmonic series. Moreover, all of these pitches are just tuned, so that none (other than the octaves of the fundamental) square precisely with the pitch levels of the same tones in EQ, leading some to reject such "natural-base" theoretical justifications entirely.[62]

---

and the sixth partial, the double octave plus fifth (1:6). The difference between the fourth and the third partial is the interval of the fourth, but *not* generated from the fundamental; the difference between the sixth and fifth partial is the minor third, again not generated from the fundamental.

62. We recall Aristoxenus's condemnation of the arithmetic of interval structure as musically irrelevant. Early in the nineteenth century Gottfried Weber and François Joseph Fétis continued the campaign, and in 1965, Milton Babbitt subjected all "natural justifications" of tonal theory to a withering critique. See "The Structure and Function of Musical Theory" (1965), reprinted in *The Collected Essays of Milton Babbitt*, eds. Peles, S., Demski, S., Mead A., and Strauss, J. Princeton and Oxford: Princeton University Press, 2003, pp. 191–201.

But, despite the discrepancies in tuning, the tradition of "natural-base theory" continued among many (including Schenker) and later, Babbitt's epistemological critique notwithstanding. With regard to tuning, the differences between the just major triad and the major triad in EQ are relatively small, but not insignificant. The 2 c. differences between the just perfect fifths and fourths and the same intervals in EQ are only hearable via close listening in the register C3–C4. The situation with thirds is quite different: the major third in just tuning is 14 c. smaller than the same interval in EQ, the minor third in just 14 c. larger. Both are quite hearable in many registers. Curiously, we have become so acclimated to large and "jangly" major thirds that beginning students of tuning often find the beatless just major third narrow and "flat" sounding. Still, there have been many (e.g., Hugo Riemann), and continue to be many (particularly among specialists today in music cognition), who contend

In fact, most natural-based theorists agree that all prime numbers beyond five are irrelevant to our tonal system. This limit seems to have represented a music-cognitive boundary for Schenker in his psychological theory of harmony (see chapter 1). Thus 1 is associated with the unison, 2 with the octave, 3 with the fifth, and 5 with the major third. All numbers beyond these are octave compounds of these tones or secondary and tertiary generations. Notice that 3 and 5, both prime numbers, are identified with the fifth and third respectively, the essential intervals of harmonic generation (1 is the fundamental, 2 and 4 are octaves). All prime numbers beyond 5, however, are irrelevant to our tonal system, a basic condition of harmonic generation that would prove crucial to Schenker. Thus the interval found between the fourth and seventh partials (4:7 = 969 c.), for example, appears to be a "minor seventh," but is considerably narrower than the minor seventh of EQ (1000 c.)—a *very* hearable discrepancy.[63] Likewise, 6:7 at 267 c. is far smaller than our (300 c.) "minor third" in EQ. Although some theorists attempted to make the seventh partial the model for the dominant seventh chord, or the eleventh partial the model for $\hat{4}$ (at a very wide 551 c. when reduced to within the range of an octave, as opposed to the 500 c. of in EQ), such attempts were doomed to failure. The tuning anomalies are the result of trying to represent the harmonic series, a series of infinitely decreasing interval sizes, in a notational system that has come to signify twelve *equal-sized* half-steps within an octave.[64]

Attempts to generate all tones and chords in our system from a single fundamental produced additional frustrations. Theorists soon found that there is no way to generate the subdominant directly from the fundamental via the harmonic series.[65] Nor is the minor triad found in the harmonic series gen-

---

that we are "hard-wired" for the just triads, and only accept the EQ triads as a compromise necessary in practice.

63. Benjamin Britten instructs the horn player to play all notes without valves in the prologue and epilogue of his "Serenade for Tenor, Horn and Strings" (1943); the intonation of the seventh harmonic is immediately recognizable.

64. Of course, potential tuning discrepancies between enharmonic "equivalents" continue to exist in many instruments: i.e., those in which pitch levels are not completely fixed (voice and strings in particular, though "bending" tones in winds can can alter EQ tuning to just). Only keyboard and fretted instruments have been locked into some kind of temperament since their invention, and into EQ since its universal adoption in Western art music, probably late in the nineteenth century.

65. The interval of the fourth (3:4) arises as a distance from the twelfth (1:3) to the double octave (1:4) (1/4 x 3/1 = 3/4). Thus it comes from the fifth, and not the

erated directly from the fundamental (to say nothing of alleged "diminished" and "augmented" triads). Schenker considered the minor triad 10:12:15, but rejected it, claiming that the overtones this high "have little effect on our ear," and that the whole system requires minor triads on the tonic, dominant and subdominant.[66]

The Rise of Figured-Bass Practices

The most important *practical* development for the study of harmony in the seventeenth century was the advent of figured bass. This notational practice, which first appeared towards the end of the sixteenth century, developed out of the purely practical demands of music making. The demand for figured bass was fueled by the appearance of thicker polyphonic textures in music of the later sixteenth and early seventeenth centuries, the notation of individual parts in book form prior to the invention of the "score" ("part-book notation"), the popularity of the solo melody with chordal accompaniment (particularly in the new form, opera), and the proliferation of keyboard and fretted instruments and their use for accompaniment. All of these conspired to create a demand for a "shorthand notation" that would turn the part book of the lowest voice (which by now had succeeded the tenor as the referential voice) into a proto-score for an accompanying keyboard, lute, or guitar player.

Thoroughbass is a notational shorthand that musicians use to transcribe complex polyphonic textures into a bass line, which is given in its entirety, and a string of Arabic numerals, which indicate the intervals between the bass and the upper parts. Thoroughbass treatises were not, of course, the only treatises to use Arabic numbers in this way: counterpoint treatises also use them to denote generic intervals. Thoroughbass notation also allows performers to fill out textures with extra strands of polyphony that are implied by the rules of tonal voice leading or by the horizontal presentation of individual chords.

Bass parts began to be published for this purpose by the turn of the seventeenth century, some of which contained Arabic figures corresponding to the most important intervals formed above the bass, while others contained none. The existence of basses without figures created a problem: the treatises of the time had to teach not only how to convert basses with figures indicating only rudimentary interval content into acceptable music (a problem not

---

fundamental.
66. *HL*, §23, 64; *HA*, 49.

unlike the one facing performers using "lead sheets" today), but also how to choose the notes to accompany basses that were partially figured, or completely unfigured. The many answers to both of these questions provided by the treatises constitute the elements of a rudimentary theory of voice leading of the period, and thus the figured bass remains of use and interest, despite later developments in harmony and the decline in continuo practice.[67] Typically, this advice consisted of catalogues of figures (see figures 3.8a and b), and practical strategies for realizing and connecting them via simple rules of voice leading that led to standardized figurations. The most famous of the latter was the so-called Rule of the Octave (*Règle de l'octave*), an exercise demonstrating the "correct" choice of figures (in example 3.1 in a form propounded by François Campion[68]) for stepwise bass lines.

The seventeenth century also witnessed the further fragmentation of musical "styles," and the new compositional techniques associated with the "vernacular" styles in particular. The music-theoretical result was that any interval could now appear in a vertical stack of figures above the bass note—i.e., dissonant "chords" were now available. By even the early eighteenth century, the full complement of figures became challenging for the aspiring accompanist to learn. As seen in figures 3.8a–b, the encyclopedic figured-bass treatise by Johann David Heinichen (1683–1729) provides a chart of thirty-two figures, while the "little" figured-bass "primer" by Johann Mattheson (1681–1763) presents a list of seventy! Such lists suggest that, for all its explanatory power, the theory of chord inversion discussed in the abstract by Harnisch and Lippius in the early seventeenth century did not filter down to the day-to-day life of the performing musician.

Schenker's Opinion of the Figured Bass

William Mitchell's article on figured-bass theory was an important corrective of the negative opinion of the figured bass that held some currency since Shirlaw's singling out of those aspects of the theory that adumbrated the theory of harmonic inversion and other more "correct" understandings of

---

67. Schenker makes precisely this point in an essay "On Voice-Leading in Figured bass" ("Von der Stimmführung im Generalbass"), 76. Though he apparently wrote this essay at the end of his life, he would probably have agreed with this statement at the time *HL* was written as well.

68. Campion, *Traité d'Accompagnement*, cited by Christensen in "'The 'Règle de l'Octave,'" 91.

Example 3.1. Campion's Rule of the Octave

Figure 3.8a. Johann David Heinichen, *Der General-Bass in der Composition* (Dresden: 1728), Chord Table Showing 32 Figures

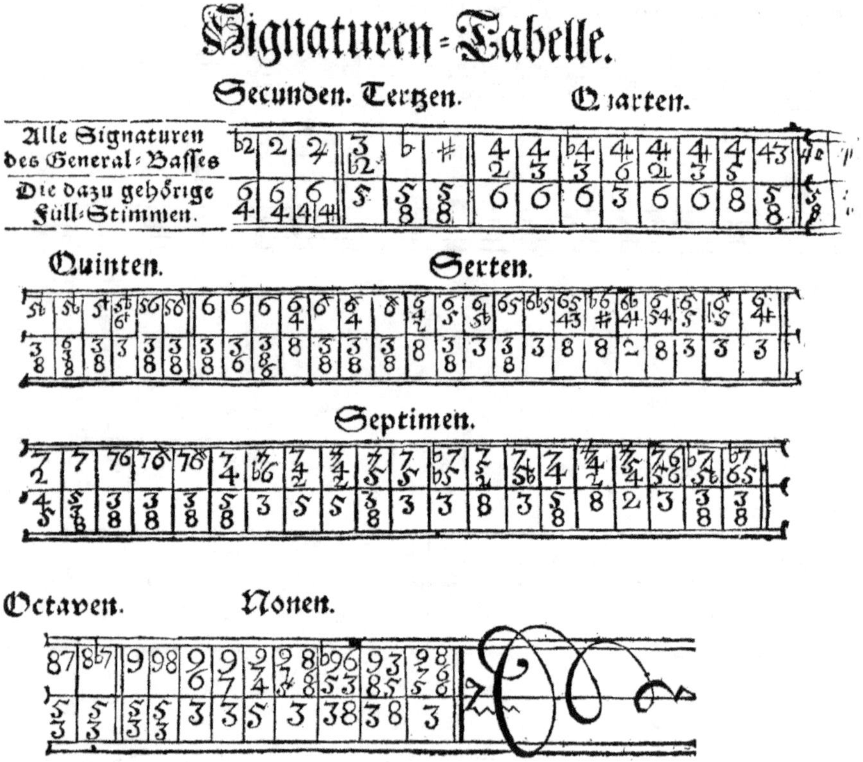

Figure 3.8b. Johann Mattheson, *Kleine General-Bass-Schule* (Hamburg: 1735), Chord Table Showing More Than 70 Figures

harmony. Mitchell takes the opposite tack from Shirlaw, and emphasizes sonorities from figured-bass theory that are treated as "fundamental" that would have been regarded as "inversions" of "root-position" seventh chords in later harmonic theory, but are clearly the governing sonorities in the particular passages discussed, thereby demonstrating the contextual sensitivity of figured-bass theory.[69] It has been assumed, since Mitchell was a well-known Schenkerian (having studied in Vienna with Schenker's student Hans Weisse), that Schenker had an unfailingly positive view of figured-bass theory.[70] In fact, his opinion is more nuanced and interesting than that.

Schenker regarded figured bass as a type of free composition ideally suited to didactic purposes, particularly chorale realization. Schenker was an avid

---

69. Mitchell, "Chord and Context."
70. Shirlaw, *The Theory of Harmony*, 7ff.

supporter of figured-bass theory and regarded C. P. E. Bach's *Versuch über die wahre Art das Clavier zu spielen* as the figured-bass treatise *par excellence*: "The theory of the voice leading of the figured bass has been discussed repeatedly in important works, but it certainly received its best and final form in C. P. E. Bach's 'Theory of Accompaniment' (the second part of his *Versuch über die wahre Art das Clavier zu spielen*)."[71] Schenker admired Bach's treatise for several reasons. Very generally, he supported the ways in which it treats figured bass as a theory of voice leading and the fact it invokes the concepts of essential counterpoint, contrapuntal chords, and composing out. And Schenker applauded Bach for encouraging performers to treat works as a single coherent whole and for invoking the concept of monotonality, and for specifically using such comments to justify his own appeal to global prototypes.

And yet, Schenker had his reservations about the power of figured-bass theory. He noted, for example, that figured-bass theory ignored many details of composition "because it can find no notation for them, and can issue none without misleading the player."[72] He backed up his claim with several examples from J. S. Bach's *Generalbaßbüchlein*. One of them is given in example 3.2.

According to Schenker, this passage should have been figured $\frac{6\text{-}6}{5}$. But Bach simply added the numbers 5-6 to show that the resolution of the tied B♭ is embellished with the upper tone C and simply left it up to the continuo player "to add the sixth of his own initiative."

Nor did Schenker believe that pieces of music are necessarily generated from the bass up. This familiar idea is almost implicit in figured-bass theory and helps to explain why Baroque theorists tended to use the bass line as the point of departure for their composition exercises. For example, when advising students how to improvise a free fantasy, C. P. E. Bach gave them the bass line shown in example 3.3.[73]

Whereas Bach simply gave the student instructions about how to elaborate the bass line, Schenker insisted that the improviser must first imagine a conceptual upper voice or *Urlinie* that would require support from such a bass line. Schenker's analysis of C. P. E. Bach's realization makes that

---

71. Schenker, "Vorwort," *KP1*, xxv–xxvi; "Author's Preface," *CP1*, xxvii.
72. Schenker, "Forsetzung der Urlinie-Betrachtungen," *MW2*, 27; "Further considerations of the Urlinie: II," tr., Rothgeb in *MM2*, 11. Also Schenker, *DfS*, §261, 171–72; *FC*, 105.
73. C. P. E. Bach, *Versuch* p. 341; *Essay*, 442f.

Example 3.2. Figured Bass from J. S. Bach's *Precepts and Principles* (Poulin, *J. S. Bach's Precepts and Principles*, p. 30, m. 7, top).

Example 3.3. Bass Line from C. P. E. Bach, *Essay*, 442f.

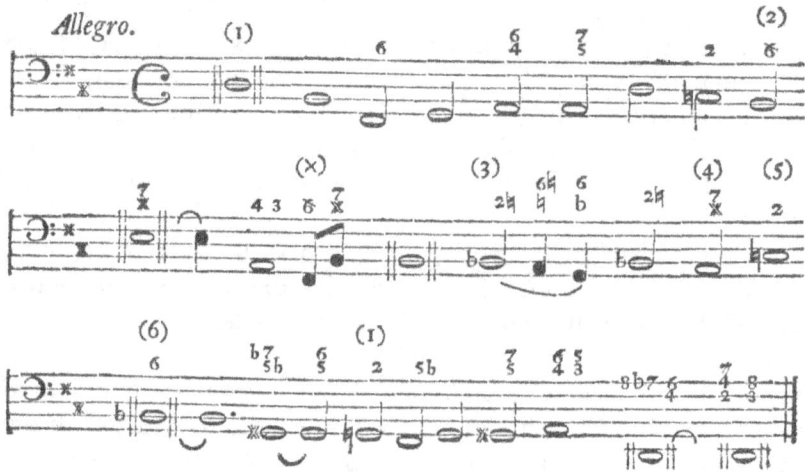

conceptual upper line clear (see Figure 3.9).[74] In this case, Felix Salzer notes that the descent A, G, F, E in Schenker's $\hat{5}$-line *Urlinie* mirrors the descent D-C-B♭-A in Bach's original bass line. According to Salzer, the beauty of Bach's realization is that it avoids creating parallel perfect fifths between the *Urlinie* and the bass line (A/D-G/C-F/B♭-E/A) by elaborating, displacing, and chromatically inflecting the two lines.[75]

---

74. Schenker, "Die Kunst der Improvisation," *MW1*, 23; "The art of improvisation," tr. Kramer, *MM1*, 8.
75. Salzer, "Haydn's Fantasia," 162.

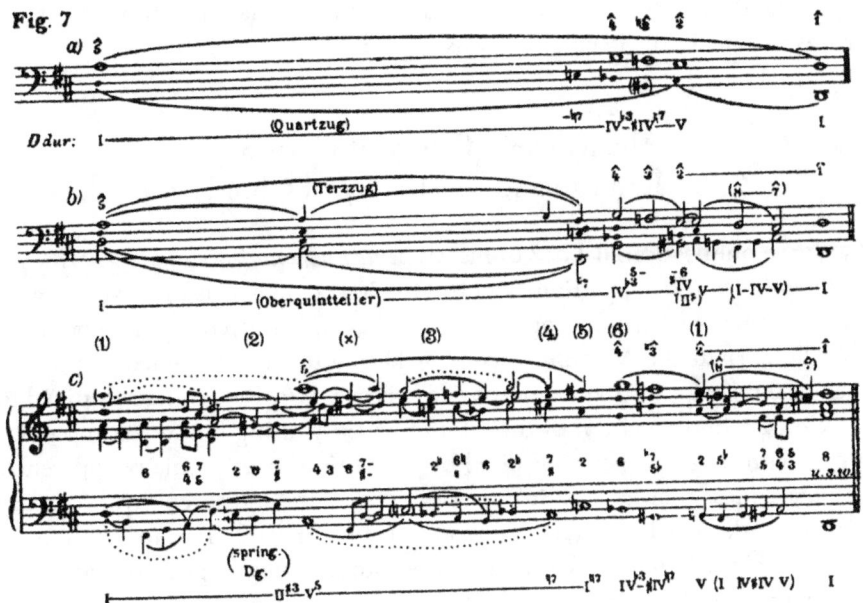

Figure 3.9. Schenker's Realization and Analysis of C. P. E. Bach's Bass Line

Much as Schenker valued figured-bass theory as a guide for teaching keyboard players how to accompany melodies, he nonetheless questioned its capacity to explain the behavior of eighteenth-century Baroque polyphony. As Schenker made clear in *KP1*, he believed theorists must not only describe what contrapuntal rules the student should follow, but they must also offer reasons for following them: "If even religion has had to cope with the fact that mankind asks "why," isn't it all the more understandable that contrapuntal theory, which in fact has long enjoyed almost the reputation of a musical religion would meet the same fate?"[76] And it was precisely C. P. E. Bach's reasons that Schenker found wanting: "The figured-bass theory of Bach was faulty because, unfortunately, problems are shown there not in their origin but in an already advanced state. Thoroughbass theory shows us prolongations of *Urformen* without having first familiarized the reader with the latter in any way."[77] He made the same point in his response to Bach's description of his free fantasy: "it is not that the musical facts of the case are falsely

---

76. "Einleitung," *KP1*, 18; "Introduction," *CP1*, 12.
77. "Vorwort," *KP1*, xxv–xxvi; "Author's Preface," *CP1*, xxvii.

represented, but that his language was as yet inadequate to supply the right words to explain the deeper relationships."[78]

The Modern Theory of Harmony: Rameau and the Theory of Chords

With the publication in 1722 of his *Traité de l'harmonie réduite á ses principes naturels*,[79] Jean-Philippe Rameau (1683–1764) emerged as the pivotal figure in the theory of harmony of his era and beyond. Indeed, many would say that he created the Modern Theory of Harmony single-handedly, but it is well recognized now that he did not do this *ex nihilo*. Rather, he continued to develop Zarlino's revision of the Classical theory, using it as a starting point along with original theory inspired by it to bring together many apparently disparate ideas that he took from various sixteenth- and seventeenth-century sources—ideas such as interval- and chord-rootedness, "chord inversion, harmonic scale-step norms, basic harmonic progressions (especially cadences), dissonance resolutions, and cadential evasion."[80] Some of these were ideas that Schenker accepted and used in *HL*, despite his famous critical diatribe against Rameau in his late work.[81] Once again, it had to have been the notion that all musical activity came down to successions of vertical "chords" that rankled him. The success and extraordinary influence of Rameau's system is the event, after all, that would culminate in Riemann's system, the "study of the meaning of harmonies (chords)."

At the most practical level, Rameau tried to solve the vexing problem of figured-bass pedagogy by fusing his new version of Zarlinian theory with the object of study of the figured bass: the vertical slice of a polyphonic texture,

---

78. "Die Kunst der Improvisation," *MW1*, 23; "The art of improvisation," tr. Kramer, *MM1*, 8.
79. Treatise on harmony reduced to its natural principles, tr. Gossett as *Treatise on Harmony*. Unless otherwise indicated, translations are taken from Gossett.
80. Lester, *Compositional Theory in the Eighteenth Century*, 90. Lester presents valuable background for Rameau's works, 90–100. To be precise, Rameau needs the number 6 to generate his intervals and the "root-position" major triad, but at other points he rejects it as a primitive, since it does not produce a new pitch class, but merely the octave of 3. The number 5 remains necessary as the source of thirds and sixths.
81. See "Rameau or Beethoven," in *MM3*, 1–9.

now a "chord" (*accord*). While $\frac{5}{3}$ and $\frac{6}{3}$ vertical combinations in counterpoint treatises were in effect "chords" when viewed through the lens of *harmonia*, any vertical slice was a chord in figured-bass theory. Rameau produced an entire work devoted to the generation, classification, and succession of chords, even managing to fold in dissonant chords, and thus conceiving a theory of all vertical pitch structures of common-practice music (which was simultaneously coming to the fore), ostensibly based on the divisions of a string and their further manipulations.[82] The inclusion of dissonant intervals in chords was truly unprecedented. Unaware of overtones when he wrote the *Traité*, Rameau soon found out about them and adopted the *corps sonore* (sounding body) as the foundation of his theories thereafter in a second work, the *Nouveau système*.[83] He would continue to develop this natural-base theory for the next forty years, alternating between theoretically and practically oriented works. Lightly edited, reinterpreted, and misinterpreted versions of his theory would become influential far and wide, and treatises using the word "harmony" in their titles would never be the same again.

In some ways, Rameau's *Traité* outwardly resembles Zarlino's *istitutioni*. Like Zarlino, Rameau wrote a work in four parts (though he called them "books"), the first pair on theory, the second on practice. However, the titles and contents of the books show how profoundly the interpretations of these categories had changed, given the rise of continuo practice, in particular.[84] "Only by means of accompaniment can one promptly acquire a

---

82. While the ancient Greeks managed to derive "steps" harmonically, it must be remembered that their constructs were analogous to "scales" abstracted from melodies. "Harmony" described the structure of a melody, *not* a vertical slice of a polyphonic texture. In the seventeenth and eighteenth centuries, the increasing prominence of accented dissonance produced downbeat accompanying "chords" with exotic-looking figures that seemed impossible to organize, beyond placing them in simple numerical order. Rameau called upon the theory of harmony as that missing principle of organization, radically transforming intervallic "derivatives" and "remainders" into "harmonies."

83. Rameau, *Nouveau système*. Soon after publication of the *Traité* Rameau became aware of the experimentation with overtones (after 1694) of the French mathematician, Joseph Sauveur (1653–1716), prompting him to get to work on his second book, in which he attempted to naturalize and extend the theory of the *Traité*. Yet he also extended the techniques of string division of the *Traité* as well in this work.

84. The development of the concept of "chord" in the eighteenth-century theory is inextricably connected to the ideal media with which to realize it, strummed instruments and the keyboard. Zarlino's vocal approach to composition survived in books

sensibility to harmony," declared Rameau in *Nouveau système*.[85] Not surprisingly, the new orientation is readily apparent in books 3 and 4, the ones dealing with practice: gone is Zarlino's vocal orientation, replaced by the keyboard. The longest of all four, "Principles of Composition" (book 3) occupies the position in the work analogous to Zarlino's *Counterpoint*, taking up many fundamental topics necessary for composition, but within a thoroughly chord-oriented approach until the brief appearance of fugue at the end. Book 4, "Principles of Accompaniment," is a primer on figured bass, apparently intended for students of modest accomplishment. But why does it end the *Traité* as a whole? Very likely Rameau regarded the brevity and accessibility of book 4 as conclusive evidence of the success of his theoretical project, for here the art of accompaniment had been reduced, from his point of view, to its very essence—with surprising efficiency, given the prolixity of the rest of the *Traité*.[86]

Books 1 and 2 on theory are of primary interest to us, the first concentrating on generating intervals and their combination into chords.[87] The consonant intervals arise from the string divisions we know well (book 1, chapter 3). Having declared the octave to be the "limit of all intervals," Rameau establishes the "rootedness" of the consonant intervals as the fundamental of the octave that encompasses them, later writing succinctly that there are "only three principal consonances, the fifth and the two thirds; from these, the fourth and the two sixths arise."[88] Thus there are "primary" intervals, and derivatives, namely intervals with roots on the bottom and their inversions with roots on top.

Dissonant intervals likewise arise "from the same divisions of the string that produced consonances."[89] But are they really the same? In fact, Rameau

---

centered on counterpoint, inevitably beginning with two parts only. Cf. Fux, *Gradus ad parnassum*, ed. and tr. Alfred Mann as *The Study of Counterpoint*.

85. This is the title of chapter 22 in Rameau, *Nouveau système*, cited and tr. Lester, *Compositional Theory in the Eighteenth Century*, 91.

86. See Christensen, *Rameau*, the most complete and up-to-date source on Rameau as theorist, esp. 51–61 on Rameau's pedagogy of figured bass.

87. Rameau would reverse this procedure in later works: ibid., 90.

88. *Treatise*, 40. Two inversionally related intervals "differ only in that the interval arising from the comparison with the lower and fundamental sound of the octave should be more perfect than the interval arising from the comparison with the upper sound of the same octave." *Treatise*, 13.

89. Ibid., 27.

follows the Greeks in finding the ratio of the major second from the difference of a fourth and fifth; but his minor second is just—the difference of a major third and perfect fourth.[90] He continues by claiming that he could derive the "harmonic dissonances" (the sevenths) from the inversions of these steps, but that they really arise from "the squares of the primary consonances or . . . the addition of two primary consonances." Of the two possibilities, Rameau prefers addition of the third to the fifth.[91] "The other dissonances [the seconds] arise from the inversion of these latter," he writes. Thus it is clear that interval inversion can be extended to dissonant intervals, and that the seventh is the primary interval.[92] But what can the "root of the seventh" be, when, from the outset, Rameau had dismissed the seventh division of the string as "out of tune"?[93] And if the sevenths do not arise directly from harmonic generation as perfect fifths and major thirds do, in what sense are they "harmonic"?

Whereas the major triad is easy to generate, the minor triad is another matter. In the *Traité*, Rameau generates the major and minor triads via arithmetic and harmonic division of the fifth. Reversing Zarlino's procedure, he claims that the two mean-proportions are equivalent within his system, thus treating proportions as he had intervals.[94] This move finesses the problem of minor for the time being: both means yield one major and one minor third, their reverse order apparently inconsequential, "for the foundation of the harmony is never in doubt in the least; on the contrary, it is that which creates all the beauty, the *major* and *minor third* being equally agreeable."[95] Just as he had casually extended the inversion of intervals to inversion of

---

90. He generates seconds of varying sizes through other interval manipulations as well.
91. Ibid., 28 and 32. The "addition" of consonant intervals will become a useful means to produce many different chords, including dissonant ones; see below.
92. Ibid., 28.
93. Ibid., 6.
94. Since Zarlino had measured divisions of strings, and Rameau is measuring string multiples, he reverses the order of proportions to x:x+1, claiming, with regard to harmonic and arithmetic proportions, that "the proof of the uniformity of these two proportions, when the object of one [e.g., major triad] differs from that of the other [e.g., minor triad] only by inversion, is so evident that it is useless to waste time on it" (ibid., 21).
95. "mais le fond de l'Harmonie n'en souffre point, c'est au contraire ce qui en fait toute la beauté, la *Tierce majeure* & la *mineure* y étant également agréables": Rameau, *Traité*, 36. Gossett's translation differs from ours: cf. *Treatise*, 42. See Christensen,

proportions, Rameau extends it to inversion of chords, allying $\frac{5}{3}$ chords with their "inversions," $\frac{6}{3}$ and $\frac{6}{4}$, via their roots.⁹⁶ But the connection between this sort of "inversion" and interval inversion is even vaguer, based as it is on the number of possible rotations of three vertical elements, the combined registral compass of which necessarily oversteps the octave, a point glossed over by Rameau.

In his generation of dissonant intervals, it was clear from his preference for sevenths over seconds that the discussion would soon turn to chords. Zarlino's use of "composite intervals" as a *de facto* method of creating triads from intervals may have prompted Rameau to add thirds above or below triads to create seventh chords. In any case, the construction of "suitable combinations of thirds and fifths" would prove to be a productive, if under-discussed, theory:⁹⁷ "To make matters simpler, we could consider thirds for the time being as the sole elements of all chords. To form the perfect chord, we must add one third to the other; to form all dissonant chords, we must add three or four thirds to one another. The differences among these dissonant chords arise only from the different positions of these thirds."⁹⁸ Rameau invents the dominant seventh chord, minor–minor seventh chord, major–major seventh chord, half-diminished seventh chord, and fully diminished seventh chord—each including all of its inversions.⁹⁹

Rameau, 96, on the appearance of substantially the same idea in *Nouveau Système*, 21.

96. *Treatise*, chapter 8, Article I, 140f.

97. The name for the theory is taken from Lewin, "Two Interesting Passages," 7; also see Christensen, *Rameau*, 98ff. Curiously, for all Rameau uses the theory as a way of generating the chords he needs that he cannot get directly via harmonic generation, he has very little to say about it, in effect leaving subsequent theorists the license to push it to extremes. Schenker is a strict constructionist when it comes to harmonic generation, finding other ways to explain the necessary chords that do not arise directly from that process.

98. *Treatise*, 39.

99. Book 1, chapter 8, Articles III–VII. The 6/5 was recognized by theorists well back into the early sixteenth century, and numerous figured-bass theorists provided instructions on usage of the figures 6/5, 4/3, 4/2 and 7. But recognition of the seventh chord as a structure worthy of specific attention (in effect, a "fundamental harmony") and capable of inversion (and thus yielding these other figures) must be credited to Rameau. See example 3b, 225, in Mitchell, "Chord and Context," for a demonstration of Heinichen's "inversions" of a 4/2 chord. In the particular passage

In *Traité* book 2 Rameau presents his most original theory: his realization that the structure of triads could be converted into laws that account for the intervals by which the roots of chords follow one another. This insight opened the door on the modern two-pronged definition of harmony: a theory of chord content and identity *and* one of chord succession or, as we say, "progression." The result was a return to the ancient Greek *harmonia* of *melos*, only this time, the temporal continuity was controlled by the abstract succession of chord roots, what Rameau called the fundamental bass (*basse fondamentale*), rather than anything approaching a "melody." The notions of chord "root" and "inversion" (which the idea of the fundamental bass also includes) had been known, if not widely used, by theorists, but Rameau's brilliant insight suggested that a theory of vertical sonorities could be made into a theory of "syntax" of tonal music happening in real time—that there could be "laws of progression" in new music at that, demonstrated analytically by the fundamental bass. This idea was essentially unprecedented. The pioneer in real-time harmonic analysis, Rameau put the fundamental bass to pedagogical and occasional analytical use throughout his works, generally creating examples to demonstrate a point at hand, but sometimes taking practical examples of real music; in both he would include an additional bass-clef system on which the fundamental bass was notated.[100]

Just what are the principles of chord progression, and how did Rameau use them? As we mentioned earlier, the laws of fundamental bass motion come down to preference rules for motion by triadic intervals: prefer descending fifths or ascending fourths (less frequently, ascending fifths and descending fourths); only then accept thirds (or sixths); seconds may occur, but they are "licenses" derived from inversions of chordal sevenths—about which Rameau is understandably skeptical—only reluctantly tolerated, and only in ascent. The same rules are still taught in many harmony classes today. Along with the preference for an economical number of fundamental bass motions, Rameau also sought a reduction in the number of chord-types, maintaining that "there are only two chords in harmony: the [consonant] perfect [i.e., major and minor triads] and the [dissonant] seventh."[101] As to *the* domi-

---

Heinichen is discussing, the 4/2 is clearly the fundamental form of the chord from which the other "inversions" depart.
100. Rameau did not use Roman numerals to indicate scale degrees, but rather notated roots of the chords on the fundamental bass staff. Roman numerals as a further generalization of the fundamental bass will arrive as our story continues.
101. *Treatise*, 53.

nant seventh of the key (*dominant tonique*), "it seems to have been made to render all the better the perfection of the consonant chord . . . since the perfect chord or its derivatives must follow it."[102] Thus the upper voices energize the fundamental bass by dissonance-to-consonance resolution, the dominant seventh chord moving to the tonic.

The result was what Rameau called the "cadence," a word used not altogether dissimilarly by Zarlino, but defined substantially as Rameau used it (without the fundamental bass) by seventeenth-century French theorists.[103] The succession that we call V^7–I is for Rameau the "perfect cadence" (*cadence parfaite*), but he defines other cadence types in the *Traité* as well, among which is what we call a deceptive cadence (*cadence rompue*, "broken cadence"), and our plagal cadence, but of a very special type: his *cadence irreguliere*, "irregular cadence," consists of an "added-sixth chord" ($^6_5$) on SD (= scale-degree in the bass) 4 proceeding directly to the tonic. In this case, the $^6_5$ "should be regarded as original" and not as an inversion of II^7.[104]

Though the term "dominant" was used by other French theorists of the seventeenth century, it was Rameau who coined the term "subdominant" (*sous-dominante*) for the chord based a fifth below the tonic.[105] Of course, we know that the chord a fifth below a generating tone cannot be derived directly from its harmonic series, but it can be derived through the cycle of fifths, which in turn can be viewed as modeled by the geometric progression we remember from our discussion of the ancient Greek theory of "means." Indeed, in the continuous progression of 3 : 9 :: 9 : 27, the tonic is not the generator, but it can be regarded as the "mean," surrounded by its two dominants. Once again, Rameau resorts to a modernized version of ancient wisdom in his effort to justify the subdominant via the "geometric triple progression."[106]

---

102. "Il semble être fait pour render plus grande la perfection des accords consonans . . . parce que le parfait ou se dérivés doivent toûjours le suivre." *Traité*, 37.

103. Christensen, *Rameau*, 113f., discusses the origin of these cadence types in French seventeenth-century theory.

104. *Treatise*, 75. Though the figured bass is the same as the one recognized by the counterpoint theorists, the resolution of the chord is very different: in Rameau's version, the 6 is treated as a dissonance to be resolved by step, instead of the 5. On Rameau's ambivalence concerning this idea, see Christensen, *Rameau*, 118.

105. Rameau invented the term in *Nouveau système*, 60–61.

106. See Christensen, *Rameau*, 178f.

Example 3.4. Rameau's *Double Emploi* (Double Employment)

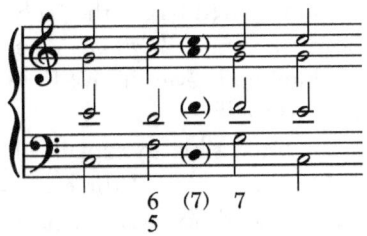

Example 3.5. Rameau's Fundamental Bass Applied to Example from Zarlino

But what if that $^6_5$ proceeds directly to V⁷, as so often happens? In such a case, the root of the $^6_5$ is in fact SD 2, and the progression is part of an "imitation of cadences" (cycle of fifths) model of progression, yielding a most attractive triple progression headed to the tonic (II⁷–V⁷–I). In a later work, *Génération harmonique*, Rameau proffers his theory of "double employment" (*double emploi*) to explain away the stepwise progression that is bound to occur as we shift from the irregular cadence to the perfect cadence: the $^6_5$ over SD 4 is interpreted as IV, heading to I in the irregular cadence, but its "real" root is reinterpreted as SD 2 just before it moves to V in the perfect cadence, signaling an "imitation of cadences," II⁷–V⁷–I (see example 3.4).

This brings two models of harmonic syntax into conflict, both in tension throughout Rameau's work. Perhaps the most important progression is this concatenation of the irregular cadence (later, in *Génération harmonique*, "imperfect cadence") and perfect cadence: IV–with added-sixth–I–V⁷–I. Chord identity and chord progression work in tandem here, for the progression is represented by three chords of different quality and figured bass—the "subdominant" (*sous-dominante*), $^6_5$ "added-sixth chord" (*accord de la grande sixte*) on SD 4; the "dominant" (*dominante-tonique*), dominant-seventh on SD 5; and the tonic (*tonique*) $^5_3$, major or minor triad on SD 1.[107]

Despite Rameau's best efforts, however, it was impossible to explain all chord-to-chord motion by these models. Consider this standard three-part stepwise cadence in the Renaissance style, taken from Zarlino (example 3.5). Rameau, in his attempt to produce a "theory of all music" (or at least the music he found of value), has added a fourth part containing the alleged fundamental bass—a way of hearing the passage that would be unlikely to have occurred to Zarlino, but is no less clever from the purely analytical perspective: the resulting interpretation of the passage is perfectly consistent with Rameau's laws of chord progression. As is clear from his analysis, a dominant-seventh chord may be operative even when its root is not present.[108]

Continuing in this vein, example 3.6 shows the bass in the upper staff of a passage by Arcangelo Corelli (1653–1713) with the composer's figures.[109] The passage is typical of the Italian Baroque. On the third staff, Rameau writes a new fundamental bass (with interpolated chords) and translates the figures accordingly. Needless to say, the new figures change the music profoundly, and show that fundamental bass interpretation is to an extent stylistically dependent, despite Rameau's efforts to make it theoretically neutral. To explain such a common succession of parallel 6/3 chords, he is forced to interpolate basses not literally in the music in order to turn a succession of steps into alternating fifths and the "imitation of cadences." Example 3.7a–b demonstrates that *ascending* stepwise motion is even more troublesome in this respect. Rameau interpolates bass tones under chords that are not their fundamentals, according to his theory of *supposition* (see below), which normalizes interval successions of the bass, but throws the whole notion of *fundamental* bass into question.

---

107. Rameau used this as the primary model in his earlier "Clermont Notes." See Christensen, *Rameau*, 23–26.

108. Grant, "The Real Relationship," 324–38, esp. 325. The example is taken from Shirlaw, *The Theory of Harmony*, 101.

109. Cited by Cohen in his "Rameau on Corelli," 441. Rameau's imitation of cadences brings the passage to a halt prematurely. Corelli's music runs two additional measures to make a standard eight-bar phrase: transposition of the arpeggiation motive down a step yields the essential C♯ in the soprano, moving to the final D.

Example 3.6. Realization of Corelli's Basso Continuo with Rameau's Fundamental Bass Added

Example 3.7a. Bass Figures of Corelli's Version of a Stepwise Ascending Bass

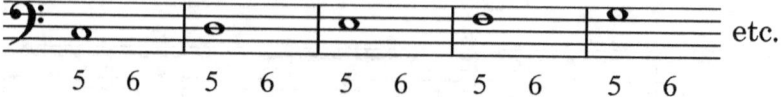

Example 3.7b. Rameau's Harmonization and Bass Figures for the Same Stepwise Ascending Progression

All of the examples we have seen demonstrate that the fundamental bass can be more than an inventory of chord roots. Thus, though many of Rameau's fundamental basses are of the simple root-inventory type, it is clear that he also used the fundamental bass as a device by which to interpret the "harmonic logic" of a chord progression, adding to the written score. Examples 3.2–3.4 also show that Rameau even "interpolated" chords not actually present to normalize "apparent" licenses in progression. We might summarize these uses in five categories that become progressively more abstract: 1. Root inventory; 2. Insertion of root not literally present (but directly implied); 3. Interpolation of root that is possible, but not literally implied; 4. Same as 3, except that harmonic rhythm is doubled with the interpolated root, leading to a more forced interpretation; 5. Double Employment: a chord may imply a choice of two roots, to be selected according to harmonic context.[110] Basses by *supposition* might be added as yet a sixth type, but they are not

---

110. Grant develops what amounts to these five categories in "The Real Relationship," 325–28.

Example 3.8. Five Types of Fundamental Basses

"fundamentals" (at least of the chords above them: see below). We shall refer to these five types of fundamental bass in what follows, citing the types, for example, as "FB 1."

However, since certain progressions fail to acquiesce to the rules of the fundamental bass even using these interpretive devices, the basic vocabulary of triads, seventh chords and the added-sixth chord does not account for all the chords in the figured basses of the period, and thus Rameau needed *supposition*. Particularly in the "Gallant Style," there remain complex figures that can occur when any chord is "displaced" via suspension in its progression to the following chord (see example 3.9).

In *Traité*, book 2, Rameau attempts to account for such figured basses via his theory of *supposition*.[111] Unlike the basic theory of the fundamental bass, which creates an imaginary "fundamental form" of a vertical slice drawn from figured-bass practice, *supposition* reverses that procedure: it takes a fundamental chord, and by "imagining" (or subposing) a bass, creates a suspension chord of figured-bass practice. Standing by his notions that the octave is the cut-off point for chord formation, and that the "major and minor dissonances" (the third and seventh of a seventh chord) are the sources of all dissonance, Rameau places new "imagined notes" (*notes par supposition*) below fully formed seventh chords, in effect transforming the sevenths of seventh chords into descending dissonances of the ninth or fourth/eleventh, or transforming the third of the seventh chord into an ascending seventh. Having come up with a figured bass in which the bass tone is not a fundamental,

---

111. *Treatise*, 88–91.

Example 3.9. Suspension Chords

Example 3.10. Rameau's Six Chord Types by *Supposition*

accord de neuvième | accord de quinte superflue | accord de onzième | accord de septième superflue | accord de quinte superflue et quarte | accord de septième superflue et sixte mineure

Rameau is forced to admit that these "chords" are not invertible, and thus not really generalizable; they are rather descriptions of particular musical contexts. And since their imagined basses are not fundamentals of the upper notes, they are merely "supernumerary." To the extent that theory of the time was focused on teaching chord-to-chord motion (including dissonant figures) in figured-bass practice (and Rameau sought an explanation of all figures according to his system), his radical simplification is certainly understandable, even ingenious. Example 3.10 shows his six chords by *supposition*. It is clear that two, four, five and six are V^7 and VII^7 in D minor suspended against the root and third of the tonic, respectively, while one and three are the same letter-name combinations as two and four, but more flexibly interpretable with regard to tonal function due to the absence of the leading tone. This theory, like implied and interpolated fundamental basses, was destined to provoke controversy and misunderstanding.[112]

---

112. Martin, "Rameau's Changing Views," 122. Our Example 3.10 is borrowed from Martin.

Despite many passages of great ingenuity, even brilliance, this first work of Rameau has its problems, as we have seen, problems that Rameau would attempt to solve throughout his career. To cite a famous example, he was obviously dissatisfied with the explanation of minor presented in the *Traité*, book 1. He puts forth a new, acoustical explanation in *Génération harmonique* (1737): strings that are *multiples* of the fundamental, instead of divisions, resonate sympathetically as well. If this were true, an "F minor" triad, the literal registral inversion of the C major triad generated by the fundamental C, would be generated by the same fundamental. (Of course, this brings up the musical question of just what the fundamental of a minor triad is![113]) But the theory turns out to be false: a longer string tuned to the same fundamental does in fact vibrate when a shorter one is set in motion, but it vibrates only in the part that corresponds to the fundamental of the shorter string; it does not produce a complete minor triad, or the subdominant scale degree, but rather only the tonic. In *Démonstration du principe de l'harmonie* (1750), Rameau admits that the minor triad does not actually sound, but continues to hang on to the idea of sympathetic resonance as a source of minor anyway. Yet he also proposes his new theory of co-generation: in A minor, for example, though A does not generate C, both A and C generate E. A, however, is the "subordinate generator," "forced to follow, in all cases, the law of the first generator" (C).[114] The idea makes some sense in a musical environment in which the major/relative minor relationship is strongly represented, but the notion of two co-existing generators is not unproblematic. Yet Rameau seems not completely convinced anyway, claiming that minor is a product of art, though "indicated" by nature.[115] Late in life he finds the just minor triad, 10:12 :: 12:15, in the harmonic series.[116] This is one of many possible examples showing that Rameau actively rethought the problematic components of his theory throughout his career.

Though Schenker is often remembered for the later wholesale condemnation of Rameau's theory we cited earlier, the theory had a strong effect on his thinking nonetheless. As we will see, Schenker's most important idea in *HL* is his notion of *Stufe* (plural: *Stufen*), translated literally as scale-degree in *HA*. One usage of the term is both idiosyncratic and seminal for all of

---

113. See Christensen, *Rameau*, 162–68.
114. *Démonstration*, 72, cited and tr. in Christensen, *Rameau*, 166.
115. *Démonstration*, 62–64, as cited by Ferris in "The Evolution of Rameau's 'Harmonic Theories,'" 236.
116. Rameau, *Code de Musique Pratique*, 202.

his later thinking, however—the one we have chosen to translate as "essential harmony." He was well aware of the importance of Rameau's ideas as he was writing his Theory of Harmony, crediting him with the invention of the notion of essential harmonies: "Almost at the same time Fux published his work [*Gradus ad Parnassum*], Rameau came out in France with a new theory of chord function, with the theory of tonic, dominant, and subdominant as main chords to which all other chords can be reduced."[117] Schenker concluded: "It was he who created the theory of essential harmonies, that theory which in musical technique . . . represents the complement of voice leading."[118]

The Reception of Rameau's Theory in German-Speaking Lands in the Second Half of the Eighteenth Century

Study of the reception of Rameau's ideas covers a vast territory, much of it still uncharted; but in general, the route his ideas took to enter German-language music theory, and thus to come to Schenker's attention, is relatively clear. Judging from the contents of Schenker's library, that knowledge of Rameau did not come from one of Rameau's works, but from intermediate sources, as we will see below. In fact, that was typical for German-speaking musicians.

After Rameau's death his harmonic ideas continued to gain interest and acceptance, finding their way into many books that dealt with figured bass and counterpoint. The ideas were likely spread by word of mouth and reviews of his work, for the books themselves were relatively unknown, and Rameau never wrote one definitive summary of his ideas.[119] The *Encyclopédie, ou dictionnaire raisonné des sciences, des arts et des métiers* (1751–72)—a grand project of the Enlightenment—began to spread the word, the editors Denis Diderot (1713/31–84) and Jean le Rond d'Alembert (1717–83) having become convinced that Rameau had found the true "science of music." They engaged the *philosophe*, writer, and composer, Jean-Jacques Rousseau (1712–78) to write over four hundred articles on music, the ones on harmonic theory often referring directly to Rameau's ideas.[120]

---

117. *CP1*, xxvii. See also Krebs, "Schenker's View of Rameau."
118. *CP1*, xxvii.
119. Lester, *Compositional Theory in the Eighteenth Century*, 150.
120. See Martin, "Rameau and Rousseau," 100, for a listing of all of Rousseau's articles on harmonic theory.

As the first volumes began to appear there was controversy almost immediately, Rameau claiming, with justification, that Rousseau had distorted his views.[121] For example, in the article "*Accord, en musique*," which appeared in the first volume (1751), Rousseau admitted all inversions of the added-sixth chord and treated the ninth and eleventh chords by *supposition* as full-fledged invertible chords.[122]

Rousseau's editor, d'Alembert, a mathematician of considerable stature but an amateur musician, was also the generator of errors in the articles *fundamental* and *gamme* (scale) that appeared in volume 7 (1757). In these, he showed his musical naiveté by inventing "new" dissonant chords merely by stacking thirds differently (or indifferently); Rameau's theory of "suitable combinations of thirds" had returned to bite him.[123] Yet before committing these and other transgressions, d'Alembert was well on the way to becoming the most important French source of Rameau for later generations, having simplified and organized the master's ideas deductively in a digest, the first edition of which received the enthusiastic approbation of Rameau himself.[124] Friedrich Wilhelm Marpurg (1718–95), the self-proclaimed authority on Rameau's theory in Germany, translated this first edition, thereby making it easily available to German speakers.[125]

D'Alembert only began to be interested in music theory in 1749 through the reading of a paper by Rameau that became his *Démonstration du principe de l'harmonie* (1750), so it is not surprising that most of *Élémens*, book I is taken from this work.[126] Yet d'Alembert asserts his independence in a separate introduction that redefines the relationship between the naturalized theory of harmony and Rameau's theory of chords, opening the way for the debate and epistemological pluralism that would characterize theories of harmony in the nineteenth century. For d'Alembert, Rameau's mysterious and all-powerful *corps sonore* (sounding body) becomes a straightforward

---

121. Rameau, *Erreurs*.
122. Rousseau's revisions of Rameau's system continued to be read by later generations, since he reworked his *Encyclopédie* articles into his *Dictionnaire de Musique*.
123. See his article *fondamental* in the *Encyclopédie*, vol. 7 (1757) and Christensen, *Rameau*, 274.
124. See d'Alembert, *Élémens* (1st ed., 1752). By the time of the second revised and expanded edition (1762), d'Alembert had fallen out with Rameau.
125. d'Alembert, tr. Marpurg, *Systematische Einleitung*.
126. See the concordance showing chapter numbers and their sources in Rameau's *Démonstration* in Christensen, *Rameau*, 256.

empirical axiom from which a series of laws can be deduced: "here, we are not interested in the physical principles underlying the resonance of sounding bodies, much less in the metaphysical basis of our emotional response to harmony . . . Our one goal is to show how the laws of harmony that Artists have found only through trial and error, so to speak, may be deduced from a single experiential principle."[127]

Chapter 1 starts with "three experiments." In the first, d'Alembert generates the major triad with no problem.[128] He adds two additional longer strings in experiment 2, failing, as Rameau had, to generate the minor triad beneath the major triad. The first experiment shows that the major triad is "a work of nature," while the second shows—so d'Alembert claims!—that "the minor mode or genre is given by nature less immediately and less directly than the major mode."[129] In experiment 3, d'Alembert explores the "natural properties" of the octave, claiming octave equivalence as a universal experience, bringing the overtones within a single octave to produce the first tones of a scale, and thus getting right to the practical implications of the three experiments.

Chapter 3 develops the possible pitches of the fundamental bass via the fifths and thirds that emerged from experiment 2, above and below the fundamental (!), while chapter 4 derives the key as a whole from the tonic, dominant and subdominant triads (assembled from the scale). D'Alembert continues in similar deductive manner throughout book I, bringing back the "elements" and techniques in a practical, compositional context in book II, in which the fundamental bass and real-time harmonic progressions are the focus, and "every rule is justified by one of the fundamental principles or elements that had been established in the first book."[130] The deductive (and reductive) structure is nowhere more apparent than in book II, chapter 5: here, d'Alembert reduces the rules of fundamental bass progression to only five, the first three of which may be substituted with three alternate rules.[131]

---

127. See d'Alembert, Élémens, v–vi.
128. In a footnote d'Alembert takes both multiples and divisions of the string, producing tones above and their parallels below the fundamental, preparing the way for experiment 2.
129. *Élémens*, chapter 2, §26, 18 and §31, 21. In the second edition (1762) d'Alembert excised the second experiment, and adopted Rameau's theory of co-vibration. Clearly, he had read Rameau's *Code de Musique Pratique* (1760).
130. Christensen, *Rameau*, 256ff. Book II is taken entirely from Rameau's *Génération harmonique*, chapter 18.
131. *Élémens*, 112–17.

Chapter 6 takes up the rules of harmonization of a melody by fundamental bass in two rules, and the following chapter, on the basso continuo, teaches the use of chord inversions. Surprisingly advanced topics turn up as well, such as *supposition*, in which d'Alembert follows Rameau closely, though he avoids the controversy over the idea via a footnote: "*Supposition* produces that which one calls the *suspension*, and is more or less the same thing."[132] Further brief chapters take up licenses of the fundamental bass, cadences, preparation and resolution of dissonance, finding the fundamental bass of a given figured bass or of a melody—all of this within a modest 172 pages. The book's clarity, accessibility, and efficiency were certainly reasons that it met with immediate success—with reviewers, the public, and even Rameau.

It was this brief digest of Rameau, deemed an oversimplification and musical impoverishment of Rameau's work by recent studies, that became, in Marpurg's translation, one of the two main sources of Rameau for German speakers of the late eighteenth and nineteenth centuries—and very likely the main source of harmonic theory that Schenker connected with Rameau's name, for he in fact owned Marpurg's translation.[133] The other was the work of Johann Philipp Kirnberger (1721–83), three of whose works are also to be found in Schenker's library, including the two that form the basis of the following discussion.

A student of J. S. Bach, Kirnberger nonetheless devised a harmonic theory that bears in some respects the stamp of Rameau, despite his claim that the "Bach-Circle" was "anti-Rameau."[134] His ideas on harmony appeared

---

132. D'Alembert, 134. He goes on to say that the category of *supposition* is broader, encompassing what we would call passing and neighboring chords as well. Rameau does not suggest suspension as a cause of *supposition* until 1760 in his *Code de Musique Pratique*.

133. Christensen, *Rameau*, chapter 9, 252, writes, "the qualities of synthesis and precision that make the Élémens such an accessible work also entail drawbacks. By reducing, reorganizing, and generally simplifying Rameau's theory, d'Alembert also distorted it." Also see Christensen, *Science and Music Theory*, 240, and Lester, *Compositional Theory in the Eighteenth Century*, 144–46.

134. In support of the latter's *Kunst des reinen Satzes*, C. P. E. Bach wrote to Kirnberger that "you can loudly declare that my principles and those of my late father are anti-Rameau." *Kunst des reinen Satzes*, vol. 2, 188, cited and tr. by Lester, *Compositional Theory in the Eighteenth Century*, 93f. In fact, Kirnberger's *Kunst* is the closest thing we have to a thorough documentation of the teaching of J. S. Bach, with whom Kirnberger studied. Wolff writes that "of all of Bach's students, he most deliberately transmitted his teacher's concepts and methods in musical composition,

in volume 1 (1771) and the first part of Volume II (1776) of his book, *Die Kunst des reinen Satzes in der Musik* (*The Art of Strict Musical Composition*), one of the most important music-theoretical treatises of the second half of the eighteenth century. Two years after the publication of the first volume of *Kunst des reinen Satzes*, another digest of a famous theorist's ideas appeared, this time summarizing Kirnberger's work.[135] Again, debts to Rameau were obvious, if unacknowledged. There is some controversy as to whether Kirnberger himself or his student Johann Abraham Peter Schulz (1747–1800) actually wrote the book, but Kirnberger's name appears as author on the title page, and there is agreement that he stood by its contents, though it uses Rameau's fundamental bass, types 2–5, more prominently than *Kunst des reinen Satzes* does, a feature that may be due to Schulz. While d'Alembert, the amateur, offered little beyond simplified Rameau in a logical and readable form, the Kirnberger–Schulz *Die wahren Grundsätze* presents an original synthesis of harmonic and contrapuntal theory clearly, accurately, and succinctly.

In fact, this brief digest of Kirnberger, who, as remarked earlier, gave us the closest thing we have to a compendium of J. S. Bach's teaching, may have had the greatest effect on the reception of Rameau's fundamental bass by German-speaking musicians. It certainly had that effect on the Viennese music-theoretical curriculum Schenker studied as a conservatory student.[136] Perhaps this study inspired Schenker to go directly to the source, and acquire three Kirnberger treatises (including *Kunst des reinen Satzes* and *Die wahren Grundsätze*) for his personal library. He owned all of the ones of greatest interest.

---

particularly in his major two-volume treatise *Die Kunst des reinen Satzes in der Musik.*" Wolff, *Johann Sebastian Bach, the Learned Musician*, 331.

135. *Die wahren Grundsätze zum Gebrauch der Harmonie*, tr. Beach and Thym as "*The True Principles for the Practice of Harmony.*"

136. The original runs to thirty pages of text and fifty-one pages of musical examples. Marpurg has been regarded as a source too in the past. Kirnberger's work was attacked by Marpurg in 1776, and a controversy ensued: not surprisingly, Marpurg held that *he* was the true transmitter of Rameau's ideas, and that Kirnberger was an interloper who had misunderstood them. Recent scholarship points to Kirnberger as the primary source of Rameau's fundamental bass (his most important doctrine) for the Austro-Germanic readership, however: Marpurg claims that only FB 1 is "authentic." See Lester, *Compositional Theory in the Eighteenth Century*, 231–57 for an excellent summary of Kirnberger and Marpurg.

Kirnberger transformed the acoustical basis of the theory of harmony into a very practical discussion of tuning and temperament—a starting point Bach likely would have taken with a student well aware of the basics of theory, as the intended reader of *Kunst des reinen Satzes* is described in the book's introduction.[137] A discussion of scales and intervals follows, the latter derived from the former. Kirnberger goes on to maintain that the two basic harmonies are the "consonant triad" and the "dissonant seventh chord." However, he admits all diatonic triads and seventh chords into these categories, showing a figured-bass orientation.[138] The only exception here is the 6/4 chord. Kirnberger speaks of both a consonant and a dissonant 6/4: the former is the product of harmonic theory; the latter a chord in which the 6 and 4 are prepared and resolved as suspensions, just as figured-bass theorists generally treated it.

In fact, suspensions prove to be of the greatest importance to Kirnberger's system, for instead of attempting to derive all figured-bass chords from the prototypical chords and their inversions by various manipulations of harmonic generation, he views the remaining bass figures as linear and temporal displacements of the two prototypical figured-bass chord-types and their inversions. Having shown the figured basses that occur when the voices of a triad and its inversions are displaced by step, Kirnberger proceeds to present example 3.11, which demonstrates the figured basses that occur when the voices of the "essential dissonant chord" and its inversions are displaced by step.[139]

The resulting dissonances are termed by Kirnberger *zufällig* (non-essential), and it is clear that the suspension is the model.[140] Thus the non-essential

---

137. *Kunst des reinen Satzes*, tr. Beach and Thym as *The Art of Strict Musical Composition*, 9.
138. Kirnberger places the chords in a hierarchy of "least to most perfect": major, minor and diminished triads; and Mm7, mm7, dm7, MM7. (*Die wahren Grundsätze*, tr. as *"The True Principles,"* §2, 169). The construction of these categories demonstrates an approach to the problem through the figured bass, not abstract harmonic theory, since each of the seventh chords or triads would have the same figured bass within the diatonic signature of a major or minor key. (Kirnberger also reads dissonant diminished triads and half-diminished seventh chords that are the upper notes of an incomplete dominant-seventh chord.)
139. Kirnberger, *Kunst des reinen Satzes*, Tabelle IV, 33.
140. Kirnberger–Schulz, *Die wahren Grundsätze*, tr. as *"The True Principles,"* §7, 176: "The essential dissonance can occur on a weak as well as a strong beat, whereas the non-essential dissonance can occur only on a strong beat."

Example 3.11. Kirnberger's Table Demonstrating Stepwise Displacements of Seventh Chords

(a) The seventh chord with suspensions.

(b) The six-five chord with suspensions.

(c) The six-four-three chord with suspensions.

(d) The chord of the second with its suspensions.

(e) The essential dissonant chord with suspensions in the bass.

dissonance is not an integral part of the chord.[141] The dissonance that is *wesentlich* (essential), on the other hand, is the seventh of a seventh chord, which, instead of resolving during the time of the chord at hand, resolves with the arrival of the next chord, and is an integral part of the prototypical dissonant chord.[142]

Though famously conservative in his musical tastes, Kirnberger recognized the "lighter styles," and had original ideas about how his categories of dissonance applied to them as well. For one thing, in these styles, resolutions of dissonances are often transferred to other voices.[143] Moreover, non-essential dissonances could also resemble essential ones, and gather together to assume the form and duration of a "chord." Yet that simultaneity does not behave like an essential harmony. With regard to examples 3.12a, in the strict style, and 3.12b,[144] in the "Gallant Style," Kirnberger writes: "In the strict style the notes marked with an asterisk would be passing notes: thus they would have to be of short[er] duration and fall on unaccented beats. But the free style is not bound to this rule, so that these sevenths can last a full measure." Clearly, Kirnberger is as concerned as Rameau with preserving a small number of allowable fundamental progressions that behave consistently, and obviously "I–II7–I6" is not one of these, particularly since the "chordal seventh" acts as a consonant pedal, while the "root" is actually a passing tone. The important point is that Kirnberger invokes a contrapuntal explanation of "passing tones" instead of a harmonic one to explain the apparent license. The result is that only the I and I6 chords are chords with harmonic value, and if a fundamental bass line were included in the examples, it would be

---

141. It is important to note that Kirnberger never applied the terms "essential" or "non-essential" to chords. He simply had no term for passing chords in *Kunst*: he only used *wesentlich* and *zufällig* to refer to the interval of the seventh, to get, by implication, the "essential seventh chord" taken from Rameau, or the seventh as a displacement of a $^6_3$ chord. In *Die wahren Grundsätze* Schulz called them *Zwischenakkorde* (intermediate chords) that connected *Grundakkorde* (fundamental chords).

142. "Essential" and "non-essential" have become fairly standard translations, though *zufällig* is more properly "accidental" or "incidental." The disadvantage of "non-essential" is that the clear reference to the duality of "essence" vs. "accident" in the Aristotelian analytical tradition is lost: "A definition is a phrase signifying a thing's essence" (Aristotle, *Topics*, Bekker 101b/37); "An accident is something which . . . may either belong or not belong to any one . . . thing" (Aristotle, *Topics*, Bekker 102b/4–7). See Barnes, ed., *Aristotle*, vol. 1, 169–70.

143. *Kunst des reinen Satzes*, tr. as *The Art of Strict Musical Composition*, 101–3.

144. Ibid., examples 5.9–5.10, 104–5.

limited to these two chords. Though fundamental bass (*Grundbass*) staves are only added occasionally in *Kunst des reines Satzes*, Kirnberger's thinking is oriented by the fundamental bass nonetheless, but with an overlay of contrapuntal thinking. For example, he sees the diminished-seventh chord as an incomplete dominant ninth chord, the seventh treated as a change-of-bass 7–6 suspension, the resolution of which is delayed until the arrival of the I chord.[145] Thus, the fundamental bass of the diminished-seventh chord is Rameau's fundamental bass, type 2.

In *Die wahren Grundsätze*, the fundamental bass is explicit, the notion of a passing chord also more fully defined: "In harmony there are passing chords [*durchgehende Akkorde*] that are not based on any fundamental harmony . . . Passing chords are intermediate chords [*Zwischenakkorde*] that are formed by the stepwise and mostly consonant progression of one or more voices from the preceding to the following fundamental chord . . . Passing chords can be further recognized by their unnatural harmonic progression."[146]

The notion of passing chords is generally limited to one at a time, though Kirnberger–Schulz recognize larger-scale alternations of passing chords and resolutions that occur against a pedal. When a pedal is not literally there and they need to explain longer progressions that we might see as "passing," they interpolate basses to normalize the progression. Examples 3.14a and b[147] show two progressions of parallel six chords, the interpretations of which resemble the opening of Rameau's interpretation of the ascending scale in our earlier example 3.7b. Yet it is also important to note the differences. Kirnberger–Schulz treat the ascending and descending scales as sopranos of the standard progression of parallel six chords, imagining a fourth-species syncopation of the soprano, 5–6, 5–6, etc. The inferred bass is a sequential alternation of ascending fourths and descending thirds in the first instance, and the cycle of fifths of diatonic seventh chords in the second. Unlike Rameau's analysis of example 3.7b, these analyses remain plausible even today, though the order of derivation might be reversed: the progression of parallel six chords without the fundamental bass certainly has priority historically, and if counterpoint is taken to be an independent generator of a musical texture and not necessarily dependent on harmony, theoretically as well.

---

145. *Die wahren Grundsätze*, tr. as "*The True Principles,*" 181, examples 12a and 12b.
146. Ibid., §18, 193.
147. Ibid., 201–2, examples 61–62.

Example 3.12a. Passing Chords in the Strict Style

Example 3.12b. Passing Chords in the Lighter Style

Example 3.13. Passing Chords in *True Principles for the Practice of Harmony*

Example 3.14a. Parallel Six Chords in *True Principles for the Practice of Harmony*

Example 3.14b. Interpolated Basses Explain Successions of Six Chords

Kirnberger–Schulz develop Rameau's use of the technique of inferring additional basses further still. Their most abstract technique might be called "harmonic ellipsis":

> When great harmonists want to express something intense or want to startle the listener, they take the liberty of omitting the resolution of the essential seventh completely. That is, the consonant chord which would result from the resolution of this dissonance is omitted, and another dissonant chord, which should have followed the omitted one and whose dissonance would have been prepared by it, is immediately taken in its place.

As in the case of *supposition*, this technique amounts to a sixth stage in Grant's analysis of Rameau's fundamental bass: both the bass and the chord inserted are not interpretable as "missing components" of a chord already there; in fact, they displace that chord, as the tonic does the dominant. It is significant that these latter analyses generally take place in the "freer styles, i.e., Kirnberger–Schulz are thinking of "strict composition" as a model from which the "licenses" of the freer styles depart, but in clearly describable ways.

This is characteristic of a northern German tradition that dates back into the seventeenth century, in the work of Christoph Bernhard (1628–92) and Johann David Heinichen (1683–1729).[148]

Harmony in the Early Nineteenth Century

In this last segment of our history of harmony, we concentrate on two very different theorists: (Jacob) Gottfried Weber (1779–1839) and François-Joseph Fétis (1784–1871). Weber and Fétis published their theories in 1817–21 and 1844 respectively, though Fétis had been working on his since the 1820s.[149] Both shifted the focus in the theory of harmony to its epistemology, Weber taking a totally empirical tack, while Fétis took a (not entirely unexpected) Cartesian starting point.

As this part of our story unfolds, the basic tenets of Rameau's theory were well known internationally, but the epistemology of the theory of harmony was very much a matter of debate, as were even some of its practical details— in particular, the use of the fundamental bass beyond FB 1. Clearly, the dogmatic presumption of natural-base theory had become untenable to many, and the search was on for a new starting point. Moreover, for many, theorizing without literal notes on the page, as Rameau had done, was suspect. Each of our theorists had a different angle on these questions, as we shall see.

Gottfried Weber, a German active in Mannheim, Darmstadt, and Mainz, was a lawyer, civil servant, and composer, largely self-taught as a music theorist. His *Attempt at a Systematically Arranged Theory of Musical Composition*, as the contemporaneous translation has it, is self-consciously compositional

---

148. Christoph Bernhard, *Tractatus Compositionus Augmentatus* and Heinichen, *Der Generalbass in der Composition*. Bernhard and Heinichen were active in Dresden, not far from Leipzig, where Kirnberger studied with Bach in 1741, or in Berlin, Kirnberger's eventual home on returning from an extended period in Poland.

149. Weber, *Versuch*, tr. Warner as *An Attempt at a Systematically Arranged Theory of Musical Composition*. Ludwig Holtmeier has characterized this book as a "fundamental work [*Urschrift*] of the German *Harmonielehre* tradition." *Die Musik in Geschichte und Gegenwart*, vol. 2, s.v. "Weber, Gottfried, Critical Appraisal." Fétis, *Traité complet*, tr. Landey as *Complete Treatise on the Theory and Practice of Harmony*. According to Landey, the book developed from Fétis's first treatise on the subject written in 1816; it was published in 1823 without most of its theory as a purely didactic work (the *Méthode élémentaire*). Landey writes that Fétis claims the *Traité* was the culmination of forty years of thought on the subject (translator's introduction, xxxiv).

and theoretical. He wrote from a critical and completely empirical point of view, rejecting the notion that certain progressions of the fundamental bass were "forbidden," as well as all of the theory of antiquity or its rebirth as acoustical theory, claiming that "most teachers of musical composition imagine that the theory of musical composition must necessarily be founded on harmonic acoustics . . . But this seems to me . . . pedantry. One may be the profoundest musical composer, the greatest contrapuntist; one may be a *Mozart* or a *Haydn*, a *Bach* or a *Palestrina*, without knowing that a tone is to its fifth as 2 to 3."[150] Perhaps, but Bach, for one, would certainly disagree.

This rejection of the natural base had profound effects on Weber. Though accepting the theories of chord rootedness and inversion as a practical heuristic in the formation of his chord categories, he went on to reject any interpretive use of the fundamental bass beyond Type 1.[151] Indeed, he attempted to theorize harmony with no preconceptions, and thus instead to evolve his own "neutral" theory of chord progression from a completely empirical examination of musical examples, propounding a descriptive and data-driven theory—a kind of naive positivism. Wiping the slate clean, he asks: how many harmonic progressions are there? The answer, 6888: "each of the fourteen harmonies appropriate to a [major] key may be followed by one of the thirteen others belonging to the same scale . . . 14 x 13 = 182."[152] After performing similar calculations to arrive at his total, he begins the exhausting task of categorizing them (during which he comes back to some standard categories, after all).

Certainly the gestation and purpose of his treatise had much to do with the approach: with no obvious pedagogical application, the work was a kind of diary, documenting his critical confrontation with the theories of harmony of the past.[153] A perspicacious critic, of our four theorists he was the least active as a pedagogue, making his living mostly as a civil servant. Yet ironically it was he who made perhaps the greatest contribution to pedagogy of the four: Roman numerals. First used analytically in the 1770s by the theorist (Abbé) Georg Joseph Vogler (1749–1814), they were popularized

---

150. Weber, *An Attempt at a Systematically Arranged Theory*, 22.
151. Curiously, the only exception was the diminished-seventh chord, which he saw rooted a third lower, even when the root was not explicitly stated.
152. Weber, *Attempt at a Systematically Arranged Theory*, vol. 2, chapter 5, 407–8.
153. See Lemke, *Jacob Gottfried Weber*, 206–19 for the background on the writing of the work.

by Weber's treatise.[154] It was through this work that they found their way into schoolbooks in conservatories in continental Europe, Great Britain, and America.[155] In fact, in analytical notation in general, Weber produced innovations that continue to be used today, such as "fake-book" notation for chord-types outside of tonal context: C, C^7, etc.; upper- and lower-case letters and Roman numerals to signify major and minor triads and seventh chords; the sign (°) to signify the diminished triad (one of his seven fundamental harmonies); or even the letter followed by a colon indicating the key of an analysis, or an analysis in one key that continues into one in another key at a different height on the page to demonstrate modulation—all were Weber's innovations. Two summary remarks are appropriate here. Firstly, Weber's Roman numerals made the fundamental bass conveniently applicable to all keys with essentially no change: the fundamental bass that had arisen from a *particular* figured bass was now abstracted from that phenomenon. Moreover, the use of both Roman numerals and letter notation left musical notation behind completely. Secondly, the result was to put the emphasis on a symbolic notation as the essence of a "harmonic analysis," an analytical direction that would be developed in the second half of the nineteenth century by the German theorists we discuss in chapter 4. In their hands, Weber's naive positivism acquired the theoretical underpinning it needed, but the analytical notation became ever more abstract at the hands of these later theorists, and the examples from the literature disappeared. It was against these developments that Schenker reacted in his return to natural-base theory, and most importantly, his restitution of musical notation as essential to the music-analytical enterprise: his treatise, in its original form, contains 376 musical examples.

Fétis, a Belgian active in Paris, lived in the political and cultural capital of France—the European center of musical "progress" of the time. A towering figure in the history of nineteenth-century musicology, he, like Weber, also composed, was a journalist, and a music theorist of considerable influence (his *Traité Complet* went through nine editions). As one of the first historians of music theory, he was well aware of competing theories of harmony. Fétis wrote from a refreshingly anthropological point of view, knowing that contemporaneous Western art music was not the only music that existed,

---

154. See Grave and Grave, *In Praise of Harmony*; the introduction (1–11) offers a useful overview. Weber was friendly with Vogler, as well as Vogler's student, Carl Maria von Weber (no relation).

155. Richter, *Lehrbuch*; Jadassohn, *Lehrbuch*. Also see Thompson, *History of Harmonic Theory in the United States*, chapter 1.

and that early European music as well as music of different cultures beyond Europe would demand different theories. He popularized the term "tonality" (*tonalité*), coined originally by Alexandre-Étienne Choron (1771–1834), for the particular system in which each type of music was composed, speaking of the "tonality of Gregorian Chant," as opposed to the "tonality" of music of his own time.[156] Yet it was always clear that the latter, which he called "modern tonality," was his real interest, and the main subject of his *Traité complet*. "Complete" did not imply a theory of all music.

In his days at the Paris Conservatoire around the turn of the nineteenth century, controversy raged over the merits of the theories of Rameau (the only ones known at the time, according to Fétis) versus those of Charles-Simon Catel (1773–1830), whose harmony book had been made the official textbook of the conservatoire by committee decision in that post-revolutionary era. Fétis claims to have rejected both, but some influence of their theories on his work is detectable nonetheless. Like Weber, Fétis rejects all starting points for a theory of harmony outside of the music itself, but he is not one to ponder examples from the literature. No naive empiricism for Fétis. Experiencing a kind of Cartesian epiphany, he claims to have found that elusive starting point in the system he has imposed on "tonality," the vague definition of which suggests the flexibility of the idea and its potential cultural relativism. In his words: "Tonality resides in the melodic and harmonic affinities of the notes in the scale, from which results the quality of necessity in their successions and aggregations. The formation of chords, the circumstances that modify them, and the laws of their succession are the necessary results of this tonality."[157] Fétis begins by detailing the relative "repose" (or its absence) residing in each scale degree. SD 1 has both repose and "knowledge of the key and mode." But how is it possible for a scale degree to carry all of this information? Is Fétis thinking of this scale degree as a generator (or at least "carrying") a tonic chord? As he continues with these assessments, it becomes clearer that he *is* thinking of them in particular tonal contexts, but essentially as "bass notes," as a figured-bass theorist would, and that the Rule of the Octave may well be lurking behind all of this. Thus SD 2 "is not a note of repose," and cannot be "accompanied" by the fifth, which is an interval of repose, without effecting a "vague change of tonality." Rather, "the intervals that preserve the tonal character of the second degree are the sixth, the third, and the fourth, which combine in various ways in

---

156. See Simms, "Choron, Fétis, and the Theory of Tonality."
157. Fétis, *Complete Treatise*, 246f. Also cited in Shirlaw, *Harmony*, 336.

the harmonies of the chords."[158] In other words, harmonize SD 2 as a bass tone with 6 or (more rarely) $\frac{6}{4}$, or 6/4/3. SD 3 "is completely opposed to any feeling of repose, and consequently excludes the harmony of the fifth ... the harmonies that, alone, belong to the third degree are the sixth, because it excludes the idea of repose ... and the third, the character of which determines the mode."[159] In other words, harmonize SD 3 as a bass tone with a 6 chord. But what if SD 3 is a soprano in a tonic chord? Or the root of a III chord? Fétis could have made the whole matter much clearer by describing his scale degrees as bass tones, unless otherwise specified.

The explanation of SD 4 is particularly interesting: it has the character of "momentary repose," and thus may be accompanied by a fifth, though more frequently it is accompanied by the sixth.[160] But there is another sort of SD 4 as well, to which Fétis devotes a separate paragraph: it may also combine with SD 7 to form the "appellative consonance" (*consonance appellative*) of the tritone, which "calls forth" scale degrees 1 and 3 (taken together, an "imperfect consonance") for resolution.[161] Thus Fétis essentially returns to Rameau's two fundamental chords (which he calls the "perfect chord" and the "natural dissonant chord"), but allegedly from a melodic point of view.[162] Once again, Fétis has a clear harmonic (or figured-bass) context in mind, though he would likely claim reverse causality: that the harmonic contexts he will gradually fill out occur because of these mysterious melodic "affinities" built into the scale. In any case, the two points of view are inextricable—though Fétis tries to separate them anyway.

Trying to characterize the melodic behavior of scale degrees in common-practice music without direct recourse to harmony proves to be hazardous, but the text gets clearer when chords become the principal topic in book II. The reader will recall that in the discussion of Rameau, we contrasted the "cadence model" with the "cycle-of-fifths model." Fétis in effect rejects both of them. With respect to any sequential chord progression he writes:

> This succession and this movement fix the mind, which holds on to the form so strongly that any irregularity of tonality [e.g., the root-position triad on

---

158. Fétis, *Complete Treatise*, 20.
159. Ibid., 21.
160. Ibid., §40, 16.
161. Ibid., §41, 16. These are more properly $\hat{4}$-$\hat{7}$-$\hat{1}$-$\hat{3}$.
162. In book II he christens them the "perfect chord" (major or minor triad in root position) and the "natural dissonant chord" (dominant seventh).

VII] is not noticed . . . Through an ascending or descending progression on all degrees of the scale, the mind, absorbed in the contemplation of the progressive series, momentarily loses the feeling of tonality, and regains it only at the final cadence, where the normal order is reestablished.[163]

Fétis concludes that "harmony" is likewise suspended in patterns of parallel six chords, in descent or ascent.[164] Even the cadential model consists only of V^7–I, for Fétis's doctrines of "substitution" and "prolongation," ideas that have their likely origin in Catel, enable him to view any II^7 pre-dominant chord as a melodic displacement of the dominant.[165] Example 3.15 shows the dominant displaced by a combination of substitution (A4 substitutes for G4), and prolonged with the seventh of the apparent II^7 serving as a suspension. Thus in Fétis's theory there are really only two harmonic "states": the music in question is either on the tonic, or (briefly) on the dominant. Or harmony has been "suspended."[166]

Very likely aware of the early evolutionary theory of Jean-Baptiste Lamarck (1744–1829), Fétis proposed an evolutionary theory of the tonality of common-practice music, based upon the salience of particular modulatory techniques.[167] The *ordre monotonique* characterized early Western music before the advent of transposition and modulation; the *ordre transitonique*, the music of the seventeenth and especially the eighteenth century, in which diatonic modulation was most prevalent; the *ordre pluritonique*, the music of Fétis's own time, in which diatonic modulation was still operative and important, but chromatic and enharmonic modulation were becoming more and more prevalent. Finally, he envisioned a future with music composed in the *ordre omnitonique*, in which all tonalities were present simultaneously. As apposite and indeed, in some respects, prescient, as these categories might appear, they remained identified with Fétis alone (though Liszt, for one,

---

163. Ibid., 27.
164. Ibid., 35.
165. Ibid., 80.
166. Curiously, there appear to be no examples of IV moving directly to V in Fétis's *Traité*.
167. Lamarck, *Recherches sur l'organisation des corps vivants* (1802); *Philosophie Zoologique* (1809); *Historie naturelle des animaux sans vertébres* (7 vols., 1815–22). Fétis devotes the four chapters of book III of the *Complete Treatise* to an exposition of each historical stage of tonality. See 149–94.

Example 3.15. Fétis's "II^7 Chord" Created by Suspension

Harmony without suspension   Same harmony with suspension

wrote a piece in what he thought of as the *ordre omnitonique*).[168] The general term "tonality," however, caught on. Modified as "monotonality" by Schoenberg,[169] it would be used often to characterize the music in which modulation to temporary tonalities was embraced by an overall tonality, the music that was of primary interest to Schenker. Moreover, Fétis's reduction of his theory of harmony essentially to the dominant and tonic is strongly suggestive of Schenker's theory. Did Schenker ever read Fétis? We do not know, but it seems most unlikely.

Some Lessons Learned from the History of Harmonic Theory

The reader who expected a lengthy discussion of voice leading to be an important part of the theory of harmony may be surprised—or disappointed. The preference for non-parallel voice motion arose relatively early and continued in full force. And once the theory of voice leading came together with the refinement of rhythmic notation in the fifteenth century, allowing for the precise control of dissonant intervals, the *essential* features of dissonance usage—preparation, dissonance and resolution—began to be clarified relatively quickly. Some vagueness with regard to their melodic profile persisted into the sixteenth century, but it dissipated with Zarlino's codification of the *prima pratica* in mid-century. By the end of the century a debate arose between theorists addressing the *prima pratica* versus those invested in the new *seconda pratica*, the defenders of the latter claiming that the expression of secular—and more dramatic—texts demanded licenses in preparation and resolution of dissonance. The advent of figured bass had much to do with

---

168. See Berry, "The Meaning[s] of 'Without.'" On the "Prélude Omnitonique" (ca. 1844), see 257f.
169. See Schoenberg, *Structural Functions*, 19f.

this controversy, since dissonant intervals of the second, seventh, ninth, and tritone supported by seventh chords were becoming "on-the-beat" components of figured-bass accompaniment—certainly in part because of demands of text expression. But once unleashed by the text, these sonorities began to take on a life of their own. This was the beginning of the modern notion of "harmony," captured in Rameau's model of dissonant-chord-to-consonant-chord "progression." As dissonant intervals became integrated into simultaneities, harmony itself gained a broader range of "harmonic fluctuation" and potential expressiveness.[170] Schenker, however, was already on the fence with regard to the status of "dissonant chords," even as he wrote *HL*, as is apparent from his insistence upon a categorical distinction between consonance and dissonance (while essentially avoiding discussion of the latter), and general downplaying of "chords."[171]

It is perhaps surprising that much of the previous discussion has to do with tuning, which, after all, may have seemed like a dead issue—once EQ presumably took over. But the "pure triad," and its tonal environment, just intonation, once valorized by Zarlino, continued to live on in theories of harmony through the nineteenth century. Indeed, the nineteenth century *in particular* witnessed many attempts to revive just intonation in practice, and to design keyboard instruments to accommodate it.[172] Whether claims that it never really existed in practice are correct or not,[173] it became an idealized pitch space in which the rules of harmony were truly at home, and continues today to be highly regarded by some music-cognition specialists. And even temperament, it has been argued, was not truly equal until around the beginning of the twentieth century, when tonal environments close to what Fétis might have heard as his *tonalité omnitonique* began to emerge.

Yet more surprising is just how much of the history of harmony is concerned with the origin and nature of the tonal system, the various means by

---

170. Hindemith, *Craft*, vol. 1, 115. Though Hindemith uses the term to describe the process in his own system, the term could conveniently apply to the fluctuation between consonant and dissonant harmony in the more conventional sense as well. That Hindemith coined such a term and appropriated the expressive "fluctuation" of consonant and dissonant harmony for his own highly original system shows how important this concept became in harmonic thinking.

171. *HA*, 131: "Only those intervals are to be considered as consonant which, either in their root position or inverted, can be reduced to the simple proportions 1, 2, 3, 5 in the series of overtones."

172. See Jackson, *Harmonious Triads*.

173. Barbour, "Just Intonation Confuted."

which it may be generated and understood, and, once alternatives to natural-base theory were imagined in the late eighteenth and nineteenth centuries, the alternative epistemologies that might come with it. Most of this seems to have been forgotten in "harmony" as taught today. Indeed, today's definition of harmony as "the combining of notes simultaneously, to produce chords, and successively, to produce chord progressions" completely ignores the attempts to build a foundation for the *theory* of harmony, attempts that were part of continuing conversation—and controversy—from the ancient Greeks to the beginning of the twentieth century, at which point the theory of harmony started its descent into "common-practice harmony," a movement already well underway in the pedagogy of harmony when Schenker began his theoretical work.

The Historical Position of Schenker's Early Theory of Harmony

Schenker's unprecedented return to the Classical theory of harmony cannot be over-emphasized. Two features that were essential to the ancient Greek view are prominent: *melos*, or the melodic content of the music, and *system*, the means of organizing that content. Schenker reinterpreted both, in light of music of his day and some elements he preserved from the Modern Theory of Harmony. They both come together right at the outset of *HL* in the opposition of motive, the creation of the artist, and system as modeled on nature (the major system) by the artist via a "hint" given by her, or developed by the artist in looser analogy to the natural system (the minor and mixed systems). In either case, the role of nature has shrunk considerably over the one accorded her by other natural-base theorists. For while Schenker attempted to preserve a highly constricted role for nature (very likely to fend off the "unnatural" music of the Viennese avant garde, in which "dissonant chords" were "emancipated"), he expended most of his effort on exploring the compositional techniques developed by the artist, the exploration of which was the *raison d'être* of the book as a whole. The combination of nature and the artist was a unique approach to the epistemology of harmony. Others accepted nature as the source and arbiter of the laws of harmony, or saw music as a cultural construct, but no one else attempted to find a place for the actual musical practitioner as creator of tonal material, compositional techniques, and the resulting language using the mere hint nature had provided. This is demonstrated by Schenker's incorporation of the "artificial" motive into the basic components of the theory of harmony (unheard of at the time), and the opposition of motive versus system that runs throught *HL*. The result is a conception of harmony equally applicable to melody as well as polyphony. Schenker's initial demonstration of harmony via examples of melody provides evidence of this fundamentally revolutionary approach to the topic. Both the combination of nature and the artist and its reflection in system versus motive may have influenced Schoenberg in the writing of his *Harmonielehre*, but we must leave such a conjecture hanging.

The question arises then, of just what, if any, components of the Modern Theory of Harmony Schenker preserved. First there is the *Naturklang*. Schenker may be considered by some as the natural-base theorist *par excellence*, but his book establishes nature's role, and moves on almost immediately to the role of the artist as inventor of the musical language. (Even the major mode, directly constructable via the hint, must be filled out by the subdominant, the invention of the artist.) While the tonal material is drawn from *Naturklänge*, generated in ascent, in a series of ascending fifths—except for the one all-important descending fifth—even these are then "adjusted" so that each letter-name inflection that results from the generative process is altered, if necessary, to be consistent with the prevailing diatonic set. And all of this is subject to temperament, the invention of the artist that makes the closed system of tonality a possibility. Second, there is the chordal vocabulary, which Schenker passes on with essentially no critical revision, until Jonas forces the text into a revision of the nature of seventh chords in *HA*. But it is surely not a revision Schenker would have accepted in 1906, before completing *KP1*. Third would seem to be Rameau's fundamental bass, for the bass always assumed a crucial role for Schenker in determining his analysis of essential harmonies, and it was very likely Rameau and a reaction against Rameau's simplistic succession of chord roots that led Schenker to think further about the nature of bass lines and their history. With Schenker that fundamental bass has been modified considerably, for instead of being a succession of chord roots with possible interpolations, the bass is necessarily a melodic entity: Schenker is interested in the melodic contour of real bass lines in compositions, looking closely at the ways in which particular spans of these bass lines mark "composings-out" (a term he uses already in *HL*, though not as a noun). Indeed, the composings-out of harmonic spans in the bass mark the birth of Schenker's most prescient idea in the treatise: the "essential harmony," descended from Kirnberger's idea, which Schenker surely knew—given his ownership of all the important works of Kirnberger—but which he developed as a primary area of interest, rather than as a way to justify progressions that Rameau had forbidden. It is this positive exploration of the "essential harmony" and indeed the notion that its use is perhaps the most important contribution of composers of genius that sets Schenker's ultimate theory apart from any other. And the seeds of that idea are clearly sown throughout *HL*.

Chapter Four

Sources of Schenker's Intellectual Methodology in 1906

The Conflict between the Human and Natural Sciences in Schenker's Education, Music Theory in the Later Nineteenth Century, and His Reaction to Both

While the technical content of music theory in the nineteenth century may be seen in many respects as evolving fairly smoothly from earlier ideas, the intellectual methodology underlying it changed quite radically, as we have seen in the cases of Weber and Fétis. This was largely a consequence of educational reforms that occurred in the aftermath of the French Revolution, and continued into the next century. The founding of the new conservatories in the first half of the nineteenth century meant that music instruction was now available to a much larger public in urban centers, a public large enough that they had to be taught in classes. "Music theorists" suddenly had the possibility of becoming classroom teachers.[1] Established in 1795, the Paris Conservatoire became a model for many others throughout Europe and

---

1. We place the job title of music theorist in quotations, since "job opportunities" were slim for such an individual before the unprecedented growth in colleges

beyond. Fétis, a Belgian, spent virtually his whole career in the conservatory environment, first in Paris, where he studied and taught from 1821 to 1833, and then in Brussels, where he became the first director of the Conservatoire royal de Bruxelles in 1833. While two other important theorists of the first half of the century, Simon Sechter (1788–1867) and Moritz Hauptmann (1792–1868), began their careers teaching privately in the eighteenth-century tradition, they were later appointed professors at the conservatories in Vienna (founded 1817) and Leipzig (founded 1843). We recall Sechter's debt to eighteenth-century theory, made clearer now after the discussion of Rameau reception in chapter 3. We take up the work of Hauptmann a bit later in this chapter.

The new research-oriented universities, which were rapidly beginning to resemble their modern counterparts, also opened up to music theory. The most important figures in German-language music theory of the latter half of the nineteenth century, Hermann von Helmholtz (1821–94) and Arthur von Oettingen (1836–1920), were based in universities, as was, ultimately, Hugo Riemann (1849–1919), the towering figure at the turn of the twentieth century. As universities expanded and changed their missions, so music theory, always a hybrid discipline, began to borrow from intellectual sources previously unavailable. While Helmholtz and Oettingen began to focus on the theory rather than the practice of music, Riemann attempted to make their work—and that of Moritz Hauptmann—"practical." To understand these competing music theories and the way that Schenker's early work fits in with them, it is helpful to consider briefly the wave of educational reforms that were enacted in the early nineteenth century and to see how they shaped Schenker's own educational experience.

Educational Reforms in the Early Nineteenth Century: The Human Sciences (*Geisteswissenschaften*) versus the Natural Sciences (*Naturwissenschaften*)

Though entirely independent of the universities, the new conservatories received their mandates during the larger movement of educational reform that began in the German-speaking countries in 1808–10, marked in particular by the founding in 1810 of the new university in Berlin—today the

---

and universities in the US after World War II. See Girard, "Music Theory in the American Academy."

Humboldt University, named for its founder, the statesman and scholar Wilhelm von Humboldt (1767–1835). The Prussian reforms, overseen by Humboldt, called for the secularization of the universities—an idea that was not well received in Austria, where the Catholic Church held great power over the curriculum. Although the reforms took time to be accepted there in the politically and educationally repressive age of Metternich, they were implemented more consistently after the revolutions of 1848, even in provincial schools.[2] Schenker's Galicia had undergone a period of intense Germanization during the first half of the century, the period in which his parents grew up. While the uprisings of 1848 brought with them a swing back to dominance of the Polish language, German language and culture surrounded him at home, and were secure among the educated—and particularly among teachers and administrators in the schools.[3] Nonetheless, his university registrations indicate that he considered Polish his native language until very late in his formal education.

Fundamental to secondary and tertiary education among German speakers was the classically inspired notion of *Bildung*, which rose to prominence during the Enlightenment and became central to Humboldt's thinking.[4] The English word "education" is insufficient as a translation, for *Bildung* denoted a broad approach that celebrated the cultural history of Europe, reaching back to ancient Greece and Rome. *Bildung* was non-careerist and lifelong: it tried to inculcate the student with the ability and desire to continue the process via self-education. The notion was fundamental to the education received by Schenker, who was always proud of the breadth of his interests.

---

2. Rothfarb, "Henryk Szenker."

3. Ibid.

4. *Bildung* is sometimes contrasted with *Erziehung*. The literal meaning of the verb *bilden* is "to form," and is often applied to the education of older students (*Studenten*), meaning "to educate culturally in the more general sense." The contrasting verb *erziehen*, from *herausziehen*, "to draw out of," is often applied to the education of younger students (*Schulern*), meaning "to train, nuture, bring up." Thus it makes sense that in the context of reforms of Austrian schools, in which the philosophy of Johann Friedrich Herbart (1776–1841) figured prominently, *Erziehung* "usually designated the process of shaping a young person's character and morals." See Coen, *Vienna in the Age of Uncertainty*, 6. On Herbart, see below. That Austrian education was essentially a moral education at all levels is underscored by Rothfarb, "Henryk Szenker," and Alpern, "The Triad."

A philosopher, historian, and linguist, Humboldt proposed that prospective university students should be taught ancient Greek, Latin, German, mathematics, physics, geography, history, and religion in secondary schools.[5] Humboldt's emphasis on learning ancient Greek and Latin as part of the general curriculum was something that he himself had learned from Friedrich August Wolf (1759–1824), the neo-humanist and founder of modern philology. With regard to Greek in particular, according to Wolf, "the study of its grammar helped develop formal mental discipline, and its literature presented the pupil with the best available examples in an original, unmixed form."[6]

Such preparation for university education was, and still is, carried out in an institution known as a *humanistisches Gymnasium*.[7] Schenker attended three *Gymnasien,* two of which were in the Galician capital, Lemberg, a cultural center with a conservatory run by a Chopin student, Karl Mikuli, from whom Schenker "received musical encouragement."[8] The state-mandated curriculum he studied followed Humboldt's model, with the addition of languages spoken in Galicia and two philosophy courses required everywhere in the Austrian Empire after 1848. When he went on to the University of Vienna in 1884, Schenker went directly to legal studies at the age of sixteen, attesting to the high level of his ability and accomplishment, and the quality of the preparation he received in his *Gymnasium* education.

---

5. See Albisetti, *Secondary School Reform in Imperial Germany*, 20.
6. Ibid.
7. The German plural is *Gymnasien*. The origin is from the Greek γυμνασιον, which originally indicated a place where the education of both mind and body took place, the Classical Greek ideal. Only the latter meaning has survived in English. Sometimes rendered as "high school for the humanities," neither the content of the education nor the age of the students are precisely comparable to Anglo-American educational models. In Austria, students typically finish the *Gymnasium* at eighteen years of age, and take the *Matura* exam to demonstrate their accomplishment. Schenker finished at sixteen! Considered the equivalent of a bachelor's degree, the Matura leads to university study that begins with work towards a masters. This was the case until recently, though the system now seems to be moving much closer to the Anglo-American model in response to the international conference in Bologna in 1999, the resulting "Bologna Declaration," and subsequent meetings. Austria was one of twenty-nine signatories of the declaration, which mandates a three-year university sequence culminating in a bachelor's degree, and only then study towards the master's and doctorate. See Austrian Ministry of Education, *Education in Austria*.
8. Federhofer, *HS*, 4.

The concept of *Bildung* also guided reforms of the universities, which were gradually transformed into modern research institutions through the efforts of Humboldt and his collegue, the theologian and philosopher, Friedrich Daniel Ernst Schleiermacher (1768–1834). In Schleiermacher's view, the function of the university was not simply to transmit "recognized and directly usable knowledge, but rather to demonstrate how this knowledge is discovered, 'to stimulate the idea of science in the minds of students, to encourage them to take account of the fundamental laws of science in all their thinking.'"[9]

One important consequence of these reforms is that the research of faculty and students became increasingly specialized. Gradually, it became necessary to distinguish between the *Geisteswissenschaften*, which we might now refer to as the "humanities" and "social sciences," and *Naturwissenschaften*, which covers the "natural sciences."[10] Although this distinction, which was already apparent in the medieval *quadrivium* and *trivium*, soon prompted debates about the status of different disciplines, "the ethic of *Wissenschaft* was the *raison d'être* of the entire modern university system."[11] It is a point

---

9. See Rüegg, ed., *A History of the University in Europe*. vol. 3, 5.

10. The term *Geisteswissenschaften*, which is now used more narrowly and usually translated as "humanities," is applicable here, but in a broader sense than "humanities," for the status of the newly rising "social sciences" (most important for this study, psychology) was not yet clear. The term was invented in the 1880s by Wilhelm Dilthey (1833–1911) as part of his ambitious research program to bring the natural and social sciences as well as the humanities together by demonstrating "eine erkenntnistheoretische Grundlage der Geisteswissenschaften," which Frederick Beiser translates convincingly—given the breadth of Dilthey's project—as "an epistemological foundation for the sciences of mind." See F. Beiser, *The German Historicist Tradition*, 323. This goal is announced is Dilthey's *Einleitung in die Geisteswissenschaften* (1883), which remained incomplete; also see Masur, "Wilhelm Dilthey and the History of Ideas," especially 96–97, and below. The reform of the *Gymnasien* and universities described here was the ideal, but in reality, old educational practices held on in the empire more tenaciously than reformers might have wished, though the reforms certainly had their impact by the time Schenker was in school. See Cohen, *Education and Middle-Class Society in Imperial Austria 1848–1918*, 20–23.

11. Beiser, *The German Historicist Tradition*, 19. It is interesting to note in this regard that though university educated, Schenker, as a theorist, was not university based, which may have given him more intellectual—and thus methodological—freedom in formulating a theory of harmony.

that Schleiermacher underscored in no uncertain terms, to cite the complete quotation from which Rüegg has abstracted a small part:

> To awaken the idea of systematic scholarship [*Wissenschaft*] in the more noble youth, who are already armed with a certain level of attainment [*Kenntnisse*]; to promote scholarship through its mastery in that area of discovery [*Erkenntnis*] to which each student wants to dedicate himself, so that it becomes instinctive to them to view everything from the point of view of scholarship [*Wissenschaft*]; to see each detail not on its own, but in its most immediate scholarly [*wissenschaftliche*] associations, and to draw it into a large context in continuous relationship to unity and totality [*Allheit*] of knowledge [*Erkenntnis*] so that the students learn to become conscious of the basic laws of scholarship [*Wissenschaft*] in all thinking and thereby gradually work out for themselves the ability to research, invent and present knowledge—*that* is the business of the university.[12]

Unfortunately, the word *Wissenschaft* is particularly difficult to translate: there is no English word that will do in all contexts in which it appears, as is apparent in our translation. Scholarship may seem too neutral, but it does capture the idea that there are underlying principles of reasoning that are common to all branches of research at the university, whereas "science," without further qualification, is too easily taken as "natural science" by the English speaker in the published translation of Rüegg.

The translation of *Wissenschaft* is not the only issue: there are also difficulties in rendering the compounds *Geisteswissenschaft* and *Naturwissenschaft*. The noun *Geist* is especially problematic: is it "spirit" or "mind"? "I conceive of the theory of harmony . . . as a world purely of the mind [*eine bloß geistige Welt*], as one of ideally moving forces," Schenker wrote at the opening of *HL*.

---

12. Rüegg's original source is Schleiermacher's "Occasional Thoughts on Universities of the German Type." "Die Idee der Wissenschaft in den edleren, mit Kenntnissen mancher Art schon ausgerüsteten Jünglingen zu erwecken, ihr zur Herrschaft über sie zu verhelfen auf demjenigen Gebiet der Erkenntnis, dem jeder sich besonders widmen will, so daß es ihnen zur Natur werde, alles aus dem Gesichtspunkt der Wissenschaft zu betrachten, alles Einzelne nicht für sich, sondern in seinen nächsten wissenschaftlichen Verbindungen anzuschauen, und in einen großen Zusammenhang einzutragen in beständiger Beziehung auf die Einheit und Allheit der Erkenntnis, daß sie lernen, in jedem Denken sich der Grundgesetze der Wissenschaft bewußt zu werden, und eben dadurch das Vermögen selbst zu forschen, zu erfinden und darzustellen, allmählich in sich herausarbeiten, dies ist das Geschäft der Universität."

The adjectival form of the word, "geistig," which, in this phrase, we translate in its modern sense as "a world purely of the mind," is often translated in earlier historical contexts as "spiritual" (as it is, incorrectly, we believe, in *HA*, where the same phrase is rendered as "a purely spiritual universe"). One consequence of the growth of psychology as a discipline in the nineteenth century was that much of what was regarded as "spiritual" early in the century was taken over into the "psychological" realm by its end.[13] Here the problem of *Geist* is exacerbated, for *Geisteswissenschaften* is essentially a catch-all, covering a number of different disciplines that range from history, which we, today, typically classify as a member of the humanities, to psychology and sociology, which are now regarded as part of the social sciences, as well as legal studies, which we usually treat as an autonomous discipline. Certainly, all three deserve the status of *Wissenschaft*, though the knowledge they produce is contingent, not transcendental, to use Kant's terms.[14] As a translation of *Geisteswissenschaften*, as Schenker understood the word, we have settled on the phrase "human sciences." It covers Schenker's frequent invocation of psychological arguments that are oriented towards the individual (composer, listener, or even the anthropomorphized tone), but also his reliance on legal arguments that are directed at larger groups (e.g., the "society of tones"). It even covers the historical narrative that underlies *HL*. Schenker clearly borrowed methodologically from the human sciences—and purposely not from the natural sciences—in the construction of his *theory* of harmony.

Surprisingly, the word *Natur*, as used in *Naturwissenschaften*, can be problematic as well, though not because of its translation *per se*, but because of the breadth of its usage, in either language. Very generally, whereas *Geisteswissenschaften* study human beings as well as their cultural and artistic products, both as individuals and as members of a society, *Naturwissenschaften* study the natural world. They do so by combining strictly controlled observations of particular phenomena with systematic analysis of the resulting data. This

---

13. The main title of Reed's *From Soul to Mind: The Emergence of Psychology from Erasmus Darwin to William James* captures this well. Though focused primarily on Anglo-American sources, the book also draws in psychological theory and experimentation in Germany, Austria and German-speaking Switzerland.

14. Immanuel Kant (1724–1804), *Kritik der reinen Vernunft*. In essence, Kant's *Critique* provided a philosophical grounding for the exact sciences, limiting a priori knowledge to only that which was based somehow on experience, and thus seriously limiting metaphysics (most of which had to be grounded in moral philosophy) and removing "values"—obviously essential to the human sciences—from the realm of "pure" knowledge.

approach, frequently referred to as the "scientific method," often involves articificially constructed experiments, carefully observed and evaluated, and sophisticated mathematical models. Although such methods can be applied to any object of study, both "natural" and "man-made," controlled experiments are much easier to carry out and more reliable for studying some phenomena, e.g., falling objects, than for others, e.g., human behavior. But "nature" can be an essential concept in the realm, for example, of aesthetics or jurisprudence (e.g., in the concept of "natural law"). We attempt to spell out the role of "nature" contextually in our use of "natural science," though on occasion, to make distinctions clearer, we use the more modern distinction between the "exact sciences" (mathematics, astronomy, optics and physics, in particular, but certainly not exclusively), the social sciences, and the "humanities," the latter two grouped together in the category of the "human sciences." We shall have more to say on these matters at the end of our discussion of Riemann, and in our discussion of Schenker and philology.

The nineteenth-century division of scholarship becomes more complex still when we consider the overall structure of the European universities as they had been since the middle ages, as exemplified by the University of Vienna (founded 1365). As was typical, it was divided into theological, legal, medical and philosophical faculties, ranked in that order within the institution's power structure. The philosophy faculty, which stood lowest in rank, was charged with preparing students during their first two years, the "philosophicum" years, and as such for many provided the foundation of their entire education. Although Schenker apparently skipped these classes for the "higher studies," he was nonetheless taught by one of the most prominent professors from the philosophy faculty; this instruction surely instilled in him the highest standards of scholarly achievement.

From what we know of Humboldt and Schleiermacher, it is not surprising that work in the human sciences—principally in "systematic" scholarship in ancient languages and texts—was in the vanguard of the new university movement.[15] However, by the second half of the nineteenth century, the exact sciences had certainly caught up with and even outpaced the human sciences, and the new social sciences gathered momentum as well, as they began to emulate the methods of the exact sciences. By now, psychology was becoming a field of research on its own. The movement towards the hegemony of exact sciences of the modern era had begun, though the direct threat had been felt at least as far back as the 1830s and 1840s in August Comte's

---

15. See Daston and Most, "History of Science and History of Philologies."

"Positivism," from which we have received the adjective "positivist[ic]" that remains popular today as a near-equivalent of "exact-scientific."[16]

But advocates of the human sciences were unwilling to give up without a fight, and they were aided by the establishment and growth of new disciplines. Historiography—a close examination of the epistemology of history—was one such discipline and would carry the banner of the human sciences into the twentieth century.[17] Since rhetoric had always been taught from Classical historical texts (Herodotus, Thucydides, Livy and Caesar), history had always been part of the *trivium* and had called for some level of philological expertise. By the seventeenth century, however, evidence was mounting that history was a *Wissenschaft*, a branch of scholarship with its own methods—a "collective memory," as it were—even if it could not lay claim to the production of transcendental knowledge. But contingent knowledge was itself vital, was it not? For historicists, nothing can escape history, including the *Naturwissenschaftler*: there was (and for many, still is) no Archimedean point outside of history from which to construct a purely formal theory.[18] The historicists began with a critique of historical method and, by the late eighteenth century, several German academies demanded that primary sources be consulted and cited in any historical studies that they published.[19] Not long afterwards, the discipline of philology emerged through Wolf's work at the University of Halle. Wolf was the first to defend the so-called "analytic theory" of Homeric poetry in which these works were seen as composites of several authors or editors.[20] And though the collecting of antiquities has a long history, archeology also developed rapidly as a discipline: for example, Pompei and Herculaneam were excavated in the late eighteenth century and sites at Troy were uncovered by

---

16. See August Comte (1798–1857), *Discours sur l'Esprit positif* (*A General View of Positivism*).

17. This presumes that one ends the historicist tradition with Max Weber (1864–1920), as Beiser does in *The German Historicist Tradition*, 511–67.

18. This is a criticism Dilthey leveled at Kant in the 1880s.

19. Beiser, *The German Historical Tradition*, 16.

20. *Prolegomena ad Homerum* (1795). See Bolter, "Friedrich August Wolf." The theory, adumbrated in a primitive form in Giambattista Vico's *Scienza Nuova* (1744), made its way to the analysis of Gregorian chant in the 1970s, via Milman Parry's and Albert Lord's work on Balkan poetry. See Lord, *The Singer of Tales*, and Treitler, "Homer and Gregory."

Heinrich Schliemann (1822–90) in the 1870s.[21] Professional geography also originated at the Berlin University with work of Humboldt and Carl Ritter (1779–1859): "The German concepts of cultural and anthropological geography and landscape (*Landschaft*) influenced the development of archeology, anthropology, and geography in many other countries ... and the distribution map, another development of this tradition, had been central to European landscape archeology, historical geography, and ethnology."[22] History also influenced the study of theology and law.[23] Faculties of theology and jurisprudence established their own chairs in history, the University of Göttingen even establishing a number of chairs in history within its law faculty.

The reforms recommended by Humboldt and Schleiermacher effectively reversed the structure of faculties, putting the philosophy faculty at the top of the hierarchy: Philosophy "alone was critical while other faculties rested on authority; it alone gave a systematic grasp of the whole extent of knowledge; it alone could teach people scientific thinking as such. The ascent of philosophy to supreme place in the hierarchy meant a corresponding elevation for its old appendage. History, once the aid of the lower faculty, now became the page of the highest."[24] With the rise of the philosophy faculty, skirmishes arose between philosophers and historians that threatened to obscure the real battle between the human sciences and the natural sciences. But by the 1860s, Idealism and the Hegelian historical method were in general disrepute, and the catchphrase was "back to Kant," and his rejection of a priori knowledge unrelated to experience. Wilhelm Dilthey (1833–1911) presented an inaugural lecture for his professorship in Basel, in which he called for a "critique of historical reason," paraphrasing Kant's titles. His dream of such a critique would set the agenda for his entire career, for he hoped to do for the human sciences what Kant had done for the *Naturwissenschaften* in his *Critique of Pure Reason* some hundred years earlier.

---

21. In evoking the severity of the situation that music found itself in at the turn of the last century, Schenker wrote, at the beginning of *KP1*, "We stand before a Herculaneum and Pompeii of music! All musical culture is buried; the very tonal material—that foundation of music which Artists, transcending the spare clue provided by the overtone series, ceated anew in all respects from within themselves—is demolished" (CP1, xvii). The "natural base" shrinks to very little in *KP1*.
22. Majewski and Gaimster, eds., *International Handbook of Historical Archeology*, 170.
23. Beiser, *The German Historical Tradition*, 21.
24. Ibid., 22.

Endeavoring "to understand human life in its own terms," Dilthey was convinced that "any attempt to force the vast field of the humanities into the strait-jacket of the so-called scientific method was doomed to failure."[25] The human sciences formed a cohesive whole, as the exact sciences did, and must have a coherent basis, but one that was very different. Dilthey's approach to that basis was through his notion of *Verstehung*, or "understanding," as opposed to the construction of law- and causality-based "explanation" (*Erklärung*) characteristic of the exact sciences.[26] Thus an introspective and descriptive psychology must be essential to the human studies: we must try to know *how* we understand. Meanwhile, philosophy "should aim to preserve the scope that idealists such as Fichte, Schelling and Hegel once gave it, but . . . must do so by recapturing the Kantian rigor that had been lost and by applying it empirically."[27]

In a second phase of his work, Dilthey wrote that "we explain through purely intellectual processes, but we understand through the cooperation of all the powers of the mind activated by apprehension."[28] Thus the immediacy of perception is essential too: the world is not some "theoretical representation," but is rather experienced as an embodiment of "values that are relevant to our purposes."[29] In his late work, Dilthey realized that inner experience was not enough, and thus stressed our access to history, and the need for such objectification, ultimately turning specifically to the history of ideas as a primary point of reference.[30] As the *Wissenschaft* of the human intellect, psychology was the basis of his enterprise, but one might see the other nascent social sciences, which stand somewhere between the human sciences and the exact sciences, as closely allied, when we move beyond personal introspection to the study of whole societies.

---

25. Masur, "Wilhelm Dilthey and the History of Ideas," 95.
26. Dilthey's approach provoked a controversy with Wilhelm Windelband (1848–1915), who stood much closer to the exact sciences with his contention that the basis of humanistic science was "idiographic" (centered on the discovery of specific facts or processes) while that of the exact sciences was "nomothetic" (focused on the discovery of general laws).
27. Makkreel, "Wilhelm Dilthey," *Stanford Encyclopedia of Philosophy*, https://plato.stanford.edu/entries/dilthey/, accessed January 10, 2018.
28. Dilthey, "Ideas for a Descriptive and Analytic Psychology" (1894); quoted ibid.
29. Ibid. "Values" had no place in Kantian science.
30. Masur, "Wilhelm Dilthey and the History of Ideas," 95.

Dilthey's work was a highpoint, but also one that epitomized the problematic relationship of the natural and human sciences in German-speaking universities in the second half of the nineteenth century. We cannot point to a document that proves Schenker knew it, but his professors certainly did and he certainly heard about it in classes. The problems Dilthey faced and solutions he formulated were essential to the environment in which Schenker's university education operated. Not surprisingly, it was from music theory of the past that Schenker derived much of the content of *HL,* though he took on some of this baggage critically and reluctantly, and certainly presented it in a very original fashion. But *HL* was also a *theory* of harmony, and, as such, Schenker drew his arguments and language primarily from the *Geisteswissenschaften,* rather than the methods and language of the *Naturwissenschaften* endorsed by Helmholtz, Oettingen, and Riemann, to whom we turn shortly. But before considering the state of music theory at the end of the century and Schenker's reaction to it, we need to examine the education that Schenker received, and his preparation for his life's mission.

Schenker's *Gymnasium* Education

Schenker was certainly inclined towards the direction he took in part because of his home upbringing and education. We have no record of his education before he was sent to *Gymnasium* at age eight, but Rothfarb goes into the "habits of mind" he would have been taught at home from a very early age, whether or not he was home-schooled.[31] His father, Johann Schenker (1828–87), was a physician who clearly brought a scholar's approach to his calling, keeping up on all the latest research.[32] Schenker's earliest memories surely included his father studying medical books in his home library. Indeed, the father clearly was an important and admired presence in the young man's life, for Schenker dedicated *KP1* "to the memory of my father." Schenker's formal education consisted of piano study, eight years in three *Gymnasien* (1876–84), four years of study of law at the University of Vienna (1884–88), and three years of musical study at the conservatory in Vienna (1887–90);

---

31. See Rothfarb, "Heinrich Schenker and ibn Ezra," 33–38.
32. "[Moriz] Violin notes that Dr. Schenker 'fled, day and night . . . to the beloved library, to his professional journals, in order to keep abreast constantly of all the new discoveries and progress made within the medical sciences.'" Translated by Kevin Karnes, in "Heinrich Schenker and Musical Thought," 35–36.

he completed his law degree in 1890, having taken time for study at the conservatory.[33]

At the age of eight, two years younger than his cohort, Schenker was sent to Lemberg, the provincial capital (today Lviv, in the Ukraine), to the Franz-Joseph Gymnasium (the Third State Gymnasium), where he spent his first three years (1876–79); he then spent a year in the Fourth State Gymnasium (1879–80), likewise in Lemberg.[34] During those years he presumably studied piano, though no details on that study are known. He transferred for his last four years (1880–84) to the Brzezany (English, "Berezhany") Gymnasium, much closer to home. There are later reports from his fellow students in Vienna of his superior intellectual prowess, but he was apparently an extraordinary student throughout his academic career, ranking first in his class throughout his time in Lemberg, despite his youth, and either first or second in Brzezany, graduating with honors at the top of his class from that institution.[35] Table 4.1 provides an overview of the *Gymnasium* curriculum he studied, and the hours of instruction in each subject.

It is clear that it was essentially Humboldt's curriculum, with the addition of local languages, and philosophy and psychology courses mandated by post-1848 Austrian educational reforms. As we expect, table 4.1 shows the curriculum to be particularly impressive for its study of classical languages:

---

33. Federhofer, *HS*, has more on Schenker's musical education than other sources. Still, Schenker's musical education in Vienna has yet to get the attention it deserves, though according to *HS*, 5, documents concerning his study at the conservatory are preserved in the library of the Gesellschaft der Musikfreunde. He studied piano at the conservatory with Ernst Ludwig, and theory with Franz Krenn (1816–97). Krenn, the author of *Generalbaß-(Harmonie) Lehre zum Selbstunterricht* (Vienna: Haslinger, 1845), and a church musician like most theory teachers of the time in Vienna, was strongly influenced by Albrechtsberger. See Wagner, *Die Harmonielehren*, 22. Krenn clearly followed in the figured-bass tradition (as late as 1845!), as is obvious from the description of chord-types in Wagner's book (38), and from the following suggestive quotation from Krenn's book: "the full cadence is a completely satisfying close; the chords of which it consists are the dominant chord and the tonic; the preparatory chords may be whatever they wish" (Wagner, 42).
34. Rothfarb ("Henryk Szenker," 20) writes that available documentation places Schenker in the sixth grade of the Franz-Joseph Gymnasium in Lemberg during the school year of 1877–78 at age nine, two years younger than fellow students, but that "he must have attended that gymnasium in the 1876–77 school year as well."
35. See Rothfarb, "Heinrich Schenker and ibn Ezra," 38.

Table 4.1. Schenker's *Gymnasium* Curriculum and Hours of Instruction

Year	1876–77	1877–78	1878–79	1879–80	1880–81	1881–82	1882–83	1883–84
Grade	5th	6th	7th	8th	9th	10th	11th	12th
Subject								
Religion	2	2	2	2	3	3	3	3
Latin	8	8	6	6	6	6	5	5
Greek			5	4	5	5	4	5
Polish	3	3	3	3	3	3	3	3
German	6	5	4	5	3	3	4	4
Ukrainian					3	3	3	3
Geography	3	2	2	4	4	3	3	2–3
History		2	1	w/Geog.	w/Geog.	w/Geog.	w/Geog.	w/Geog.
Math	3	3	3	3	4	3	3	2
Nat. Hist.	2	2			2	2		
Nat. Sci.			2	2				
Physics							3	3
Phil. Prop.							2	2
TOTAL	27	27	28	29	33	31	33	32–33

Source: Rothfarb, "Henryk Szenker," 24.

Schenker learned the full complement of Latin grammar and syntax, with accompanying selected readings, in the lower division, and in the upper read literature by numerous Latin authors, among them Livius, Vergil, Cicero, Tacitus, and Horace, and selected passages in verse from Ovid's Metamorphoses ... The Greek curriculum, which starts halfway through the lower division (in grade 7), begins with an intensive study of grammar (word forms and inflections, verb forms and conjugations, regular and irregular), reinforced by translation exercises from Greek into Polish and, unusually, Polish into Greek! Upper-division studies continue with advanced work in grammar and syntax, and introduce excerpted passages from Greek literature as well as, later, the reading of complete plays, for instance Sophocles's King Oedipus and Philoctetes, readings from Demosthenes, and selected chapters from Homer's The Iliad and The Odyssey. In assessing the depth of instruction in Latin and Greek, we can compare with modern-day university study of classical languages, and conclude that Schenker's course of study would satisfy the requirements of today's undergraduate major in both languages.[36]

Schenker subsequently put his Latin study into practice in his legal study, reading all primary sources in Roman law in the original language during his first two years of study. Examining his *Gymnasium* curriculum as a whole, of particular interest are the courses in logic and the "propaedeutic philosophy" course that he studied in his last two years. One result of the civil strife of 1848 was the *Entwurf der Grundzüge des öffentlichen Schulwesens in Österreich* (Draft of the Essential Features of Public Instruction in Austria), which, among many demands, called for two years of university-level study of philosophy to be moved back to the *Gymnasium*. This may be one reason why Schenker started directly with the legal curriculum at the university. The first course dealt with formal logic, rather than presenting a chronological survey of philosophers or philosophical trends. The state saw the logic course as a "neutral" path that trained the mind while avoiding "dangerous" ideas from Kant or Hegel. As Rothfarb describes it,

> The course, following Kremer's text [Józef Kremer, *Poczatki logiki dla szkól srednich* (Beginnings of Logic for Secondary Schools, Kraków: Drukarni Uniwersytetu Jagiellonskiego, 1876], begins with chapters on the foundations and laws of thought and reasoning, on differentiating logic and psychology, on the law of identity, of contradiction/non-contradiction, and of excluded

---

36. Rothfarb, "Henryk Szenker," 38. Rothfarb cites the opinion of classicist and historian of music theory Thomas Mathiesen in this regard.

middle, the notions of simple and complex concepts and their scope, etc. With the foundations in place, the instruction introduces classic Aristotelian syllogisms using Euler diagrams ... the course would prove to be an ideal introduction for Schenker for the study of law at the University of Vienna, in which the analysis and refinement of an argument was a central discipline.[37]

The second course was an introduction to psychology—at the time, a very young science in its ascendency, and surely an exciting one for a student of Schenker's caliber. The book that he studied was Johannes Crüger's introductory text, in Polish translation.[38] The course focused on empirical psychology, and was based upon ideas from the philosophy of Herbart. His philosophy had been established as the "official" philosophy taught in Austria by Franz Exner (1802–53), a philosopher, advisor to the minister of education in the post-revolutionary period after 1848, and teacher (at the University in Prague) of Robert Zimmermann.[39] Zimmermann, who had himself studied with Herbart as well, was one of Schenker's professors in his legal studies.

Among Herbart's main interests was education, and thus it is not surprising that his ideas would form the basis of a beginning course in psychology. His educational philosophy set Austrian education on a new course, for he had "modified Leibniz's term 'apperception' to denote assimilation of new presentations ["mental images" or "ideas"] by old ones of a similar kind. This notion underlay a pedagogy that prized teaching by means of association rather than by rote."[40] Thus the philosophical doctrine of associationism found practical application in the Austrian educational system. It would also find its way into *HL*, so it is appropriate that we return to it and explore its history more deeply here.

Associationism first arose in antiquity. The notion that the essential connection of ideas is via similarity, contrast, contiguity or frequency of occurrence dates back to Aristotle's "On Memory," though the modern history of the doctrine is often said to have begun with the chapter "On the Association

---

37. Rothfarb, "Henryk Szenker," 12–15.
38. Crüger, *Grundriss der Psychologie*. See Rothfarb, "Henryk Szenker," 53.
39. Franz Exner was also the father of Adolf Exner, Schenker's teacher of Roman law. See Coen, *Vienna in the Age of Uncertainty*, which centers on the extraordinary Exner family.
40. Johnston, *The Austrian Mind*, 282.

of Ideas" by John Locke (1632–1704).[41] Locke's means of associating ideas by "natural correspondence," and "chance or custom" seem hardly an improvement on Aristotle, however. The idea, this time much closer to Aristotle's view, was picked up and developed by David Hume (1711–76), who adds, most significantly, cause and effect, and drops frequency of occurrence: "to me, there appear to be only three principles of connexion [sic] among ideas, namely, Resemblance, Contiguity in time or place, and Cause or Effect . . . Contrast or Contrariety is also a connexion among Ideas: but it may perhaps, be considered as a mixture of Causation and Resemblance."[42] The British empiricist development of the idea reached its apex in the eighteenth century in David Hartley's weighty *Observations on Man* (1749), "which proposed a complete associationistic account of human mind and behavior."[43] Hartley's ideas held sway for at least the next seventy-five years, influencing even those of Wordsworth and Coleridge.[44]

By the middle of the nineteenth century associationism had become an area of research within the nascent field of experimental psychology. In Germany, it was taken up by such luminaries as Helmholtz, and the father of German experimental psychology and founder, in 1879, of the first laboratory dedicated to empirical study of psychology and experimentation in Leipzig, Wilhelm Wundt (1832–1920). Wundt received the idea not from British writers, but from Herbart.[45] However, he accepted it critically as one of many alternative directions.[46]

Crüger's *Gymnasium* textbook adds detail to the theory of associationism through the notion of *Reproduktion*, also taken from Herbart.[47] Reproduction is specifically directed to the temporal extension of associations.

---

41. Barnes, ed., *Aristotle*, vol. 1, 714–21, esp. 717. Also see https://en.wikipedia.org/wiki/Association_of_ideas accessed September 17, 2016; Locke, *Essay*, vol. 1, 527–35. This chapter was added to the end of book II in the fourth edition (first edition, 1690; fourth edition, 1700). Locke was actually not the first "modern" to take up the idea. Among others, Thomas Hobbes (1588–1679) speaks of the succession, sequence, series, etc., of ideas, but Locke appears to be the first to propose specific types of associations of ideas.
42. Hume, *Enquiry Concerning Human Understanding*, 22.
43. Leahey, *A History of Psychology*, 162.
44. Hartley, *Observations on Man*, v.
45. Rieber, ed., *Wilhelm Wundt*, 78.
46. Wundt, *Grundriss der Psychologie*, 15ff.
47. Herbart, *Lehrbuch der Psychologie*, 44.

"Reproduction occurs when mental images that have 'faded' (*verdunkelt*) over time are recalled to ('reproduced' in) immediate consciousness by new ones related in specific ways to faded ones."[48] Four types of reproduction turn out to bear resemblances to types of associations from past theories: "images that were in consciousness together (simultaneity); that occur immediately after one another (succession); that resemble one another (similarity; analogy); and that are opposed to one another (contrast)."[49] We note that three of the four—similarity, contrast and succession (contiguity)—are from Aristotle, whose contribution to the topic, as we see by now, simply cannot be overstated. We also note their similarity to Schenker's approach to "likeness." Crüger's idea that "images that ... occur immediately after one another [repetition]; that resemble one another [*Gleichnis*, similarity or analogy]; and that are opposed to one another [counter-image or contrast]" are related by "association" surely influenced Schenker's ideas on ways to treat motives presented in WEG in the section "On Motive Itself" and elsewhere.

Schenker's Study at the University of Vienna

Schenker arrived in Vienna, the capital and seat of the central bureaucracy of the Austro-Hungarian Empire (so-called after the 1867 *Ausgleich* with Hungary) in the fall of 1884 to study at the University of Vienna, the flagship institution. It was the year that the university's new main building, constructed in the Italian Renaissance style, opened for the first time.[50] With the razing of the old city walls by the Emperor Franz Josef in 1857, a ring of real estate surrounding the old city was now available, and the *Ringstrasse* began to take shape, a process that would continue through the rest of the century. By the time of Schenker's arrival, many new and imposing structures existed, built in the prevailing historicist styles of the day—many Greco-Roman, but not exclusively so: aside from the Renaissance-style university building, the City Hall (built 1872–83) and Votivkirche (built 1879, close to the university), for example, are both neo-Gothic. The *Ringstrasse* must have been

---

48. Crüger, *Grundriss der Psychologie*, 36–39 (§11), quoted in Rothfarb, "Henryk Szenker," 54.
49. Rothfarb, "Henryk Szenker," 54f. See Crüger, *Grundriss der Psychologie*, 42–46 (§12).
50. For a short history of the university and photos of the main building, see http://www.eshe.eu/static/eshe/files/History_University-of-Vienna.pdf

an extraordinary sight for a sixteen-year-old from the provinces; it remains impressive today, though important structures were damaged or destroyed in World War II, and thus are actually reconstructions of historical replicas.

Schenker studied law at the urging of his father (on scholarship), all the while pursuing his first love, music. Still, his legal education would have important effects on his music theory. Whether or not law would have been his first choice, it turned out to have been the best choice, since he rejected "scientific" music theory of the sort promoted by Helmholtz, and had serious disagreements while writing *HL* with the relatively new study of music in the university, *Musikwissenschaft*—modeled by Guido Adler (to whom we return later) on "scientific" research.

Before we turn to the law curriculum, it is important to point out that contributions from professors outside of the law faculty to Schenker's education were considerable too. For example, two of his four professors during his first term were from the philosophical faculty: the course in "practical philosophy," to which we turn shortly, was taught by Robert Zimmermann (1824–98), and Schenker also took a course in Austrian history with Heinrich von Zeißberg (1839–99), who, though born in Vienna, was an expert in Polish as well as Austrian history. Not surprisingly, Zeißberg had taught in Galicia at the University of Lemberg before moving on to Innsbruck and finally back to Vienna, later becoming director of the Vienna Institute for Historical Research (1892), and of the Imperial Court Library (1896).[51] Apparently Schenker had finished most of the law requirements by his last semester. It was then that he took a course with Zeißberg again, this time on history of the middle ages; one hopes that the two spoke of their Polish cultural connection. Also during his last semester Schenker took a course in "Austrian Statistics" with Theodor Sternegg (1843–1908), who had studied law and economics at the University of Munich, taken a doctorate with a dissertation entitled "The Economic Consequences of the Thirty Years' War," and joined the faculty there; he would go on to a very high profile career in Innsbruck, Prague, and finally as "honorary professor" in Vienna.[52] Alpern's claim that Schenker took a course in "finance" with the philosopher "Franz Brentano"—peculiar, given the alleged instructor's specialty—is in fact in error. In checking Schenker's eighth-semester university registration (December 6, 1887), it is clear that the instructor of the

---

51. See https://geschichtsforschung.univie.ac.at/en/, accessed February 21, 2018.
52. "Die wirtschaftlichen Folgen des Dreisigjährigen Krieges," in *Historisches Taschenbuch*, 1864.

course was Lujo Brentano, Franz's brother, an expert in social economics.[53] We return to Franz Brentano shortly. We move now to the law curriculum, shown in figure 4.1.

Alpern emphasizes the course in "practical philosophy" that Schenker took in his first year with Robert Zimmermann, and the potential influence Zimmermann and his course may have had on Schenker's thinking.[54] Without doubt, Zimmermann was one of the most gifted and accomplished *Geisteswissenschaftler*—and *Naturwissenschaftler*—in the philosophical faculty, eventually serving two terms as head of the department, and one as *Rektor* of the university.[55] It is impossible that he did not make a deep impression on the young Schenker. Born in Prague to an intellectually enlightened family, his early education in philosophy and mathematics was entrusted to Bernard Bolzano (1781–1847), "(as some would have it) *the* greatest logician who lived in the long stretch of time between Leibniz and Frege."[56] Clearly, Zimmermann, off to a prodigious start, continued on the same trajectory, studying philosophy in Göttingen with Herbart and in Prague with Franz Exner, and finishing a doctorate in the philosophy faculty in Vienna at twenty-two, having studied philosophy, mathematics, physics, chemistry—and astronomy, the subject area of his PhD dissertation. After professorial appointments in Olmütz (1852–61)—today, Olomouc, in Moravia, in the east of the Czech Republic—and Prague, at the German-speaking Charles University, he moved back to Vienna and served as professor there for thirty-five years (1861–96). A close friend of Hanslick's, and the dedicatee of at least two editions of *Vom musikalisch-Schönen*, he wrote the first history of aesthetics, which remains a standard work on the topic, following it with his most substantial and original

---

53. "Lujo" was in fact his given name at birth, not a nickname. It was a composite of a "Ludwig" and a "Joseph" for whom he was named. See Lujo Brentano, *Mein Leben im Kampf um die soziale Entwicklung Deutschlands* (Jena: Diederichs. Reprint Marburg: Metropolis, 2004) 18. Korsyn first pointed this out in his review of Cook's *Schenker Project*. Thanks to Lee Rothfarb for his further research on the matter.
54. See Alpern, "The Triad of the True, the Good, and the Beautiful," 7–48.
55. Peter Stachel, "Zimmermann, Robert von," in *Oesterreichisches Musiklexikon*, http://www.musiklexikon.ac.at/ml/musik_Z/Zimmermann_Robert.xml, accessed February 22, 2018.
56. *Stanford Encyclopedia of Philosophy*, https://plato.stanford.edu/entries/bolzano/, accessed February 21, 2018.

Semester I Fall 1884		Semester II Spring 1885	
Course	*Professor*	*Course*	*Professor*
History of Roman Law	Adolph Exner	Roman Family Law	Frederic Maassen
German Legal History I	Heinrich Siegel	German Legal History II	Heinrich Siegel
Practical Philosophy	Robert Zimmermann	Roman Law of Possession	Gustav Demelius
Austrian History	Heinrich Zeissberg	Roman Law of Obligation	Adolph Exner
III Fall 1885		IV Spring 1886	
Roman Law of Succession	Franz Hofmann	Canon Law II	Joseph Zhismann
Roman Civil Process	Gustave Demelius	**Legal Philosophy**	**Georg Jellinek**
Private Law	Johann Tomaschek	Legal Methodology	Johann Tomaschek
Canon Law I	Joseph Zhismann		
V Fall 1886		**VI Spring 1887**	
Civil Law	Franz Hofmann	Law of Obligation	Leopold Pfaff
Law of Possession	Leopold Pfaff	Law of Succession	Franz Hofmann
Family Law	Leopold Pfaff	Criminal Procedure	Salomon Mayer
Criminal Law	Wilhelm Wahlberg	Economics	Gustav Gross
VII Fall 1887		**VIII Spring 1888**	
International Law	Georg Jellinek	Finance	Franz Brentano
Civil Process	Emil Schrutka	Litigation Procedure	Anton Menger
Commercial Law	Carl Grünhut	History of Middle Ages	Heinrich Zeissberg
Administrative Law	Wenzel Lustkandl	Austrian Statistics	Theodor Sternegg

Figure 4.1. Schenker's Curriculum of Study at the University of Vienna (from Alpern, "Music Theory as a Mode of Law," p. 1460, with correction: the instructor of "Finance" in the last term is not Franz Brentano, but Lujo Brentano.)

contribution, a treatise entitled *General Aesthetics as a Theory of Forms*—a development of basic ideas from Herbart.[57] The irony is that Hanslick's pamphlet *Vom musikalisch-Schönen* has come to epitomize music aesthetics as a theory of form in the nineteenth century, while his friend at the same time wrote a weighty tome on the topic, all but unknown today.

Surely, as Alpern writes, Zimmermann and Schenker shared an interest in aesthetics, but the course Schenker had with Zimmermann was "Practical Philosophy," the philosophy of action rather than thought. The question is, did aesthetics have any part in it? If "pure reason" (Kant's first critique, 1781, 2nd edition 1787) tells us how we should—and what we can—think, "practical reason" (Kant's second critique, 1788) tells us how to act, and how these actions affect the actions of others. This is the work in which Kant presents the "categorical imperative" as the overriding principle. Thus this study usually consists essentially of ethics (also known as moral philosophy). In the absence of direct evidence of Zimmermann's curriculum, we can speculate, fairly safely, that he would have followed Herbart, since he had actually studied with him and was regarded as the primary Herbartian in Austria. It is important to emphasize that as a philosophy of "values," moral philosophy was for Herbart a subset of aesthetics, though his *Allgemeine Praktische Philosophie* does not take up conventional aesthetic questions *in extenso*. Table 4.2 presents a translation of the table of contents of Herbart's work.

It cannot be denied that the door was open for Zimmermann, primarily an aesthetician as a philosopher, to work in his own ideas. Thus Alpern's contention that Zimmermann "introduced [Schenker] to the idea of Artistic, moral, and rational monism: that aesthetics, ethics, and reason share a common nexus through the intermediary of form," what Alpern calls "the triad of the true, the good and the beautiful," may well be correct, but we have no real documentation with which to prove it. It is important to differentiate the probable content of Zimmermann's course from what is readily available in print by him in English—his work on aesthetics.[58] Herbart's treatise on the subject of Zimmermann's course is strong testimony against Zimmermann's

---

57. See Payzant, "Eduard Hanslick and Robert Zimmermann." Also see Rothfarb, "Nineteenth Century Fortunes of Musical Formalism," especially 181–86, where he goes into detail on how Zimmermann developed Herbart's aesthetics. Our bibliography lists the major works of Zimmermann.

58. See the segment from Zimmermann's *Allgemeine Aesthetik* in *Music in European Thought 1851–1912*, ed. Bujić, 40–50.

Table 4.2. English Translation of the Table of Contents from Johann Friedrich Herbart's *Allgemeine Praktische Philosophie*

Introduction	
I	Of Moral Taste
II	To What Extent Can Universality Be Attributed to Practical Philosophy?
Book One: The Theory of Ideas	
Ch. 1	The Idea of Personal Freedom
Ch. 2	The Idea of Perfection
Ch. 3	The Idea of Benevolence
Ch. 4	The Idea of Law
Ch. 5	The Idea of Equity
Ch. 6	More Precise Applications of the Ideas of Law and Equity
Ch. 7	Transition from Original to Derivative Ideas
Ch. 8	Social Law
Ch. 9	The System of Reward
Ch. 10	The System of Government [*Verwaltung*]
Ch. 11	The System of Culture
Ch. 12	The Living [*Beseelte*] Society
Book Two: The Idea and the Human Being	
Ch. 1	Virtue and Its Opposite
Ch. 2	The Expression of Virtue in Action and Suffering
Ch. 3	Life as a Succession of Moral Action and Suffering
Ch. 4	The Limits of Humanity
Ch. 5	The Theoretical Idea of Society
Ch. 6	The Limits of Society
Ch. 7	Principles of Progress and Regress
Ch. 8	Duties of the Individual Person
Ch. 9	Duties of Society for Its Members
Ch. 10	The Future, to the Extent that It Is Dependent on Private Will
Ch. 11	The Future, to the Extent that It Is Dependent on Forms and Power
Ch. 12	Limits of Activity

(continued)

Table 4.2.—*(concluded)*

Appendix
Explanation
Analytical Elucidation of Natural Law and Moral Philosophy
Preface
Introduction
Historical Preparation (§§1–14)
Initial Overview of Natural Law and Moral Philosophy (§§15–34)
Part One: The Foundation of Practical Philosophy
Ch. 1   The Foundation According to the Followers of Spinoza (§§35–44)
Ch. 2   The Foundation According to Kant and Fichte (§§45–54)
Part Two: Analytical Elucidation of Natural Law at the Time of Kant (§§75–107)
First Observation: On the Laws of Punishment
Second Observation: Over Types of Contracts
Part Three: Analytical Elucidation of Moral Philosophy
Ch. 1   The Outlines of Moral Philosophy (§§109–25)
Ch. 2   On the Main Points of Moral Philosophy (§§126–91)
Ch. 3   On the Teleological Direction of Moral Philosophy (§§192–213)

direct influence on Schenker's view of artistic aesthetics, though it shows Alpern to be correct in his claims regarding ethics.[59]

In any case, it seems probable that Zimmermann, like Herbart, would not have made questions of artistic judgement prominent in a course in "practical philosophy," and would instead have tailored the course to fit in with the legal curriculum, in which questions of moral philosophy loomed largest. Clearly, Zimmermann was a profoundly educated aesthetician, and would have had much in common with Schenker. And we can hardly deny that Schenker the music theorist had a deep conviction of the moral dimension of music, yet another neo-Hellenic aspect of his music theory. We question, however, the practical consequences of this view for his Theory of Harmony, and the extent to which it is related to his interaction with Zimmermann: it is difficult to imagine the sixteen-year-old recently arrived

---

59. The second part of Herbart's work on practical philosophy consists of shorter and disconnected, occasional lectures, none of which are on aesthetics.

Schenker approaching the formidable sixty-year-old Universitäts-Professor Dr. Dr. Zimmermann for an after-class chat on musical aesthetics, though of course it is not impossible, and Schenker may well have attended a lecture (or more) given by Zimmermann on his own research.[60] Finally, there is the question of whether Zimmermann might have introduced Schenker to his friend Hanslick. It seems more likely, however, that Schenker knew Hanslick through classes he visited.[61] Hanslick—by all reports a dull lecturer—was nonetheless a full professor beginning in 1870, and in charge of musicology (though his doctorate was in law) throughout Schenker's time as a student and beyond, only succeeded by Adler in 1898. Clearly, this was the very beginning of musicology as we know it, and the proper approach to it was a contentious matter for discussion that surely would have interested Schenker.

Historicism and the University of Vienna Law Faculty

In looking at the Vienna law curriculum, we note immediately its strong historical bent. Indeed, all courses in the first year except for the one in practical philosophy are historically oriented, and the study of Roman law is prominent, continuing into the second year as well. The focus on Roman law was in fact a primary characteristic of the so-called "historical school of law" at the new University of Berlin. The founder of the movement, Frederick Karl von Savigny (1779–1861), from an old family of lawyers and legal scholars, was the author of a famous article "The Right of Possession" (*Das Recht des Besitzes*, 1803) that made his reputation at age twenty-two. A specialist in Roman law, he insisted that his students be thoroughly trained in it, and that they possess the linguistic and philological equipment necessary to read and interpret everything in the original texts.[62] Savigny, with two other colleagues, was a founding edi-

---

60. In formal circumstances, Austrian academics are often addressed using all titles, including the PhD doctorate as well as the habilitation doctorate; moreover, it is important to differentiate a "university professor" from a mere "professor." In any case, the social gap between the young Schenker and the sixty-year-old Zimmermann was extreme.

61. It is important to point out that during his time at the university Schenker would likely have "signed up" (*inskribierte*) for a variety of courses which he only "visited," and for which he did not take a proof-of-completion exam (*Abschlussprüfung*). That remains typical. The list of the courses Schenker finished is thus insufficient to provide a complete sense of his university experience.

62. Beiser, *The German Historical Tradition*, 234.

tor of the *Zeitschrift für geschichtliche Rechtswissenschaft* (Journal for Historical Jurisprudence), which first appeared in 1815. The basic features of the "historical school of law" were announced in the first issue's preface: 1. Rather than a generation being able to remake itself anew (the general assumption during the Enlightenment), each one "finds its world given to it by history"; 2. While the notion of "natural law" loomed large in the eighteenth century, "positive law" (law posited by particular societies) was now regarded not as some arbitrary creation of society, but as "the necessary result of its *Volksgeist* [collective consciousness]"; indeed, Savigny began his career as an advocate of the idea of "natural law," but by the time of his teaching in Berlin, rejected it entirely; 3. Individuality and self-sufficiency were part of the Enlightenment ethic; "the historical school, however, claims that the individual derives its identity entirely from its place in society and history."[63]

A younger colleague of Savigny who wrote a dissertation and became a tenured professor at the University of Berlin would become one of the most important legal scholars of the next generation: Rudolph von Jhering (1818–92), author of an essay entitled *Der Kampf um's Recht (The Struggle for Law)*. If Schenker's teacher Jellinek espoused von Jhering's idea, which Alpern has also claimed, his view of law as conflict is certainly suggestive of Schenker's notion of the struggle of the tones for personal freedom (a natural law dictated by the harmonic series), the positive law of tonality superimposed over them to limit that freedom.[64] Von Jhering accepted the chair in Roman law in the Vienna law faculty, and taught there from 1868 to 1872. In 1872 he moved on to Göttingen and was replaced by Franz Exner's son (1841–94), who would become Schenker's professor for Roman law in 1884. Having studied law in Vienna, Exner went on to further studies in Leipzig, Heidelberg, and Berlin before returning to the University of Vienna to teach, creating yet another connection from Vienna to the Berlin historical school of law. A number of Exner's legal papers are available.[65] These include his notes for a curriculum in Roman law that he likely taught Schenker. As in the case of Savigny's students, Exner's too would have had to have the linguistic and

---

63. Ibid., 234–35.
64. Alpern, "Music Theory as a Mode of Law," 1469–70.
65. Among the available legal papers by Exner is his discussion of the principle of "an act of God" as a way of avoiding liability (its Roman origin is "vis major," "higher power"). Deborah Coen sets this in the context of the new industrial age of the 1880s (e.g., as a basis on which to avoid the potential legal predicaments of railroads): see *Vienna in the Age of Uncertainty*, 111–15.

philological tools necessary to read all the original texts; Schenker undoubtedly put his *Gymnasium* study to good use in his work with Exner.

As Alpern has shown, the strongest influence on Schenker during his legal studies was his professor of legal philosophy, Georg Jellinek, one of the most important and prolific legal scholars of the later nineteenth century. As did many legal scholars of the period, Jellinek accepted the basic tenets of the historical school, writing that "the true principles of law were 'taught not by jurisprudence but by history,' and required 'careful historical analysis, which will show different results for different epochs.'"[66] Late in his career he was especially well known for his original contributions to international law, though one legal scholar dismisses his system of international law as "nothing more than law built on a community of legal consciousness, the formation of which corresponded with Savigny's teachings about the creation of positive law."[67] Jellinek clearly remained the historicist throughout his career.

According to Alpern, "Jellinek's chief concern was the polarity between the social order and individual freedom, and the role of law in mediating its reconciliation."[68] "To recognize the true boundaries between the individual and the community is the highest problem that thoughtful consideration of human society has to solve," Jellinek wrote.[69] He had specific historical examples in mind that represented the range of possible relationships between the community and the individual. The two extremes were represented by Roman law, which to Jellinek erred on the side of excessive authoritarianism of the state, and democracy, which erred on the side of excessive libertarianism of the individual.

"The fatal defect of democratic equality, Jellinek asserted, was its faulty assumption of social homogeneity, which he regarded as empirically false . . . Treating all citizens as equals by superficially tallying up their votes on the basis of mere numbers alone not only disregarded their innate differences, but abrogated each person's unique individuality."[70] Moreover, it suppressed

---

66. Alpern, "Music Theory as a Mode of Law," 1469–70. The embedded quotations are from Georg Jellinek, *The Declaration of the Rights of Man and of Citizens*, 97, footnote 6.

67. In Roben, "The Method behind Bluntschli's 'Modern' International Law," 267; quoted in Kelly, "Revisiting the Rights of Man," http://www.jstor.org/stable/4141687, accessed February 26, 2018.

68. Alpern, "Music Theory as a Mode of Law," 1467.

69. Jellinek, *Declaration of the Rights of Man*, 98.

70. Alpern, "Music Theory as a Mode of Law," 1475–76.

the rights of minorities—who, in Jellinek's view, were often the source of much creative thinking and social renewal—in favor of the majority, regardless of whether the collective opinion was consistent with the social good or not. It must be noted, however, that Jellinek's opinion of modern democracy was certainly colored by its origin in the notion of "inalienable rights" and the eighteenth-century heritage in "natural law," which could scarcely have appealed to a proponent of historical jurisprudence, given the latter's preference for historical analysis of positive law.

The ideal balance between the excesses of authoritarianism and libertarianism was achieved, according to Jellinek, by medieval Teutonic law, "a hierarchical meritocracy based on the selective principle that 'votes should be *weighed*, not counted.'"[71] Here, "individual freedom was conceived neither as 'the product of state concession' as in Roman law, nor as an independent 'right' higher than and opposed to the state as it was under democracy. It was rather a natural preexisting 'condition of liberty' prior to the state's formation that 'was not created but recognized . . . in the self-limitation of the state.'"[72]

It is not hard to imagine Schenker's interpretation of the end result of a "democracy of tones," though an "authoritarian regime of the tones" (perhaps some humdrum tonal exercise) is more difficult to conceive. In any case, we can predict the victor in the conflict of political systems: the Teutonic law of tonality represented a balance of musical oppositions, in which dissonance was sublimated to consonance, chromaticism to diatonicism, etc. In short, as we learned in chapter 1, political "concordance" and musical "harmony" are strongly analogous.

Beyond Formal Education: Psychological Research at the University of Vienna and Schenker's Music Theory

What are the sources of the appeals to psychology that permeate [DTS], and emerge with some frequency in both *HL* and *KPI*? Surely Schenker's formal study of psychology in the *Gymnasium* is one. But the extent to which

---

71. Ibid., 1476; the embedded quotation is from Jellinek, *The Rights of Minorities*, 5f. Of course, Jellinek's lionization of medieval Germanic law is consistent with Savigny and the Romantics. See Patterson, *Jurisprudence*, 413. And Jellinek says no more about the actual process of "weighing."
72. Alpern, "Music Theory as a Mode of Law," 1473; embedded quotations from Jellinek, *Declaration of the Rights of Man*, 97.

psychology would have come up in the "Practical Philosophy" course with Zimmermann is questionable, since he had written a *Gymnasium* textbook on it earlier in his career, thereby clearly assigning the topic to that level after the school reforms.[73] Nevertheless, it, like the Crüger book, demonstrates the relatively sophisticated level of psychological studies that would already be covered in the *Gymnasium*. In any case, as mentioned earlier, "practical philosophy" was generally recognized as ethics and moral philosophy.

Yet another source may have been the work of the same Friedrich Schleiermacher we met earlier as a founder of the new research university. Schleiermacher's exegesis of biblical texts (of the New Testament) was especially influential (though there is actually earlier work that is not dissimilar). Schenker may have heard about Schleiermacher's work while studying to produce his own interpretations of historical legal texts. Indeed, Schleiermacher has been considered by many the founder of "hermeneutics," a hotly debated approach to text exegesis that continues to the present day.[74] Very briefly, Schleiermacher distinguished two ways into a text: the "grammatical" (a completely "objective" or "positivist" approach borrowed from the natural sciences), and the more subjective "psychological" approach (that has since been dismissed by many), by which he meant an attempt to understand the "intentions" (i.e., the "psychology") of the author in the writing of the text—an attempt via "divination" by the interpreter to "become" the author during the act of interpretation. Karnes demonstrates Schenker's use of the subjective approach in a review of Brahms's songs, Op. 107, from October 1891.[75] The approach was controversial at the time, and, given the growth and influence of the exact sciences, would become ever more so in the twentieth century. Indeed, as Karnes shows, Schenker himself was always ambivalent about it, and would move into a more "objective" method later, of which, we claim, his pioneering musical philology is an important part, and one closely related to his music theory. And we would add that his move to music theory may

---

73. Zimmermann, *Philosophische Propaedeutik*. The first edition, published in 1853, had been a two-volume book, the first on logic, which it has been alleged, was completely dependent on Bolzano. Zimmermann replaced this treatment of the topic with original material in the second edition. See Künne, ed., *Bolzano and Analytic Philosophy*, 57.

74. See Schleiermacher, *Hermeneutics and Criticism*. For an introduction to more recent developments, see Hoy, *The Critical Circle*.

75. On Schenker's work as a music critic, see Karnes, *Music, Criticism, and the Challenge of History*: Brahms analysis, 86ff.

have been part of this search for objectivity, while, in his view, not sacrificing artistry. In any case, Schleiermacher's subjective method of text exegesis is certainly one resonance of "psychology" that may have prompted Schenker's many appeals to it in his music theory. Schenker clearly imagined himself as the "composer's advocate"—if not the composer himself—in interpreting the extraordinary number of musical examples in *HL*, and very likely in his interpretation of composers' manuscripts as well.

However, the most important source of Schenker's knowledge of psychology is very likely one that dates from after his formal education. Like his Viennese cohort, who were famously interested in all aspects of intellectual life, Schenker was very likely aware of the research and writing in psychology taking place in the university's Philosophy Faculty long before psychology separated itself from philosophy—at least it is highly unlikely that he would be unaware of it, given that he read a version of GEIST as a lecture before the University of Vienna Philosophical Society, where talks about psychology occurred frequently, and he expressly promised in SPIRIT "to explain the nature of harmonic and contrapuntal prescriptions almost solely in terms of their psychological origins and impulses" (324). In understanding this, it is important to separate the much better known field of post-Kantian German philosophy, for which metaphysics still played some role, from Austrian philosophy of the period, which is strongly related to more recent developments in analytic philosophy. Work on ontology at the University of Vienna by students of Franz Brentano (1838–1917) "proceeded always in tandem with work on the cognitive processes in which the corresponding objects are experienced, and it is in thus spanning the gulf between ontology and psychology in non-reductionistic fashion that the members of the Brentano school can be seen to have anticipated certain crucial aspects of contemporary cognitive science."[76] Schenker's appeal to psychology should be seen in this light: his attempt to understand our *mental processing* of music is at the heart of the matter.

Brentano was also a co-founder of the Philosophical Society. By 1894, Schenker's mysterious *Geschichte der Melodie*, which survives only in the form of GEIST (or, as we contend, most likely became a part of *HL*), provided some of the material for the lecture that Schenker read before the society in 1895. In fact, the lecture generated enough interest that Schenker was invited back for a discussion session a month later. Among his colleagues in the society were early proponents of what would eventually become *Gestalt*

---

76. Smith, *Austrian Philosophy*, 6.

psychology.[77] Christian von Ehrenfels (1859–1932), who would go on to teach Max Wertheimer (1880–1943), studied with Brentano at the university in the early 1880s and wrote his dissertation under another Brentano student, Alexius Meinong (1853–1920), in 1885.[78] All four were major contributors to the earliest stages of *Gestalt* psychology, Wertheimer going on to be one of its most important figures early in the next century.[79] Interestingly, three of the four (excepting Brentano) were educated musicians as well, and the study of melody figured prominently in the discussion.[80] Ehrenfels, a composer who had studied with Bruckner in 1880–82, received his habilitation in philosophy in 1888, and two years later (the year Schenker received his law degree) published his famous "On *Gestalt* Qualities" ("Über Gestaltqualitäten"), often cited as *the* founding paper of *Gestalt* psychology.[81]

Here, Ehrenfels reacted to work by the famous physicist—and University of Vienna colleague—Ernst Mach (1838–1916), the other co-founder of the society, whom many see as the true founder of *Gestalt* psychology and father of the Vienna Circle of so-called Logical Positivism.[82] To judge from Mach's remarks on musical perception and cognition in his popular and extremely accessible *Analysis of Sensations* (still in print), Mach, like so many who lived (and live) in Vienna, had much more than a passing acquaintance with

---

77. See Tan, "Beyond Energetics" for more on the beginnings of musical gestaltism, in particular, 103–12.
78. Meinong was a friend of Guido Adler, and may have influenced the structural vision for musicology presented in Adler's, "Scope, Method, and Goal of Musicology." See Karnes, *Music, Criticism, and the Challenge of History*, 29, footnote 17. See below, and Eder, ed., *Alexius Meinong*.
79. Charles Seeger recognized the psychological tack of Schenker's theory in his review of *HA*: "His work is a music-theoretical counterpart of the Gestalt psychology evolved by his contemporaries Koffka, Wertheimer, and others (among them Von Hornbostel!)."
80. See Ash, *Gestalt Psychology*, chapter 6, esp. 88ff.
81. See Ehrenfels, "On *Gestalt* Qualities."
82. See Blackmore, *Ernst Mach*, 47. For Mach's own lucid introduction to his work in psychology, see his *Analysis of Sensations*. Mach was an extraordinary polymath, Janik and Toulmin writing that "seldom has a scientist exerted such an influence upon his culture" (*Wittgenstein's Vienna*, 133); they go on to detail a long list of Viennese scientists and artists who followed Mach's work closely. Schenker may well have been one of them.

music.⁸³ Central to Mach's account of sensations is, once again, the familiar notion of association, which presupposes that the mind bundles individual phenomena and thoughts together in order to create specific ideas and memories. To quote Mach: "Colors, sounds, temperatures, pressures, spaces, times, and so forth, are connected with one another in manifold ways; and with them are associated moods of mind, feelings, and volitions. Out of this fabric, that which is relatively more fixed and permanent stands prominently forth, engraves itself in the memory, and expresses itself in language."⁸⁴ In the case of music, Mach specifically mentions repetition as a means for association: "The fact that a repetition of sensations is productive of pleasant effects is not restricted to the realm of the visible. To-day, both the musician and physicist know that the harmonic or the melodic addition of one tone to another affect us agreeably only when the added tone reproduces part of the sensation which the first one excited," an idea that is clearly on the way to the gestaltist point of view, and with which Schenker would surely have agreed.⁸⁵ Mach also believed that associations can be achieved through recognizing that certain patterns are arranged via symmetry, e.g., melodic inversion, melodic retrogrades, and so forth. But he insisted that such relationships are often silent. In his words: "the symmetry is there for the mind, but is wanting for sensation. No symmetry exists for the ear, because a reversal of musical sounds conditions no repetition of sensations."⁸⁶ Mach uses this argument to reject completely Oettingen's theory of dualism.⁸⁷

> The tonal series occurs in something which is an analogue of space, but is a space of one dimension limited in both directions and exhibiting no symmetry like that, for instance, of a straight line running from right to left in a direction perpendicular to the median plane . . . That the province of tone-sensation offers an analogy to space, and to a space having no symmetry, is unconsciously expressed in language. We speak of high tones and deep tones, not of right tones and left tones, although our musical instruments suggest the latter designation as a very natural one.⁸⁸

---

83. Mach, *Analysis of Sensations*, esp. 262–309, "The Sensations of Tone." Ehrenfels reacted to §13, 283–87.
84. Mach, *Analysis of Sensations*, 2.
85. Ernst Mach, "On Symmetry," 99.
86. Mach, "On Symmetry," 103.
87. Ibid., 278.
88. Mach, *The Analysis of Sensations*, 297.

278   CHAPTER FOUR

Like Helmholtz, Mach adhered to the predominant "elementarist" school of psychological research (see below), but with the important difference that he championed the notion of perceptual *Gestalten* (from personal experience that went back to his childhood) and tried to reconcile them with elementarism through his particular interpretation of that doctrine: to the idea that the sum total of individual perceptions formed the sole content of our experience, Mach added "muscle sensations" in an attempt to account for our sense that there is something that transcends the individual perceptions of a melody, a geometrical figure, etc. Ehrenfels enthusiastically accepted Mach's observation that a particular melody might have no tones in common with another, be played on a different instrument, at a different tempo, etc., but yet be recognized as the "same." But he jettisoned Mach's attempt to extend elementarism, claiming instead that the mind gathered, remembered and interpreted—essentially "added to"—the "psychic elements," leading to our sense that something more—his *Gestalten*—were there:

> for whoever has truly become convinced that something new is created through the combination of psychic elements will award the latter an incomparably higher significance than he who sees in psychic life only the continual displacement of eternally recurring components . . . Every temporal instant of every one of the numberless unities of consciousness therefore possesses its own peculiar quality, its individuality, which sinks, unrepeatable and irreplaceable, into the bosom of the past, while at the same time the new creations of the present step in to take its place.[89]

Ehrenfels was particularly active in the Philosophical Society, giving ten presentations between 1892 and 1901.[90] In light of Schenker's interests and original thoughts on melody (very evident in *HL*, of all places), it seems likely he would have been aware of Mach's popular work and perhaps even of Ehrenfels's more specialized response.[91] Throughout [DTS] and

---

89. "On *Gestalt* Qualities," 116.
90. See Blackmore et al., eds., *Ernst Mach's Vienna*, chapter 12, "The University of Vienna Philosophical Society," 277–314.
91. The various connections between Mach's and Schenker's ideas that we detail here are all the more suggestive when we realize that a card from Mach to Schenker exists, dated December 2, 1896, the content of which indicates that Mach was familiar with Schenker's recently published GEIST or had heard his lecture before the Philosophical Society. Mach writes to Schenker: "It seems to me that the views you have broached have a healthy kernel and deserve to be pursued. In any case

HL, Schenker's thoughts seem compatible with such a "holistic" approach to psychology. Moreover, the tune that Ehrenfels used to demonstrate his ideas in his critique of Mach was a folk tune "Muß i denn, muß i denn zum Städtele hinaus?" ("Must I, must I leave the town?") When, in *HL*, Schenker demonstrates how melodies project their underlying harmonic structure by outlining members of the tonic triad, he uses precisely the same tune.[92] It is difficult not to find this an implicit critique of what Schenker would no doubt have regarded as a naive reading of the tune—the notion that a tune is the "same" when transposed could not have impressed him as an original thought, after all. Though Schenker does not remark on Ehrenfels, this seems hardly a chance occurrence.

But perhaps the clearest connection to *Gestalt* psychology in [DTS] and *HL* is Schenker's invocation of the law of least action (also known as the law of least expenditure of effort): the notion that we take the simplest and most direct path to understanding any phenomena. Schenker effectively invokes it in [DTS] §[4] in his claim that "we give preference to simple relationships as opposed to complicated ones," and many times in *HL*. Although its origins can be traced back to antiquity, the law of least action resurfaced in the second and third decades of the twentieth century as a basic tenet of *Gestalt* psychology—the law of Prägnanz.[93] But it was not until 1914 that Max Wertheimer, founder of the Berlin School of *Gestalt* Psychology, announced the law, formulated in language "that could not possibly have been clear."[94]

---

the discussion will be beneficial and stimulating" (tr. by Korsyn; see his "Schenker's Organicism Reconsidered," p. 111ff.). Korsyn cites the card as evidence that GEIST had an impact on the society, and that Schenker and Mach were personally acquainted. Federhofer speculates, on the basis of the card, that Mach may have taken part in the session (or sessions) during which Schenker presented GEIST. If so, the paper made a lasting impression, for Mach's card is dated more than a year after Schenker's lecture on February 15, 1895 and discussion session March 18, 1895. See Blackmore et al., eds., *Ernst Mach's Vienna*, 254.

92. See Ehrenfels, "On *Gestalt* Qualities," 90ff., and *HL*, §76, 176; *HA*, 133. Also see Zelton, *Deutsche Volkslieder*, 495.

93. According to a recent account: "The *law of Prägnanz*, similar to the *law of simplicity*, states that people have a tendency to see things in the simplest form possible. Consistent with the *law of Prägnanz* is the *Gestalt* principle called the *law of least action*, which states that an organism will tend to follow the course of action that requires the least effort or expended energy under prevailing conditions." Roeckelein, *Dictionary*, 209f. Also see Brown, *Explaining Tonality*, 215–16.

94. Ash, *Gestalt Psychology in German Culture*, 133.

Clarification took nearly ten more years. Schenker is thus a pioneer in his use of the law in the psychology of music. Pierre Louis Maupertuis (1698–1759) was the first to champion it publicly, proclaiming it as a universal teleological principle in the early eighteenth century.[95] Maupertuis "was supported by Leonhard Euler (1707–83), its real discoverer, who first presented the principle in a serviceable form."[96] Its status as an alleged fundamental law of physics became a source of controversy shortly after Maupertuis made his claim, discussion heating up by the late nineteenth and early twentieth centuries. Among the many physicists to react to the law, Helmholtz made it a leading principle, Mach also adopted a variant that he called the "law of economy of thought" as fundamental to the scientific enterprise in general, and much later Max Planck (1858–1947) also wrote about it. The law of least action's emergence into the new field of psychology is more difficult to reconstruct; it seems to have occurred around 1900. Gibson attributes the introduction of the law into the study of psychology to Guillaume Ferrero, but notes that Ferrero's version of the law is particularly severe: the mind is essentially inactive, unless prompted by outside stimuli.[97] Gibson rejects this view.

"Scientific" Music Theory in the Second Half of the Nineteenth Century and Schenker's Reaction to It

The Philosophical Basis: Moritz Hauptmann (1792–1868)

Foundational to the movement in German-language music theory that dominated the late nineteenth century when Schenker began his music-theoretical career was the work of a theorist born in the latter half of the eighteenth century who was very much part of the intellectual world of the early nineteenth century. Moritz Hauptmann, in almost all ways the opposite of the theorists of harmony who centered on the keyboard, and dominated the field in the eighteenth and early nineteenth centuries, was a violinist, his theory of harmony very unlike those penned by the keyboardists. An intellectual, his outlook was likewise very different from the practically minded organists and pedagogues.[98] Even a quick perusal of

---

95. See Gibson, "The Principle of Least Action."
96. Ibid., 470.
97. See Ferrero, "L'Inertie Mentale et La Loi du Moindre Effort."
98. See the collection of Hauptmann's essays, *Opuscula*.

his major work, *Die Natur der Harmonik und der Metrik* (*The Nature of Harmony and Metre*) reveals, by virtue of its clever dialectical recasting of fairly conventional harmonic theory, an intellect to be reckoned with.[99] If the general tendency of the most interesting European theorists of the first half of the nineteenth century was to look for a new and more convincing starting point for the theory of harmony—indeed, if the right approach to the history of theory of the century as a whole is epistemological, as Rummenhöller has argued—then Hauptmann has to be seen as the major figure of mid-century, for the way in which he told the story of harmonic theory was unique, powerful, and of its time methodologically.[100] Even if he contributed little or nothing to harmony as a practical, analytical or compositional study, he is essential to our story precisely because *theory* loomed so large in the second half of the century, and it was as much against that as against the pedagogy of practical harmony that Schenker reacted. Both were in a sorry state as far as he was concerned.

Hauptmann's status at mid-century was impressive. After some twenty years of private teaching in Cassel (while also performing as a violinist in the Court Orchestra under Louis Spohr), he was called to Leipzig in 1842 as Cantor of the Thomasschule, the prestigious job J. S. Bach held some hundred years earlier. He began to teach at the Leipzig Conservatory on the recommendation of Mendelssohn with the conservatory's founding in 1843. And with the founding of the Bach Gesellschaft in 1850, he became the editor of the monumental *Bach-Gesellschaft-Ausgabe*. Having been working on a book on harmony as early as 1831, he published *Die Natur der Harmonik und der Metrik* ten years into his conservatory teaching, in 1853.[101] It was surely not unrelated to his teaching, but it is also the least pedagogically oriented of any book on harmony of the period and beyond, presenting pure theory, and containing not a single musical example, contrived or actual—or even a reference to some actual piece. Indeed, the section on harmony contains no musical notation—only diagrams. (A primitive rhythmic notation proves to be unavoidable in the section on meter.) Hauptmann was also working on a practical *Harmonielehre* when he died, but even it has a paucity of examples,

---

99. Hauptmann, *The Nature of Harmony and Metre*.
100. Rummenhöller, *Musiktheoretisches Denken im 19. Jahrhundert*. In saying "of its time," we assume again that the theory was essentially formed before the death of Hegel (1831).
101. See the letter to Franz Hauser in Jorgenson, *Moritz Hauptmann of Leipzig*, 110–11.

all in the treble clef—suggestive, given his instrument—and hardly typical of the many books written by the keyboardists.[102] Unfortunately, the last three chapters—"Modulation," "Enharmonic Reinterpretation," and "Conclusion"—merely parallel the last three sections of *Die Natur der Harmonik und der Metrik*, and were written and added to the book by his student Oscar Paul (1836–98) after Hauptmann's death.[103] Given the master's famously conservative tastes (late Beethoven left him cold), it would have been interesting to know if he had changed his views on these more "advanced" topics. In fact, his system could be made into a point of departure in the investigation of music of the New German School (Liszt, Wagner, and others), as his student Carl Friedrich Weitzmann (1808–80) would show.

Like the system of Simon Sechter, Hauptmann's was based on just intonation.[104] Indeed, this was made quite clear by the way in which he presented it in an original notation, widely adopted, and developed further by others to show the explicit presence of the syntonic comma (or multiple commas) and tone generation in multiple octaves.[105] The tonal system appears as a string of thirds dividing fifths:

$$F - a - C - e - G - b - D$$

The pitches notated in capitals are tuned in just-fifths apart, as are those notated in lower case letters, the latter placed just-thirds above the former.

---

102. Seen in this light, it is interesting that Hauptmann would appeal to two physicists writing about harmony, who, despite their amateur musical backgrounds, were dominant influences in the second half of the nineteenth century.

103. Hauptmann, *Die Lehre von der Harmonik*.

104. In tuning "just intonation" starting on C, begin by locating the roots of major triads on F and G as 3:2 fifths above and below C. Tune triads on C, F and G with perfect 3:2 fifths and 5:4 major thirds. This procedure automatically tunes the minor triads on E and A to 3:2 fifths and 6:5 minor thirds, but the triads on D and B are problematic: the fifth D-A will be 22 c. (a "syntonic comma") narrower than the same interval in EQ, while the tritone B-F will be 10 c. larger than the same interval in EQ (though, as a smaller deviation, and a dissonant interval anyway, this is less worrisome to most writers on tuning). Zarlino's "mean-tone" temperament, which he advocates for keyboard instruments, preserves many pure major and minor triads in the most frequently used transpositions. For more detail on tuning, see chapter 3.

105. The notation is suggestive of the two-dimensional *Tonnetz* diagrams that have resurfaced in current Neo-Riemannian theory. That technique was invented by the eighteenth-century mathematician and music theorist, Leonhard Euler.

The notation shows immediately that all fifths formed of letters of the same case are just, as are thirds formed of opposite-case letters.[106]

Yet surprisingly, having developed a clear notation of the tuning assumed by many theorists, and having presented a sophisticated discussion of acoustics and harmony, Hauptmann is quite explicit about *not* founding his system on the harmonic series. In the long run, this will turn out to be a wise decision: adopting the dialectic as a "universal" idea that offered a more secure foundation than acoustical theory, Hauptmann also found a much more flexible one. Indeed, it was so flexible that the music theory endured even when its dialectical overlay went out of fashion (almost by the time the book appeared in print), mainly because the book contained music-theoretical ideas suggestive of further development, independent of their mode of presentation.

In simplest terms, the dialectic consists of three transformative steps, leading to higher levels of abstraction. Commonly referred to as "thesis, antithesis, and synthesis" (though both their history and use by Hauptmann are considerably more subtle than this oversimplification),[107] the stages are often expressed by Hauptmann as Roman numerals. We have added these to the following quotation: "The Octave is the expression of unity [I]; the Fifth expresses duality or opposition [II]; the Third, unity of duality or union [III]. The Third is the union of Octave and Fifth."[108]

Hauptmann's interval designations refer specifically to the octave, perfect fifth and major third: "there are three intervals directly intelligible: I. Octave. II. Fifth. III. Third (major). They are unchangeable."[109] The idea that these three intervals (which, it will be remembered, correspond to the primes 2, 3 and 5 in tuning theory) are primitives of the system, needing no justification, would form an axiom of later systems of harmony. Though the basic idea was there, in essence, in Rameau, it was Hauptmann who focused on it and brought it to the attention of later generations of German-speaking theorists in particular, for whom Rameau's *Traité*, book I, and his later speculative works were terra incognita.

---

106. Both the perfect fifth formed of mixed cases (D/a) and the minor third formed of the same cases (D/F) are a syntonic comma narrow of just. The two tritones are, properly speaking, "just," despite their mixed-case representation. The "diminished fifth" is 10 c. wide of the EQ 600 + 600 c. division, while the "augmented fourth" is 10 c. narrow of it.
107. Rummenhöller, *Musiktheoretisches Denken im 19. Jahrhundert*, 39–44.
108. Hauptmann, *The Nature of Harmony and Metre*, 6.
109. Ibid., 5.

Like theorists before him, Hauptmann has no trouble generating the major triad with these intervals: the acoustical root happily corresponds to I, the fifth to II and the third to III: acoustical and dialectical order of generation agree completely! Generating the whole major system via the dialectic proves to be a little more challenging. (A word to the wise: Hauptmann also uses the terms "octave, fifth and third" metaphorically throughout his work to indicate "unity, duality and higher unity," even though the application of the dialectical terms changes): "First, the given triad is *unity, Octave*; then through its two dominant chords it falls apart within itself into opposition, *duality*, and becomes *Fifth*; lastly it is restored as uniting *Third* element in the correlation of the other two, as higher unity, as *unification* or *unity of union*."[110]

"Unity," and especially "duality" and "unity of duality," are certainly used quite differently than they were in the explanation of the major triad! And they will continue to be used many different ways as the book progresses. Nonetheless, Hauptmann manages to keep the reader hanging on by offering reinterpretations that are usually plausible, and almost always inventive, though the significance of any of these "derivations" for real-time analysis remains dubious. It was left to Riemann to attempt to remedy that defect.

The notion of the major key system ultimately encompasses modulation as well. Hauptmann represents the relationship of a key to its dominant key and subdominant key as follows:

B♭ d F a C e G b D f♯ A

In his words: "This triad of keys has a link, or element of relationship [*Verwandtschaft*], in the tonic triad of the middle key, which appears in it as tonic chord, in the subdominant key as dominant chord, and in the dominant key as subdominant chord."[111] The notion of tonal *relationship* would

---

110. Ibid., 10. Given the difficulty of interpreting the above quotation, we depart from our usual practice and provide the original German: "Der gegebene Dreiklang ist erst *Einheit, Octav*, zerfällt durch seine beiden Dominantaccorde in sich selbst zu entgegengesetzter Bestimmung, zur *Zweiheit*, wird *Quint*, und stellt sich in der Vermittlung dieser Beiden als verbindendes *Terz*moment, als höhere Einheit, als *Eigenkeit*, oder Einheit der Verbindung daraus wieder her" (*Die Natur der Harmonik und der Metrik*, 27)." The difficulty does not reside in the translation, which is generally reliable and as clear as possible.
111. Ibid., 13.

become a major interest of Helmholtz, who obviously knew his Hauptmann; indeed, the third and most musically relevant part of his treatise is titled "The Relationship [*Verwandtschaft*] of Musical Tones."

As might be expected, the generation of the minor triad is vexing, even given the flexibility of the system. Yet, by rejecting a natural base, Hauptmann has moved the discussion away from the confines of acoustic generation to the "logic" of theory, and can apply his three dialectical steps starting most anywhere he wants. Still, in offering two possible explanations of the minor triad's origin, he presents nothing really new. The first is familiar as Rameau's "co-generation" theory presented in *Démonstration du principe de l'harmonie* (1750): the acoustical root generates the fifth, which is doubly generated by the third as well. The question that remains, of course, is just where the third comes from. The second is the one Rameau put forth in *Génération harmonique* (1737), but was forced to retract in *Démonstration* when he found that the minor triad did not vibrate in its entirety when its fifth was sounded! Did Hauptmann read Rameau? He does not credit him with these ideas, and it is most unlikely that he would have had any access to *Génération harmonique* or *Démonstration du principe de l'harmonie*. Most likely, the ideas came from intermediate sources, or they may even have been "reinvented" by Hauptmann, as Riemann claims in his essay, "The Nature of Harmony."[112]

Hauptmann goes on to generate the minor key, in which the dominant must be a major triad to produce the "positive" element necessary. But then, not altogether surprisingly, he produces a third key system, the synthesis of major and minor: the "minor–major key," in which the tonic is a major triad, the dominant also major, but the subdominant minor. This idea is a significant and original contribution by Hauptmann that characterizes much music of the late nineteenth century, and would be picked up and developed by Oettingen (minor–major and major–minor), Riemann (major–minor), and many, many others.[113]

All of these ideas were influential, but surely Hauptmann's most influential idea was his second explanation of minor, amazing as this may seem, given its earlier reception with Rameau. But Hauptmann, freed from an acoustical root in his choice of the dialectic, can make either explanation of minor plausible, and the second, picked up first by Oettingen and then Riemann had immense influence: it spawned the movement known as

---

112. Riemann, "The Nature of Harmony," 80.
113. See Matthew Riley, "The 'Harmonic Major' Mode."

"Dualism" that was particularly powerful in German music theory in the latter half of the nineteenth and early twentieth centuries (and against which Schenker reacted strongly), and has reemerged in American music theory almost exactly a century later, now that American theorists seem to have renounced any interest in acoustically grounded tonal theory. Hauptmann's oft-quoted theoretic/hermeneutic explanation of minor forms an apt ending to our inquiry:

> The minor triad thus being of passive nature, and *having its starting-point above (not its most real starting-point, yet that which is determined as unity), and forming from it downwards*, [emphasis added] there is expressed in it, not the upward driving *force*, but the downward drawing *weight, dependence* in the literal, as well as in the figurative sense of the word. We therefore find in the minor chord the expression for *mourning*, the hanging boughs of the weeping willow as contrasted with the aspiring arbor vitae.[114]

The Physicists

The efforts of Dilthey and others not withstanding, natural science had an especially strong impact on music theory late in the nineteenth century largely due to the efforts of Helmholtz and Oettingen. The outstanding scientist of his day, Helmholtz had the broader impact, but Oettingen's work was the more interesting and suggestive for future developments in the field of music theory.

For Helmholtz, *tonal sensations*—argued by some to be the lowest level of psychological activity—became the physiological basis of the theory of music, that basis designated explicitly as "theory" (*Theorie*)—not *Musiklehre* or *Harmonielehre*.[115] This is a big claim and an important change in the epistemology of the theory of harmony.[116] Thus the Pythagorean and Platonic theory, first naturalized as the physical science of acoustics in the seventeenth century and updated by Helmholtz in parts I and II of his book, was now taken as well into the latest research in physiology, providing the impetus to research into music psychology. The success of the book was striking: from

---

114. Hauptmann, *The Nature of Harmony and Metre*, 17.
115. Hermann von Helmholtz, *Die Lehre von den Tonempfindungen* (*On the Sensations of Tone*). Schenker owned a copy of this book.
116. Rummenhöller, *Musiktheoretisches Denken im 19. Jahrhundert*. See "Der sensualistisch-kritische Theoriebegriff Hermann von Helmholtz," 61–68.

the beginning of its writing Helmholtz had hoped to appeal to a broad audience, and succeeded in doing so.[117] In contrast to Hauptmann's book, which was never reprinted (and translated fairly late into English), Helmholtz's went into a second edition within two years of its appearance, French and English translations followed, and the English translation itself went into a second edition. The book also went through further editions revised by Helmholtz, a fifth and sixth edition (essentially unrevised reprints) appearing after his death.[118] Given the size and technical detail of the work, this is simply extraordinary.

Helmholtz's theory was essentially a mechanistic view of musical sensation that set the stage for a conservative music theory (part III) bound to provoke responses from music theorists.[119] In the words of Mitchell Ash, Helmholtz was "unquestionably the leading sensory physiologist of his time," and one of the chief proponents of "elementarism," which required, in Helmholtz's own words, a "universe as consisting of elements with unalterable qualities." Ash continues, "only in such a world would it be possible to explain natural phenomena mechanically—by referring only to the motions of objects treated as point-masses having [in Helmholtz's words] 'unalterable motive forces that are dependent only on spatial relations.' [Helmholtz's] theories of vision and hearing were, in essence, attempts to employ this mechanistic and deterministic language in the study of the senses."[120]

Though the research on the physics of sound and physiology and of hearing looms large, part III, "The Relationship of Musical Tones," is arguably the point of the book—and certainly the part to which music theorists reacted.[121] Helmholtz clearly regarded the application of everything that went before to the way we hear and judge music to be an essential matter for investigation. But the problem is that by experience and profession the author was much less prepared to address this aspect of his overall project and had to rely more heavily on secondary sources. Thus the notation of many examples is derived from Hauptmann, and the discussion of the relationship of tones (*Verwandtschaft der Töne*, which Steege translates as "affinities

---

117. See Steege, *Helmholtz*.
118. Ibid., 19ff.
119. Helmholtz would counter by invoking his status as a Neo-Kantian who spoke against the materialist philosophy of those such as Gustav Fechner, but he surely did not go far enough into psychology for Schenker.
120. Ash, *Gestalt Psychology*, 52.
121. Helmholtz, *On the Sensations of Tone*, 234–371.

of tones") and tonality is beholden to Fétis,[122] as are, apparently, occasional ethnomusicological excurses.

Particularly influential was Helmholtz's conception of a musical sound as a "*Klang*" (which most translate as "compound tone"), and the effect of this idea on the consonance or dissonance of chords; it is one that would be adopted, developed, and revised by Oettingen and Riemann.[123] On the other hand, Helmholtz's theory that dissonance was caused by the phenomenon of "beating" would provoke much criticism, and ultimately, the separation of "consonance" as a music-theoretical, interpretive concept from "concordance" as an acoustical one.[124] Even more problematic was Helmholtz's silence in part III on the music of his own time. Part III contains virtually nothing that might be read as "compositional," and includes no music analyses of any sophistication; in short, it ignores what musicians normally look for in a book on "harmony."

Harrison points to major problems that doom Helmholtz's harmonic theory from the start.[125] First, his requirement of just intonation affects virtually everything he says, and he is quite rigid in holding to it (much more so than Hauptmann or Sechter), making much of the theory irrelevant to music in EQ.[126] This means, for example, that he rejects all enharmonic activity, which, given music of the time, produces a theory that must have seemed

---

122. See the quotation from Helmholtz selected by Steege (131) to summarize Helmholtz's "central historical claims." The notions that European "tonality" was developed "from a *freely chosen* principle of style [and] that beside it, and before it, other tonal systems have been developed from other principles" would have been—and essentially were—embraced by Fétis.

123. A sounding fundamental and its upper partials together make up the "compound tone." Such tones are emitted by all acoustic instruments, excluding experimental ones—tuning forks, etc.—designed to produce only the fundamental.

124. "Beats" are perceivable impulses caused by the interference of partial tones of one harmonic series with a partial tone (or tones) in dissonant relationship in another, simultaneously sounding, harmonic series. The frequency of the beats is equal to the difference in frequencies of the fundamentals of the two series. A key figure in this development was the psychologist, Carl Stumpf (1848–1936), author of, among many works, the two-volume (unfinished) *Tonpsychologie* (Leipzig: S. Hirzel, 1883–90).

125. Daniel Harrison, *Harmonic Function in Chromatic Music*, 234–42.

126. He was so serious about this that he and his students worked on complex keyboard instruments that could produce the large number of pitches required for multiple just-tuned scales and modulation between them.

irrelevant to musicians of the time—if they read it. Second, and most important, Helmholtz sees minor as highly inferior to major: "minor triads are generally inferior in harmoniousness to major triads . . . in the minor chords, the Third does not belong to the compound tone of its fundamental note, and hence cannot appear as a constituent of its quality; so that the relation of all the parts of a minor chord to the fundamental note is not so immediate as that for the major chord."[127] Though Helmholtz's system presupposes a relative view of consonance and dissonance (cf. the "beating theory") and thus requires some qualification to account for minor, it ultimately presumes that minor chords remain and will always remain questionable as tonics and as the basis for systems built on them.[128] This rejection of minor by the most famous scientist of his time was the main provocation for Oettingen and Riemann. In the case of Oettingen, it was a scientist answering a scientist. But for Riemann, the musician, it underscored all of the things that Helmholtz did not say about music—including anything relevant to music of the New German School of the 1850s and 60s.[129]

Both Hauptmann and Helmholtz provided fundamental ideas for the system of harmony propounded by Oettingen; but in many respects, the originality of that system deserves more attention than Neo-Riemannians have given it so far. Though Rameau provided the two familiar explanations of the minor triad as co-generated by two intervals, and inversionally equivalent to major, Oettingen seems to have received them directly from Hauptmann and done his historical homework later.[130] In an attempt to counter Helmholtz's critique of the minor triad, Oettingen endeavors to raise its status to equal major in his "System of Harmony in Dual Development," to translate the title literally.[131] This is the first version of "dualism" (Oettingen invented the musical use of the term), and since the concept is so important both

---

127. Helmholtz, as quoted in Harrison, *Harmonic Function in Chromatic Music*, 241.
128. Harrison, *Harmonic Function in Chromatic Music*, 240–42.
129. This is a topic that surely interested Riemann, who dedicated his Sketch of a New Theory of Harmony (*Skizze einer neuen Methode der Harmonielehre*) to Franz Liszt.
130. Oettingen in fact cites d'Alembert's *Elémens*, and thus knew the origin of these ideas in Rameau.
131. Arthur von Oettingen, *Harmoniesystem in dualer Entwicklung* (1866). There is no English translation.

today, and in understanding Schenker's reaction to harmonic theory of his time, we describe Oettingen's idea in some detail.

Oettingen starts with a subtle revision of Hauptmann's distinction between "being" and "having." This account runs as follows:

> By tonicity of an interval or a chord, I understand its property *to be able to be interpreted as a compound-tone-component of a root* [*Grundton*].[132] I call this root the *tonic root* . . . By phonicity of an interval or a chord, I understand its property to possess whichever of the partial tones common to all tones [in the interval or chord]. The lowest of the complete collection of common partial-tones I call the coinciding or *phonic overtone*, because all [voices] sing the tone, so to speak, that is, actually state it.[133]

Thus, the major triad contains two intervals that may be interpreted as components of the harmonic series over the root: in Hauptmann's terms, they "have" a root, though the acoustical root—an octave below our pitch-class "root"—does not actually sound! Meanwhile, the minor triad consists of two intervals that possess common overtones, the lowest of which is the *phonic overtone*: that tone is a *sounding overtone* that is possessed by the acoustical interval roots (none of which actually sound). In the case of a C major triad C4 E4 G4, the imagined root of E4 is C2, that of G4, C3, neither of which is actually sounding. In the case of the minor triad C4 E♭4 G4, however, G4 is the actually sounding lowest common overtone of imagined intervals E♭2/G4 and C3/G4, the "coinciding" or *phonic* overtone. Thus Oettingen adopts Rameau's co-generation explanation of minor, as reinvented by Hauptmann, as his basic (and quasi-acoustical) explanation. He is also quite clear as to what actually sounds and what does not sound.

But Oettingen proceeds to investigate "reciprocal relations," with which we are familiar from earlier work with string division versus the harmonic series.[134] And then he turns to Hauptmann, who writes that "in the major triad, unity [I] is the positive determining [feature], while in the minor triad, it is the positively determined [feature]"—determined by the fifth, that is, a fairly typical Hauptmannian reversal. The reader may remember that Hauptmann's F minor triad example is either F (I) C (II, III) A♭ (I)—the co-generation explanation, or F (II) A♭ (III) C (I), the symmetrical-inversion

---

132. Oettingen writes *Klang*, which he conceives according to Helmholtz.
133. Oettingen, *Harmoniesystem in dualer Entwicklung*, 31f.
134. Ibid., 35–37.

explanation. In the above description, Hauptmann clearly refers to the explanation via symmetrical-inversion. In Oettingen's opinion, however, this is consistent with his notation: c+ = a tonic C chord; c° = phonic C chord ("F minor," in more common parlance). Providing an important insight into his theoretical apparatus, Oettingen writes:

> With the same right by which we generalized the principle of the relationship [*Verwandtschaft*] of chords above and saw it as not dependent on the *real existence* of overtones, we must now attribute the *phonically* consonant property of minor chords to them in all cases. The interpretation that developed originally from physiologically grounded phenomena is now, in the case of the minor chord, even more understandable, for the phonic overtone really exists, while the tonic overtone does not, or—to use explanations normally used in optics—the root of the tonic is *virtual*, the phonic overtone a *real* sound. On the other hand, the tonic chord [major triad] produces a B-chord [= E minor], since C E G = C⁺ + b° [i.e., B is an actually sounding overtone of E/G], while the tonic root A♭ in c e♭ g only exists virtually. When it actually sounds, we hear C E♭ G as components of an A♭ chord. In all structures of the major and minor keys we find such a duality of chords as a fully formed, symmetrically structured opposition.

Oettingen's version of "dualism" is thus a highly textured and subtly thought-out concept in which symmetrical inversion is only part of the story—regardless of what one might think of dualism's potential musical value. It was Riemann who believed that he heard a series of "undertones" and thus oversimplified the matter by going right to the explanation of major and minor via symmetrical inversion.[135]

As is clear, Oettingen often agrees with Hauptmann, to whom he is always deferential, though he criticizes the dialectic, which he clearly regards as outmoded metaphysics. And yet, because of the new "real natural–scientific foundations" available from Helmholtz, he believes that he can construct a more effective system than Hauptmann by substituting physical, physiological, and to an extent, psychological principles for Hauptmann's purely philosophical ones.[136] The move towards psychology is important. We cite a single example, taken from both Hauptmann and Helmholtz: the ever-appealing just intonation. According to Oettingen, "tempered tuning is invaluable for practical music. The theory of harmony deals with just intonation . . . when

---

135. See Rehding, *Hugo Riemann*, 15–19.
136. Rummenhöller, *Musiktheoretisches Denken im 19. Jahrhundert*, 84f.

tempered intervals sound, we conceive just intervals. Thus we possess the ability to restore the purity of impure intervals interpretively."[137] Oettingen is quite clear on the necessity of temperament in practice, but equally clear in transferring just tuning to the psychological domain.

Oettingen also draws on a third idea from Helmholtz: that "everything must be worked out "scientifically" (*wissenschaftlich*). "All concepts which enter into the system must be justified scientifically; likewise, their terminology and symbolic representation. The same basic determining factors will be met both in music and acoustics."[138] In other words, he *seems* to demand the method of the exact sciences. But, given the breadth of *Wissenschaft*, it is fair to ask, just what kind of science? It is certainly not the empirical brand endorsed by Helmholtz. Rather, as Oettingen gradually introduces a host of new terms necessitated by a system that is virtually unprecedented, he develops an analytical notation for them that essentially constitutes a "harmonic analysis," clearly modeling the terms and their precise definitions on symbolic logic. This amounts to an attempt to "reduce musical events to their formal-logical dimension through progressive abstraction, and to make them expressible and understandable through symbols."[139] Thus, whether or not Oettingen was aware of the work of Gottfried Weber, his attempt is reminiscent of Weber's analytical notation, brought to yet a higher level of abstraction and precision. Real music had been first reduced to the figured bass, then the fundamental bass, then, by Weber, to the fundamental bass with Roman numerals substituting for actual notes (so that a particular fundamental bass progression appeared exactly the same in all keys), and now to a succession of symbols that point up as many dualistic relationships as possible. Oettingen's penchant for notational innovation was already apparent in the 1866 *Harmoniesystem in dualer Entwicklung*. It ultimately leads to numbered "instructional paragraphs" (*Lehrsätze*) in the second half of *Das duale Harmoniesystem* (1913) while his last book, *Die Grundlage der Musikwissenschaft* (1916) consists of numbered logical statements. Indeed, the work has been compared to Ludwig Wittgenstein's *Tractatus logico-philosophicus* (1918) as a representative of "Neo-positivism."[140]

---

137. Arthur von Oettingen, *Das duale Harmoniesystem* (1913), 6.
138. Oettingen, *Die Grundlage der Musikwissenschaft* (1916), first two numbered statements.
139. Rummenhöller, *Musiktheoretisches Denken im 19. Jahrhundert*, 83.
140. Rummenhöller, *Musiktheoretisches Denken im 19. Jahrhundert*, 83.

Oettingen stands firmly in the tradition of theorists we have been examining since the ancient Greeks: the theorist preoccupied with the fundamental nature of tonal systems. The four foldout tables that he presents at the end of *Harmoniesystem in dualer Entwicklung* summarize the larger contribution of the book, an exhaustive investigation of the modulatory relations of the 12 major and 12 minor systems.[141]

Schenker contra Riemann

The works of Helmholtz and Oettingen—as well as Hauptmann (including the dialectic)—shaped the work of Hugo Riemann, who defined the theory of harmony at the beginning of our story in chapter 1 and the state of music theory at the turn of the last century. The most important and prolific music theorist of the time, Riemann was a musician who pursued a path to the university. Having published his first music-theoretical article in 1872 at the age of twenty-three, he completed his PhD at Göttingen soon after with a dissertation on "musical hearing" (*Über das musikalische Hören*, 1873). The dissertation, which was a clear entry into the territory occupied by Helmholtz, investigates the question of consonance and dissonance, and it comes down firmly on the side of Aristoxenus and the "musical ear," not Pythagorean canonics.[142] But its language is "a kind of verbal polyphony—a blend of Oettingen, Helmholtz, and Hauptmann—that gave him a greater range than the *Hegelei* of Hauptmann alone."[143]

Except for Helmholtz's derivation and negative view of the minor triad, Riemann largely agrees with his analysis of musical tone, though he did not think that his view of "tonal sensations" went far enough in the direction of true musical cognition. Since he was influenced by the philosopher Hermann Lotze (1817–81) while studying at Göttingen, Riemann always regarded musical hearing as "more than a passive reception of tonal stimuli." Over the years, he described it variously as a "comparative perception, a 'choice of tonal material brought to the ear,' a 'logical activity,' [and] a 'mental imaging [of tones]' [*Vorstellen*]."[144] Schenker would probably have disagreed with only one of these characterizations, but that disagreement

---

141. Unfortunately, these are missing in Internet copies, but they are preserved and developed in *Das duale Harmoniesystem*.
142. Seidel, "Die Harmonielehre Hugo Riemanns," 43.
143. Mooney, "Hugo Riemann's Debut as a Music Theorist," 82.
144. Seidel, "Die Harmonielehre Hugo Riemanns," 43.

is crucial: just as he rejected the notion that harmony was a psychological processing of successions of chords, so he would also have rejected the idea that musical hearing was a "logical activity"—which is to say reducible either to dialectical logic à la Hauptmann, or to Oettingen's positivistic symbolic notation—the most abstract forms of "chord progression." Yet that idea was obviously crucial to Riemann, for he used the title "musical logic" in his 1872 article, a gloss on Hauptmann that attempts to turn his theory into a system of real-time musical analysis (though it contains only three artificial musical examples), as well as for the republished (and presumably revised) version of his dissertation.[145] Clearly, Riemann regarded the task of defining the exact nature of that "musical logic" as central to his work in music theory; along with the unremittingly vertical view of harmony as the "science of musical hearing," it is something that Schenker found utterly repugnant.

Riemann confronted Oettingen's work directly in his *Musikalische Syntaxis* (Musical Syntax, 1877), this time using his forebear's terminology to create dualistic categories of two-chord progressions and an analysis of Schubert's Impromptu, Op. 90, No. 3. Schenker owned a copy of this book and was doubtless suspicious of the Schubert analysis; he also owned the next work—the *Handbuch zur Harmonielehre* (Handbook of Harmony, 1887)— Riemann's attempt to apply his abstract theory to music pedagogy.[146] Both

---

145. The dissertation was first turned down by the University of Leipzig in 1873, and then accepted that year by the University of Göttingen. It was published twice as *Über das musikalische Hören* (Göttingen: Vandenhoeck & Ruprecht, 1874; Leipzig: F. Andrä, 1874), and then republished as *Musikalische Logik, Hauptzüge der physiologischen und psychologischen Begründung unseres Musiksystems* (Leipzig: C. F. Kahnt, 1874). Riemann's 1872 publication, the one that develops Hauptmann's theory, was entitled "Musikalische Logik: ein Beitrag zur Theorie der Musik," and appeared under the pseudonym of Hugibert Ries in the *Neue Zeitschrift für Musik* (no. 28ff) in 1872. To make matters more complicated still, this article was revised and appeared in a collection of Riemann's articles published in 1901, *Präludien und Studien*. See Mooney, "Riemann's Debut as a Music Theorist," to which this publication data is indebted, for important background on all of these works. Also see his translation of Riemann's essay "Musikalische Logik" in the same issue, 100–26.

146. Riemann was still in his ascendency when Schenker studied the Sechter/Bruckner system of harmony at the conservatory in the late 1880s. He likely knew Riemann's work by then, for Riemann's reputation was growing, his published output already prodigious. Of all the music books in Schenker's library, the ones by Riemann far outnumber those by any other single author. Schenker owned eight works having to do with theory or composition besides the two already mentioned,

books date from Schenker's student years; it is likely that this is when he acquired them. But Schenker apparently did not own *Harmony Simplified*, the book in which Riemann outlined his well-known theory of "tonal functions," a kind of "formalized" Rameau that has inspired American "Neo-Riemannians." Perhaps Schenker had lost interest by this point. Here, Riemann tries to navigate the divide between theory and practice by attempting to account for all progressions within a key by placing each chord into one (or more) of Rameau's three categories, "tonic" (T), "dominant" (D), and subdominant (S). He even presents this "new" theory as a pedagogy of harmony.[147] Towards the end of his life, Riemann returned to the psychology of music and "musical logic," his interest all along, and something about which he had changed his mind very little.[148]

While Schenker was clearly upset about the music theory of "the physicists," his particular *bête noire* was Riemann—as the most powerful representative of this way of thinking. There are many reasons why this was so. When Schenker wrote *HL*, he was already in his mid-thirties; he was a professional pianist, composer, essayist, music editor, and philologist, academically trained principally in the human sciences. Moreover, he had developed a view of the theory of harmony that was profoundly different from the one endorsed by Riemann and his circle. As the theorist who tried to synthesize theories of Hauptmann, Helmholtz and Oettingen into a pedagogically and commercially acceptable form, Riemann no doubt epitomized a whole movement that Schenker rejected. Riemann was, above all, the conduit by which those ideas reached the musical public, the people on the front line, so to speak.

Schenker's antipathy may also have stemmed from the fact that his background and motivations were not dissimilar to those of Riemann: it was precisely those points of intersection that made Riemann a bigger threat than any of "the physicists." For starters, both men were educated in classical *Gymnasien*, and both studied law at university, though Riemann ultimately switched to philosophy and history. Since the university study of music was still in its infancy, it was from philosophy that he forged an unusual and courageous path to "music theory" (in the modern sense—virtually unknown as

---

as well as the *Musik-Lexicon* and seven additional works on other musical topics. He clearly was interested in Riemann's ideas, even if he rejected them.

147. Riemann, *Vereinfachte Harmonielehre*, tr. as *Harmony Simplified*.

148. Riemann "Ideen zu einer 'Lehre von den Tonvorstellungen,'" tr. by Wason and Marvin as "Ideas for a Study 'On the Imagination of Tone.'"

a university subject of study) via the psychology and aesthetics of music. He legitimized his work by reacting to one of the most eminent authorities of the time, Helmholtz.

Like Schenker, Riemann was a well-trained musician: he not only studied piano from his early years with a student of Liszt, but he also enrolled at the Leipzig Conservatory (and later taught there). Like Schenker, Riemann was also a composer, though he followed models that Schenker would have found problematic (particularly the second): Robert Schumann (1810–56) and Joachim Raff (1822–82). Whereas Schenker eventually gave up composing, Riemann continued to write music through the rest of his career, creating a substantial catalogue of nearly seventy opus numbers, most of them published.[149] In this, he was thoroughly in step with contemporary music theorist–composers, though subsequently eclipsed by his student Max Reger. Although no study of Riemann's musical works yet exists, it would be surprising if they were entirely irrelevant to his theory.

There were personal issues as well. By the turn of the twentieth century, Riemann exerted an extraordinary influence on German-language music theory, an influence of which a younger aspiring music theorist could not but feel some envy. He was, in this respect, far more of a target than "the physicists," who were of an earlier generation. Moreover, Riemann had a pronounced tendency towards self-aggrandizement, something that was probably a reaction to the difficulty he had earning a living as a music theorist.[150] Riemann's inflated view of himself was most evident in the section on *Harmonielehre* in his *Geschichte der Musiktheorie* (History of Music Theory, 1898), but also in his reviews of works of other theorists, which were regularly published in the most prestigious music periodicals of the day.

But the main source of Schenker's antipathy was one particular doctrine that Riemann promulgated throughout his career: dualism. As it happens, Riemann's views about dualism certainly changed during the course of his career: at first, he tried to emulate Helmholtz by searching for its physical basis, believing that he had actually found it in an audible series of "undertones," but by 1905 he gave up that quest and simply claimed that the

---

149. See the list of Riemann's compositions in Michael Arntz, *Hugo Riemann*, 341–44.

150. Relying on his writing and part-time teaching appointments, he was not offered a full professorship until 1901 at the University of Leipzig, where he eventually became director of the Institute of Musicology in 1914.

reciprocity between wave length and frequency was a sufficient basis.[151] Either way, he remained a firm believer. When Schenker offered his most comprehensive response to dualism in [DTS], he may well have had Riemann's essay on "The Problem of Harmonic Dualism" in mind, given that it had appeared in a well-known general musical periodical.

One immediate result of these critiques is that Schenker asked Cotta not to send the manuscript of *HL* to Riemann or his disciples for review before publication:

> If I may at this point express one wish, it is that you not let too many specialists examine my manuscript. The issue is really one of the priority of my idea, which I should like to be sure is safeguarded as completely as possible. . . . In particular, I fear lest Professor Riemann or any "Riemannian" might get his hands on it. It is precisely against "musical mathematics" as represented by Riemann that my book is expressly directed. No one in the world is more eager than Professor Riemann to appropriate every new idea to himself alone, to present it as coming from himself alone. He currently commands the market place, and no longer allows anyone even a small patch.[152]

Despite its many historical resonances, the reference to "musical mathematics" in this passage was surely code for "musical logic," and all the machinery of Riemann's many, many works.

Art and the Sciences

> An act of the imagination, in the broadest sense, is the essential element in all invention. Independent thought in the sciences involves just as much creativity [*Phantasie*] as the products of poetic thought, and it is quite doubtful whether Newton or Shakespeare possessed more.[153]

The plot thickens as we draw in Schenker's appeal to "art," as well as his status as a *Wissenschaftler*. His approach to harmony was very different

---

151. Riemann, "Das Problem des harmonischen Dualismus," tr. as "The Problem of Harmonic Dualism."
152. Schenker, letter to Cotta Verlag, November 22, 1905, *SC*, 78.
153. Johann Friedrich Herbart, *Lehrbuch der Psychologie*, 46. "Das Dichten, im weitesten Sinne, ist das Wesentliche bey allem Erfinden. Zum Selbstdenken in den Wissenschaften gehört eben so viel Phantasie, als zu poetischen Erzeugnissen; und es ist sehr zweifelhaft, ob Newton oder Shakespeare mehr Phantasie besessen habe."

from Riemann's, and he proclaimed as much in the title he had originally planned for his first book: "New Musical Theories and Creative Ideas of an Artist" (*Neue musikalische Theorien und Phantasien von einem Künstler*).¹⁵⁴ By "art" we refer of course to the *schöne Künste*—the "fine arts" in general, which will be the rather surprising subject of the opening of *Harmonielehre*. Ultimately, the phrase became the overall title of his triptych *Harmonielehre*, *Kontrapunkt I–II*, and *Der freie Satz*, but, as we saw earlier, it is an apt title for *Harmonielehre*—perhaps even more correctly descriptive of the content of the book (which presents quite a radical interpretation of its topic) than the perennial title he finally settled on—or was counseled to accept.

Schenker's original title is telling on several counts. First, by stressing that the author is an "artist," Schenker calls upon his careers in performance and composition and tries to distance his work from contemporary music theory, be it promoted by the physicists or the pedagogues. This strategy is clear to see both from his vigorous rejection of dualism, especially as promulgated by Riemann, and his frequent critiques of music pedagogy from Fux and C. P. E. Bach to Bruckner, Riemann, and Reger.¹⁵⁵ Second, by juxtaposing the terms "theory" and "creative idea," Schenker underscores two very different sides of intellectual life, in the fine arts or the sciences—both of which are necessary for significant and original work: in the fine arts, the ability to envision creative ideas and the compositional technique (in whatever medium) to realize them; in the sciences, the ability to envision creative ideas and the systematic and theoretical means to develop them.

In the first part of his title, Schenker acknowledges the systematic aspects of theorizing about music. Those aspects, which are manifest in the highly organized layout of his text and in its constant appeals to music psychology, law, and history, clearly place the book within the tradition of *Musikwissenschaft*, rather than that of conventional music theory pedagogy. Moreover, they interpret *Wissenschaft* in a broader sense than is the case with the exact sciences, which is consistent with Schenker's rejection of purely physical theories of harmony (Helmholtz) and any notion of a "musical logic" (Oettingen and Riemann). Schenker simply found other ways to "naturalize" music theory.

In the second part of the title, he uses the German word *Phantasie* to convey the imaginative aspects of his project as a music theorist, but also as an

---

154. *Neue musikalische Theorien und Phantasien von einem Künstler*. See *SC*, 76, footnote 2. On the problem of translating *Phantasie*, see below.

155. For details, see chapter 3.

appeal to the creativity of the artist. As we learn at the end of the title, he is also one of the latter, and we infer that his music theory attempts to model their thinking. Here, it is important to make sure that the English reader does not get the wrong idea, for the German word *Phantasie* essentially means imagination or creative thinking (or the ability to summon both): hence, our opening quotation from the familiar Herbart.[156] Although imagination is obviously an essential feature of creativity in the arts, it is an equally important component of scientific inquiry—both in the natural sciences, and in the human sciences. Whether we are speaking of creativity in the fine arts, or inquiry in the natural and human sciences, the artist must constantly imagine new possibilities and be prepared to carry them out in the work at hand, while the researcher must balance the need for accurate observations and careful systematization with some broader and more speculative vision. Both of these traits are on full display in Schenker's Theory of Harmony.

Geisteswissenschaft and Schenker's Editorial Projects

Schenker's interest in the human as opposed to the natural sciences is also apparent in his fascination with the emerging science of philology. Like psychology, philology exploded as a discipline during the course of the nineteenth century, especially in German-speaking universities. Indeed, just as scientists grappled with the problems of accounting for variations and errors in the observations they used to support their experiments, so philologists wrestled with the problems of dealing with textual variants and errors in their editions of works by Homer, Virgil, and other ancient authors. Those problems stemmed from the fact that the texts in question were written thousands of years earlier, at a time when the only means of transmission was to copy them by hand, either by a single scribe or groups of scribes. This process inevitably introduced discrepancies of one sort or another: the more the text was copied, the more discrepancies were introduced. The task of the philologist was to recover the original version or *Urtext* from later

---

156. When used in the phrase "er hat Phantasie," the word means "he has the capacity to be imaginative," or "is imaginative." *Phantasie* is not "the faculty or activity of imagining things, especially things that are impossible or improbable: *his research had moved into the realm of fantasy.*" This is the first meaning of the English cognate given by the Oxford American Dictionary.

incarnations that have "been obscured by a cloud of witnesses."[157] In part, that task required the application of rigorous philological methods that could be applied in an objective fashion. And yet it also called for more: it demanded "judgment informed by deep knowledge of the subject," judgements that allow the scholar "to discard an outlying observation or to emend a specious reading."[158]

As it happens, the basic methods for identifying discrepancies were well known before the nineteenth century and involved collating different sources (*emendatio ope codicum*) and appealing to the scholar's own knowledge and insight (*emendatio ope ingenii*).[159] In the late eighteenth and early nineteenth centuries, however, philologists such as Friedrich August Wolf and Karl Lachmann called for "more rigorous procedures that would enable [philologists] to both reduce the number of variants to choose from and make that choice without having to have recourse to personal taste."[160] Among other things, they distinguished between variants and errors: the former are alternative but plausible readings of a given passage, whereas the latter are grammatical mistakes that may occur systematically, in which case they are habitually introduced by a particular scribe or particular group of scribes, or randomly, in which case they are haphazardly added by the scribe or scribes. Drawing an analogy between scientific laws and grammatical rules, philology not only emerged as *a* science, but as *the* science: "the discoveries of the philologists, whether concerning the authorship of the *Iliad*, the decipherment of hieroglyphics, or the ancestry of modern languages, counted alongside those of the chemists and the physicists as among the most spectacular of the age and their methods as among the most rigorous."[161]

The science of philology appealed to Schenker on several counts. On the one hand, it resonated with his training in classics and the law, two disciplines that put a premium on both the accuracy and interpretation of texts. As a classics student, Schenker was obviously familiar with the problems of text criticism and of translating texts from one language to another, and the thorough understanding of Greek and Latin grammar such work entailed.

---

157. Daston and Most, "Focus: History of Science and History of Philologies," 381.
158. Ibid.
159. Pfeiffer, *History of Classical Scholarship from the Beginnings to the End of the Hellenistic Age*; Pfeiffer, *History of Classical Scholarship from 1300 to 1850*; and Reynolds and Wilson, *Scribes and Scholars*.
160. Daston and Most, "History of Science and History of Philology," 380.
161. Ibid., 384.

Moreover, he clearly would have put all of this into philological practice many times in the six (!) classes he took in Roman law.

Surprisingly, Schenker's background in Judaism seems have been a negligible philological influence, contrary to what we might expect. The *Wissenschaft des Judentums* (Jewish Studies) was, from at least 1820 on, only to be found outside the University of Vienna in rabbinical schools, though some study of biblical Hebrew likely took place in the university departments of theology or oriental studies. Still, it is clear that Schenker knew no Hebrew,[162] and thus those departments are unlikely to have been a source from which he learned even elementary philology.[163] Nonetheless, it is clear that he did know ibn Ezra, and thus seems to have known at least basic biblical exegesis, most likely from religious training in his youth.[164]

But as a law student, Schenker was well aware of the difficulties that arise in establishing the reliability of different testimonies. He was taught how to distinguish first-hand testimonies from eyewitness accounts and other forms of forensic and circumstantial evidence.[165] Indeed, by the time he graduated, Schenker may well have known about the recent developments in forensic science, such as the system of fingerprint analysis devised by Alphonse Bertillon and the methods of handwriting analysis cultivated by Jean-Hippolyte Michon, Jules Crépieux-Jamin, Alfred Binet and others.

Schenker, however, was also drawn to philology for purely pragmatic reasons: he wanted to have accurate scores of the pieces that he and his students wished to play. This latter issue, of requiring accurate performance editions, had come to the forefront in the 1890s when the Berlin Academy of Arts published a series of famous compositions, including the piano sonatas of Mozart and Beethoven, that claimed to eliminate all arbitrary accretions to those scores. These scores were published under the rubric "Urtext

---

162. Rothfarb, "Henryk Szenker," 30, footnote 103: "Heribert Esser, longtime friend of Schenker disciple Oswald Jonas, reported to me by email (April 18, 2012) that Jeanette Schenker's brother, Victor Schiff, who embraced his Jewish heritage and learned Hebrew, used to write letters in Hebrew to her and Heinrich, and that they had to have them translated into German."

163. Email from Lee Rothfarb to R. Wason on January 17, 2018, containing a message from Dieter J. Hecht of the University of Vienna. Rothfarb provided the information on ibn Ezra, while Hecht wrote of the status of the *Wissenschaft des Judentums*.

164. Abraham ibn Ezra, about whose identity there is some controversy, was a biblical commentator of the middle ages.

165. See Alpern, "The Triad of the True, the Good, and the Beautiful."

of Classical Musical Compositions" (*Urtext classischer Musikwerke*).[166] Spurred on by the success of these editions, Schenker prided himself on making "his students use exclusively *Urtext* and original editions, insofar as they are available."[167] And thanks to the efforts of Ernst Rudorff and Joseph Joachim, Schenker even decided to make editions of his own, starting with a selection of keyboard works by C. P. E. Bach in 1902.[168]

Schenker's main goal in making the C. P. E. Bach edition was to reconstruct Bach's conception of his own music, thereby removing the numerous emendations found in earlier editions, such as the one by Hans von Bülow.[169] Schenker claims that, instead of recreating C. P. E. Bach's *Urtext*, Bülow actually translated "the keyboard language of the eighteenth century to that of the nineteenth—from the clavichordistic to the pianofortistic."[170] He did so by adding "appropriate inner voices to the all too meager accompaniment," filling "some gaps and pauses," enlivening "certain transitory sketchy outlines," and including "careful and detailed dynamic markings."[171] As a result, Schenker dismisses Bülow's editions as "trivial" and completely denounces their "alleged historical basis."[172] He voices similar reservations in *HL* and suggests that the approach adopted by Bülow depends upon the whim of the editors, some of whom are not "as gifted and as learned as is required by the task."[173] The bellicose tone of such comments calls to mind Lachmann's equally harsh review of an edition by Gottfried Hermann. Having claimed that Hermann's tolerance for the judgement of others was simply "laziness" and amounted to "criminal leniency," Lachmann added that textual critics must be wary of those "who do not strive above all for a

---

166. See the Wiener Urtext website http://www.wiener-urtext.com/en/wiener-urtext-edition, accessed December 30, 2017.

167. Cited by Oswald Jonas, "Ein textkritisches Problem der Ballade op. 38 von Frédéric Chopin," 156–57, footnote 6, in "Translator's Foreword," *CFF* (1984), vii–viii.

168. See Schenker's letters to Theodor von Frimmel (June 17, 1912, and August 4, 1912) cited by Federhofer, *HS*, 30–31.

169. C. P. E. Bach, *Sechs Klavier-Sonaten*, ed. Hans von Bülow (Leipzig: C. F. Peters, 1862). Schenker discussed Bülow's edition in *EBO*, 4–6; *CSO*, 16–20. See also Cook, "The Editor and the Virtuoso," 78–95.

170. *CSO*, 17.

171. C. P. E. Bach, *Sechs Klavier-Sonaten*, ed. Bülow, 3–4; *CSO*, 17.

172. *CSO*, 19–20.

173. *HL*, 88–89; *HA*, 69.

documentary text and who venture to get to work all too quickly, without having severely interrogated the witnesses."[174]

Schenker's desire to reconstruct the composer's own conception of a given work prompted him to prioritize sources that either came from the composer's original hand, such as sketches, autographs, teaching materials, letters, and so on, or that could be authenticated by some other means, such as early editions, reliable secondary sources, and so forth—all techniques of the human sciences pioneered by the historicists. Such texts not only provided him with the primary sources for his *Urtext*, but they also provided him with vital information about "the principles of art, the creation of musical coherence, the individual style of notation, etc."[175] The latter was especially important to Schenker: whereas the standardized appearance of printed editions often indicates the publisher's individual house style, the idiosyncracies in beaming, slurring, and even fingering found in composers' sketches and autographs often reveal insights about the ways in which those authors actually conceived of the piece structurally. By basing his editions on close readings of individual manuscript sources, Schenker could legitimately claim to be "the true founder of the discipline of autograph-study" and the "forefather of the Wiener Urtext Edition."[176]

When autographs were unavailable, however, Schenker focused his attention on the first edition and early prints, often interpreting them in terms of other historically relevant documents. This was precisely the strategy he used when editing C. P. E. Bach's keyboard music. Since he did not have access to the autographs for these pieces, Schenker relied on early editions, supplementing his readings with material taken from C. P. E. Bach's keyboard treatise *Versuch über die wahre Art das Clavier zu spielen*.[177] Above all, he used the latter to address the issue of ornamentation: by adding decorations in the manner suggested by C. P. E. Bach in the *Versuch*, he could avoid the nineteenth-century "pianofortistic" excesses introduced by Bülow and present a text more in line with the eighteenth-century "clavichordistic" style of the original score.

Enthusiastic as he was about the status of *Urtexte*, Schenker was nonetheless critical of the fact that such editions often fail to make the music

---

174. Daston and Most, "History of Science and History of Philologies," 380.
175. *DfS*, 23–24; *FC*, 7.
176. Ibid. See also Wiener Urtext website http://www.wiener-urtext.com/en/wiener-urtext-edition.
177. C. P. E. Bach, *Versuch*; Mitchell, *Essay*.

in question accessible to the modern-day performer, surely their ultimate *raison d'être*. A good case in point was E. F. Baumgart's edition of C. P. E. Bach's keyboard works. Although Schenker admits that this edition offers an accurate representation of C. P. E. Bach's original text along with a lengthy account of the latter's approach to ornamentation, he nonetheless complains that it fails to explain how performers might translate the signs on the page into sounds in the ether.[178] Since Baumgart ignores the "practical purpose" in making an edition, namely to help musicians perform the work, Schenker laments that his edition will simply gather dust in the library and do little to make C. P. E. Bach's music known to concertgoers. Schenker amplifies this point in *HL*: while the "historical approach" may have the advantage of strict neutrality, "its disadvantage is that of misleading public opinion." He continues: "Our audience, trained to trust its artists and scholars and wont to impute to rediscovered works an artistic value which alone would warrant their revival, transfers this assumption, in itself justified, to the assessment of any work. Unaware of the purely historical motivation of the revival, this audience is inclined to corrupt its own judgment, to force upon itself the conviction of the justice of its prejudice, rather than to admit a truth less pleasant. By this process, the formation of good taste suffers severely."[179]

There are, of course, good reasons why Schenker was so concerned about the differences between recreating what composers notated in their scores and understanding what composers intended by those notations. The fact is that each task requires slightly different types of information and skills: the former is, of course, a largely philological task and depends on a careful reading of the original sources; the latter, however, is a largely psychological task and depends on determining the stylistic and structural concerns of the composer. In legal terms, this is analogous to the distinction between specifying what someone may or may not have done and explaining why that person did or did not do it. They also call to mind the so-called Chinese Room Argument. Devised by the philosopher John Searle, this thought experiment raises doubts about whether computers are inherently capable of genuine understanding.[180] Searle, who does not understand how to speak or read Chinese, imagines himself locked in a room with a set of syntactic rules in English that enable him "to correlate one set of formal symbols with another set of formal symbols." These rules allow him to respond in Chinese

---

178. C. P. E. Bach, *Clavier-Sonaten, Rondos, und freie Fantasien*; CSO, 2–4.
179. *HL*, §88–89; *HA*, 69.
180. John Searle, "Minds, Brains and Programs."

to questions also written in Chinese. Although Searle's answers are syntactically correct and satisfy interrogators who are fluent in Chinese, they do not reflect any genuine understanding on his part because Searle cannot explain what the symbols actually mean or why they were originally written.

Schenker's response to this dilemma was simple: to supplement the work's *Urtext* with additional information, thereby creating an "elucidatory edition" (or *Erläuterungsausgabe*).[181] Some of this additional information is historical in nature and includes insights from letters, treatises, and other relevant documents. It is the sort of thing that can be found in many so-called critical editions (*kritische Ausgaben*). In the case of Schenker's edition of C. P. E. Bach's *Klavierwerke*, his critical report became so lengthy that it appeared as an independent Monograph entitled *Ein Beitrag zur Ornamentik* (1903, rev. 1908).[182] But Schenker went further to add an array of relevant analytical observations in his elucidatory comments. Since those observations inevitably reflected his own theoretical predispositions, his early editions, such as those of C. P. E. Bach's *Klavierwerke* (1902) and J. S. Bach's *Chromatische Phantasie und Fuge* (1910), include insights about the works' themes, phrase structure, modulations, and formal structure, and largely mirror the sorts of theoretical concerns outlined in *HL* and *KP1*.

As Schenker's theoretical perspectives expanded, however, so the analytical comments in his elucidatory editions developed in response. Indeed, as table 4.3 shows, there are often close chronological and conceptual connections between Schenker's editions and his theoretical and analytical projects. The left-hand column of table 4.3 lists Schenker's published editions, which range from editions of standard repertory (e.g., Beethoven's *Klaviersonaten*) and facsimiles of autograph manuscripts (e.g., Beethoven's "Moonlight" Sonata Op. 27, No. 2) to piano transcriptions (e.g., his four-hand version of G. F. Handel's *Zwolf Orgel-Concerte*, Op. 4) and even more comprehensive endeavors (e.g., Beethoven's *Die letzten fünf Sonaten* vol. 1–4).[183] The right-hand column then lists Schenker's major theoretical writings, starting with *EBO*, *HL*, and *KP1*, and ending with *TW*, *KP2*, *MW*, *FT*, and *DfS*.

---

181. Drabkin, "The New *Erläuterungsausgabe*"; Bent, ""That Bright New Light"; Marston, "Schenker's Concept of a Beethoven Sonata Edition."
182. Schenker, *EBO/CSO*.
183. After editing the first six concerti in 1905, Schenker intended to complete another six in 1908, but was replaced by Jan Brandts Buys because he wanted a higher honorarium; see *SDO*.

Table 4.3. Schenker's Editions and Theoretical Writings

Editions	Treatises
C. P. E. Bach, Klavierwerke (Vienna: UE, 1902).	Ein Beitrag zur Ornamentik (Vienna: UE, 1903/1908).
G. F. Handel, Zwolf Orgel-Concerte (Vienna: UE, 1905).	HL (Stuttgart & Berlin: Cotta, 1906).
J. S. Bach, Chromatische Phantasie und Fuge (Vienna: UE, 1910).	KP1 (Stuttgart & Berlin: Cotta, 1910).
L. Van Beethoven, Die letzten fünf Sonaten, Op. 109 (Vienna: UE, 1913; 2/1923). Die letzten fünf Sonaten, Op. 110 (Vienna: UE, 1914; 2/1924).	TW1–10 (Vienna: A. Guttman, 1921–24).
Die letzten fünf Sonaten, Op. 111 (Vienna: UE, 1915; 2/1925). Die letzten fünf Sonaten, Op. 101 (Vienna: UE, 1920; 2/1928).	KP2 (Vienna: UE, 1922).
Sonate Op. 27, Nr. 2 Facsimile (Vienna: UE, 1921); Klaviersonaten (Vienna: UE, 1923).	MM1–2 (Munich: Drei Masken Verlag, 1925, 1926). MM3 (Munich: Drei Masken Verlag, 1930).
Johannes Brahms, Oktaven und Quinten u. A. (Vienna: UE, 1933).	FT (Vienna: UE, 1932).
	DfS (Vienna: UE, 1935).

Perhaps the most significant example of the interrelationships between Schenker's editing and his theorizing involves the concept of the *Urlinie*.[184] Although Schenker anticipated this term in his references to *Urideen* in *HL* and *Urformen* and melodic fluency in *KP1*, he used it explicitly for the first time with appropriate graphic analyses in his editions of Beethoven's Piano Sonatas, Op. 101 (1920) and Op. 27, No. 2 (1921).[185] He subsequently refined the idea in the first volumes of *TW* (1921–22) and introduced the concept of an *Ursatz* for *TW5* (1923) in connection with his analysis of J. S.

---

184. See Urchueguía, "Wie kam die 'Urlinie' in den 'Urtext'?"
185. William Pastille, "The Development of the *Ursatz*." See Schenker, *HL*, XXX and *HA*, 306; *KP1*, *CP1*, and bass motives in *EBO*.

Bach's Little Prelude No. 5 in D minor, BWV 926.[186] Schenker's decision to invoke *Urlinien* in his editorial commentaries is especially striking because it underscores the term's conceptual links to the idea of an *Urtext* and because it conveys important information about the composers' psychological motivations for writing a piece.[187] Since Schenker believed that *Urlinien* or *Ursätze*, voice-leading transformations, and voice-leading levels are constrained by the rules of strict counterpoint and that composers such as Bach, Beethoven, and Brahms, internalized those rules through their own training, teaching, and improvisation, he also believed that his graphic analyses reconstruct the thought processes going on inside the composer's head.

Schenker highlighted this point in his essay "Forsetzung der Urlinie-Betrachtungen" in *MW1* (1925). Having placed his foreground sketch of measures 1–4 of the first movement from Mozart's Piano Sonata in A major, K. 331 above rather than below the middleground prototype, Schenker notes: "The voice-leading strata are deliberately viewed from the perspective of the observer, not from that of the composer—that is, they are presented, as an exception, from the foreground to the background."[188] The same idea was apparently behind Schenker's claim in *DfS* that it is the composer, rather than the performer or the listener, who must experience their works "as entities which could be heard and perceived as a whole."[189]

For Schenker, then, the task of creating an "elucidatory" edition is ultimately a complex process that encompasses two different branches of *Geisteswissenschaft*, calling to mind Schleiermacher's distinction between the "grammatical" and the "philosophical" approach to a text that we described earlier. The first, or philological, stage is encapsulated in the concept of an *Urtext* and recreates what composers actually notate in their scores. As such, it presents the composers' external actions. The second, or psychological, stage is eventually enshrined in the concepts of an *Urlinie* or *Ursatz* and reconstructs what structural concerns might have been in the back of the

---

186. Pastille, "The Development of the *Ursatz*" 79. See Dubiel trans., 180–81. The Commentary appears in the section "Miscellanea" (or Vermisches) trans. Joseph Lubben, 212–13.
187. Urchueguía, "Wie kam die 'Urlinie' in den 'Urtext'?"
188. Schenker, "Forsetzung der Urlinie-Betrachtungen," *MW1*, 189; "Further consideration of the *Urlinie*: I," 105.
189. *FC*, "Introduction," xxiii. Schenker even mentioned parallels with Greek drama: see *FC*, chapter 1, section 1, "The Concept of the Background in General," and appendix C, 159.

composers' minds when they were writing particular pieces, concerns that prompted them to use their musical material in some ways but not in others. In this respect, Schenker wanted to explain the motivations behind a composer's musical actions, the internal mental decisions that prompted their external behavior. In the spirit of *Geisteswissenschaft*, the philological and the psychological endeavors require editors to balance their use of systematic methods with their own individual judgements and imagination. In other words, they must balance *Theorien* with *Phantasien*.

Part Three

Harmonielehre: The Future

Chapter Five

A "New Edition" for a New Audience and an "American Version" for a New Country

Problems of Editing and Translating *Harmonielehre* (1906)

The Revised Edition of *HL*

Introduction

Earlier, we examined the origins of *HL,* showing how the book was a product, in many respects, of ideas that Schenker had originally learned while a *Gymnasium* student in Galicia and an aspiring lawyer at the University of Vienna. The genesis of the revised abridged edition (in English only) was far more complex, taking place over a span of nearly fifty years, across two continents. The impetus for that edition occurred in Europe, and in this chapter we discuss, first, the motivations behind it, and the problems with creating it. We then turn to the problem of language, for both the purpose and audience of the book had changed completely.

There were four main protagonists behind the movement towards a revised edition: Heinrich Schenker, Otto Vrieslander, Manfred Willfort, and Oswald Jonas. Each one of them had slightly different reasons for supporting the project: Schenker wanted to correct some mistakes in the original publication and create a version of his treatise that he could teach from; Vrieslander wanted to make the text more amenable to classroom teaching and to add some suitable written exercises; Willfort wanted to improve on Vrieslander's abridged edition; and Jonas wanted to update Schenker's original material in light of his later thinking and to correct common misunderstandings about his theoretical ideas. The revised text not only reflects these different concerns, but it also highlights Schenker's belief in the affinity between editing and theorizing.

To show how the revised edition actually came into being, this chapter begins by winding the clock back to the first decade and a half of the twentieth century, when Schenker originally completed *HL* and developed his own innovative approach to editing. The focus of the chapter then shifts to Vrieslander and his twenty-year quest to produce a revised edition of Schenker's treatise. In particular, it discusses some of Vrieslander's other editorial projects and shows how they were directly influenced by Schenker's ideas. Next, the spotlight turns to Willfort and his attempts to produce an alternative abridgement to Vrieslander's. Finally, the discussion turns to Jonas, his version of what an introduction to Schenker's work should look like, his relationship with Schenker, his experiences as an editor, and his decision to continue Vrieslander's work after emigrating from Vienna to Chicago. The first part of the chapter ends by showing how the revised edition differs from the first and how those differences resonate with ideas that Schenker had taught Vrieslander and Jonas many years before.

Heinrich Schenker

As noted in chapter 2, Schenker had a long and illustrious career as an editor and is widely regarded as one of the leading music editors of the early twentieth century. His approach to editing was guided by two of the most significant branches of *Geisteswissenschaft*: philology and psychology. Schenker's interest in philology was motivated by a desire to recreate the original version of the masterworks. Such *Urtext* editions favor readings found in a work's autograph and first edition, and they systematically remove any readings that were added in an ad hoc fashion by later hands. Schenker was especially keen to remove the "over-abundant" expression marks that can be found in so many nineteenth-century musical editions.[1] Meanwhile, Schenker's interest in psychology was prompted by a desire to reconstruct what authors or composers intended to convey when they created specific works. In the case of musical scores, this desire meant not only addressing issues of performance

---

1. *HL*, §17, 52; *HA*, 38.

practice, especially as regards ornamentation, but also understanding the internal structures of the works in question. However diverse the works in question may be, these structures are determined by certain fundamental laws of tonal harmony and voice leading: "The fact that all of the masterworks manifest identical laws of coherence in no way precludes a diversity in essential nature among the masters. That is, the masters achieved variety and newness without seeking new principles of coherence."[2]

Since Schenker's editorial projects were always closely entwined with his theoretical work, it goes without saying that he had these concerns in mind when, soon after completing *HL* in 1906, he contemplated producing a revised edition.[3] The most pressing matter was, of course, that of correcting the many mistakes that found their way into the text during the process of publication. Such slips are easy to make and just as simple to correct. Fortunately, Schenker had help in finding the culprits: after studying the first edition of *HL* in great detail, his student Otto Vrieslander sent him a comprehensive list of typographical errors in 1915. This list provided a perfect starting point for preparing a revised edition.

But, whereas the task of correcting typographical errors was straighforward enough, our task of pinning down Schenker's intentions is far more difficult to accomplish. The problems here are two-fold. For one thing, Schenker never stopped thinking about tonal harmony once he had completed *HL*: on the contrary, he came up with new insights about the contrapuntal function of chords while he was working on his next treatise *KP1* (1910). Perhaps the most significant revision in this regard concerns his treatment of seventh chords: in *HL* Schenker acknowledges that essential harmonies can be expressed by independent seventh chords, but in *KP1* he insists that essential

---

2. Schenker, *DfS*, 22; *FC*, appendix 4H, Omissions from the Original German Edition, 160.
3. Although Schenker mainly edited musical scores, he also tried his hand at editing other theoretical texts. The most famous, of course, is his elucidatory edition of Johannes Brahms's study *Oktaven und Quinten u. A.* (Vienna: UE, 1933; Mast, tr., *Johannes Brahms*). Schenker also wrote commentaries on J. S. Bach's *Generalbaßbüchlein* and C. P. E. Bach's *Versuch*. As regards the former, see "Von der Stimmführung," in FS 51/6/231-2 (copy in OC/6, 1), and Siegel, "A Source for Schenker's Study of Thorough-Bass." As regards the latter, see "Kommentar zu Ph. E. Bachs 'Versuch,'" in FS 52/10 (copy in OC/6, 1), and Schenker, "Die Kunst der Improvisation," *MW1*, 11–40; tr. Richard Kramer, "The art of improvisation," *MM1*, 2–19.

harmonies can only exist as root position or first inversion triads and that seventh chords are byproducts of contrapuntal motion.

For another, Schenker seems to have changed his mind about the overall goals of *HL*. When preparing the original treatise, though he offered the book to Cotta as a "textbook," what he really produced was a book to instruct teachers rather than to teach students of tonal theory.[4] This goal prompted him to make some telling decisions. First, he constantly condemns the state of contemporary music theory pedagogy and openly criticizes many other authors. In the preface, for example, he rebukes Hugo Riemann for his mistaken appeal to undertones as the source of the minor system: "This very conclusion leads the whole theory *ad absurdum*."[5] Later in the book, he takes pot shots at Fux and other counterpoint theorists for not realizing that the rules of strict counterpoint must be modified to explain tonal voice leading (*HL*, §91); C. P. E. Bach and other figured-bass theorists for treating every verticality as an interval (*HL*, §53) and for failing to explain why one harmony actually follows another (*HL*, §92); Ernst Friedrich Richter, Peter Tchaikovsky, and Nikolai Rimsky Korsakov for confusing harmony and counterpoint (*HL*, §90); his former teacher Anton Bruckner for his cavalier attitude towards rules (*HL*, §90); and Salomon Jadassohn and Max Reger for not realizing that modulating and preludizing are ultimately free exercises in composition (*HL*, §181).[6] The belligerent tone of such attacks is not only confusing to ordinary music students, but is also extremely off-putting to potential publishers and reviewers. Those fears had already surfaced when Schenker negotiated the original publication of *HL*: on October 21, 1905, Universal Edition (UE) contacted Schenker about softening its strident and polemical tone. When the editors at Breitkopf und Härtel turned down the book a couple of months earlier, they claimed "works in the same vein published by Riemann make a sure success of the work questionable."[7]

---

4. Halm says as much in his review in *Der Merker* xi (1920), 414–17.
5. *HL*, Preface, VII–VIII; *HA*, xxvi. What was the recent treatise? Very likely it was Hugo Riemann, *Harmony Simplified*.
6. *HL*, §53, §§90–92, and §181, 151–53, 175–236, 445–47; *HA*, 117–19, 178–81, and 336–38. See C. P. E. Bach, *Versuch*, tr. *Essay*; Richter, *Lehrbuch*; Tchaikovsky, *Guide to the Practical Study of Harmony*; Rimsky Korsakov, *Practical Manual*; Jadassohn, *Die Kunst zu modulieren und präludieren*; and Reger, *Beiträge zur Modulationslehre*, tr. *On the Theory of Modulation*.
7. OJ/59, 9.

Second, Schenker's decision to write *HL* for teachers rather than for students led him to organize his material in ways that are not obviously suited for classes at a music conservatory. For one thing, the division of the book into two parts—one theoretical and the other practical—recalls the Aristotelian division of knowledge into theoretical, practical, and poetic, especially since the "practical part" ends with some thoughts on form, which would have been identified with *Musica Poetica* in the eighteenth century. For another, it is hard to imagine average music students responding favorably to Schenker's arcane derivation of the tonal system at the start of the theoretical part and it is unlikely that they would have had the patience to read through Schenker's explanation of intervals or the relationship between essential harmonies and counterpoint. And the fact that the book has no exercises whatsoever makes it look more like a book for aspiring music theorists than a primer for music students in general. This particular point is exacerbated by Schenker's idiosyncratic choice of musical examples, which are often far too advanced for the uninitiated. Again, this problem did not escape Halm's notice.

And yet, while Schenker originally wrote *HL* for other music theorists rather than for conservatory students, his motivations for the revised edition were quite different: he was keen to secure a stable academic job and have a version of the book to use in the classroom. And with good reason: having reviewed the second impression of *HL* in 1908, Schenker's student Ludwig Karpath attempted to have him appointed a professor of music theory at the Vienna Conservatory in 1908/09. But Karpath's efforts came to naught and, adding insult to injury, the job eventually went to Schoenberg—who actually turned it down!![8] Schenker's subsequent bids for appointments in Munich, Berlin, and Leipzig likewise fell short. Last-ditch efforts were made to hire him at his alma mater in 1933. Among his most vocal supporters was Wilhelm Furtwängler: "I hold it for strongly desirable that Dr. Schenker be engaged, at the very least, for a lecture-course (or something of that ilk) at the *Akademie*."[9] This position, like all the others, was not forthcoming; Schenker had to rely yet again on wealthy patrons to support his endeavors as a scholar and a teacher.

---

8. See Simms, "Schoenberg ... Commentary," 156 in particular. Also see Violin, *Zustände*, 22–26.

9. Federhofer, *HS*, 41.

Although Schenker began to contemplate a revised edition almost as soon as the first edition had rolled off the press in 1906,[10] those plans went off the boil during World War I and did not resurface until the early 1920s while he was preparing *KP2* for publication.[11] During negotiations in 1920 to publish the third part of his *Neue musikalische Theorien und Phantasien*, UE acquired the rights to publish *HL* from Cotta, along with existing stocks of *HL* and *KP1*.[12] UE subsequently reprinted 531 more copies of *HL* on February 21, 1921. On September 25, 1929, however, the publishing house notified Reinhard Oppel that the book was "essentially out of print."[13] Schenker was furious at the news: he complained to his friend Moriz Violin (November 24, 1929) that UE's owner and director, Emil Hertzka, concealed the fact that *HL* had in fact been "out of print" for three years.[14] Once his anger had subsided, Schenker contacted Hertzka again on December 19, 1929, to inquire about the possibility of issuing a revised edition. Hertzka replied that he "was not very hopeful at the moment."[15] Schenker received the same response a couple of years later when, on November 1, 1931, he refloated the idea, citing interest for the book in Hamburg, New York, and Oberlin.[16] Alfred Kalmus, who succeeded Hertzka as co-director of UE in

---

10. Vrieslander confirms that Schenker had already started to make emendations in 1906 in an announcement for the revised edition of *HL* in *Der Dreiklang* 8/9 (November 1937, February 1938), 207–11. See also Federhofer, *HS*, 37ff.

11. See the letter from Schenker to August Halm, *SDO*: DLA [Deutsches Literaturarchiv] 69.930 9; January 18, 1920; transc. Ian Bent and Lee Rothfarb; transl. Lee Rothfarb. (There is also a partial transcription by Federhofer in *HS*, 141–43.) The book also included material that would ultimately appear as *DfS*, and *Von der Stimmführung des Generalbaßes*. See Siegel, "When 'Freier Satz' was part of *Kontrapunkt*,'" 13.

12. The paste over of the Universal name on some copies demonstrates this point.

13. UE to Oppel, OC/52, 856. Since Oppel was teaching at the Leipzig Conservatory at that point, it seems likely that he might have checked into the availability of the book for use in his teaching. The card may have come to Schenker in a letter from Oppel, or perhaps UE sent a copy to Schenker at the same time as it notified Oppel.

14. *SC*, 373.

15. Hertzka (UE) to Schenker, December 20, 1929, Wiener Stadt- und Landesbibliothek, 418:2; see also OC/52, 857. See Kosovsky, "Levels of Understanding," 7; and the introductions to *WT*. In particular, see the introduction to *WT2*, v–xii. See also a letter of November 4, 1930, in which UE estimated printing costs of *HL*: OC/52, 863.

16. Wiener Stadt- und Landesbibliothek, 442.

1932, claimed this time that the "enormous costs" of such a venture made such an edition impossible.[17] In retrospect, this reaction is hardly surprising. Schenker's relationship with UE in general and Hertzka in particular had been deteriorating for years and had essentially fallen apart by the mid-1920s due to his threatened lawsuit over the publication of *TW*. That project was actually published in Vienna by A Gutmann Verlag and his next one, *MW*, in Munich by Drei Masken Verlag.

The impasse between Schenker and UE was apparently broken, however, by a chance meeting between Kalmus and Josef Marx in October or November 1932. Marx (1892–1964), a *Lieder* composer of note, taught theory and composition at the conservatory from 1914 until 1952 and served both as *Direktor* and *Rektor* from 1922–25 and 1925–27 respectively. In his conversation with Kalmus, Marx expressed his desire to use *HL* in his own classes. As Schenker explains in a letter to Jonas from the fall of 1932, Marx intended to use the book "for the 'composition' class" alongside the current text, Richard Stöhr's *Praktischer Leitfaden der Harmonielehre*.[18] But such a plan would not work, Marx lamented, because the costs would be prohibitively high and because the volume contained far too much material to cover in such a course. Kalmus urged Schenker either to make an "extract" of *HL* that would contain the essence of his theory or to assign this task to one of his students.[19] This "extract" should contain "at most 100 pages" and include "an "appendix" with concise references to *chorale, form*, and *modulation*."[20] Thus the possibility of a "student edition" emerged, one that was quite different from the original one.[21] Preoccupied with putting the finishing touches on *DfS*, Schenker immediately wrote to his former student Otto Vrieslander for help with the project.

---

17. See letter dated November 3, 1931, Kalmus (UE) to Schenker, Wiener Stadt- und Landesbibliothek, 443; OC/18, 4).
18. Vienna: UE, 1909. See OJ/5, 18, 17, November–December 1931.
19. See letter from Alfred Kalmus (UE) to Schenker, November 3, 1932, OC/18, 6.
20. See *SDO*: OJ/5, 18, 24; letter of March 22, 1933; transc. and transl. John Rothgeb and Heribert Esser.
21. The two most important harmony books of the period, by Schoenberg and Louis/Thuille, were likewise abridged for the classroom. The abridgement of Louis/Thuille was called *Grundriss der Harmonielehre*, and written by Louis, after Thuille's death; Schoenberg's student, Erwin Stein, wrote the *Praktischer Leitfaden zu Schönbergs Harmonielehre*.

Otto Vrieslander (1880–1950)

There were, in fact, good reasons why Schenker was so keen to approach Vrieslander to perform this task. Vrieslander first encountered *HL* as an up-and-coming *Lieder* composer, soon after its original publication, and was so impressed with the book that he compiled his first commentary in 1910.[22] Figure 5.1 shows example 324 from Schenker's *HL*; figure 5.2 shows a page from Vrieslander's commentary on that example (starting in the second paragraph). This commentary (of 472 pages!) was probably written early in the period 1910–25. During the years 1911–12, Vrieslander actually came to Vienna to study with Schenker. Documents indicate, however, that the main focus of these studies was not on tonal harmony, but rather on completing exercises in voice leading (counterpoint) and on more general musical questions.[23] One immediate result was that Vrieslander contacted Schenker in 1915. His purpose this time was two-fold: first, to present Schenker with an exhaustive list of typographical errors that he found in *HL*; and second, to start work on a new edition that would also include practical exercises and assignments. Schenker's response runs as follows:

> Don't forget that I really wanted to bring out *KP1 first*, and that I was forced to reorder the [appearance of the] volumes only for important reasons. *HL* is and remains the higher plateau; even if I lay it out in a more practical way after publication of II^2, it will, I fear, still presuppose a brilliant guide and teacher. We must be clear from the outset that a theory of such ideal character, which speaks only of the mystery-forces of free composition, presupposes

---

22. Heribert Esser, letter to Wason, August 1, 2004: "Kommentar zu Schenkers Harmonie-Lehre" (472 pp.). Florian Vogt has recently discussed one of Vrieslander's commentaries on Schenker's *HL*. The commentary is from a source once owned by Hedwig Reischauer (presumably a student of Vrieslander's) and discovered at an *Antiquariat* in Freiburg by Ludwig Holtmeier. It probably dates from 1917–18, the same period as the commentaries owned by Esser. The Holtmeier/Vogt source also contains an incomplete commentary on *KP1* and "Lehrbriefe." See Vogt, "Otto Vrieslanders Kommentar zu Heinrich Schenkers *Harmonielehre*; Ein Beitrag zur frühen Schenker-Rezeption," http://www.gmth.de/zeitschrift/artikel/0101/0101.html#fn_2. From Vogt's description, the commentary on *HL* (which runs 470 pages) seems similar to the two larger ones owned by Esser (these run 468 and 472 pages). Indeed the close correspondence in date and size of all three commentaries suggests that they may all be variants of a single commentary.

23. Heribert Esser to Wason, letter of August 1, 2004. Esser possesses Vrieslander's lesson materials.

a knowledge of voice leading, [and] can never be reduced to the state of an exercise-collection in the manner of the Richters and Regers.[24]

Schenker certainly understood the practicality of such a "student edition" and the "material costs" for not providing the sorts of student exercises that Vrieslander had suggested.[25] In a letter to Oswald Jonas written many years later (March 22, 1933), Schenker even recalls how in 1918 or so, Vrieslander had already "put such a project before Director Hertzka" and how, "as a matter of course," he had "referred Dr. Kalmus to Vrieslander."[26] Much to Schenker's chagrin, Marx wanted to include exercises, thereby making the book look like "a:—'Stöhr'!" For his part, Jonas sides with Schenker on this matter and does not include any in *HA*.

But Vrieslander was not simply an enthusiastic advocate of *HL*, he was also inspired by Schenker's editorial work and published an "elucidatory" edition of C. P. E. Bach's *Kurze und leichte Clavierstücke* in 1914.[27] This text was clearly modeled on Schenker's own editions of J. S. Bach (*CFF*, 1910), and the late Beethoven sonatas, Op. 109 (1913) and Op. 110 (1914). Like them, it includes numerous analytical insights about the individual compositions. Schenker responded enthusiastically to Vrieslander's edition and published his own graphic analysis of the first piece in *TW4*.[28] Vrieslander's interest in C. P. E. Bach continued in the following years and resulted in a monograph on the composer (1923), an edition of his songs (1922), and an article about his theoretical writings.[29] According to Esser, between about 1910 and 1925

---

24. The passage is from an undated letter (late in 1915) to Vrieslander. Schenker summarizes the letter and records sending it in his diary, November 13, 1915. See Federhofer, *HS*, 214. The English translation is by John Rothgeb, in his review of Federhofer, *HS*; see 154.

25. Rothgeb, Federhofer, *HS*, 154.

26. *SDO*: OJ/5, 18, 24; letter of March 22, 1933; transc. and transl. John Rothgeb and Heribert Esser.

27. C. P. E. Bach's *Kurze und leichte Clavierstücke: Neue kritische Ausgabe mit erläuterndem Nachwort* (Vienna: UE, 1914).

28. See Schenker, "Ph. Em. Bach: Kurze und leichte Klavierstücke mit veränderten Reprisen, Nr. 1, Allegro," 10–11 (graph in appendix), *TW4*; tr. William Drabkin, "C. P. E. Bach's Allegro in G Major," in *WT1*, 148–49.

29. Otto Vrieslander, *C. P. E. Bach: Lieder und Gesänge*; *Carl Philipp Emanuel Bach*; and "Carl Philipp Emanuel Bach als Theoretiker." As regards Vrieslander's survey of Schenker's *Kontrapunkt*, see Schenker's letter to Jonas: *SDO*: OJ/5, 18, 24; March 22, 1933; transc. and transl. John Rothgeb and Heribert Esser.

hinausschiebt: so fühlen wir uns denn einer Tonika zugleich fern und nah, wodurch eine eigentümliche Schwebesituation entsteht.

Figure 5.1. Schenker, *Harmonielehre*, 373, Example 324

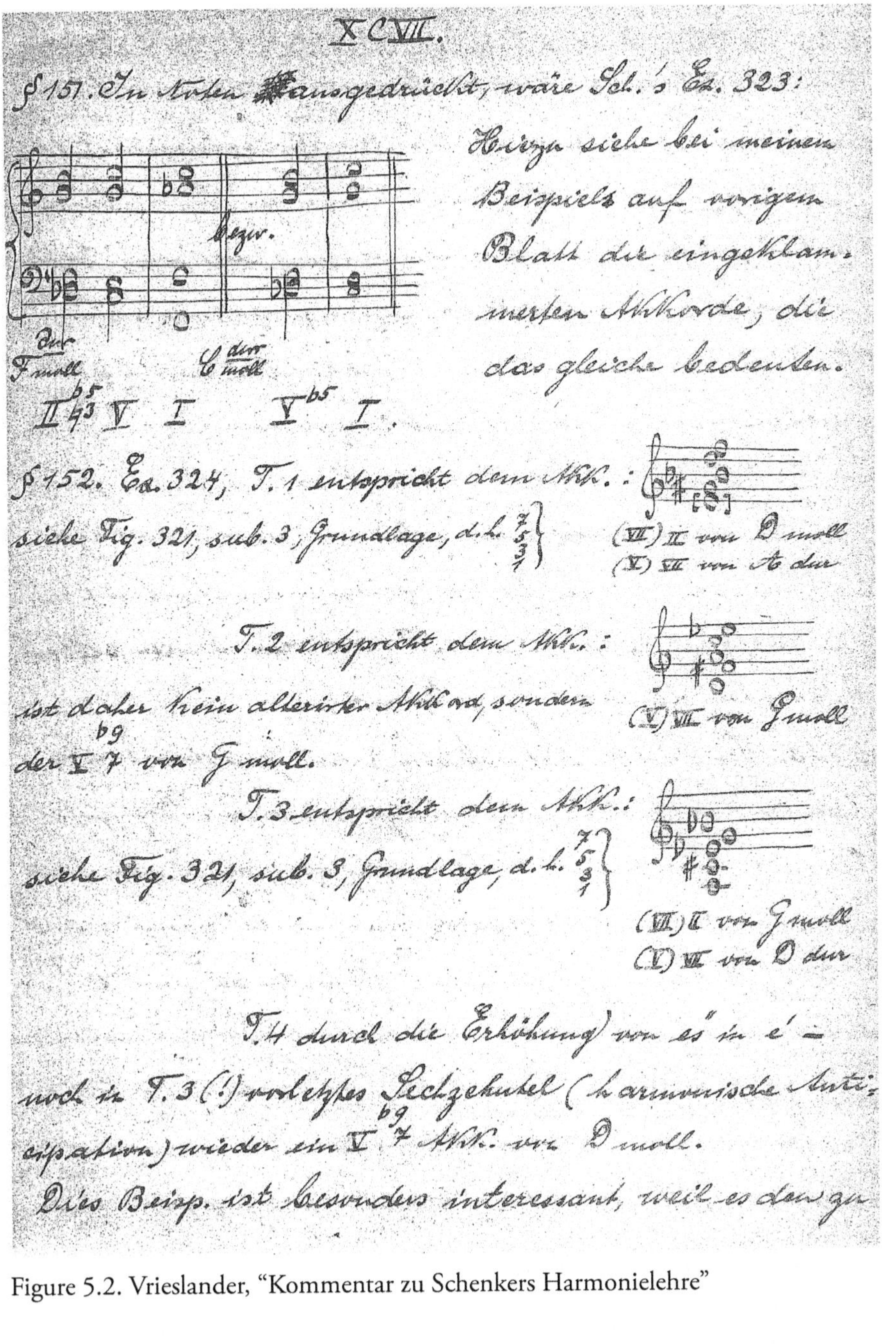

XCVII.

§ 151. In Noten ausgedrückt, wäre Sch.'s Ex. 323:

Hiezu siehe bei meinen Beispiels auf vorigem Blatt die eingeklammerten Akkorde, die das gleiche bedeuten.

§ 152. Ex. 324, T. 1 entspricht dem Akk.: siehe Fig. 321, sub. 3, Grundlage, d.h. 7 5 3 1 }

(VII) II von D moll
(V) VII von A dur

T. 2 entspricht dem Akk.: ist daher kein alterirter Akkord, sondern der V b9 7 von G moll.

(V) VII von G moll

T. 3 entspricht dem Akk.: siehe Fig. 321, sub. 3, Grundlage, d.h. 7 5 3 1 }

(VII) II von G moll
(V) VII von D dur

T. 4 durch die Erhöhung von es'' in e' — noch in T. 3 (!) vorletztes Sechzehntel (harmonische Anticipation) wieder ein V b9 7 Akk. von D moll.

Dies Beisp. ist besonders interessant, weil es den zu

Figure 5.2. Vrieslander, "Kommentar zu Schenkers Harmonielehre"

Vrieslander wrote two further commentaries on *HL*, a synopsis of *KP1*, and several articles about Schenker and his work.[30] He even served as an intermediary first with Cotta (1920) for delivering to them the manuscript of *KP2* and then with Drei-Masken-Verlag (1924) for helping to produce *MW*.[31]

It was against this backdrop that Schenker contacted Vrieslander about helping him with the "student edition" of *HL*. On November 9, 1931, Vrieslander replies and mentions that he has already produced a "commentary" on *HL* running at around 450 pages and is currently working on another "concentrated" version.[32] To follow up on Marx's suggestion, Vrieslander recommends that he continue the concentrated version, using some examples from the commentary when and where they are appropriate. He also advises against introducing ideas from Schenker's later work, on the grounds that it would be "too complicated and confusing for beginners." After several exchanges, Vrieslander offers a fairly detailed description of his plan for the edition: it would include 6660 lines of text and would fit on 185 pages, including tables, and would require around another 100–125 pages for examples (chosen from the original and the commentary).[33] But UE still seemed unsure about whether Vrieslander would really produce the student edition they had in mind. Vrieslander writes to Schenker in utter frustration on December 17, 1932, wanting to continue with the project regardless of whether they had a publisher, saying that Schenker could always keep the materials for his own personal use.[34]

Following Schenker's death in January 1935, his widow Jeanette urged Vrieslander to continue working on the new edition and sent him her husband's personal copy of *HL* to complete the endeavor. Schenker's *Handexemplar* is bound in two volumes (the first containing pages 1–278, the second, pages 279–460); the printed pages are interleaved with white sheets, which, like the margins of the print pages, are covered with examples that Schenker

---

30. Esser, letter to Wason of August 1, 2004: "Schenkers Harmonielehre kommentiert von Otto Vrieslander (erster Versuch)" (468 pp.); "Kommentar zu Schenkers Harmonie-Lehre" (472 pp.). See also Vrieslander, *Musikblätter des Anbruch* (February–March 1923); *Die Musik*, xix/1 (October 1926), 33–38; *Deutsche Tonkünstler-Zeitung* (March 5, 1928); and *Der Kunstwart* xliii (1930), 181–89.
31. See *SDO*/Profiles/Person/Vrieslander, Otto.
32. Vrieslander to Schenker, OC/18, 5.
33. OC/18, 8.
34. OC/18, 11–12.

had assembled over the years.[35] Vrieslander immediately set to work copying, identifying, and commenting upon these extra examples, ultimately producing an elegant 156-page fair copy entitled "Nachträge zu Schenker's Harmonielehre." According to Esser, Vrieslander's original plan was to leave Schenker's text as is and to publish the "Nachträge" as an appendix.[36] Figure 5.3 shows example 324 from Schenker's *HL*, which appeared in figure 5.1, but this time from Schenker's *Handexemplar*—hence, the preceding page of commentary. Figure 5.4 shows Vrieslander's transcription of that commentary (again courtesy of Esser); figure 5.5 shows the fair copy of this material that Vrieslander prepared for publication and is now part of the "Nachträge zu Schenker's Harmonielehre."

Among the documents associated with the revised edition are two sets of cut-pages that Vrieslander used to enter his corrections and changes to the text of *HL*.[37] From newspaper print used to paste up these pages, it is clear that Vrieslander began to work on them prior to 1933. The fact that they do not contain substantial cuts in the text seems to indicate that the idea of an abridged edition was ultimately abandoned, perhaps because of the wishes of Jeanette Schenker. A number of sources show that the project continued after Schenker's death. Indeed, as late as the final issue of *Der Dreiklang*, the editors could still optimistically promise the appearance of the work—edited by Vrieslander, and now containing the notes from Schenker's *Handexemplar*. They promised this in a "Notice" (*Anzeige*) that appears almost at the end of *Der Dreiklang* 8–9, dated November 1937–February 1938 (see figures 5.6a and b).

Unfortunately, the terrible events of history intervened, and both *Der Dreiklang* and work on the revised edition came to an abrupt halt. Jeanette Schenker had signed a contract with Vrieslander on November 16, 1937,

---

35. This is the "working copy" mentioned by Jonas in *HA*, 5, footnote 5. It is also in the possession of Heribert Esser, to whom we owe this detailed description. Thus the examples in Schenker's *Handexemplar* and Vrieslander's three earlier studies came into existence completely independently. Esser believes that Vrieslander did not see the *Handexemplar* during Schenker's lifetime and that Schenker had not seen Vrieslander's earlier studies.

36. According to Federhofer, Vrieslander offered an *Erläuterungen zur 'Harmonielehre'* (presumably this work) to Hertzka for publication; see Federhofer, *HS*, 25. The OJ catalogue also describes this source as "prepared for the press but never published." OJ/18, 6.

37. AW/1, 3–5.

Figure 5.3. Schenker's *Handexemplar* of *HL*, With Commentary Interleaved

formally designating him as editor of the new edition. She also signed another contract with UE for both of them on January 17, 1938: this document resulted in an advance of 500 Swiss Francs for Vrieslander. But the Germans marched into Vienna on March 13, 1938, and UE canceled the deal about a month later.[38]

---

38. A letter of April 12, 1938, from "Dr. Roth" of UE to Jeanette Schenker reviews the dates of the earlier contracts and continues by stating that "the situation now is such that, given the very different conditions for publication (as opposed to what was foreseen on January 17, 1938), we would like to do away with the contract." The writer is probably Ernst Roth, who was later forced into exile himself. (We would like to thank Christopher Hailey for this information.) Roth goes on to say that since the SF 500 were figured against future royalties, "nothing stands in the way of a simple dissolution of the contract." Heribert Esser kindly provided a copy of this letter.

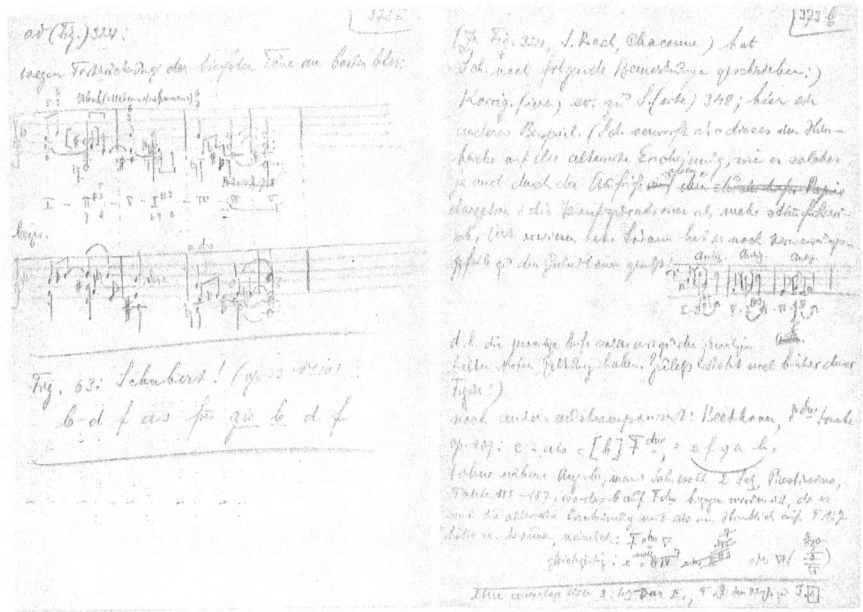

Figure 5.4. Vrieslander's Draft Copy of Schenker's Commentary on *HL*, Example 324

Manfred Willfort (1909–82)

As it happens, Vrieslander was not the only member of Schenker's circle to be interested in creating a compressed version of *HL*. Soon after Schenker's death on January 13, 1935, Kalmus approached Manfred Willfort to produce a similar abbreviated edition. A noted composer, conductor, and pianist, Willfort had studied with Weisse in the late 1920s prior to the latter's emigration to New York in September 1931, and then with Schenker himself.[39] Between 1931 and 1932, he became a member of Schenker's "Friday Seminar" with Trude Kral, Greta Kraus, and Felix Salzer, and as such helped prepare *FT* for publication in 1932.[40] Willfort left the seminar in June 1934.

---

39. *SDO*/Profiles/Person/Willfort, Manfred. He may have studied with Schenker from as early as 1927 (cf. OJ/15, 22, 9).
40. He appears in Schenker's set of lesson notes for the seminar October 9, 1931 to May 23, 1932 (OC/16, 39–42). *SDO*/Profile/Organization/Seminar 1931–34 (Schenker), by Ian Bent and Hedi Siegel. "The publication was planned as the first of a series of similar publications, but no further volumes were issued. Analyses

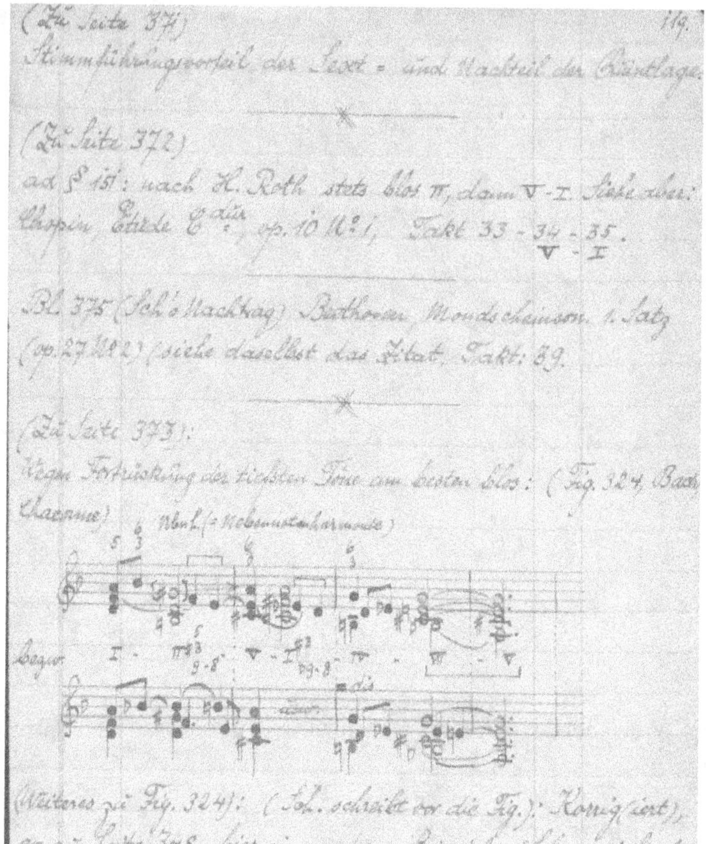

(Zu Seite 371) 119.
Stimmführungsvorteil der Sext = und Nachteil der Quintlage.

(Zu Seite 372)
ad § 151: nach H. Roth stets blos II, dann V - I. Siehe aber: Chopin, Etude C dur, op. 10 No. 1, Takt 33 - 34 - 35.
V - I

Bl. 375 (Sch.'s Nachtrag) Beethoven, Mondscheinson. 1. Satz (op. 27 No. 2) (siehe daselbst das Zitat, Takt: 39.

(Zu Seite 373):
Wegen Fortrückung der tiefsten Töne am besten blos: (Fig. 324, Bach Chaconne)

(Weiteres zu Fig. 324): (Sch. schreibt vor die Fig.): Konig(iert), so zu Seite 348; hier ein anderes Beispiel. (Sch. verweist also dieses im Hinblick auf die alterierte Erscheinung, wie er dies auch durch obigen Aufriß dargetan und die Konfigurationen als mehr stimmführerischer Art erwiesen hat. Sodann hat er noch Verweisungsteile zu den Grundtönen gefügt): d. h. die jeweilige Stufe sollte erst zu der jeweiligen hal. ben Note gehören. – Zu letzt steht noch hinter Fig. 324): noch anders auskomponiert: Beethoven, E dur Sonate, op. 109: c-ais [?] F dur, e f g a h (ohne Angabe, entweder 2. Satz Prestissimo, Takte: 156 - 159, wo das h auf F dur bezogen ist, anstatt vermittelst ais zur

Figure 5.5. Fair Copy of Commentary that Vrieslander Prepared for Publication and is now Part of the “Nachträge zu Schenker’s Harmonielehre”

ANZEIGE.

Die Schriftleitung gibt den Beziehern und Lesern bekannt, daß die seit Jahren vergriffene Harmonielehre von Heinrich Schenker (Band 1 des Serienwerkes „Neue musikalische Theorien und Phantasien") neu aufgelegt werden wird mit dem Untertitel: „Neudruck mit allen Zusätzen aus dem Handexemplar des Autors, herausgegeben von Otto Vrieslander."

Die Zusätze reichen vom Erscheinen des Werkes im Jahre 1906 bis in die letzten Lebenstage des Autors, und es könnte scheinen, als wäre manches durch die später erschienenen Werke überholt. Interessant aber und auch belehrend wird es bleiben, das harte Ringen mit dem Stoff zu beobachten vom Aufkeimen der neuen Erkenntnisse in der Musik bis zu ihrer letzten Fassung und plastischen Darstellung, das auch einem genialen Menschen nicht erspart bleibt.

Möge das Werk — es kann noch ein Jahr vergehen bis zu seinem Erscheinen — bei Musikern und Musikfreunden freundliche Aufnahme finden.

Figure 5.6a. The Notice in *Der Dreiklang* that a New Edition of Schenker's *HL* was Scheduled

Notice

The editors notify subscribers and readers that the Harmonielehre of Heinrich Schenker (Volume I of the Series, "New Musical Theories and Creative Ideas"), which has been out of print for years, will be newly published with the subtitle, "reprinted with all addenda from the personal copy of the author, edited by Otto Vrieslander."

The addenda date from the first publication of the work in the year 1906 to the last days of the author's life, and it might seem as though much was revised due to work that appeared later. In any case, it remains interesting and also instructive to observe the difficult struggle with the material from the first budding of new insights about music to their last version and graphic representation—a struggle from which even a brilliant mind was not spared.

May the work find a friendly reception by musicians and music lovers. (Up to a year may elapse before its appearance.)

Figure 5.6b. Translation of Figure 5.6a

On July 5, 1935, he wrote a letter to Jeanette Schenker in which he described his meeting with Kalmus, who claimed that the new edition must contain no more than 200 pages to garner the required profits.[41] Willfort writes to her that "by my calculations, [the printing of] at most about 120 pages can be spared (into which is reckoned the laying out of some score examples on two systems). Since the Theory of Harmony has 476 pages, that still falls [far] short of the goal [of an edition of] 200 pages."

In his letter to Jeanette Schenker, Willfort insists that the remaining text would be "an abbreviated but faithful reprint of the 1906 [edition] as an organic whole." And in claiming that "everything that remains of the text will be reproduced in precise, diplomatic form," he tries to distance his proposed edition from Vrieslander's "adaptation" of Schenker's original text and Jonas's "introduction" to Schenkerian theory, *Das Wesen des musikalischen Kunstwerks* (1934). In the first case, Willfort remembers Schenker's private complaints about Vrieslander's text: "I clearly recall—and on this you will in any case be better informed [than I]—having once heard a conversation by Schenker himself about the [*HL*], [in which] he (Schenker) did not wish the publication of this adaptation." In the second case, Willfort admits that, despite paying special attention to *HL*, Jonas's monograph does not capture the power of Schenker's original: "Lastly, even Dr Jonas's book, in which ample space is indeed granted the theory of harmony, may qualify as an attempt at an 'adaptation and introduction.' I cannot, however, help myself saying that precisely Jonas's paraphrase arouses in anyone who knows well the original a powerful longing for the crystal-clear text of Schenker." To judge by Willfort's description, his edition would seem ideal, except for the practical problem: with the removal of only 120 pages, prospective publishers might still question the practicality of a book on harmony between 300 and 400 pages. The following outline paraphrases the description of the edition that Willfort sent to Jeanette Schenker in a "supplement" (Beilage):

- Not an "adaptation" or "introduction" to Schenker's theory taking into consideration his later works.
- Not a collection of selected chapters, but an abbreviated but faithful reprint of the 1906 edition as an organic whole.

---

for the second volume prepared in the seminar—including graphs and sketches of Beethoven, Sonata, op. 27, No. 2; Mozart, Fantasy in D minor, K. 397; Chopin, Etude, op. 10, No. 3; Brahms, *Auf dem Kirchhofe*, op. 105, No. 4; and Brahms, Paganini Variations, op. 3—are preserved in FS (FS 28)."

41. We would like to thank Ian Bent for forwarding this letter to us before publishing it.

- The editor will change nothing, and will add nothing other than a short afterword. Everything that remains of the text will be reproduced in precise, diplomatic form.
- The work will be shortened essentially as follows:
  a) Deletion of short sections, paragraphs (exclusively whole paragraphs that, without compromising intellectual and linguistic relation, can be deleted): 1) dispensable detailed supporting evidence; 2) detailed elaboration of a preceding idea; and 3) polemical footnotes.
  b) Individual chapters of a more theoretical-systematic nature will be presented in abridged form: e.g. "Transpositions"; "Theory of Triads"; "Modulatory Meaning [of Triads]"; "Inversion [of Triads]," etc.
- I believe I can show that all important chapters, such as "Association and Repetition," "System," "Derivation of Minor and Mixture," the crucially important sections "Essential Harmony and Harmonic Theory," "Essential Harmony and Counterpoint" (including the profound historical deviations!), and "Critique of Current Teaching Methods," are retained in their entirety. Furthermore, the "Practical Part" ("Psychology of Content and of Essential Harmony," "Closures of Content," the wonderful chapter, "Form on a Large Scale," etc.), which will never lose its value as an introduction to music, remains virtually untouched. Finally, the method permits individual chapters, tables, and schemata to be presented in excerpted form, leaving room to spare without sacrificing the tight structure of the succession of ideas.[42]

Significantly, Willfort was not alone in voicing reservations about Vrieslander's edition: Hans Weisse shared the same view, as he made clear in a letter to Schenker dated March 17, 1933: "In your [*HL*], so much seems to me to require such thorough revision that I ask myself: how can Vrieslander undertake this? The concept of the essential harmony belongs above all to the middleground and background. The harmonies in the foreground (in fact, you yourself usually indicate these, in parenthesis) are only illusory essential harmonies. Your [*HL*], however, makes no distinction whatever in this regard."[43] Weisse exaggerates, of course, as we saw in chapter 2 with Schenker's analysis of example 2.6, which clearly suggests a middleground reading. Weisse concludes: "I would almost say that your [*HL*] is no longer yours.

---

42. This paraphrase of the supplement was conceived before the SDO translation appeared. The earlier quotations from the body of the letter are from the SDO translation at *SDO*, OJ/15, 22, 10, transcr. Ian Bent and William Drabkin, transl. Ian Bent, William Drabkin, and Hedi Siegel.

43. *SC*, 472–73. This is Drabkin's translation, with "harmony" and "essential harmony" substituted for "scale-step," as context dictates.

And precisely now, to invoke this very book for use in schools! It's a real tragedy. Only those in the know will be able to recognize, with a special emotion, the passages in [*HL*] in which the seeds of your entire theory took root."[44] But, despite such reservations, Weisse was convinced that a revised edition should appear: on October 22, 1935, he wrote to Jeanette Schenker that it should be a "shortened edition" starting from Schenker's "working copy" (she had come out against making any cuts in an earlier communication).[45] For Weisse, the book's lack of availability was ultimately a more serious problem than its questionable relationship to Schenker's later work. Even he recognized that cutting portions of the text was simply an unavoidable fact of life.

Oswald Jonas (1897–1978)

Whereas Weisse remained skeptical about Vrieslander's capacity to edit *HL*, he was surely more confident about Jonas taking over the job. Indeed, Jonas was not only a leading authority of Schenker's work and former student of Weisse's, but he was also the one disciple of Schenker "who specialized early and extensively in [manuscript] studies."[46] Jonas's work in this area was as diverse as it was voluminous. Like Schenker before him, he published editions of specific manuscripts (e.g., facsimile edition of Beethoven's Piano Sonata, Op. 109) and other compositions (e.g., J. S. Bach, C. P. E. Bach, Mozart, Haydn, Beethoven, Brahms). Jonas likewise wrote philological essays about specific manuscripts and, like Schenker, was an ardent supporter of the Archiv für Photogramme musikalischer Meisterhandschriften.

There can be little doubt that Jonas's approach to editing was profoundly influenced by his teacher, especially his attempt to balance accuracy with accessibility. Jonas explains the philological task as follows: "Misunderstandings of the composer's writing may occur, or misprints may easily slip into the first edition—misprints not to be recognized as such unless we are able to go back to the manuscript as our source; but the manuscript could be lost or inaccessible for various reasons."[47] Since composers are "not infallible," he continues: "discrepancies between the manuscript and the first edition raise the question of whether the printed version represents a mistake or an intended correction made by the composer himself in the proofs, which are

---

44. Ibid.
45. OJ/15, 16.
46. John Rothgeb, "Schenkerian theory and manuscript studies," 4.
47. Jonas and Podolsky, *Mozart: Authentic Editions*, 3.

rarely preserved." Jonas was also committed to the psychological issues of understanding why composers produced a specific text: "there are hurdles and endless difficulties to be overcome in order to bring out an authentic edition in accordance with the intention and will of the composer. Knowledge of the sources and their correct use, knowledge of specific ways of writing[,] habits of the composer in question, well-rooted musical knowledge and insight—yes, a certain amount of intuition—all are necessary to cope successfully with the task."[48] As regards Beethoven's piano sonatas, he even wrote a valuable introduction to the composer's distinctive approach to keyboard technique, especially fingering.[49]

Given his profound knowledge of Schenker's work and his love of text criticism, Jonas was in many ways the perfect person to take over the job of making an abridged revised edition of *HL*. He made it clear in his Introduction to *HA* that he was spurred on to do so both because the subject of tonal harmony was still in "a state of hopeless confusion" and because Schenker's book, which was long out of print, was of "the greatest importance."[50] According to Jonas, its chief merit is that it "disentangled the concept of the essential harmony (which is part of the theory of harmony) from the concept of voice-leading (which belongs in the sphere of counterpoint)," something that "had been confused for decades." By separating the two, Schenker was able to devise the conceptual framework for his later theories, albeit "in their embryonic stage." As noted earlier, Jonas had made the same point twenty years before in the Preface to *Das Wesen des musikalischen Kunstwerks*, where he completely endorses Schenker's derivation of the tonal system from the opening part of *HL* in chapter 1, but summarizes Schenker's later views about essential harmonies, composing out, levels, and fundamental structures in chapters 2–4.

While Jonas remains adamant about the lasting value of *HL*, he nonetheless claims that the text needs to be updated in significant ways. For one thing, he wants to change the book's tone. Although he acknowledges the inherent "difficulty of the subject matter," he concedes that there was "the need for a more objective grappling with the problems." Instead of presenting his work in a "belletristic" style, Schenker ruthlessly stood his ground, "no matter whether this put him into shrill contrast with all his contemporaries." The same issue resurfaces when Jonas edits *DfS* (1956) and Schenker's

---

48. Ibid.
49. Jonas "Wisdom from the Past," 9–11.
50. Jonas, "Introduction," *HA*, vi and vii. All the following quotations come from this source, v–xi.

editions of *CFF* (1910) and *Die letzten fünf Sonaten Beethovens*. Once again, he softens the tone of Schenker's prose considerably. Jonas also wants to update the contents of *HL* so that they conform to Schenker's later thinking: "Schenker's doctrine . . . was in a continuous process of growth and development; and the author, always occupied with the completion of new work, was never in a position of even considering the revision of older works." To explain this "hypothetical development," Jonas adds an extensive introduction, copious footnotes, and a long appendix replete with numerous voice-leading graphs. In point of fact, Jonas revises the contents of *HL* in ways that reflect his own experiences in finding ways to present Schenker's ideas in his book, *Das Wesen des musikalischen Kunstwerks*. Sometimes he finds Schenker's ideas "immature" and insists that they "found their final and clear expression only in a subsequent volume." A good case in point is Schenker's discussion of essential harmonies, which is framed locally in *HL* and globally in *MW* and *DfS*. Jonas also regards some of Schenker's earlier ideas as unnecessary and claims that they became "obsolete when the later work appeared." The "mysterious number five" is one such idea: whereas Schenker discusses it at great length in *HL* (cf. §§11, 15, 17, 113), he minimizes its role in his later writings.[51] And Jonas even suggests that some sections of *HL* were either half-baked or completely wrong-headed. For him, this was the case with the sections on seventh chords (*HL*, §§52) and modulation (*HL*, §§171ff.), both of which were "completely remodeled in Schenker's later work."

Besides updating Schenker's early text so that it conforms with his later thinking, Jonas also believes that a revised version of *HL* might correct some "common misconceptions" both about music theory in general and about Schenker's work in particular. He had two specific misconceptions in mind. First, Jonas was keen to underscore the significance of species counterpoint and figured bass to Schenker's work, while at the same time downplaying the impact of Rameau's theory of the fundamental bass. His main point was simple: although Schenker was skeptical about the value of using species counterpoint and figured bass as methods of teaching tonal harmony, his doubts stemmed from the fact that neither one was designed to achieve this goal. According to him, species counterpoint "was a study of voice-leading in its purest form, totally free of any considerations of harmony" and, as

---

51. In light of our discussion of the "mysterious number five" in chapter 1, we would observe that the influence of contemporaneous psychological thinking in general waned as Schenker developed his own alternative ways of thinking about music theory.

such, "never could lay claim to the teaching of advanced composition." Figured bass was likewise "a discipline of voice-leading" and, though it "served as a preparation and introduction to the study of composition," it "was the obligatory gateway to any musical performance."

But whereas species counterpoint and figured bass were of limited value because they were never intended as tools for explaining the nature of tonal music, fundamental-bass theory raised far more serious problems, problems that Schenker regarded as devastating. To quote Jonas:

> In broadest terms, Rameau's great error was to interpret harmonically, or vertically, a bass that was composed horizontally, according to contrapuntal principles. The possibility of *Auskomponierung* was totally overlooked. The bass line of a thorough-bass composition represented a happy attempt at horizontal construction. The upper voices, whose movement was directed by the continuo numerals, moved along similar lines. To reduce this living bass line to the so-called "fundamental" bass was the fundamental error of Rameau's doctrine.

Since Jonas believes that Schenker's *HL* was still "under the influence" of fundamental bass theory, he sets out to eliminate Rameau's influence completely and, in so doing, to bring the text in line with the very different perspective taken by Schenker in his later writings. Such issues were sufficiently serious that Jonas even included a lengthy critique of Rameau's accounts of triadic inversion, seventh chords, and chord function, in chapter 3 of *Das Wesen des musikalischen Kunstwerks*.[52] The material from this chapter clearly served as a model for his preface to *HL*.

It is clear that Jonas was particularly concerned with the status of the seventh: he hoped to eradicate any suggestion that seventh chords could serve as free-standing harmonies and to affirm, once and for all, that they are always byproducts of contrapuntal motion. As noted earlier, Schenker took this step in *KP1* (1910), just a few years after completing *HL*. Given Schenker's claim that intervals are defined by their harmonizability, the change in his attitude to harmony entailed a change in his definition of interval. When Jonas edits *HL*, he opts to downplay or remove entirely much of Schenker's original discussion of intervals and seventh chords from part I, division II. Table 5.1 demonstrates these cuts.

---

52. Jonas, *Das Wesen*, Abschnitt II, chapter 3, 166–74; *Introduction to the Theory of Heinrich Schenker*, 122–28. See also Oswald Jonas, "Die Krise der Musiktheorie," 67–74.

Table 5.1. Deletion of Material on Intervals and Seventh Chords from *HL*

Passage Number from Appendix C; Section Number in *HL*	Pages in *HL*	Page in *HA* that lists cuts	Examples and Tables cut
7–10; §§58–61	157–60	123	Ex. 111; Tables IV, V, and VI
11–12; §§66–67	164–71	127	Exx. 112–31; Table VII
16–22; §§100–106	243–49	189	Exx. 190–213

By rejecting Rameau's claim that seventh chords could serve as free-standing harmonies, Jonas does not simply challenge the tenets of fundamental-bass theory; he also casts doubt on the idea of using Schenkerian theory to explain the structure of late nineteenth and twentieth-century music.[53] Jonas's main target in this regard was Felix Salzer, though he may have had Adele Katz in mind as well.[54] He pulls no punches on this matter: "Recently [1952] an attempt was made to offset this objection by applying Schenker's ideas to modern music and its interpretation: *Structural Hearing* by Felix Salzer. Such an attempt was possible only through misinterpretations of Schenker's basic theories, first of all his concept of tonality, and therefore is doomed to fail."[55] Jonas underscored the fact that Schenker's theory was grounded "in the principles of tonality as he found them elaborated in the works of the great masters from Bach to Brahms."[56] To remove any possible doubt about the limits of Schenker's work, Jonas goes so far as to remove several examples from *HL* that already begin to test those boundaries: example 94 (Franz Liszt, B minor Sonata); example 173 (Max Reger, Quintet, Op. 64); examples 242–43 (Anton Bruckner, Symphony No. 7); example 262 (Richard Strauss, *Don Quixote*, Op. 35); and example 345 (Franz Liszt, *Ricordanza*). He also excises an important figure cataloguing the full range of chromatic degrees in the major–minor system given earlier in chapter 2 as figure 2.5a and b.[57]

---

53. Jonas shared Schenker's dislike of most new music: see his essay "Über neue Musik."
54. Felix Salzer, *Structural Hearing*; Adele T. Katz, *Challenge to Musical Tradition*.
55. Jonas, "Introduction," *HA*, viii, footnote 2.
56. Jonas, "Introduction," *HA*, viii.
57. *HL*, §160, 395.

These are, of course, by no means the only modifications made by Jonas: on the contrary, there are countless other alterations, some of them already noted in preceding chapters. The size of appendix C provides a sense of just how much text (and nearly all of the tables) was removed from *HL* in the creation of *HA*. The extent of these changes, however, leaves the reader wondering why someone as committed to modern text criticism as was Jonas would have interfered so egregiously with a historical text. The answer may, in fact, lie with Schenker himself and his enthusiastic response to Jonas's *Das Wesen des musikalischen Kunstwerks*. As mentioned earlier, Schenker was extremely supportive of Jonas and his project, even volunteering to promote the book himself. It was at precisely the same time when Jonas was putting the finishing touches on his book in the fall of 1932 and spring of 1933 that Schenker was approached by Kalmus and Marx about producing the "student edition" of *HL*. Besides calling on Vrieslander to help produce this edition, Schenker wrote to Jonas describing Marx's request and suggesting to him that he should send Marx a copy of *Das Wesen des musikalischen Kunstwerks*.[58] Nothing came of this suggestion, but the very fact that Schenker believed that Jonas's introduction could have served Marx's purposes was sufficient incentive for Jonas to make the text of *HL* conform with his own introduction to Schenkerian theory. We will never know for sure, of course, whether Schenker would have approved of Jonas's revised edition had he lived to see it published. Certainly, he would have been pleased to see a shortened version of his original text and a complete lack of student exercises. But Jonas's extensive and often unidentified changes seem at odds with the high standards of editorial technique that Schenker established for himself. And Jonas's "elucidatory" comments in his "Introduction" and its appendix have little to do with the original work itself.[59] The result is something of a mishmash: unsuitable both as a primer on tonal theory or as an introduction to Schenker's later thought. To paraphrase Weisse, the revised edition no longer looks like Schenker's book.

The Problem of Translating Schenker's Theory

Introduction

At the same time as work on a revised German-language edition of *HL* was gaining momentum, interest in Schenker's work, especially *HL*, was picking

---

58. OJ/5, 18, 17.
59. "Introduction," *HA*, v–xxvi and "Appendix to *Harmony*," 343–52.

up steam in the English-speaking world. In Edinburgh, Scottish pianist and music theorist John Petrie Dunn (1878–1931) became enthralled with Schenker's work and, though he never studied with Schenker in person, began to correspond with him in the late 1920s. During this time, Dunn even prepared an abbreviated translation of *KP2* for use in his classes at the University of Edinburgh.[60] He apparently shared his translation with von Cube who, in turn, suggested to Schenker that it was more suitable for use in the classroom than Vrieslander's abridged translation of *HL*.[61] Across the Atlantic, there were likewise moves to make an English translation of *HL*. These started with Arthur Waldeck (1899–1965), who approached Schenker directly about undertaking such a project and finally got the latter's approval in 1932. Around the same time, other budding Schenkerians made similar requests. These all came to naught and when Waldeck's translation was eventually turned down for publication by University of Chicago Press, it was left to Borgese to transform Jonas's revised edition of *HL* into what we now know as *HA*. That was in 1954 when two important books about Schenkerian theory had been published in English: Adele Katz's *Challenge to Musical Tradition* (1945) and Felix Salzer's *Structural Hearing* (1952).

There are, of course, many reasons why it took so long to create an English translation of *HL*. Some were clearly beyond anyone's control, such as Schenker's death in 1935, the annexation of Austria in 1938, the outbreak of war in 1939, and the general disruption of normal life during the war years, until 1945. But others included the confusion regarding just who was to produce the revised edition, and delays in completion of the German text. Yet the fact that the project took a quarter-century to complete raises a number of other questions of a more technical nature. What is it about Schenker's work that made it difficult to translate into English? To what extent are these difficulties exacerbated by the fact that Schenker originally wrote his book in German, rather than his native language of Polish? To what extent do the numerous problems with Borgese's translation stem from the fact that she was not an expert in Schenkerian theory and Jonas, who edited her work, was not a native English speaker?

The following section addresses some of these questions. It begins by reconsidering some of the general problems that arise in translating texts from one language to another and suggests that in many ways they are akin

---

60. See *SDO* and Federhofer, *HS*, 102–4. Schenker mentioned Dunn's translation in a letter to Violin, February 16, 1927, OJ/6, 7, 320.
61. See letter from von Cube to Schenker, October 29, 1927 (OJ/9, 34, 9).

to the problems Schenker encountered in editing texts. Indeed, like editing, translating involves the "philological" task of determining what individual words mean and a "psychological" aspect of determining what the author intended to convey by using those particular words and placing them in one place but not in others. The text will then turn to the specific problems that arise in translating Schenker's *HL* into English. In particular, it discusses the issue of deciding when particular words should be treated in their everyday sense and when they should be treated as technical terms within Schenker's intended theoretical framework. Finally, the chapter will describe the specific ways in which Waldeck and Borgese set about creating their own translations and some of the critical reaction that readers have had to their work.

Problems of Translating from German to English

Dieses Buch habe ich von meinen Schülern gelernt.

The foreword to the *Harmonielehre* of Arnold Schoenberg begins with this one-sentence paragraph that grabs the reader immediately. Literally, it reads, in English: "This book have I from my students learned." When the book was translated (in full, for the first time) in the late 1970s, one reviewer—excellently qualified for the job, it should be noted, being an accomplished composer who had worked in Schoenberg studies, and bilingual in German and English—tossed around a number of alternative translations, composed by him and his Princeton colleague, Milton Babbitt. These included: "The content of this book was learned from my teaching," "The content of this book was made necessary for me to learn by my pupils," "The content of this book was inspired by my work with my pupils," etc.[62] We would suggest that other more literal translations could include: "I have learned this book from my students"; or, better yet, "My students taught me the essence of this book." Which of these should we choose? How "free" can we get? And is there a better rendering? These questions have larely been ignored in the past: though there has been writing on translation, the discussion of this art in academia has hardly been as deep as it deserves, translation generally being regarded as a "service," and not an "original contribution." In short, it is a

---

62. Spies, "Review."

worthy art, and deserves more. Fortunately, it now seems to be getting some of the attention it deserves.[63]

In the recent translation of Hanslick's *Vom musikalisch-Schönen* (1854), the authors distinguish between an approach to translation they call "formal," which "attempts to preserve the lexical and grammatical structure of the text" (the philological approach), and one that is "functional," which "strives to give a more natural, user-friendly rendering, though at the expense of lexical and grammatical details."[64] (It is certainly akin to the psychological approach, attempting to write "what the author really said, but as he or she would have said in English," regardless of the resulting structure.) Clearly, Spies goes straight to the "functional," trying to produce a readable and even stylish translation of the original text at the expence of its structure and vocabulary. A composer and fluent speaker, he improvises variations on the original text from our point of view—but variations that render the (fairly obvious) meaning faithfully. This could not be clearer, since our additional examples stay quite close to the original text (which, in this unusual case, is not difficult to do). Even the literal "I have learned this book from my students" is, after all, not unidiomatic, if it is elliptical in its preservation of "book" as a metaphor for "teachings" or "course content." Not unlike Hanslick's translators, we prefer to start with a formal translation, and fine-tune it using elements of a functional approach.

By focusing on a simple and direct sentence, Spies made two points wonderfully: on the one hand, translation is difficult, and its end result will always be "different" from the original in some respects; on the other, translation from German to English can be particularly difficult—especially, we could add, when dealing with notoriously complicated German prose from the turn of the twentieth century written by a writer who, at least for a time, considered himself a non-native speaker. True, a simple sentence such as our first example is relatively straightforward: in the present instance, every word

---

63. See "Translators Strive to Prove Their Bona Fides," *Chronicle of Higher Education*, January 17, 2010, on the continuing struggle for recognition of translation as a legitimate academic field of study. We are happy that the University of Rochester is in the vanguard of fostering translation, having both a master's degree in translation, and the Open Letter Press, which publishes a series of translations of fiction. The translation of a relatively unrecognized "harmony book" in German between and after the world wars of the twentieth century, in the days when even the American PhD in musicology was quite new, would have been impossible to support in American academia.

64. Hanslick, *On the Musically Beautiful*, vii–viii.

is cognate with the corresponding English word in a "direct" translation. The reader simply needs to take into account: first, consonants shifted as English arose from earlier German (the German "d" becomes the English dental "th" in "dies[es]" = "this"; "b" becomes "v" in "habe" = "have"; "v" becomes "f" (as it is pronouncd in German anyway) in "von" = "f[r]om"; second, spellings of vowel sounds changed, as their exact pronunciations differed and spelling conventions changed (German "u" in Buch becomes "oo" in book); third, German word "inflections," the "case endings" of nouns, pronouns, articles and adjectives, and the "ge" signaling the past participle of the verb, were dropped in English (remove "es" from "dieses," "en" from "meinen"; "ge" from "gelernt").[65] After these adjustments are made, we wind up quite close to the word-for-word translation above: "Thies book have I fon mein Schülern (= literally "school-ers") lernt."

Before developing this thought, it is important to remember that Schoenberg's simple and direct beginning is a rhetorical device: it should not lead us to believe that English words will generally be visible behind German words. Indeed, the more abstract the discussion becomes (as it tends to do in music-theoretical writing), the more the vocabularies of the two languages diverge. And once grammar and syntax are well understood, and one has experience with them, translation comes down largely to vocabulary. And that is never easy, even with considerable experience. Indeed, there is, from the point of view of the native English speaker, a bewilderingly large vocabulary of abstract German words that were not taken over into English, most of which are "compounds" made from German root-words strung together, as well as French and Latin derivatives. Most have slightly different meanings in different contexts, and finding the exact word that captures that particular contextual meaning sends many an experienced translator back and forth between the thesaurus and dictionary—German–English, English–German, and purely German. (We all have large collections.) The result may be that the word in question *still* does not map onto some one-to-one "equivalent" in English. Add to this the standard German practice of creating neologisms from root-words (a practice virtually unknown in English), and vocabulary can easily offer more vexing difficulties in translation than grammar and syntax. Thus our opening example should not lead to a false sense of security.

---

65. "Sound shift" (*Lautverschiebung*) was first studied and documented by the Grimm brothers, Jacob and Wilhelm, pioneering linguists of the nineteenth century (and incidentally compilers of fairy tales). Consistent shifts in consonant sounds occurred as early English evolved from German.

Rest assured that it would disappear quite quickly with more experience in translation.

To return to our opening example: if we ignore small details that still need attention where we left off, was our initial literal translation really acceptable English? The answer is no: we would not say it that way; the words are out of order. Using precisely those words, we could only say our literal translation: "I have learned this book from my students." In German, however, as our reviewer of Schoenberg points out, using the precise wording of the first sentence, any of the following are idiomatic:

> Ich habe dieses Buch von meinen Schulern gelernt.
> Von meinen Schulern habe ich dieses Buch gelernt.
> Gelernt habe ich dieses Buch von meinen Schulern.[66]

Except for the last and most colloquial, the finite verb (here the auxiliary) comes second, and the past participle comes at the end of the sentence (as they should), but the appearance of subjects and objects is flexible in Germanic languages in general, as these four ways of saying the same thing with precisely the same words show. Though the "same," the stress on particular words (and hence the meaning) is slightly different in each. Yet all are acceptable German, while not one is acceptable English.[67]

The point is that German is an *inflected* language, in which endings to words—not just the position of the words in the sentence field—indicate their grammatical function. English is primarily a *positional* language, in which the position of words in the sentence field is essential in assigning grammatical function. Thus German is flexible with respect to word order, something that can be called upon to adjust meaning and emphasis, but English much less so. A major difficulty in translating from German into English, then, is word order; the trick is to preserve some of the stresses in meaning that can arise in a particular German word order (i.e., *this* book, as Schoenberg stresses—not just *some* book), while converting it into one of the relatively fewer available patterns in English prose that are at least grammatically clear and acceptable—and, one hopes, idiomatic, as well.

The problem of word order is a profound one; it points to the very different ways we think in the two languages, and different deeper-level structures

---

66. Spies, "Review," 181.
67. The past participle must remain next to the auxiliary verb in an English construction.

of the languages themselves. It also means that what we can say about one language is not necessarily the case with the other. For example, in introducing his notion of *Inversion*, Schenker writes that the reversal of order of the two tones of a melodic interval is "similar" to "a common process in language"—in the German language in which he is writing, obviously.[68] He starts his discussion with a simple example at about the same level as our Schoenberg sentence. If one says "Der Vater ritt durch den Wald" (The father rode through the forest), alternate locutions such as "Es ritt der Vater durch den Wald" (untranslatable; see below) or "Durch den Wald ritt der Vater" (Through the forest rode the father) do not change the essential meaning, but offer different "nuances" of "tension" with respect to the subject: in the second two, which do not start with the subject, as the sentence begins we ask "who rode: friend, enemy, someone known to us, someone unknown"?[69]

Unfortunately, Borgese plunges on as if the three sentences could be "translated" literally into English, and renders them as: "Father rode his horse through the woods," "His horse rode father through the woods," and "Through the woods father rode his horse."[70] Only the first is English that we might consider acceptable; the third expression is hardly idiomatic, though possible in some archaic or poetic rendering. The second, on the other hand, is completely farcical: the horse certainly did not ride father through the woods! First of all, there is no "horse" (Pferd) in any of the German versions. In "es ritt der Vater," "es" (it) does not refer to some imaginary "horse" (*das* Pferd), but simply indicates that the act of riding took place: starting with a "neuter subject" is a common German idiom that is seldom used in English.[71] In other words, "Es ritt der Vater" is another way of saying "Der Vater ritt" = "The father rode." It does not tell us what he rode, or rode on. Indeed, in German one could say "Der Vater ritt das Pferd" or "Das Pferd ritt der Vater" and mean the same thing: "the father [nominative subject] rode the horse [accusative object]," or "the horse [accusative object] rode the father [nominative subject]." For the latter, English needs the passive construction, "The horse *was ridden by* the father." In German, we would know that the father must be the rider in both because he appears in the masculine

---

68. *HL*, §16, 44ff.; *HA*, 31ff.
69. *HL*, 44–45. Spies makes similar points concerning German in his review.
70. Schenker, *HA*, 31–32.
71. In English, an introductory clause may put off the sentence's beginning in a similar manner: "It happened one day that the father was riding his horse through the woods, when . . ."

nominative – the accusative would be *den* Vater. (Admittedly, the neutral nominative or accusative of the horse would both be *das* Pferd.) The father is necessarily the subject of the sentence. In any event, "Es ritt der Vater durch den Wald" does not mean "It [the horse] rode father through the woods," thankfully. This last translation is the way to get a laugh.

The upshot of this comical discussion, however, is serious: Schenker's notion that his invention of *Inversion* has an analogy in "language" works well in German, but is, at best, problematic in English. Indeed, linguists—including German linguists—do use the Latin-derived word *Inversion* to describe changes in word order.[72] When discussing translations of the Song of Songs by Johann Gottfried Herder (1744–1803), John Baldwin writes, "as we shall see, Herder inverted many normal clauses in the Hebrew to accord with his preconception of the frequency of inversion in primitive poetry. The original manuscripts show how often Herder translated with a normal clause before crossing out and changing words around in favour of inversion."[73] Perhaps Herder's native language had some influence on *his* translations as well. At any event, inversion occurs less frequently and is of less consequence in English. In other words, the reason behind Schenker's choice of the term *Inversion* is impossible to understand without a brief explanation of the way it works in German, or at least a note that it does work in German, but not really in English. We return to this problem shortly in discussion of our translation of Schenker's German usage of *Inversion*.

The inflected grammar of German can also support long and complex sentence structures, another major problem in translation. Although it is impractical to give examples of sufficient size here, it can easily be imagined that if word order is flexible and a clear system of inflections governs grammar, then grammatical relationships are interpretable even over long spans in the sentence field. This is surely one of the sources of Schenker's preoccupation with musical connections that are non-contiguous and ultimately, long-range: such long-range connections abound in German, the grammar of which Schenker must have studied in great detail, given that he had a German course in each of his eight years of *Gymnasium*, while speaking Polish

---

72. For a lucid treatment of subject–verb inversion (SVO—VSO), by which interrogatives are formed from declarative statements, see Christian Lehmann: http://www.christianlehmann.eu/ling/lg_system/grammar/morph_syn/Inversion_der_Hauptkonstituenten.html accessed August 22, 2016. This linguistic notion of inversion is not to be confused with music-theoretical usage.

73. John D. Baldwin, *Paradisal Love*, 224.

with his fellow students. This relationship also suggests that Schenker may not be far from a correct understanding of the source of such long-range connections in the music of German composers, though we are perhaps dangerously speculative in making that claim.

We begin with a very brief example of such longer-range grammatical connections. The question here is where is the subject and where is the verb? If we were to attribute Schenker's *HL* to him in English as part of a longer sentence, we might write, "*HL*, which Schenker published in 1906, contains . . ." *HL* is the subject, "contains" is the verb, and the parenthetical clause is set off in commas. In German, on the other hand, it would be possible to express the same thing in quite compact form: "die von Schenker 1906 publizierte Harmonielehre enthält . . ."—literally "the from-Schenker-[in]-1906-published *HL* contains . . ." The subject does not enter until just before the verb, and the relative clause is compressed into an extended modifier of that subject. This is possible because the grammatical connections "*die . . . veröffentlichte* Harmonielehre . . ." are clear: "Harmonielehre" is feminine, and "die" and the "e" at the end of "veröffentlicht*e*" clearly modify it. Imagining this and other "interruptions" of grammatical connections used frequently provides some idea of the grammatical complexity and sentence length possible. Now a German lesson from Mark Twain, the master of teaching German via satire. Here he complains about (and lampoons) precisely this feature of the German language hilariously in his essay, "The Awful German Language," the title of which plays wonderfully on two meanings in the title: "horrible," and "awe-inspiring."

> Yet even the German books are not entirely free from attacks of the Parenthesis distemper . . . Now here is a sentence from a popular and excellent German novel—with a slight parenthesis in it. I will make a perfectly literal translation, and throw in the parenthesis-marks and some hyphens for the assistance of the reader—though in the original there are no parenthesis-marks or hyphens, and the reader is left to flounder through to the remote verb the best way he can: "But when he, upon the street, the (in-satin-and-silk-covered-now-very-unconstrained-after-the-newest-fashioned-dressed) government counselor's wife *met*," etc., etc. (Wenn er aber auf der Strasse der in Sammt und Seide gehüllten jetzt sehr ungeni[e]rt nach der neusten Mode gekleideten Regierungsrät[h]in begegnet.)[74]

---

74. Found at https://www.cs.utah.edu/~gback/awfgrmlg.html, accessed August 6, 2019. Archaic spellings indicated in square brackets.

"He" is the subject and "met" is the verb, and the mass of parenthetical information is thrown in between them. The example is all the more confusing because *die* . . . Regierungsräthin appears in the dative (indirect object) as "der . . . Regierungsräthin," because "begegnen" takes the dative, as they say: "to run across [someone]." When the noun finally arrives, as English speakers we naturally think of it as a direct object and unconsciously expect "die"! Many longer sentences, and more complex grammatical connections can easily be imagined. This brings up a nagging problem in German translation: to what extent can—or should—we cut long sentences into shorter ones? And when do we reach the point that the original source is no longer identifiable? In the present instance, we must guard against making Schenker speak a kind of English that may be clear, but that he no doubt would have found simplistic and even telegraphic: that is emphatically not the Schenker we know in German. Schenker's native language, after all, is even more heavily inflected than German: there are four cases in German, but seven in Polish!

Problems of Translating Schenker's *HL*

To what extent should particular words be treated in their everyday sense and when should they be interpreted as technical terms within Schenker's intended theoretical framework? This is surely one of the main questions to ponder when translating Schenker's work, but fortunately, at the early point in his career at which he wrote *HL*, the problem of terminology is not nearly as critical as it became by the end of it, when many completely original ideas had emerged, necessitating terms to denote them, and occasioning the glossaries that often accompany translations of Schenker's work. But the problem exists nonetheless. Indeed, early on there is the question of just what qualifies as a technical term. Although technical terms tend to proliferate in academic prose, such was not necessarily the case at the time Schenker wrote *HL*: a strong case can be made that Schenker adopted much of the standard vocabulary of harmony books, placing it over the eclectic, but largely untechnical, vocabulary in which he expressed his theory. The most problematic example of this is his continual use of *Stufe*, ubiquitous in Austro-Germanic writings on harmony of the nineteenth century. To express his own very original idea—one that certainly cannot be boiled down to a "scale-step"—he nonetheless turned to a ubiquitous term in the very theory of harmony he rejected! We return to this problem shortly.

The classic example of the terminological problem in Schenker studies is of course the word *Zug*. Read any German–English dictionary entry on it (which will run nearly a page or more), or Mark Twain's classic essay claiming that it is one of three all-purpose German words one must know to get along in the language.[75] The word's basic meaning is "motion." The famous example is "train": the German word for train (*der Zug*) refers simply to the motion the "train" makes, while all the Latin-derived names (*le train*, *il treno*, etc.) refer to the succession of cars. English follows the Romance languages in this case. When Schenker says *Quintzug*, any German reader with a modicum of music theory quickly gets the idea that it means "motion through a fifth." "Linear progression of a fifth" or "linear span of a fifth" turns this everyday word into an English "term." The result is wordier and less handy; the consequence is that many teachers of Schenkerian analysis find themselves saying *Zug* instead of one of the recommended translations. Besides being quicker and easier, *Zug* preserves some of the sound of the original source. German speakers have no problem simply taking over English terms when they need them in a technical discussion.[76] Perhaps we should think of adopting a similar strategy. It certainly works in the case of *Zug*! Or, if a translation is sought regardless of the price paid, we should say "motion through a fifth" for *Quintzug*, a solution that is not all that awkward.

Unfortunately, the answer is not that simple. The most difficult term to translate in *HL*—and it is a "term"—is the word *Stufe*, which simply means "step" or "degree"—or even simply "chord." In fact, it has a long history of meaning "step" in the theory of harmony. Once Rameau's theory of harmony was further generalized by Weber—once Rameau's fundamental bass in a particular key became a succession of transposable Roman numerals, that is—the word *Stufe* began to appear regularly in Austro-Germanic theories of harmony. Yet, in that word (or term) resides perhaps the most original idea in Schenker's *HL*, namely the idea that a "step" (scale-degree?) may assume temporary superiority and exist beyond the level of the single chord it appears to support—that it may assert its natural desire to be tonic, so to speak, and gather chords around it that relate directly to it, and only through this temporary tonic to the overall tonic. The traditional term's meaning is *completely* transformed. At this stage in Schenker's development, the process

---

75. Ibid. The other two words are *Schlag* and *also*, the latter of which you can utter while "reloading" with another *Zug* or *Schlag*. There are also a number of very funny German translations of "The Awful German Language," the first having appeared in 1891.

76. This was the course of action recommended to Wason by his teacher in Vienna, Franz Eibner (1914–86).

is essentially his notion of *Tonikalisierung*, which, early on, was translated literally into English as "tonicalization," but was shortened by Roger Sessions into the word "tonicization," by which it is generally known now.[77] It is also present in relatively brief "composed-out" progressions of chords—developments of the Kirnberger–Schulz "passing chords." Borgese has chosen to render the term *Stufe* as "scale-step" (on Jonas's advice?), and it has caught on in virtually all writings about Schenkerian theory and analysis in English. But it may be objected that scales are entirely absent from Schenker's theory of harmony. Indeed, these "steps" are generated by a continuous cycle of fifths, not a scale. The fifth-generated triads are then supported by copies of the *Naturklang* that are brought under control of the tonic via "diatonicization" of all chromatic degrees. Thus their appearance as major triads is their *more fundamental* state—hence, their continual attempts to break free of the diatonic order and assert themselves as tonics. These apparent "scale-degree triads" are not constructed of diatonic scalar material initially, as they are in the theory of Sechter, for example, among many others.

In fact, *Stufe* (plural, *Stufen*)—one form or another of which occurs 888 times in *HL*—is surely the most used term in the book, and its status is quite different from that of *Zug*. While the word *Zug* remains stable in its standard meaning in Schenker's later work, *Stufe* does not mean the same thing every time it is used, even in *HL*. Thus it must be translated in order for the English-language reader to know precisely the meaning intended. Fortunately, its usage is relatively simple to explain: it has, in essence, only two meanings. Its most important meaning is "broad, directive harmony" (Mitchell's recommended translation), "controlling" harmony—or, as we have chosen, "essential harmony." This last translation puts Schenker in the tradition inaugurated by Kirnberger and passed on by Sechter, albeit in oversimplified form, but developed by Schenker in new and creative ways throughout his career.

But of its 888 appearances in *HL*, far and away the most common meaning of the word is simply "chord," "local harmony," or, very often what we have chosen to render as "degree" instead of "step." In other words, it is a "degree" and a chord attached to it, without any scales around. Why "degree?" This meaning may be nothing new, but Schenker's usage certainly is. During his gathering of pitches generated in register by a cycle of fifths occupying 3 1/2 octaves, and then compressed into a one-octave span via either *Abbreviation* or the "vocal principle," what most readers will recognize as "scales"

---

77. Roger Sessions, *Harmonic Practice*, xvii.

(unacknowledged) necessarily arise, but Schenker in fact calls them *Reihen*. Indeed, neither the Latin term *scala* nor its Germanized spelling, *Skala*, appears even once in *HL*, and the German translation of it, *Tonleiter*, occurs only once (87), regarding Brahms's (mistaken) belief that his Op. 62, No. 7 choral work was composed "in the dorian scale [*Tonleiter*]." (Why Schenker did not use the Latin *modus* is difficult to understand.) *Leiter* appears twice as part of compounds that are best translated as "diatonic" (103, 394), and once in a compound that means the "diatonic circle of fifths" (*Quintenleiter*, or "[diatonic] ladder of fifths," 198.)

Why does Schenker say *Reihe* and what does he mean by it? In everyday speech the word means "line," and very often "things in a line"; the image is primarily a horizontal one, in contrast to an "ascending" or "descending," "diagonally" conceived *Skala*. Taken as a technical term in mathematics, it also means "series," putting the accent clearly on the purely consecutive ordering of elements in the *Reihe*.[78] Thus, the Jonas–Borgese "scale-degree" is simply wrong and misleading in a system in which fifth generation *in register* is essential, the *Reihe* a later consequence, and "scales" simply do not exist, at least in name. Still, though directionality may be de-emphasized, Schenker cannot avoid it completely. The "series" implied must consist of those "degrees" that occur within the octave span, and it is of necessity "diagonal" in orientation in its simplest registral representation: not the completely horizontal *Reihe* (represented musically by the "purely" horizontal held or repeated pitch), nor the vertical simultaneity, the chord. In the (inevitable) ascending order in which the degrees occur, the list of chord names is the ordinal: I, II, III, IV, V, VI, VII, well-known to almost all of Schenker's readers, and surely one reason why he adapted them from Weber. Interestingly, though Sechter and Bruckner placed much stock in scales, they more often used letter names to designate scale degrees as chord roots. But even the avoidance of musical notation will not solve the problem, since the letters are also ordinal (originating in the medieval *scala*), just as the numbers are. Of course, we could throw both out, and preserve merely the notion of "interval," which Schenker goes into in great detail in *HL*, since his intervals, like Riemann's (and other nineteenth-century theorists) signify incomplete

---

78. See, for example, the extensive article "Reihen" in Richard Knerr, *Mathematik: Lexikon für jedermann* (Stuttgart: Parkland, 1991), 337–43, where the English translation would surely be "series," or even "set." These features made it ideal for twelve-tone theory to take it over as *Tonreihe*—"tone row," "series" or, in the terminology pioneered by Babbitt, simply "set."

chords. (Of course, most of this discussion was removed from *HA*.) But in order to calculate the magnitudes of intervals, we need something to count, and those degrees of measurement inevitably have directionality, or collapse intervals in register to the six interval classes, which oversimplifies, since Schenker has plenty to say about intervals in register. We might replace all of these names with "order-of-generation-names," assuming *that* is what *Reihe* meant to Schenker. But the pitches arising from fifth generation range through an indefinite span of the pitch space, and when the 3 1/2 octave span of generators is compressed into the one-octave span, and the Roman numerals translated into the order of generation, their number-names (with G for generation and R for reversion—(this latter, our translation of Schenker's use in German of the Latin *Inversion*) would be G1, G3, G5, R1, G2, G4, G6—directly opposed to the ordering of scale-degree chords in register, and very difficult to conceive of as chord names. Directionality is simply impossible to avoid. The nice thing about *Reihe* for Schenker is that its (forward) direction is completely secondary: the word signifies merely the consecutiveness of the components. Hence, we have decided that *Stufen in einer Reihe* will become "degrees in a series," and *Stufe* in the narrowest sense will sometimes be simply "chord," or, depending on context, "degree," while *Stufe* in its largest and most important sense will be "essential harmony."

Another strategy that has been tried in translation of terminology is to retain German neologisms, and translate them directly. The verb a*uskomponieren*—newly minted by Schenker in *HL*, and surely the second most important term, despite its small number of appearances (19)—is *the* case in point. The term is at home in German, where neologisms made of German root words fused to Latinate words are completely acceptable; and it is marginally admissible as a Germanized English-language locution, especially when dealing with technical terminology. Both words are cognate with the direct English translation, "to compose-out," the meaning of which is clear and commonly used by English-speaking teachers of Schenkerian analysis. Thus we recommend keeping the literal translation in this instance. Fortunately, in *HL* Schenker never uses the term in its nominal form (*Auskomponierung*, or *Auskomponierungszug*), as he would do later. Finding a solution for a translation of the word as a noun would be much more difficult, and we do not propose one here.

The word *Inhalt* ("contents," as in *Inhaltsverzeichnis*—"table of contents") is an example of a noun that works in German, but whose *usage* is quite different in English: the word is simply too vague in English to be used without a modifier, in isolation from context. Rendering Schenker's heading "Von der Psychologie des Inhalts und des Stufenganges" as "On the Psychology of Contents and of Step Progression," as we read in *HA*, leaves the reader wondering whatever the noun "contents" might mean. Our solution of "On the Psychology of Harmonic Progression and Its Realization" avoids the problem of "step," uses words associated with the Modern Theory of Harmony very much in their "normal" meaning, is immediately understandable to the knowledgeable reader of music theory, and denotes the essence of what Schenker wants to say, even though it borders on a "functional" translation. In our estimation, its positives far outweigh the negatives.

Indeed, the problem of a term whose exact form changes—based on its part of speech in the text at that point—exists in *HL*, and we know of no general solution. Neither did reviewers of Borgese's translation, who were quick to point out its defects in translations of difficult nouns nonetheless. For example, beginning in the works of Vogler and Weber (from the late eighteenth century), the notion of *Mehrdeutigkeit* (literally, "multi-meaningness") emerges more and more frequently in theories of modulation: harmonies "change their meaning" at critical junctures in a modulation. These theories also begin to take up more and more space in works on harmony. Fortunately, a word exists that is not specifically connected to chemistry or biology (as some of Borgese's choices were). "Multivalence" is defined by the *Oxford American Dictionary* first as "having or susceptible of many applications, interpretations, meanings or values" (as opposed to "polyvalence," which is first of all a scientific term). Though its "scientific" reverberations would need to be reined in with a footnote, multivalence is serviceable nonetheless, and would be most useful in any translation of a German harmony book from the nineteenth or early twentieth century. Offshoots of the word also arise—*eindeutig*, which we translate easily as "unique." For *zweideutig* we recommend "amphibolous," though the familiar "ambiguous" is also possible; however, the latter carries negative connotations that the rarely used amphibolous does not. With either solution a footnote is needed pointing out that the word will attribute specifically two possible meanings to the noun it modifies; though this is the less used of the dictionary definitions of "ambiguous," it is etymologically correct in both cases.[79]

As mentioned earlier, another serious problem is Schenker's use, in German, of the Latin "inversion." The word certainly existed in English and in German linguistic theory. But clearly this is not "inversion" as it is commonly

---

79. "Amphibolous" and the noun "amphibol" are Oettingen's choices in his dual system of harmony.

meant in English-language music theory, nor in then-current harmonic theory in German. Schenker seems to mean "order inversion," as opposed to the normally assumed "inversion in pitch or pitch-class space," as theorists would say today, though his *Inversion* is restricted to the reversal of "natural" fifth-generation upwards. Then there is the term's opposite, *Entwicklung*. By rendering *Entwicklung* as "development" and *Inversion* as "inversion," *HA* creates confusion between Schenker's idiosyncratic ideas and the standard meanings of these terms. When Schenker means "inversion" in the conventional sense, he says *Umkehrung* (= "around-turn") as we would expect. The translation of *Inversion* and *Entwicklung* is equally vexing in [DTS], and of critical importance there, where the processes are central to the essay. Thus we had to take *our* decision into [DTS] as well. While it would have been ideal for the sake of consistency to have been able to follow *HA*, the translation there is unsatisfactory.

By the word *Entwicklung*, Schenker refers to the overall process of generating tones in the *ascending direction* on the model of the overtone series as part of the "natural" system, not "development" in the music-theoretic sense or otherwise. We have chosen the translation of *Entwicklung* that most directly describes that process in English, which is surely the "generation" of tones, rather than their "development"—or "evolution." One disadvantage of this choice is that when Schenker refers to generation *by a specific interval*, he usually calls it a *Zeugungsgesetz*, which can only be rendered as a "law of generation." But then he also speaks occasionally of an *Entwicklungsgesetz*. We have rendered both as "law of generation"; to distinguish between the two by including the German in parentheses would have been both pedantic and too distracting for the reader. The problem occurs relatively seldom.

By his notion of *Inversion*, Schenker refers to the artist taking control and reversing the order of *Entwicklung*. In other words, instead of moving from the generator to the tone generated, we move in the reverse direction: from the tone generated to the generator. He is careful not to confuse his notion of *Inversion* with the common theories of harmonic or melodic inversion by choosing the Latin cognate instead of the German *Umkehrung*, the usual term for those processes (which he in fact uses, when he refers to the conventional meaning of "inversion"). We have already seen how Schenker probably got the idea to use the word *Inversion* from German linguists.[80] Schenker

---

80. Interestingly, Halm found the whole comparison of linguistic inversion with the musical process Schenker wishes to explain unconvincing: review of *HL*, *Der Merker* xi (1920), 414–17.

was fortunate in his choice, given that the cognate *Inversion* was not common in German-language music theory. Choosing an English translation is another matter. We have chosen "reversion" because it indicates well the notion of *reversal* (in this case, of generation), and has no prior music-theoretical meaning. Reversion also has the benefit of *not* giving the impression of pitch-space (Riemannian) *in*version. Schenker makes his meaning of reversal of *Entwicklung* clear enough that later on in [DTS], when he gets close to the Riemannian notion, he has to describe it—he cannot assume that the new meaning is contained in the word *Inversion*: "yet, as was said repeatedly earlier, an oppositional interpretation that is defensible may be justified therewith: namely, that reversion finds its true opposing basis in generation, which is given by nature."

Even here, "oppositional interpretation" (*entgegengesetzte Auffassung*) and finding "its true opposing basis" (*seinen reallen Gegengrund*) may refer to the opposed *origins* of the processes—not the resulting pitch-space directionality. Regardless, there can be no doubt that the principal meaning of *Inversion* as Schenker uses it is of a motion backwards, a retracing of one's steps— in music-theoretical terms, a motion back to a generator. Thus the familiar cycle of *descending* fifths is a continuous search for the prime generator, the fundamental. "Reversion" captures that meaning quite well, while avoiding a word that already has a standard music-theoretical meaning.

Who Should Translate *HL*?

So far, we have described some of the general problems that arise in translating German texts, such as Schenker's *HL*, into idiomatic English, as well as the more specific matter of terminology. There were, however, other pragmatic problems that had to be overcome in order to produce *HA*, some involving the general increase in interest in Schenker's work—particularly in the US—and the varying levels of support given by Schenker's circle of students in the early 1930s to potential translators. Just as there were various interpretations of what a new edition of *HL* should look like, so there were at least three different people who came forth to vie for the rights to translate *HL*. The first and the winner of this initial "contest" was Arthur Waldeck, who wrote to introduce himself to Schenker in 1929.[81] Figure 5.7a shows the letter itself, while figure 5.7b provides a translation.

---

81. OJ/15, 7.

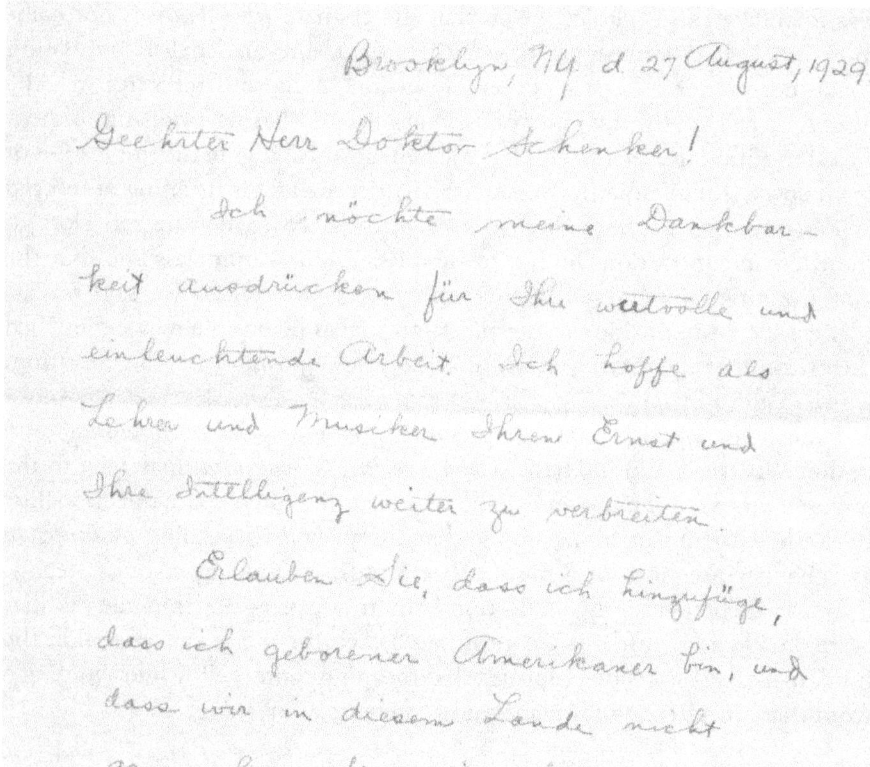

> Brooklyn, NY d 27 August, 1929.
>
> Geehrter Herr Doktor Schenker!
>
> Ich möchte meine Dankbarkeit ausdrücken für Ihre wertvolle und einleuchtende Arbeit. Ich hoffe als Lehrer und Musiker Ihren Ernst und Ihre Intelligenz weiter zu verbreiten.
>
> Erlauben Sie, dass ich hinzufüge, dass ich geborener Amerikaner bin, und dass wir in diesem Lande nicht ganz ohne Sinn sind für das ewige ~~Gute~~.
>
> Ich hoffe Sie werden noch lange in Gesundheit tätig sein.
>
> Achtungsvoll
> Arthur Waldeck
>
> 767 Lincoln Place
> Brooklyn, N.Y.

Figure 5.7a. First Handwritten Letter from Waldeck to Schenker, dated August 27, 1929. AW 1/1.

Brooklyn, N.Y., August 27, 1929

Dear Dr. Schenker,

I would like to express my thanks for your valuable and enlightening work. As a teacher and a musician, I hope to disseminate your serious and intelligent approach further.

Please allow me to add that I am a native-born American, and that we in this country are not completely devoid of any sense of eternal values.

I hope you will be healthy and active for a long time to come.

Respectfully,
[*signed:*] Arthur Waldeck
767 Lincoln Place
Brooklyn, N.Y.

Figure 5.7b. Translation of Figure 5.7a.

Clearly Waldeck is proud of the appropriately formal (and correct) German he had acquired, noting at the beginning of the second paragraph that he is a native American. A New Yorker, he studied at Carnegie Hall with a piano teacher named Israel Citkowitz, the guru of an important, though largely forgotten, New York circle of Schenkerians, a group that also included musicologist Nathan Broder, and was probably unknown to Schenker before Weisse mentioned Citkowitz's interest in his work in a letter of March 15, 1934.[82] Waldeck's personal collection of Schenker's published work—nearly complete and covered with copious marginalia (AW)—shows that he engaged with Schenker's published work directly, undertaking translations of each part of the *Neue musikalische Theorien und Phantasien*.

Waldeck followed up on the first letter with one dated September 22, 1932 to find out if an English translation of *HL* was planned, and, if not, for permission to undertake the work.[83] After consulting with Universal Edition, Schenker gave his permission gladly in a letter of November 8, 1932, which included Universal's details regarding rights, credit-lines and

---

82. OJ/15, 16. Also see SC, 476–78. Almost all of the pre–World War II history appearing here on pp. 351–56 was conceived directly from sources in OC and OJ before these letters were available at SDO. All letters cited in notes 81–91 are now available either in SC (as noted), or at SDO.
83. OC/18, 34.

royalties.⁸⁴ Some five months after Waldeck's second letter, however, another American, this time a student of Hans Weisse, Frederick Auslander, wrote to Schenker asking for permission to translate his work.⁸⁵ But the request came to little: Weisse met Auslander a month later on the matter of translation and started to have doubts about the latter's ability to do the job.⁸⁶ Two months later Auslander wrote to Schenker (in English) saying that he and Weisse had adjusted their sights to a more modest goal: "to translate certain sections of your works, individually, and publish them if possible as separate articles in an accepted widely circulated Music [sic] magazine."⁸⁷ This alternate plan also failed, or, at least, we have yet to find such a publication.

In the meanwhile, Waldeck sent a "test translation" that Schenker received on December 27, 1932; a letter from Vrieslander seems to indicate that Schenker sent this translation on to him as well, Vrieslander responding that given the "characteristic manner of expression of this excellent American," a translation of the shortened version would work best.⁸⁸ Despite such support, Waldeck was apparently unable to muster much other interest in the work. In a letter to Schenker sent about eighteen months later, Waldeck reports that, since it was impossible to find a publisher, he would write an article with Broder in which they would introduce Schenker's work to American musicians. That strategy worked.⁸⁹ Though unsuccessful in securing a contract, Waldeck seems to have kept up his translation of works by Schenker.

Interest in Schenker's work was obviously expanding rapidly in New York during the early 1930s and other aficionados were clearly interested in translating it or portions of it into English. On March 15, 1934, for example, Weisse notified Schenker of "a certain Mr. Cobb, who was briefly a pupil of mine and who has been in touch with Associated Music Publishers [the American representative of Univeral Edition] without saying anything about this to me." Evidently Cobb wrote to Schenker, proposing the idea

---

84. AW 1/1; also at SDO.
85. Auslander to Schenker, January 5, 1933, OC/18, 29.
86. Weisse to Schenker, February 15, 1933, OJ/15, 16; see SC, 468.
87. Auslander to Schenker, April 8, 1933, OC/18, 30.
88. Vrieslander to Schenker, February 1, 1933, OC/18, 20. When Vrieslander refers to the author as a "student of Dr. Weisse's" he must be referring to Waldeck, who, Weisse says, also attended his lectures. Weisse to Schenker, November 28, 1932, OC/18, 32 ; see SC, 468. Apparently, Auslander never got a translation underway.
89. Waldeck to Schenker, June 3, 1934, AW/1, 1; OC/18, 36. The article is "Musical Synthesis as Expounded by Heinrich Schenker."

of "Americanizing the [*HL*]." However, there is no extant evidence of it.[90] Weisse was clearly embarrassed by the situation and quickly added: "The person concerned is no longer my pupil, and the little that he showed me had so little to do with your work that I would never have allowed or advised him to undertake the task. About his relationship to the publisher, I know absolutely nothing."

We come now to the most obscure part of the chronology, for there is a gap of some ten years in documentation between the late 1930s and 1948. A passage in a letter from Ernst Oster to Jonas could be interpreted to mean that Oster found out about Waldeck's translation from the letters he had written to Schenker.[91] Arthur Waldeck's son claimed, however, that Oster and his father had known one another from the point when Oster first arrived in the United States in 1938, and that both had worked with Citkowitz.[92] It is most likely through Oster (if not through Schenker himself) that Jonas got to know of Waldeck's translations of Schenker's work. The experience with UE regarding the stillborn revised edition was certainly also known to Jonas, and clearly influenced his ultimate decision to make significant cuts in *HL* before presenting it to the University of Chicago Press. No doubt, the previous rejection of what, apparently, was a translation of the whole of *HL* without Jonas's critical apparatus (see below) had its effect too.

According to Heribert Esser, the connection between the failed revised edition and the translation grew stronger right after World War II when Oster visited Vrieslander at his home in Tegna, Locarno, in Switzerland. By this time, all hope for the revised edition was lost and Oster, very likely acting as Jonas's representative in what was by then probably the "Waldeck–Jonas edition–translation project," induced Vrieslander to turn over his working materials for the revised Viennese edition project.[93] Aside from the edited

---

90. *SC*, 477. William Drabkin writes in the notes to the Weisse letter of March 15, 1934 that "the name of Cobb is not known to appear elsewhere in the Schenker correspondence" (*SC*, 478).

91. OJ/36, 199. The letters from Waldeck and Auslander to Schenker are preserved in OC/18, 29–30, 34–36.

92. Lewis E. Waldeck (1935–2004), son of Arthur Waldeck, in private communication to Wason, May 2003.

93. These are in AW/1, 3–5.. Reused typescripts on which a couple of the pages are mounted date them to the early 1930s; the corrections are clearly in Vrieslander's (easily identifiable) hand.

cut-pages, Vrieslander gave Oster his "Nachträge" and Schenker's *Handexemplar* for use in preparation of the English translation.[94] Jonas made a highly abridged copy of these examples—fewer than five typewritten pages—entered in the checklist of OJ as "Ergänzungen zu Schenkers Harmonielehre (auf eingebundenen leeren Blättern)." Despite its brevity, this document seems to be complete as he intended it. Figure 5.8 shows the final page from this source: it preserves Schenker's figured bass for example 324, but nothing else in the immediate vicinity. Did these five pages preserve examples from Schenker's *Handexemplar* that Jonas found of particular interest, and hoped to include in the translation? Whatever the answer to this question might be, neither Schenker's *Handexemplar*, Vrieslander's "Nachträge," nor even Jonas's "Ergänzungen" made any impact on, or appearance in, the final translation.

The correspondence picks up again in the late 1940s. On November 13, 1948, Jonas writes to Oster, saying that he has found the time to type the "Anmerkungen"—his elucidatory introduction and commentary, described at the end of the first part of this chapter—and hopes to be finished in two weeks.[95] Since Jonas originally conceived the introduction and annotations in German, the "Ergänzungen" are perfectly in keeping with his editorial commentary, also conceived in German.[96] From various documents, it is clear that Waldeck translated everything Jonas wrote. The project was submitted to Princeton University Press (precise date unknown), but rejected, despite an introductory letter by Roger Sessions of August 30, 1950.[97] On December 5, Oster reported to Jonas that Waldeck wanted to submit the project to Simon and Schuster, and that it would be better "if he had your

---

94. After Vrieslander's death in 1950, his widow asked Oster to return her husband's things to her. Oster sent Schenker's *Handexemplar*, but held on to the "Nachträge," which she failed to notice, since she did not have a detailed knowledge of all the items he had taken. Thus, the "Nachträge" ended up in OJ, while the *Handexemplar* made its way back to Europe, where it was given to Heribert Esser by Vrieslander's widow, as were the other commentaries on *HL*, which never left Vrieslander's possession. (These details come from Esser's letter to Wason of August 1, 2004.) Waldeck apparently kept the edited pages he had acquired during the first stages of the Jonas–Waldeck translation project; as relations with Jonas disintegrated (documented by a stream of frustrated letters from Waldeck to Jonas), he held onto them, and they are now with his effects in AW.
95. OJ/36, 45.
96. Both are preserved in OJ/18, 7.
97. OJ/18, 7.

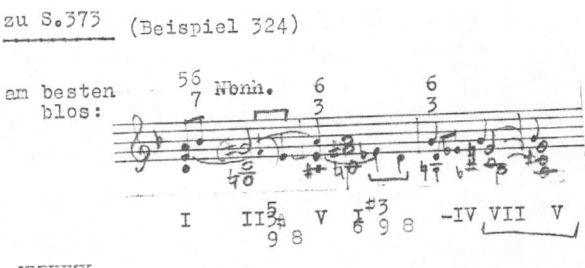

Figure 5.8. The Last Page of Jonas's Addenda to *HL*

introduction, or some of your annotations," so presumably they had yet to be completed when the project went to Princeton, which, in turn, must have occurred before December 5, 1950.[98] This conclusion is further supported by a letter from Waldeck to Jonas of December 11, 1950, which laments the rejection by Princeton, and also counsels Jonas not to bring Milton Babbitt into the matter.[99]

Apparently, the project was not submitted to the University of Chicago Press until 1952, implying perhaps that the translation underwent substantial revision after the Princeton episode. If so, however, no evidence of it has survived. More likely, the edition was still being formulated by Jonas,

---

98. OJ/36, 45.
99. OJ/36, 241.

and they had simply submitted the whole of Waldeck's translation to test the waters.[100] In the spring of 1952, two outside readers, Siegmund Levarie and probably William J. Mitchell, recommended publication by University of Chicago Press, but called for substantial revisions to the translation; Mitchell was critical of the introduction and annotations as well.[101] Waldeck had, in fact, translated these sections from Jonas's German original.[102] Although the University of Chicago Press took over the project, the editor, Hayden Carruth, called for a new translation: "We wonder whether it might be necessary to put another translator to work right from scratch."[103]

Over the next two months, Jonas and Oster discussed the fate of Waldeck's translation; almost immediately a new name surfaced in the letters— Elisabeth Mann Borgese. Oster writes to Jonas on June 26, 1952, suggesting that he look very carefully at her translation of the introduction before allowing her to continue with the work. But on July 9, Oster received a letter from her saying that it would require more work to revise Waldeck's translation than to start over; "that's it for Waldeck," he informs Jonas the next day.[104] Although doubts persisted about Borgese's suitability as a translator, she seems to have undertaken the project very soon afterwards, Oster reading extracts by September 1953 and Jonas receiving proofs of the title page by September 1954, the year of *HA*'s publication.[105]

---

100. The only surviving document relating to the Princeton submission is the Sessions letter (OJ/18, 7).

101. These reviews may be found in OJ/18, 7.

102. Waldeck translated the introduction, but that translation seems to be lost. Two copies of Waldeck's translation of the book are now in AW/1, 14, but neither contains the translation of the introduction and notes. In a letter of April 18, 1953, Waldeck complained to Jonas that the translation of the notes and introduction had been removed from the copy that was returned to him: OJ/36, 241. An incomplete (six-page) typescript of the opening of the introduction (almost certainly by Waldeck and very different from the published version) is contained in OJ/18, 7, where the bulk of materials for the translation may be found.

103. Letter of May 20, 1952, in OJ/36, 103.

104. "so ist damit W[aldeck] wohl erledigt"; OJ/36, 199.

105. As regards Borgese, Oster wrote to Jonas (November 8, 1952) that he had gone to visit Auslander: "We can't use him—not a professional musician, and very neurotic, bordering on mentally disturbed" ("er ist nicht zu gebrauchen. Nicht Berufsmusiker, and schwer neurotisch, grenzend an Geistesgestörtheit"), OJ/36, 199.

Arthur Waldeck's Translation of *HL*

While Borgese was a native German speaker, Waldeck was an American—a native speaker of the target language, with that advantage, one would think. What of his German training? We suspect that he had indeed studied German, most likely in a course specializing in the spoken language, but not translation of German, an art in itself. Furthermore, since he later made a living as a voice teacher, it is likely that he specialized in German diction. True, Waldeck's son remembered his grandmother, an amateur violinist, fondly as 'an old Viennese anarchist,"[106] and thus it is likely that Arthur heard German spoken in the home, and participated. But that does not mean he was a skilled translator: indeed, he may even have learned his German "by ear." As a singer who heard German around the house, his skill with the spoken language may well have appealed to Jonas, but his basic approach to translation was problematic. On the plus side, however, Waldeck had actually studied Schenker's work seriously, and clearly had a general background in music theory, to the extent that he avoided elementary errors in technical terminology (despite some complaining from pre-publication reviewers in Chicago, who disagreed with his non-literal translation of some terminology). Glaring errors in the translation of elementary music-theoretical terms marred the final published version.

Unfortunately, the pre-publication reviews were neither positive nor helpful. One of the Chicago reviewers, Siegmund Levarie (a native German speaker with great fluency in English), came out strongly in favor of Chicago publishing an English translation of *HL* based on the work's importance and the lack of availability of the original at that time, but concluded that "neither the translation nor the present state of the submitted copy meets the high editorial standards of the University press. I therefore suggest that the press accept the book for publication with the provision that the translation be revised and the text edited in accordance with Press standards." Unfortunately, he did not go into further detail. The other review is anonymous. That author spot-checked the translation, and found fault with a few word choices, but was toughest on the editor, writing of the introduction that "the case with . . . the editor is a sad one. He is a dedicated Schenker disciple, but he cannot express himself in English . . . [he] should write in German and engage a translator, but not Waldeck." Little did the reviewer know that

---

106. Conversation of Wason with Lewis Waldeck, May 2003.

Jonas had in fact written the introduction in German, and that the translator *was* Waldeck.

To judge from Waldeck's own testimony, he began what was to become the first English translation of *HL* after the war. Ultimately, that claim is puzzling, however, for the sources clearly show that Waldeck had been translating works of Schenker, at least partially, since the 1930s. Waldeck writes that it is a complete translation, made from a copy of *HL* given to him by Vrieslander (see figure 5.9). That copy must have been the cut pages that Oster got from Vrieslander during his visit to him in Locarno in 1948. (Waldeck in fact had his own copy of the book.) Perhaps he completed a partial translation, or edited a complete translation, according to the directions Vrieslander had inserted in the page cuts—not that difficult to do, since Vrieslander corrected errors, but cut relatively little of the text. Thus, Waldeck very likely began to edit and complete what he already had of the translation at the request of Jonas and Oster after the latter returned from Locarno in 1948. The paragraph claiming completeness is marked by Waldeck for omission, however. Surely this was entered in the early 1950s as a result of Jonas's editing, during which Waldeck's complete translation (preserved in two copies) moved ever closer to the abridgement envisioned in Vienna. As figure 5.9 shows, copy 1 has been gone through by Waldeck himself; black penciled-in notes are in his hand, as are a few notes in red pencil. That the hand is Waldeck's emerges from a comparison of figure 5.9 with the signed letter to Schenker, figure 5.7a. Most of the remarks amount to passages circled and marked "omit," probably on orders from Jonas. Indeed, there are many such "omissions" marked, among which is the one given in figures 5.10a and b. Jonas seems to have apprised Waldeck of the cuts he wanted as he went through his complete manuscript. Many of these are preserved in a letter from Waldeck to Jonas, in which Waldeck provides a long list of Jonas's cuts, and argues that many of the passages should be reinstated.[107] This brings up the question of the status of Jonas's "revised edition": did it actually exist in any real sense prior to his reacting to Waldeck's manuscript? It apparently does not exist as a finished document in OJ, though there are a number of loose pages that record possible cuts, and are clearly sketches contributing to such a document. That Waldeck's translation was complete, and was the translation in which the cuts were made initially is demonstrated by figures 5.10a and b, which show the exact same deletions as were ultimately

---

107. OJ/36, 241. December 11, 1950.

made by Jonas and Borgese.[108] Apparently, Waldeck's complete translation with numerous passages circled for deletion served as Borgese's guide as she decided just *what* to translate.

Figures 10a and b also provide samples of the two extant manuscripts of Waldeck's translation of *HL* in AW. By virtue of the sharpness of the image as well as the use of Eaton's "corrasable bond" (i.e., erasable bond) paper, the manuscript which at this writing is named by the New School University Archive Administration as "copy 2" appears to be the typed master from which a copy (copy 1) was made. Whether that copy was a carbon or photographic copy is unclear, though it appears more likely to be the latter. The typed content of copy 1 is in fact a duplicate of copy 2, but interestingly, Waldeck's remarks, on both copies, to "omit" the circled passage and example 14, are the same, but not *duplicates*. Note that they have been re-entered. Thus, the copy apparently was made before any editorial activity. In any case, the master (the circulating copy, copy 2) preserves Waldeck's original editorial remarks (entered for the first time, or re-entered), where they are apparently underneath a complicated editorial overlay from more than one hand, in pencil and blueish-purplish ink. Waldeck's complaints about that editorial activity (see figure 5.11) turn out to be not unjustified, for most of these suggestions are indeed of little use, and none of the nitpicky changes of wording gets to the real problems in the translation, which are obvious in his treatment of §1, as we shall see.

The Translation War: Waldeck versus Borgese

Figures 5.12 a and b show, in both manuscripts, Waldeck's translation of the very first section of *HL*. Table 5.2 aligns Schenker's original text of this passage with Waldeck's and Borgese's translations. A comparison of Schenker's text of this brief opening section that we know well with two alternative translations will suffice to show the differences in approach.

First, we remember that what Rothfarb and Landerer called a "formal" approach should be the starting point—or at the very least the translator should keep that alternative in mind, even when introducing elements of the "functional approach" right from the beginning (as Spies and Babbitt

---

108. Compare figure 5.10 to passage 1 from appendix B and *HL*, 23–25; these pages were removed (*HL,* ex. 14 and accompanying text). Ex. 16, 27–9 was also removed. Both would have been inserted between *HA* pages 15 and 16.

did with the Schoenberg opening). Understanding the grammar and syntax as well as the vocabulary is essential. The point is to stay as close to the original text as possible, while rendering it in idiomatic English, to the extent possible.

Starting with the first sentence, a literal translation would read, "all of the arts, music excepted, are basically only associations of ideas of nature and reality—great and universal ideas, to be sure." This is in fact relatively simple to translate: we would go so far as to claim that this literal translation might be written by many students in American graduate programs taking reading tests, with modest preparation in the language, though perhaps with the aid of a dictionary and some practice in translation. Borgese, not surprisingly, comes close to this, writing: "All art, with the exception of music, rests on associations of ideas, of great and universal ideas, reflected from Nature and reality." We ask, why not "all of the arts"? It *does* work. But perhaps "all art," which can be taken to mean "art, period," has the greater impact. Other than that minor matter, however, she deftly rearranges two clauses, so that the referent of the clause, "of great and universal ideas," is clearer in English, the positional language, thus rendering the separation of the final clause via the em-dash unnecessary, a distinct improvement over our literal version. Curiously, Waldeck, in effect, presents a brief summary: "All of the arts except music have underlying them a reference to something in the world about us." That's all? What has become of "associations of ideas," an essential concept in the whole opening section, as we saw in chapter 1? Moreover, the distinction of "nature" and "reality" is a most important modification of the mimetic theory, and that's gone too! Schenker in fact needs both: nature, as the source of ideas for the "natural system" (major), and (human) reality, as the source of ideas for the "artistic system" (minor). Waldeck's shortened version thus damages Schenker's argument immeasurably. What a way to start! With sentences 2 and 3, Waldeck combines them, inexplicably. Once again, Borgese stays right with the original. Skipping to the last sentence, we see that Waldeck writes: "Obviously no human activity can unfold without the aid of references, or, in other words, idea associations." But that is not what Schenker wrote. Read Borgese's translation for a faithful rendering. Once again Waldeck has left out part of the sentence "Offenbar kann . . . keine menschliche Tätigkeit sich entfalten, sei es Fassungs-, sei es Schöpfungskraft," which Borgese renders quite literally as: "It seems that ["sei" is the subjunctive, rendered here with the vacillating "seems"] . . . no human activity can unfold either in comprehension or in creation." (According to

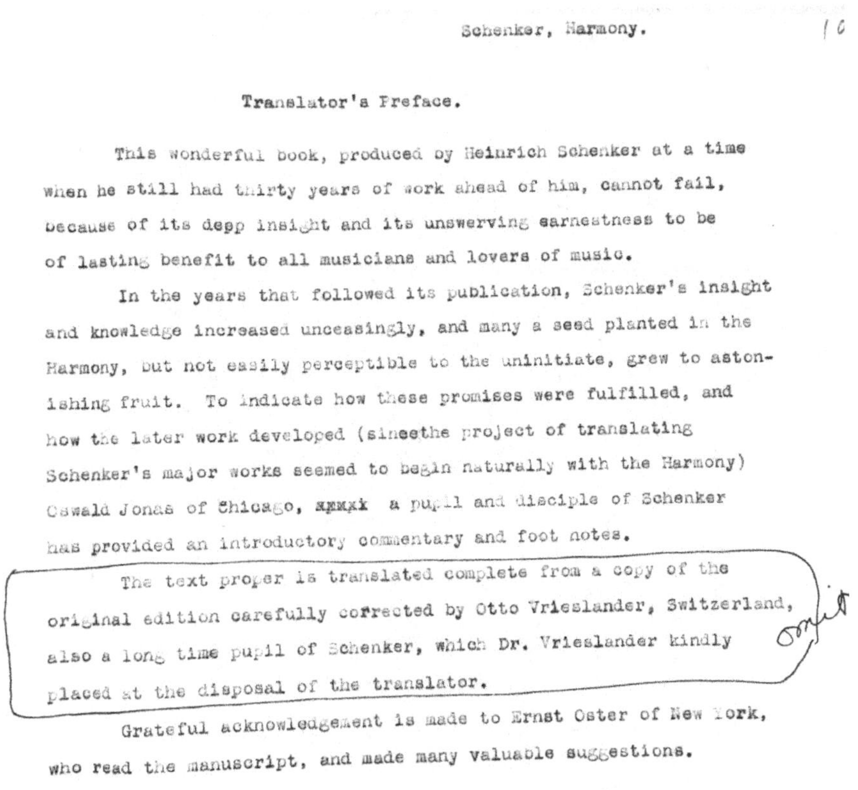

> Schenker, Harmony.
>
> Translator's Preface.
>
> This wonderful book, produced by Heinrich Schenker at a time when he still had thirty years of work ahead of him, cannot fail, because of its deep insight and its unswerving earnestness to be of lasting benefit to all musicians and lovers of music.
>
> In the years that followed its publication, Schenker's insight and knowledge increased unceasingly, and many a seed planted in the Harmony, but not easily perceptible to the uninitiate, grew to astonishing fruit. To indicate how these promises were fulfilled, and how the later work developed (since the project of translating Schenker's major works seemed to begin naturally with the Harmony) Oswald Jonas of Chicago, a pupil and disciple of Schenker has provided an introductory commentary and foot notes.
>
> The text proper is translated complete from a copy of the original edition carefully corrected by Otto Vrieslander, Switzerland, also a long time pupil of Schenker, which Dr. Vrieslander kindly placed at the disposal of the translator.
>
> Grateful acknowledgement is made to Ernst Oster of New York, who read the manuscript, and made many valuable suggestions.

Figure 5.9. Translator's Preface from Waldeck's Translation of *HL* (Copy 1 of two preserved copies), providing proof that his translation is of the complete book

the dictionary definition, "offenbar" seems to oscillate between "obviously" and "apparently," so Borgese's choice is fully defensible.) We could go on, but these instances, in the very first section, demonstrate that Waldeck had no idea of what a "formal" (or we might say, "structural") translation was; he headed purely for the functional, and thus produced in many instances a summary or paraphrase of the original source rather than a translation. To judge from the editorial overlay of example 5.12b, it would seem to be the vocabulary that the readers found fault with. If so, they missed the mark: it is not the diction that is at fault, but the overly "free" approach to structure in his rendering of the German original, and his arbitrary deletion of essential parts of Schenker's argument that often distorts its meaning.

Harmony, Schenker.

Section 7 - continued.

composer then pays belated tribute to the principle of repetition.

Ex. 14

[bracketed, marked "omit"]
Here too, because of the length of the passage, one might have expected a two or three part grouping (a1:a2 or a1:b:a2). However, the material goes straight forward, without any of the five parts (I have indicated the beginning of each by an asterisk) being repeated as such. The condition is not changed by the many miniature repetitions which occur within the individual parts. It is obviously the activity of the single tiny motives which saved the composer the need of a higher order of repetition in structuring the whole.

Ex. 15

In this example the composer is even more daring. The He covers much territory, even changes the key (so as to present new ideas) and yet finds sufficient therefore only a modest reference. He repeats a few tones (see the first bracket) in other places (the following brackets) in a not necessarily rigourous sequence.

It is mostly in transition and cadencing parts of same compositions that it is appropriate to oust the principle of repetition. Quite inimitable in this rhetorical art - an inheritance from Philipp Emanuel Bach - is Haydn, whose works are full of such inspired free passages. The asterisks in examples 16, 17 and 18 denote the places where the content unexpectedly gets virtually a push forward.

Ex. 16 *omit!*
Ex. 17
Ex. 18

See Note by O.J.

Figure 5.10a. Copy 1, Discussion of Example 14 from *HL*, omitted from *HA*, as indicated

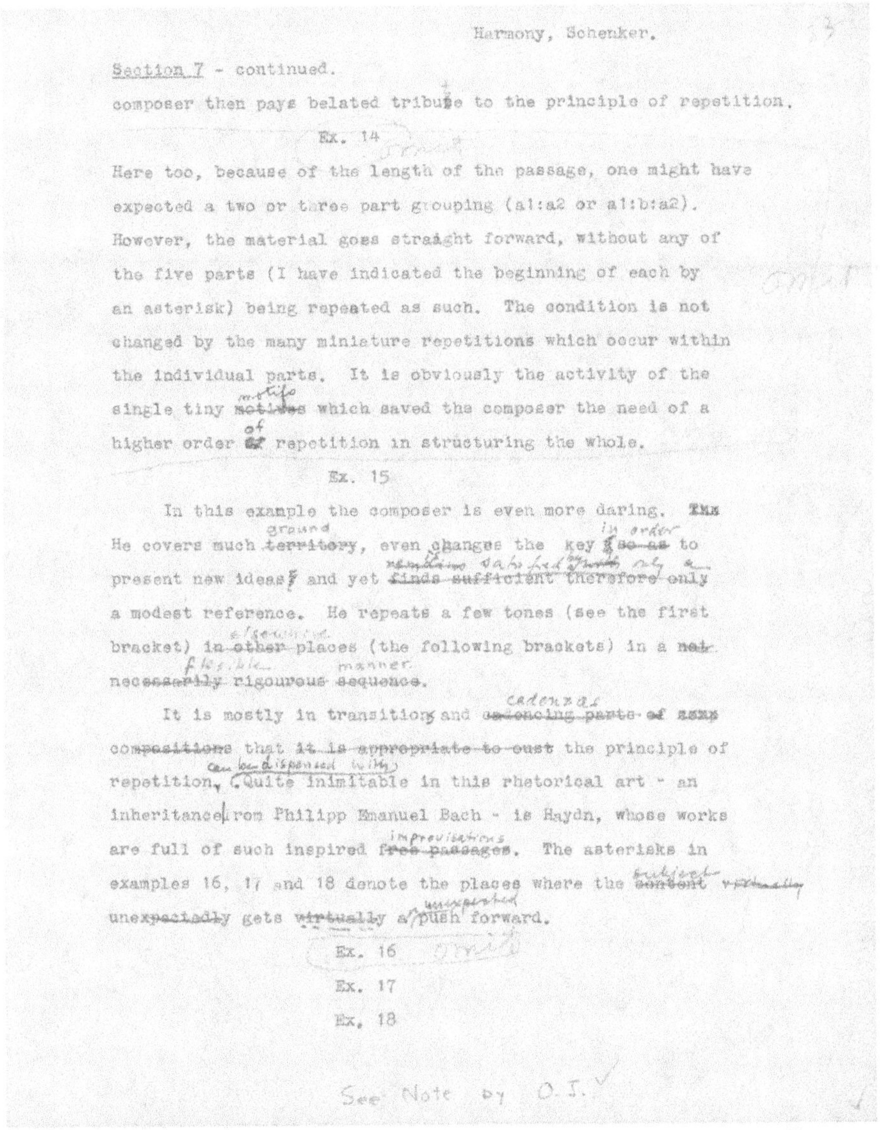

Harmony, Schenker.

Section 7 - continued.

composer then pays belated tribute to the principle of repetition.

Ex. 14

Here too, because of the length of the passage, one might have expected a two or three part grouping (a1:a2 or a1:b:a2). However, the material goes straight forward, without any of the five parts (I have indicated the beginning of each by an asterisk) being repeated as such. The condition is not changed by the many miniature repetitions which occur within the individual parts. It is obviously the activity of the single tiny motifs which saved the composer the need of a higher order of repetition in structuring the whole.

Ex. 15

In this example the composer is even more daring. He covers much ground, even changes the key in order to present new ideas, and yet reaching back only a modest reference. He repeats a few tones (see the first bracket) elsewhere (the following brackets) in a flexible manner.

It is mostly in transition and cadenzas that the principle of repetition can be dispensed with. Quite inimitable in this rhetorical art - an inheritance from Philipp Emanuel Bach - is Haydn, whose works are full of such inspired improvisations. The asterisks in examples 16, 17 and 18 denote the places where the subject unexpectedly gets a push forward.

Ex. 16

Ex. 17

Ex. 18

See Note by O.J.

Figure 5.10b. Copy 2, the same page showing more editorial content in different handwriting, pencil and ink colors, apparently involving additional editors

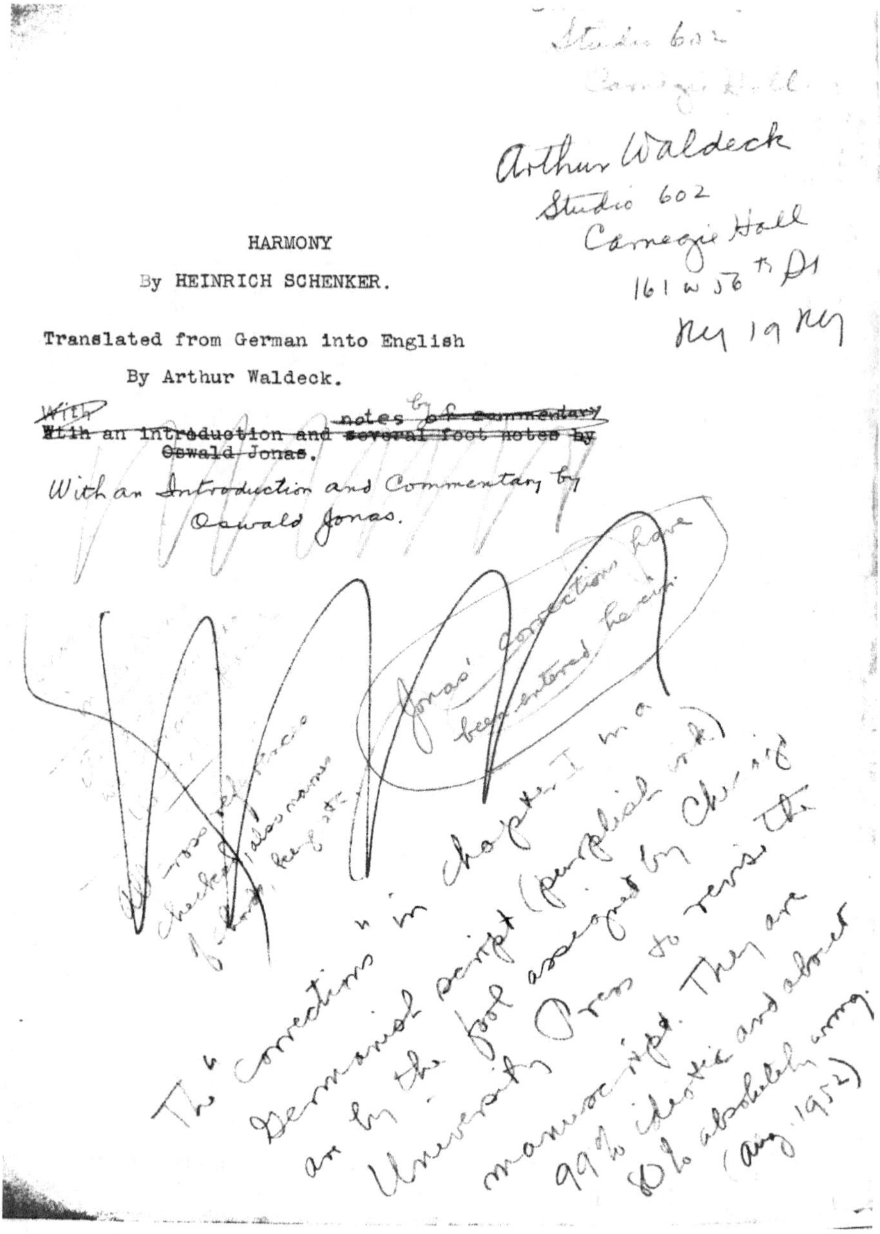

HARMONY

By HEINRICH SCHENKER.

Translated from German into English
By Arthur Waldeck.

~~With an introduction and several foot notes by Oswald Jonas.~~

With an Introduction and Commentary by Oswald Jonas.

Arthur Waldeck
Studio 602
Carnegie Hall
161 W 56th St
NY 19 NY

[Handwritten annotations, partially legible:] Too depressing — checked the names — foot ref. p. 35 — Jonas' corrections have been entered, he — The "corrections" in chapter I was a demand script (purplish ink) an by the fool assigned by Chicago University Press to revise the manuscript. They are 99% idiotic and about 80% absolutely wrong. (Aug 1952)

Figure 5.11. Waldeck's complaints about the treatment of his work, on the title page

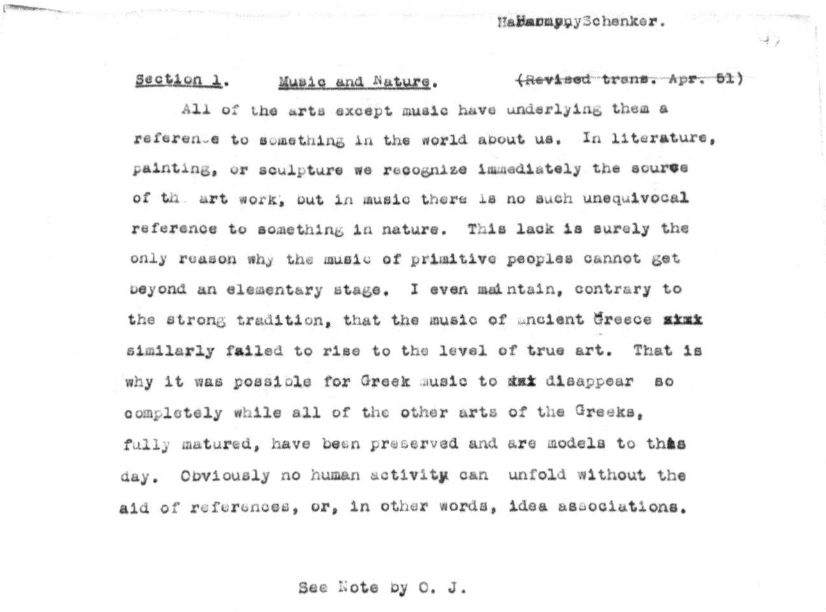

HaHarmpnyySchenker.

<u>Section 1.</u> <u>Music and Nature.</u> ~~(Revised trans. Apr. 51)~~

All of the arts except music have underlying them a referen.e to something in the world about us. In literature, painting, or sculpture we recognize immediately the source of th. art work, but in music there is no such unequivocal reference to something in nature. This lack is surely the only reason why the music of primitive peoples cannot get beyond an elementary stage. I even maintain, contrary to the strong tradition, that the music of ancient Greece ~~xxxx~~ similarly failed to rise to the level of true art. That is why it was possible for Greek music to ~~xxx~~ disappear so completely while all of the other arts of the Greeks, fully matured, have been preserved and are models to this day. Obviously no human activity can unfold without the aid of references, or, in other words, idea associations.

See Note by O. J.

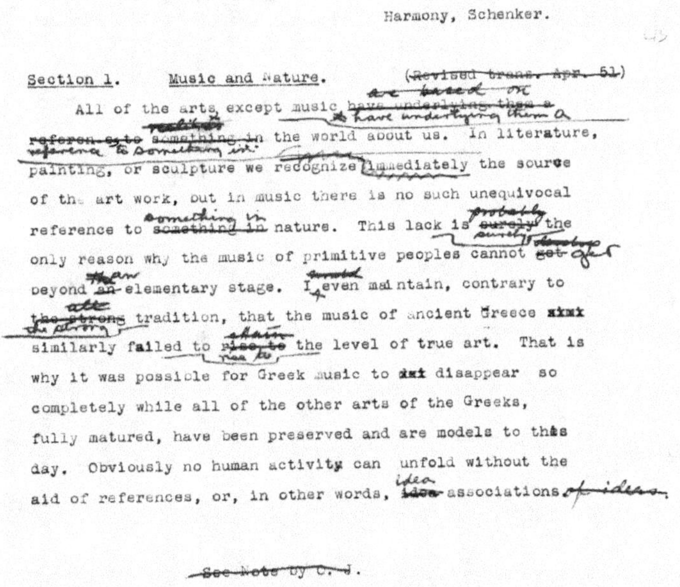

Harmony, Schenker.

<u>Section 1.</u> <u>Music and Nature.</u> ~~(Revised trans. Apr. 51)~~

All of the arts, except music ~~have underlying them a~~ are based on ~~referen.e to something in~~ realities in the world about us. In literature, painting, or sculpture we recognize immediately the source of th. art work, but in music there is no such unequivocal reference to ~~something in~~ something in nature. This lack is ~~surely~~ probably the only reason why the music of primitive peoples cannot ~~get~~ get beyond ~~an~~ than elementary stage. I would even maintain, contrary to ~~the strong~~ the tradition, that the music of ancient Greece ~~xxxx~~ similarly failed to ~~rise to~~ attain the level of true art. That is why it was possible for Greek music to ~~xxx~~ disappear so completely while all of the other arts of the Greeks, fully matured, have been preserved and are models to this day. Obviously no human activity can unfold without the aid of references, or, in other words, ~~idea~~ idea associations ~~of ideas~~.

~~See Note by O. J.~~

Figure 5.12a–b. Waldeck's translation of *HL*, §1, in both copies

Table 5.2. Comparison of Schenker's Original Text with the Waldeck and Borgese Translations

Schenker	Waldeck	Borgese
§1	§1	§1
1 Alle Künste, die Musik ausgenommen, sind im Grunde nur Ideenassoziationen der Natur und der Wirklichkeit, allerdings große und weltumspannende Ideenassoziationen. 2 Allemal ist die Natur Vorbild, die Kunst deren Nachbild, sei es in Wort, Farbe oder Form. 3 Wir wissen sofort, welchen Teil der Natur das Wort, welchen die Farbe und welchen das plastische Werk bedeutet. 4 Anders in der Musik. 5 Hier fehlt von Haus aus jede derartige unzweideutige Assoziation zur Natur hinüber. 6 Dieser Mangel allein ist wohl der einzige Grund, weshalb die Musik bei Naturvölkern nicht über ein primitives Stadium hinausgelangen kann. 7 Ich möchte sogar allen Überlieferungen und Geschichtsnotizen entgegen behaupten, daß ebensowenig je die griechische Musik schon wirklich Kunst gewesen; daß sie nur, weil sie eben	All of the arts except music have underlying them a reference to something in the world about us. In literature, painting, or sculpture we recognize immediately the source of the art work, but in music there is no such unequivocal reference to something in nature. This lack is surely the only reason why the music of primitive peoples cannot get beyond an elementary stage. I even maintain, contrary to the strong tradition, that the music of ancient Greece similarly failed to rise to the level of true art. That is why it was possible for Greek music to disappear so completely while all of the other arts of the Greeks, fully matured, have been preserved and are models to this day. Obviously no human activity can unfold without the aid of references, or, in other words, idea associations.	All art, with the exception of music, rests on associations of ideas, of great and universal ideas, reflected from Nature and reality. In all cases Nature provides the pattern; art is imitation—imitation by word or color or form. We immediately know which aspect of nature is indicated by word, which by color, and which by sculptured form. Only music is different. Intrinsically, there is no unambivalent association of ideas between music and nature. This lack probably provides the only satisfactory explanation for the fact that the music of primitive peoples never developed beyond a certain rudimentary stage. Against all traditional and historical notions I would go so far as to claim that even Greek music never was real art. It can only be ascribed to its very primitive stage of development that Greek music has disappeared without leaving any traces or

erst in den Anfängen war, so laut- und spurlos verschwinden konnte, während alle übrigen Künste des griechischen Volkes uns bis auf den heutigen Tag als Vorbilder erhalten geblieben sind. 8 Offenbar kann ohne Zuhilfenahme von Ideenassoziationen keine menschliche Tätigkeit sich entfalten, sei es Fassungs-, sei es Schöpfungskraft.

echoes, while all other branches of Greek art have been preserved as inspiration and paradigm for our own arts. It seems that without the aid of association of ideas no human activity can unfold either in comprehension or in creation.

Borgese's Translation of *HL*

Given her lack of experience in Schenkerian theory, Borgese is an unusual choice as the translator of *HL*. Born in Munich in 1918, she was the fifth of six children born to Katia Pringsheim and Nobel Prize-winning author Thomas Mann.[109] Her parents brought her up in exile in Zurich, where she earned a Bachelor of Arts degree in Classics and studied piano and cello at the conservatory. In 1938, the family eventually immigrated to the US, where her father accepted a position at Princeton University. It was there that she met Giuseppe Antonio Borgese (1882–1952), an Italian writer and academic, whose anti-Fascist opinions had forced him to flee from Italy to the US in 1931. Though she was thirty-six years younger, she married him in 1939 and they both moved to Chicago, where he became Professor of Italian Literature at the University of Chicago. She then worked as an editor and translator for various organizations such as the Ford Foundation, UNESCO, and the *Encyclopaedia Britannica*. From 1945 to 1952, she also assisted her Giuseppe on the Chicago Committee to Frame a World Constitution. During their time in Chicago, the couple became part of a close-knit circle of European émigrés that also included Siegmund Levarie and Oswald Jonas. It was surely through this circle of friends that Jonas came up with the idea of having her translate his abridged version of Schenker's *HL* that he had created from Waldeck's complete translation. But, with the rise of McCarthyism in the US, Giuseppe moved back to Italy with his family in 1952. Tragically, he suddenly died three months after their arrival. She remained in Florence until 1964, where she completed her translation of *HL* and undertook various other translations and editorial projects.

Despite her lack of background in Schenkerian theory, Borgese used her skills as a professional editor and translator and trained musician to produce an English translation of *HL* that reads surprisingly well and is usually more reliable than Waldeck's. And yet, there are nonetheless problems with her rendition, as William J. Mitchell was quick to point out in his review for *The Musical Quarterly*.[110] After an introductory section that offers excellent and much-needed context for Schenker's achievement, Mitchell launches into the core of his review in a restrained tone that suddenly turns into one

---

109. For details of Elisabeth Mann Borgese's life, see the extensive collection of documents at the IOI – Canada (http://internationaloceaninstitute.dal.ca/emb.htm).
110. William J. Mitchell, "Review: Harmony by Heinrich Schenker," *The Musical Quarterly* (1955), 256–60.

of the classic one-liners in a negative review: "The jacket of the present, abridged translation carries the information that this is 'The Only English Translation of a Classic in Musical Theory.' If the statement should prove to be prophetic, which seems likely, it is much to be hoped that a painstaking revision will soon make its appearance." The question is what was the main problem that set Mitchell off, the editing or the translating? In some cases, Borgese's translations are simply wrong, admittedly. But such errors are more often music-theoretical, a result of staying too close to a dictionary with insufficient music-theoretical knowledge and experience with Schenker's theory—and clearly no assistance from the editor. As Mitchell points out, an obvious example is the phrase "Von der Psychologie der Chromatik und der Alteration," which is incorrectly rendered as "On the Psychology of Chromatic Alteration."[111] As becomes clear during the course of Schenker's treatise, the terms *Chromatik* and *Alteration* had different connotations for him: he associated the former with tonicization and the latter with mixture. Earlier we alluded to the difficulty of translating headings that appear out of context. To wind up with a translation that misses the point of the theory just will not do. At another point, *Dreistimmigkeit* becomes "three-phony"—a strange-sounding neologism if there ever was one, though there is no easy answer to that problem.

However, Mitchell is also tough on the non-music-theoretical aspects of the translation, claiming that both translator and editor suffered from a basic unfamiliarity with idiomatic English: "The result is an over-all awkwardness which often flirts with mistranslation." He then cites several pertinent examples: "*Es geht nicht an*," a universally used phrase in very basic German, meaning "it doesn't work," or "you can't do that," etc., becomes "it is illicit" (*HL,* 20; *HA,* 13), where, as far as Mitchell is concerned, Schenker meant simply "it is wrong" or "it is erroneous." It is difficult to believe that Borgese was unfamiliar with the idiomatic translation of "*Es geht nicht an*," and easier to write off her translation as an attempt to maintain the "elevated tone" of the treatise. But Mitchell also pointed to the fact that Borgese was inconsistent in translating the German pitch name H as B throughout the text—a demonstration of music-theoretical incompetence that causes great problems for the poor reader! Although he was certainly sympathetic to the challenges posed by "Schenker's frequently turgid and unliterary German,"

---

111. Ibid., 256–57.

Mitchell recommended that any revisions should be performed "by a native editor with a working knowledge of music and German."[112]

Jonas was irate when he read this review—both the opening and the fact that it was written by a Salzer partisan must have done the trick. He complained to various people, with some justification. Mitchell was overly harsh with respect to the translation of much of the book, with the exception of the technical discussions, which he picked at quite justifiably—perhaps even insufficiently. But the problems don't simply stem from Borgese: some also stem from Jonas, on whom Mitchell was particularly tough. Indeed, many of Borgese's infelicities could have been corrected if Jonas had intervened more heavily in the translation, a task that was made all the more difficult by the fact that she was in postwar Italy and he was in Chicago (mail service could not have been quick!)—and that both were non-native speakers, though she was clearly the more sophisticated one. Her confusion may have been compounded by his inadequate editing of the original German text. Almost every chapter has an unidentified cut, alteration, or error of one sort or another. In *HL*, §41, for example, Schenker constructs an elaborate chart to show the different ways in which mixture operates within the tonal system. As shown in chapter 2, figure 2.2a, the major and minor systems are given at the top and the bottom and the six possible combinations of natural and lowered degrees are given in between. In his original edition, Schenker places arrows along the right-hand side to highlight the fact that mixture can occur to varying extents between the purely major and the purely minor. These arrows are inexplicably absent from Jonas's revised edition. Other proof-reading errors can cause frustration to the inattentive reader as well. In §5, for example, Schenker explains how the law of immediate repetition is sometimes violated in two-part forms (a1–a2) by inserting a digression to produce the scheme a1–b1–a2.[113] Unfortunately, the English translation contains a typographical error: the text on page 11 should read a1–a2 and not a1–b2. This was hardly the way to introduce an unknown theory by a virtually unknown author to a new reading public. Schenker deserved better.

༄ ༄ ༄

During the course of this chapter, we have seen that the task of editing and translating Schenker's *HL* to produce what ultimately became an American

---

112. Ibid., 258.
113. *HL*, §5, 12.

revised edition was a complex one that was impeded by both the failure of Vrieslander and Jonas to produce an adequate revised edition of the text in German, and by the fact that Waldeck and Borgese had very different ideas about what constituted a successful English translation (of *HL*, in Waldeck's case, and of Jonas's "edition" of it, in Borgese's case). Yet, as complex as the story was, the contending editors quickly dwindled to two, Vrieslander and Jonas, due to Schenker's death, and what seems to have been purely tentative inquiries of Willfort by Universal, his acknowledgement that he could not reach Kalmus's two-hundred-page limit, and Jeanette Schenker's support of Vrieslander for the job. This is unfortunate, since Willfort may have had the most promising ideas for the edition. Of course, the end of the editorial competition in Vienna was about to occur without a settlement anyway, due to the larger events of history. They seem also to have brought about the end of any dream of an Austro-German revised edition by Vrieslander, certainly in part because of the musicological and music-theoretical brain-drain after the war.

But only one of the two contending editors moved to the US—Oswald Jonas—so there was no longer any question as to who would do the job there. Though three translators vied for it initially, Waldeck quickly rose to the top. He was well versed in Schenkerian theory and likely appealed to Jonas as an American with a good sense of spoken German; but, unfortunately, he was not qualified to be a professional translator. His inexperience should have been clear from the beginning: our brief look at *HL* §1 certainly demonstrates that there would be problems down the road. The switch to Borgese changed matters entirely: she had impeccable credentials as an editor and translator but, though a trained musician, was completely unfamiliar with Schenkerian theory, Schenkerian terminology, and perhaps even music theory in general beyond an elementary level. From the musical point of view, her inclusion in the project was probably more an accident of her presence in Jonas's social circle of European émigrés to the Chicago area. Moreover, the transition from Waldeck to Borgese was hardly well handled by Jonas. His acceptance of Oster's abrupt dismissal of Waldeck was heavy-handed at the very least—hardly fair treatment of a pioneering student and supporter of Schenker's ideas in a new land. But getting rid of Waldeck immediately simplified Jonas's life in two respects: first, Waldeck was never really on board with Jonas's ideas for the edition in the first place, pleading continually for reinstatement of his "favorite passages." Clearly, he had no idea what this edition really entailed—if indeed that was documented, and the editor was not formulating it on the fly. Once the abridged translation met critical resistance from two university presses, Jonas probably had no other choice except to find another translator, but he surely could have gone about doing so more diplomatically. The new division of labor between Jonas and Borgese and the gulf that existed between their knowledge of the work meant that she was in little position to challenge some of his dubious editorial decisions, if indeed she was really invested in the project to that extent. He simply retained possession of the two copies of Waldeck's manuscript, apparently with the latter's acquiescence (until he failed to return them, despite Waldeck's repeated pleas for their return when the project was complete!). Presumably Jonas had one copy and Borgese the other, so that her translation was partial from the beginning.

And new this translation was—indeed, probably brand new, since Borgese and Waldeck very likely never met, and she wrote to Jonas that it would be easier to start over than to correct Waldeck's work. Since we know that Jonas held on to a copy of Waldeck's translation after they had terminated his role in the whole affair, it seems likely that Borgese used that copy, but most likely it was used merely to instruct her on just what to leave out. At least there is no evidence in the final translation that she used Waldeck's work for suggestions on the translation of problematic terminology, which, one would think, might have been useful to her. The prospective publishers do not emerge from this mess unscathed either, for they were apparently of little assistance. Unfortunately, we do not know what happened at Princeton, but the Chicago reviews were perfunctory at best (though each reviewer stressed the importance of translating Schenker's works into English), and worse yet, it appears that the final translation was never vetted before it was published. Given its history, it surely should have been sent to pre-publication reviewers. But all of this work was probably rushed along towards the end anyway, as the historical distance between the appearance of Felix Salzer's *Structural Hearing* in 1952 and the publication of Schenker's first major work increased by the hour. That confrontation and what Jonas (and perhaps the University of Chicago Press) surely regarded as an unassailable victory for "Bach-to-Brahms" Schenker was certainly uppermost in his mind.

Finally, we might ask why, given all of these serious shortcomings, Borgese's translation has not been replaced—just why that "painstaking revision" Mitchell called for never appeared. First, the publication of Borgese's translation with all of its inadequacies did put Schenker's name out there for the first time for non-German readers, allowing even some reviewers to celebrate his most original ideas. No less an authority than Charles Seeger wrote that "in spite of its many faults . . . the book remains, I hold, the most important contribution to the theory of harmony 1700–1900."[114] And, despite the book's roasting in Mitchell's review, much of it is well and accurately done, as both its continual use by scholars in the field and our little sample suggest. Indeed, it shows that the work of an expert translator can stand the test of time, even when that translator knows little about the field of the work translated; it was the expert in the project whose work was most problematic in this case. And of course, there is the practical problem of convincing a publisher to take a chance on a book that apparently has a limited readership. But the 1950s were very different from the present in that regard. One hopes that the outpouring of translations of Schenker's works over the last forty years has paved the way for a scholarly translation of his first major work in music theory. It is certainly about time for it.

---

114. Review in *Notes* 13, No. 1 (December 1955), 53–55. In fact Seeger wrote almost nothing about the book as an edition and translation, addressing almost exclusively Schenker's ideas, available in English for the first time.

Chapter Six

The Twilight of the Masters

Schenker's Reinterpretation of the Classical Concept of Harmony

One of the main goals of this project has been to demonstrate that Schenker's *Theory of Harmony* (1906) is unlike other music theory treatises of the period or, for that matter, of any other period, past or present. The book and its satellite texts stand out on several counts. For one thing, they show that Schenker was less concerned with the nuts and bolts of chord structure and chord progression and more with showing how studying harmony enhances our appreciation of music as art.[1] Gone are the model harmonizations and student exercises found in rival books about harmony; instead, Schenker set to illustrate "every verbally abstracted experience or proposition" with "a living example from the great masters themselves."[2] For another, the book and its satellite texts underscore the contempt that Schenker felt towards the works of other theorists and pedagogues, especially Jean-Philippe Rameau, Hugo Riemann, Ernst Friedrich Richter, Salomon Jadassohn, and Max Reger, and, to a more moderate degree, even his own teacher, Anton Bruckner.[3] Schenker was clearly on a mission to correct what he regarded as fundamental errors in the way harmony was normally studied. His purpose in writing *HL* was to push the study of harmony in another direction and, as such, he wrote the

---

1. "Vorwort," *HL*, V; *HA*, xxv.
2. *HL*, V–VI; *HA*, xxv–vi.
3. *HL*, VII–VIII; *HA*, xxvi–vii.

book as much for professional music theorists as for beginners, despite his claim to the contrary.

Perhaps the most obvious way in which Schenker redirected the study of harmony was by reviving and reinterpreting the Classical meaning of the term, the one conveyed so evocatively by De Morgan in her canvas *Cadmus and Harmonia*. According to this definition, the word "harmony" refers not to individual chords or chord progressions, but rather, denotes the conceptual glue that binds together the disparate elements of a musical composition as a coherent whole. In this sense, the term is more closely related to the notions of organic unity and synthesis, ideas that Schenker no doubt absorbed from his classes in Greek and Latin at the *Gymnasium*.[4] An obvious source for such ideas was surely Aristotle's *Poetics*, the most important treatise on aesthetics ever written and a work that Schenker doubtless encountered in his studies of Greek drama. In particular, he would have read Aristotle's celebrated discussion of plot:

> Just as in other imitative arts the imitation is unified if it imitates a single object, so too the plot, as the imitation of action, should imitate a single unified action—one that is also a whole. So the structure of the various sections of the events must be such that the transposition or removal of any one section dislocates and changes the whole. If the presence or absence of something has no discernible effect it is not part of the whole.[5]

Aristotle famously supported this statement by comparing the plots of Homer's *Odyssey* and *Iliad* with those of plays by lesser poets; whereas the latter often recount every conceivable incident that might befall a given character, Homer judiciously selected specific events, in an effort to unify his works into "a single action."[6] Aristotle's decision to focus on specific works by one of the world's greatest authors (or oral traditions, if one chooses to interpret Homer via Wolf's analytic theory) surely provided a precedent for Schenker, when he decided to base *HL* solely on examples taken from tonal

---

4. Schenker referred to studying Greek drama at the *Gymnasium* in a discussion of the concept of organic depth: "As little as a dull schoolboy tends to blame himself rather than Homer (or the teachers) for not having learned to read Homer at school, so little does it occur to the democrat to blame mankind—an eternally dull schoolboy—for not having learned in the school of the genius." *KP2*, "Vorwort," XI; "Author's Preface," *CP2*, xv.
5. Aristotle, *Poetics*, tr. and ed. Heath, 15.
6. Ibid.

masterworks by composers such as Bach, Beethoven, Brahms, Chopin, Haydn, Mozart, Schubert, and Schumann, and to show their superiority over works by Wagner, Reger, and Bruckner. It is striking that Schenker himself mentioned the names of Homer, Aeschylus, and Sophocles, along with those of Orpheus, Marsyas, Pythagoras, Aristotle, and Aristoxenus near the beginning of WEG.[7]

Aristotle's claim that tragedies should unify several specific events into "a single action" likewise had a profound effect on Schenker's approach to musical form and to his strident attacks on traditional *Formenlehre*. As he made clear in §308 of *DfS*, he rejected the ways in which music theorists typically classify the formal scheme of a composition by subdividing it into small units:

> Coherence in language does not arise from a single syllable, a single word, or even from a single sentence; despite the correspondence of words and things, every coherent relationship in language depends upon a meaning hidden in a background. Such meaning achieves no fulfillment with mere beginnings. Similarly, music finds no coherence in a "motive" in the usual sense [*DfS*, §50, 51–53; *FC*, 26–27]. I reject those definitions of song form which take the motive as their starting point and emphasize manipulation of the motive by means of repetition, variation, extension, fragmentation, or dissolution. I also reject those explanations which are based upon phrases, phrase-groups, periods, double periods, themes, antecedents, and consequents.[8]

Instead, he focused on the ways in which the individual elements of a work are glued together to create a single unified whole: "Be they two-, three-, four-, or five-part forms, all receive their coherence only from the fundamental structure, from the fundamental line in tone-space."[9] According to him: "My theory of form replaces all of these with specific concepts of form which, from the outset, are based upon the content of the whole and of the individual parts: that is, differences in prolongations lead to differences in form."[10] Form, for Schenker, was thus intimately related to the Classical concept of harmony.

---

7. OC/83, 4; Hooper, "Heinrich Schenker's Early Approach to Form," 369–70.
8. *DfS*, §308, 212; *FC*, 131.
9. *DfS*, §25, 39; *FC*, 16.
10. *DfS*, §308, 212–13; *FC*, 131.

Similarly, Schenker would have been well aware of Aristotle's claim that poets should focus on the universality of human actions: their goal should not be "to say what *has* happened," but rather "to say the kind of thing that *would* happen, i.e., what is possible with probability or necessity."[11] According to Aristotle, poets were able to do this because they recognized that there are general patterns in the ways people normally behave in given situations: they did not invent these patterns, they merely exploited them for their own purposes. As he explained, the ability to perceive these patterns comes from a natural desire to understand what causes things to be the way they are: "We do not understand something until we know why it is what it is: and the cause gives us 'the why.'"[12] This idea clearly resonates with Schenker's observations about the natural tendencies of the tone: "In this study [*KP1*], the beginning Artist learns that tones, organized in such and such a way, produce one particular effect and none other, whether he wishes it or not. One can predict this effect: it *must* follow."[13] Schenker continues: "Thus tones cannot produce any desired effect just because of the wish of the individual who sets them, for nobody has the power over tones in the sense that he is able to demand from them something contrary to their nature. Even tones must do what they do."[14] Again, like Aristotle before him, Schenker believed that people have a natural desire to understand why tones produce some effects and not others: "all the contrapuntal rules must be supported by good reasons . . . if even religion has had to cope with the fact that mankind asks "why," isn't it all the more understandable that contrapuntal theory, which in fact has long enjoyed almost the reputation of a musical religion, would meet the same fate?"[15]

Aristotle's insistence that plots are determined by causally related actions influenced Schenker's thinking in other ways as well. In particular, Aristotle believed that successful plots, such as those guiding great tragedies, are determined by actions that are motivated by human psychology: "tragedy is an imitation of an action, and the action is performed by certain agents."[16] Schenker picked up on these ideas when he was writing the final portions

---

11. Aristotle, *Poetics*, tr. and ed. Heath, 16.
12. Aristotle, *Physics*, II.3, 194^{b}17–20, cited in Lear, *Aristotle*, 15.
13. *KP1*, "Einleitung," part 4, 21; *CP1*, "Introduction," 14.
14. Ibid.
15. *KP1*, "Einleitung," part 4, 18–19; *CP1*, "Introduction," 12.
16. Aristotle, *Poetics*, tr. and ed. Heath, 11.

of WEG, agreeing that in creating true art, composers may imitate stimuli drawn from daily life:

> Only in possession of this means of [making intrinsic] likenesses may artists now attend to other influences and motivations, which may be taken into their art zealously, the more the artist feels that music made from these points of departure can produce true Art. The better they understand how to produce their art, the more assured they use such foreign stimuli [*fremde Anregungen*]. Among these stimuli we understand stimuli from true—indeed the most genuine—daily life. Thus mental states—but not simply those of a general nature, like love, anger, revenge, vehemence, sadness, excitement, or exuberance, seriousness or joy, but rather—what is more wonderful—especially states of mind, and even motions of the body, motions of the hands, the eyes, a peculiar tone of voice, or peculiar feeling, etc. With all of these, life itself, the completeness and diversity of human life, enters into likeness with the art of music. This is thus a second, new likeness, that distinguishes itself clearly from inner musical likeness. From this point on music could also approach Nature, like the other arts, which it also approached thereby.[17]

He adds: "Music had merely to remain true to the basic principle of its essence as a higher category, while its sister arts were satisifed—perhaps even more than that—with likeness to Nature."[18]

A decade or so before completing *HL*, Schenker specifically invoked the Classical concept of harmony in his essay GEIST (1895) in order to highlight the organic coherence of ancient Greek melodies. His account of the topic, which was already cited at the beginning of this book, is worth quoting again:

> I am prepared to restore to the word "harmony" . . . what was and still is its original and finest meaning. By "harmony" the imaginative Greeks understood *the melody itself*, that is, the succession of tones as a whole, together with all the particular elements at work in that succession. In this broad sense, the concept of harmony ceased to exist quite some time ago, yet even today the concept seems to strive innately toward the broad significance that it had for the Greeks at the start of its existence. All too often we forget that every succession of tones, every melody, carries its own harmonic credo within itself, and that it expresses this conviction autonomously. That which the plan of the melody imparts directly

---

17. Hooper, "Schenker's Early Approach to Form," 386; OC/83, 24–25.
18. Ibid.

to Feeling can be easily interpreted by Reason, which always strives directly to articulate what it sees, from the melody's focal points.[19]

In other words: "every melody possesses a harmony of its own, and so Greek melody too must have had its own sort of harmony." Schenker lamented not only the disappearance of "this primal, proper, broad, and beautiful conception of harmony . . . from the province of theory," but also the dominance of the modern "chordal" conception of harmony promulgated by Rameau and his followers.[20]

In connecting the concept of harmony so explicitly with melody, Schenker underscored his belief that melody is the primary element of musical composition. Indeed, the opening sections of GEIST clearly show that, in Schenker's mind, melody actually played a central role in the origins of music and its role in human evolution.[21] According to him, music originally evolved for purely extrinsic reasons to express "a sudden spontaneous outburst of accumulated emotional or physical delight." Soon, however, "the joy of singing must have become an end in itself."[22] Stripped of any extrinsic associations, songs were "in a state of naïve aimlessness, much like the wandering melodies piped by shepherds in their fields." Schenker suggests that melodies tried to organize themselves intrinsically by imitating the syntax of natural language: "music strove to liken its cadences to the cadences of language and in order to do so . . . had to suggest convincingly the impression of a self-contained thought."[23] But this impression was ultimately illusory: Schenker believed that melodies did not become self-contained entities until they emancipated themselves from language. For Schenker, this step only occurred when melodies embraced the concepts of repetition, which gave them their form, and harmony, which gave them their overall coherence.[24]

Jumping ahead a decade, Schenker reaffirmed Aristotle's remarks about art, imitation, and organic unity in *HL*, his most extensive accounts of the

---

19. GEIST, 143; SPIRIT, 325.
20. Ibid.
21. For a summary of Schenker's views on the origins of music, see Hooper, "Schenker's Early Conception of Form," 38; also see GEIST, 136; SPIRIT, 320. Schenker's discussion fits in well with Darwin's accounts of the origin of music; see Kivy, "Charles Darwin and Music."
22. GEIST, 135; SPIRIT, 319.
23. SPIRIT, 320.
24. GEIST, 137–38; SPIRIT, 320–21.

role harmony plays in music. He opened the book in Aristotelian fashion by declaring that "art is imitation—imitation by word or color or form. We immediately know which aspect of Nature is indicated by word, which by color, which by sculptured form."[25] Again following his illustrious forebear, Schenker even claimed that imitation rests on the association of ideas: all art is "grounded only in the association of ideas, indeed, the profound and universal association of ideas, from Nature and Reality."[26] Later in *HL*, during a discussion of large-scale composition, he insisted that composers should synthesize their diverse themes and theme groups in a coherent manner: "By never wasting any harmony, it spares each one for whatever effect it may yield. The essential harmonies and the themes motivated by them are assured, in any case, their desired effect, and there rises the image of organic unity which is so essential to a cyclic [i.e., sonata form] movement."[27]

But how precisely did Schenker reconcile his endorsement of Aristotle's organicism and mimetic theory of art, both of which intersect with the Classical definition of harmony, with the fact that most instrumental music of the common-practice period does not, in fact, have any obvious extramusical or "extrinsic" associations?[28] Although he could not resolve this issue for ancient Greek music and was forced to deny that it was ever "real art," Schenker did so for common-practice music by suggesting that musical material becomes associative if it is repeated: in *HL*, he suggests that it was by repeating motives that composers turned music into art: "Fortified by the quiet possession of a principle which was subject no longer to change or loss, music could now subordinate those extrinsic associations, such as, for example, of word or dance, from which it had benefitted for brief moments in the past."[29] As it happens, Schenker's treatment of motives was actually quite liberal: any series of tones can be regarded as a motive by virtue of rhythm, melody, or harmony, provided that the series is repeated, preferably immediately, and possibly varied. Harmony provided Schenker with an abstract conceptual backdrop against which these motivic repetitions and variations might take place: "I conceive of the theory of harmony . . . as a world purely of the mind [*eine bloß geistige Welt*], as one of ideally moving forces."[30]

---

25. *HL*, §1, 3; *HA*, 3.
26. Ibid.
27. *HL*, §129, 325; *HA*, 245.
28. *HL*, §1, 3; *HA*, 3.
29. *HL*, §§2–3, 4; *HA*, 4.
30. *HL*, "Vorwort," V–VI; *HA*, "Introduction," xxv.

In §6 of *HL*, Schenker alludes to Aristotle's concept of plot, when he compares the ways in which playwrights develop characters in their dramas to those in which composers repeat and vary motives in their musical compositions. In the case of plays, he suggests that "men are led through situations in which their characters are tested in all their shades and grades, so that one characteristic feature is revealed in each particular situation. And what is a character as a whole, if not a synthesis of these qualities which have been revealed by such a sequence of situations?"[31] In the case of musical compositions, "the life of a motive is represented in an analogous way. The motive is led through various situations. At one time, its melodic character is tested; at another time, a harmonic peculiarity must prove its valor in unaccustomed surroundings; a third time, again, the motive is subjected to some rhythmic change." Again, following Aristotle's advice, Schenker implored composers to select only those versions of a motive that contribute to a work's overall plot: "No composer could hope to reveal through overloaded, complicated, and unessential matter what could be revealed by few, but well-chosen fatal moments in the life of a motive. Everyone knows that [the hero] must have lunched daily; [but] the poet can [therefore] omit the dramatic presentation of these quite unessential lunches in order to concentrate the drama on the essential moments of his hero's life."[32]

Although Schenker ultimately changed his mind about the status of Greek melody as art between GEIST and *HL*, he nonetheless remained completely firm in his belief that melody is the principal element in music and that, to paraphrase GEIST, it should possess a harmony of its own.[33] Leafing through the pages of *HL* and its related texts, *EBO*, *CFF (1984)*, *KP1*, and *NdK*, we come away with a fairly coherent picture about what this idea actually entails. Harmonically, Schenker insisted that tonal melodies should be anchored triadically and that they become "fluent" when they rise and fall in a wave-like manner, combining repeated tones, stepwise successions, and leaps.[34] According to him, stepwise successions stem from neighbor and, above all, passing tones, whereas leaps often arise from shifting between one "latent voice" and another.[35] These ideas even extend

---

31. *HL*, §6, 19–20; *HA*, 12–13. Schenker gives his discussion a German rather than an ancient Greek flavor by citing Friedrich Schiller's plays about Wallenstein.
32. *HL*, §6, 20; *HA*, 13.
33. *HL*, §88, 214; *HA*, 168.
34. *HL*, §76, 176–77; *HA*, 133; and *KP1*, part 1, chapter 2, §20, 133–34; *CP1*, 94–95.
35. *KP1*, 135–36; *CP1*, 95–96.

to bass lines, which are not only melodic in conception, but are potentially motivic as well.[36] Schenker also believed that successful melodies should create a balance between the repetition and variation of particular motives and the infusion of new material: according to him, ornamentation and embellishment are vital aspects of melodic construction and are manifestations of music's improvisational impulse.[37]

Schenker even proposed that composers should use the integrative powers of harmony and tonality to arrange together diverse themes into larger groups (*Gruppenbildungen*).[38] And, in *KP1* and *CFF* (1984), he even showed that successions of surface motives might be coordinated in some large sense by some hidden melodic line. These foreshadow the concept of fundamental line or *Urlinie*, which Schenker formulated in his editions of Beethoven's late piano sonatas (1913–20) and clarified in the early volumes of *TW*. After quoting the "Introduction" to his *Erläuterunsausgabe* of Beethoven's Sonata Op. 101, he noted in *TW1*: "A piece of music comes into the world alive, woven out of Urlinie, harmonic degree (*Stufe*), and voice-leading. The method of observation in which one must initially become aware of each factor in isolation should not obscure the fact that all these sources and forces (from the Urlinie there issues motive and melody) constantly weave together and work on one another."[39]

Besides using the concept of harmony to shed light on the organic structure of tonal melodies, Schenker also invoked it to inform his views about music history. As regards the distant past, he claimed that plainchants and Renaissance melodies lacked the levels of coherence, fluency, and triadicity typical of successful tonal melodies.[40] Schenker maintained, for example,

---

36. *HL*, §88, 218; *HA*, 172–73. For Schenker's discussion of Beethoven's "motivic use of bass tones," see *EBO*, 42.
37. *EBO*, 28.
38. *CFF* (1984), 25; *EBO*, 28ff.; *HL*, §§129ff.
39. "Die Urlinie: eine Vorbemerkung," *TW1*, 23; tr. Robert Snarrenberg, "The Urlinie: A Preliminary Remark," *WT1*, 22. *Stufe* could certainly be rendered by our "essential harmony" in this quotation.
40. *HL*, §88, 217–18, *HA*, 171–72; *NdK*, 115–16, *DAC*, 121; *KP1*, "Vorwort," XXIV–XXV, *CP1*, xxvi. Schenker presented the same general views about the prehistory of tonality in "Noch ein Wort zur Urlinie," *TW2* (1922), 3–6, tr. Robert Snarrenberg, "Yet Another Word on the Urlinie," *WT1*, 54; "Rameau oder Beethoven?" *MW3* (1930), 12, tr. Ian Bent, "Rameau or Beethoven?" *MM3*, 2; *DfS*, §§251–66, 150–74; *FC*, 131–32, and "Von den Diminution," *Der Dreiklang* 4–5 (1937), 93–98.

that they were unnecessarily complicated because they tend to repeat motives rather than generate new ones.[41] Around 1600, Caccini, Viadana, and others tried to remedy the situation by writing monodies in a quasi-improvised manner and by liberating the bass from its strict dependence on the melody. But, since they were unable to assimilate individual ideas into larger formal units, the bass lines still did not pass muster, according to Schenker. In his view, tonal melodies first came of age in Germany during the seventeenth and eighteenth centuries, thanks to the proliferation of chorales: "The invention of synthesis from the Urlinie and the melody of the whole [*aus Urlinie und Gesamtmelodie*] is German, German to the core—historically considered, a victory over short-nerved Italian monody incapable of widely spaced goals—and generates from the depth and breadth of the German spirit." Earlier, Schenker had remarked that the "Urlinie leads directly to synthesis of the whole. It is synthesis. Since it offers grounds for deciding upon harmonic degree and form in doubtful cases, it makes it possible, above all, to get proper insight into synthesis."[42]

As regards the immediate past, Schenker likewise used the concept of harmony to explain what he saw as a precipitous decline in German composition after its zenith in the music of Handel, J. S. Bach, C. P. E. Bach, Haydn, Mozart, Beethoven, Schubert, Schumann, and Mendelssohn. It is a view that Schenker certainly hinted at in his works up to and including *HL*, but he did not address it head on until he wrote NdK, which he ultimately never published. Schenker nonetheless conceived of it as a supplement to *HL*, saying so in the "Vorwort" to that volume.[43] He renewed his promise to complete this new project in the "Vorwort" to *KP1*: "I plan to discuss more precisely in a later volume the decline [of musical composition] and its causes. The seriousness of the task to which I introduce the reader in the volume at hand, however, demands that I deal with these circumstances even here, if in a brief and perfunctory manner."[44] As William Drabkin notes, Schenker even removed material from *HL* and *KP1* and placed it in NdK.[45]

---

41. *DfS*, §254, 161; *FC*, 99.
42. "Noch ein Wort zur Urlinie," *TW2*, 5; tr. Snarrenberg, "Yet Another Word on the Urlinie," *WT1*, 54.
43. *HL*, "Vorwort," VII; *HA*, xxvi.
44. "Author's Preface," *KP1*, xvii.
45. Drabkin notes that Schenker's page proofs for *HL* (OC/31, 154–55) contain "pejorative remarks on the repetition of themes in the Tristan prelude, on Bruckner's appropriation of classical form, and on harmonic coherence in Richard Strauss's

Dismayed by what he regarded as the "twilight of the masters," Schenker was hardly surprised by the current plight of German music: on the contrary, he believed that it was perfectly analogous to periods of exhaustion that occurred "in Greece after the death of Euripides, or the decline in Italy after Michelangelo or in England After Shakespeare."[46] With the exception of Brahms, whom he regarded as the last great German composer, Schenker was critical of virtually every late nineteenth-century composer of the German school: Franz Liszt, Richard Wagner, Anton Bruckner, Antonín Dvořák, Hugo Wolf, Richard Strauss, Hans Pfitzner, Engelbert Humperdinck, Gustav Mahler, Max Reger, as well as Nicolai Rimsky-Korsakov, Peter Tchaikovsky, and even Edward Elgar.[47] For the sake of brevity, however, he limits his harshest criticism in NdK to attacks on Berlioz, Liszt, Wagner, Bruckner, Wolf, and Strauss.[48]

Schenker despised late nineteenth-century composers for many reasons, but his chief complaint was that they were unable to synthesize the diverse elements of their works into unified entities in the manner advocated by Aristotle in the *Poetics*. As he explained in NdK:

> While the masters wrote their individual themes and their groups of themes in a joined-up way, the modern cyclic [i.e., sonata] composer writes his melodies straight as an arrow and without connectedness, from a single idea and as far as possible without groups. He is still proud of this mistake beyond all measure, and does not realize how much it ruins his plan. There arises in this way, first of all, the monotonous construction of the modern long melody, which

---

portrayal of his critics in *A Hero's Life*" that eventually made their way to NdK, 113–14. Similarly, Drabkin observes that Schenker's handwritten draft of the foreword to *KP1* (OC/31, 169–90) includes passages praising the achievements of Chopin, Mendelssohn and Brahms "as the last great 'legislators' [*Gesetzgeber*] of music" (OC/31, 180): these resemble material in NdK, 45. See Drabkin, DAC, 21–22.
46. Schenker, NdK, 2; DAC, 34 and 35.
47. Schenker, KP1, "Vorwort," XVII and "Einleitung," 22–23; CP1, "Author's Preface," xxii and "Introduction,"15. For Schenker's criticisms of these composers, see Matthew Brown, ""Polyphony and Cacophony?," and Pastille, "Schenker's Value Judgements."
48. For Schenker's critiques of: Hector Berlioz, see NdK, 46–56 and DAC, 70–77; Franz Liszt, see NdK, 56–59 and DAC, 77–79; Wagner's music dramas, see NdK, 84–91 and DAC, 97–102; Anton Bruckner, see NdK, 107–11 and DAC, 114–17; Hugo Wolf, see NdK, 111–12 and DAC, 117–18; and Richard Strauss, see NdK, 112–14 and DAC, 118–21.

proceeds ad infinitum in superfluous repetitions—and only in such repetitions—and additionally gives the impression of a foolish sentimentality.[49]

No longer organically unified, their large-scale works were "a potpourri comprising three melodies that seem to have been locked up in cages; and since it otherwise lacks any Artistic effect of a higher order, on account of its all too regular construction and philistinism, it is clear that it cannot give rise to that irrationality that draws us to a true work of art in the first place."[50]

Furthermore, just as Schenker became skeptical about the artistic value of ancient Greek melodies because they were marred by "extrinsic" associations, so he became increasingly critical of nineteenth- and early twentieth-century composers because they were inclined to base their music on programs or other extramusical ideas rather than purely musical relationships. In NdK, for example, he declared:

> Objectively, programmatic music reveals internal associations being set aside, in order to be replaced by external ones. When one considers that our music first became an art only by the victory of purely internal musical associations (see *HL*, §3), and in this respect is perhaps to be reckoned as at most five or six centuries old—compared to the other arts, music is much the youngest—then the damage that music suffers from programmatic music must be described as all the more terrifying.[51]

In making such claims, it is important to stress that Schenker did not reject the idea that pieces of music can be used to express extramusical ideas; he simply insisted that such works can only do so by means of the fundamental laws of tonal harmony and voice leading. Schenker expresses his view in no uncertain terms at the start of his analysis of "The Representation of Chaos" from Haydn's oratorio *The Creation*. To quote Schenker:

> The representation of Chaos is inseparably linked with a surge of light and life—to perceive in Chaos only an eternal non-fulfilment would be to think chaotically—thus music, an art which unfolds in time, is well-placed to reproduce the effect of Chaos: the first tremblings and movements; the first rumbling of dark forces; the becoming, the giving birth; finally the light, the light of day, the Creation! But it is only with strict principles that art is able to

---

49. NdK, 42; DAC, 68.
50. NdK, 43; DAC, 69.
51. NdK, 49–50; DAC, 50.

convey the meaning of Chaos! Thus Haydn, in his portrayal of Chaos, remains faithful to his basic artistic principles; but he is, of course, committed to stretching the means of art, to increase the tension to the point that they—mysteriously—suggest the very mysteries of Chaos.[52]

Nevertheless, Schenker's contempt for program music was so strong that he even found fault with Mozart's operas. Much as he enjoyed Mozart's stage works, Schenker insisted that they were but mere shadows of his instrumental music: "In the whole of *Don Giovanni* one finds absolutely nothing of the artifice with which [Mozart's] absolute music is so extravagantly conceived; nothing of the complexities of voice-leading, which become concentrated by embracing the learned forms, from the simplest imitation right up to a fugue, and nothing of the indescribable wonders of his synthesis."[53] He went so far as to suggest that the music is so simple "that it is hard to believe that the same composer also wrote that Artistic body of music."[54]

Having rebuked nineteenth- and early twentieth-century composers for writing too little music, especially in genres without extrinsic associations, Schenker also complained about the ways in which they deliberately shunned the fundamental laws of tonal harmony and voice leading in order to develop their own idiosyncratic methods of organization. Once again, he left absolutely no doubt about his contempt for such trends:

> We must be all the more amazed by the fact that the present generation, as it arrogantly proclaims, actually works without any preconceptions. If the Artists of today are so proud of having freed themselves from all tradition and no longer feel obliged to cart about with them technical ballast from the past, why is their productivity not at the same time even more fluid and greater than that which we have already seen from the masters? If, as it seems, one has merely to follow one's own individuality, or, as is often said, merely to work by following one's nose, how does it come about that such lack of preconceptions—which, as is well known, has become the proud fanfare of all contemporary

---

52. "Haydn: Die Schöpfung. Die Vorstellung des Chaos," *MW2*, 161–70; translated by Drabkin, "The Representation of Chaos from Haydn's *The Creation*," 97–105.
53. NdK, 67; DAC, 84–85. During his discussion of Mozart's operas, Schenker analysed the "Introduction" from Act 1 (NdK, 67–73; DAC, 85–89), the "Churchyard Duet" from Act 2 (NdK, 73–75; DAC, 89–91), and the "Finale" from Act 2 (NdK, 75–77; DAC, 91–92).
54. NdK, 67; DAC, 85.

composers' guilds and individual 'masters' among the 'moderns'—promotes productivity so little, so very little?[55]

For Schenker, the craft of musical composition is something composers ignore at their peril: "there is a mechanical, purely technical something, a workmanlike ingredient, which each and every Artist must possess. Unfortunately, the acquisition of these technical elements is not merely a mechanical act, as one might perhaps like to expect. Although it appears to be given objectively, so that no one can bypass it, whether they will or not, instinct is in truth accessible only to the eyes and ears of those who are in any event led and compelled by an inner instinct and Artistic imagination."[56]

The Classical concept of harmony and the primacy of melodic construction are not only essential features of Schenker's early thinking about tonal music: they also inform his theoretical writings of the late 1920s and early 1930s. At the end of *MW3* (1930), for example, Schenker again compared the decline in nineteenth-century German composition to the demise of ancient Greek civilization: "Greek civilization has fallen into decay ever since the days of Socrates and Plato, its luminaries; and yet, their ideas have stood the test of time for millennia, and still dominate man's thinking today. German music of genius will dominate man's thinking in the same way, however fatally the German people may be in decline."[57] And, at the start of *DfS*, he blamed their common misunderstandings about Greek dramas on their failure to appreciate the background structures of particular works: "Every drama presents a content whose meaning truly reveals itself to the audience only if they perceive the fundamental [*wurzelhaft*] significance of the inner connections which find expression in it according to the background, middleground, and foreground. Whenever we lose even the background of a drama, we possess the drama no more, as in the case, for example, with Greek drama."[58]

Schenker's late writings likewise recall his earlier arguments from GEIST, *HL*, *EBO*, *CFF* (1984), *KP1*, and NdK, about the connections between harmony and melody, albeit filtered later through the lens of *Ursätze*, voice-leading

---

55. NdK, 6–7; DAC, 38.
56. NdK, 11; DAC, 41–42.
57. Schenker, "Vermischtes: Gedanken über die Kunst und ihre Zusammenhänge im Allgemeinen," *MW3*, 107; tr. Ian Bent, "Miscellanea: thoughts on art and its relationships to the general scheme of things," *MM3*, 70.
58. *DfS*, chapter 1, §1, 14; *FC*, appendix C, 159.

transformations, and levels. Schenker now insisted that the overall melodic motion of an entire piece is controlled by an *Urlinie*, "the fundamental determinate melodic succession, the primal design of melodic content."[59] Just as he had already suggested in GEIST that *"every melody possesses a harmony of its own,"* Schenker insisted that *Urlinien* are always anchored triadically: "The fundamental line (*Urlinie*) is the name which I have given the upper voice of the fundamental structure (*Ursatz*). It unfolds a chord (*Klang*) horizontally while the counterpointing lower voice effects an arpeggiation of this chord through the upper fifth."[60] Since it unfolds a single chord, the *Urlinie* projects "the space of a third, fifth, or octave" and fills these spaces with passing tones."[61] These passing motions are the most basic of all melodic patterns and are "the source of all coherence in music."[62] Although *Urlinien* proceed exclusively by step, part 2 of *DfS* describes how, through the application of different voice-leading transformations, they can be composed-out with leaps: some of these leaps arise from shifting between one harmonic tone and another (e.g., register transfer and arpeggiation), while others arise from shifting between one essential voice and another (e.g., unfolding, motion to and from an inner voice, and voice exchange).[63] And, in part 3, Schenker includes a long section devoted to diminution, in which he describes a wide range of issues connected with melodic construction.[64] Especially interesting are his discussions of so-called "concealed repetitions" and bass diminutions.[65]

Similarly, Schenker continued to invoke the concepts of harmony and melody to support his attacks on contemporary music. In *DfS*, for example, he recycled arguments that he had already rehearsed in *HL*, *EBO*, *CFF* (1984), *KP1*, and NdK. Such is clearly the case in §266, "Vom Zusammenbruch der Diminution" ("The decline of diminution").[66] Recalling the opening

---

59. *DfS*, 17; *FC*, 5.
60. *DfS*, 16; *FC*, 4.
61. *DfS*, 32–33; *FC*, 12.
62. *DfS*, 33; *FC*, 12.
63. *DfS*, §§125–55, 79–88 and §§230–41, 133–39; *FC*, 46–52 and 82–86.
64. *DfS*, §§251–66, 150–74; *FC*, 131–32.
65. *DfS*, §§254 and 257, 161–64 and 166–67; *FC*, 99–100 and 102.
66. *Untergang* or *Niedergang* are approximately equivalent to "decline." "Collapse," "breakdown" or "disintegration" are common dictionary definitions given for *Zusammenbruch*. *Zusammenbruch* is not "decline": Oster has toned down Schenker's diction considerably in this instance.

paragraph of NdK, he immediately compared the monumental achievements of Handel, J. S. Bach, C. P. E. Bach, Haydn, Mozart, and Beethoven with those of nineteenth-century composers: "German musical genius gave greater depth for diminution by creating an especial abundance in the middleground, which, in return, made still greater abundance of foreground relationships organic. Schubert, Mendelssohn, and Chopin still revealed a genius for diminution, each expressing it in his own personal way. But their followers and imitators could equal neither the older nor the younger masters."[67] Once again, Schenker specifically blamed the decline of diminution on composers' inherent mastery of tonal composition and on their obsession with programs and other extrinsic associations. This time, however, Wagner was his main *bête noire*:

> Wagner's inability to achieve diminutions like those of the masters made it necessary for him to turn away from diminution, and, in the service of drama, to make expressiveness, indeed overexpressiveness, the guiding principle of music. His very helplessness with respect to purely musical diminution appealed to the musical world, which likewise prefers to stay clear of all hidden relationships. In the final hour Brahms appeared with a masterful capacity for synthesis and with his special mode of diminution. But in the meantime the musical community in Germany had been disrupted, and Brahms's diminution was unable to exercise the same extent of influence that was granted the older masters. Then came the World War—and since that time the German ear has been lost in chaos. Wagner's train of imitators were stillborn, as were the imitators of the great masters.[68]

In short: "Today there is neither ability for compositional synthesis nor any art which has expressiveness as its central principle. There are no models—only imitators of misunderstood models.[69]

By the time he wrote this paragraph, Schenker had already encountered the works of more radical composers, such as Schoenberg, Stravinsky, Ravel, and Debussy.[70] He was sufficiently appalled by their music that he took the opportunity in *MW3* (1930) to rebuff the recent attempts to claim that certain atonal pieces actually expressed some new form of tonality:

---

67. *DfS*, §266, "Vom Zusammenbruch der Diminution," 174; *FC*, "The decline of diminution," 106.
68. *DfS*, 174; *FC*, 106–7.
69. *DfS*, 174; *FC*, 107.
70. See, for example, *MW2*, 34–39; *MM2*, 15, 16–18, 130.

How can the atonalists not see that they merely make themselves look ridiculous today by denying their past? How on earth can they make out of any old rubbish-heap of notes to be arbitrarily atonal on one occasion and tonal on another, like dealers playing the stock market? Is the reversing of "tonality" and "atonality" anything like a religious conversion? Or, to pick an example from the unhappy period of inflation, anything like the random, fraudulent racking-up of the prices on goods?[71]

According to Schenker, there was only one possible explanation: "He who is born an atonalist—as if in penance—is denied a musical ear at birth. He is oblivious of tonality. This is demonstrable and the evidence is right there in his own new theories, in which he consciously dissociates himself from the music of the masters, thereby disavowing and denying the very tonality they practised. The atonalist can of course bank on the applause of the born atonalists among the public. But this seems—as we have seen—not entirely to satisfy them. He wants to convert musicians, too, to faith in a tonal atonality."[72]

Schenker's pessimism about the state of music during the first few decades of the twentieth century was not, however, confined to that of compositional practice: it encompassed the field of music theory as well. This is something that Schenker explored in greater detail in his essay "Fortsetzung der Urlinie-Betrachtungen," *MW2* (1926).[73] Having cited the famous "Tristan Chord" from the opening of Wagner's *Tristan und Isolde*, Schenker ridiculed the ways in which composers and theorists tried to classify "every vertical stack of notes" (*Ton-Übereinander*).[74] The prime culprit was Arnold Schoenberg, whose *Harmonielehre* (1911) attempted "to clothe the misunderstanding in theoretical robes."[75] In particular, Schenker denounced the ways in which Schoenberg invoked the idea of "emancipated dissonances" in order to explain certain vertical configurations in the music of J. S. Bach: "Thus Schoenberg is incorrect in describing the seventh and ninth as 'emancipated dissonances'; it is rather the case that,

---

71. "Vermischtes: Gedanken über die Kunst und ihre Zusammenhänge im Allgemeinen," *MW3*, 120; tr. Ian Bent, "Miscellanea: thoughts on art and its relationships to the general scheme of things," *MM3*, 78.
72. Ibid.
73. *MW2*, 11–44, esp. 29ff.; tr. John Rothgeb, "Further considerations of the Urlinie: II," *MM2*, 1–22, esp. 12ff.
74. *MW2*, 29; *MM2*, 12.
75. *MW2*, 30; *MM2*, 12–13.

in spite of their externally chordal trappings, they highlight the melodic aspect of the voice leading."[76] And Schenker rejected Schoenberg's claims that "there are no limits to the possibilities of notes sounding together, to harmonic possibilities," that "[the limits are] at most to the possibilities of fitting harmonies into a system that will establish their aesthetic valence," and that it might be possible to attain "a system embracing all phenomena, establishing the value of each."[77] For Schenker, such proposals completely misunderstand the absolute distinction between consonance and dissonance, and mistakenly attribute chordal functions to contrapuntal phenomena, especially those arising from passing tones: "Schoenberg's new chords are nothing but old-fashioned passing sounds!"[78] Schenker added: "The passing tone certainly has always been free, always 'emancipated'—so free, I repeat, that it has not yet been recognized in any textbook. What can it mean, then, to want to liberate it for the first time?"[79]

Schoenberg's suggestion that composers can create their own systems of harmony that can embrace all phenomena is, of course, extremely controversial from a theoretical point of view, as Schenker already made clear in NdK. Edward Laufer has stated the methodological issues in even clearer terms:

> There is no triad to be prolonged: some contextually derived associative sonority must take its place. The concepts of consonance and dissonance, as technically defined, therefore cannot exist, nor can, strictly speaking, the notions of passing or neighbor notes where these were dissonant events. Their attendant constraints, which provided motion and delays, must be compensated for by other kinds of embellishing and traversing motions. There is probably no generalized fundamental line: it could not now be diatonic. If there is no technically consistent, non-speculative basis, then anything goes, and likewise nothing.[80]

And Leonard B. Meyer has objected to Schoenberg's suggestion from a psychological point of view in his well-known critique of radical contextualism.[81] As Meyer notes: "an absolute and arbitrary (in the sense of non-dependence

---

76. *MW2*, 34–35; *MM2*, 13.
77. *MW2*, 35–36; *MM2*, 16.
78. *MW2*, 36; *MM2*, 16.
79. Ibid.
80. Laufer, "Review: Heinrich Schenker, *Free Composition*," 161.
81. Meyer, *Music, The Arts, and Ideas*, 280ff.

on any established tradition) contextualism precludes not only the possibility of communication but also the possibility of any but fortuitous perception and cognition." Like Schenker before him, Meyer implicitly invokes associationism when he insists that "our ability to perceive relationships depends in part upon what our past experience has told us constitutes a relationship. In other words, meanings and relationships are functions not merely of what *exists* in the world but of the habits, dispositions, and traditions which competent observers or listeners bring into play when they perceive and organize the world."[82]

Schenker's hostility towards Schoenberg is important, then, not only from a historical perspective because it pits one giant of Viennese music theory against another, but also from a theoretical perspective because it juxtaposes two very different conceptions of music theory. In writing his *Harmonielehre*, Schoenberg's purpose was to justify his own approach to musical composition by finding precedents for his own harmonic practices in the works of earlier composers. He wanted to show how his own methods of composition were extensions of those employed by earlier composers. In writing *HL*, however, Schenker's goal was to explain how the masterworks of tonal music exemplify the Classical conception of harmony and hence how they can be regarded as unified works of art. Schenker's explanations were grounded in what he regarded as fundamental laws of human cognition, many of which have been updated and confirmed by contemporary music psychology, and various general laws of tonal voice-leading and harmony.[83] As he explained near the beginning of *DfS*: "There is but one grammar for tonal motion [*Züge*]—the one described here in connection with the theory of coherence in music. It sufficed for the masters; therefore those without knowledge or capabilities felt it necessary to seek newer forms of coherence. But I repeat here what I have often said before: the fact that all of the masterworks manifest identical laws of coherence in no way precludes a diversity in essential nature among the masters."[84] Given such different views of music theory, it is small wonder that theorists have had such a hard time reconciling the theoretical claims of the one with those of the other.

For Schenker, then, the Classical theory of harmony provided a powerful antidote to the theory of harmony promoted in eighteenth- and nineteenth-century music treatises and conventional approaches to musical form as

---

82. Ibid., 280.
83. See Brown, *Explaining Tonality*, 209–33.
84. *DfS*, 22; *FC*, Appendix H, 160.

amplified in nineteenth-century treatises on *Formenlehre*. The basic elements of that theory—the primacy of melody, associationism, universality, causation, explanation, and organic unity—were ideas that he first encountered as a student of Classics in the *Gymnasium* and in his training as a lawyer at the University of Vienna. Prior to completing *HL* and NdK, Schenker explored many of these ideas in projects such as GEIST, [DTS], WEG, and *EBO*; after finishing *HL* and NdK, he cultivated them further both in his theoretical writings, such as *KP1–2*, *TW*, *MW*, and *DfS*, and in his many elucidatory editions, such as *CFF* (1984) and *Die letzten fünf Sonaten von Beethoven*. Drawing on the Classical definition, he no longer believed that harmonic theory should be concerned exclusively with the purely vertical aspects of musical composition; on the contrary, Schenker maintained that tonal harmony always involves projecting chords horizontally as well as vertically, and coordinating surface melodic and motivic details with the structure of the entire composition. By the time *DfS* was written, Schenker had devised a way to demonstrate graphically the interrelationships between line and chord, and between the local and the global through the concepts of the *Ursatz*, voice-leading transformations, and transformational levels. And, just as Aristotle tried to show the fundamental principles that made the dramas of Homer, Sophocles, Euripides, and Aeschylus great art, so he used these ideas to show what made the works of Handel, J. S. and C. P. E. Bach, Scarlatti, Haydn, Mozart, Beethoven, Schubert, Schumann, Mendelssohn, Chopin, and Brahms, tonal masterworks.

Since Schenker's reinterpretation of the Classical concept of harmony was motivated by his desire to explain how tonal masterworks of the common-practice period are bound together as organic wholes, one might be forgiven for assuming that it is entirely backward-looking and promoted a completely pessimistic picture of the future of music. Certainly, there is much evidence to support this assumption and for acknowledging what William Benjamin has described as Schenker's elegiac tone.[85] And yet, there are also a few moments of hope. One such moment appears in a letter from Schenker to Salzer from December 31, 1933, in which he comments on Béla Bartók's *Hungarian Folk Tunes* for violin and piano: "For the first time this is something by Bartók that commands downright respect: different from Liszt and Brahms and others, and yet in regard to the line, beautiful, very beautiful!"[86]

---

85. William E. Benjamin, "Schenker's Theory and the Future of Music."
86. See *SDO*, FS 40/1/19; handwritten letter from Schenker to Salzer, undated [December 31, 1933]; transc. and transl. Hedi Siegel. The letter is discussed by

Another occurs in his essay "Der Kunst der Improvisation" (*MW1*, 1925). Having described with great enthusiasm the structure of several improvisatory works by Handel and C. P. E. Bach, Schenker ends on an surprisingly optimistic note: "How much newer than all the latest novelties of today would a creative musical personality be if he were able to bring to pass a realization of the fundamental chord (*Grundklang*), and all the individual sonorities (*Einzelklänge*) that are drawn from it, with the strength of a Handel, a C. P. E. Bach, or another of the great masters! Nothing in the art and life of the future genius will likely call to mind our present time. This genius will be similar, rather, to the great masters of the past—would to God only that he might soon be summoned to the German people!—but surely as different from them as they all differ from one another."[87] The prospect of encountering such a genius is exciting indeed.

Siegel, "Schenker's letters to Felix Salzer," and Koslovsky, "Tonal Prolongation in Bartók's Hungarian Folktunes."

87. Schenker, "Der Kunst der Improvisation," *MW1*, 40; tr. Richard Kramer, "The art of improvisation," *MM1*, 19.

Appendix A

"The Path to Likeness"

Translation of OC/83, 2–43, with Introduction

Introduction

The problems with Schenker's essay "Der Weg zum Gleichniss" begin with the title. Just what is *Gleichnis*?[1] The authoritative nineteenth-century German dictionary begun by the brothers Grimm (important linguists as well as compilers of fairy tales) provides a list of meanings that include the pictorial notion of image (*Bild*), symbol (the word is often used today to indicate "metaphor"), similarity (it can also mean "analogy"), example, and means of comparison.[2] Schenker essentially invokes all of these, and thus choosing among them seems futile. For him, *Gleichnis* is both a process and a product. The meaning may be broad, but the purpose of the idea in Schenker's longer-range research plan is clear: firstly, it connects music to the arts as a whole via the mimetic theory: the arts "imitate"; music imitates (itself, as it turns out); therefore music is one of them; second, and more narrowly, *Gleichnis* includes "repetition" and all of its ramifications, a concept Schenker had already begun to explore in GEIST, and one which would become essential to the opening of *HL*. It is impossible to encapsulate all

---

1. The second "s" in *Gleichniss* is antiquated, so, except for the title, we use *Gleichnis* whenever the German word is called for.
2. We thank Martin Eybl for reminding us of the Grimm dictionary. Begun by Jacob and Wilhelm Grimm in 1854, the *Deutsches Wörterbuch*, not finished until 1961, is now available digitally. The entry for *Gleichnis* is at http://woerterbuchnetz.de/cgi-bin/WBNetz/wbgui_py?sigle=DWB&mode=Vernetzung&lemid=GG18604#XGG18604), accessed September 3, 2019.

of this in one word. For practical reasons, we have elected to follow Bent, Marston and others and retain the neutral cognate, "likeness."

The handwritten text of Schenker's essay itself presents the greatest difficulty. The only known copy, it has an extensive editorial overlay, and suffers from numerous passages that will continue to be controversial, or simply deemed illegible by even the most knowledgeable of readers. There exists one published transcription.[3] While a pioneering and useful effort, it does have significant problems, and, as with any transcription—though especially in this case—it should be used in conjunction with a parallel reading of the original manuscript.[4] Indeed, there may never be a "definitive" transcription, given the severity of the editorial problems.

Nonetheless, the transcription by Nicholas Marston comes close. Thus we are very much in his debt for allowing us to use this unpublished transcription in the preparation of the present translation. Certainly *the* expert on this manuscript, Marston has studied it over a long period of time, as is obvious from his transcription, and is the author of the recent prize-winning article on it.[5] The translation that follows is based essentially on his transcription. Departures are noted when they are significant, but passed over when minor in order to keep the notes unobtrusive. Needless to say, Professor Marston bears no responsibility for errors that may exist in our translation, nor would he necessarily agree with all of our speculations about Schenker's essay (both here and in chapter 1). But we can guarantee that our translation is much the better for the work we were able to do as a consequence of his generosity, and are most thankful for that.

Marston describes the manuscript as follows:

> The 'Gleichniss' manuscript consists of thirty-six numbered pages in Schenker's handwriting, in ink and pencil or crayon, with three pages interpolated non-sequentially at certain points and three others, consisting of notes and other material, following at the end. The essay is incomplete and breaks off at the bottom of page 36 with a sentence that may itself be incomplete. Whether the remainder is preserved, unidentified, elsewhere among Schenker's papers, or whether it has not survived (if indeed it ever existed), is at present unclear. As it stands, the surviving text runs to some 6,500 words. Complete decipherability is sometimes impossible, and there are extensive revisions, rewordings,

---

3. Hooper, "Heinrich Schenker's Early Approach to Form," 368–94.
4. In viewing the OC microfilm, bear in mind that the nuances of the editorial overlay show up much more clearly on a screen than in a printout.
5. Marston, "'. . . nur ein Gleichnis.'"

and restructurings of sentences . . . supplemented by numerous music examples written on hand-drawn staves.[6]

We add that the OC numbering system can cause confusion. Because OC/83, item number 1 is an inventory of file 83, irrelevant to the essay, Schenker's page 1 starts on OC/83, item number 2. OC numbers and Schenker's page numbers draw farther away from one another as the essay moves on and the three non-sequential pages enter the picture. Moreover, there are relevant notes on the reverse side of two other pages that are obviously in sequence, though we do not know if they were written in sequence (Schenker may have used the back of a page to pencil in a note at a later time, for instance). Of course, the big question with regard to the interpolated pages is whether their OC item numbers (given to an unattached piece of paper) have anything to do with Schenker's page numbering of the essay as he worked on it, for all of the Oster Collection went through a lot before it ended up as a library collection. Thus the "correct position" of the interpolated pages will continue to be debated.

These mechanical difficulties with the manuscript aside, there remains the question of interpretation of the editorial overlay as well as the interpolated pages and verso notes, not to mention discussion of the editorial decisions made during our reconstruction of Schenker's text. That is a project for another time, and perhaps for another author. We believe that the reader of this book should experience Schenker's essay first-hand now, and without delay, since it and [DTS] are the two papers foundational to *HL*: that is our number one priority.

Since many interpolated additions are relatively minor, some producing redundancies, we had to make decisions (most often, silently) as to which alternatives to choose. Here, faithfulness to text and idiomatic translation come into conflict: there is no way to include all—or even most—of the editorial additions without either destroying the flow of the English, or overburdening the reader with footnotes consisting of many redundant snippets of text. Nor do we discuss the relevance of the interpolated pages, with the exception of one of them that was of significance in chapter 1. However, we include translations of these in the footnotes where they occur in the pagination of the OC file, perhaps leading to their discussion by others. In order to help the reader keep Schenker's compositional sequence straight while still being able to find positions in the microfilm of the OC Collection, we include both numbering

---

6. Ibid., 8.

systems adjacent to one another: OC item numbers are in curly brackets, Schenker's page numbers in square brackets. The result is a rendering of Schenker's complete text minus editorial redundancies with interpolated passages placed in footnotes so that the reader who so chooses may read the essential content of Schenker's essay in continuity throughout without interruption.

❧ ❧ ❧

One of the most interesting features of this essay is its possible relationship to [DTS] (translated as [FTS] in appendix B). Like [DTS], if we exclude the editorial overlay of WEG, mostly in lighter pencil or the same ink, the copy of the essay in OC looks neat enough that it may have begun life as a fair copy of an earlier version. However, it becomes rough at numerous points—rougher than [DTS] does. Always the indefatigable reviser, Schenker continued his copious editing to the point that the relatively neat manuscript ultimately became quite crowded. But it never went through a final editing. Nonetheless, he thought enough of the work to preserve it incomplete and edited inconclusively as it was.

Interestingly, we can make similar statements about [DTS], though we can make them more securely in the latter case, for here there exists a typescript preserving the *Handschrift* with its lighter editorial overlay. Both suggest that [DTS] is much closer to a finished product than WEG, despite its ending in mid-sentence. Comparison of the manuscripts of [DTS] and WEG shows that the two are very likely "fraternal twins": i.e., that they were likely written at nearly the same time, though their topics are very different. The writing of both essays in *Lateinschrift* is only one of several features that point to a close relationship. Indeed, perhaps the abrupt endings of both announce the beginning of *HL*. The paper of each is exactly the same size, and both were written on pieces from sheets of double size that were torn in half—certainly suggesting strongly that the paper came from a common source. Both essays contain between twenty-one and twenty-three lines per page, suggesting that Schenker used the same straight edge in their preparation. And it appears that the same red and green pencils were used in editing both. Both essays draw on psychology quite heavily in their music-theoretical and analytical observations, justifying the origin of any music-theoretical phenomenon not taken from nature as "a form of our consciousness" (*eine Form unseres Bewußtseins*), a Kantian phrase that occurs in both, but not in *HL*.⁷ (Schenker does not even mention "consciousness" in *HL*.) Indeed, there are many other idiosyncratic phrases in common, considerably stretching the possibility that they are simply the result of chance. WEG is more music-analytical than [DTS], which deals with theoretical problems at the very foundation of the theory of harmony, suggesting that Schenker was farther along in his thinking about motives than he was in his work in harmony when the papers were conceived. This is consistent with our belief that WEG is closer, both chronologically and in content, to GEIST than [DTS] is—that Schenker thought about the attributes of melody long and hard before turning to the systematic details of harmony.

The Path to Likeness
[Heinrich Schenker]

{2}[1] To a greater extent than the other arts, music deserves to be conceived of and evaluated as the most personal creation of humanity. Today, just as at the beginning of her destiny, she alone among the other arts does without any purpose or model in nature. If poetry, painting, and sculpture have collectively the task of transferring phenomena of nature to human consciousness—the first revealing the individual's deepest thoughts to the mind's eye, the latter two the colors and outlines of all phenomena of the world, and architecture (to mention this art as well) holding fast to dwelling places as its initial crux—then music, on the contrary, has unfortunately found no helpmate in nature in the expected sense of the word. Thus those arts appear to be assigned, according to nature's intention (if one may say so), to carry out the distinction between humans and animals, plants, rocks, and the rest of the environment through self-consciousness; thus the other arts appear to be, most of all, arts of consciousness—of the greatest gift of nature to humanity. Since there is only one nature, the single "All," and there is only one consciousness, that of the human, there is thus one {3}[2] single task in this regard, namely, to bring nature into harmony with consciousness [*die Natur im Bewusstsein aufzulösen*]. Another, second duty could not be in the offing,⁸ for with such an assignment nature certainly would have overstepped herself. And it appears, at the outset, that the opportunity to establish another art was out of the question, to the extent that such an art was not already called

---

7. See below and appendix B.
8. We follow Hooper here in the reading of "anstehen" instead of "entstehen."

upon to partake in the original mission. Yet such an art was there from the beginning, and it was music. Music communicates neither the inner nor the outer world of human consciousness. It does not reveal the depth of thought, like poetry—at least not to the same degree of definition. Neither does it depict the green of the meadow nor the foliage of the forest like painting—nor preserve the form of human or animal, as sculpture does. It pays no heed to any of that—neither to nature nor consciousness. Yet it appeared among us, and soon shared the honors of the other arts. How could this be?

II.

Nature had no reason to invent music, and humans, themselves a product of nature, had just as little reason to do so. She had no private interest in music; therefore, neither did they. Thus it took a long time—centuries, even millennia—until humans, finally, through beautiful playing, refined that art born of both practical need and nature to an art on its own, {4}[3] finally mature and ready for practice and cultivation. Wonderful poetry had long existed, and indeed classical sculpture and architecture developed, as well as delightful painting. Yet, at the same time, there was no music that we justifiably would be able to call art in the same sense. Does anyone really believe that, for example, the music of the Greeks was as much an art as their poetry or sculpture? Or does anyone really believe that the music disappeared merely because the notation was faulty, or for this of that other reason?[9] No, it is truly not because of external impediments that no Greek music became an art in the true sense, despite Orpheus, Marsyas, Homer, Aeschylus, Sophocles, Pythagoras, Aristotle, and Aristoxenus, among others.

If not art in general—not to mention art at the highest level—the activity of the Greeks in the area of music was at least evidence that art could already be practiced at that time without the model of nature or any sort of

---

9. Schenker had some evidence of notation in the early fragments, some important ones having been discovered in the 1890s. The earliest notation treatise (Alypius's "Introduction to music") is quite late, however, dating from the fourth century CE. It was also known in the 1890s, and Schenker may have read it. It appeared just as his research on melody was getting underway in the compilation of musical-technical sources by Karl von Jan (Carolus Janus), *Musici scriptores graeci* (Leipzig: Teubner, 1895). Jan later published a small volume of all the notated Greek melodies then known: *Musici scriptores graeci,* supplementum, *melodiarum reliquiae* (Leipzig: Teubner, 1899).

goal compelling humanity towards it.[10] Thus the basis of music was there, but not yet art. This would only arrive when music was completely free of the servitude to poetry and dance, from which it received its model and purpose until then, this materially driven element that was so foreign to it. Only music made this self-referentiality without obfuscation by model and purpose into true art. {5}[4] I would beware of placing the beginning of true musical art earlier than the sixteenth century. However, there were positive signs even before then.

III.

Unlike music, the other arts had the advantage of starting with a model, and as vast, lofty, and inexhaustible as it may have been for them, its steady presence offered security, and a certain comfort and ease in artistic practice. The artist could always know that for which he had to strive, for the eternal goal—nature—stood before him. Even his error was illuminated by the light of the goal shining through.

However, from the same invaluable advantage arose a deeper fulfillment of the human mind, which had its basis in the following: it is an idiosyncrasy of the human mind that it can grasp the world, including itself, only through likeness—i.e., through all the appearances of the world, which it must place against one another to compare and distinguish. And it must conceive of them with particular names: thus it names that person "king" who is not a vassal; "rich," one who is not poor; "sun," that which is not moon; "man," that person who is not woman; "day," that which is not night; "love," that which is {6}[5] not hate, and so forth. If there were only love—love alone in the world—there truly would be none! Goethe expresses this with the famous words, "Alles Vergängliche ist nur ein Gleichnis."[11] The manner in which a likeness is conceived then is a form of our consciousness.[12] Nature,

---

10. Hooper's reading of this sentence is problematic.
11. From the end of Goethe's *Faust*, part II. The statement is a Platonic belief fundamental to Schenker's thinking: i.e., that the "real" is in back of the transitory appearances of the world. Goethe might be paraphrased and elaborated as, "All appearances of the world are but metaphors for something deeper."
12. Schenker refers to the Kantian notion of "form," i.e., the logical connective of substances. Here, "form" of consciousness is literally the means by which it works. Cf. Kant, "for metaphysics has the peculiar good fortune, not characteristic of any other branch of knowledge, that it deals with objects (for *logic* deals with the *form*

which granted us consciousness, also gave us its form. Thus it appeared to be in nature's interest that she did not bring her gift to us for naught. Since she provided herself to the arts as the model, she spawned in that way a likeness of herself, just as, on the other hand, she ordered the arts [to pursue] likeness themselves. The model became likeness: nature as a likeness of the arts, the arts a likeness of nature. Thus nature fulfilled our consciousness by preserving its form with all the content of the world, and its fundamental goal: to raise us above the animal world through our consciousness.

Poetry became the likeness of man himself: the model and likeness of his being. Whether in the lyric or dramatic genre, man represented himself everywhere, made himself into the likeness of himself in order to understand himself and others. "Know thyself" the ancients said in this sense.[13] {7}[6] Similarly, painting and sculpture received the whole large world of visible and colorful phenomena as likeness: line and color of a picture became likeness of nature, just as nature was a likeness of the picture.

But we saw music excluded from all of these advantages. Nature could not use music, for she organized the practice of the arts vis-à-vis consciousness, and thus necessity, purpose, model, and likeness all fell away for music. First of all, even access to consciousness was completely blocked for her, since likeness was lacking. Therefore, as we showed above, she was chained to poetry at the beginning so that she would receive the likeness to nature through that art at the very least. The word, prepared in humanity as a condition of the mind, and thus even as a first likeness, was to bear the second likeness from itself, the likeness from word to tone. Even if the original likeness of tone to world went no further, a derivative, borrowed idea should at least appear. Nonetheless, poetry, the first likeness, held on to its superior power, and as much as musicians of yore liked to deceive themselves, music could in no way lay claim to the rank of first likeness, and beyond that, it could not in any sense become art, as long as it bore that deficiency {8}[7][14] within it, namely that it did not know how to accord with the form of our consciousness, the demand for likenesses. So first of all this deficiency had to be removed. But humans—here artists—had to advise themselves on how this was to be done, for nature was silent. Without the guidance of nature, the

---

[our emphasis] of thought in general)." Immanuel Kant, *Kritik der reinen Vernunft, Vorrede zur zweiten Auflage*, 35.

13. Motto inscribed in the temple of Apollo at Delphi, and often quoted from Socrates.

14. {8, verso} "Likeness – Contrast."

artists, simply following instinct, began coming to terms with the difficult riddle: they began in that quest for new means, developed many experiments that they systematized, only to throw them out the next day. It was a fearful struggle with an unknown mystery, which, as was said, lasted to the beginning of the Modern Period. Finally, however, it was a genius who emerged from humanity or the power of instinct that sensed the way, and even here was unable to find it. But the discovery was made. Man found the principle, the basic law of music, and knew it in words and intention. The period of experimentation was closed: what music needed to become art was known, and with that art itself began. Music had received likeness.

Artists had found the idea that fortunately came to the rescue: to search for the likeness of music not outside of music {9}[8]—since it was nowhere to be found, as they must have experienced. Rather, they placed the likeness of music in the music itself—a clever stroke of genius that awards the human intellect perhaps the greatest honor. Even if it was artificial to elevate the art to its own likeness, the demand of our consciousness, which may not be avoided under any circumstances, was met well enough. All the parts were in place now: the art had gotten its likeness, and on that account we could only now comprehend and develop it. What a huge step!

Nature herself was elevated thereby, for the artist, under his own power, knew to model the artificial likeness within music herself after the natural likenesses of the other arts in so felicitous—yes, even clever—a way. {10} [9] A new art was erected artificially, and with it a second, artificial, and higher nature that was comparable to the first. [illegible sentence].[15] What a proud creation of humanity, of the artist. What a triumph: nature, finally conquered by the mind of man, even if this artificial art must be placed next to the other arts as child of her children!

On Likeness Itself

This likeness is called "motive."

When, in the course of the following discussion, we attach a more comprehensive and thorough definition to this much used term, we hope less to make ourselves guilty of subordinating artists and theorists, and more to cast greater light on their true intentions. By motive, we understand all and everything in music that may be raised to the level of a model for an

---

15. See OC/83, 9, middle of second paragraph; Hooper: 373, line 16ff.; Marston, [8]: line 20ff.

imitation, or counter-image.[16] Conceptually and materially, motives possess two properties: the model, and its opposite, the likeness, which we call imitation or contrast. Without likeness there is no model, and more obviously, without model, no likeness. Therefore, likeness and contrast are included in the concept "motive."

Music offers us in all of its facets the occasion to deploy motives in this sense: in the melodic, rhythmic, harmonic, and contrapuntal [sense] {11} [10] of the notes. The motive—melodic likeness—contains the best known and typical meaning: when one speaks of motive, the melodic motive is almost always meant. There is no great difficulty to contrast the melodic motive, along with everything that belongs to that idea; the widespread usage of the idea alone speaks for that. Whether the likeness is read in an exact repetition or contained in a freer one, whether it be for example in a transposition by octave or another interval, or even [in] more or less limited variations of the same [motive], it is everywhere to be heard as a likeness, whereby the motive is made understandable to our consciousness. Even the number of notes that are raised to the level of a motive is inconsequential. Small as well as large groups may attain this status. Rather than describing everything that belongs to this material in this context, we introduce a few examples, leaving the further study of the works of the masters to the industry of the reader:

Example A.1. J. S. Bach, Prelude in D Minor, *Well-Tempered Clavier I*, BWV 851

Example A.2. J. Brahms, Two Rhapsodies, Op. 79, No. 2

---

16. Schenker writes literally *Nachbild* (imitation, copy) or *Gegenbild* (contrast, counterpart), and stands by this terminology, which we have translated "imitation" and the literal "counter-image." "Contrast" is already taken as a musical process, and "counterpart" carries with it the notion of "correspondence" in everyday speech, not "opposition." Schenker may have thought about using "contrast": he writes "Gleichniss – Contrast" on OC/83, 8 verso (otherwise unused), two pages in advance of this paragraph. At one point in the essay he writes *Gegen-Theil*, but he is speaking more generally about an "event" and its "opposite."

{12}[11]

Example A.3. Beethoven, Sonata in E Minor, Op. 90

Such a representation or development of likeness, especially in reference to the cyclic form of the sonata, is often called *thematic*, whereby, as is easy to see, the motive is called "theme." Both designations in the melodic sense in general are easily conflated, even to the point of complete identity; or they are separated, sometimes consciously, sometimes unconsciously, with intention, or none. The sum of all likenesses, all thematic material, including the motive, and other types to be treated later, is also often designated by the eminent word, "organic." This is exactly the same situation as with the motivic element—i.e., with likeness itself. Just as this is of artificial origin and not modeled by nature, but corresponds to a form of our consciousness, so too the sum of all of this cannot be designated as anything more than artificial. The characteristic "organic" therefore must be used and understood only in the free, analogous, and artificial sense of the word. When one takes this word out of its own domain of validity, {13}[17]{14}[12] where it indicates the ultimate mystery of nature, and applies it to art in order to award it the highest praise—a complete equalization with nature—one should always remain conscious nonetheless that poetry, painting, and sculpture earn their designation via that word more than music. This said, we do not snub the latter art, for music, resting on artificial postulates, does not pretend to bring about consequences that are other than artificial. In its origin, as in its development, music is a completely different art than the others: exactly this word [organic] may fit all of those other arts, at the very least, not to mention [fitting them] in the same sense.

To create motivic likeness to perfection is the supreme power only of the geniuses. Often they succeed in concealing the motivic element a thousand ways, to the extent that even the most practiced listeners cannot find it again, and to silence it for unpracticed listeners, who, much to their own detriment, cannot ever perceive it. And it is not infrequent that one stands before

---

17. {13} Printed form "An die Valueten Cassa," with indistinct notes related to the essay.

an unsolvable situation, perplexed and in doubt as to whether a likeness is present here or not. To give only one example, who would want to claim definitively that {15}[13] m. 67 of the E minor Sonata of Beethoven is a likeness of the earlier bass in m. 54 and the following, a diminution of the eighth-notes B C♯ D?

Example A.4. Beethoven, Sonata in E Minor, Op. 90, First Movement, mm. 67–8

Example A.5. Beethoven, Sonata in E Minor, Op. 90, First Movement, mm. 55–6

Or, to introduce another example, the question is whether in the following measures 24–5 of the Sonata in A♭, Op. 110[18]

Example A.6. Beethoven, Sonata in A-flat Major, Op. 110, First Movement, mm. 23–5

---

18. Schenker fails to number this example, and thus the reader will find that the example numbers on the manuscript are one off from our example numbers from here on.

the likeness that spans the two groups enclosed in brackets was recognized consciously by Beethoven, or whether no likeness at all exists between the bracketed groups, and, on the contrary, the author consciously limited himself to the likeness in the descant alone?

The examples just given may serve to establish the concept and value of likeness for now, for it is definitely not a matter of pinpointing the compositional meaning of a motive in a particular artwork. Thus, also in the following, we want to present the motive briefly in its rhythmic, harmonic, and contrapuntal sense, and show its meaning in small examples—always {16} [14] with reference only to art in general.

By rhythm, we understand the temporal phenomenon, the temporal form of the melody itself, in contrast to the pure and eternally invariable time that exists behind rhythm, which is sometimes called meter. An example in which we will develop rhythmic likenesses will make this clear: it is the beginning of the great B-flat major Sonata of Beethoven, Op. 106:

Example A.7. Beethoven, Sonata in B-flat Major, Op. 106 ("Hammerklavier"), First Movement

The first eighth-note, B♭, provides us with the measure of time, for up to then, all time remained virtual. Now, with this unit of time we measure the first dotted quarter, which contains three eighths, and thus, the first temporal model also originates on one, bound initially to the melodic dimension. We obtain the feeling for time not through an abstract, {17}[15] so-called "metric" scheme, but only through true, embodied duration, which we have borrowed from the first eighth-note.

Even [when assessing] time we conceive an "event" only when we set an "opposition" [*Gegen-Theil*] against it. [As to] what a half of a quarter-note may be, only a second, next [half] can tell us, and without that there would be absolutely no "[first] half." For also in the temporal dimension our consciousness demands the assistance of likeness, without which nothing can be understood. Thus we set one part against the whole as a likeness, which produces a third part (1 : 3). Here once again there would be no third, if two other parts did not follow; this time they would express the likeness of the parts to the whole, as to one another. Thus our [temporal] feeling sets up the time for us instinctively, such that it appears to us as two or three. Our feeling does not create other likenesses; and when occasionally an artist whimsically demands that we feel in five, it resists our feeling, and is always extended in relation to the first, because the simpler likenesses two and three, already experienced, return.[19] Our feeling for time would be led back only to the last [likeness], and thus to all that which we call meter. {18}[16] According to my view, there is no other meter than the likenesses contained in this feeling [*Gefühl*]. Now, this feeling [for time] is the basic one that we always have; it is even the manner in which we hear time itself, and thus a form of our [temporal] feeling that we always have and that never leaves us. However, this constant growth of form in us is obviously the reason that in the parsing of time in the artwork itself, it is better to abandon it and observe only the form of the temporal phenomenon that the melody itself presents. Our feeling for time is not suspended because the melody articulates time in its own way; on the contrary, that [articulation] does not itself suffice to understand the temporal form of the melody. These [melodies] want to be interpreted on their own as a new and higher likeness. Applied to the example above, we feel on that account something that in the general likeness of time we express with the number two; yet the result we have does not emerge from that, for our eye is fixed on the way the melody brings it forth as active, always living. Therefore, with rhythm, we have enriched only {19}[17] this living temporal likeness, not the basic [rhythmic] feeling in general.

To return to the rhythmic likeness that we took from the above example, we see the first eighth-note with the following dotted note raised to a model in the purest sense, thus as motive in the [music] following:

Example A.8. Beethoven, Sonata in B-flat Major, Op. 106 ("Hammerklavier"), First Movement, mm. 39–40

---

19. Here Schenker invokes the "law of least action," as he does often in [DTS] and *HL*.

But more as a contrasting model in the following bass figure:

Example A.9. Beethoven, Sonata in B-flat Major, Op. 106 ("Hammerklavier"), First Movement, mm. 47–8

[This is] most interesting, because it is immediately bound to a further rhythmic figure from the beginning itself:

Example A.10. Beethoven, Sonata in B-flat Major, Op. 106 ("Hammerklavier"), First Movement, m. 1

where it first appears as though a similar dotted quarter-note wants to follow the eighth-note. Furthermore, the realization [*Inhalt*] of the piano B♭ is raised to be a model, and indeed such that a counter-image [*Gegenbild*] in doubled [metric] values is set against it:

Example A.11. Beethoven, Sonata in B-flat Major, Op. 106 ("Hammerklavier"), First Movement, mm. 17–19

{20}[18] However, in a way that Beethoven alone [could do] (this stood as an imperative only to him), the complete content of bracket c is raised to become a rhythmic model, which can be succeeded by the following counter-image [*Gegenbild*]:

Example A.12. Beethoven, Sonata in B-flat Major, Op. 106 ("Hammerklavier"), First Movement, mm. 91–5

One sees how the motive, taken rhythmically so large, to describe it, begins with a *sf*, which aspires to be a sign of brilliance, not for [its] mechanical strength (a mechanical forte), but for passion and defiance, as this effects the change of the first eighth into a quarter. Furthermore, both quarters (the content of the little b [bracket]) have the effect of a model, which only now is embellished so wonderfully with the *sf* on the second-beat quarter [in the counter-image]. This is a likeness, but a rest stands in place of a quarter-note, after which the second quarter follows with *sf*. What a rhythmic likeness! And what soul and passion with it!

Example A.13. Beethoven, Sonata in B-flat Major, Op. 106 ("Hammerklavier"), First Movement, mm. 112–13

Who knows whether both quarters do not want to be felt as a counter-image and likeness {21}[19], as though the *sf* has merely been augmented, after which—its longing now put to the test—it goes back to the opening. What more, then, is the *sf* on the second beat than a psychological syncopation, so to speak, in contrast to a physical, or material one, which is the only one known under this name.

We add, finally, that this is much more a rhythmic likeness than the creation of a large number of the same likenesses one after the other. In this regard, to refer to these measures and the following in the sonata,

Example A.14. Beethoven, Sonata in B-flat Major, Op. 106 ("Hammerklavier"), First Movement, mm. 62–4

we believe we have said what is most important regarding the nature of the rhythmic motive, to the extent that it may serve as clarification of likeness, this fundamental concept in music.

In feeling, then, not to persist with our clarification, we want to speak only briefly regarding harmonic likeness, and say that here also antecedent and consequent (or counter-image) formations may follow immediately. In this regard we provide the following {22}[20]

Example A.15. Beethoven, Sonata in B-flat Major, Op. 106 ("Hammerklavier"), First Movement, mm. 100–11

as an example of how the minor subdominant (mm. 2–4) contrasts the diatonic major subdominant (mm. 8–10) even in the melodic dimension. If desired, one might compare example A.3 [above] in a similar manner, where the melodic model in minor is the basis of the counter-image of a G major triad.

The following from the same sonata is an example of the so-called genuine harmonic sense:

Example A.16. Beethoven, Sonata in B-flat Major, Op. 106 ("Hammerklavier"), First Movement, mm. unidentified

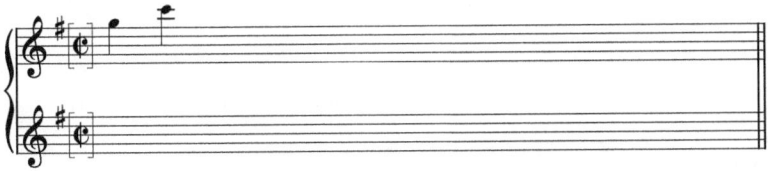

Here, as a result of a clever mixture with F minor, instead of D-F-A of F, the listener suddenly gets to hear D♭-F-A♭.[20] Practical music teems[21] with harmonic alterations exactly of this nature, with which artists—for the most part of lesser stature and with a deficit of the necessary talent—love to run riot with motivic and rhythmic likenesses, in which constant, monotonous or sterile motives {23}[21] live. Indeed, they can always produce harmonic excitement with which they do not disappoint the knowledgeable, and so much the more lure and amaze the ignorant.

In keeping with the notion from which we later will have to develop sustenance—that counterpoint in the truest and most genuine understanding of the word is only contained in two parts—we allow finally a couple of examples of contrapuntal likenesses taken from Beethoven, though reduced simply to two-part structure, as they occur in the two outer parts.

Example A.17. Beethoven, Sonata in E-flat Major, Op. 81a, Second Movement, mm. 1–3, 10–11

---

20. No measure in the sonata corresponds to this description.
21. Here we follow Hooper, 384, who reads "wimmeln."

Example A.18. Beethoven, Sonata in B-flat Major, Op. 106 ("Hammerklavier"), Third Movement, mm. 13–16, 21–2.

{23, verso}[22]

{24}[22] Conclusion and Transition. The Second and Less Important Likeness: The Poetic Element[23]

Embracing such a likeness, music became a true art. This happened in the course of time —not at the very beginning as in the case of the other arts, to whom nature offered likeness through and with herself a priori. Since likeness in music is a pure, inner, and abstract one, it may be said, if one wishes, that this art is an abstract one: of all the arts, music, on the basis of its origin, is the most abstract art, the art κατ' εξοχην.[24] If one wants, music can also be conceived as the art *per analogiam*, as long as one pays tribute to the fact that this likeness is only an analogy and artificial replica of the likeness that nature offers us.

Only in possession of this means of likeness were the artists permitted henceforth to dare to attend to other influences and sources of inspiration,

---

22. "*Gesang-Rom.*" = chant? "On Motive/chant as motive."
23. Schenker initially called this section "Conclusion and Transition." An important question is whether it links with the fragmentary "transition" (OC/83, 29) to be found in the midst of this section. We believe that it does. See chapter 1 above.
24. In ancient Greek, "most eminent, greatest, mightiest . . ." (Liddell and Scott, *Intermediate Greek-English Lexicon*, 276).

which they so eagerly exploited in their art, the better to feel the power of granting the music emanating from these sources the status of true art. The better they understood how to make their art, the more assuredly they used such foreign sources of inspiration. Among these sources, however, we understand {25}[23] real—even the most real—daily life. Thus we understand states of the heart [*Seele*], etc. and not just those of a general nature, such as love, anger, calm, tempestuousness, sadness, cheerfulness or exuberance, the serious or the comic, but rather, more amazingly, particular conditions of the human mind [*Seele*]—even movements of the body, the hands, the eyes, a peculiar tone of voice or peculiar feelings, etc. With that, life itself entered—the whole breadth of human life entered into likeness in musical art. It was a second and new likeness, which distinguished itself from the first, inner-musical one clearly enough. From this point on music could nourish itself with life and nature just as the other arts, which she approached. Only she had to satisfy as well her basic principle of existence as a likeness of a higher category, while the sister arts had enough—perhaps even more than enough—with only one likeness, the likeness of nature. Whether it is now apposite to say that by such a view of the matter music has a double weight to bear—namely two types of likenesses—remains to be seen. It appears to us, {26}[24] at least, that what belongs to the essence of an art cannot at the same time be a burden to it. For, in that case, eating and sleeping would have just as much a right to be valued as a burden of humanity, which is certainly not the case. Music must be art first of all; then comes whatever may—humanity, nature, the whole, wide world—but only secondarily.

How easy it is to guess what is meant when we speak here of the species of music always referred to improperly by that special name, program-music. It is used improperly because all good (and indeed the best) music can be in this sense program-music, without ceasing to be artistic music—that is, true music and true art. On the other hand, the unique character of the name would have to indicate much less an accolade than a criticism of the species, if one wanted to say thereby that the program moves to the foreground in front of the music itself. What else would one want to venture by this if one were not convinced, as we are, that Beethoven or Haydn had already written program music before Berlioz, Liszt or Wagner, {27}[25] and indeed better than they? He, who, like us, believes on the best evidence that, for example, the A Major Sonata of Beethoven Op. 101 shelters within it the most sublime program music ever reached—or that ever will be reached—should be careful using the word program-music in the sense of a new and special species of art, to be used first with regard to Liszt's music in "Tasso."

What would he acknowledge or say that is uniquely new about the music of Liszt that could not also be said a thousand times even before Beethoven? Or is this game merely about the fact that Beethoven's work is simply called a "sonata," while Liszt's opus appears with the name Tasso written above it, which indicates a human being, his character, perhaps even an event from a well-known life? Does one have to call all music of this sort that has a particular title with whatever name—or even a previously printed story, saying or legend—does one have to call that program-music? Is the whole world really so obtuse that merely at the beck and call of some trifle they decree a distinction between the last string quartets of Beethoven and the overtures of Berlioz *within* the [same] species? {28}[26]

Now, however, even a Beethoven—who could do a lot (indeed everything that one could wish for from art and an artist)—was not able to give the poetic likeness of his work the explicitness and physicality that people love to cling to today, even in the music of the lesser masters. The country folk, whose life he described in his Sixth Symphony, are not nearly as graspable and visible, as, for example, the peasant folk that Tenier[25] paints, or of which Anzengruber[26] writes poetry. The "farewell" that [Beethoven] cries out to his dear friend does not have the physicality nor even the simplest taking of leave. And it would be useful if the tones (two words) "lebe wohl" could fall out of the mouth, so to speak (please excuse this image). Is this not all too little—much too little—when set against the reality of parting? Where is the faltering heart, the blanching cheeks, the wringing of the hands, the anxious beating of the blood, the blank staring of the eyes after the friend drawing away? Oh, where is all of this—the whole body, as though drunk in the pit of anger, the soul, as though stuck in an instant without a future? How would music {29}[27]{30}[27] be able to describe all of this?

---

25. Either David Tenier (1582–1649), or his son, David ("the Younger," 1610–90). It was surely the latter, a Flemish Baroque, minor master, who was known for developing the "tavern scene," and his depictions of peasants.
26. Schenker refers to the Viennese novelist, dramatist, and poet, Ludwig Anzengruber (1839–89).
27. {29} Inserted page, deleted in green crayon:

Transition [*Überleitung*]

However, in order to fulfill the task of the art of music, the tonal material had to be created first. The tonal system had to be found, in which it was possible to demonstrate musical as well as poetic likenesses. To find this was

Yet it is also, fortunately, not her calling to do everything, and [if] pictures do not speak, statues do not walk, and words do not [speak], then the tones, like the words, do not need to speak, to paint with color, or to embody by carving. Every art has its own task, and with that its boundaries and its own means of production. Only faithfulness to its task is the same for all: the loyalty to likeness is the same. Just as poetry, painting and sculpture must remain true, so music must remain true to its own. Likeness is everything.

However, loyalty to musical likeness means creating endless melodic, rhythmic, harmonic, and contrapuntal likenesses, and following only these assiduously and tirelessly, with likenesses and counter-images. If a person—or nature—sees him or herself as well in one likeness or another, so much the better, as long as the counter-image is not lacking.

Pereat mundus, vivat musica![28]

However, woe to him who defiles such a beautiful calling of loyalty with the disgusting name "formalism." For he appears to have no sense of how terribly his {31}[29]{32}[28] lack of knowledge compromises true art. To be sure, we are happy to recognize his right to feel bored by the likenesses of composer X or Y. However, having become really annoyed by the matter, as often as he may sense the desire to run down the whole system of likenesses, he should simply remember the system of Beethoven or Bach, each on his own in that system, which guarantees the marvels of art as well as of the soul, indeed which even appears to become a human system of likenesses. What can Beethoven and the system do about it, anyway, if a lesser talent is not capable of following them?[30]

Or what if that person wants to take the formalism of Beethoven seriously, but sets it against the musically impoverished poetic likenesses of a Berlioz,

---

almost more difficult than to find the internal musical principle [of likeness], and centuries went by—indeed millennia—until what we have was finally created.

To p. 27

To Likeness

IX Symphony – Finale

Tone – Word, second time

Wagner program

Repetition with regard to the finale

28. "[Though] the world perish, long live music!"

29. {31} "to 28. Goethe 'rules poetry'" [*Poesie*, archaic].

30. The passage "To be sure . . . following them?" was arrived at in consultation with Lee Rothfarb, who receives a special thank you for this one.

for example, as something newer and more progressive—as the longed-for "non-formalistic"? He would have to say that he is the enemy of the arts in general, because the arts present a unified phenomenon. For art will never lose that unity! And how topsy-turvy also, that nature, hidden in eternity, will never have to enter by the power of her inexhaustible fecundity.[31]

{33}[29] If every art can only be conceived as bounded by time and space, and therefore suffer many and manifold limitations, the problem can only be how such external and essential constraint [*Gebundenheit*] can be pervasive in the face of more important inner constraint. How does it occur that both—restrictions as well as freedom from such—may together become requirements and preconditions, while on the other hand, that in greater restriction, a more extensive space for greater freedom from restriction is forecast and assumed—that the most characteristic design of the human psyche [is freedom], and yet, in the greatest freedom, the greatest restriction is forecast and preordained. This alone is the basic problem of art; and among the creative, the most artistic will always be those who solve this problem in the greatest moderation—that is, those who want to understand it as directing us to express psychological freedom through the means of formal restriction, and to deploy in formal restriction the greatest freedom. And under no circumstances are we permitted to doubt whether such is truly possible, for we had {34}[30] one who could [do this] and who proved it, and it was Beethoven!

When we follow his traces, how he treated a likeness, for the use and piety of all that follow him!

From Beethoven himself we first take an example of poetic likeness that is beyond any doubt: from the "les adieux" Sonata Op. 81a. The title alone tells that he wishes to say unconditionally that here he has used poetic likenesses in the large and small, and we have no right to punish him for lying. "Lebe wohl,"[32] the first words, set by the first tones, stand for pathos:

Example A.19. Beethoven, Sonata in E-flat Major, Op. 81a, First Movement, mm. 1–2

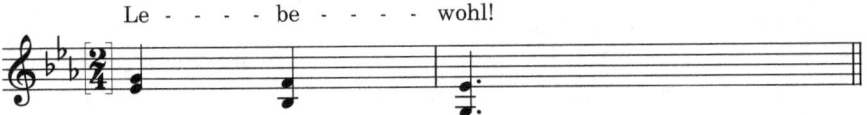

---

31. With this last sentence, we follow Hooper.
32. "Goodbye" or, in approximate English, "stay well."

Now we ask, has influence on a sequence of tones via the model of a poetic word or situation really occurred here, or not? Further, have we the obligation to believe him by virtue of his personal written assurance that stands above the music, or also the right, in spite of this assurance, to reject this as a likeness?

{35}[31] No, we think: the word of the master must be believed, above all since the impression of the succession of tones born under the influence of likeness is such as to be better able to support rather than rebut the word of the master. However, once we have assumed that what Beethoven has assured us is really true, and indeed true in word and tone, do we not have the obligation through this alone to grant the music a right to poetic likeness at the same time? If likeness in Beethoven's art was carried out, and we even believed this because we were unable to deny it, how might we claim the opposite: music could not express likeness? Should—and must—it not be enough that the music had expressed likeness to him, the author, irrespective of what goes on for listener, the art, and the artist? If likeness were an actuality and an event for him alone, it is not something to be dismissed once and for all, whether we have a part in it or not. And we may not be hesitant when we say that music can {36}[32] express poetic likeness and it expresses it whether we perceive it or not. All of this follows from the fact that it is real to the artist, and indeed from that alone. With him, who has created and experienced likeness, we must agree and say, music can very well also express poetic likeness.

For even we, who simply listen, and do not create, likewise have rights to the hearable [*Thatsachen* = *Tatsachen*], if need be only in our direction with respect to the artist, just as earlier he had the same rights with respect to us. Our right consists in being permitted to say that this or that series of pitches appears to us as a likeness to this or that mental activity, a likeness to this of that dramatic gesture, etc. If it occurs that a series of tones makes us think of something definite from real life, then the likeness is already there, since it came about as every association of ideas—uncalled for, unwanted, and unable to be prevented.[33] We can do nothing to make something from real life occur to us as a consequence of the power of an act of likeness to a series of tones. {37}[33] If it happens, who wants to take that right for himself to deny this particular feature of the hearable or even to reject the whole of it? And why should it be denied us? Whom does is harm[34] that this hear-

---

33. Cf. chapters 1 and 4 on "associations of ideas."
34. Here we follow the reading of Hooper, 392.

able feature is our exclusive intellectual property, and perhaps must remain so? An example: as often as we listen to the so-called "development section" of the sonata mentioned above, we always have the definite impression of life, and believe that we see and hear sobbing, to which all thoughts and feelings want to go, like an emotional breakdown before the end, as though the cruelty of parting does not think to come to an end—does not feel the end mostly because of the lack of courage in the face of pain, or because, more comfortingly, it pushes him to hope, before he has fallen prey to pain. We hear plainly how all the last words fall into emptiness for him—into emptiness beyond, where feeling and spirit appear to disconnect, and the moment becomes so hollow and eternal, the body, alone and so unfeeling, consumed thoughtlessly by the conflagration of pain. {38}[34] We hear that part approximately as follows, to express it in notes:

Example A.20. Beethoven, Sonata in E-flat Major, Op. 81a, First Movement, mm. 73–89

If the fragment of a second, lower staff containing notes were taken away, and it were to be lacking in the sonata—itself instead of those other musical and poetic likenesses actually being there—is it not now as though the first motive, as though from impotence or pain, could not be brought to an end? And if it were we alone who hear it this way, is this interpretation on that account any less true? Is the certainty of our hearing not just as vital to us as that of others is vital to them, or the artist's vital to him? We do not aim to convert anyone to a similar feeling just because we feel in such a way. Even Beethoven could not prevent our feeling in that way, especially if we were as defenseless {39}[35] against such an idea as he was with respect to his ideas that came to him. Our feeling insists also on its right, whether or not the master even proposes another poetic likeness (of which we know nothing).

[Here Schenker apparently changes the penpoint, perhaps returning to writing at a later time.][35]

To move to still other cases from this point on is not difficult, and thus in general, the following cases arise. First, the artist creates a poetic-musical likeness, of which the listener knows nothing, but instead the listener imagines another poetic one than the one imagined by the artist, connected to the musical one. 2. The listener imagines a poetic-musical likeness without the artist having thought of any at all, but it is the same one nonetheless. From this may be seen that a poetic-musical likeness may take aim at two subjects—the artist and the listener—and is anchored when it is acceptable by one side or the other, and that it is not necessary that it be valid in the same meaning for artist and listener, notwithstanding the rarest and best of cases, in which both sides are in complete agreement regarding the likeness.

{40}[36] There can be no more doubt that the "double subjectivity" of poetic-musical likeness on the side of the artist, as well as on the other side of the listener, may, if anything, count as the basis of why music can express yet another likeness than the purely musical, and even should, but not the other way around. We have already said that the poetic-musical likeness must be presented only by means of the first, inner-musical likeness, and thus by means of the melodic, rhythmic, harmonic, and contrapuntal motive, its counter-image and replication included. We only add that the better the poetic merges into the purely musical—that is, the more that the second goes into the first likeness—the better the purpose of art in general is fulfilled. Beyond that, the desired effect of the poetic is aspired to better and more assuredly when on the way to pure musical likeness than when poetic excesses are piled on one another in [various] note-values without the succession being conventionalized according to the binding laws of art.

---

35. Ian Bent kindly double-checked this spot in the manuscript, confirming that the new section continues to be in Schenker's handwriting; email to Wason of August 31, 2019.

One experiences this best also in [the music of] Beethoven.[36]

Introduction and translation by Robert W. Wason

---

36. {41} Added page on two-, three- and four-part counterpoint.

{42} Added page:
[sheet headed "Form" in pink crayon]
"Because the Lied stands in the relationship of a likeness to the word, it no longer needs the further likeness—that is, the pure musical likeness."
Program music
{43} Added page:
[ink, pink crayon underlining s and deletion]
Selection. Likeness
"The law of selection directs the treatment of motives, and, in short, all likenesses of all categories. The strongest and most characteristic [likeness] must assert itself.
Thus, selection.
Abbreviation recalls the drama and other art forms."

Appendix B

"[Foundations of Tonal Systems]"

Translation of OC/31, 360–417, with Introduction

The Theory of Systems: its Genesis in [DTS] and Revision in *HL*

Schenker starts the discussion of systems in *HL* with what amounts to the conclusion of the investigation of the harmonic series he had presented in [DTS], namely that it is only a "hint" (*Wink*) that has been vastly overrated. This seems to indicate that the discussion in [DTS] is preparatory for *HL*, for in [DTS] Schenker carefully considers the harmonic series as a source of tonal material, as well as the influence of human perceptual limitations on just how much of it can be used (§§3–6). In *HL*, on the other hand, he seems to describe the harmonic series quite neutrally and even perfunctorily (§9), ending the section by deriving the just minor triad (10:12:15), from the proportion 3:4, and even the chordal seventh from the seventh overtone. But in *HL*, §§10–11, Schenker criticizes and rejects all of these "derivations" other than the one he started with, the major triad. Clearly, in reworking this material, Schenker strove for the greatest rhetorical impact, constructing the argument as a critique of accepted harmonic dogma rather than a neutral investigation of the phenomena.

Crucial to the critique presented in *HL*, §10 is Schenker's notion that the generative process is essentially "successive" (*Nacheinander*), not "simultaneous" (*Nebeneinander*); these terms and attendant explanation appear in

[DTS], §6. Schenker anthropomorphizes the process by briefly mentioning family trees in [DTS], §6, but to drive the point home in *HL*, he presents the Bach "family tree," demonstrating both "successive" (generations) and "simultaneous" progeny (siblings).[1] He then proceeds to reject all harmonic relations that do not issue directly from the fundamental, such as , the minor third, the minor triad, etc., all of which are only relations between "siblings." In *HL*, §11, however, he continues by rejecting all of the "out-of-tune" overtones, contending that the fifth overtone is the limit on the usefulness of the harmonic series (cf. [DTS], §5). Whereas *HL*, §§12 and 14 emphasize the supremacy of the fifth (cf. [DTS], §§9–10), *HL*, §13 (on the status of the major triad in nature and in the system) has no parallel in [DTS]. Here, once again, Schenker invokes his psychological principle of *Abbreviation* to limit harmonic generation: the major triad is to be conceived as a "conceptual abbreviation of nature," thereby collapsing the indefinite dimensions of pitch space into a one-octave pitch-class space. The notion of *Abbreviation*, like Schenker's earlier notion of *Assoziation*, is something he discusses in connection with art in the largest sense in *HL*, but that would not have come up—or perhaps had not yet occurred to him—within the narrow purview of [DTS].

While *HL*, §15 makes *Abbreviation* the first process to which the artist turns to limit the generation of usable tones, *HL*, §16 introduces another—*Inversion*, which we translate as "reversion," as discussed in chapter 5, in order not to confuse Schenker's idea with the standard music-theoretical meanings of "inversion." Reversion is the process by which the artist reverses the direction of the infinite "generation" (*Entwicklung* and *Zeugung*) of ascending fifths provided by nature to produce the succession of descending fifths, and thereby the missing $\hat{4}\flat$, at which point he stops the process in the "natural system"; in [DTS] he allows it much freer rein in the "compositional system," which he limits considerably in *HL*. In revising the presentation from [DTS], Schenker collapses [DTS], §§13–25 essentially into *HL*, §16 ("Reversion as the Opposite of Generation") and §17 ("The Discovery of the Lower Fifth as the Consequence of Reversion and Its Incorporation into the System"); *HL*, §18 acts as a summary ("The Ultimate Resolution of Oppositions and Foundation of the System"). It is interesting that in [DTS] the presentations of generation and reversion are more nearly balanced, while in *HL* the latter has shrunk noticeably. Certainly, crucial elements from the earlier presentation were reused, particularly the closing ([DTS], §§24–25), which

---

1. *HL*, §10, 36; *HA*, 23f.

demonstrates Bach's use of the subdominant to "anchor" opening phrases (cf. *HL*, §17), and generation and reversion as analytical categories in the analysis of melody (cf. *HL*, §16). But, as noted earlier, Schenker goes further in [DTS], writing of the generated fifths that "what goes up can also go down."[2] Perhaps this last formulation came a little too close to Riemann's version of dualism, for given Schenker's singling-out of Riemann and dualism for criticism in the *Vorwort* of *HL*, it seems likely that his dualism of generation and reversion was—or at least became during the writing of *HL*—a conscious revision of Riemann's.[3]

The Sources and Critical Apparatus

[DTS] exists in two versions in OC, file 31: a hand-copied manuscript of twenty-eight numbered pages, items 360–87 (HS); and a typescript of fifty-nine numbered pages, items 388–417 (TS).[4] The twenty-five sections of the essay (each indicated by §) are unnumbered in both; the last stops in mid-sentence at precisely the same point in both HS and TS. In HS it stops at the end of a full page, suggesting that there was more to the essay, but that it is lost, or that Schenker simply stopped writing in mid-sentence after he had filled the page, which seems most unlikely. In either case, it is clear that TS, which stops at the same place as HS but only halfway down the page, is

---

2. [DTS], §21.
3. It is interesting that what might be regarded as Riemann's most important article on dualism appeared shortly before *HL*. See Riemann, "Das Problem des harmonischen Dualismus," and "The Problem of Harmonic Dualism: A Translation and Commentary," by Ian Bent. The near coincidence of publication dates suggests that "Das Problem" was the impetus for Schenker's critique, but on the other hand, in *HL*, §9, Schenker writes that he "rejects the derivation of the minor triad from the series of undertones," which form the basis of Riemann's theory. In fact, Riemann gave up on defending the theory of undertones in "Das Problem," and settled for the reciprocity of frequency versus wave length as justification for his dualism.
4. Both HS and the editorial additions to TS are definitely in Schenker's hand, but the provenance of TS is uncertain. The typeface is an italic variant of "Bookman" (also called "Bookman Old Style"), designed in the 1850s. *It is simulated very closely by the typeface of this sentence, in Bookman Old Style Italic from the MS Word character set.* The inclusion of this typeface in the MS Word character set suggests that the typeface was widely used, and thus probably not helpful in identifying the typewriter or the approximate date of TS.

a copy of HS in its incomplete state. This suggests that the copy was made later, though not much later, since the paper of both is the same, except that Schenker uses half-sheets in the HS. Perhaps Jeanette Schenker made the copy at Heinrich's behest (see below), from the incomplete HS. It also suggests that either Schenker or his wife made a special effort to preserve what existed of the essay.

Though we get little in the way of larger organizational clues in either manuscript, two editorial additions to TS in the same handwriting as HS read "Section I: The Principle of Generation," inserted before the third section, and "Section II: The Principle of Reversion," inserted before the thirteenth. These are not in HS, indicating that, at least in this respect, TS is a further editorial "stage" of HS and not just a copy made at a later date (though TS itself is a verbatim copy). Most likely, this implies that HS and TS date from approximately the same time, and not from some later time when Jeanette may have been attempting to preserve Heinrich's legacy. Indeed, even the two added headings are products of at least two editing stages: in the first case, "Haupt" has been affixed to the beginning of "Abschnitt" in green pencil; it is also an addition to the second heading in a blacker pencil overlay. This addition of two headings (in two stages) constitutes the only important editorial feature of TS—though perhaps the most important one of all the editorial activity.[5] It seems that the larger two-part organization, or at least its precise articulation, occurred to Schenker at a later stage in the composition of the essay, but still while the essay was on his mind, so to speak. The near balance of these two large sections as well as subtler features that emerge from content alone make it likely that we have almost all of the essay, despite the mid-sentence ending, which occurs just as Schenker is about to tell an anecdote about Brahms. Even before that point, the manuscript had wandered off from its nominal subject into a polemic against the naive attribution of musical ideas of the great composers to "inspiration," which Schenker rejects out of hand, preferring to see them as the products of hard work and extraordinary mastery. The polemic began with an interesting discussion of the use of generation and reversion as important in opening themes, which Schenker develops further during the discussion of reversion in *HL* §16.

---

5. Besides correcting a few typographical errors, Schenker crossed out a few words, and added an insertion or "break" mark on p. 10, though he did not include any additional text.

HS is written in an extremely neat and legible *Lateinschrift* on high-quality paper, the pages of which are half sheets (ca. 6 11/16 x 8 1/4 inches) of the paper used for TS (ca. 13 3/8 x 8 1/4 inches). The pages of TS are folded in half in the same way, though they are not separated. The fact that they are written on the same paper may also suggest that HS and TS were conceived close in time to one another, though it is possible that Schenker kept the paper over some time. HS seems to have started life as a fair copy of an earlier draft, and was probably designed, initially, for presentation to a patron or publisher, most likely the latter.[6] The extreme mark-up of the text surely destroyed its original purpose. Though the editing of HS consists mainly of additions of single words to clarify or intensify the text, two large text blocks were deleted (reinstated in square brackets, below) and a few other clauses were added or deleted. A detailed discussion of the editorial process from HS to TS is clearly of interest, but beyond the scope of this introduction.

Given that HS likely started as a fair copy of a previous version (not preserved), much of the editorial activity on it, all in Schenker's hand and ink, seems not to have occurred while Schenker was making this copy, but at a "second stage," as he made another editorial pass over the copy; otherwise, why not abandon the fair-copy procedure earlier on, as the editorial changes mounted? In fact, HS retains its integrity as a "fair copy" right to the end. Still, a number of corrections in the middle of a sentence (otherwise free of correction) change its further course. Such changes may have occurred to Schenker as he made the copy, before the editorial pass. Five words added to the first paragraph of HS in light pencil and not transferred to TS may constitute a third layer, or perhaps the tentative start of the second layer.[7] Whatever the case, the untidy appearance of HS meant that it could no longer serve as a final copy; this no doubt prompted Schenker (or Jeanette Schenker) to create TS.

The following translation is primarily based on TS, though informed by readings from HS. For readers wishing to compare the translation with the

---

6. Robert Kosovsky reports: "I do recall that [the essay] was written on well-preserved paper, which is . . . unusual for Schenker's time. The meaning of that could be either nothing, or it could be that he had intended it for something special and used high-quality paper." Personal email of June 3, 2000, to Wason, who agrees, based on his own inspection of both manuscripts.

7. Page numbers 10–12, 14–16, 18–20 and 22–25 were added in red pencil; page numbers 26–28 were added in green pencil—apparently the same green pencil used to add the heading "Haupt" to part I.

typescript, all page numbers in TS are given in bold between curly brackets. For those interested in comparing the translation to Schenker's handwritten manuscript, the NYPL item number for each page of HS is given in bold between angle brackets.[8] Editorial interpolations in square brackets have been kept to a bare minimum. All footnotes, which are also kept to a minimum, are editorial.

[Foundations of Tonal Systems]
[Heinrich Schenker]

§[1]

<360> {1} The tonal system, as it has developed over the course of recent centuries—indeed, since Johann Sebastian Bach, it has remained essentially immutable—represents, to be exact, a *mixture* of two systems, which may be examined independently. Knowledge of the independence of these two systems—in particular of their independent origin—is, in my estimation, absolutely the single key to a theoretical and artistic understanding of music. Such knowledge provides first of all a provisional viewpoint from which to distinguish the two systems, the better to see where and how the mixture, to which we owe the whole, is accomplished. One of the two systems is the property of nature, the other the original and beautiful property of artists alone. Therefore, I would propose that the latter be called the "compositional system," since it arose directly from the drive to compose, in {2} contrast to the former, which may continue to carry the venerable name "natural system."[9] Granted, theorists up to now have put forth a certain "natural system" in their writings and instructional works as the main justification of the tonal system. However, my conception of that which might be called a "natural system" diverges from the usual one, as the next section of this essay will show.[10]

---

8. We have used the item numbers rather than the HS page numbers as the latter are often quite difficult to read.

9. The terms suggest the dualism of natural law versus positive law. Schenker continues by identifying the former system with nature, and the latter with artists, "the drive to compose," and then with culture, making the analogy all the more convincing.

10. Schenker assumes the knowledge of competing accounts of tonal systems on the part of the reader and continues to describe his version of the "natural system"

For general purposes as well as for orientation, remarks will be made here on the relationship in which the two systems stand to one another. They relate to one another as nature does to culture, and completely so. Just as culture, basically, can never deny nature (and should not be permitted to do so), just as little can the compositional system deny the natural system. Thus the compositional system represents, in relation to nature, what culture does: it is less a contradictory force than a continuation and extension—a {3} second nature, so to speak. One has the impression that nature would have reached the same conclusions regarding the artistic system, had she intended to produce sonatas or symphonies, or to allow them to be produced by the human mind (which of course is not the case). She found it sufficient to endow the tone with a few primitive urges, just as she endowed humans with a few urges (though certainly a sufficient number, given their power), such as, for example, the urge to live, eat and procreate. She was essentially unconcerned with what else humans did with these. It is <361> so much the better to see, then, what humanity has accomplished, apparently following nature as a mature child follows its own mother, and yet remaining in the most mysterious relationship to her, only elaborating upon and extending what she herself no longer provides. It is as though she wanted to rest, so to speak, from {4} the first difficult, creative act, which appeared to exhaust her!

§[2]

The laws of nature are embedded in the cosmos of tones. Nature has not encountered musical laws other than those contained in the tones. On that account, the physicists, most importantly Helmholtz, have promoted them to the front rank of science, and have not allowed themselves to make any objections against what these laws have witnessed and described.[11] What followed as a consequence was understandable—namely, that scholars and music theorists felt the urge to derive all phenomena throughout our musical system from the laws of nature alone, chiefly because it would have meant solace and security if the works of humans had permitted themselves to be seen as completely accountable to these laws. This urge culminated at the point when nature, in her beneficence, even made overtures that seemed

---

throughout part I of the essay.

11. Most likely Schenker is referring to the laws of "the relationship of compound tones," to use Ellis's translation of *Verwandtschaft der Klänge* (see Helmholtz, *On the Sensations of Tone*, tr. Ellis, part III, esp. 254–57, "Relationship of Compound Tones").

to accommodate the wishes of the theorists, such that {5} they could flatter themselves that they had reached the goal of their strivings. But soon things changed, and after fleeting joy, a cruel riddle long bewildered these learned scholars. And even though they had received a wonderful victory from nature's hand, it happened then that in their helplessness they became ungrateful to her, and foisted interpretations upon her that, far from all truth, only served to preserve—at any price—the illusion that the tonal system, as it arose historically, was completely compatible with nature—the illusion, that is, for whose sake alone they had deigned to worship her as the one and only provider of laws. Yet the same drama is played out over and over: if nature runs counter to the scholar, the scholar sets himself instantly against nature, as though, so to speak, secretly wounded by her vile and false counsel. We need not be alarmed, however, for {6} nature always shows herself to be stronger than the vanity of the scholars.

<362> §[3]

Part One: The Principle of Generation[12]

It can certainly be said colloquially, and, at the same time, metaphorically, that the eternal law of reproduction presides in the cosmos of the tones just as it does in the organic world. And further, in one as in the other, there occurs an endless series of familial generations and cross-breedings, within which what happens once does not happen a second time.[13] If we substitute frequency ratios for organic essences, as a consequence of the previous imagery the organic drive of nature may be imagined in these ratios as well. The infinitely varied types of reproduction that produce the organic world and secure its survival for eternity may be compared with the various divisions of the vibrating body that produce {7} the so-called overtones as eternally new and different species. As is well known, we express an overtone-generating division of a vibrating body with a fraction whose denominator indicates the number of parts into which, for example, a string divides, and we say 1/2 denotes an octave, 1/3 a fifth, etc. On that account, the same denominator, alone, may be used, in short, as a symbol of the particular overtone whose

---

12. Later editorial addition; see introduction.
13. The German is *Generationen* and the translation should be taken as "generations" in the biological sense—as "the offspring of a certain parent or couple, considered as a step in natural descent" (*Webster's New Universal Unabridged Dictionary*).

mysterious origin is carried in that number, in the sense that we can say that 2 is the law of generation of the octave, 3 the law of the fifth, etc. There are infinitely many laws of generation in the cosmos of tones, just as there are in the real organic world, which has the result that nature imposes no limits in that regard. The {8} generative laws of nature regarding the species of overtones are contained in the prime numbers (1, 2, 3, 5, 7, 11, 13, 17, etc.)—as understood in the sense discussed above, and indeed only in this sense. Yet, as an autonomous individual, so to speak, each overtone can also be assigned to the same laws of generation, whereby the total of the generations then multiplies again and gains diverse content. As a result, <363> the fifth (represented by the number 3 above), for example, can now be assigned in its own right to the law of generation 2, 3, or 5. From this, then, arises the octave of the fifth, the fifth of the fifth, or the third of the fifth, corresponding to the symbol 3 x 2, 3 x 3 or 3 x 5, respectively.

§[4]

In general, a consequence of our limited capacity to comprehend is that we give preference to simple relationships as opposed to complicated ones merely because we comprehend the former better and more easily. If, for example, a length or an area has only few units, so that we {9} can orient ourselves right away to its number, then that strikes us more agreeably than the reverse, when the feeling of orientation abandons us because the length or area is too large or complicated to be estimated on first glance. And there will be a substantial distinction for us in the first and more favorable case when the length measures 4 meters, not 5; or 8 meters, not 7, etc. Likewise, it causes us greater pleasure when we quickly assess, for example, thoughts or artworks as complete wholes, or the organizational plan of buildings, animal- or plant-forms; on the other hand, our aesthetic perception is perplexed and thus unsatisfied when complexity prevents us from quickly grasping these phenomena. Not taxing our senses is thus a higher life-principle for us than straining them, from which arises the necessity of an easier and quicker view of all things and relationships, respectively, and for the fulfillment of this necessity as an aesthetic {10} rule, and as a means by which pleasure in general is regulated.

This describes our state as we confront the phenomena of the tonal universe described in the previous section (§). That is, here we also tend, for innate reasons, <364> to prefer the simple to the complicated, as, so to speak, closeness to distance, an earlier generation to a later one, or the stronger to the weaker. And we even went so far that we accepted only the first three species of overtones—the first and most strongly generated—into our practical tonal system.

(We did this unconsciously, of course, which demonstrates the dependability of our instincts as well as the overwhelming force of nature.) These species result from the laws of generation, 2, 3 and 5—and thus, to take the cosmos of C as an example, would be the octave c, fifth g and third e.[14]

{11} §[5]

But our instinct rejected the distant species of overtones (those that originated from the laws of generation of 7, 11, 13, 17 etc.) as clearly too complicated and incomprehensible. Not one of them found inclusion in the tonal system, and so it is today. The question would be whether this territory will ever open up for us—whether such an extension and redefinition will confront music and a genius will ever find himself strong enough to release us from our bonds—or whether, on the contrary, the limitations on our powers of conceptualization will remain an eternal and definitive human inheritance.

§[6]

Following on what has been said previously, this is the place to indicate emphatically once again that it would be an unpardonable error and madness to look at the sixth of our tonal system a, or a {12} minor third e-g, for example (when we relate these to C), *as such*—which is to say, as a sixth or a minor third on its own and directly grounded in the tonal system simply because it is found in the cosmos of tones, i.e., in the harmonic series with the others <365>, in the most peaceful and allegedly meaningful coexistence.[15] We must never forget that nature, in her capacity as *natura naturans*, moves forever forward only through generative acts whose chain cannot be broken.[16] Nor should we forget that the father divides whenever he spawns a son, as the mother divides whenever she gives birth, as the cell divides whenever it generates a second cell, as does each living essence, every

---

14. This translation follows Schenker's use of upper or lower case pitch designations throughout. Schenker speaks of specific pitches he is generating rather than pitch classes, though he often fails to give their precise octave registrations. In general, he uses the upper-case letter C to designate the fundamental, and lower-case letters for all generations from C. Though incomplete, this is consistent with the so-called "Helmholtz System." When we introduce more precise octave registrations in square brackets in order to clarify a specific generating algorithm, we will follow that system as well, but with Arabic superscripts standing for ', ", '", etc.
15. Emphasis added.
16. That is, nature as an active agent: nature "naturing."

wave, etc. What this means, however, is that we have the right to observe nature according to this eternal generative process, and at the most, only this one. When we occasionally have to provide a descriptive word for this, we may rather call it a succession, but never a simultaneity, since this word {13} would merely reflect an instance of our way of seeing, according to which we readily project onto a plane that which conceptually has nothing to do with it. Only that particular mode of seeing things, just mentioned, satisfies us, for example, when we set up or view family trees; indeed, then we love to take in the full effect, given the clearly arranged manifoldness of both the simultaneity of generations of procreation as well as their successions. Of course, it would be foolish to forget for a moment that the family tree basically represents nothing other than a huge sum of successive relationships—that is, of imagined procreations. Nature as such can therefore have nothing further in common with the simultaneity of the same relationships demonstrated on a plane with such alluring power to our eye. Rather, she creates all and everything independently, in a single act of creation that is completely independent, with an ever fresh and renewed display of the law of creation, so to speak {14}: thus, human by human, animal by animal, leaf by leaf, stone by stone etc., each is always a direct creation, and never merely a relative connection (which is to be regarded merely as an idiosyncratic creation of our consciousness—not as a reality of nature). Consequently, in nature's creation there always lies an element of generation <366> that must have nothing to do with relationship and simultaneity. Thus, also in the cosmos of the tones, we see nature only producing according to her eternal task: that is, creating and developing, but not formulating relationships. The octave (2), fifth (3), and third (5) arise out of direct generation, and still others after them do as well—always new and autonomous species of overtones according to the laws of generation 7, 11, 13, etc. We did not even bother to consider these, since we were not obligated to use them, but all of them—exactly like those which were mentioned first—are distinguished by the characteristic {15} and deciding property of *generation*. Thus, the sole task of researchers and theorists, when correctly comprehended, could have been only that of examining whether and to what extent the remaining intervals of our tonal system (our second, d, if C is the fundamental, fourth, f, sixth, a, and seventh, b) are also derived from the system of nature exactly as the octave, fifth, and major third are—that is, whether the element of generation, from which nature simply does not desire to depart, belongs to those former as well as to these latter intervals. The union of the practical system with the natural system (that is, the justification of the former via the latter), which is so ardently desired, was only obtainable when one demonstrated that, for example, our seventh degree b is based just as much on direct procreation and generation as is, for example, the fifth g. The erroneous derivation darkened every other trail, however, including therefore the one the scholars blazed, as they, despite passionate efforts, could not spot the seventh or the fourth from our system in nature. {16} In this situation, they rescued themselves by means of a very shoddy method, and simply explained that, for example, the seventh overtone served as an approximate model for our seventh degree, the eleventh overtone for our fourth degree, and so on. In their need, they allowed an approximation rather than an absolute identity to be valid. And if an intellectual capitulation already lay therein, the mistake was more disastrous yet: to confuse a direct, independent, and separate origin of the octave, fifth or third with the seventh or thirteenth overtone (all of which, in essence, are of equally high birth), and thus to confuse what the seventh or fourth of our system represents in reality.

<367> §[7]

To summarize in a few words, it can thus be said that neither the overtone 7, nor 11, nor the others, make any pretense of wanting to be that which our seventh or fourth is; and it certainly does not occur to them, so to speak, to encourage that understanding in any way. They remain, {17} both before and after, independent phenomena that our instincts have simply rejected, based on a comparatively larger complexity than that of the octave, fifth or third. We arrive at the aforementioned critical intervals of our system, however, as well as the other degrees (with the exception of the fourth), when we remain on the track of nature and make do with the generative laws of 2, 3, and 5, whose comprehensibility has already been proven and established—without suggesting our own conceits to her. As I earlier had the opportunity to suggest, in the cosmos of the tones, each overtone, though hardly self-generating, allows itself to be a fundamental of the generative laws of 2, 3, 5, 7, 11, 13, etc., to have a new effect, released, so to speak, from its own species, as it never was before and never will be again. Also here, however, the ultimate law of nature prevails, according to which {18} she herself granted precedence to the generative law of 2 before the generative law of 3, 5, and so forth. Thus our instinct seems to understand better—according to nature's instruction, so to speak—the species of overtone that originates from the generative law of 2, than those that originate from the other, clearly complicated generative laws. The series of old and new species may be stated with their symbols thus:

Table B.1: Sample of Tones Resulting From the "Generative Laws" of 1, 2, 3, and 5

1	the fundamental	C	1
2	Octave	c	2
3	Fifth	g	[3]
5	Third	e[1]	[5]
2 x 2	Octave of the Octave	c[1]	
2 x 3	Fifth of the Fifth	d[2]	
3 x 5	Third of the Fifth	b[2]	
5 x 5	Third of the Third	g♯[3]	and so forth
2 x 2 x 2		c[2]	up to
3 x 3 x 3	third Fifth	a[3]	and so forth

<368> {19} Obviously, from this series, our tonal system has taken its elements, which, according to their value (a true reality of nature and not merely a form of our perception) must be ordered as follows: C (1), c (2), g (3), e[1] (5), d [2] (3 x 3), b[2] (3 x 5), and finally a[3] (3 x 3 x 3).

§[8]

From this it follows, furthermore, that what we call second, seventh and sixth with respect to the fundamental really must be understood, correctly assessed, as independent and newly originating phenomena on the path of generation—that is, each as a direct (if more remote) creation, etc., and indeed by means of the generating law of the fifth or that of the third, as we may finally name these laws. At the same time, the essence of dissonance, as we call it, may find its final explanation (perhaps even exclusively) therein: namely, that each tone demands to be conceived first of all as it originated according to the generating law of the third or fifth, to which it owes its existence, and most of all {20} to the law of the fifth, which represents the fundamental. Furthermore, it must portend misfortune for our senses (whose stimulation otherwise it is out of place to consider here), when we are put in a position of hearing two tones against one another, which, in that moment of simultaneous sounding, must necessarily leave that natural need unsatisfied because the one has not generated the other as fundamental of its fifth through the law of fifth generation, or, vice versa, the one is not dependent upon the other through the same law. Thus, for example, b necessarily sounds dissonant against c as a fundamental, because their sounding against one another does not express the relationship of unmediated ascending or descending fifths,[17] and the question of this relationship, our first question, remains just as nature herself had put it initially through the direct act of creation—the unmediated relationship. {21} In this regard it may be added that by logical consistency the so-called resolution of the dissonance occurs when either one of the two dissonant tones is assisted to a connection by fifths <369> (that is, to a pure, unmediated, unambiguous and unified relationship); this has to be sufficient under all circumstances, no matter what means should be applied. The b of the example must get away from the c, or vice versa, no matter how. With dissonance, it is as with a drowning man who is served if one pulls him from the water, no matter how. And just as it would be stupid (and, above all, impossible) to issue regulations for the rescuers to whom one would have to cling in the moment of danger, it would be madness to prescribe to an artist how to liberate dissonance from its plight. It is enough that he separates them, {22} and thereby place each into a different relationship. Thus, for example, b can be brought into a pure fifth-relationship with e as root (presuming, naturally, that the new relationship is demonstrated clearly and unmistakably through the melody alone), or, the melody can fall into the province of the C triad, where c has gained a pure fifth-connection to g. Or, it can often be the case that one of the tones forming the dissonance escapes in order to provide itself with a more conducive relationship, but encounters a new tone in this process of escape with which it once again gets into just as impure a situation as the one from which it was able to escape in the first place. Here, it must suffice that the tone forming the dissonance took the step toward freeing itself *bonae voluntatis*, and thus may not be held responsible for what now befalls it from the other side under such circumstances.[18] Once again it is the same as with the drowning man, when he—indeed willingly—{23} actually delays the rescue while trying to allow himself to be saved, by needlessly getting his head caught under the lifeboat, as is known to happen so often. In short: the tones forming the dissonance must, first of all, seek to flee from each other; all manners of escape prove themselves hereby as virtuous and good, regardless of their success. There is no exception to this. One might be able to consider how many possibilities this means

---

17. I.e., G as fundamental mediates between C as fundamental and the pitch b.
18. Italics added; "Of good will." Cf. the Gloria of the Mass: "Gloria in excelsis Deo. Et in terra pax hominibus bonae voluntatis."

(viewing all, without exception, as essentially good), provided that one bears in mind the infinity of their number, which accrues (aside from the diatonic) from our chromatic and modulatory drives. To characterize them all would be just as impossible <370> as it is to continue to preserve the old rule (a fiction, really) of the "downward resolution of the seventh." Equipped with all the qualities of those fraudulent teachings and dogmas that control the world {24} all the more constantly and compellingly the more obscure they become to the teacher and student, the ancient rule of the "downward resolution of the seventh" still dominates all theory to the present day. Only the most recent theorists have finally dared to affirm so many exceptions even in the venerable masterpieces that the rule has become almost invisible.[19] And not without horror do I recall my teacher, a widely admired symphonist, who used to teach the preparation and downward resolution of the seventh for the whole semester in a public conservatory class, and in this regard, used to say, as though justified: "of course in composition, everything is different." Now, it soon became clear to me, that his theory was rather poor composition, but his composition on the other hand was indeed good theory.[20]

{25} *§[9]*

One may explain the fifth as a musical aural-unit, just as one could consider the meter to be a unit of length, or the gram as a unit of mass etc. There is, however, one notable difference here: that the two latter units are totally arbitrary contrivances invented by the minds of people, in contrast to the fifth, which as an aural-unit, appears to our instinct to be compelled by nature. One can easily provide confirmation of this innate character of the fifth when one attempts to examine a given melody according to its own intrinsic content, removed from a harmonic sub-structure; here, one would perceive that beyond all chromatic

---

19. Schenker likely refers to Cyril Hynais, "Die Harmonik R. Wagners in Bezug auf die Fundamentaltheorie Sechter's" [The Harmony of R. Wagner in Relation to the Fundamental-Bass Theory of Sechter], *Neue Musikalische Presse* x (1901), 50–52, 67–69, 81–82, 97–100. A former student of Bruckner's, Hynais follows Sechter's theory in most respects, but writes on page 97 that "the rising seventh plays a significant role in Wagner's voice leading, in which there are many instructive examples that modern theory should attend to." He cites an example from *Meistersinger* to support his contention.
20. The passage is reminiscent of Schenker's quotation of Bruckner in *HL* "Segn's meini Herrn, dos ist die Regl, i schreib' natirli net a so." See *HL*, §91, 228. ("Look gentlemen, this is the rule. Of course, I don't compose that way. *HA*, 177).

pitches the melody might have, our ear manages to make the melody intelligible almost exclusively with the fifth-relationship, and only where this is not attainable, does it make do with the vague third-relationship.[21] {26} Never can a melody be heard on its own, and absolutely never, abstractly, in sevenths. As is remarked incidentally in another context, this amounts to a confirmation of what is said about the seventh in §[5].[22]

<371> *§[10]*

In continuation of the main topic, it needs yet to be expressly mentioned that to the root itself (1) in the course of generation, belongs its third (5), and to this third (5) its g♯ (5 x 5), and so on; to our second degree, d—that is, the second fifth (3 x 3)—its own third (3 x 3 x 5), that is f♯; and to our seventh degree, b, that is, the third of the fifth (3 x 5), its own third (3 x 5 x 5), d♯; likewise to our third fifth, that is, the sixth degree, a, belongs a third c♯, with the symbol (3 x 3 x 3 x 5). I will have later opportunity to show how the artist heeded well the obligatory opinion of nature in a wholly marvelous way, and used it practically in composition.[23]

{27} To return to the technical details, I must mention then that the fifth e of our sixth degree a (with the symbol 3 x 3 x 3 x 3) [= 81]—which because of its fifth-generation remains separate from the one generated by the octave or third—can stand in no relationship whatsoever to the first third-generated e (5), or to the e (80) [= that produced from this first e through further octave-generation: 5 x 2 x 2 x 2 x 2]. As I already have said repeatedly, each generation in the cosmos proves itself to be something new, not something former and recurring, and the repetition of a phenomenon is just as out of the question here as in the whole organic world in general, in which, for example, there are not two men, two animals, two trees, or two leaves to be found alike. That is the true sense of the so-called comma.[24]

---

21. This passage may be the origin of the more highly developed discussion (*HL*, §76) of "The Realization of the Triad," in which Schenker's discusses the folk tune "Muß i denn?" (see above, chapter 2).

22. The paragraph reference is blank in HS and TS. In §5, Schenker rejected the seventh overtone.

23. All of these arise in the precise octave indicated by the law of generation. Thus f♯3, for example, is *not* an octave duplication of the eleventh partial, which is unusable in our system.

24. It will be recalled that the syntonic comma is the difference between four stacked perfect fifths [(3/2 x 3/2 x 3/2 x 3/2) = 81/16], and one pure third + 2 octaves [(5/4

§[11]

But f, [understood] as the fourth in our tonal system, certainly may not be deduced from the fundamental C on the path of generation. For, quite apart from the fact, {28} first of all, that we have not come across the fourth as an autonomous generative law (one co-equal with the laws 2, 3, 5, 7, 11, 13 etc.), and second, that we hear only by means of fifths, the fourth can be heard as a fifth, especially when we take the latter fact into account. In the sense of generation, this fifth can only be heard, unfortunately, <372> such that the fundamental character of f and the fifth-character of C would then have to be recognized, which stands in contradiction to our postulate. One would have to hold the peculiar opinion that it is possible for a son occasionally to back-create his own father, which surely will not be permitted to happen any time soon. How, on the other hand, it came to pass that we have incorporated the f into our tonal system, and to which purposes, will soon be shown.

§[12]

The creative artists based {29} their practical artistic activity—correctly even if unconsciously—on the principles of generation that have been demonstrated here. Without knowing it, they created everything from this unending supply of generations, which nature knew to suggest to them so forcefully by using the artistic instinct as a medium. Thus, not only do they accept the octave, fifth, and major third from nature (and, indeed, in the meaning recognized in them by nature) but also, more broadly speaking, all the later generations and lineages—that is, the more remote overtones together with their own fifths and thirds. In short, they accept the entire infinite sum of eternally new phenomena and contradictions, but always consistently retaining the generational character peculiar to each. So great was the instinct to appropriate that which was correct from nature, and so little did we know of it when we actually met it, that, conversely, we even incorrectly interpreted that which we had achieved all too well, as though through a secret mission of nature.[25]

---

x 2/1 x 2/1) = 20/4 = 80/16] That difference is 81/80 (= 21.5 c.). As Schenker points out well, the comma (syntonic or Pythagorean) marks a conflict in modes of generation—in the latter case, for example, 3/2 fifths (or 9/8 whole tones) versus 2/1 octaves.

25. Though the message is coded, Schenker certainly speaks of the potentially false origin of the subdominant he has described in the previous section.

{30} Thus, without our knowledge, our tonal system took shape such that within boundaries established by the nature of the material itself it had to count as the result of our practical artistic efforts and at the same time as a true echo of the tonal cosmos. As with the tonal cosmos, our system contains the series of three fifths, of which each earlier fifth generated a later one in a direct act of generation, thus C g d[2] a[4]. And also without our knowledge, the same three fifths 1 3 9 27 retained, in their ascending generation, the <373> law of generation, which they have in their nature and through which they came to be, and which, to use a free metaphor, appeared to run freely like blood in their veins. In spite of all theoretical misinterpretation on our part, they even asserted their characteristic generation, {31} and continue to assert it today, where we have learned in the meantime through increasing artistic experience to neutralize, so to speak, every other law of nature temporarily (even this law of generation) through a stronger one—that is, to switch to the extent that we use a law in accordance with a plausible purpose in the natural sense, or suppress it in favor of another law. In such transactions, essentially the cultural activity that is so related to other cultural works exists in the field of music (as was mentioned earlier), which, rather than wounding nature, or contradicting her, rather raises and improves her.

The fact that our system did not also include the fourth fifth E (81) came as a result of this fifth being forced, above all, to accommodate the first-born third (5); it was not allowed simultaneously to incorporate its contradiction as well within a frame that, as we have said, was in no way {32} permitted to expand if it did not want to overstep the purely conceptual purpose of the system. However, that which was not admitted into the system as the shortest, simplest, and at the same time strongest expression (if one wants the epitome and emblem of the cosmos as well as of practical art), did come all the more sharply to its right in developed composition itself. Thus, we see all those overtones that the system could not accommodate recurring here— namely, the more distant fifths and thirds with all of their allure of independent appearance and, at the same time, mild contradiction: that is, the third E (5) with its third G♯ (5 x 5) in contrast to the fifth G (3); the second fifth D (9) with its third F♯ (9 x 5) as a contradiction to F (to be explained later) <374>; the distant fifth A (27), with its third C♯ (27 x 5) as a conflict against the fundamental C itself, etc. And as in the cosmos, they are also found in composition purely on {33} account of an independent generation. They arose in the cosmos through procreation and generation, and they absolutely want to be heard as having arisen and having been generated in this way in composition as well. In the practical system, then, we restored to the overtones of the fundamental their own independent generative capacity according to nature's wish and treated them entirely as if they were their own fundamentals and rulers of their own domains. However, as in the cosmos of the tone, it happens that all conflicts dissolve in the majesty of the fundamental, by virtue of the law of the stronger. Thus, we knew to emulate this regal appearance of high nature as we created tonality, whose central and most natural force subdues all contradictions to which she gives birth from her womb. That alone is the true meaning of tonality.

Tonality is therefore the most complete and accurate image of the cosmos of the tones.

{34} Its first principle is, as in the universe, living generation from a fundamental. Hence, it reveals itself only in the living generation and unfolding from a given fundamental. Tonality does not yet exist, as long as the fundamental that initiates the drive for generation is doubtful or unknown. This is the component to watch.

All chromatic tones also find their origin in tonality, to the extent that it is called upon to help the more distant overtones appear completely independent (entirely in the natural sense). The final resolution of these tones into the central fundamental constitutes the substance of tonality.

One can say that the tonal system relates to tonality such that the former contains only the foreground, so to speak, of the latter—the very first and at the same time all-powerful component.

<375> {35} Tonality, and along with it, the musical artwork as a whole, is, in the final analysis, very much comparable to the state. The state also forms, in a similar manner, a powerful unity and indeed a unity of human beings, to each of which it grants (or at least should grant) individual growth, whose independence it even desires. The intrinsic and moral splendor of the state appears all the greater to us; [indeed the countless individualities combine in the state as a unity, and the countless generations merge, each completely different afterwards than before;] the more that the individual grows, the greater the freedom the various generations are guaranteed, without the idea of the state as a unity being damaged, or even split apart.[26] How beautiful it is when equilibrium prevails between the demands of the individual on the state and, vice versa, those of the state on the individual. Likewise, it is beautiful when a similar equilibrium emerges between the rich expansion of the independent overtone generations on the one hand and the collective idea of tonality on the other. {36} In the richness and the independence of the overtones lies the

---

26. The bracketed passages here and on p. 448 appear in HS and not TS.

splendor of tonality, and consequently also of the artwork. One can even call this splendor color. Therefore, for example, chromaticism does not have to appear to us as a harmful poison (as many conservative cranks opine); on the contrary, it is to be conceived as an essential postulate, and the most beneficial vehicle of tonality. Naturally, moderation must be maintained in these matters in the sense discussed above. And if our old masters from Bach to Beethoven (and among the more recent masters, Schubert and Brahms) serve us mainly as models in this regard, then the most recent composers (including, all too often, Richard Wagner) unfortunately confuse tonality with modulation. These concepts are in no way identical as they maintain, since it is the task of modulation only to seek a tonality; in this task alone lies its essence—an {37} essence wholly different from that of tonality. <376> One can say that only out of and upon the foundation of tonality can chromaticism become that which it wants to become—that it is only apparent and not real as soon as any doubt concerning the tonality prevails. Thus to the same extent that chromaticism is a means of expressing tonality, tonality is a condition of being for chromaticism. This also explains, for example, many passages in Wagner's works, since they do not function in the sense of a safely retained tonality (which they would like), and chromaticism, despite its glitter and overabundance, appears not even as genuine chromaticism but only creates the impression of an overly long, spun-out modulation (in which, as was said, doing without a firm tonic as a primal basis for generation is permitted and necessary). Of what use would be all the glitter of the stars, if the central force of the sun were not to hold them together?[27]

{38} *§[13]*

Part Two: The Principle of Reversion[28]

Unfortunately, it is not given to us mortal humans to completely follow the rigorous direction of nature, who amasses one creative act after another in her generations and explains such infinitudes and eternities in this way. We much prefer not to lose the ground under our feet, to maintain the point of origin well in our eyes and senses, and we soon long for the place from which we have

---

27. The problem with Schenker's analogy is that all celestial bodies exert gravitational force on other objects proportional to their mass. Schenker, of course, needs a gravitational center for his tonal universe.
28. Later editorial addition in Schenker's hand (cf. heading at §[3]). Recall the discussion of problems in the translation of *Inversion* in chapter 5.

just recently departed. Such is human nature. Perhaps we never really understood what generation, purpose, or such motion forward would be, if we had to forget the point of origin and did not have the confidence to return to it. When we climb the tower, we do so, to be sure, with the feeling and knowledge of our distance from the ground. When we finally climb back down to the ground, we enjoy the descent as a sort of corroborative audit of the ascent. Such is also the case for us when we climb mountains: we measure all paths and elevations from the bottom, from sea level up; <377> {39} we look forward to the descent because we already anticipate it. Thus, we always long for the security of the point of origin, as of a future point of return. And how it oppresses us when we behold a generation whose beginning we are unable to find. How tormented we are by the conundrum of the person who may have been the initial one before the first Adam, the mystery of the beginning of the world, and the creator of all worlds. We cannot content ourselves just with seeing that something has come; we also want to know from where it comes; and that is why we like to trace all generation back to its origin. Nothing mollifies us to such an extent as knowing the origin. Might this suggest, perhaps, that if we were to know it, we would also be thereby equipped to conquer infinity? Meanwhile, as of today, infinity has not yet become home to us, and dense and ominous {40} clouds still lie in front of eternity. After as before, we contrast every forward motion of generation with a backward one of our own perspective. Whether one takes this proclivity of ours merely as a peculiarity of our view, or as a form of our consciousness, it is given to us all the same, and as an expression of our circumferentially limited finiteness, it demands its rights.[29] As we have seen, we already paid the toll of our finiteness: that was when we rejected the species of overtone 7 and those beyond it as unintelligible to us, because the finiteness in us demands that we contemplate any generation in reverse and seek its point of origin.

<378> §[14]

I call the reverse view of generation and the pursuit of a fundamental tone from one of the overtones by virtue of an inborn necessity {41} reversion. Because, with the act of reversion, we accomplish what nature did not accomplish, I call reversion a purely compositional act. This is also the first component of the compositional system, which will be called upon to mix with the

---

29. As we noted in appendix A, Schenker uses the Kantian phrase "a form of our consciousness" (*eine Form unseres Bewusstseins*) in both essays translated here, meaning the way in which consciousness "works."

natural system. We have seen how nature, through the unfolding of its generation, actually provided the impetus and foundation for such a reverse view, and to that extent, one may not consider reversion as a completely arbitrary act. Rather, it should be said that an extension of nature according to idiosyncratic human sensation and capability has taken place here.

§[15]

In the tonal system, and in practical composition, the following is expressed: we still retain the feeling of the fundamental, though we are carried along by the sense of generation {42}. Thus, when we arrive, for example, at the first fifth G (5),[30] we know we are at the first; progressing further, we are also aware when we reach the second or third fifth. In the reverse process, we satisfy our root-awareness when we move back toward it, first from the third to the second fifth, from here to the first, and then finally reaching the root. In the sense of reversion, the tonal system presents itself thus:

$$a - d - g - C, \text{ next to} \quad b - e - C$$
$$27 - 9 - 3 - 1 \quad\quad\quad 15 - 5 - 1$$

It is enough that we feel and know whether the fifth is the first, second, or third. For because we know which fifth is present, we express our constant root-awareness as an element that we always feel. The presence of the root in the intuition [*Gefühl*] is the moral basis for reversion; it is this that urges us <379> {43} to carry out reversion. In this we do what nature does not, since it is not at all in her power to do so. Reversion is thus our own property, but born from a righteous basis.

§[16]

It is the same presence of the fundamental in our intuition that generates a tension in us, which is certainly not the case with the [tonal] cosmos. Moreover, since we keep the fundamental C always in our intuition even when we distance ourselves from it via the paths of generation (and head up to the fifth, g, and then to the more remote fifths, d and a), a tension emerges which corresponds to the degree of displacement. The farther up we climb, the greater the tension. Arriving at the top with the third fifth, we feel the greatest tension. To resolve this tension, on the other hand, is the job of

---

30. *Sic.* Schenker must mean 3 here, though both HS and TS clearly say 5.

reversion. In the tension, however, we find the greatest attraction, so that we may dare to consider it as one of the primary engines of all art.

{44} *§[17]*

However, the tonal system, as it represents generation dictated by nature:

C	g	e	d	b	a
1	3	5	9	15	27

can be used directly as the representation of reversion as well.[31] We merely read in reverse, naturally in falling fifths. It is essentially the act of generation and that of reversion (which are combined in the feeling of tension) that cause us always to move in a piece with a sense of measurement, back and forth, so to speak, as though wandering through a room or any other space with measuring eyes and ears.

<380> *§[18]*

If generation from a fundamental tone is by its very nature unlimited (and it is simply a matter of when we, in our own interest, limit it arbitrarily), then reversion in the tonal system, on the other hand, comes up {45} against a boundary all too soon. For when it attains the fundamental tone itself from above, it must stop as though at the last lower border. To overshoot this border, and thus the fundamental tone, must mean abandoning the tonal system of C—that is, its natural system.

And yet we have also dared to do this.

Compelled by the character of reversion itself, in whose nature it lies to question each tone as to its origin, we allowed ourselves to be misled even by the fundamental tone, questioning it as to its origin. And here our curiosity appeared all the greater, the better we knew that we had the fundamental tone before us. The question of which might be the progenitor and creator of all the fifths and thirds was precisely the one that tantalized us to experience it. It was now easy to answer this question, if one did not simply dismiss it right at the outset: it could only be f, which, as a fundamental, created the fifth C.

[Once the border was breached, what was to stop us from investigating the succession of further ascents of the fundamental? Essentially, nothing; however, the next ascent (B♭, the fundamental of F) could not be taken into

---

31. I.e., in the order of their generation as overtones.

the system.] {46} It is this f, for which we have made a place in our tonal system in so unique a manner.

<381> *§[19]*

This *f* acts as a proper fundamental, so that in comparison to it, C loses all its dignity. C is no longer regarded, in the face of f, as generator of all generations, but rather as the first fifth (3). That is exactly what we wanted, however: C was to be described in greater detail through f, so that we became all the more precisely aware of what that tone was that bore, in succession, the remaining generation. This means explicitly that before or after, the emphasis and our interest remain on C—that is, on that which develops itself upward, and then falls back again upon itself. F is only to be understood as an artificial psychological aid through which we essentially {47} seek to explain and envision the nature of the fundamental. Incidentally, it was not in our power, despite the assumption of a second fundamental, to modify or debase our interest in the first fundamental and all of its content presented to us, since this interest rests on the incontrovertible and compelling power of the fact that generation is the stronger and the primary process, while reversion by contrast is only secondary, and so to speak its reverse side. First of all, generation is the stronger (in this case the generation from the bass note C), and furthermore, on that account our interest in it had to survive undiminished, in spite of the addition of a new, second bass note f through the method of reversion. The truth of this is shown best by the fact that we stemmed the enthusiasm for reversion, which would have led us necessarily to B♭ and so forth, only because the b that arose from the generation of C {48} could not possibly tolerate its contradiction in B♭. Therefore, it follows that we came to a stop with the reversion of **<382>** C at f and no longer searched in the first ascending series, and that we rejected that B♭ (the fundamental of f), because the natural system of C produced by generation could not accommodate it simultaneously with its own b (15).

§[20]

The acceptance of f into the system therefore proved to be—as reversion itself, whose fruit it is—the second component of the compositional system mentioned above. After the establishment of f it is right to understand and to evaluate the system like this:

f,	C	g	e	d	b	a
		3	5	9	15	27

As we see, our tonal system therefore in reality actually contains two fundamentals, f and C. All significance rests only on the one C; indeed, f {49} cannot dislodge it at all, for reasons that are described above.

§[21]

In practical composition, however, beyond the narrowly restricted tonal system, we certainly gave reversion its fullest course once again, just as we awarded generation all its power in practical composition, where, namely, it had to exceed the tonal system. Thus, in practical composition, B♭, E♭, A♭, and all other roots that may be found through the process of reversion return—in short, everything [returns] that the tonal system could not demonstrate within its narrow framework. What occurred upward can also occur downward. The freedom is the same; only the directions are different, as implied by generation and reversion, which run in different directions.

<383> In this sense, tonality supplements itself through {50} a tremendous supply of possibilities that derive from reversion. The fact that this occurs purely for compositional reasons will disturb us just as little as the concept of reversion in general or the acceptance of f disturbed us, though compositional grounds alone governed in the latter regard as well.

§[22]

Whoever is of the opinion that all reversion (that is, the centripetal force of all overtones towards the fundamental) is merely a mirroring of our subjective sensation [*Gefühl*], an idiosyncratic form of our consciousness, and not a reality of nature—to him, the comparison between reversion and the rainbow may be welcome. This is also merely an illusion of our eyes, and not a reality of nature: nevertheless, as long as the eye remains the eye, one will always see rainbows, and likewise, one will accept reversion as something that {51} truly exists as long as consciousness remains consciousness.[32]

---

32. The exact dimensions and color distribution of the rainbow—light refracted through water droplets—are dependent on the particular observer: "since the rainbow is a special distribution of colors (produced in a particular way) with reference to a definite point—the eye of the observer—and as no single distribution can be the same for two separate points, it follows that two observers do not, and cannot, see the same rainbow." W. J. Humphreys, *Physics of the Air* (New York: McGraw-Hill Book Co., 1929). For a recent and extraordinarily clear account of our perception of rainbows, see Richard Dawkins, *The Magic of Reality: How We Know What's Really True* (New York: Free Press, 2011), 153–56. In Schenker's view, the subdominant is likewise a psychological phenomenon: though based on the reality of fifth

§[23]

Yet, as was said repeatedly earlier, a somewhat oppositional interpretation[33] may be justified therewith: namely, that reversion finds its true opposing basis in generation, which is given by nature. One might say that it has become, even if derived compositionally, a new phenomenon of nature, so to speak, incorporated into nature as such, and, by this point, fully coordinated with all of her other components. Permit me to give an example from everyday life. The telephone and the electric train are by no means original to nature: in fact, they were until recently not present at all, and what was present in nature was actually, exclusively and solely, the power of electricity. However, as people {52} drew the remaining new consequences from the power of nature that remained unknown to her, <384> nature admittedly must have allowed herself to be in accord with these on behalf of her own laws, as extensions and enhancements, so to speak. Thus the telephone and the electric train have now become genuine parts of nature—as much a part of her as the sun, the tree, the stone, or water, etc. So it is similarly with reversion: since it drew from the law of generation, it is now just as much an element of nature as this phenomenon. Of course, the two had to be separated initially and each explored according to its first origin, since it was a question of the psychological evaluation of these elements, which is different in each case.

§[24]

It is a favorite practice of J. S. Bach's {53} to begin his pieces, almost as a rule, by first circling the fundamental—that is, by turning it into a fifth of the second fundamental, and then immediately letting it return back to its own fundamental status, whereby he achieves the greatest possible definition

---

generation, it is a product of our mode of perception, and not really "there" in the outer world.

33. Does this *entgegengesetzte Auffassung* represent a revision of the *duale Auffassung*? The subdominant seems to be a "dual" of the dominant since Schenker goes on to say that it has become co-equal, despite its origin via reversion. Indeed, it has become "just as much a product of nature" as the "telephone and the electric train" (!) are now, simply because they were made possible because of the natural phenomenon of electricity—a questionable argument, it would seem, though Schenker essentially repeats it unaltered in *HL*, §24. For whatever reason, however, most of *HL*, §24 was excised by Jonas in the preparation of *HA*.

of the fundamental tone. Generation begins only after complete circling of the fundamental.

§[25]

Reversion plays a large role even in the formation of melody. Quite apart from the harmonic element, it makes a big difference whether melody opens its course in the sense of generation or reversion. When the melody starts with a reversion (that is, it begins by falling from a fifth to the fundamental), it has a characteristic charm. And it was our great masters, <385> in particular, who loved to use this opening gambit regularly. The opening of their works {54} shows only too clearly that the masters intentionally sought such a melodic formation. Obviously they were convinced of the beautiful effect that diversity had to have, even when represented by the formation of melody within one and the same piece. For an example of this, one might look at any piano sonata by Mozart, even the simplest. In any of these, one finds a rich diversity in the way a melody begins, which has a great influence on its further course. And from this method that Mozart uses so freely in all the various openings (among which, as was said, he cultivates the one using reversion in particular), it is certainly to be assumed that he consciously intended them all, and, much less likely, that he merely allowed himself to fall upon them via the path of free association, that is, "inspiration." To be more explicit, an opening of a melody—for example, with a reversion—creates a {55} particular harmonic and motivic situation that is set down as a condition: it is only possible contingently. And since we see that Mozart concerns himself to create such prerequisites and conditions, we also have the full right to say that he intended each opening. Here I choose the example of Mozart only because I can show best directly through him, the eternal Ganymede of the muses, how even the most fluent genius, so to speak, does not place all of his stock in the beneficence of inspiration, <386> but rather searches, with the most accomplished awareness, for every means to create diversity, in the correct belief that this alone can satisfy our desire for aesthetic pleasure. To the extent that this diversity always supplies our aesthetic sense with something new, entertaining it with change, and only thereby with, at the very least, constant (if not increasing) freshness, {56} it puts it in a position to follow the inner destiny of a work. This is not to mention the fact that contrast, which appears as a parallel or non-parallel phenomenon, can be expressed only through diversity. In short, all laws are fulfilled, of which the thematic law (that is, the motivic aspect) must hold, if the work is to appear clear and cogent to us. Mendelssohn and Brahms were the last composers who showed in their work that they could understand and at the same time fulfill this law that lies both outside and within us, and therefore they alone have earned the right to be placed worthily in the line of the Classical Masters, as, provisionally, the last masters. All other authors show such an ignorance in this regard, and, consequently, such a carelessness that it is difficult to determine which is more severe: their lack of talent, or their lack of study of human nature in general, {57} and of the masters.[34] Of these three beautiful things, the one that anyone can still obtain most easily is the exact knowledge of the masters. For this, a diligent and energetic observation of their works can suffice, and that even this is absent is most unpardonable of all. Following upon the knowledge gained merely through observation, a halfway talented artist might possibly succeed now and then merely in imitating the life-force of the masters and composing a living cyclical work. But how should such a miracle occur when the artist's talent is neither strong enough <387> to lead to the source of nature, nor, beyond that, is his desire to learn great enough that it would force him to imitate models? They are content to have neither talent nor desire for study, and only howl all the more the joyful hymns of praise to "inspiration" {58} as the single source of holiness that comes from God. It is obvious that no prize-song has ever been written through inspiration.[35] He who refuses to believe this, may he be convinced by the fact that despite hymns, these lazy and stupid enthusiasts of "inspiration" will not succeed in approaching the muse in any other way than through blackmail. Yes, in reality, that is the opposite side of their Alleluias, namely that the enthusiasts of "inspiration" extort ideas either from God or the muse, each according to his religious confession, and even more ironically, rejoice most gratefully over it when the extortion has worked for them. But "inspiration" remains forever foreign to them, and they have not even an inkling that one can also sow ideas just like corn and wheat; that, if the seed is to germinate, the ground must be well plowed beforehand; and that only then, when one has plowed well and seeded much, may one hope (indeed, with the help of God) to have a good harvest. They do not sense that the entire {59} secret of the geniuses consists in the fact that they do not merely "have" ideas (as though they childishly cultivate them to express themselves), but rather have also learned to sow their ideas and then to harvest them. God can help only him who

---

34. Their "lack of study of human nature in general, and of the masters" reinforces our points made earlier with regard to the importance of the psychological and historical modes of argumentation.

35. Cf. Walther's *Preislied* in Wagner's *Meistersinger*.

sows, however. In contrast, the authors who all believe that everything comes from God and from the "inspired musical thought" that He dispatches from Himself (and that hence also comes down of its own accord and blesses the artists so magnificently through no doing of their own)—they seem to me to be like farmers who—without plowing or sowing—simply say: "All wheat comes from God; if He wants, He will make it with or without us," and in such trust, would not even bother to sow. Sad to say, a characteristic anecdote from Brahms' life, which I want to tell, is appropriate here. It was after the appearance of a larger, cyclic work of his, since . . .

Introduction and translation by Robert W. Wason

Bibliography

Entries of authors, editors, and multiple sources under the same author or editor are in alphabetical order, except for the works of Schenker, which are listed chronologically, following the earlier list of his major works. The bibliography contains books and articles only. The bibliographic information for scores, correspondence not in *SC,* and incidental writings cited once only, is given in the text proper.

Adler, Guido. "Guido Adler (1855–1941) 'Umfang, Methode und Ziel der Musikwissenschaft.'" Partial translation by Martin Cooper in Bojan Bujić, ed., *Music in European Thought, 1851–1912,* 348–55.
———. "Guido Adler's 'The Scope, Method, and Aim of Musicology' (1885): An English Translation with an Historico-Analytical Commentary." Complete translation by Erica Mugglestone. *Yearbook for Traditional Music* 13 (1981): 1–21. Available at: http://web.ff.cuni.cz/ustavy/mus/pdf/gabrielova/Mugglestone_AdlersTheScopeMethodAndAimOfMusicology.pdf.
———. *Der Stil in der Musik.* Leipzig: Breitkopf & Härtel, 1911.
———. "Studie zur Geschichte der Harmonie." *Sitzungsberichte der Philosophisch-Historischen Klasse der Wiener Akademie der Wissenschaften* 98 (1881): 781–830. Available at https://ia800207.us.archive.org/33/items/sitzungsberichte98stuoft/sitzungsberichte98stuoft_bw.pdf.
———. "Umfang, Methode und Ziel der Musikwissenschaft." *Vierteljahresschrift für Musikwissenschaft* 1 (1885): 5–20.
Albisetti, James. *Secondary School Reform in Imperial Germany.* Princeton, NJ: Princeton University Press, 1983.
Alembert, Jean le Rond d'. *Élémens de musique, theorique et pratique, suivant les principes de M. Rameau.* Paris: David/Le Breton/Durand, 1752.
Alpern, Wayne. "Music Theory as a Mode of Law: The Case of Heinrich Schenker, Esq." *Cardozo Law Review* 20 (May–July 1999): 1459–1511.
———. "The Triad of the True, the Good, and the Beautiful: Schenker's Moralization of Music and His Legal Studies with Robert Zimmermann and Georg Jellinek." In *Essays from the Fourth International Schenker Symposium,* vol. 2. Edited by Poundie Burstein, Lynne Rogers, Karen M. Bottge, 7–48. Hildesheim: G. Olms, 2013.

Antonicek, Theophil. "Musikwissenschaft in Wien zur Zeit Guido Adlers." *Studien zur Musikwissenschaft*, 37 (1986): 165–93.
Aristotle. *The Complete Works of Aristotle*. 2 vols. Edited by Jonathan Barnes. Princeton, NJ: Princeton University Press, 1984.
———. *Poetics*. Translated with an introduction and notes by Malcolm Heath. Oxford: Oxford University Press. 1996.
Aristoxenus. *Elementa Harmonica*. In *Greek Musical Writings*, vol. 2. Translated and edited by Andrew Barker, 126–84. Also see Macran, 165–222.
Arntz, Michael. *Hugo Riemann (1849–1919): Leben, Werk und Wirkung*. Cologne: Concerto Verlag Johannes Jansen, 1999.
Ash, Mitchell G. *Gestalt Psychology in German Culture 1890–1967: Holism and the Quest for Objectivity*. Cambridge: Cambridge University Press, 1995.
Austrian Ministry of Education (Bundesministerium für Bildung). *Education in Austria*. Available at https://www.bmb.gv.at/enfr/school/bw_en/bildungswege2016_eng.pdf?61ec3r.
Bach, C. P. E. *Clavier-Sonaten, Rondos, und freie Fantasien für Kenner und Liebhaber*. Edited by E. F. Baumgart. Breslau: F. E. C. Leuckart, 1863.
———. *Essay on the True Art of Playing Keyboard Instruments*. Edited and translated by William J. Mitchell. New York: Norton, 1949.
———. *Versuch über die wahre Art das Clavier zu spielen*, 2nd edition. Berlin: George Ludewig Winter, 1759 (part I) and 1762 (part II); reprint, Leipzig: Breitkopf & Härtel, 1978.
Bach, J. S. *J. S. Bach's Precepts and Principles for Playing the Thorough-Bass or Accompanying in Four Parts*. Translation with Facsimile, Introduction, and Explanatory Notes by Pamela L. Poulin. Oxford: Clarendon Press, 1994.
Baldwin, John D. *Paradisal Love: Johann Gottfried Herder and the Song of Songs*. Sheffield England: Sheffield Academic Press, 1999.
Barker, Andrew. *Greek Musical Writings*, vol. 2, *Harmonic and Acoustic Theory*. Cambridge: Cambridge University Press, 1989.
———. *The Science of Harmonics in Classical Greece*. Cambridge: Cambridge University Press, 2007.
———. *Scientific Method in Ptolemy's "Harmonics."* Cambridge: Cambridge University Press, 2000.
Barbour, J. Murray. "Just Intonation Confuted." *Music and Letters* 19 (1938): 48–60.
Beiser, Frederick C. *The German Historicist Tradition*. New York: Oxford University Press, 2011.
Benjamin, William E. "Schenker's Theory and the Future of Music." *Journal of Music Theory* 25 (1981): 155–73.
Bent, Ian. "'That Bright New Light': Schenker, Universal Edition, and the Origins of the *Erläuterung* Series, 1901–1910." *Journal of the American Musicological Society* 58 (2005): 69–138.

———. *Music Analysis in the Nineteenth Century*. Cambridge: Cambridge University Press, 1994.

———. "Schenker as Teacher: The Pre-Lesson Book Years." *International Forum for Schenkerian Research* Vol. 1 (2025), 111–46.

Bent, Ian, and Anthony Pople. "Analysis." In *Oxford Music Online*, part II, History, §4, 1910–45.

Berger, Karol. *Musica Ficta: Theories of Accidental Inflections in Vocal Polyphony from Marchetto da Padova to Gioseffo Zarlino*. Cambridge: Cambridge University Press, 1987.

Berry, David Carson Berry. "Hans Weisse and the Dawn of American Schenkerism," *Journal of Musicology*, 20 (Winter 2003): 104–56.

———. "The Meaning[s] of 'Without': An Exploration of Liszt's *Bagatelle ohne Tonart*." *Nineteenth-Century Music* 27 (Spring 2004), 230–62.

Bernhard, Christoph. *Tractatus Compositionus Augmentatus*. Edited by Joseph Maria Müller-Blattau, in *Die Kompositionslehre Heinrich Schützens in der Fassung seines Schülers Christoph Bernhard*. Leipzig, Breitkopf & Härtel, 1926; reprint, Kassel: Bärenreiter, 1951.

———. *Tractatus Compositionus Augmentatus*. Translated into English by Walter Hilse, and collated with a related text by Bernhard as "The Treatises of Christoph Bernhard." In *The Music Forum III*. Edited by William J. Mitchell and Felix Salzer, 1–196. New York: Columbia University Press, 1973.

Blackmore, John T. *Ernst Mach: His Work, Life and Influence*. Berkeley and Los Angeles: University of California Press, 1972.

Blackmore, J. T., R. Itagaki, and S. Tanaka, eds. *Ernst Mach's Vienna 1895–1930*. Dordrecht: Kluwer Academic Publishers, 2001.

Blasius, Leslie David. *Schenker's Argument and the Claims of Music Theory*. Cambridge: Cambridge University Press, 1996.

Bolter, Jay. "Friedrich August Wolf and the Scientific Study of Antiquity." Available at http://grbs.library.duke.edu/article/viewFile/7001/5017.

Bower, Calvin. "Boethius and Nicomachus: An Essay Concerning the Sources of *De institutione musica*." *Vivarium* 16 (May 1978): 1–45.

Brahms, Johannes. "Brahms's Study, Octaven u. Quinten u. A., with Schenker's Commentary Translated." Edited and translation, with additional commentary, by Paul Mast. In *The Music Forum V*. Edited by Felix Salzer and Carl Schachter, 1–196. New York: Columbia University Press, 1980.

———. *Oktaven und Quinten u.[nd] A.[nderes]*. Edited with commentary by Heinrich Schenker. Vienna: Universal Edition, 1933.

Breuer, Benjamin. "The Birth of Musicology from the Spirit of Evolution: Ernst Haeckel's *Entwicklungslehre* as Central Component of Guido Adler's Methodology for Musicology." PhD diss., University of Pittsburgh, 2011.

Broder, Nathan, and Arthur Waldeck. "Musical Synthesis as Expounded by Heinrich Schenker." *The Musical Mercury* 11, 4 (December 1935), 56–64. Reprinted in *Theory and Practice* 10 (1985), 63–73.

Brown, Matthew. "The Diatonic and the Chromatic in Schenker's Theory of Harmonic Relations." *Journal of Music Theory* 30 (1986): 1–33.

———. *Explaining Tonality: Schenkerian Theory and Beyond*. Rochester, NY: University of Rochester Press, 2005.

———. "Polyphony and Cacophony? A Schenkerian Reading of Strauss's 'Dance of the Seven Veils.'" In *Explorations in Schenkerian Analysis*. Edited by David Beach and Su Yin Mak, 283–302. Rochester, NY: University of Rochester Press, 2016.

Brown, Matthew, Douglas Dempster, and Dave Headlam. "The #IV Hypothesis: Testing the Limits of Schenker's Theory of Tonality." *Music Theory Spectrum*, 19, 2 (1997): 155–83.

Bruckner, Anton. *Vorlesungen über Harmonielehre und Kontrapunkt an der Universität Wien*. Edited by Ernst Schwanzara. Vienna: Österreichischer Bundesverlag für Unterricht, Wissenschaft und Kunst, 1950.

Bujić, Bojan, ed. *Music in European Thought, 1851–1912*. Cambridge: Cambridge University Press, 1988.

Burkhart, Charles. "Schenker's 'Motivic Parallelisms,'" *Journal of Music Theory* 22 (1978), 145–75.

Campion, François. *Traité d'Accompagnement et de Composition selon la règle des l'octaves de Musique*. Paris: 1716.

Chew, Geoffrey. "The Spice of Music: Towards a Theory of the Leading Note." *Music Analysis* 2 (1983): 35–53.

Christensen, Thomas, ed. *The Cambridge History of Western Music Theory*. Cambridge: Cambridge University Press, 2002; paperback rdition, 2004.

———. *Rameau and Musical Thought in the Enlightenment*. New York: Oxford University Press, 1993.

———. "'The 'Règle de l'Octave' in Thorough-Bass Theory and Practice." *Acta Musicologica* 64, fasc. 2 (July–December 1992): 91–117.

———. "Science and Music Theory in the Enlightenment: d'Alembert's Critique of Rameau." PhD diss., Yale University, 1985.

Citkowitz, Israel. "The Role of Heinrich Schenker." *Modern Music* 11, 1 (1933): 18–23. Reprinted in *Theory and Practice* 10 (1985): 15–22.

Clark, Suzannah. "Schenker's Mysterious Five." *Nineteenth-Century Music*, 23 (Summer 1999): 84–102.

Coen, Deborah R. *Vienna in the Age of Uncertainty: Science, Liberalism, and Private Life*. Chicago: University of Chicago Press, 2014.

Cohen, Albert. "Rameau on Corelli." in *Convention in Eighteenth and Nineteenth Century Music: Essays in Honor of Leonard G. Ratner*. Edited by Wye J. Allenbrook, Janet M. Levy, and William P. Mahrt, 431–45. Stuyvesant, NY: Pendragon Press, 1992.

Cohen, Gary B. *Education and Middle-Class Society in Imperial Austria 1848–1918*. West Lafayette, IN: Purdue University Press, 1996.

Cohen, H. F. *Quantifying Music: The Science of Music at the First Stage of the Scientific Revolution, 1580–1650*. Dordrecht: D. Reidel Publishing Company, 1984.
Comte, August. *Discours sur l'Esprit positif*. Paris: Carilian-Goeury et V. Dalmont, 1844.
———. *A General View of Positivism*. Translated by J. H. Bridges. London: Trübner and Co, 1856, 1865; reprint, Cambridge University Press, 2009.
Cook, Nicholas. "The Editor and the Virtuoso, or Schenker versus Bülow." *Journal of the Royal Musical Association* 116 (1991): 78–95.
———. *The Schenker Project: Culture, Race and Music Theory in* fin-de-siècle *Vienna*. Oxford: Oxford University Press, 2007.
Corry, Leo. *A Brief History of Numbers*. Oxford: Oxford University Press, 2015.
Corwin, Lucille. "*Le Istitutioni Harmoniche* of Gioseffo Zarlino, part 1: A Translation with Introduction." PhD diss., City University of New York, 2008.
Coussemaker, Edmond de. *Scriptorum de Musica Mediiaevi*. Paris: Durand, 1864–76.
Cowan, Nelson, Candice C. Moray, and Zhijian Chen. "The Legend of the Magical Number Seven." In *Tall Tales about the Mind and Brain: Separating Fact from Fiction*. Edited by Sergio Della Sala, 45–59. Oxford: Oxford University Press, 2007.
Crocker, Richard. "Aristoxenus and Greek Mathematics." In *Aspects of Medieval and Renaissance Music: A Birthday Offering to Gustave Reese*, 96–110. New York: Norton, 1966; Pendragon, 1978.
———. *A History of Musical Style*. New York: McGraw-Hill, 1966.
———. "Pythagorean Mathematics and Music." *Journal of Aesthetics and Art Criticism*, 22 (Winter 1963; Spring, 1964): 189–98; 325–35.
Crüger, Johannes. *Grundriss der Psychologie für den Unterricht und die Selbstbelehrung* (Introduction to Psychology for Class Instruction and Independent Study). 2nd rev. edition. Leipzig: G. W. Körners Verlag, 1881. The Polish translation of this edition studied by Schenker was: "Crüger, Johannes. *Dra Jana Crügera Zarys psychologii do uzytku szkolnego i nauki prywatné*. Translated by Zygmunt Sawczyński. Kraków: J. M. Himmelblau, 1878. The 4th German edition was used in the present study: Leipzig: C. F. Amelangs Verlag, 1892.
Dahlhaus, Carl. *Foundations of Music History*. Translated by J. B. Robinson. Cambridge: Cambridge University Press, 1993.
———. *Studies on the Origin of Harmonic Tonality*. Translated by Robert O. Gjerdingen. Princeton: Princeton University Press, 1990.
Danziger, Kurt. *Constructing the Subject: Historical Origins of Psychological Research*. Cambridge: Cambridge University Press, 1990.
Daston, Lorraine, and Glenn W. Most. "History of Science and History of Philologies." *Isis* 106 (2015): 378–90.
Drabkin, William. "The New *Erläuterungsausgabe*." *Perspectives of New Music* 12 (1973–74): 319–30.

Eder, Gabriele Johanna, ed. *Alexius Meinong und Guido Adler: eine Freundschaft in Briefen.* Amsterdam; Atlanta, GA: Rodopi, 1995.

Encyclopedia Britannica https://www.britannica.com/topic/Marsyas-Greek-mythology.

Eggebrecht, H. H., F. A. Gallo, M. Haas, and K-J. Sachs, eds. *Die mittelalterliche Lehre von der Mehrstimmigkeit.* Darmstadt: Wissenschaftliche Buchgesellschaft, 1984.

Ehrenfels, Christian von. "On Gestalt Qualities." Translated by Barry Smith. In *Foundations of Gestalt Theory.* Edited by Barry Smith, 82–116. Munich: Philosophia Verlag, 1988.

———. "Über Gestaltqualitäten." *Vierteljahrschrift für wissenschaftliche Philosophie* 14 (1890), 249–92.

Exner, Adolf. *Grundriß zu Vorlesungen über Geschichte und Institutionen des römischen Rechts.* 2nd edition. Vienna: Manz'sche k. k. Hof-Verlags- and Universitäts-Buchhandlung, 1885.

Eybl, Martin. *Ideologie und Methode: zum ideengeschichtlichen Kontext von Schenkers Musiktheorie.* Tutzing: Hans Schneider, 1995.

Federhofer, Hellmut. *Heinrich Schenker als Essayist und Kritiker: Gesammelte Aufsätze, Rescensionen und kleinere Berichte aus den Jahren 1891–1901.* Hildesheim: Olms, 1990.

———. "Heinrich Schenkers Bruckner-Verständnis." *Archiv für Musikwissenschaft* 39 (1982): 198–217.

Ferrero, Guillaume. "L'Inertie Mentale et La Loi du Moindre Effort." *Revue Philosophique de la France et de l'Etranger* 37 (January–June 1894): 169–82.

Ferris, Joan. "The Evolution of Rameau's 'Harmonic Theories,'" *Journal of Music Theory* 3 (1959): 231–56.

Fétis, François-Joseph. *Complete Treatise on the Theory and Practice of Harmony.* Translated with introduction and commentary by Peter M. Landey. Hillsdale, New York: Pendragon Press, 2008.

———. *Esquisse de l'Histoire de l'Harmonie* (1840). Translated, edited and annotated by Mary I. Arlin. Stuyvesant, NY: Pendragon, Press, 1994.

———. *Méthode élémentaire d'harmonie et d'accompagnement.* Paris: Petit, n.d.

———. *Traité complet de la théorie et de la pratique de l'harmonie contenant la doctrine de la science at de l'art.* Paris: Maurice Schlesinger; Brussels: au Conservatoire [royal de musique de Bruxelles], 1844. Enlarged edition, Paris: Brandus, 1849.

Fiecconi, Elena Cagnoli. "*Harmonie, Melos,* and *Rhythmos*: Aristotle on Musical Education." *Ancient Philosophy* 36 (Fall 2016): 409–24.

Flotzinger, Rudolf. "Bruckner als Theorielehrer an der Universität." In *Anton Bruckner in Lehre und Forschung,* 39–46. Regensburg: Bosse Verlag, 1976.

Forte, Allen. *The Harmonic Organization of the* Rite of Spring. New Haven: Yale University Press, 1978.

Fuller, Sarah. "Theoretical Foundations of Early Organum Theory." *Acta Musicologica* 53 (1981): 52–84.

Fux, Johann Joseph. *Gradus ad parnassum*. Vienna: Johann Peter van Ghelen, 1725.
———. *The Study of Counterpoint*. Translation only of material on species counterpoint, edited and translated by Alfred Mann. New York: Norton, 1973.
———. *The Study of Fugue*. Trnslation of material on fugue, edited and translated by Alfred Mann. New Brunswick, NJ: Rutgers University Press, 1958.
Gaffurius, Franchinus (Franchino Gaffurio, Gafurius, Gafori). *Practica musicae*. Milan: 1496.
———. *Practica musicae*. Translated and edited by Clement A. Miller. Dallas: American Institute of Musicology, 1968.
———. *The* Practica Musicae *of Franchinus Gaffurius*. Translated by Irwin Young. Madison, WI: University of Wisconsin Press, 1969.
Gerbert, Martin, ed. *Scriptores Ecclesiastici de Musica Sacra Potissimum*. Vol. 1. San Blasian, 1784. First publication of Hucbald "Musica": 104–52, entitled *harmonica institutione*; of the anonymous "Musica Enchiriadis": 152–73; and "Scolica Enchiriadis": 173–212. Both attributed to Hucbald.
Gibson, W. R. Boyce. "The Principle of Least Action as a Psychological Principle." *Mind* (New Series) 9, 36 (October 1900), 469–95.
Grant, Cecil Powell. "The Real Relationship between Kirnberger's and Rameau's Concept of the Fundamental Bass." *Journal of Music Theory* 21 (1977): 324–38.
Girard, Aaron Robert. "Music Theory in the American Academy." PhD diss., Harvard University, 2007.
Grave, Floyd K., and Margaret G. Grave. *In Praise of Harmony: The Teachings of Abbé Georg Joseph Vogler*. Lincoln, NE and London: University of Nebraska Press, 1987.
Graves, Robert. *The Greek Myths*. Baltimore: Penguin Books, 1955.
Gushee, Lawrence. "Questions of Genre in Medieval Treatises on Music." in *Gattungen der Musik in Einzeldarstellungen: Gedenkschrift Leo Schrade* 365–453. Bern and Munich: Francke Verlag, 1973.
Halm, August, two-part review of Schenker's *HL* in *Der Merker* 11.17 (1920), 414–17, and of *KP1* in *Der Merker* 11.21 (1920), 505–7.
Hanslick, Eduard. *On the Musically Beautiful*. Translated by Lee Rothfarb and Christoph Landerer. Oxford: Oxford University Press, 2018.
Harrison, Daniel. *Harmonic Function in Chromatic Music: A Renewed Dualist Theory and an Account of Its Precedents*. Chicago: University of Chicago Press, 1994.
Hartley, David. *Observations on Man, His Frame, His Duty, and His Expectations*. Gainesville, FL: Scholar's Facsimiles and Reprints, 1966.
Hauptmann, Moritz. *Die Lehre von der Harmonik, mit beigefügten Notenbeispielen*. Edited by Oskar Paul. Leipzig: Breitkopf & Härtel, 1868; 2nd edition, 1873.
———. *Die Natur der Harmonik und der Metrik*. Leipzig: Breitkopf & Härtel, 1853.

———. *The Nature of Harmony and Metre*. Translated and edited by W. E. Heathcote. London: Swan Sonnenschein, 1888; New York: Novello, Ewer, 1888; reprint, 1893; New York: Da Capo Press, 1991.

———. *Opuscula: Vermischte Aufsätze*. Leipzig: F. E. C. Leuckart, 1874.

Heinichen, Johann David. *Der General-Bass in der Composition*. Dresden: self-published, 1728.

Helmholtz, Hermann von. *Die Lehre von den Tonempfindungen als physiologische Grundlage für die Theorie der Musik*. Braunschweig: Vieweg und Sohn, 1863.

———. *On the Sensations of Tone as a Physiological Basis for the Theory of Music*. Translated by Alexander J. Ellis. New York: Dover Publications, 1954.

Hempel, Carl G. *Aspects of SCIENTIFIC EXPLANATION and other Essays in the Philosophy of Science*. New York: The Free Press, 1965.

Herbart, Johann Friedrich. *Allgemeine Praktische Philosophie* (1808). Reprint in *Johann Friedrich Herbart's Sämtliche Werke, Achter Band, Schriften zur Praktischen Philosophie, erster Theil*. Edited by G. Hartenstein. Leipzig: Leopold Voss, 1851.

———. *Lehrbuch der Psychologie*. Königsberg und Leipzig: August Wilhelm Uuzer, 1816.

———. *Psychologie als Wissenschaft, neu gegründet auf Erfahrung, Metaphysik und Mathematik*. Königsberg: Unger, 1824.

———. *A Text-Book in Psychology: An Attempt to Found the Science of Psychology on Experience, Metaphysics, and Mathematics*. Translated by Margaret K. Smith. New York: D. Appleton and Company, 1891; reprint, Whitefish, MT: Kessinger Publishing, 2010.

Hindemith, Paul. *Craft of Musical Composition*. Vol. 1, Theory. New York: Associated Music Publishers, Inc., 1942.

Hooper, Jason A. "Heinrich Schenker's Early Approach to Form (1895–1921): Implications for His Late Work and Its Reception." PhD diss.: The City University of New York, 2017.

———. "Heinrich Schenker's Early Conception of Form 1894–1914." *Theory and Practice* 36 (2011): 35–64.

Hornblower, Simon, Antony Spawforth, and Esther Eidinow, eds. *Oxford Classical Dictionary*. 4th edition. Oxford: Oxford University Press, 2012.

Hoy, David Couzens. *The Critical Circle: Literature, History and Philosophical Hermeneutics*. Berkeley: University of California Press, 1978.

Hucbald, Guido, and John on Music: Three Medieval Treatises. Translated by Warren Babb and edited with an introduction by Claude V. Palisca. New Haven, CT: Yale University Press, 1978.

Hucbald. *L'oeuvre musicale d'Hucbald de Saint-Amand: les compositions et le traité de musique*. Edited and translated by Yves Chartier. Saint-Laurent, Québec: Bellarmin, 1995.

Huemer, Wolfgang, and Landerer, Christoph. "Mathematics and Laboratories: Herbart's and Brentano's Role in the Rise of Scientific Psychology." *History of the Human Sciences* 23, no. 3: 72-94.

Huemer, Wolfgang. "'Vera philosophiae methodus nulla alia nisi scientiae naturalis est': Brentano's Conception of Philosophy as Rigorous Science." *Brentano Studien* 16, no. 1 (Brentano Centennial). Dettelbach: J. H. Röll Verlag, 2018: 53–71.

Hume, David. *An Enquiry Concerning Human Understanding*. Chicago: Open Court, 1907.

Jackson, Myles W. *Harmonious Triads: Physicists, Musicians and Instrument Makers in Nineteenth-Century Germany*. Boston: MIT Press, 2006.

Jadassohn, Salomon. *Die Kunst zu modulieren und präludieren*. Leipzig: Breitkopf & Härtel, 1890.

———. *Lehrbuch der Harmonie*. Leipzig: Breitkopf & Härtel, 9th edition, 1906; 1st edition, 1883.

Jan, Carl von. *Musici scriptores graeci*. Supplementum. *Melodiarum reliquiae*. Leipzig: Teubner, 1899; reprint, Hildesheim: Olms, 1962.

Janik, Allan, and Stephen Toulmin. *Wittgenstein's Vienna*. New York: Simon and Schuster, 1973.

Jelensperger, Daniel. *L'harmonie au commencement du dix-neuvième siècle et une méthode pour l'étudier*. Paris: Zetter, 1830.

Jellinek, Georg. *Allgemeine Staatslehre*. Berlin: Häring, 1900; 2nd and 3rd editions, 1910 and 1915.

———. *The Declaration of the Rights of Man and of Citizens*. Translated by Max Farrand. New York: Henry Holt and Company, 1901.

———. *The Rights of Minorities*. Translated by A. M. Baty. London: P. S. King and Son, 1912.

Jhering, Rudolph von. *The Struggle for Law (Der Kampf um's Recht)*. Translated by John J. Lalor. Chicago: Callaghan and Company, 1915.

Johannes de Garlandia (John of Garland, Johannes Gallicus), *Concerning Measured Music: De mensurabili musica*. Translated by Stanley H. Birnbaum. Colorado Springs: Colorado College Music Press, 1978.

———. *Johannes de Garlandia: De mensurabili musica: Kritische Edition mit Kommentar und Interpretation der Notationslehre*. Edited with commentary and interpretation by Erich Reimer. Beihefte zum Archiv für Musikwissenschaft, 1972. Vols. 10 and 11. Wiesbaden: Franz Steiner Verlag, 1972.

Johnston, William M. *The Austrian Mind: An Intellectual and Social History, 1848–1938*. Berkeley and Los Angeles, University of California Press, 1972.

Jonas, Oswald, ed. *Beethoven. Die letzten Sonaten. Sonate A Dur Op 101. Erläuterungsausgabe von Heinrich Schenker*. Vienna: Universal Edition, 1972.

———, ed. *Beethoven. Die letzten Sonaten. Sonate As Dur Op 110. Erläuterungsausgabe von Heinrich Schenker*. Vienna: Universal Edition, 1972.

———, ed. *Beethoven. Die letzten Sonaten. Sonate E Dur Op 109. Erläuterungsausgabe von Heinrich Schenker*. Vienna: Universal Edition, 1971.

———, ed. *Beethoven. Die letzten Sonaten. Sonate C Moll Op 111. Erläuterungsausgabe von Heinrich Schenker*. Vienna: Universal Edition, 1971.

———, ed. *Chromatische Fantasie und Fuge D moll von Johann Sebastian Bach: Kritische Ausgabe mit Anhang*. Edited by Heinrich Schenker. Vienna: Universal Edition, 1969.

———, ed. Heinrich Schenker, *Der freie Satz*. Universal Edition: Vienna, 1956.

———. *Introduction to the Theory of Heinrich Schenker*. Translated by John Rothgeb. New York: Longman, 1982; 2nd edition, Ann Arbor, MI: Musicalia Press, 2005.

———. "Die Krise der Musiktheorie." *Der Dreiklang* 3 (June 1937): 67–74.

———. "Preface" to Ludwig van Beethoven, *Piano Sonata Opus 109*. New York: Robert Owen Lehman Foundation, 1965.

———. "Ein textkritisches Problem in der Ballade op. 38 von Frédéric Chopin." *Acta Musicologica* 35 (1963): 155–58.

———. "Über neue Musik." *Der Dreiklang* 6 (1937), 133–38.

———. *Das Wesen des musikalischen Kunstwerkes*. Vienna: Saturn-Verlag. 1934.

———. "Wisdom from the Past: Beethoven's Piano Technique." *The Piano Teacher* 3, 2 (1960): 9–11.

Jonas, Oswald, and Leo Podolsky. *Mozart: Authentic Editions of Four Works for Piano*. Chicago: Clayton F. Summy, 1955.

Jorgenson, Dale A. *Moritz Hauptmann of Leipzig*. Lewiston, NY: Edwin Mellen Press, 1986.

Judd, Cristle Collins. *Reading Renaissance Music Theory: Hearing with the Eyes*. Cambridge: Cambridge University Press, 2000.

Kant, Immanuel. *Critique of Pure Reason*. Translated and edited by Paul Guyer and Allen W. Wood. Cambridge: Cambridge University Press, 1998.

———. *Kritik der reinen Vernunft. Werke in Sechs Bänden*, vol. 2. Cologne: Könemann, 1995; 1st edition, Riga: 1781; 2nd edition, 1787.

———. *Metaphysical Foundations of Natural Science*. Translated by John Ellington. Indianapolis: Bobbs-Merrill, 1970.

———. *Die metaphysischen Anfangsgründe der Naturwissenschaft*. Riga: 1786.

Karnes, Kevin C. "Heinrich Schenker and Musical Thought in Late Nineteenth-Century Vienna." PhD diss., Brandeis University, 2001.

———. *Music, Criticism and the Challenge of History: Shaping Modern Musical Thought in Late Nineteenth-Century Vienna*. Oxford: Oxford University Press, 2008.

Katz, Adele T. *Challenge to Musical Tradition: A New Concept of Tonality*. New York: Alfred Knopf, 1945.

Kelly, Duncan. "Revisiting the Rights of Man: Georg Jellinek on Rights and the State." *Law and History Review*. Published by American Society for Legal History. 22 (Autumn 2004): 493–529.

Kilmer, Anne Draffkorn. "A Music Tablet from Sippar (?): BM 65217 + 66616." *Iraq* 46, 2 (Autumn 1984): 69–80.

Kirnberger, Johann Philipp. *The Art of Strict Musical Composition.* Translated by David W. Beach and Jürgen Thym. New Haven: Yale University Press, 1982. (Translation of volume I, and part I of volume II of *Kunst des reinen Satzes*).

———. *Die Kunst des reinen Satzes in der Musik.* 2 vols. Berlin and Königsberg: Decker und Hartung, 1771–79. Vol. 1: Berlin: Christian Friedrich Voß, 1771; reprint, Berlin: Decker und Hartung, 1774; corrected edition, Berlin: H. A. Rottmann, ca. 1776. Vol. 2, in 3 parts: Berlin: Decker und Hartung, 1776, 1777, 1779.

———. "*The True Principles for the Practice of Harmony* by Johann Philipp Kirnberger: a Translation." Translated by David W. Beach and Jürgen Thym. *Journal of Music Theory* 23 (1979): 163–226.

———. *Die wahren Grundsätze zum Gebrauch der Harmonie.* Berlin: Decker und Hartung, 1773.

Kivy, Peter. "Charles Darwin and Music." *Journal of the American Musicological Society* 12 (1959): 42–48.

Kline, Morris. *Mathematical Thought from Ancient to Modern Times.* Vol. 1. New York: Oxford University Press, 1972.

Korsakov, Nikolai Rimsky. *Practical Manual of Harmony.* Edited by Nicholas Hopkins. The Masters Collection. New York: Carl Fischer, 2005.

Korsyn, Kevin. "Schenker's Organicism Reconsidered." *Intégral* 7 (1993): section V, 109–16.

———. "Schenker's Vienna: Nicholas Cook on Culture, Race and Music Theory in *fin-de-siècle* Austria." *Music Analysis* 28 (2009): 153–79.

Koslovsky, John Charles. "The Early Schenkerians and the "Concept of Tonality." *Gamut* 7, 1 (2014): 155–85.

———. "From *Sinn und Wesen* to *Structural Hearing*: The Development of Felix Salzer's Ideas in Interwar Vienna and Their Transmission in Postwar United States." PhD diss., University of Rochester, 2009.

———. "Tonal Prolongation in Bartók's Hungarian Folktunes for Violin and Piano: A Case Study." *Theory and Practice* 37–38 (2012–13): 1–45.

———. "Tracing the Improvisatory Impulse in Early Schenkerian Theory." *Intégral* 24 (2010): 57–79.

Kosovsky, Robert. "Levels of understanding: an introduction to Schenker's *Nachlass.*" In *Schenker Studies II*, 3–11. Edited by Carl Schachter and Hedi Siegel. Cambridge: Cambridge University Press, 1999.

Kraft, Victor. *Foundations for a Scientific Analysis of Value.* Edited by Elizabeth Hughes Schneewind, translated by H. L. Mulder. Dordrecht: Reidel, 1981.

———. *Die Grundlagen einer wissenschaftlichen Wertlehre.* Vienna: Springer-Verlag, 2nd ed., 1951.

Krebs, Harald. "Schenker's View of Rameau: A Comparison of Remarks in *Harmony*, *Counterpoint*, and *Rameau or Beethoven*." *Theoria* 3 (1988): 59–72.
Künne, Wolfgang, Mark Siebel and Markus Textor, eds. *Bolzano and Analytic Philosophy*. Grazer Philosophische Studien, 53. Amsterdam: Brill Rodopi, 1998.
Kuhn, Thomas. *The Structure of Scientific Revolutions* (1962). 2nd edition. Chicago: University of Chicago Press, 1970.
LaRue, Jan. *Guidelines for Style Analysis*. New York: W. W. Norton, 1970.
LaRue, Jan, and Marian Green, eds. *Guidelines for Style Analysis*. Sterling Heights, MI: Harmonie Park Press, 2011.
Laufer, Edward. "Review: Heinrich Schenker, *Free Composition (Der freie Satz)*, translated by Ernst Oster." *Music Theory Spectrum* 3 (1981): 158–84.
Leahey, Thomas Hardy. *A History of Psychology*. Upper Saddle River, NJ: Prentice Hall, 1997.
Lear, Jonathan. *Aristotle: The Desire to Understand*. Cambridge: Cambridge University Press, 1988.
Lemke, Arno. *Jacob Gottfried Weber: Leben und Werk*. Mainz: Schott's Söhne, 1968.
Lester, Joel. *Between Modes and Keys*. Stuyvesant, NY: Pendragon Press, 1989.
———. *Compositional Theory in the Eighteenth Century*. Cambridge, MA: Harvard University Press, 1992.
Lewin, David. "Two Interesting Passages in Rameau's *Traité de l'harmonie*." *In Theory Only* 4, 3 (1978): 3–11.
Liddell and Scott, *A Greek-English Lexicon*. Oxford: Clarendon Press, 1958.
———. *An Intermediate Greek-English Lexicon*. Oxford: Clarendon Press, 1992.
Locke, John. *An Essay Concerning Human Understanding*. 2 vols. New York: Dover, 1959.
Lord, Albert B. *The Singer of Tales*. Edited by Stephen Mitchell and Gregory Nagy. Cambridge, MA: Harvard University Press, 2000.
Louis, Rudolf. *Grundriss der Harmonielehre von Louis und Thuille*. Stuttgart: Klett, n.d. [1914].
Louis, Rudolf and Thuille, Ludwig. *Harmonielehre*. Stuttgart: Carl Grüninger [Klett & Hartmann], n.d. [1907].
Lubben, Robert Joseph. "Schenker the Progressive: Analytic Practice in *Der Tonwille*." *Music Theory Spectrum* 15 (1993): 59–75.
McAlpine, Fiona. *Tonal Consciousness and the Medieval West*. Bern, New York: Peter Lang, 2008.
Mach, Ernst. *The Analysis of Sensations and the Relation of the Physical to the Psychical*. Translated by C. M. Williams, and revised and supplemented from the fifth German edition by Sydney Waterlow. New York: Dover Publications, 1959.
———. *Beiträge zur Analyse der Empfindungen*. Jena: Gustav Fischen, 1886.
———. "On Symmetry." in *Popular Scientific Lectures*. 3rd rev. edition. Translated by Thomas J. McCormack. Chicago: Open Court, 1898.

Macran, Henry S. *The Harmonics of Aristoxenus*. Edited, translated, notes, introduction, and index of words by Henry S. Macran. Oxford: Clarendon, 1902; reprint, Hildesheim: Olms, 1974.

Majewski, Teresita and David Gaimster, eds. *International Handbook of Historical Archeology*. New York: Springer, 2009.

Makkreel, Rudolf. "Wilhelm Dilthey." In *The Stanford Encyclopedia of Philosophy*. Fall 2016 Edition. Edited by Edward N. Zalta. Available at https://plato.stanford.edu/archives/fall2016/entries/dilthey/.

Mann, Alfred. *Theory and Practice*. New York: Norton, 1987.

Marpurg, Friedrich Wilhelm. *Systematische Einleitung in die Musikalische Setzkunst: nach den Lehrsätzen des Herrn Rameau / Hrn. D'Alembert; aus dem Französischen übersetzt und mit Anmerkungen vermehret von Friedr. Wilh. Marpurg*. Leipzig: J. G. I. Breitkopf, 1757.

Marston, Nicholas. "'. . . nur ein Gleichnis': Heinrich Schenker and the Path to 'Likeness.'" *Music and Letters* 100 (2019): 1–31.

———. "Schenker's Concept of a Beethoven Sonata Edition." in *Essays from the Fourth International Schenker Symposium*, vol. 2. Edited by Poundie Burstein, Lynne Rogers, Karen M. Bottge. Hildesheim: G. Olms, 2013.

Martin, Nathan John. "Rameau and Rousseau: Harmony and History in the Age of Reason." PhD diss., Schulich School of Music, McGill University, 2008.

———. "Rameau's Changing Views on Supposition and Suspension." *Journal of Music Theory* 56 (Fall 2012): 121–67.

Masur, Gerhard. "Wilhelm Dilthey and the History of Ideas." *Journal of the History of Ideas* 13, 1 (January 1952), 94–107.

Mathiesen, Thomas. "Problems of Terminology in Ancient Greek Theory: 'ARMONIA.'" In *Festival of Essays for Pauline Alderman*, 3–17. Provo, UT: Brigham Young University, 1976.

Maus, Fred Everett. "Hanslick's Animism." *Journal of Musicology* 10, no. 3 (Summer, 1992): 273–292.

———. "Music as Drama." *Music Theory Spectrum* 10, 10th Anniversary Issue (Spring 1988): 56–73.

Meyer, Leonard B. *Music, The Arts, and Ideas: Patterns and Prediction in Twentieth-Century Culture*. Chicago: The University of Chicago Press, 1967.

———. *Style and Music History, Theory and Ideology*. Philadelphia: University of Pennsylvania Press, 1989.

Miller, George A. "The Magical Number Seven, Plus or Minus Two: Some Limits on Our Capacity for Processing Information." *The Psychological Review* 63 (1956): 81–97.

Mitchell, William J. "Chord and Context in Eighteenth-Century Theory." *Journal of the American Musicological Society* 16, 2 (Summer 1963): 221–39.

———. "Review: Harmony by Heinrich Schenker." *The Musical Quarterly* (1955), 256–60.

Monahan, Seth. "Action and Agency Revisited." *Journal of Music Theory* 57, no. 2 (Fall 2013): 321–71.

Mooney, Kevin. "Hugo Riemann's Debut as a Music Theorist." *Journal of Music Theory*, 44, 1 (Spring 2000), 81–99.

Morgan, Robert P. *Becoming Heinrich Schenker: Music Theory and Ideology*. Cambridge: Cambridge University Press, 2014.

Musica et scolica enchiriadis. Critical edition by Hans Schmid. Munich: Bavarian Academy of Sciences, 1981.

Musica et scolica enchiriadis. Translated by Raymond Erikson and edited by Claude V. Palisca as *Musica enchiriadis and scolica enchiriadis*. New Haven and London: Yale University Press, 1995.

Neumeyer, David. "The Three-Part *Ursatz*." *In Theory Only* 10 (1987): 3–29.

Oettingen, Arthur von. *Das Duale Harmoniesystem*. Leipzig: Siegel's Musikalienhandlung, 1913.

———. *Die Grundlage der Musikwissenschaft*. Leipzig: Abhandlungen der königlichen-sächsischen Akademie der Wissenschaften, 1916.

———. *Harmoniesystem in dualer Entwicklung*. Dorpat: W. Gläser, 1866.

Palisca, Claude V. *Humanism in Italian Renaissance Musical Thought*. New Haven and London: Yale University Press, 1985.

Pastille, William. "The Development of the *Ursatz* in Schenker's Published Works." In *Trends in Schenkerian Research*. Edited by Allan Cadwallader, 71–85. New York: Schirmer Books, 1990.

———. "Heinrich Schenker, Anti-Organicist." *Nineteenth-Century Music* 8 (Summer 1984): 29–36.

———. "Schenker's Value Judgements." *Music Theory Online* 1, 6 (1995): 1–8.

Patterson, Edwin W. *Jurisprudence: Men and Ideas of the Law*. Brooklyn: The Foundations Press, 1953.

Payzant, Geoffrey. "Eduard Hanslick and Robert Zimmermann: a Biographical Sketch." available at https://www.rodoni.ch/busoni/cronologia/Note/hanslick.pdf.

Peles, Stephen, ed. *The Collected Essays of Milton Babbitt*. Princeton: Princeton University Press, 2003.

Pfeiffer, Rudolf. *History of Classical Scholarship from the Beginnings to the End of the Hellenistic Age*. Oxford: Clarendon Press, 1968.

———. *History of Classical Scholarship from 1300 to 1850*. Oxford: Clarendon Press, 1976.

Pöhlmann, Egert and Martin L. West. *Documents of Ancient Greek Music: The Extant Melodies and Fragments*. Oxford: Oxford University Press, 2001.

Poulin, Pamela L. *J. S. Bach's Precepts and Principles for Playing the Thorough-Bass or Accompanying in Four Parts, Leipzig, 1738*. Oxford: Clarendon Press, 1994.

Proctor, Gregory. "Technical Bases of Nineteenth-Century Chromatic Tonality: A Study in Chromaticism." PhD diss., Princeton University, 1978.

Rameau, Jean-Philippe. *Code de musique pratique, ou méthodes pour apprendre la musique . . . avec de nouvelles réflexions sur la principe sonore.*
———. *Démonstration du principe de l'harmonie, servant de base à tout l'art musical théorique et pratique.* Paris: Durand, 1750.
———. *Erreurs sur la Musique dans l'Encyclopédie.* Paris: Sébastien Jorry, 1755.
———. *Nouveau système de musique théorique, où l'on découvre le principe de toutes les règles nécessaires à la pratique, pour servir d'introduction au traité de l'harmonie.* Paris: Ballard, 1726.
———. *Traité de l'harmonie réduite à ses principes naturels.* Paris: Ballard, 1722.
———. *Treatise on Harmony.* Translated by Philip Gossett. New York: Dover, 1971.
Reed, Edward S. *From Soul to Mind: The Emergence of Psychology, from Erasmus Darwin to William James.* New Haven: Yale University Press, 1997.
Reger, Max. *Beiträge zur Modulationslehre.* Leipzig: Kahnt, 1903.
———. *On the Theory of Modulation.* Translated by John Bernhoff. New York: Dover, 2007.
Rehding, Alexander. *Hugo Riemann and the Birth of Modern Musical Thought.* Cambridge: Cambridge University Press, 2003.
Rehding, Alexander and Edward Gollin, eds. *The Oxford Handbook of Neo-Riemannian Music Theories.* New York: Oxford, 2011.
Reynolds, L. D. and N. G. Wilson, *Scribes and Scholars: A Guide to the Transmission of Greek and Latin Literature.* 4th edition. Oxford: Oxford University Press, 2013.
Richter, Ernst Friedrich. *Lehrbuch der Harmonie* (1st edition, 1853). 23rd edition. Leipzig: Breitkopf & Härtel, 1902.
Rieber, R. W. *Wilhelm Wundt and the Making of a Scientific Psychology.* New York: Plenum Press, 1980.
Riemann, Hugo. *Geschichte der Musiktheorie im IX.–XIX Jahrhundert.* Berlin: Max Hesse Verlag, 1898.
———. *Grundriß der Musikwissenschaft* (1st edition, 1908). Leipzig: Quelle & Meyer, 1928.
———. *Harmony Simplified, or the Theory of Tonal Functions of Chords.* Translated by Henry Bewerunge. London: Augener, 1895.
———. "Ideas for a Study 'On the Imagination of Tone.'" Translated by Robert Wason and Elizabeth West Marvin. In *Journal of Music Theory* 36 (Spring 1992): 81–117.
———. "Ideen zu einer 'Lehre von den Tonvorstellungen.'" *Jahrbuch der Musikbibliothek Peters* 21–22 (1914–15; reprint Vaduz, 1965), 1–26.
———. *Musik-Lexikon.* 5th edition. Leipzig: Max Hesse's Verlag, 1900.
———. "The Nature of Harmony." Translation and commentary by Benjamin Steege. In *The Oxford Handbook of Neo-Riemannian Music Theories.* Edited by Alexander Rehding and Edward Gollin, 55–91. New York: Oxford University Press, 2011.

———. "Das Problem des harmonischen Dualismus." in *Neue Zeitschrift für Musik* 51 (1905): 3–5, 23–26, 43–46, 67–70.

———. "The Problem of Harmonic Dualism: A Translation and Commentary." By Ian Bent. In *The Oxford Handbook of Neo-Riemannian Music Theories*. Edited by Alexander Rehding and Edward Gollin, 167–93. New York: Oxford University Press, 2011.

———. *Skizze einer neuen Methode der Harmonielehre*. Leipzig: Breitkopf und Härtel, 1880.

———. *Vereinfachte Harmonielehre; oder, die Lehre von den tonalen Funktionen der Akkorde*. London: Augener, 1893.

Riley, Matthew. "The 'Harmonic Major' Mode in Nineteenth-Century Theory and Practice." *Music Analysis* 23 (2004): 1–26.

Roben, Betsy Baker. "The Method behind Bluntschli's 'Modern' International Law." *Journal of the History of International Law* 4 (2002): 249–92.

Roeckelein, Jon E. *Dictionary of Theories, Laws and Concepts in Psychology*. Westport, CT: Greenwood Press, 1998.

Rosenthal, Carl A. "Reminiscences of Guido Adler (1855–1941)." *Musica Judaica* 8, 1 (5747/1985–86): 19.

Rothfarb, Lee. "Heinrich Schenker and ibn Ezra: Literal and Interpretive Meaning in Music." *Musiktheorie* 29 (2014): 33–49.

———. "Henryk Szenker, Galitzianer: The Making of a Man and a Nation." In *Journal of Schenkerian Studies* 11 (2018): 1–51.

———. "Nineteenth-Century Fortunes of Musical Formalism." *Journal of Music Theory* 55 (Fall 2011): 167–220.

Rothgeb, John. "Review of *Schenker, Nach Tagebüchern und Briefen*, by Hellmut Federhofer." *Journal of Music Theory* 45 (Spring 2001): 151–62.

———. "Schenkerian Theory and Manuscript Studies." In *Schenker Studies*. Edited by Hedi Siegel. Cambridge: Cambridge University Press, 1990.

Rothstein, William. "On Implied Tones." *Music Analysis* 10 (1991), 289–328.

Rousseau, Jean-Jacques. *Dictionnaire de Musique*. Paris: veuve Duchesne, 1768.

Rüegg, Walter, ed. *A History of the University in Europe. Vol. III: Universities in the Nineteenth and Early Twentieth Centuries (1800–1945)*. Cambridge: Cambridge University Press, 2004.

Rummenhöller, Peter. *Musiktheoretisches Denken im 19. Jahrhundert: Versuch einer Interpretation erkenntnistheoretischer Zeugnisse in der Musiktheorie*. Regensburg: Bosse, 1967.

Sachs, Klaus-Jürgen. "Zur Tradition der Klangschritt-Lehre. Die Texte mit der Formel 'Si cantus ascendit' und ihre Verwandten." *Archiv für Musikwissenschaft* 28 (1971), 233–70.

Salmond, John W. *Jurisprudence*. 7th edition. London: Stevens and Haynes, 1924.

Salzer, Felix. "Haydn's Fantasia from the String Quartet, Opus 76, No. 6." In *The Music Forum IV.* Edited by Felix Salzer and Carl Schachter. New York: Columbia University Press, 1976, 161–94.

———. *Sinn und Wesen der abendländischen Mehrstimmigkeit.* Vienna: Saturn-Verlag, 1935.

———. *Structural Hearing.* New York: Charles Boni, 1952.

Schachter, Carl. *The Art of Tonal Analysis.* Edited by Joseph N. Straus. New York: Oxford University, 2016.

———. "Introduction." *Beethoven, Complete Piano Sonatas.* Edited by Heinrich Schenker. New York: Dover, 1975.

Schenker, Heinrich. *Beethovens Neunte Sinfonie.* Vienna: Universal Edition, 1912.

———. *Beethoven's Ninth Symphony: a Portrayal of its Musical Content, with Running Commentary on Performance and Literature as well.* Edited and translated by John Rothgeb. New Haven: Yale University Press, 1992.

———, ed. *Erläuterungs-Ausgabe. Die letzten fünf Sonaten von Beethoven Op. 101.* Vienna: Universal Edition, 1921; 2nd printing, with corrections, 1925.

———, ed. *Erläuterungs-Ausgabe. Die letzten fünf Sonaten von Beethoven Op. 109.* Vienna: Universal Edition, 1913; 2nd printing, with corrections, 1923.

———, ed. *Erläuterungs-Ausgabe. Die letzten fünf Sonaten von Beethoven Op. 110.* Vienna: Universal Edition, 1914; 2nd printing, with corrections, 1924.

———, ed. *Erläuterungs-Ausgabe. Die letzten fünf Sonaten von Beethoven Op. 111.* Vienna: Universal Edition, 1915; 2nd printing, with corrections, 1925.

———, ed. *G. F. Händel, Sechs Orgelkonzerte.* Vienna: Universal Edition, 1905.

———, ed. *L. Van Beethoven, Sonate Op. 27, Nr. 2* Facsimile. Vienna: Universal Edition, 1921.

———, ed. *L. Van Beethoven, Klaviersonaten: Nach den Autographen und Erstdrucken rekonstruiert von Heinrich Schenker.* Vienna: Universal Edition, 1921–23.

———, ed. *Piano Sonata in A♭ Major, Op. 101. Beethoven's Last Piano Sonatas: An Edition with Elucidation. Volume 4.* Translated, edited, and annotated by John Rothgeb. New York: Oxford University Press, 2015.

———, ed. *Piano Sonata in A♭ Major, Op. 110. Beethoven's Last Piano Sonatas: An Edition with Elucidation. Volume 2.* Translated, edited, and annotated by John Rothgeb. New York: Oxford University Press, 2015.

———, ed. *Piano Sonata in C Minor, Op. 111. Beethoven's Last Piano Sonatas: An Edition with Elucidation. Volume 3.* Translated, edited, and annotated by John Rothgeb. New York: Oxford University Press, 2015.

———, ed. *Piano Sonata in E Major, Op. 109. Beethoven's Last Piano Sonatas: An Edition with Elucidation. Volume 1.* Translated, edited, and annotated by John Rothgeb. New York: Oxford University Press, 2015.

———. "Vom Hintergrund in der Musik." *Der Dreiklang* 1 (April 1937): 12–13.

———. "Von der Stimmführung im Generalbass." *Der Dreiklang,* 3 (June 1937): 76.

Schleiermacher, Friedrich D. E. *Gelegentliche Gedanken über Universitäten im deutschen Sinn, nebst einem Anhang über eine neu zu errichtende*. Berlin: 1808. Available at http://edoc.hu-berlin.de/miscellanies/g-texte-30372/123/PDF/123.pdf.

———. *Hermeneutics and Criticism, and Other Writings*. Translated and edited by Andrew Bowie. Cambridge: Cambridge University Press, 1998.

Schoenberg, Arnold. *Harmonielehre*. Vienna: Universal Edition, 1911; 3rd edition, 1922.

———. *Structural Functions of Harmony*. New York: W. W. Norton, 1954.

Searle, John. "Minds, Brains and Programs." *Behavioral and Brain Sciences* 3 (1980): 417–57.

Sechter, Simon. *The Correct Order of Fundamental Harmonies: A Treatise on Fundamental Basses, and Their Inversions and Substitutes*. Translated and edited by Carl Christian Müller. New York: Wm. A. Pond, 1871.

———. *Die Grundsätze der musikalischen Komposition*. 3 vols. Leipzig: Breitkopf and Härtel, 1853–54. Vol. 1: *Die richtige Folge der Grundharmonien, oder vom Fundamentalbass und dessen Umkehrungen und Stellvetretern*. Vol 2: *Von den Gesetzen des Taktes in der Musik; Vom einstimmigen Satze; Die Kunst zu einer gegebenen Melodie die Harmonie zu finden*. Vol. 3: *Von drei- und zweistimmigen Satze; Rhythmische Entwürfe; Von strengen Satze, mit kurzen Andeutungen des freien Satzes; Vom doppelten Contrapunkte*.

———. *Practische Generalbaß-Schule, bestehend in 120 progressiven und mehrfach ausgeführten Übungen im Generalbasse, mit besonderer Rücksicht auf jene, welche sich im Orgelspiele vervollkommnen wollen*. Vienna: Joseph Czerny-Witzendorf, [1830].

Seeger, Charles. Review of *HA*. *Notes* 13, 1 (December 1955): 53–55.

Seidel, Elmar. "Die Harmonielehre Hugo Riemanns." In *Beiträge zur Musiktheorie des 19. Jahrhunderts*. Edited by Martin Vogel, 39–102. Regensburg: Gustav Bosse Verlag, 1966.

Sessions, Roger. *Harmonic Practice*. New York: Harcourt, Brace & World, 1951.

Shannon, John R. *The Evolution of Organ Music in the Seventeenth Century: A Study of European Styles*. Jefferson, NC: McFarland, 2012.

Shirlaw, Matthew. *The Theory of Harmony: An Inquiry into the Natural Principles of Harmony, with an Examination of the Chief Systems of Harmony from Rameau to the Present Day*. London: Novello & Company, 1917; reprint, New York: Da Capo Press, 1969.

Siegel, Hedi. "Schenker's letters to Felix Salzer: A Nod to the Future." In *Essays for the Fourth International Schenker Symposium*, vol. 2. Edited Poundie Burstein, Lynne Rogers, and Karen M. Bottge, 73–83. Hildesheim: Olms, 2013.

———. "A Source for Schenker's Study of Thorough-Bass: His Annotated Copy of J. S. Bach's *Generalßbüchlein*." in *Schenker Studies*. Edited Hedi Siegel. Cambridge: Cambridge University Press, 1990.

---. "When 'Freier Satz' was part of *Kontrapunkt*: a preliminary report." in *Schenker Studies II*. Edited Carl Schachter and Hedi Siegel, 12–25. Cambridge: Cambridge University Press, 1999.

Simms, Bryan R. "Arnold Schoenberg, *Theory of Harmony*, translated by Roy E. Carter: Commentary by Bryan R. Simms," *Music Theory Spectrum* 4 (1982), 155–62.

---. "Choron, Fétis, and the Theory of Tonality." *Journal of Music Theory* 19, 1 (1975): 112–38.

Smith, Barry. *Austrian Philosophy: The Legacy of Franz Brentano*. Chicago: Open Court, 1994.

---, ed. *Foundations of Gestalt Theory*. Munich: Philosophia Verlag, 1988.

Spengler, Oswald. *Der Untergang des Abendlandes*. 2 vols. Munich: Oskar Beck, 1918 and 1922.

Spies, Claudio. "Review of *Theory of Harmony* by Arnold Schoenberg, tr. Roy E. Carter (Berkeley and Los Angeles: University of California Press, 1978)." *Journal of the Arnold Schoenberg Institute* 3, 2 (1979): 179–86.

Steege, Benjamin. *Helmholtz and the Modern Listener*. Cambridge: Cambridge University Press, 2012.

Stein, Erwin. *Praktischer Leitfaden zu Schönbergs Harmonielehre*. Vienna: Universal Edition, 1923.

Stöhr, Richard. *Praktischer Leitfaden der Harmonielehre*. Vienna: Universal Edition, 1909.

Tan, Daphne. "Beyond Energetics: Gestalt Psychology in Ernst Kurth's *Musikpsychologie*." *Theoria* 22 (2015), 99–129.

Tchaikovsky, Peter. *Guide to the Practical Study of Harmony*. Moscow: P. Jurgenson, 1872.

Thompson, David M. *A History of Harmonic Theory in the United States*. Kent, OH: Kent State University Press, 1980.

Thomson, Ulf. *Voraussetzungen und Artungen der österreichischen Generalbasslehre zwischen Albrechtsberger und Sechter*. Tutzing: Hans Schneider, 1978.

Tinctoris, Johannes. *The Art of Counterpoint*. Translated, edited and introduced by Albert Seay. n.p. [Rome]: American Institute of Musicology, 1961.

---. *Liber de arte contrapuncti*. In *Johannes Tinctoris opera theoretica*. In vol. 2 of 3 vols. Edited by Albert Seay. n.p. [Rome]: American Institute of Musicology, 1975–78.

Treitler, Leo. "Homer and Gregory: The Transmission of Epic Poetry and Plainchant." *The Musical Quarterly*, 60 (July 1974), 333–72.

---, general ed. *Source Readings in Music History*. Edited by Oliver Strunk. Revised Edition. New York: W. W. Norton, 1998.

Urchueguía, Cristina. "Wie kam die 'Urlinie' in den 'Urtext'? Aporien musikalischer Schrift im Denken Heinrich Schenkers." *Schweizer Jahrbuch Für Musikwissenschaft* Neue Folge 32 (2012): 237–52.

Violin, Moritz. *Die Zustände an der k. k. Akademie für Musik und darstellende Kunst: Ein offenes Wort über die Leiter der Anstalt Herren v. Wiener und Bopp*. Vienna: Self-published, 1912.

Vogt, Florian. "Otto Vrieslanders Kommentar zu Heinrich Schenkers *Harmonielehre*; Ein Beitrag zur frühen Schenker-Rezeption." *Zeitschrift der Gesellschaft für Musiktheorie* 3, 2 (2006), 183–207.

Vrieslander, Otto. *C. P. E. Bach: Lieder und Gesänge*. Munich: Drei Masken Verlag, 1922.

———. *Carl Philipp Emanuel Bach*. Munich: Piper, 1923.

———. "Carl Philipp Emanuel Bach als Theoretiker." In *Von neuer Musik*, 222–79. Cologne: Mercau, 1925.

Wagner, Richard. *The Artwork of the Future*. Translated by Emma Warner. Edited by Tash Siddiqui. London: The Wagner Journal, 2013.

———. "Das Kunstwerk der Zukunft." In *Gesammelte Schriften und Dichtungen*, vol. 3. 3rd edition. 10 vols. Leipzig: Fritzsch, 1897–98.

Wagner, Manfred. *Die Harmonielehren in der ersten Hälfte des 19. Jahrhunderts*. Regensburg: Gustav Bosse Verlag, 1973.

Waldeck, Arthur and Broder, Nathan, "Musical Synthesis as Expounded by Heinrich Schenker." *The Musical Mercury* 11, 4 (December 1935), 56–64; reprinted in *Theory and Practice* 10 (1985): 63–73.

Wason, Robert. "From *Harmonielehre* to *Harmony*: Schenker's Theory of Harmony and Its Americanization." In *Schenker-Traditionen: Eine Wiener Schule der Musiktheorie und ihre internationale Verbreitung*. (A Viennese School of Music Theory and Its International Dissemination.) Edited by Martin Eybl and Evelyn Fink-Mennel, 171–201. Vienna: Böhlau Verlag, 2004. A version with revised examples is printed in *Essays from the Fourth International Schenker Symposium*, vol. 1, edited by Allen Cadwallader, 213–58. Hildesheim: G. Olms, 2008.

———. "Schenker's Notion of Scale-Step in Historical Perspective: Non-Essential Harmonies in Viennese Fundamental Bass Theory." *Journal of Music Theory* 27 (1983): 49–73.

———. *Viennese Harmonic Theory from Albrechtsberger to Schenker and Schoenberg*. Ann Arbor, MI: UMI Research Press, 1985; Rochester, NY: University of Rochester Press, 1995; digital edition, 2008.

Wason, Robert, and Elizabeth West Marvin, "Riemann's Ideen zu einer 'Lehre von den Tonvorstellungen'": An Annotated Translation." *Journal of Music Theory* 36 (1992): 69–117.

Weber, [Jacob] Gottfried. *An Attempt at a Systematically Arranged Theory of Musical Composition Treated with a View to a Naturally Consecutive Arrangement of Topics*. 2 vols. Translated by James F. Warner. Boston: J. H. Wilkins and R. B. Carter, 1842–46; see also the later edition augmented by John Bishop, London: Robert Cocks, 1851.

———. *Versuch einer geordneten Theorie der Tonse[t]zkunst zum Selbstunterricht mit Anmerkungen für Gelehrtere*. 3 vols. Mainz: Schott, 1817, 1818, 1821.

West, M. L. *Ancient Greek Music.* Oxford: Clarendon Press, 1992.

Westphal, Rudolf. *Aristoxenos von Tarent: Melik und Rhythmik des classischen Hellentums übersetzt und erläutert von Rudolf Westphal.* Leipzig: A. Abel, 1883, 1893; reprint, Hildesheim: G. Olms, 1965.

Wharton, J. J. S. *The Law Lexicon, or Dictionary of Jurisprudence.* Littleton, CO: Rothman, 1987; reprint of Harrisburg, PA: I. G. M'Kinley & J. M. G. Lescure, 1848.

White, Hayden. *Metahistory: The Historical Imagination in Nineteenth-Century Europe.* Baltimore, ML: Johns Hopkins University Press, 1973.

Wolff, Christoph. *Johann Sebastian Bach, the Learned Musician.* New York: W. W. Norton, 2000.

Wulstan, David. "The Tuning of the Babylonian Harp." *Iraq* 30, 2 (Autumn 1968): 215–28.

Wundt, Wilhelm. *Grundriss der Psychologie.* Leipzig: Verlag von Wilhelm Engelmann, 1897.

Zarlino, Gioseffo. *The Art of Counterpoint: Part Three of* Le Istitutioni Harmoniche, *1558.* Translated by Guy A. Marco and Claude V. Palisca New Haven: Yale University Press, 1983.

———. *Dimostrationi Harmoniche.* Venice: 1571.

———. *Le istitutioni harmoniche.* Venice: 1558; revised edition 1573. For a translation of part 1, see Corwin, Lucille; there is no published English translation of part 2.

———. *On the Modes: Part Four of* Le Istitutioni Harmoniche, *1558.* Translated by Vared Cohen, with an introduction by Claude V. Palisca. New Haven: Yale University Press, 1983.

Zeleny, Walter. *Die historischen Grundlagen des Theoriesystems von Simon Sechter.* Tutzing: Hans Schneider, 1979.

Zelton, Heinrich. *Deutsche Volkslieder.* Wilhelmshaven: Florian Noetzel Verlag, 1988.

Zimmermann, Robert. *Allgemeine Aesthetik als Formwissenschaft.* Vienna: Braumüller, 1865. Translation of selections from the work in Bujić, *Music in European Thought,* 40–50.

———. *Geschichte der Aesthetik als philosophische Wissenschaft.* Vienna: Braumüller, 1858.

———. *Philosophische Propaedeutik: Prolegomena. – Logik. – Empirische Psychologie. Zur Einleitung in die Philosophie.* 2nd improved and greatly expanded edition. Vienna: Braumüller, 1860.

Index

Adler, Guido, 62, 69–82, 100n51, 264, 270, 276n78
Aeschylus, 7, 378, 395, 402
aesthetics, xxvn27, 70, 71n198, 118n97, 180, 199–200, 253, 265–70, 296, 393, 433
agency, 2n3, 6, 7, 22, 25, 37
Alembert, Jean le Rond d', 89, 224–28, 289n130
Alpenhorn, 77
Alpern, Wayne, xxivn25, 46n119, 248n4, 264–69, 271, 272, 273n72, 301n165
Archimedes, 254
Archiv für Photogramme musikalischer Meisterhandschriften, 330
Aristotle, xix, 6, 7, 8nn20–21, 29, 47, 69n191, 108, 187, 198n56, 231n142, 261, 262, 263, 377–83, 386, 395, 402; *Poetics*, 6, 7, 47, 377–80
Aristoxenus, 7, 8, 9n24, 69n191, 179, 187, 188, 201n62, 293, 378, 402; *Elementa harmonica*, 187–88
art and science, 275, 297–99, 303
artist: product (or "property") of, vs. Nature, product of, 4, 6, 8, 16, 21, 22, 23, 26, 31, 34, 36, 37, 39, 42, 43, 44, 57, 59, 60, 62, 90, 138, 143, 154, 226, 243, 244, 252, 255n21, 350, 362, 380, 403, 404, 405, 430, 431, 438, 440, 441, 442, 452, 453; creative ideas (*Phantasien*) of, vs.

scientist (*Wissenschaftler*), theories of, 28, 70, 74, 80, 81, 94n29, 298, 299, 304
associationism, xix, 6, 14, 25, 26, 28–31, 138, 261, 262, 368, 395
associations (*Assoziationen*): extrinsic, xix, 6, 138, 381, 382, 387, 391; intrinsic, 30, 138, 139
atonality, atonalists, 178, 391, 392
Auskomponierung, 80, 109, 136, 162n227, 165, 166, 171, 173, 333, 348
Auslander, Frederick, 354, 355n91, 358n105

Babbitt, Milton, 37n96, 201n62, 337, 347n78, 357, 361
Bach family tree, 33, 426
Bach, C. P. E., 128, 130, 227n134, 330, 391, 395, 427; Collection 1, Sonata IV [in *Kenner & Liebhaber*, No. 5 in Schenker edition], 1st mvt, 128; Collection 1, Sonata IV [in *Kenner & Liebhaber*, No. 5 in Schenker edition], 3rd mvt, 128; Collection 1, Sonata VI, [K&L; No. 9 in Schenker edition], 128; *Klavierwerke* (1902) ed. Schenker, 302–6 table 4.3; *Kurze und leichte Clavierstücke*, 319; *Versuch über die wahre Art das Clavier zu spielen*, xxvii, 46, 66, 67, 93, 207–9 ex. 3.3, 298, 303, 313n3, 314, 396

Bach, J. S., 10, 33, 227, 228, 229, 235n148, 236, 281, 307, 330, 334, 374, 378, 385, 391, 392, 395, 418, 427, 430, 444, 450; Chorales, 68; *Chromatische Phantasie und Fuge*, BWV 903, xiii, 10, 104 ex. 2.10, 154, 319; Fugue in D Minor, *WTC I* BWV 851, 106–8 ex. 2.12, 406 ex. A.1; Fugue in B minor, *WTC I* BWV 869, 148–49; *Generalbaßbüchlein*, 65, 207–8 ex. 3.2, 313n3; Little Prelude No. 5 in D minor, BWV 926, 166–68 fig. 2.16, 306–7; Prelude, *English Suite* in D minor, BWV 811, 152–53 ex. 2.18a–b, 154–55 ex. 2.19b; Prelude in A minor, *WTC II*, BWV 889, 149; Prelude in E-flat Minor, *WTC I*, BWV 853, 121, 123 ex. 2.15

Bach-Gesellschaft, 281

background (*Hintergrund*), 125, 168, 169, 171

Baldwin, John, 342

Barker, Andrew, 8nn21–22, 179, 181n8, 182n12, 187nn25–27, 188nn29–30

Bartók, Béla, 395

bass arpeggiation (*Baßbrechung*), 168

Baumgart, E. F., 304

Beeckman, Isaac, 199

Beethoven, Ludwig van, 10, 12–13, 68, 134, 154 (piano sonatas), 165, 282, 301, 305, 307, 330, 331, 332, 378, 384, 385, 391, 395, 416, 417, 418, 419, 420, 423, 444; Piano Concerto in E-flat major, Op. 73, 132–33, 168n239; Piano Sonata, Op. 27/2, 1st mvt, 156, 159 fig. 2.13, 305, 306 table 4.3, 328n40; Piano Sonata, Op. 53, 1st mvt, 159–62 fig. 2.14; Piano Sonata, Op. 57, 1st mvt., 161–64 fig. 2.15; Piano Sonata A-flat major, Op. 110, 319; Piano Sonata A-flat major, Op. 110, 1st mvt., 129 table 2.2, 155–56 fig. 2.11a, 408 ex. A.6; Piano Sonata A-flat major, Op. 110, 2nd mvt., 155–59 figs. 2.11b–2.13; Piano Sonata in A major, Op. 101, 2nd mvt., 159 fig. 2.13; Piano Sonata in B-flat major, Op. 106, 1st mvt., 409–14 exx. A.7–A.16, 414–15 ex. A.18; Piano Sonata in E-flat major, Op. 81a, 1st mvt, 417, 419–22 exx. A.19–20; Piano Sonata in E-flat major, Op. 81a, 2nd mvt., 414 ex. A.17; Piano Sonata in E major, Op. 109, 319, 330; Piano Sonata in E minor, Op. 90, 1st mvt., 406–7 ex. A.3, 408–9 exx. A.4, A.5; String Quartet in F major, Op. 59, No. 1, 129 table 2.2; String Quartet in E minor, Op. 59, No. 2, 129 table 2.2; String Quartet, Op. 95, 1st mvt., 125–30 ex. 2.16; String Quartet, Op. 132, 1st mvt., 105n70; Symphony 3 [Op. 55], 1st mvt., 129 table 2.2; Symphony 4 [Op. 60], 1st mvt., 129 table 2.2; Symphony 4 [Op. 60], 4th mvt., 129 table 2.2; Symphony 5 [Op. 67], 1st mvt., 129 table 2.2; Symphony 6 [Op. 68], 1st mvt., 129 table 2.2; Symphony 7 [Op. 92], 1st mvt., 129 table 2.2; Symphony 8 [Op. 93], 1st mvt., 129 table 2.2; Symphony 9 [Op. 125], 1st mvt., 129 table 2.2; Symphony 9 [Op. 125], 4th mvt., 13; Variations in C minor WoO 80, 96 ex. 2.7

Benedetti, Giovanni Battista, 198

Benjamin, William, 157, 395n85

Bent, Ian, 12n35, 17, 18n46, 57n155, 100n50, 119n98, 125n116, 149n199, 305n181, 316n11,

325n40, 328n41, 329n42, 384n40, 389n57, 398, 422n35, 427n3
Berlioz, Hector, 10, 386, 416, 418; Overtures, 417
Bernhard, Christoph, 235
Bertillon, Alphonse, 301
Bildung, 248, 250
Binet, Alfred, 301
Biological nature of tones, 2n3, 22, 53, 138
Blasius, Leslie, xxvin30
Boethius, 188, 189, 190, 191
Borgese, Elisabeth Mann, xviii, xix, 38, 39n103, 90n18, 102n54, 57, 108, 118n97, 120n102, 132n133, 336, 337, 341, 346, 347, 349, 358n105, 359, 361, 362, 363, 368–69, 370–74
Borgese, Giuseppe Antonio, 370
Brahms, Johannes, 10, 57, 70n195, 75n208, 129–30 table 2.2, 134, 307, 330, 334, 374, 378, 386, 391, 395, 428, 444, 452, 453; *Auf dem Kirchhofe*, Op. 105, No. 4, 328n40; *Oktaven und Quinten*, 306, 313n3; Paganini Variations, Op. 3, 328n40; Piano Quartet No. 1 in G minor [Op. 25], 1st mvt., 129; *Seven Songs*, Op. 62, No. 7, 347; Songs, Op. 107, 274; String Quartet in C minor [Op. 51, No. 1], 1st mvt., 129; Symphony in D major [Op. 73, No. 2], 1st mvt., 129; Symphony in F major [Op. 90, No. 3], 1st mvt., 129; Symphony in E minor [Op. 98, No. 4], 1st mvt., 129; Two Rhapsodies, Op. 79, No. 2, 406 ex. A.2
Breitkopf und Härtel, 17, 314
Brentano, Franz, xxv, 264–66, 275–76
Britten, Benjamin, 202n63
Broder, Nathan, 353, 354
Brown, Matthew, xviii, xxn20, 39n104, 56n154, 117n95, 144n180,
157n221, 166n235, 171n250, 172, 279n93, 386n47, 394n83
Bruckner, Anton, 4, 10, 11–12n33, 18, 36n92, 69, 70, 76, 83–84, 85, 86, 89, 90n17, 100n51, 276, 294n146, 298, 314, 347, 376, 378, 385n45, 386, 439nn19–20; Symphony 7 in E major, WAB 107, 1st mvt., 334
Bülow, Hans von, 302, 303
Buys, Jan Brandts, 305n183

Caccini, Guilio, 64, 65n181, 103, 385
Caesar, 254
Campion, François, 204, 205 ex. 3.1
Carruth, Hayden, 358
Catel, Charles-Simon, 238, 240
causality, 16n40, 47–50, 55–56, 74, 239, 256
Chew, Geoffrey, 171n250
Chinese Room Argument, 304–5
Chopin, Frédéric, 10, 75n208, 249, 378, 386n45, 391, 395; Ballade No. 2 in F major, Op. 38, 302n167; *Etude* in E major, Op. 10, No. 3, 328n40; *Etude* in A minor, Op. 10, No. 4, 121–22 ex. 2.14c; Prelude in B Minor, Op. 28/6, 105–6 ex. 2.11, 109–11 ex. 2.13
Choron, Alexandre-Étienne, 238
Christensen, Thomas, 21n51, 192n45, 199n57, 204n68, 212n86, 213–14n95, 216nn103–4, 216n106, 218n107, 223nn113–14, 225n123, 225n126, 226n130, 227n133
chromaticism, 20, 21, 24–25n58, 34, 39, 49, 50, 85, 88–90, 91, 95–96, 97n40, 103, 104, 108, 115–17, 118–24, 132, 134, 144, 147, 160–64 table 2.4, 166, 185n20, 193, 240, 273, 334, 346, 371, 439, 443, 444. *See also* tonicization (*Tonikalisierung*)
Chrysander, Friedrich, 75

Cicero, 260
Citkowitz, Israel, 353
Clarke, Suzannah, 36n96
Cobb, Mr, 354–55
Comte, August, 254
concealed fundamental, 86–87
consonance-dissonance, 3–4, 50, 88, 93–95, 100, 102, 115n93, 142, 145–46, 147–48, 163, 165–66, 182–83, 191–94, 199, 200, 212–13, 215–16, 229, 231–32, 234, 239, 242, 273, 288–89, 291, 293, 339, 393
content (*Inhalt*), 25, 108–9, 348–49, 411
Cook, Nicholas, xiin5, xiiin10, xxivn24, xxivn28, 9n25, 265n53, 302n169
Corelli, Archangelo, 218–20 ex. 3.7a
corps sonore, 211, 225
Cotta Verlag, xviin16, 10, 11, 17–18, 32n79, 297, 306 table 4.3, 314, 316, 322
counter-image (*Gegenbild*), 31, 406n16, 411
Crépieux-Jamin, Jules, 301
Crüger, Johannes, 30n73, 261–63, 274
Cube, Felix-Eberhard von, 336
cyclic composition (*zyklischer Satz*). See form, sonata

Danziger, Kurt, 26, 27nn63–65
Darwin, Charles, 381n21
Daston, Lorraine, 253n15, 300nn157–58, 300nn160–61, 303n174
Debussy, Claude, 391
De Morgan, Evelyn: *Cadmus and Harmonia* fig. 1.1, 1, 377
Dempster, Douglas J., 39n104
Descartes, René, 199
diatony (*Diatonie*), 168–69
Diderot, Denis, 224

Dilthey, Wilhelm, 250n10, 254n18, 255–57, 286
double emploi, 217, 220
Drabkin, William, xivn13, 11, 17, 305n181, 319n28, 329n42, 355n90, 385, 386n14, 388n52
Drei Masken Verlag, 306 table 4.3, 317, 322
Dreiklang, Der, 143n170, 316n10, 323, 327 fig. 5.6, 384n40
dualism, 15, 22, 277, 286, 289, 291, 296, 297, 298, 427, 430n9
Dunn, John Petrie, 336
Dvořák, Antonín, 10, 386

edition, critical (*kritische Ausgabe*), 305, 319n27
edition, elucidatory (*Erläuterungsausgabe*), 305, 307–8, 313n3, 319, 335, 356, 384, 395
edition, *Urtext*, 299–307, 312
Ehrenfels, Christian von, xxv, 100, 276–79
Eibner, Franz, 345n76
Einstein, Albert, 41
Elgar, Edward, 386
essential (*wesentlich*) dissonance, 229–32
essential harmony. See *Stufe*
Esser, Heribert, 301n162, 317n20, 318n22–23, 319, 322n30, 323, 324n38, 355, 356n94
Euclidean geometry, 51, 188
Euler, Leonhard, 261, 280, 282n105
Euripides, 386, 395
Exner, Franz, 261, 265, 271–72
explanation, 4, 23, 45–47, 48, 55–57, 183, 256, 290–91
explanation, theoretic-hermeneutic, 286
Eybl, Martin, 75n208, 397n2

Ezra, ibn, 257n31, 258n35, 301

Federhofer, Hellmut, xiin5, 5, 57n155, 69n193, 74n206, 249n8, 258n33, 279n91, 302n168, 315n9, 316n10–11, 319n24–25, 323n36, 336n60
Ferrero, Guillaume, 280
Fétis, François Joseph, 21, 42, 68n188, 94n32, 201n62, 235, 237–41, 242, 246–47, 288
Fichte, Johann Gottlieb, 256, 269 table 4.2
figured bass, (thoroughbass, *Generalbaß*), 3, 36, 65–67, 84, 85, 93, 95, 96 fig. 2.1, 108, 179, 194, 203–10, 210–12, 214n99, 216n104, 218, 221–22, 224, 227, 229, 237, 238, 239, 241–42, 258n33, 292, 314, 332–33, 356
five, magic or mysterious number, 36–42, 54 table 1.1, 332
foreground (*Vordergrun*d), 125, 168, 169 fig. 2.17, 171, 307, 329, 389, 391, 416, 443
form: four-part, 131, 170, 378; fugue, 131, 170; global, 30–31, 131–35; Lied (song), 131, 170, 378; local, 124–31; rondo, 170; sonata (cyclic composition, *zyklischer Satz*), 10, 31n76, 54 table 1.1, 130, 131, 133–35, 170, 382, 386, 407; three-part, 30–31, 131, 170; two-part, 30–31, 131, 170; undivided, 170; variations, 170
free composition (*freie Satz*) as an extension of strict counterpoint (*strenger Satz*), 44n117, 47, 56–57, 98, 101–3, 135, 143, 146, 165–66, 172, 307, 314
Friday Seminar, 325
Frimmel, Theodor von, 302n168
Frisius, Rudolf, xviin16

fundamental bass (*basse fondamentale*), 16, 23, 53–54, 85–88, 112n86, 145–46, 148, 206, 214n99, 215–22, 226–28, 231–39, 292, 332–34, 345, 439
fundamental line. See *Urlinie*
Furtwängler, Wilhelm, 315
Fux, Johann Josef, xxvii, 84, 94n32, 101, 103–4 ex. 2.9, 212n84, 224, 298, 314

Gaffurius, Franchino, 192, 193n47
Garland, John of, 191
Geist, 8, 251–52, 382
Geisteswissenschaft (human science) 81, 247–57, 299–308, 312
Geisteswissenschaft (human science) vs *Naturwissenschaft* (natural science) 26, 42, 44, 45, 46, 72, 178, 197, 247–57, 265, 274–75, 297–99
Gesellschaft der Musikfreunde (Society for the Friends of Music), xin4, 17n43, 84n2, 258n33
Gestalt psychology, xxv, 24n54, 32n79, 100, 275–79, 287n120
Gibson, W. R., 280
Glarean, Heinrich: *Dodecachordon*, 19n49, 62nn169–70
Goethe, Johann Wolfgang von, 46, 403, 418n29
Gogava, Antonio, 9n24
Graves, Robert, 1n1
Greater Perfect System, 183, 186
Greek civilization, 3, 389, 402
Greek drama, 5, 307n189, 377, 383, 389, 395
Greek harmony (Classical theory), xvi, xix, 1–9, 16, 71n1, 90, 130, 177–201, 210–11, 215, 243, 376–96
Greek language, 3n5, 8, 249–50, 258–60, 300, 377, 415n24
Greek legend, 1

Greek melody, 2–5, 7–9, 60–61, 68, 181, 187, 189, 211n82, 215, 368–69, 380–83, 387, 402
Greek music, 2, 5, 7, 60–62, 181, 187, 198n56, 243, 368–69, 382, 402
Greek system, 15n39, 190
Greek theory, 8–9, 15n39, 60, 62, 93, 181–86, 180–89, 192, 200–201, 211n82, 213, 215–16, 243, 293
Gregorian chant, 63, 68, 238, 254n20
Grimm, Brothers, 339n65, 397
group construction (*Gruppenbildung*), 10, 125–33, 384
Guido of Arezzo, 190–91
Gushee, Lawrence, 20n50
Guttman Verlag, 306
Gymnasium, xi, xxv, 3, 30, 249, 257–63, 272–75, 311, 342, 377, 395

Halm, August, 18n45, 57n155, 314n4, 315, 316n11, 350n80
Handel, G. F., 10, 65n181, 385, 391, 395, 396; "Air and Variations," *Suites de pièces*, 2nd collection, No. 1, 154–55 ex. 2.19; *Zwölf Orgel-Concerte*, 305–6
Hanslick, Eduard, xxvi, 5, 7n15, 17n43, 30, 70, 72, 265, 267, 270, 338
harmonic ellipsis, 234
harmonic (overtone) series, 3, 16, 22–23, 32–33, 36–38, 77, 90, 93n29, 94, 112, 137 table 2.3, 142–43, 172, 179, 182n14, 195n52, 197, 199–202, 216, 223, 226, 242n171, 255n21, 271, 277, 283, 288n124, 290–91, 350, 425, 426, 432, 434, 436, 442
harmony of spheres, 179, 182n12
Harnisch, Siegfried, 194, 204
Harrison, Daniel, 288n125, 289nn127–28
Hartley, David, 262

Hauptmann, Moritz, 18, 63, 95n34, 247, 280–86, 287–91, 293–95
Haydn, Franz Josef, 10, 130, 134, 208n75, 236, 330, 378, 385, 391, 395, 416; *The Creation*, "The Representation of Chaos," 387–88; Piano Sonata in A-flat major No. 8 [Hob. XVI:46], 1st mvt., 128 table 2.2; Piano Sonata in E-flat No. 1 [Hob. XVI:52], 1st mvt., 128 table 2.2; String Quartet in A major, Op. 55, No. 1 [Hob. III:60], 1st mvt., 128 table 2.2; String Quartet in D major, Op. 20, No. 4, [Hob. III:34], 1st mvt., 128 table 2.2; String Quartet in D major, Op. 20, No. 4, [Hob. III:34], 4th mvt., 128 table 2.2; String Quartet D major, Op. 50, No. 6 [Hob. III:49], 1st mvt., 128 table 2.2; String Quartet in D major, Op. 71, No. 2 [Hob. III:70], 1st mvt., 128 table 2.2; String Quartet in E-flat major, Op. 64, No. 6 [Hob. III:64], 1st mvt., 128 table 2.2; Symphony in D major [Hob. I:104], 1st mvt., 128 table 2.2; Symphony in D major [Hob. I:104], 4th mvt., 128 table 2.2
Headlam, Dave, 39n104
Headtone. See *Kopfton*
Hegel, Georg Wilhelm Friedrich, 255, 256, 260, 281n100
Heinichen, Johann David, 204, 205 fig. 3.8a, 214–15n99, 235
Helmholtz, Hermann von, 24n54, 42, 247, 257, 262, 264, 278, 280, 285, 286–93, 295–96, 298, 431, 434n14
Hempel, Carl, 55–56
Herbart, Johann Friedrich, xxiv–xxv, 27–28, 30, 248n4, 261–62, 265–69, 297n153, 299
Herder, Johann Gottfried, 342

Hermann, Gottfried, 302
Herodotus, 254
Hertzka, Emil, 316, 317, 319, 323n36
Hindemith, Paul, 242n170
history, historicism, 57–67, 270–73
history of compositional technique, 67–69, 69–82
history of melody, 5, 8, 58, 67, 78–79, 99, 181
history of music, 57, 58, 67, 75, 79–82
Homer, 7, 254, 260, 299, 377–78, 395, 402
Hooper, Jason, xivn11, 16n40, 49n138, 50n139–41, 105n65, 131n126, 131n129, 378n7, 380n17, 381n21, 398n3, 401n8, 402n10, 405n15, 414n21, 419n31, 420n34
Horace, 260
Hucbald, 189–90
Humboldt, Wilhelm von, 248–50, 253, 255, 258
human vs natural sciences, 26, 42, 44, 45, 46, 72, 178, 197, 247–57, 261–75, 297–99, 303
Hume, David, 31, 262
Humperdinck, Engelbert, 386
Hynais, Cyril, 439n19

illusory *Stufen*, 168, 329
imagined notes, 86, 165, 221, 222, 243
imitation (*Nachbild*), 31, 368, 406n16
Intellectual style, 20n50
interpolated bass, 222, 234
interpolated chord, 86, 218, 220
inversion. *See* reversion, 23n53, 35n90, 51, 348–51, 426, 444–46

Jadassohn, Salomon. 19, 134, 237n155, 314, 376
Jelensperger, Daniel, 19n49
Jellinek, Georg, 43, 73, 98n42, 271–73
Jhering, Rudolph von, 271

Joachim, Joseph, 302
Johnston, William, xxvn26, 261n40
Jonas, Oswald, xix, xxiii, 37n96, 39n105, 67n186, 81n225, 82, 130, 136–45, 149–51, 157, 165, 168n241, 244, 301n162, 302n167, 311–12, 317, 319, 323n35, 328, 330–35, 336, 346, 347, 355–58, 359–61, 370, 372–74, 450n33
Judaism, 301
Judd, Cristle Collins, 19n49
Just intonation, 193, 194, 197, 202n64, 242, 282, 288, 291

Kalmus, Alfred, 316, 317, 319, 325, 328, 335, 373
Kant, Immanuel, 26–27, 30, 118n97, 252, 254n18, 255, 256, 260, 267, 269 fig. 4.2, 400, 403n12, 445n29
Kantian, neo-, 287n119
Kantian, post-, 275
Karnes, Kevin, 71, 73, 75, 76n211, 78n216, 257n32, 274, 276n16
Katz, Adele, 334, 336
Ketter, Daniel, 100n51
Kirchentonalität, 76
Kirnberger, Johann, xxvii, 76, 85, 86–90 ex. 2.1, 91–92, 149, 227–35 exx. 3.11–3.14, 244, 346
Kivy, Peter, 381n21
Kline, Morris, 182, 183n15
Kopfton (headtone), 166
Korsyn, Kevin, xxivn24, xxvn28, 265n53, 279n91
Koslovsky, John, 75n209, 80nn220–22, 81, 82n227, 125n116, 118, 143n170, 395–96n86
Kosovsky, Robert, 316n15, 429n6
Kraft, Viktor, 118n97
Kral, Trude, 325
Kraus, Greta, 325
Krebs, Harald, 224n117

Krenn, Franz, 258n33
Kuhn, Thomas, 67–68

Lachmann, Karl, 300, 302–3
language, ancient, 2, 15n39, 71, 249, 253, 415n24
language, coherence, 170, 378, 381
language, grammar, 46–47, 49–50, 260, 300, 339, 342, 362
language, theoretical, xviii, xxvi, 59, 109, 178, 190, 210, 243, 257, 311
language and music, 46, 59–60, 71, 109, 138, 170, 178, 190, 210, 244, 257, 277, 287, 293, 342, 381
latent voices (*latente Stimmen*), 154, 163, 165, 383
Laufer, Edward, 393
law, jurisprudence, xxvi, 52–57, 267–69
law, natural vs positive, xxvi, 21, 29, 33, 38, 42, 43, 45, 46, 53–57, 253, 271–73, 297–98, 430, 443, 450
law of abbreviation, 34–35, 51–52, 53 table 1.1
law of least action, 25, 32–34, 34–36, 36–42, 118, 279–80, 410n19
laws (rules) of counterpoint, 44n117, 45, 46, 47, 51–54, 98, 135, 146–48, 165–66, 171–72, 191–93, 203, 215, 307, 314
Lemarck, Jean-Baptiste, 240
Lester, Joel, 145nn183–84, 146n185, 194n49, 210n80, 212n85, 224n119, 227nn133–34, 228n136
Levarie, Siegmund, 358, 359, 370
Lippius, Johannes, 194, 204
Liszt, Franz, 10, 240, 282, 289n129, 296, 386, 395; *Tasso*, 416–17
Livy, 254, 260
Locke, John, 262
Lotze, Hermann, 293

Louis, Rudolf, and Thuille, Ludwig: *Harmonielehre*, xiiin9, 19n49, 24, 118n96, 317

Mach, Ernst, xxv, 91, 276–80
Mahler, Gustav, 70n195, 386
major and minor systems, 14, 15n39, 23, 35–36, 44, 61–63, 79, 90, 112–17, 120–24, 133, 137, 142–45, 180, 296, 200, 202, 243, 284, 289, 291, 293, 334, 362, 372, 426, 435, 441
Mandyczewski, Eusebius, 17n43
Mann, Thomas, 370
Mannes, David, 81
Mannes College of Music/The New School, 81
Marpurg, Friedrich Wilhelm, 89, 225, 227, 228n136
Marston, Nicholas, xivn11, 2n3, 9, 12, 29n70, 36n95, 305n181, 398, 405n15
Marsyas, 7, 378, 402
Marx, A. B., 11n33
Marx, Josef, 317, 319, 322, 335
Mattheson, Johann, 206 fig. 3.8b
Maupertuis, Pierre Louis, 280
mean proportions, 184–86, 213
mean-tone temperament, 194, 195n51, 282n104
Meinong, Alexius, 276
melodic fluency (or *fliessender Gesang*), 151–54, 306, 384
memory, 40–41, 254, 261, 277
Mendelssohn, Felix, 10, 130, 134, 281, 385, 386n45, 391, 395, 452; String Quintet in A major [Op. 18, No. 1], 1st mvt., 129; String Quintet No. 3 in D major [Op. 44, No. 1], 1st mvt., 129; String Quintet No. 5 in E-flat major [Op. 44, No. 3], 1st mvt., 129; Symphony in A minor [Op. 56, No. 3], 1st mvt., 129

mental image (*Vorstellung*), 30, 261, 263
Mersenne, Marin, 199
Meyer, Leonard B., 74n205, 393, 394
Michelangelo, 386
Michon, Jean-Hippolyte, 301
middleground (*Mittelgrund*), 139, 144, 168–72, 307, 329, 389
Mikuli, Karl, 249
Miller, George, 38n100, 40, 193n47
mimetic theory of art, 5, 29, 60–61, 104, 200, 362, 382, 397
Mitchell, William, 93n25, 204, 206, 214n99, 303n177, 346, 358, 370–75
mixture (*Mischung*), 14, 37, 39n103, 50, 53, 62, 95, 112–17, 119, 123, 134, 137, 144, 160, 329, 371, 372, 414, 430
modes, church, 14, 39n103, 61–63, 79, 101n53, 112–15, 137, 143–45, 181, 193, 194–96, 200
modulation, 20, 21, 35, 39, 49, 50, 53, 85, 91, 103, 119, 120, 131–34, 144, 157–63, 237, 240, 241, 282, 284, 288n126, 293, 305, 314, 317, 329, 332, 349, 439, 444
modulation, enharmonic, 35–36, 85, 132, 162, 240, 282
monody, 53 table 1.1, 64–65, 68, 385
monotonality, 207, 241
Most, Glenn W. 253n15, 300nn157–58, 300nn160–61, 303n174
Motive, xiii, xiv, xix, 4–9, 12, 14–16, 29–31, 34–36, 44, 47, 52n145, 53 table 1.1, 59–62, 67, 72, 103–10, 124–30, 134–39 table 2.3, 154–56, 166, 170, 218n109, 243–44, 263, 287, 306n185, 329, 378, 381–85, 401, 405–15, 419–22
Mozart, W. M., 10, 75n208, 130, 134, 236, 301, 330, 378, 385, 391, 395,

451; *Don Giovanni*, K. 527, 388; Fantasy in D minor, K. 397, 139–42 ex. 2.17, 328n40; Piano Sonata in A major, K. 331, 1st mvt., 307; Piano Sonata in C major, K 309?, 1st mvt., 129; Piano Sonata in C major, K. 330?, 1st mvt, 129; String Quartet in C major, K 465?, 1st mvt., 118–19n98, 129; String Quartet in E-flat major, K 428?, 1st mvt., 128; String Quintet in C major, K. 515, 1st mvt., 128; String Quintet in G minor, K. 516], 1st mvt., 128; Symphony in C major, K. 551, 1st mvt., 128; Symphony in C major, K. 551, 4th mvt., 128; Symphony in E-flat major K. 543, 1st mvt., 128; Symphony in G minor K. 550, 1st mvt., 128
Musica Enchiriadis, Anonymous, 189–90
musica poetica, 315
musica practica, 179, 190, 193n47, 197
musica theorica, 179, 190, 193
musical laws, xxvi, 22, 28, 33, 42–49, 51–52, 70, 109, 154, 177, 215, 243, 313, 387, 394, 422, 431
Musikwissenschaft, 17n43, 68, 70, 71, 72n200, 74, 75n209, 79, 80, 81, 264, 292n138, 298
"Muß i denn, muß i denn, zum Städtele hinaus," 100, 101, 279

Natur, problem of translation, 252–53
naturalization, 38, 71n198, 93, 95, 179–80, 211n83, 286, 298
Nature vs Art, 4, 6, 8, 12, 16, 21, 28–31, 33, 35, 36, 37, 42, 44, 104, 124, 134, 136–43, 172, 180, 200, 223, 243, 244, 253, 351, 362, 368–69, 380, 382, 400, 401–5, 407, 414–16, 418, 430

Naturklang (Chord of Nature), 3. 35,
  193, 200, 226, 242, 244, 346, 426
Naturwissenschaften, 68, 247–57, 265
Neo-Hellenic, 269
Neo-humanist, 249
Neo-Platonist, 182, 194
Neo-Positivism, 292
Neo-Riemannians, 282n105, 289, 295
Neumeyer, David, 171n250
New German School, 282
Newton, Isaac, 21n51, 41, 297
Nichomachus, 188
Nietzsche, Friedrich, 73
non-essential dissonance (*zufällig*), 229–32
normal science, 67

Oettingen, Arthur von, 24n54, 42, 247,
  257, 277, 285, 286, 288–95, 298,
  349n79
Oppel, Reinhard, 316
ordre pluritonique, 21, 240–41
ordre transitonique, 21, 240–41
Orpheus, 7, 378, 402
Oster, Ernst, xix, 168n241, 355–56,
  358, 360, 373, 390n66
Oster Collection, 399

passing chord, 48, 54, 76, 86–88, 92,
  122, 147, 149, 157, 165, 182–83,
  231–33, 346, 390, 393
Pastille, William, 2n3, 153n209,
  155n214–16, 306n185, 307n186,
  386n47
Paul, Oscar, 282
pedal point, 25, 48, 54 table 1.1, 103,
  104 exx. 2.9–2.10, 125, 153, 156,
  168, 231, 232
Pfitzner, Hans, 386
Phantasien vs. *Theorien*, 28, 298, 308
philology, xiv, 12n34, 17n43, 57–58,
  73, 249, 253, 254, 270, 272, 274,
  295, 299–308, 312, 330, 337, 338

Planck, Max, 280
Plato, 3, 29, 181–82, 188, 286, 389,
  403n11
Podolsky, Leo, 330n47
polyphonic melody, 153–54
positivism, 71, 75, 81, 236, 237, 254,
  274, 276, 294
prelude, 25, 67, 134
Pre-Raphaelite, 1
prima pratica vs *seconda pratica*, 241
Proctor, Gregory, 163n229
Prosdocimo de Beldomandis, 192
psychology, xxv, 7n15, 8, 15–16,
  20–21, 24–42, 44–45, 60, 71n198,
  99, 100n51, 108–10, 118, 132, 134,
  178, 250n10, 252–53, 256, 258,
  260–63, 273–80, 286, 287n119,
  288n124, 291, 292, 294–98, 307–8,
  312, 331–32, 337, 338, 349, 371,
  379, 394, 400
psychology of tones, 2n3, 25–26 30,
  44, 45, 108, 110, 118, 132, 134,
  178, 202, 252, 273, 295–96, 329,
  349, 379
Ptolemy, Claudius, 188, 194n50
Pythagoras, 3, 7, 41, 93, 181–88, 190–
  91, 286, 293, 378, 402
Pythagorean comma, 35n92, 441n24

quadrivium, 179, 250

Raff, Joachim, 296
Rameau, Jean-Philippe, xviin15, 16,
  19n49, 21n51, 23, 42, 48, 84,
  85, 86, 89, 145–49, 179n5, 194,
  199n57, 210–24, 224–35, 238, 239,
  242, 244–45, 247, 283, 285, 289,
  290, 295, 332–34, 345, 376, 381,
  384n40
ratios and proportions, 2, 3, 7, 94, 181–
  88, 192, 195–96, 199, 200, 213–14
Ravel, Maurice, 391

Reality, [*Wirklichkeit*], 6, 22, 28–30, 91, 93, 100, 362, 368, 382, 435, 437
Reger, Max, 11, 18, 97n40, 134, 296, 298, 314, 319, 376, 378, 386
Rehding, Alexander, 291n13
Reihe, 62, 63n172, 95, 114–15, 347–48
repetition, xiii, xiv, xix, 9, 14, 30–31, 47, 53 table 1.1, 59–63, 65, 75, 103–10, 124–31, 131–35, 137–39 table 2.3, 154, 170, 172, 263, 277, 329, 372, 378, 381–85, 387, 404–15, 419–23
repetition, concealed (or *verborgene Wiederholung*), 138–42, 390
repetition, transformation, 139, 154, 157, 160
reversion *see* inversion
rhythm, 30, 61, 65, 70, 71, 86, 92, 98, 105, 125, 134, 135, 136, 169, 170, 187n26, 188n29, 192n45, 193, 220, 241, 281, 382, 383, 406, 409–14, 418, 422
Richter, Ernst Friedrich, 19, 65, 99, 237n155, 314, 319, 376
Riemann, Hugo, xxii, 11n33, 15, 17, 22, 23, 24, 28, 38, 42, 49, 63, 71, 86, 94n29, 95n34, 177n1, 178, 201n62, 210, 247, 253, 257, 284, 285, 288, 289, 291, 293–99, 314, 347, 351, 376, 427
Rimsky Korsakov, Nikolai, 314, 386
Ritter, Carl, 255
Roman law, 3, 98n42, 260, 270–73, 301
Roman numerals, 12, 86n8, 115, 149, 215n100, 236, 237, 283, 292, 348
Rore, Cipriano de, 198
Rothfarb, Lee, xinn2–3, xxii, xxivn25, xxvn27, 7n15, 21n51, 57n155, 248n2, 248n4, 257, 258nn34–35, 259, 260, 261nn37–38, 263nn48–49, 265n53, 267n57, 301nn162–63, 316n11, 361, 418n30

Rothgeb, John, xxiii, 81n225, 136nn149–50, 148nn194–95, 151n204, 153nn206–7, 154n212, 155n217, 207n72, 317n20, 319nn24–25, 29, 330n46, 392n73
Rothschild, Baron Alphons von, 17
Rothstein, William, 16n40, 49n138, 161
Rousseau, Jean-Jacques, 224–25
Rudorff, Ernst, 302
Rüegg, Walter, 250n9, 251n12
Rule of the Octave (*Règle de l'octave*), 123–24, 204–5
Rummenhöller, Peter, 281, 283n107, 286n116, 291n136, 292nn139–40

Salzer, Felix, xxii, 69, 75n208, 79–82, 208, 325, 334, 336, 372, 374, 395, 396n86
Samarotto, Frank, 129
Savigny, Frederick Karl von, 270–71, 272, 273n71
scale, 85, 91–99, 144, 180–81, 183n15, 185, 189, 195–96, 200, 225, 226, 229, 238, 288n126
scale degree, xviii, 62n169, 63, 90n18, 91–99, 118n97, 210, 211n82, 215n100, 223, 239–40, 329, 344–46
Scarlatti, Domenico, 395
Schachter, Carl, 159–62
Schelling, Friedrich Wilhelm Joseph von, 256
Schenker, Heinrich, critique of: figured bass, 66–67; *Formenlehre*, xiv, 125n114, 133–34, 378, 394–95; music pedagogy, xiii, 11, 57, 98–90, 93, 243, 295, 298, 314–17; physicists, 286–93, 295; Rameau and fundamental bass, 148–51; Riemann and dualism, 286, 293–97, 298, 299

Schenker, Heinrich, editions: C. P. E. Bach, *Klavierwerke* (1902), 302–6; J. S. Bach, *Chromatische Phantasie und Fuge* BWV 903 (1909), xiii, 10, 104 ex 2.10, 154, 305–6, 319; Beethoven, *Klaviersonaten* (1923), 305–6; Beethoven, *Die letzten fünf Sonaten* vol. 1–4 (1913–20), 154, 155–9, 305–6, 319, 332, 384, 395; Beethoven, *Sonaten*, Op. 27, No. 2 (1921), 156, 159, 305–6; Brahms, *Oktaven und Quinten* (1933), 306, 313n3; Handel, *Zwölf Orgel-Concerte* (1905), 305–6

Schenker, Heinrich, education and teaching: *Gymnasium*, 257–63, 395; legal training, xi, xxvi, 2, 3, 18n48, 42–57, 258, 263–70, 270–73; music conservatory, xi, xiin5, 83–84, 89, 90, 178, 228, 257–58, 294n146, 376, 439; desire for position at conservatory, xvii, 68–69, 311, 314–15, 317–18; private teaching, xii, 19, 59, 69, 74

Schenker, Heinrich, writings: "Der Geist der musikalischen Technik," xiii, xxv, xxvi, 4n6, 5, 9, 15–16, 24, 30n72, 58, 59n152, 60, 90, 179, 275, 278n91, 279n91, 380, 381, 383, 389, 390, 395, 397, 401; "Der Weg zum Gleichniss," xiii–xiv, xxi, 6–7, 8–16, 24, 29n70, 30, 31, 34, 36, 59nn161–62, 61, 263, 378, 380, 395, 397–423 appendix A; "Das Tonsystem," xiv, 6, 8, 9–16, 19, 22, 23, 24, 25, 27, 29n70, 32 33, 34, 36–39, 42–45, 51–52, 53, 94, 180, 273, 278, 279, 297, 350–51, 395, 399–401, 410n19, 425–53 appendix B; "Über den Niedergang der Kompositionskunst: eine technisch-kritische Untersuchung," xiv, 10–11, 17, 31n76, 32n79, 43n114, 57, 81, 131–35, 383, 384n40, 385–95; *Ein Beitrag zur Ornamentik* (1904/1908), xiii, 10, 105n70, 125n116, 302n169–172, 304n178, 305–6, 318n22, 384n36–38, 389, 390, 395; *Harmonielehre* (1906), xii–xxvi, xxvii, 2, 4–9, 9–16, 17–20, 23n53, 24–54, 57–67, 69n192, 71, 73n202, 74–75, 79–81, 82n228, 88n15, 90–135, 135–38, 142–46, 149–51, 160, 168, 170, 172, 178n4, 193, 203n66, 204n67, 210, 223, 242–45, 252, 257, 261, 264, 273, 275, 278–79, 289, 295, 297, 302, 304, 305–6, 311–30, 330–37, 341n68–69, 343, 344–58, 359–69, 370–75, 376–77, 380–85, 387–90, 394–95, 397, 399–401, 425–27, 428, 439n20, 440n21, 450n33; *Kontrapunkt 1* (1910), xiii, xiv, xxiiin23, 9–12, 16, 18n45, 24, 37, 44, 45, 46, 47n123, 48, 49, 50n139, 52, 54, 64n179, 66, 67n185, 137 table 2.3, 144, 146, 147n193, 148, 151, 153n207, 154nn210–11, 166n234, 207n71, 209, 224nn117–18, 244, 255n21, 257, 273, 305–6, 313, 316, 318, 322, 333, 379, 383, 384, 385, 386n45, 386n47, 389, 390, 395; *Kontrapunkt II* (1922), xvi, 12, 49, 97, 98n41, 147, 153n206, 208, 154n214, 305–6, 316, 322, 336, 377n4, 395; *Der Tonwille* (1921–24), xvi, xxii, 30n74, 65n181, 81n226, 153n209, 154n214, 165–68, 305–6, 316n15, 317, 319, 384, 385n42, 395; *Das Meisterwerk in der Musik*, (1925–30), xvi, xxii, 100n50, 147, 148n194–95, 151, 153n209, 154n214, 165, 207n72, 208n74, 210n78, 81,

305–6, 307, 313n3, 317, 322, 332, 384n40, 388n52, 389, 391, 392, 393n76–79, 395, 396; *Fünf Urlinie-Tafeln* (1932), 306; *Der freie Satz* (1935), xvi, 12, 30n74, 65n181, 82, 103n58, 120n103, 136, 137 table 2.3, 138, 139, 142, 143n170, 144, 145n182, 148, 149, 151, 154n214, 157, 160–61 table 2.4, 162n227, 163n230, 165, 168, 169 fig. 2.17, 170, 172, 207n72, 303n175, 305–6, 307, 313n2, 316n11, 317, 331, 332, 378, 384n40, 385n41, 389, 390, 391n67–69, 394, 395
Schiller, Friedrich, 7, 34n86, 383n31
Schleiermacher, Friedrich Daniel Ernst, 250–51, 253, 255, 274–75, 307
Schliemann, Heinrich, 254–55
Schoenberg, Arnold, 70n195, 95n34, 241, 315, 391; *Harmonielehre*, xiiin9, xviin15, xx, 95n34, 244, 337, 340–41, 362, 392–94
Schubert, Franz, 10, 75n208, 80, 84, 130, 378, 385, 391, 395, 444; Impromptu, Op. 90, No. 3, 294; Octet [D. 803], 129 table 2.2; String Quintet in C major [D. 956], 129 table 2.2
Schultz, Johann Abraham Peter, 85n7, 228
Schumann, Robert, 10, 296, 378, 385, 395
Scolica Enchiriadis, Anonymous, 189–90
Searle, John, 304–5
Sechter, Simon, xxvii, 11, 12n33, 18, 24, 36n92, 69n194, 76, 83–90, 91, 92, 112n86, 119n99, 247, 282, 288, 294n146, 346, 347, 439n19
Seeger, Charles, 276n79, 374, 375n114
Sessions, Roger, 346, 356, 358n100

Schenker, Jeanette, 136, 301n162, 322, 323, 324n38, 328, 329n42, 330, 373, 428, 429
Schenker, Johann, 257, 264
seven, magical number, 40–42
Shakespeare, William, 297, 386
Shirlaw, Matthew, 204, 206, 218n108, 238n157
Siegel, Hedi, 44n117, 49n138, 105n70, 313n3, 316n11, 325n40, 329n42, 395–96n86
society, 42, 78n216, 268 table 4.2, 271, 272
society of tones, 22, 252, 273
Socrates, 389, 404n13
Song of Seikilos, 60
Sophocles, 7, 260, 378, 395, 402
Spengler, Oswald, 80–81
Spies, Claudio, 337n62, 338, 340n66, 341n69, 361
Spitta, Philip, 75
Stein, Erwin, 317n21
Sternegg Theodor, 264
Stimmführungsschichten (*Verwandlungsschichten*, or voice-leading levels), 136, 157, 160–61, 168–73
Stimmführungsverwandlungen (or voice-leading transformations), 136, 157, 160–61, 168–73
Stöhr, Richard, 319; *Praktische Leitfaden der Harmonielehre*, 317
Strauss, Richard, 10, 11, 18, 386; *Ein Heldenleben*, Op. 35, 385–86n45
Stravinsky, Igor, 391
Stufe vs. scale step, scale degree, xviii, 34, 62n169, 86n11, 90n18, 118n97, 215, 223, 239, 240, 329, 344–48
Stumpf, Carl, 27–28, 71n198, 94n29, 288n124
style, musical, 58, 59, 68, 74–75, 80, 180, 204, 218, 221, 231, 233, 234, 263, 288

supposition, 48, 218, 220, 221–22, 225, 227, 234
Sweelinck, J. P., Psalm 1, 66 ex. 1.1
synthesis, 2, 16n40, 31, 42, 50, 74, 109, 180, 354n89, 377, 383, 385, 388, 391
system, tuning, 194
system, Greek, 186, 189–90, 243

Tacitus, 260
Tchaikovsky, Peter, 314
tetrachords, 183, 185, 186 fig. 3.3, 188–90 fig. 3.5
tetraktys, 183, 184 fig. 3.1, 185, 193
Thesis-antithesis-synthesis, 283
Thucydides, 254
Thuille, Ludwig *see* Louis, Rudolf
Thym, Jürgen, 85n7, 153nn206–7, 228n135, 229n137
Tinctoris, Johannes, 192
tonal system, xiv, 4, 12–15, 20–23, 24, 27, 32–39, 42–44, 51–54, 58, 61–63, 66, 79, 90, 95, 101, 112–17, 118–24, 133, 136–38 table 2.3, 142–48, 180, 185n20, 196–97, 200, 202–3, 242–43, 243–44, 282, 314–15, 329, 331, 334, 350, 362, 372, 417, 425–53
tonalité omnitonique, 242
tonality (or *Tonalität*), 22, 39, 43, 49, 50, 71, 76, 78, 82, 163, 168, 200, 207, 238, 240–41, 244, 271, 273, 288, 334, 384, 391–92, 443–44, 449
tonicization (*Tonikalisierung*) 20, 39, 88, 95, 118–24, 132, 137, 144, 145, 157, 160–61, 163, 346, 371. *See also* chromaticism
transposition, 14n38, 15, 35, 53 table 1.1, 62, 66, 119n99, 137, 144, 181, 190, 195, 218n109, 240, 279, 282n104, 329, 345, 377, 406

Treitler, Leo, 101n53
trivium, 250, 254
Twain, Mark, 343, 345

understanding (*Verstehung*) vs explanation (*Erklärung*), 256
undertone series, 22, 291, 314, 427n3
unending melody (*unendliche Melodie*), 386–87
Universal Edition, xviin16, 11, 18, 81n225, 82n228, 314, 316–17, 353–54, 373
Ur, Tombs of, 77
Urchueguía, Cristina, 306n184, 307n187
Urformen, 67, 209, 306
Urideen, 105, 306
Urlinie, 10, 65n181, 136, 139, 143, 148nn194–95, 151n204, 153n209, 154–59, 161, 165–73, 207–8, 306–7, 384–85, 390, 392
Ursatz, 136, 144, 153n209, 155nn215–16, 161, 165–73, 306–7, 389–90, 395
Urtext, 299–303, 305, 306n184, 307, 312

Viadana, Lodovivo Grossi da, 64, 103, 385
Vico, Giambattista, 254n20
Vienna Circle, 276
Vienna, Conservatory [in], xi, xvii, 84, 247, 257–58, 294n145, 315–17
Vienna, University of xi, xxv, 32n79, 70–75, 83–84, 248–49, 253, 257, 261, 263–70, 270–73, 275–80, 294, 301, 311, 395
Vienna, University of, Philosophical Society, xxv, 5n11, 275–78, 279n91
Violin, Moritz, 136, 257n32, 315n8, 336n60
Virgil, 260, 299

Vogler, Georg Joseph, 236–37, 349
Vogt, Florian, 318n22
voice-leading levels (*Stimmführungsschichten*), 136, 138, 139, 144, 151, 171–72, 307, 389–90, 395
voice-leading transformations (*Stimmführungsverwandlungen*), 136, 139, 157, 160–61, 163, 171–72, 307, 389–90, 395; arpeggiation (*Brechung*), 157, 161 table 2.4, 390; displaced tones (*uneigentliche Intervalle*), 157, 161 table 2.4; linear progressions (*Züge*), 157, 160 table 2.4; mixture (*Mischung*), tonicization (*Tonikalisierung*), 157, 160 table 2.4; motion to/from an inner voice (*Untergreifen* and *Übergreifen*), 157, 160 table 2.4, 390; neighbor motion links repeated neighbor tones (*Nebennoten*), 157, 160 table 2.4; reaching over (*Übergreifen*), 157, 160 table 2.4, 171, 390; register transfer (*Höherlegung, Tieferlegung, Koppelung*), 157, 160 table 2.4, 390; repetition (*Wiederholung*), 157, 160 table 2.4; substitution (*Vertretung*), 157, 161 table 2.4; unfolding (*Ausfaltung*), 157, 160 table 2.4, 171, 390; voice exchange (*Stimmentausch*), 157, 160 table 2.4, 171, 390
Vrieslander, Otto, xvii, 311, 312, 313, 316n10, 317, 318–30, 335, 336, 354–56, 360, 373

Wagner, Manfred, 258n33
Wagner, Richard, 10, 68, 79, 258n33, 282, 378, 386, 391, 392, 416, 418n27, 439n19, 444, 452n35; *Das Rheingold*, 48; *Faust* Overture, 48; *Tristan* chord, 392; *Tristan* Prelude, 385n45

Waldeck, Arthur, xix, xxi, xxiii, 336, 337, 351–61, 361–69, 370, 373–74
Wallis, John, 199
Wason, Robert, xviii, 12n35, 70n194, 84n2, 84n6, 85n7, 86n11, 119n99, 301n163, 318n22–23, 322n30, 345n76, 355n92, 356n94, 359n106, 422n35, 429n6
Weber, Carl Maria von, 237n14
Weber, Gottfried, 11n33, 18n48, 19n49, 119n98, 201n62, 235–37, 238, 246, 292, 345, 347, 349
Weber, Max, 254n17
Weisse, Hans, 74, 75n208, 81, 82, 136, 168, 206, 329–30, 335, 353–55
Weitzmann, Carl Friedrich, 282
Wertheimer Max, 276, 279
West, Martin, 60n165, 61n166, 181n9, 187n25
White, Hayden, 57n156
Wiener Urtext Edition, 302n166, 303
Willfort, Manfred, 311–12, 325–30, 373
Willner, Channan, 171n250
Wittgenstein, Ludwig, *Tractatus logico-philosophicus*, 292
wolf fifth, 195
Wolf, Friedrich August, 249, 254, 300, 377
Wolf, Hugo, 10, 70n195, 386
Wundt, Wilhelm, 26, 27, 262

Zarlino, Gioseffo, 19, 33n80, 38, 93–95, 192–98 fig. 3.6, 210, 211, 212, 213, 216–18 ex. 3.5, 241, 242, 282n104
Zeleny, Walter, 84n6, 85n7
Zeißberg, Heinrich von, 264
Zimmermann, Robert, xxv, 30, 261, 264–65, 267, 269, 270, 274
Zuckerkandl, Viktor, 75n208

www.ingramcontent.com/pod-product-compliance
Lightning Source LLC
Chambersburg PA
CBHW072109010526
44111CB00038B/2407